A CONSTITUTIONAL HISTORY
OF BRITISH GUIANA

COPYRIGHT

A
CONSTITUTIONAL HISTORY
OF BRITISH GUIANA

BY

SIR CECIL CLEMENTI

Formerly
COLONIAL SECRETARY AND THRICE OFFICER
ADMINISTERING THE GOVERNMENT
OF BRITISH GUIANA

MACMILLAN AND CO., LIMITED
ST. MARTIN'S STREET, LONDON
1937

> Yet unspoiled
> Guiana, whose great city Geryon's sons
> Call El Dorado.
>
> MILTON, *Paradise Lost*, xi. 409.

O to climb up to the mountains,
  Where the strength of God abides!
O to cleanse my soul at fountains
  Gushing from their giant sides!

For my heart is in the highlands
  At the border of Brazil,
Where my straining eyes espy lands
  That Guiana's hope fulfil:

And in splendid revelation
  There is flashing into view
El Dorado's consummation—
  Walter Raleigh's dream come true!

61 *Main Street, Georgetown.*
June, 1918.

DEDICATED
WITH AFFECTIONATE GOOD WISHES
TO ALL WHO LIVE IN
EL DORADO

PROLOGUE

THE constitution of British Guiana, as it existed for more than a century prior to 1928, was, in the words of Mr. E. F. L. Wood (now Lord Halifax), "unique in the Empire." [1] It was a freakish by-product of the Napoleonic Wars and the creature of pure mischance; but it well deserves special study as a signal illustration of the danger involved in the premature grant of representative institutions and in the control of finance by elected legislators not charged with administrative responsibility. Moreover, in British Guiana we may watch the wheel of constitutional change turn full cycle, from strict control by the Crown to a system which was a parody of self-government, and thence back again to an advanced form of Crown Colony government. Here we may learn how the commercial adventure of a Dutch trading company grew to be a colonial administration, how Dutch methods of colonizing were gradually modified under British rule, how representative institutions on too narrow a basis proved incapable of healthy growth, how an oligarchy of sugar-planters came to be a negro demagogy, how an autocratic executive was by degrees so emasculated that it could no longer rule, and how at last the scandal became such that Parliament was obliged to intervene, in order to sweep away the constitutional eccentricities which impeded the progress of British Guiana, and restore to its Government the power of governing.

The strange story of this constitution is little known even in the Colony itself, and is wholly unknown elsewhere. But in it may be found, writ small, and thus more easily examined, many of the problems which beset colonial administration throughout the world, as well as a salutary object-lesson in the futility of any endeavour to cram the political education

[1] See "Command Paper" No. 1679, p. 87. Report by the Hon. E. F. L. Wood, M.P., Parliamentary Under-Secretary of State for the Colonies, on his visit to the West Indies and British Guiana in 1922.

of a people.   So I have not shrunk from telling the story in full detail, hoping that the errors of the past, when clearly seen, may be warning signals for the future.   I have also felt strongly that a record should be preserved of this unique system before knowledge of its working has faded from the memory of those who had actual experience of its anomalies.

It is, indeed, to be feared that in British Guiana itself the lessons of the past have not yet been sufficiently laid to heart. There were die-hards who strenuously resisted the reforms of 1928; and, four years after those reforms, the elected unofficial members of the Colony's new Legislative Council moved, on the 1st September, 1932, for a Committee to be appointed, to revise the Colony's constitution once again, upon the grounds that it did not satisfy the local community and that the Government, with the power to govern, had been given an opportunity of showing what they could do for the Colony and had accomplished nothing.   The nominated unofficial members did not give this motion their support, but expressed the view that the local community as a whole did not show any desire for a change and that in any case the new constitution had not yet been given a fair trial, because the reforms had practically coincided with the beginning of a world-wide economic depression.   The motion was therefore amended and accepted as no more than an expression of " the unanimous opinion of the elected members."   In that form it was transmitted to the Secretary of State for the Colonies, who refused to entertain the proposal for the appointment of such a committee.   Nevertheless, the fact that the fourteen elected members unanimously pressed for this committee is ominous; and, if the matter should hereafter come up for reconsideration, it is essential that the inhabitants of British Guiana and those charged with the duty of decision should have before them a detailed description of the old constitution, now abolished. No such description at present exists, and my object in these pages is to supply it.   I write from experience gained as Colonial Secretary of British Guiana between 1913 and 1922, during which period I thrice administered its Government : and, although Coleridge has said that " to most men experience is like the stern lights of a ship, which illumine only the track it has passed," I trust that in this case experience may prove to be a pilot light, which will both mark out the rocks to be avoided and indicate the course to be steered.

C. CLEMENTI.

Holmer Court,
26th September, 1936.

CONTENTS

PART II

CONSTITUTIONAL HISTORY OF THE COLONY OF BRITISH GUIANA

PART III

CRITICAL ANALYSIS OF THE CONSTITUTION OF BRITISH GUIANA PRIOR TO THE YEAR 1928

CONTENTS

PART IV

APPENDICES

TABLES

ABBREVIATIONS

B.G. British Guiana.

B.G.B.A. *British Guiana Boundary. Arbitration with Venezuela :
the Case on Behalf of the Government of Her Brittanic Majesty.* London : printed at the Foreign Office, 1898.

B.G. Laws. *The Laws of British Guiana : A New and Revised Edition
prepared under the authority of the Statute Laws (Revised Edition)
Ordinance, 1904.* By Sir Thomas Crossley Rayner, Kt., K.C.,
Attorney-General. In five volumes. London : printed by
Waterlow & Sons, Ltd., London Wall, for the Government of
British Guiana, 1905.

B.G. Laws (1870). *New and Revised Edition of the Laws of British
Guiana, chronologically arranged from the year 1773 to 1780.*
Demerara : printed and published by L. McDermott at the *Colonist*
Office, Water Street, Georgetown, 1870.

E.B. *Encyclopædia Britannica*, 11th edition. Cambridge : at the
University Press, 1910.

PART I

CONSTITUTIONAL HISTORY OF THE THREE RIVERS
BEFORE THE UNION

B

CHAPTER I

EARLY SETTLEMENTS IN ESSEQUEBO AND BERBICE (1598–1648)

THE Union of Utrecht, signed on the 29th January, 1579, by the representatives of the provinces of Holland, Zeeland, *Dutch Revolt* Utrecht, Gelderland and Zutphen, laid the founda- *against Spain.* tion upon which the Republic of the United Nether- lands was raised; and from that year the national existence of the Dutch people may be said to date. By this famous compact the northern provinces of the Netherlands bound themselves together, " as if they were one province," to maintain their rights and liberties " with life-blood and goods " against foreign tyranny. Till then, however rebellious, they had been subjects of the King of Spain; and although by an Act of Abjuration the Dutch people formally declared, in 1581, that the King of Spain had forfeited his sovereignty over them, and that they held themselves thenceforth absolved from their allegiance to him, this declaration of independence did not of itself release them from the Spanish yoke. Not until the year 1594 was the soil of the northern Netherlands free from the presence of Spanish garrisons; nor was it until the 9th April, 1609, that a truce was concluded by Spain with the Dutch provinces " in the quality of free States," the *uti possidetis* being recognised as regards territorial possessions, in whatever continent they might be situated. This truce lasted until 1621, and thereafter war between the two countries continued until, by the Treaty of Münster, signed on the 30th January, 1648, the independence of the Netherlands was finally recognized.

In those days America was but a Spanish island. No other European state, save Portugal, had yet planted a colony on *Dutch Cruise* its shores; and Portugal was then one of the *along Coast of Guiana in* dominions of the King of Spain.[1] Yet if the *1598.* English, though nominally at peace with the King

---

[1] Portugal did not sever itself from the crown of Spain until 1641.

3

of Spain, might " singe his beard " in the West Indies, so with far better warrant might the Dutch, his bitter enemies. The traders of Holland and Zeeland throve mightily by the war. Their ships penetrated to the East and West Indies and were to be found in every sea. It was in these circumstances that, in 1598, two Holland ships cruised along the coast of Guiana and brought back a report that " between the rivers Curetyn and Worinoque are these rivers : Berbice, Apari, Maychawini, Maheyca, Demirara, Dessekebe, Pauroma, Moruga, Wayni." [1] They did not, however, visit or trade in these rivers, because they were pressed for time, and because the Indians informed them that " not much was to be found there," and also because their provisions were growing scant; so they " did no more than to coast along the land, in order to have some idea of it, as far as the river Worinoque." [2]

This venture of the province of Holland was followed by the voyages of other Dutchmen, for Sir Walter Raleigh's *Discoverie of Guiana*, published in 1596, had set the imagination of all adventurers on fire; and, in the opening years of the seventeenth century, Willem Usselinx of Antwerp, the originator of the Dutch West India Company, urged upon his fellow-countrymen the colonization of America in general and of Guiana in particular.[3] From Spanish records we learn that in 1613 the Dutch were settled at various points upon the coast between the Orinoco and the Amazon;[4] but it seems probable that these settlements were for many years nothing more than trading-posts, rendered necessary by the fact that traffic with the Indians was subject to great delay, while negotiable articles were being collected, and that, therefore, it became usual for merchant-ships to leave a few men in

[1] The modern spelling of these river-names is as follows : Courantyne, Orinoco, Berbice, Abary, Mahaicony, Mahaica, Demerara, Essequebo, Pomeroon, Moruka, Waini.

[2] *U.S.E.*, p. 17. Report to the States-General of the earliest Dutch voyage to the coast of Guiana (3rd December, 1597, to 28th October, 1598), written by A. Cabeliau, clerk of the expedition, and submitted by him on 3rd February, 1599.

[3] Usselinx wrote in 1608 his " Exposition, how necessary, useful and profitable it is to the United Netherlands to preserve the freedom of trading to the West Indies, in the Peace with the King of Spain." See Professor J. F. Jameson's biography of Usselinx.

[4] *B.G.B.A.*, appendix, vol. i, pp. 31, 32.

charge of a little store at suitable points along the coast of Guiana until the return of the vessel, when the small party was picked up again and possibly other members of the crew were left in its place.

In 1621, the Twelve Years' Truce with Spain came to an end.   Meanwhile the seven provinces of the United Nether-

Constitution of the United Netherlands. lands had, since their abjuration of Spanish rule, been formed into a republic, which was, however, by no means a democracy.   The governing body was differently constituted in different provinces; and it is true that in Friesland and Groningen the provincial States were chosen by a method closely approaching popular election, while in some of the other provinces the nobility, and in one the clergy, enjoyed a greater or less degree of representation.   But for the most part the provincial States consisted of deputies, who represented the city corporations.   As a rule, therefore, the municipal councils were the ultimate authority; and these were, under some limitations, self-electing.   The municipal council chose all the officers of the city and usually sent, to represent it in the provincial States, one or two burgo-masters, several town councillors and the pensionary.[1]   The number of persons deputed might be greater or smaller, as in any case each city had but one vote.

For example, the States of the province of Holland consisted of nineteen members.   The nobility of the province formed one " member," being represented by one of their number; and the other " members " were the eighteen chief towns, each represented in the manner already mentioned. The pensionary of the province presided over their deliberations and arranged their business.   Their meetings took place at the Hague.   Through this assembly the sovereign powers of the province were exercised, but the sovereignty itself resided in the nineteen " members," and not in their deputies. Accordingly, many of the most important matters of deliberation were subjected to enormous delay, because the deputies

[1] A name given to the leading functionary and legal adviser of the principal town corporations of the Netherlands.   The pensionary conducted the legal business of the town, and was the secretary of the town council and its representative and spokesman at the meetings of the provincial States.   The post was permanent and the influence of the pensionary was great.   (*E.B.*, vol. xxi, p. 122.)

in the provincial States were obliged to refer to their principals, the city councils.

Each of the seven provinces regarded itself as an independent and sovereign State; but the loose union, in which they were joined, had as its organ an assembly known under the title of " The High and Mighty Lords the Lords States General of the United Netherlands." This assembly, called for brevity's sake " the States-General," was not a sovereign legislative and executive body. It is better described as a permanent congress of ambassadors, deputed by the provincial States to represent them in deliberations at the Hague upon common affairs, but with little power of decision save with the unanimous consent of the assemblies, which deputed them, and of the municipal councils and other ultimate repositories of sovereignty, which deputed those assemblies. Each province fixed the form of its representation to suit itself, since the voting was by provinces.[1]

The King of Spain had, when absent, been represented in the Netherlands by a " stadtholder ";[2] but, when the northern Netherlands revolted, six of the seven States forming the confederation of the United Netherlands took as their Stadtholder William of Orange-Nassau, called " the Silent," and his descendants during three generations. The seventh, Friesland, had for Stadtholder William's brother, John " the Old," and his descendants. The younger line became stadtholders of the other States as well, after the extinction of the elder line, and were the ancestors of the present royal family of the Netherlands.[3] But, although the stadtholders of the house of Orange-Nassau were of princely rank and intermarried with the royal families of Europe, they were not sovereign princes. They exercised large administrative powers and commanded the land and sea forces, but it was with delegated authority given them by each of the provincial States in domestic affairs, and by the States-General in all common and foreign affairs. The States-General and some of the provincial States

---

[1] See Professor J. F. Jameson's *Usselinx*, pp. 23–5.
[2] Dutch *Stadhouder*. The word *stad* has the force of the kindred English " stead." Thus the *stadhouder* was in the place, or stead, of the sovereign.
[3] *E.B.*, vol. xxv, p. 750.

not only claimed, but exerted, the right of suspending the stadtholdership.[1]

When war with Spain broke out afresh in 1621, a company, known as the Dutch West India Company, was formed to *Dutch West India Company formed in 1621.* regulate and protect the contraband trade already carried on by the Dutch in the American and African possessions of Spain and Portugal, and to establish colonies on both continents and their islands. Letters patent, dated on the 3rd June, 1621, were issued by the States-General to this Company, which by the terms of its charter was to be composed of five " chambers," established in Amsterdam, Zeeland, Rotterdam, the North Department (Friesland and Hoorn) and Groningen. Each chamber was to be represented on the general governing board according to the capital contributed by it. Thus Amsterdam, which contributed four-ninths of the capital, had eight directors on the board; Zeeland, which subscribed two-ninths, had four. Rotterdam was represented by two directors, though it contributed only one-ninth; while the North Department and Groningen, which each contributed one-ninth, appointed one director each. Another director was appointed by the States-General. In 1629 a ninth representative was given to Amsterdam, and the strength of the whole board was fixed at nineteen.[2] This governing board was, therefore, commonly called " The Nineteen "; and, as we shall see, it exercised a considerable influence on the early fortunes of Guiana.

The States-General granted to the *Geoctroyeerde Westindische Compagnie* for a term of twenty-four years the monopoly of *Charter and Privileges of Dutch West India Company.* Dutch trade with the whole American coast and with the African coast between the Tropic of Cancer and the Cape of Good Hope. The Company was authorized to plant colonies; and the policy of the Nineteen was to use the monopoly on the coast of Africa in order to secure the cheap and regular supply of negro labour necessary for the development of the possessions which the Company hoped to acquire in America. The general governing body was endowed with ample power to negotiate treaties

---

[1] As, for instance, after the death of William II in 1650, and of William III in 1702.
[2] *E.B.*, vol. viii, p. 735.

with native princes, to make war and peace with them, and to appoint its officials, generals and governors, under a very limited supervision by the States-General, such as approving the appointment of, and the instructions issued to, the Company's governors.   It also had power to legislate in the Company's possessions, subject to the laws of the Netherlands. The States-General undertook to secure the trading rights of the Company; to support the Company by a subvention of one million guilders (about £100,000); and in case of war to contribute sixteen vessels of 300 tons and upwards for the defence of the Company, which was, however, to bear the expense of maintaining them.   In return for these aids, the States-General claimed a share in the Company's profits, stipulated that the Company must maintain sixteen large vessels [1] and fourteen " yachts," [2] required that all the Company's officials should take an oath of allegiance to themselves as well as to the board of directors, and ordered that a duplicate of all despatches to the board should be sent to themselves.

The history of the Dutch West India Company is a chequered one.   In early days the trade was not sufficient to meet the heavy expense of the armaments raised against Spain and Portugal.   A compensation was, however, found in the plunder of Spanish and Portuguese galleons : and, in 1628, the Company's admiral, Piet Heijn, captured a vast booty in Spanish treasure-ships.   But this source of profit was dried up by the success of the Company's cruisers in destroying their enemy's trade.   Profit had therefore to be sought in the development of colonies established on the American continent.   Accordingly, in 1629, chiefly to encourage agriculture, the Company

Company issues Charter of Privileges and Exemptions.   issued a Charter of Privileges and Exemptions, which provided that any member of the Company might obtain an area of unoccupied land extending sixteen miles along the sea-coast or on one side of a navigable river, or eight miles along both banks of a navigable river, " and so far into the country as the situation of the occupiers will permit," by purchasing such area from the Indians and planting upon it a Colony of fifty persons, upwards

---

[1] *I.e.*, ships of 300 tons and upwards.
[2] *I.e.*, small craft of 50 to 100 tons or so.

of fifteen years old, within four years from the beginning of the undertaking, one-fourth part within one year. The founder of a Colony was styled a " patroon "; and, although the colonists were bound to him only by a voluntary contract for specified terms, the relations between them and the patroon during the continuance of the contract were in several important respects similar to those under the feudal system between the lord of the manor and his serfs. The patroon received his estate in perpetual inheritance; and each colonist not only paid him a fixed rent, usually in kind, but also had to share with him the increase of the stock and to use his mill. The patroon was the legal heir of all his colonists, who died intestate. He had a civil and a criminal jurisdiction within the boundaries of his estate. He could create offices, found cities, and appoint officers and magistrates.[1]

Even after the grant of the letters patent in 1621, the Company was long in organizing. The stock had first to be *Earliest* taken up. The Zeeland shareholders did not meet *Mention of* to choose the directors of the Zeeland Chamber until *Dutch Settle-* the 26th May, 1623;[2] and the governing board of *ment in* *Essequebo.* the Company first came together on the 3rd August, 1623.[3] The first volume of the minutes of the Zeeland Chamber has long been lost; but from the 4th May, 1626, to the 31st May, 1646, these minutes are preserved intact; and in them, on the 26th November, 1626, occurs what is apparently the earliest mention in extant records of any Dutch settlement in Guiana. The passage is as follows :

> " The committee on wares is authorized to make up a suitable cargo to the Amazons for the yacht [4] *Arnemuyden.*
> " *Resolved*, to send with the aforesaid yacht *Arnemuyden* 20 ripening youths, in order to land them in the Amazon, the Wiapoco,[5] or the Essequebo—wherever the folk of our Chamber may be found—for the purpose of being employed there. And each of them shall be granted two, three, or four guilders a month, according to their capacities." [6]

[1] *E.B.*, vol. xix, pp. 603–4.
[2] See the minutes of the shareholders : Hague, Rijksarchief, *West India Papers*, vol. 470.
[3] See the minutes of the Nineteen : *West India Papers*, vol. 51.
[4] See note 2, p. 8, *supra*.
[5] Now spelt Oyapock.   [6] *U.S.E.*, p. 42.

Again, in the minutes of the 10th December, 1626, we read :

> " *Resolved*, to let Jacob Canyn come home from Esse-
> quebo,[1] as he asks to do, and to fill his place with another."[2]

And two days later, on the 12th December, 1626 :

> " Johannes Beverlander is taken into the service of the
> Company for three years, to be in the river of Essequebo
> along with Jan van der Goes; and that for 21 guilders a
> month." [3]

It is more than six months before there is again in these
minutes any mention of Essequebo. Then, on the 23rd
August, 1627, it was, on the report of a committee :

> " *Resolved*, to raise the wages of Jan van der Goes in
> Essequebo, after his first three years (for which he is
> bound to the Company), to five pounds Flemish a month,
> and to send the supplies asked by him, as is set down in
> the request, together with the other necessaries, and to
> authorize him to retain five or six men out of the ship
> *Arent*, and that by next [ship] we shall send him 30 men
> and cause a fort to be made." [4]

Thereafter there is no further entry, in 1627, relating to
the Essequebo trade.

From these minutes it is reasonable to conclude, in the first
place, that the Zeeland Chamber had specially concerned itself
with trade in the Essequebo river; in the next place, it may
perhaps be conjectured that Jan van der Goes was at the
head of the first Dutch occupation of the Essequebo, and
that the occupation began in, or about, the year 1625.
This occupation was still in the nature of a trading-post rather
than a settlement, and no fort had as yet been built. The
post was under the command of an agent, who (it seems) was
without a title and had, in August, 1627, not yet completed
the third year of his service. It further appears that from
the outset the Company reserved the Essequebo to itself and

---

[1] It seems plausible to infer from this and the following passage that
Canyn was clerk of the Essequebo post, that Beverlander was sent
out to take his place, and that Jan van der Goes was in command of
the post.

[2] *U.S.E.*, p. 43.   [3] *U.S.E.*, p. 41.   [4] *U.S.E.*, p. 45.

had no mind to entrust the trade in that river to patroons :
for the Zeeland Chamber stated, in 1751, in a memorial
resulting from a search through its own records, that

> " the Colony of Essequebo from the beginning on, down
> to the year 1656 was inhabited only by such persons as
> were employés of the Zeeland Chamber, and who at that
> time were called ' colonists ' and were kept there for the
> carrying on of trade, which soon grew to such proportions
> that in some years a hundred barrels or more of annatto
> dye came over at once." [1]

Meanwhile, on the 22nd April, 1627, the Zeeland Chamber
accorded to Abraham van Pere permission to " carry men
Origin of to the number of forty, and twenty youths—in
Settlement in all, sixty individuals—as settlers over to the main-
Berbice. land (called the Wild Coast) [2] of West India, in
the river Berbice, situate at the latitude of $6\frac{1}{3}$ degrees north,"
stipulating, however, that his colonists should " not be at
liberty to come into the river Essequebo, nor into any other
river where the Company, whether of this or of other Chambers,
has its colonists or folk, whether many or few in number."
But the Berbice colonists were, subject to this proviso, expressly permitted " to build a fort in the aforesaid river, at
such convenient place as they shall think fit, to carry on
their trade with the natives of the land, to fell forests, sow,
plant, seek minerals, and, in general, to do all other things
which they shall judge good and profitable for their colony ;
also to explore other neighbouring rivers and transfer themselves thither, if they should think to find better profit there." [3]
Abraham van Pere arranged with the Chamber to establish
the Berbice settlement at his own expense ; and, having been
given entire control over it as patroon, he despatched for the
Berbice river on the 31st July, 1627, two small vessels.   On
arrival the settlers built Fort Nassau, and a regular trading-
post was established ; but it is not probable that any cultivation began.   The trade only concerned the mercantile house of
Van Pere, and therefore very little is known of it.   The post

---

[1] *Nederlandsche Jaerboeken*, 1751, p. 1097.
[2] *Wilde Custe* was the name given to the stretch of coast between the
Amazon and the Orinoco ; and is a sort of generic name for Guiana.
[3] *U.S.E.*, pp. 46–7.

must, however, have given a profit, otherwise it would have been abandoned.

On the other hand, trade in the Essequebo river did not prosper. The promised fort appears not to have been erected, and, in 1632, the Nineteen decided to give up this trading-post.[1] The colonists seem to have come home in a body, Jan van der Goes at their head. But, after conference with him, the Zeeland Chamber, in spite of the decision of the Nineteen, resolved on the 8th April, 1632, " not to abandon the colony at Essequebo ";[2] and, having thus made itself responsible for maintaining that colony, the Chamber proceeded to consider an offer of Abraham van Pere to carry on the trade to Essequebo in connexion with that to the settlement, of which he was patroon, in the Berbice river. On the 16th July, 1632, at a meeting of the Zeeland Chamber with Abraham van Pere, held at Middelburg, articles and conditions were agreed upon " regarding the trade on the Wild Coast and the continuation of his colony in the river Berbice and that of Essequebo for the Company ";[3] and in August Jan van der Goes was re-engaged, with two assistants, to take charge of the Essequebo trading-post.[4] It is not surprising to find, in view of the responsibilities thus incurred by the Zeeland Chamber and Abraham van Pere, that the Chamber, on the 29th June, 1634, instructed the deputies sent to the meeting of the Nineteen to " request, and even insist, that no colonists or other persons shall be at liberty to navigate to the Wild Coast except this Chamber and Confrater van Pere alone ";[5] and again, on the 21st May, 1635, " it was unanimously resolved that the trade to the Wild Coast shall be done by the Company alone, and by no private individuals : and this shall be brought by this Chamber before the Board of Nineteen."[6] It is probable, however, that the Nineteen rejected this request of the Zeeland Chamber for a monopoly.[7]

The Zeeland Chamber becomes responsible for Essequebo Settlement. (margin note)

[1] *Nederlandsche Jaerboeken*, 1750, p. 1494.
[2] *U.S.E.*, p. 65.   [3] *U.S.E.*, pp. 67–8.
[4] *U.S.E.*, p. 67.   [5] *U.S.E.*, p. 69.
[6] *U.S.E.*, pp. 69–70.
[7] The Zeeland Chamber itself, in its memorial of 1751 (*Nederlandsche Jaerboeken*, 1751, p. 1092), mentions the request made in 1634, and

Still the Essequebo trade—apparently mainly in annatto dye—did not succeed: and on the 16th April, 1637, the *Precarious* Chamber instructed its Committee on Commerce and *Nature of the* Finance " to inspect and determine whether the trade *Essequebo* *Trade.* to Essequebo is profitable to the Company or not, in order at an early date to make report, so as to know whether the wares, for which they ask, shall be ordered or not." [1] The report was presumably favourable, for the trade continued; and on the 30th June, 1642, there was drawn up by the Zeeland Chamber, and inserted in its minutes, a standard list of supplies to be shipped to Essequebo at each of the infrequent consignments to that colony.[2] This list throws much light on the size and aims of the post. It would seem to indicate that there were then employed in Essequebo not more than thirty men, and that their business was wholly the gathering of dyes; for the articles on the list are such as would be bartered to the Indians or used in the gathering of these products and in supplying the colonists with food. On delivering these supplies, the ship was to " take in such dye and letter-wood as at the time shall be ready " and return directly home.

Meanwhile it is interesting to note the first mention of agriculture in the Colony, and a suggestion of that industry *First Men-* which was later to be its greatest source of wealth. *tion of Sugar-* On the 14th May, 1637, " Confrater van Pere was *cane Cultiva-* *tion.* authorized to turn over two kegs of syrup, or sap of sugar-cane, arrived from Essequebo from Jan van der Goes, to Sr. Segers, in order that he may try to reduce it to sugar." [3] Not, however, until the year 1664 was the first sugar-mill established in the Colony, at Brouwershoek, on the north bank of the mingled Cuyuni and Mazaruni, near their junction with the Essequebo.[4]

The waters-meet of the Cuyuni and Mazaruni rivers is known as Cartabo Point, and to a small island off this point the

---

repeated in 1635, without claiming the acquiescence of the Nineteen, though such acquiescence would have been of the utmost value to the memorial and though its authors had access to the minutes of the Nineteen, now lost.

[1] *U.S.E.*, p. 71. [2] *U.S.E.*, pp. 100–2.
[3] *U.S.E.*, p. 72. [4] *U.S.E.*, pp. 132–3.

Dutch settlers gave, because of its commanding situation, the name Kijk-over-al (" Look over all "). Here the seat of *Seat of Government at Kijk-over-al.* government in Essequebo was established and in the proceedings of the Zeeland Chamber, on the 5th May, 1644, we find the first contemporary mention of a fort at Kijk-over-al.[1] The fort, as we saw, had been promised in 1627; and it was presumably built during the interval, although the exact date of its construction is not on record. Moreover, on the 21st February, 1639, the Chamber had granted Jan van der Goes the rank of " Commandeur,"[2] a title by which the principal officer of the Company in charge of the Essequebo settlement was thenceforth known. Here, then, are the first beginnings of the evolution of a commercial agency into an organized government.

Still, however, the Essequebo establishment was not a success, as appears from the fact that, when the charter of the *Company's Charter renewed.* Dutch West India Company, which had been granted for twenty-four years from 1621, was about to expire, and it was necessary to put its affairs in order, a committee of the Zeeland Chamber, submitting suggestions to that end, reported on the 29th May, 1645 :

> " As concerns the river of Essequebo, the committee's opinion is that now for some time it has been traded to with small profit to the Company, and for the reason that individual colonists are permitted to trade there as well as the Company, so that the goods coming from there cannot fetch their proper price. On this point they are of advice that, at the expiration of the charter, either the trade there ought to be held exclusively for the Company, or it were better that the aforesaid place should, subject to proper fees, be thrown open to free trade."[3]

Neither alternative seems to have been adopted; but the Company's charter was renewed for a period of twenty-five years from the 1st January, 1647.

In the following year by the Treaty of Münster, signed on the 30th January, 1648, the independence of the Netherlands *The Treaty of Münster.* was finally recognised. The treaty also provided that navigation and trade to the East and West Indies should be maintained pursuant to, and in con-

---

[1] *U.S.E.*, p. 102.   [2] *U.S.E.*, pp. 96–7.   [3] *U.S.E.*, p. 104.

formity with, the charters granted, or to be granted, in that behalf : while the King of Spain and the States-General were respectively to remain in possession and enjoyment of such lordships, towns, castles, fortresses, commerce and country in the East and West Indies, in Brazil, and on the coasts of Asia, Africa and America as they then respectively held in possession.   Thus the Dutch tenure of the Berbice river with Fort Nassau, and of the Essequebo river with Fort Kijk-over-al was definitely regularized.   Hitherto these colonies had, at all events from the Spanish point of view, been rebellious attempts to establish trading-posts in " the land of Guiana situate in the Kingdom of Peru." [1]   Now, however, Berbice and Essequebo were formally recognized by Spain and by the world at large as Dutch possessions; and from this point onwards it will be convenient to describe separately the development of the two settlements until their amalgamation, in 1831, into a single colony.

[1] " Het Landt van Guiana gelegen in het Coninckryck van Peru," *U.S.E.*, pp. 11–12.

CHAPTER II

SETTLEMENT IN POMEROON AND ITS DESTRUCTION ; AND GROWTH
OF ESSEQUEBO FROM THE TREATY OF MÜNSTER TO THE
RISE OF DEMERARA (1648–1746)

THE conclusion of a lasting peace with Spain and the renewal
for a quarter of a century of the charter of the Dutch West
Arrival of India Company might have been expected to result
First Free in rapid colonial development. But the Company
Colonists in was now deprived of the privateering, which had been
Essequebo. its chief source of revenue, and incurred heavy loss from the
long and fruitless struggle for Brazil. Nothing, therefore, was
done to assist Essequebo until, in 1655, the hopelessness of
the recovery of Brazil having become apparent even to the
Company itself, the Zeeland Chamber threw open the Guiana
coast to colonization, on condition that the colonists should
draw all their supplies and wares from Zeeland and ship
thither their cargoes. Then, on the 12th October, 1656, the
Chamber issued a provisional prospectus inviting settlement of
the " Wild Coast," [1] " under the sovereignty of the States-
General and the authority of the West India Company," upon
tempting conditions ; [2] and in the following year was prepared
a new body of " liberties and exemptions offered by the West
India Company (Zeeland Chamber) to patroons of colonies in
Guiana." [3] As a result, " on the 22nd March, 1657, the first
free colonists, to the number of twelve persons, some with,
and some without, family, wife, children and slaves, arrived "
in Essequebo.[4]

The Zeeland Chamber, however, being reluctant itself to
assume direction of the enterprise, entered into a contract,

---

[1] The connotation of the words *Wilde Custe* had now shrunk to mean
Essequebo only : cf. *U.S.E.*, p. 127, *Wilde Custe ofte Isekepe* (" Wild
Coast, otherwise Essequebo ").
[2] *U.S.E.*, pp. 113–17.   [3] *U.S.E.*, pp. 120–3.
[4] *Nederlandsche Jaerboeken*, 1751, p. 1093.

on the 24th December, 1657, with the Burgomasters and Rulers of the three great trading towns of Zeeland, namely, the Walcheren cities—Middelburg, Vlissingen and Vere— "to establish and plant colonies, on the continental Wild Coast between the first and the tenth degrees " of north latitude : while, subject to the supremacy of the States-General and to the Company, " in so far as the latter is by charter entitled thereto," the contract conceded to these three cities " high, middle and low jurisdiction, in order the better to maintain the necessary authority over their subordinates." [1]   The cities thereupon appointed a managing committee, which consisted of two representatives from Middelburg and one each from Vlissingen and Vere, with four directors of the Zeeland Chamber of the West India Company.[2]   They re-christened the Wild Coast " Nova Zeelandia," drafted instructions for a " director " and a " commissary " of the settlement, and, on the 2nd February, 1658, despatched the ship *Joannes* from Vlissingen to " Nova Zeelandia." [3]   This new settlement was not, however, established in the Essequebo, but in its neighbouring river to the westward, the Pomeroon, and in an adjoining stream, the Moruka.

Colonization under Direction of Three Walcheren Cities.

On the Pomeroon was expended most of the energy of this new effort at colonization : but the means of the three cities were unequal to the task.   As early as 1660, Vere was unable to pay its stipulated share of the cost; and before the end of 1663 the managing committee in Zeeland had become so embarrassed that it broke up altogether.[4]   Nevertheless, during the brief six years which the settlement lived, colonists poured in and negro slaves were liberally supplied, so that Lieut.-General Byam, a contemporary governor of the neighbouring British colony of Surinam, wrote in his " exact narrative of the State of Guiana as it stood Anno 1665 " [5] that " there, greatest of all they [the

Settlement in the Pomeroon River.

---

[1] *U.S.E.*, p. 125. [2] *U.S.E.*, p. 126.
[3] *U.S.E.*, p. 128. [4] *U.S.E.*, p. 179.
[5] The British Museum manuscript known as "Sloane MS. 3662 " (more fully, " 3662 Plut. cii. G ") contains Major John Scott's draft of his " Description of Guiana," and also, at fol. 27 *sqq*. Byam's narrative.   The handwriting is the same throughout.   Surinam, now a Dutch colony, was given to the Dutch by England in exchange for New York in 1674.

Dutch] ever had in America, was Bowroom [1] and Moroco,[2] alias
New Zealand,[3] a most flourishing colony, 16 leagues leeward
of Discecabe." [4] The Essequebo, however, was not abandoned. There, still at Kijk-over-al, was stationed the Commandeur of the entire Colony, of which Pomeroon was only a
district; and the erection of a sugar-mill at Brouwershoek,
in 1664,[5] points to the growth of agriculture in the Essequebo
valley.

But disaster was at hand. The two maritime states,
England and Holland, though eyeing France distrustfully, had
Destruction of greater and growing grudges against each other.
Pomeroon and The true cause was doubtless commercial jealousy,
Essequebo
Settlements. and the conflict sprang immediately from collisions
between trading companies. In October, 1663, a British
squadron was sent to attack the Dutch in West Africa and
in America; and war was formally declared in February,
1665. The Dutch claimed the support of France in virtue of
a defensive treaty made in 1662. Louis XIV allowed the
claim, but unwillingly; and the still young navy of France
gave little help in the wholly maritime warfare which ensued.
One of the minor operations of this war was an attack, made
in the winter of 1665, by Major John Scott, at the head of a
British force from Barbados, upon the Pomeroon Colony,
which was captured and its little fort destroyed. Major Scott
then went up the Essequebo river, seized Fort Kijk-over-al,
and, leaving small garrisons both in Pomeroon and Essequebo,
returned to Barbados in April, 1666. But the Indians refused
the English all supplies; and the starving garrisons, after being
harassed and shut up in their forts by the French, who came
to the help of their Dutch allies, surrendered within a few
months to Matthijs Bergenaar, Commandeur of Berbice.[6]
Thus " Essequebo and Pomeroon, first taken by the English,
then plundered by the French " and thereafter " by the whole
world abandoned "—to use the phrases of the Zeeland States
themselves—passed again into Dutch hands.[7]

The Peace of Breda, signed on the 31st July, 1667, left the

[1] Pomeroon.   [2] Moruka.   [3] Nova Zeelandia.
[4] Essequebo. And see *U.S.E.*, p. 137.   [5] See above, p. 13.
[6] *U.S.E.*, p. 179.
[7] *Nederlandsche Jaerboeken*, 1750, pp. 1496–1501; and 1751, pp.
1102–3.

United Provinces in possession of all settlements in Guiana
occupied by them before the war: but the Pomeroon Colony,
Zeeland
Chamber   destroyed in its infancy, remained unpeopled
again   for a score of years.   The Commandeur of Berbice
becomes re-   would have liked to retain both the Pomeroon and
sponsible for
Colony of   the Essequebo settlements as his capture.   But the
Essequebo.   provincial authorities of Zeeland ignored his claim
and took charge of both settlements " as *res nullius*," till
they could find an owner who would meet the cost of the
expeditionary force sent by the Province, with the approval
of the States-General, to re-occupy the Colony.   Late in 1668,
the Province offered Pomeroon and Essequebo to the three
Walcheren cities : but these, dismayed at the expense of a
fresh beginning, would have no more of them and thought of
selling the Colony.   There was only the West India Company
to fall back on.   That Company was slow to come to terms;
but, on the 11th April, 1670, its Zeeland Chamber concluded
with the States of Zeeland a compromise, by which it should
again receive " the Fort and the Colony of Essequebo," on
condition of paying the cost of the garrison, which had occupied
it, and of undertaking that " the Colony of Essequebo "
should henceforward be open to all Zeelanders, " excepting
that the trade in annatto dye shall be carried on by the
aforesaid Chamber alone " :   and on the 15th October, 1670,
the States-General sanctioned the transfer upon these
conditions.[1]

This agreement being concluded, the Chamber appointed
Hendrick Rol,[2] a good skipper and trader, to be Commandeur
Hendrick Rol   at Kijk-over-al, where he arrived at the close of 1670
appointed   with a secretary and six other servants of the
Commandeur.   Company.   As Commandeur, Rol was governor of
the little settlement, captain over the few soldiers, storekeeper, and, last but not least, Indian trader.   It may here
be noted that the Commandeurs with the assistance of a
secretary and of one clerk (first appointed in 1672) did all
administrative work for nearly a century.   At the commencement of Rol's administration there were but three plantations
in Essequebo, two of them worked by some twelve or fourteen

[1] *Nederlandsche Jaerboeken*, 1750, pp. 1501–8.
[2] *U.S.E.*, p. 138.

slaves apiece, and the third, lying an hour above Kijk-over-al (probably on the Mazaruni), by twenty-eight or thirty. But it is not unlikely that the virtual abandonment of the Pomeroon was advantageous to Essequebo. The former settlement had been well supplied with slaves, and 1,200 of these, seized by the English, were turned over by them to Essequebo at their surrender, and were doubtless put to good use in cleaning the land and laying it out for sugar-cane cultivation. The garrison of Kijk-over-al was now strengthened, and the prospects of the settlement brightened.

In 1671 a dispute took place between the settlers in Essequebo and Berbice as to the right of trading in the Demerara river; and it was amicably decided by an agreement that the Abary creek should be the boundary between the two colonies. For some fifteen years previously the Berbice authorities appear to have had in the Demerara river a trading-post of fifteen or sixteen men; but the control of this post now passed to Rol, and we find him in 1673, if not earlier, trafficking also in the Barima and just opening a trade with the Orinoco.[1]

Boundary settled between Colonies of Berbice and Essequebo.

However, in 1672, King Charles II, in pursuit of a policy arranged between himself and his cousin, Louis XIV, had declared war on the Netherlands, the avowed object of the two monarchs being the partition of Holland. Spain became involved in the war; and for a time all colonies in the West Indies were in jeopardy, England and France being pitted against the United Provinces and Spain. Fortunately for Essequebo and Berbice, they were not worth plundering; but, when on the 19th February, 1674, peace was signed between England and the United Provinces, the Dutch West India Company had become hopelessly insolvent and was obliged to go into liquidation. Its debts were taken over by a new company, to which the States-General granted a charter on the 20th September, 1674, under the same name, but with territorial limits widely different. Instead of the entire coast of America, there were granted to the new West India Company on that continent " the places of Essequebo and Pomeroon " only. The directorate of the new Company

West India Company reorganized in 1674.

[1] *U.S.E.*, p. 140.

now became known as " the Ten," being composed of four
directors from Amsterdam, two from Zeeland, and one each
from the Maas, South Holland and North Holland, with a
president appointed by the States-General. The constitution
of the different Chambers remained as before, and again the
Chamber of Zeeland took upon itself the entire control of the
trade to Essequebo.

Having received its charter, the new West India Company
drew up a document known as the Articled Letter,[1] which
The Com- was confirmed by the States-General on the 12th
pany's April, 1675, and which, although more comparable
Articled
Letter. to ships' articles than to a code of laws, is interesting as containing the regulations under which the Commandeur
governed. It provided that all servants of the Company
should be engaged for four years; that none of them, whatever their position, should be allowed to carry on any private
trade or business; and that no one should be entitled to claim
an increase of salary during the term of his engagement, not
even for extra services. No person was allowed to have or
use cards or dice. For curses, oaths, blasphemy or mockery
a fine was imposed; and anyone absent from morning and
evening prayers without sufficient cause was also liable to a
fine. Some of the attempts " to make the punishment fit
the crime " are curious. Thus it was provided that " whoever shall draw a knife with intent to stab another shall be
fastened by the knife through his hand to the mast and left
to free himself. Whoever shall wound another shall be keel-
hauled and lose a month's wages. If anyone shall murder
another, he shall be tied to the corpse and with it thrown
overboard, and all his wages and prize-money shall be forfeited." Wages and prize-money depended on a ship getting
home safely; and it was shrewdly laid down that, " if the
vessel is destroyed in an action with the enemy, wages will
be paid; but if it is captured, the servants will lose everything." [2]

Hendrick Rol died at Kijk-over-al on the 31st March, 1676;

---

[1] Articul-Brief van de Geoctroyeerde West Indische Compagnie;
S'Gravenhague, 1675.

[2] The quotations are taken from " a free translation of the substance
of the Articled Letter " in Rodway, vol. i, pp. 23–8.

and as his successor the Ten appointed on the 25th July, 1678, Abraham Beekman, giving him a proper commission *Commission and Instructions given to Commandeur.* and full instructions for his guidance. The commission [1] appointed Beekman to be " Commandeur and Governor over the fort of Kijk-over-al, situated in the River of Isekepe [2] on the Great Wild Coast of America, also to command the sailors and soldiers on that coast who are in the service of the said Company." The instructions [3] required the Commandeur on his arrival in Essequebo to " make all the Company's servants take anew the proper oath, in the name and on behalf of Their High Mightinesses the States-General, the Prince of Orange, and the West India Company." He was directed to " keep all his subordinates in good order and under discipline, and exact from them the punctual fulfilment of the contents of the Charter, and punish all those who disobey the Articled Letter, and other orders, instructions and ordinances, made or yet to be made." " In matters concerning justice," he was " bound to assume as his councillors the Sergeant of the garrison and the Captains of vessels," which might be present at the time; and he was instructed not to " administer justice but with the aforesaid Council, and in their presence," it being understood, however, that cases involving capital punishment should always be referred to the high authorities in the Netherlands, for them to judge and award such punishment as might be suited to the case. Moreover, the Commandeur was " earnestly recommended to take care that the religion adopted by the public authorities in these territories be maintained as far as possible in its usual form, at the fort and in the ships, and that the inhabitants of the country, as well as their children, are brought through a holy life into the knowledge of God and the true reformed religion." Throughout the instructions there is no mention of " free colonists," as distinguished from the Company's servants; and it is therefore probable that the former were as yet few in number and of little importance in the Colony.

Unlike his predecessor, the new Commandeur was not a skipper. In fact, he may be regarded as the first Governor

---

[1] Rodway, vol. i, pp. 34–5.   [2] Essequebo.
[3] Rodway, vol. i, pp. 32–4.

de carrière of the Essequebo colony; but his chief occupation was doubtless that of manager of the Company's estates,
Revival of the Pomeroon Settlement. which were now four in number—namely, " Vryheid " on the site of Bartika Grove, " Duynenburg " and " Fortuin " south of Kalacoon, and " Poelwijk " on Caria Island. The provision grounds were at Cartabo. Thus the whole Colony still clustered for safety near Fort Kijk-over-al. The Pomeroon settlement had disappeared; but the Commandeur, thinking that the region " promised some profit," sent thither in August, 1679, one of his soldiers to barter for annatto dye.[1] The soldier was temporarily recalled because of a raid of the Caribs; " but the scare being now over," writes Beekman to the Company on the 20th October, 1679, in the earliest extant letter from Essequebo,

> " I shall send him back there within four or five weeks; . . . and, if the trade prospers, it would not be a bad idea to build there a hut for two or three men, so that they may dwell permanently among the Indians and occupy that river. Thus these would be stimulated to furnish a deal of annatto—for the place is too far off for them to bring it here to the fort. In that event, you ought to send me more men from the fatherland." [2]

This post, which was speedily established, is often mentioned in the letters of the next few years. The annatto trade flourished there; but in 1686 the Company found a better use for the Pomeroon. An Essequebo planter on a visit to Holland—one Jacob Peterzoon de Jonge—persuaded the Directors to open the Pomeroon river to himself and other settlers. After satisfying themselves that the Walcheren cities and the States of Zeeland no longer had any valid claim there, the Ten granted the petition, created the new settlement into an independent colony, and appointed De Jonge to be its Commandeur. De Jonge arrived in Pomeroon and began operations in April 1686. Colonists followed, and the settlement was in a hopeful way, when again a European
Pomeroon Settlement again destroyed by War. war—that of the League of Augsburg—proved fatal. On the 30th April, 1689, just three years after the Colony's birth, the French, guided by Caribs through the water passage leading from the Barima,

[1] *U.S.E.*, p. 144.   [2] *U.S.E.*, p. 145.

and reinforced by those savages, fell upon the settlement in the night and utterly dispersed it.[1]   No attempt to re-establish the Pomeroon Colony was ever made.   The Ten, on receiving news of the disaster, instructed the Essequebo Commandeur on the 15th November, 1689, to leave there the Company's flag, with a post of three men, in order to retain possession. The post was established and maintained; but the Pomeroon was not again thrown open to settlement until the very last years of Dutch occupation, and it remained subject to the Essequebo Commandeur.[2]

The War of the League of Augsburg, in which France without a single ally faced England and Holland, not only

War of the League of Augsburg. united under the same chief, but supported by a coalition of half Europe, continued until exhaustion compelled Louis XIV to sign the Peace of Ryswick in 1697.   But the Essequebo Colony seems to have escaped attack, and its territorial growth continued slowly and without interruption.   During the war, on the 9th December, 1690, Samuel Beekman, one of the principal planters of Essequebo, was appointed by the Ten to succeed Abraham Beekman as Commandeur.   By this time the Company's plantations had become important enough each to require a

Origin of Essequebo Council. manager; and these managers, with the Commandeur and Secretary, formed a Council (Raad), which sat occasionally as a Court of Justice, or to consider the Company's affairs.   The " free planters " had no voice in these matters and did not attend the Council meetings, in which nevertheless is to be found the origin of the subsequent Court of Policy.   In the first muster-roll preserved in the colonial records, and dated the 6th September, 1691,[3] it is stated that the list of " those in Rio Essequebo in the Company's service " numbered at that date only forty-three men, and included therein are the men stationed in the two subsidiary trading-posts in the Pomeroon and the Demerara

Essequebo Muster-rolls. rivers.   The next muster-roll sent by Samuel Beekman to the West India Company in his letter of the 17th July, 1701, included two additional trading-posts in the

---

[1] *U.S.E.*, pp. 174, 181, 188; Blue Book, "Venezuela No. 3," 1896, pp. 60–6.

[2] *U.S.E.*, pp. 190–2.   [3] *U.S.E.*, pp. 192–3.

Mahaicony and Wacupo creeks, and gave the total European population of the Colony, including the " free settlers," as 67.[1] By 1703 there had been added a post in the Cuyuni " up in the savannah, six weeks by boat " from Kijk-over-al.[2]

Meanwhile it is interesting to note that, after the Peace of Ryswick, the Ten resolved on the 10th September, 1698, to *Head-tax and* impose an annual head-tax of $2\frac{1}{2}$ guilders (4s. 2d. *Acreage Tax.* or \$1·00) for each slave, and to levy annually one stiver (one penny) *per* acre on the private plantations. The former tax, being confirmed by the States-General, was collected annually under the name of the Company's (or later the King's) taxes up to the time of the abolition of slavery; but, for some reason which does not appear, the acreage tax was not enforced. It is perhaps allowable to conjecture that the Company, being in control of the supply of slaves, could insist upon payment of head-tax, whereas the passive resistance of the free planters to an acreage tax was difficult to overcome. Thus taxation was at first imposed in Essequebo without any representation. The number of free planters at this time was about thirty, and their slaves would amount to some eight or nine hundred, while the expenses of the Colony to the Company were 872 guilders (£72 13s. 4d. or \$348.80) *per mensem*, besides the cost of rations. These figures show that the head-tax did not go far towards paying the colonial expenditure, which was provided for by the profit on Indian trading and on the produce of the Company's plantations.

Samuel Beekman died at Kijk-over-al on the 10th December, 1707; and here may be noted the origin of the custom that the Secretary should provisionally succeed the Commandeur at his death, or act for him in his absence. Samuel Beekman, just before his death, called the members of Council to his bedside and desired them to acknowledge the Secretary, Pieter van der Heyden Resen, as his successor. This they did; and on the 4th October, 1710, the Ten confirmed him in office.[3] But the

---

[1] *U.S.E.*, p. 199.   [2] *U.S.E.*, p. 206.

[3] This procedure was formally adopted for future cases by a resolution of the Ten, dated 12th April, 1721, which authorized the Secretary to assume command at once, in case of death or any accident to the Commandeur, in order to prevent confusion or possible discord.

new Commandeur was not fortunate in the circumstances under which he took up his duties. The War of the *War of the Spanish Succession: Essequebo plundered.* Spanish Succession had broken out in 1702, and once more England and Holland were allied against France. Hostilities continued during eleven years, and the disaster which destroyed Pomeroon in 1689 now befell Essequebo. In the autumn of 1708, a French privateer leader, Captain Antoine Ferry, pillaged the Essequebo settlements and attacked Kijk-over-al, which was obliged to surrender. The settlers and the Company had to pay a heavy ransom. Then, in the following February, two more French privateers came up the river and plundered the plantations. After their departure only two sugar-mills remained in the whole Colony, and most of the private planters were ruined.

The Peace of Utrecht was not signed until the 14th April, 1713; but, even during the last years of the war, Essequebo *Recovery of Colony after Peace of Utrecht.* had been recovering; and from 1713 to 1715 the profits of the Company on the trade with the Colony averaged 17,000 guilders annually. There remained, however, a feeling of insecurity; and from this time begins the agitation which led to the transfer of the fort, in 1743, to Flag Island, a point nearer the mouth of the river. It was in any case clear that the islet on which Fort Kijk-over-al stood was much too small to accommodate the steadily increasing number of the Company's soldiers and servants; so, in 1716, the Commandeur was given permission to build a Colony House on the mainland just opposite Kijk-over-al, on the Mazaruni side of the point formed by the junction of that river with the Cuyuni. This house went by the name of Huis Nabij,[1] and the hamlet which gathered about it was called Cartabo, from the plantation occupying the point. Kijk-over-al was now left to the garrison, while the Commandeur and the civil servants lived at Cartabo Point, one of the rooms of the Huis Nabij being used as a council chamber and church, while the lower floor was utilized as the Company's store.

In 1718 the constitution of the Essequebo Council was altered, and its designation was changed to " Raad van

---

[1] *Anglice* " house near-by ".

Politie en Justitie " (Council of Policy and Justice).   It was still a single Council, and was composed of the Commandeur, the Secretary and two managers of the Company's plantations, meeting once a quarter.[1]   The private planters, whose number had fallen to fifteen, were not represented.   The ultimate authority, however, still vested in the Ten and in the Directors of the Zeeland Chamber, the Company being absolute and sending out instructions, which the Commandeur was bound to enforce, on the most petty matters.

The Council of Policy and Justice.

Van der Heyden was succeeded by Laurens de Heere, who was appointed Commandeur on the 5th April, 1721.   The new administrator was well acquainted with Essequebo, and knew that the land near the mouth of the river was more fertile than that in the neighbourhood of Kijk-over-al, where the soil was already becoming exhausted.   Accordingly he laid out a new Company's plantation, which he named " Pelgrim," at the mouth of the Bonasika Creek, near Flag Island, thus taking the first step in the slow, but general, migration towards the coast.   This steady migration continued under Hermanus Gelskerke, who succeeded De Heere as Commandeur on the 9th March, 1729. Its significance is twofold.   It determined that the future of the Colony should depend on sugar cultivation, for which the coast-lands are particularly suitable; while at the same time, there being no natural drainage on the coastal flats, as there had been among the low hillocks around Kijk-over-al, canals had to be dug to drain the plantations.   Work such as this could not be undertaken by poor settlers with only a few slaves each.   Thus the migration to the coast laid the foundation of the wealthy plantocracy which ultimately, after a long struggle, overthrew the Company.

Migration to the Coast begins.

The work of removing the fort from Kijk-over-al to Flag Island was now seriously commenced; and, in 1733, Gelskerke reported to the Directors that the new structure, although not yet finished, was able to defend itself. It was finally completed in 1739, and named Fort

Seat of Government moved to Fort Island.

[1] The minutes of the Council of Justice, as far as they have been preserved in the colonial records, open on the 12th July, 1735.   The minutes of the Council of Policy open on the 5th July, 1744.   The meetings were held early in January, April, July and October.

Zeelandia. The seat of government was then removed from Huis Nabij to Flag Island, thereafter known as Fort Island; and the first meeting of the Council in Fort Zeelandia took place on the 5th October, 1739. In completing this fort Gelskerke had the energetic help of Laurens Storm van 's Gravesande, who had arrived in the Colony as its Secretary in 1738.

The year following the new Secretary's arrival was marked by an important change in the constitution. At a meeting *Free Planters* of the Council held on the 2nd January, 1739, *given Representation in* there being present the Commandeur, the Secre-*the Council.* tary, and two managers of Company's plantations —namely, Cornelis Boter and Jacobus van Roden—a communication from the Directors was read ordering that the number of Councillors should be increased from four to six, one of the two additional members to be a free planter. Gelskerke, then, on the part of the Company, chose Johan Hendrick Muncx, a servant of the Company, and, at the request of the other Councillors, nominated two free planters, from whom the Council chose Abraham Philipus Heraut to be the first representative in the Council of such colonists as were not servants of the Company.

It had always been considered a matter of course that all citizens, or burghers as they were called, would do their best *Origin of* to protect the Colony against internal enemies, such *College of* as Indians and revolted slaves, and even, if neces-*Kiezers.* sary, defend it against privateers. From an early date a burgher militia system, on the lines of that of Holland, appears to have been in existence : and, when the seat of government was moved to Fort Island, an attempt was made to improve that system. Essequebo was divided into two districts, the upper one being centred at Kijk-over-al and the lower at Fort Zeelandia. A burgher company was enrolled for each district; and every new settler, whatever his nationality, was required to take the oath of allegiance, on which he became entitled to the rights and privileges of a citizen, and was assigned to one or other of the district companies. The companies in each district were commanded by a captain, a lieutenant and an ensign, these officers performing the duties of justices of the peace and even constables, as well as being the medium of communication between the settlers and the Government. At first these officers appear to have been elected by the burghers, but afterwards they were nominated by the Commandeur and his Council. The six Burgher Officers met together occasionally, forming a Court Martial for the trial of offences and to discuss matters of importance; and, in 1743, Gravesande, who had in the previous year succeeded Gelskerke as Commandeur, formed these six Burgher Officers into a College of Kiezers (electors) for the purpose of nominating the representatives of the free planters in the Council. Their first nomination was made in the same year, when the membership of the Council was increased to seven, of whom two were now representatives of such colonists as were not servants of the Company.

CHAPTER III

(a) *From the Rise of Demerara to the Fall of the Dutch West India Company* (1746–91)

THE first Dutch traders in the Demerara river appear to have come from Berbice; but as early as 1671 it was, we have seen, *The Rise of* agreed that the Abary Creek should be the boundary *Demerara.* between the colonies of Berbice and Essequebo, and that the control of trade in the Demerara river should therefore vest in the Commandeur at Kijk-over-al. Not, however, until the 3rd April, 1746, were the first concessions of land on the banks of the Demerara river granted by the Essequebo Council of Policy. Progress then was rapid, for on the 10th July in the same year, Gravesande wrote : " In Rio Demerara lands have already been allotted for eighteen sugar plantations, as well as for a few small ones." [1] Two years later, on the 2nd December, 1748, he reported that " the success, far beyond all expectations, of Demerara, its crop of sugar, for the abundance of which God be praised, and the reasonable price thereof, afford very good hope of the flourishing growth of that Colony " ; [2] and he indicated that the time had come when it was necessary to appoint someone to administer the affairs of this new district. In that year a " brandwagt," or guard-house, was built on the site of what is now Stabroek market, near the mouth of the Demerara river; and on the 15th August, 1750, the Directors of the Zeeland Chamber appointed Gravesande's own son, Jonathan Samuel, to be the first Commandeur of Demerara, and the father himself to be Directeur-General of the Two Rivers. These appointments were duly confirmed by the Ten and afterwards by the Stadt-

---

[1] Gravesande, vol. i, p. 218.
[2] *Ibid.*, p. 237.

holder, as Governor and Chief Director of the Dutch West
India Company.

In the same year it was further arranged that the Council of
Policy should consist of the Directeur-General, the Commandeur
Council of of Demerara, the Secretary, the Captain of the
Policy separ- Troops, and three managers of the Company's
ated from
Council of plantations in Essequebo : and that the members of
Justice. the Council of Justice, which was now separated from
the Council of Policy, should be the Directeur-General, the Commandeur of Demerara, the Secretary, the Captain of the Troops,
three managers of the Company's plantations in Essequebo,
and two free planters chosen by the Essequebo College of
Kiezers. Thus the principle of representation of colonists,
other than those who were servants of the Company, was
admitted with respect to the Council of Justice, but not in the
Council of Policy, which was still mainly concerned with the
administration of the Company's property.

From this time onwards the story of Essequebo merges in
that of Demerara, which soon became the more important of
Origin of the two. Indeed, we already find Gravesande
British Settle- writing on the 31st August, 1752 : " that Colony
ment in the
Two Rivers. [Demerara] will begin to hold up its head and will
in a short time, I think, surpass this " [Essequebo].[1] Such
rapid development must in part be attributed to the fact that
both rivers had been opened to all nations, with ten years'
exemption from head-tax for everyone who took up a new
plantation. A fair number of settlers from Barbados, Antigua
and other West Indian islands were thus attracted ; and in
this connexion it is interesting to note the origin of British
settlement in the Two Rivers. On the 2nd October, 1743,
Gravesande had reported that there were then seven English
plantations in Essequebo ;[2] and, with the rise of Demerara,
plantations were soon occupied by Englishmen in that river,
notably by Gedney Clarke of Barbados, who appears, in 1752,
to have erected two sugar-mills in Demerara.[3] A year later
Gravesande reported in a letter, dated the 14th April, 1753,
that of the inhabitants of Demerara " by far the greater number
consisted of English or of those understanding the English
language," and that he had granted a request from them to

[1] Gravesande, vol. i, p. 286.   [2] *Ibid.*, p. 204.   [3] *Ibid.*, p. 281.

hold divine service in their mother tongue.[1] Later on, from a register compiled and forwarded to the Company by Gravesande on the 9th January, 1762, it appears that Essequebo then had sixty-eight plantations, eight of which were owned by Englishmen, while Demerara in the same year had ninety-three plantations, of which no fewer than thirty-four —over one-third—were owned by Englishmen.[2] Moreover, it is probable that many of the Dutch plantations in Demerara were either not occupied or left in the hands of English attorneys; for Gravesande had written on the 17th December, 1760, that the English were in the majority there.[3] To this immigration of English planters the subsequent cession of the colonies of Essequebo and Demerara to the British Crown must, no doubt, be mainly ascribed.[4]

Encouraged by the success which attended the experiment of throwing Essequebo open to all nations, the Ten resolved on the 11th August, 1750, to invite all the Chambers to participate in the trade with the Two Rivers, thus re-affirming a resolution to allow free trade with Essequebo to all the Dutch provinces, passed in 1685, and left a dead letter, partly because the Zeeland Chamber opposed it, but principally on account of the pettiness of the trade. There had always been rivalry between the Chambers of Amsterdam and of Zeeland; and the latter claimed that, when in 1632 the Nineteen proposed to abandon Essequebo, the Zeeland Chamber had resolved to continue the Colony at its own cost; that this resolve had been carried out until, in 1657, finding the Colony too heavy a charge, the Chamber had transferred Essequebo to the patronage of the three Walcheren cities, by whom the Colony was, in 1669, handed over to the States of Zeeland, who in their turn restored it to the Zeeland Chamber in 1670; and that the development of the Two Rivers was entirely due to the Chamber's care and attention. On the other hand, the Ten claimed that under the Company's charter no particular Chamber could have a monopoly apart from the other Chambers; that they, the Ten, had always held the supreme power and exercised the right of commissioning the Commandeur

Dispute between the Zeeland Chamber and the Ten.

---

[1] Gravesande, vol. i, p. 292.   [2] *Ibid.*, vol. ii, pp. 398–400.
[3] *Ibid.*, p. 379.   [4] Netscher, p. 115.

and the Directeur-General, only allowing the Zeeland Chamber
to manage the Colony as their vicegerents; and that the
arrangement of 1670 had been annulled by virtue of the reconstruction of the Company and by the new charter, granted in
1675, and renewed in 1700 and from time to time thereafter.

The Zeeland Chamber, as claimant of the monopoly, appealed
to the States-General in a memorial dated the 30th September,
Arbitration by 1750; and the dispute dragged on wearily for twenty
the Stadt- years, until the States-General finally resolved, on
holder. the 17th August, 1770, to submit it to the arbitration
of the Stadtholder, who gave his decision on the 15th October
following. His Highness ruled that no monopoly of trade
and navigation in the Two Rivers could belong to any one
Chamber of the Company to the exclusion of the others, unless
a law to that effect had been passed by the States-General :
and, as no such law existed, he decided that every inhabitant
of the Dutch Republic was entitled to trade in the Essequebo
and Demerara rivers, free and unhindered, without first seeking
the permission of the Zeeland Chamber; but that nevertheless
the Zeeland Chamber, on account of its interest in the Colony,
ought to have a reasonable share of the trade assured to it;
and that, therefore, the Company might not grant permits for
such trade until the Zeeland Chamber had, in the spring of
each year, despatched sixteen vessels to the Colony. This
decision was accepted by both parties; and thenceforth the
monopoly, claimed by the Zeeland Chamber, became a
preferent right only.

Meanwhile, in 1753, the seat of government for Demerara,
to which the burgher militia system was extended, had been
Alterations in established in Borsselen Island; and the Council of
Administra- Essequebo resolved on the 3rd July, 1753, that the
tive System of Commandeur with two Burgher Officers should be
the Two
Rivers. empowered to try petty offences in Demerara. A
further step was taken in 1766, when the settlements had
become so numerous that the Demerara river was divided, as
the Essequebo river had already been divided, into two districts,
the East bank and the West bank, with one company of
burgher militia for each district and three Burgher Officers in
each company. These six officers, with the Commandeur as
president, were, by a resolution of the Essequebo Council,

D

dated the 6th October, 1766, constituted a Council of Justice
for Demerara. In the absence of the Commandeur, one of the
Essequebo Councillors was to preside; and if none of these
could attend the meetings, the senior Burgher Captain took the
chair. Meetings were held at Borsselen on the first Mondays
in March, June, September and December; and all civil
disputes, when the amount in question did not exceed 150
guilders, as well as all criminal matters, could be decided by the
Demerara Council, subject to a right of appeal to the Essequebo
Council of Justice, which was itself reconstituted, in 1767, by
substituting for the three managers of the Company's plantations in Essequebo, two free planters, chosen by the six
Burgher Officers in Demerara, who formed a College of Kiezers
for that purpose on the model of that already existing in
Essequebo. In the same year, 1767, the Chamber of Zeeland
decided that only the senior manager of the Company's plantations in Essequebo should have a seat in the Council of Policy,
the other two being replaced by burghers, one from each river,
nominated by the respective Colleges of Kiezers. Thus the
first representatives of the burghery were admitted into the
Council of Policy, which, instead of being exclusively concerned
with the executive control of the Company's affairs, now
became a legislative and executive body for the whole Colony,
while the Councils of Justice confined themselves to the functions of a civil and criminal court. None of the Councillors
received any remuneration for their services; but when those
from Demerara went to Fort Island, they were entitled to free
board and lodging during the session.

On the 27th November, 1772, George Hendrick Trotz, a
planter and Councillor of Essequebo, succeeded Gravesande as
Further Re- Directeur-General of the Two Rivers, while on the
organization same day Paulus van Schuylenburg became Com-
of the Admini-
stration by the mandeur of Demerara. The dispute between the
Ten. Ten and the Zeeland Chamber had now been settled;
and the former took advantage of the simultaneous change in
the holders of the two highest posts in the Colony to effect a
thorough re-organization of the administrative system and to
issue detailed instructions for all officials in Essequebo, from
the highest to the lowest. In the first place, the Ten declared
that the supreme control of the Colony was in their hands, and

that the Zeeland Chamber had no greater rights in respect of the Two Rivers than any other Chamber. This declaration was confirmed by the States-General and notified to the Zeeland Chamber on the 17th March, 1773, when the Directors of that Chamber were informed that they would be allowed to superintend the Colony in the name of the Company, but that the Ten reserved their right to general supervision. In the next place, the Ten created four new posts in the Colony—namely, Fiscal, Vendue-Master, Captain Commandant, and Predicant.

The necessity for a legal functionary had long been felt in Essequebo and Demerara, where the duties of public prosecutor had hitherto been divided between the Commandeurs and the Secretaries; and in the appointment of a Fiscal, now made, is to be found the origin of the present office of Attorney-General. The title *advocatus fisci*, or fiscal advocate, is as old as the Roman Empire, and was given to an officer whose function, like that of a solicitor of taxes at the present day, was connected with the collection of revenue. In the time of the Cæsars the word *fiscus* [1] denoted the imperial revenues, as distinguished from *ærarium*, the public chest—a distinction which was perpetuated in Essequebo and Demerara under the form of Company's (or afterwards King's) chest on the one hand and Colony's chest on the other, and which is of great importance in the constitutional history of the Two Rivers. Many of the institutions of Rome were adopted in the Netherlands, and among them the office of Advocate Fiscal, whose duties, however, were extended in course of time from those of solicitor of taxes to include all the functions of law officer of the government. The instructions [2] drawn up for the Fiscal by the Ten enjoined him to observe scrupulously " the placaats, ordinances, resolutions, articled letter, etc., of their High Mightinesses the States-General and of the Company ": to take action against all who contravened them : to " keep, protect and maintain with all diligence, earnestness and zeal all the Company's rights, domains, jurisdictions and authority ": to " proceed in law against anyone found violating the rights of

---

[1] " Res fiscales quasi propriæ et privatæ principis sunt." *Dig.*, 43, 8, 2, § 4.

[2] A translation of the instructions to the Fiscal is given in Rodway, vol. i, pp. 238–9.

the Company and confiscate the goods of the guilty parties ":
to see that all criminal sentences were carried out properly :
and not to " compromise any suit, either criminal or civil."
As a precaution, however, he was instructed not to " make any
private or preliminary inquiry into a case without the consent
of the Directeur-General and Councillors."

The Vendue-Master was a personage of much importance
in the Colony, because under the Dutch regulations no one but
the Vendue-Master could offer anything for sale publicly. A
merchant might keep a store and sell in a semi-private manner;
but anything like a shop was not allowed. As official auctioneer
the Vendue-Master may be regarded as in some sense the
predecessor of the subsequent Administrator-General; but the
Vendue Office, as such, was abolished in 1844.

The Captain Commandant relieved the Directeur-General
and the Commandeur of their military duties, and was the predecessor of the present Commandant of the Local Forces; while
the Predicant became the chief religious dignitary in the Colony.

The planters of Demerara had complained of the necessity
of going to Essequebo to attend the Council of Policy, and had
Separate urged in April, 1772, that when required to go to
Council of Fort Island compensation should be paid them.
Policy ap- Accordingly the Ten now decided that there should
pointed for be a Council of Policy, as well as a Council of Justice
Demerara.
for each river. It was ordered that the Council of Policy for
Essequebo should consist of the Directeur-General, the Fiscal,
the Captain Commandant and the Vendue-Master, who were
all servants of the Company, and of " four other persons chosen
from the most important, capable and pious of the inhabitants,
members of the Reformed Church." [1] Thus the representation
of the interests of the Company and of the free planters now
became equal, while the Directeur-General, as President of all
Councils which he attended, had a casting vote. The Council
of Policy for Demerara consisted of the same representatives
of the Company, together with the Commandeur of Demerara,
who presided in the absence of the Directeur-General, the latter
continuing to reside at Fort Island. In this Council also there
were four elective members. The electives were nominated

---

[1] See instructions given by the Ten to the Director-General, translated
in abstract, Rodway, vol. i, pp. 236–8.

both in Essequebo and in Demerara by the College of Kiezers for their respective river; and, although the Ten thought it desirable that Councillors, other than servants of the Company, should serve for a term of six years only, this was never carried out, the representatives of the free planters being elected for life or for so long as they remained in the Colony. It will be noticed that the Secretary, who, under the directorate of the Zeeland Chamber, had been the most important official next to the Directeur-General and had in some cases corresponded with the Directors, being in that respect above the Commandeur of Demerara, now lost his place as a Councillor. He was, however, instructed to assist at the meetings of all Councils, write the minutes, and take care that the arguments in the Councils of Justice were properly recorded. The Councils of Justice for each river consisted of the same persons as the Councils of Policy, save that the Fiscal, being public prosecutor, had no seat in the former. It was further laid down that no resolution or decision should be arrived at unless a majority of the Councillors were present, and that " the Councils of Policy and Justice shall not only deal with such matters as may be brought before them by the Directeur-General, but also with all matters of civil and criminal justice." The criminal ordinance of Philip II, published on the 9th July, 1570, now became the authority of the Councils of Justice; and by resolution of the States-General, dated the 4th October, 1774, " all the laws of Holland in general," in addition to those of the States-General and of the Company, were to guide their judgments.

All these changes were opposed by the Chamber of Zeeland in a memorial to the States-General, on the ground that the *Earliest Form of Combined Council.* action taken by the Ten had separated the Two Rivers; and the States-General, while giving general approval to the reorganization, which had been effected, made a small concession to the Zeeland Chamber by ordering that the Directeur-General should have the superintendence of both rivers; and that the Commandeur and two Councillors of Demerara should go to Fort Island once or twice a year to meet the Councillors of Essequebo in Combined Council, and consider such matters as affected both rivers. This Combined Council was called together by the Directeur-General, who was its President, at irregular intervals, whenever there was business to transact; and its first meeting was held on the 26th June, 1775.

Attempts were made, in 1779, by the Company to increase the taxes payable in Demerara and Essequebo; but to these *Attempts made to increase Taxation.* attempts the colonists opposed a firm resistance. The head-tax of 2½ guilders (4s. 2d. or $1) *per* slave had become a regular impost; and the Company exacted a customs duty of 2%, called *recognitie*, on exports and imports to and from Demerara and Essequebo, besides which 0.5% was charged for convoy and a small amount was received from stamps. This was all the Company could collect to defray the expenses of the local administration. But the planters, now that they had representatives in all the Councils, were willing from time to time to pay extraordinary taxation, known as the Colony's *ongeld*, which was always imposed by their consent and kept quite distinct from the funds in the Company's chest. In fact, several disputes took place between the Councils and the Ten as to whether certain expenses should be defrayed from the Colony's *ongeld* or the Company's chest. Thus, in 1776, an expedition was sent to Spanish Guiana to bring back some runaway slaves; and the expenses of this expedition were provisionally paid out of the Colony's *ongeld*. Thereupon the Essequebo Council of Policy petitioned the Ten for a refund of the amount from the Company's chest; but this was refused on the ground that the expenditure had been incurred for the benefit of the planters. The acreage tax, imposed by resolution of the Ten in 1698, had not been enforced.[1] Now, however, in 1780, the Ten ordered the Directeur-General to collect it without further consultation with his Councillors, and to prosecute those who did not pay. But the events of the following year rendered these orders of no effect.

The controversy between Great Britain and her North American colonies, which began in 1765 and led to the *War between England and Holland.* American War of Independence, ultimately involved France in 1778, and Spain in 1779, both as enemies of England. During this war the action of England in seizing enemy's goods in neutral ships bore hard upon the neutral Powers, and especially upon those of the Baltic and

---

[1] See p. 25, *supra.*

upon Holland; for the war had diverted into Dutch vessels much of the European carrying trade, while the products of the Baltic, naval stores and grain, were those which England was particularly interested in forbidding to her enemies. Finally, in 1780, the famous agreement known as the " Armed Neutrality " was entered into by Russia, Sweden and Denmark, who bound themselves to support with a combined armed fleet of a fixed minimum number certain declarations made by them as to the rights of neutrals. The attitude of the United Provinces was undecided. They had been asked to join the Armed Neutrality. They hesitated; but the majority of the Provinces favoured it. A British officer had already gone so far as to fire upon a Dutch man-of-war, which had resisted the search of merchant-ships under its convoy; and it was determined by the British Government, who, without meeting the declarations of Russia, Sweden and Denmark by a direct contradiction, had decided to disregard them, that, if the States-General joined the Armed Neutrality, war should be declared on Holland. On the 16th December, 1780, the British Ministry was informed that the States-General had resolved to sign the declarations of the Armed Neutrality forthwith. Thereupon orders were at once sent by the British Government to Admiral Sir George Rodney to seize the Dutch West Indies; and four days later England declared war on Holland. The additional enemy was of small account to Great Britain, whose geographical position effectually blocked the junction of the Dutch fleet with those of her other enemies. But the colonies and commerce of Holland fell everywhere a prey to the British cruisers.

Demerara and Essequebo were quite helpless. Four British privateers, then in the West Indies, hearing of the declaration of war, made for the coast of Guiana, and, arriving in Demerara on or about the 21st February, 1781, seized all vessels, and interrupted communication between the east and west banks of the river. The Commandeur and Council of Policy decided that nothing could be done to defend the Colony. They accordingly surrendered. A few days later, on the 27th February, His Majesty's ships *Surprise* and *Barbuda* reached Demerara, and to them the Commandeur and Council of Demerara made a fresh surrender,

Capitulation of Demerara and Essequebo to Great Britain.

while the Directeur-General and the Councillors of Essequebo similarly surrendered on the 3rd March. Joseph Bourda and John Haslin, two Councillors of Demerara, were then sent to arrange Articles of Capitulation with Admiral Rodney and General Vaughan at St. Eustatius. These articles, which were signed on the 14th March, 1781, permitted the " Commandant and other officers " to go to Holland in a cartel; required the remaining inhabitants to take the oath of allegiance to His Britannic Majesty; stipulated that all the property, stores, etc., belonging to the Dutch West India Company should be delivered up to the British officers; but " granted to the inhabitants to remain in full possession of their property and to be governed by their present laws until His Majesty's pleasure be known." The supreme authority in the Two Rivers vested temporarily in the senior British Naval Officer there present, Captain E. Thompson; but in October, 1781, Lieut.-Colonel R. Kingston was appointed Governor of Essequebo and Demerara.

A number of English settlers now arrived from Barbados, some of whom received land-grants; and, owing to the rivers *Subsequent* being open to English merchants, trade increased *Capitulation* to a considerable extent, especially in Demerara, *to France.* which was now the more important river of the two. But the British occupation lasted less than a year; for France, then an ally of Holland, recaptured the lost rivers by means of an expedition, which sailed from Rochefort on the 8th October, 1781. On the 31st January, 1782, six French ships, commanded by the Comte de Kersaint, were sighted off the mouth of the Demerara. The English had no prospect of beating off so large a force. A parley was arranged; and on the 3rd February, 1782, Articles of Capitulation were signed in the house of John Haslin at Plantation " Friendship." Essequebo surrendered on similar terms. Thus the Two Rivers passed for a short period under the French flag; for, although nominally retaking the Colony on behalf of an ally, the French placed officials of their own nationality in all the chief posts, leaving the Directeur-General, the Commandeur and the Councillors as mere puppets. On the 15th July, 1782, the Marquis de Lusignan arrived in Demerara as Governor, and under him an *Ordonnateur* was appointed for each river. The

Councils were rarely consulted; and the method of government was very autocratic, until, the war having been ended by the Peace of Paris, signed on the 3rd September, 1783, the French Government declared on the 16th February, 1784, their intention of evacuating the Colony.

Meanwhile, when the negotiations which led to the Peace of Paris were set on foot, the Dutch West India Company seriously *Reorganiza-* considered what should be done with the Two *tion of Two* Rivers, and certain radical changes in the con-*Rivers con-* *templated by* stitution were proposed. The supreme control of *Company.* both rivers was to be vested, as before, in a Directeur-General, but his residence was to be shifted from Essequebo to Demerara, now officially recognized as the more important of the two rivers. The post of Commandeur of Demerara was abolished; and instead a Commandeur of Essequebo was appointed, subordinate to the Directeur-General. The Councils of Policy were to remain distinct for each river, but were to consist solely of servants and nominees of the Company; namely, in Demerara, of the Directeur-General, the President of the Council of Justice, the Fiscal, the Receiver of Taxes, the Commissary of Military Stores, and of three colonists nominated by the Directeur-General; and in Essequebo, of the Commandeur, of the four servants of the Company next him in rank, and of three colonists nominated by the Directeur-General. Each river was to have its own Council of Justice consisting of six Protestant members to be chosen by the Directeur-General, with the approval of the Ten, from a nomination by the Burgher Courts-Martial of three persons from among the colonists for each vacancy. Properly qualified legal gentlemen were to be appointed Presidents of these Councils, and to be suitably remunerated. Combined Councils were to be held occasionally in Demerara, two members attending from the Council of Policy in each river.

On the 6th March, 1784, the Two Rivers were formally restored by France to the Dutch authorities; and next day *Two Rivers* Joseph Bourda was appointed Commandeur of *restored to* Demerara *ad interim*. The Council took the oath *Holland :* *Stabroek* of allegiance to the Netherlands, and at once set *founded.* about restoring the *status quo ante bellum*, but with one important alteration; for it was resolved to transfer the seat of government from Borsselen Island to the house lately occupied by the French Governor near the Brandwagt at the mouth of the river. A town, even a village, there never was at any time in Essequebo; and this fact seems to have much impressed the Comte de Kersaint, for in a proclamation issued on the 22nd February, 1782, he said :

> "This is perhaps the only instance of a European colony, among thousands throughout the world, which has arrived at some magnificence without the establishment of either town or village. But, if it is considered under what circumstances and at what cost this state of things has obtained, it will be seen that there is no reason why the colonists of Demerary should refuse to co-operate to the best of their means in carrying out what we now propose to establish on the land formerly known as the Brandwagt."

When the French occupation ceased, the beginnings of a town had already been constructed on this site; and by a resolution of the Ten, dated the 14th September, 1784, this new town, destined to become the seat of government not only for Demerara and Essequebo, but for Berbice as well, was named Stabroek, in honour of Nicolaas Geelvink, Lord of Castricum, Backum and Stabroek, who was then representative of the Stadtholder in the Company and President of the Ten.

In September, 1784, Jan l'Espinasse was commissioned as Directeur-General of the Two Rivers; and in December of the same year, J. C. Bert was appointed Com- *Attempt by Company to reorganize the Constitu- tion.* mandeur of Essequebo. This news was received in the Colony on the 4th January, 1785, together with the resolution of the Ten as to the changes in the constitution. The proposed changes caused considerable dissatisfaction; and at a Council meeting on the 20th January, 1785, Joseph Bourda and three other Councillors protested against the new constitution, pointing out that under the constitution of 1773 the votes of the servants of the Company and of the colonists had been equal, whereas the Company now wanted to have five of its servants to three colonists, and these latter only nominees of their own. The new Directeur-General arrived at Stabroek on the 2nd February, 1785, and was at once presented with a memorial complaining of the proposed changes, while Councillor A. P. Swaen added a strong protest against the arbitrary doings of the Company. The Directeur-General then proceeded to read the new appointments—namely, Antony Meertens to be Fiscal and Councillor, M. B. Hartsinck to be Receiver of Taxes and Councillor, D. H. Macare to be Commissary of Vendues and Councillor, after which came the nominations of Joseph Bourda and Pieter van Helsdingen as representatives of the colonists in the Council. Both refused to sit as nominees of the Company; and, there not being a quorum, the meeting could not go on. The Directeur-General then nominated H. Jonas and H. Reim, who, however, on the 8th February, both sent letters declining the honour. The Fiscal now proposed to convene the Burgher Officers and deliberate with them as to what should be done; but the Directeur-General refused to do anything of the sort, and nominated C. J. Hecke, A. Lonck and J. Bastiaanse. All three declined to serve. At last, however, on the 10th February, C. J. Hecke was persuaded, on reconsideration of the matter, to accept nomination, and the Council proceeded to business with one colonial member only, among its earliest acts being a resolution that, in view of the difficulty of getting Councillors, any person refusing to serve as Councillor without lawful excuse should be fined 3,000 guilders.

Meanwhile, in Essequebo the government had, since the departure of the French, been administered by Councillor Broodhagen; and, as the new Commandeur, J. C. Bert, did not arrive in the Colony until the 4th August, 1785, the Deirecteur-General went to Fort Island on the 25th February to inaugurate the new constitution, and nominated Van Doorn and Milborn as representatives of the colonists in the Essequebo Council. Both refused to serve. Next day Albertus Backer and Paul W. Jansen were nominated; and, as they accepted office, the Council was duly constituted. A protest, however, was entered against the action of the Company by ex-Councillor Broodhagen and others, while the colonists of Essequebo joined in the petitions, memorials and protests, which now began to pour in, but with less determination than did the colonists of Demerara.

A great struggle between the colonists and the Company now commenced. The new Council of Demerara imposed, by order of the Company, a head-tax of six guilders on slaves.

The planters, almost to a man, refused to pay. They were willing to contribute the old head-tax of 2½ guilders, which had

Struggle between Colonists and Company as to Taxation. been in existence since 1698, and also the *ongeld*, if imposed by consent of colonial representatives; but they absolutely refused to go further. The Fiscal was ordered to prosecute some of the leaders of the opposition; but they would not even attend his summons, telling him to wait until they heard from the Stadtholder, and adding that in the meanwhile they were not going to trouble themselves about the actions of the " pretended Council." At an extraordinary meeting of the Council, held on the 28th November, 1785, to consider the matter, the Directeur-General expressed the view that the Fiscal should proceed to execution on the property of defaulters; but on consideration the Council decided not to incur the responsibility of further action until instructions had been received from the Company. The result was that for the years 1784 to 1786 no taxes were paid in the Colony.

The multitude of petitions, memorials and protests from Demerara and Essequebo to the Ten, the States-General and

" Concept Plan of Redress." the Stadtholder, praying for redress of grievances, led to the appointment of a Committee, composed of delegates both of the States-General and of the Ten. This Committee, after many sittings in Holland during 1786, drew up on the 19th March, 1787, a report to the States-General embodying a " Concept Plan of Redress," [1] which was considered by the States-General in 1788 and referred to the Stadtholder to take what action he deemed advisable. Accordingly, on the 25th December, 1788, the Stadtholder appointed two Commissioners, Baron van Grovestins and William Cornelis Boey, to proceed to the Colony with full power to make the changes in the government necessary to give effect to the Plan of Redress, as well as to appoint and dismiss officials, administer oaths, and do everything possible to restore peace and concord in the Two Rivers.

The Plan of Redress provided that there should be over both rivers one Council of Policy, and in each river provisionally one Council of Justice, " it being the intention of the Company, after having consulted the Council of Policy, to report to Their

[1] See Appendix A.

High Mightinesses whether the administration of justice for both rivers might not in future be executed by one Council, holding its session in the chief town of Demerary." The number of members in the College of Kiezers for Essequebo as well as in that for Demerara was increased to seven, " the said increase and further vacancy to be supplied by a plurality of voices of the inhabitants, who must possess five-and-twenty negroes or upwards." The Council of Policy was to consist of the Directeur-General over both rivers, the Commandeur of Essequebo, the Fiscal of Essequebo, the Fiscal of Demerara, two colonists of Essequebo and two colonists of Demerara : that is to say, the voices of the representatives of the Company on the one hand and of the colonists on the other were equal, but the Directeur-General, as President of the Council of Policy, was given a casting vote. The Council of Justice in Essequebo was to consist of the Commandeur of Essequebo and six colonists besides one Adviser; and in Demerara of the Directeur-General and six colonists besides one Adviser, the Fiscals in each river being expressly excluded from membership. As regards the method of electing colonists to the Councils, it was laid down that the Council of Policy, as well as the Councils of Justice, should, " for the first time, be chosen by ballot from among a double return of members to be nominated by the Kiezers of both rivers, who shall be assembled by the Directeur-General "; that, " after a lapse of two years, and afterwards yearly, during the course of the present charter, one of the members of Policy, chosen from the colonists, shall retire—the first year the senior in rank in Essequebo, and the second year the senior in rank in Demerary, and so on, successively. From each Council of Justice one-third shall retire every two years, to begin with the senior in rank; it being nevertheless understood that the members, both of Policy and of Justice, on retiring, shall be re-eligible." With respect to qualification of Councillors, it was provided that the Councils of Policy and Justice should be chosen " from among the principal, most capable and most religious inhabitants, above twenty-five years of age, professing the Protestant religion and perfectly acquainted with the Dutch language "—the language test being doubtless aimed at the large body of British colonists in the Two Rivers ; that a colonist, in order to be eligible, must have resided at least three years within the Colony; that, with regard to consanguinity, the 6th article of the instructions to the Directeur-General, issued in 1773, should remain in full force;[1] and that servants of the Company should be eligible to all the Councils. Finally, the Kiezers, before proceeding to a nomination, were bound to swear before the Directeur-General that they would nominate such persons as, to the best of their knowledge and opinion, were duly qualified agreeably to the regulations.

The two Commissioners, appointed by the Stadtholder, arrived in Demerara on the 26th May, 1789. Jan l'Espinasse *Inauguration* at once resigned; and the new Council, under the *of Plan of* Plan of Redress, sat for the first time on the 29th *Redress.* May, 1789, Joseph Bourda being one of its members. After a thorough inquiry into all matters in dispute and the inauguration, much to the satisfaction of the colonists, of the system contained in the Plan of Redress, the Commissioners left Demerara in August, having provisionally appointed Albertus Backer to be Directeur-General with effect from the 18th of that month.

On their arrival in the Netherlands, the Commissioners reported very unfavourably on the Dutch West India *Downfall of* Company. That Company, since the last war *the Company.* with England, had been heavily in debt and had paid no dividend for many years. Its creditors were clamouring for payment and asked the States-General to intervene on their behalf. The trouble in Demerara and Essequebo brought matters to a head, as it was evident that, for want of funds, the Company would not be able to carry out satisfactorily the recommendations of the States-General in respect of that Colony. The Company's charter was due to expire at the end of the year 1791; and the Ten, on applying to the States-General for a renewal, were informed that no renewal would be granted. The directors and shareholders protested, but to no purpose. The States-General took over the Company's liabilities and gave the shareholders Govern-

---

[1] This article reads : " Two or more persons related, either in the ascending or descending line, shall not be permitted to be Councillors at the same time, nor yet a father-in-law and his son-in-law, two brothers, or two brothers-in-law " (Rodway, vol. i, p. 237).

ment bonds, bearing 3% interest, to the amount of 30% of the face value of their shares. So the Company's control of the Two Rivers came to an end on the 31st December, 1791, after having lasted 170 years and survived the fortunes of six European wars.[1]

(b) *Between the Fall of the Company and the Cession to Great Britain* (1792–1803)

Proclamation was duly made in the Colony on the 1st January, 1792, that the Two Rivers, under the title of " the *The States-* United Colony of Demerary and Essequebo," would *General as-* in future be governed by the States-General, who *sume Direct* *Control of the* would exercise their control over this as over other *Two Rivers.* colonies through a Colonial Council. The office of Directeur-General was replaced by that of Governor; and Baron van Grovestins, who had been one of the two Commissioners in 1789, assumed the duties of that office on the 31st March, 1793, while Albertus Backer became Commandeur of Essequebo. No radical changes were made, the Plan of Redress being adopted as the basis of the constitution.

By this time the whole coast-line, from the Abary on the east almost to the Pomeroon on the west, had been granted to colonists; and, in 1794, a survey and map were completed, on the basis of which the Pomeroon itself, with the adjacent territory as far as the Moruka, was to be thrown open to settlement once more. The plan included a reservation of ground for a town at the mouth of the Pomeroon river and provided for fortifications at both sides of the estuary.[2] But the fortune of war again interrupted the development of this district.

When the War of the French Revolution broke out, the United Provinces remained neutral as long as they could. The *The War of* " patriot party," as the anti-Orange republicans *the French* styled themselves, sided with the French; but for *Revolution.* various reasons the conquest of the Low Countries was delayed until, in the closing months of 1794, Pichegru at

---

[1] *I.e.*, Spanish war (1621–48); war with England (1665–7); war with France and England (1672–4); War of League of Augsburg (1689–97); War of Spanish Succession (1702–13); American War of Independence (1765–83).

[2] *U.S.E.*, pp. 607–8, 612–32.

the head of a large and victorious army invaded Holland. Town after town fell before him; he occupied Amsterdam; and, crossing the ice with his cavalry, he took the Dutch fleet as it lay frost-bound in the Texel. The Stadtholder and his family fled to England early in 1795; while the " patriots " received the French with open arms and public rejoicings, and the Government was reorganized so as to bring it into close harmony with that of Paris. The stadtholderate and all the ancient constitutional system of the United Netherlands were abolished and were transformed into the Batavian Republic, the bosom ally of France. But the Dutch had soon cause to regret their revolutionary ardour. French alliance meant French domination and participation in the wars of the Revolution. Its consequences were the total ruin of Dutch commerce and the seizure of all the Dutch colonies by Great Britain.

The probability of war had been discussed in Demerara by the Council of Policy as early as the 17th March, 1793. Baron *Effect of War in the Two Rivers.* van Grovestins was a partisan of the Prince of Orange; and, on the assumption that France was the enemy, measures were taken to improve the defences of the Colony, the English planters heartily co-operating with the Dutch colonists. Even an extraordinary head-tax of ten guilders met with no protest. However, on the 27th April, 1795, despatches from the States-General announcing the restoration of friendly relations with France reached Demerara; while a few days later a British man-of-war brought the Governor a letter from the Prince of Orange, dated at Kew on the 7th February, 1795, and commanding that any British forces or squadron sent to Demerara or Essequebo should be admitted and considered " as forces and vessels of a power in friendship and alliance with Their High Mightinesses the States-General of the United Netherlands, coming there to prevent the Colony from being invaded by the French." Confronted with these contradictory instructions, the Council of Policy decided to obey the States-General, as being the *de facto* Government of the Netherlands, and not the Stadtholder, who was a fugitive in England. Thereupon Baron van Grovestins at once left the Colony; and, as Commandeur Backer was absent, the Council urged Antony Beaujon, the Secretary, to accept office as Governor *ad interim*. Beaujon absolutely refused; and in these circumstances, as from the 5th May, 1795, it was decided that the government should be administered for periods of eight days in rotation by two Councillors, one from Demerara and one from Essequebo, acting jointly. This provisional form of government lasted until despatches were received and published on the 27th June, 1795, announcing the establishment of the Batavian Republic and appointing Antony Beaujon to be Governor of the Two Rivers.

The constitution of the Colony had by this time been virtually settled on the basis of the Plan of Redress; but in that plan *Complaints as to the Method of Taxation.* the question of taxation had been left unsettled. It will be remembered that there were two sets of taxes with the corresponding " chests," into which they were paid. The one formerly belonged to the West India Company, and now to the States-General, while the other was the Colony's *ongeld*. The latter was in origin an extraordinary tax, imposed by general consent of the colonists for special purposes, for which the Company or the State would not provide, and was payable for one year only; but, as the Colony developed, it became an annual impost, varying according to the estimated requirements of the coming year. Now, under the scheme of government based upon the Plan of Redress, the official and the unofficial sections of the Council of Policy having four votes each, the latter could always be overruled by the Governor's casting vote; and the colonists complained that, as a result, expenses were paid from the Colony's chest which ought to have been met from the State chest. As early as the 5th August, 1790, application had been submitted to the States-General, inviting attention to a report made in the Assembly of the States-General on the Plan of Redress, from which report the following sentence was quoted : " The whole of this not affecting the contributions towards the Colony fund, which are to be regulated by the inhabitants themselves "; and their High Mightinesses were requested to " determine in which class of persons the report above quoted vested the right of imposing and raising taxes, and in what mode this was to be carried into effect." The application was referred for the consideration of certain commissioners, but no answer to it was ever made. However, on the 12th April, 1793,

E

Baron van Grovestins, yielding to the remonstrances of the colonial members of the Council of Policy, laid before them his private instructions as Governor, wherein it was directed that he

> " should carefully watch every public administration and, so far as the same immediately concerns the Colony, shall leave the superintendence thereof not only to the Colony Councillors, but shall call and admit thereto a greater number of colonists, for instance, the College of Kiezers, separating moreover these funds from those which belong to Government, and submitting the latter-mentioned to the oversight of the Councillors and Bookkeeper-General."

These instructions were too indefinite in their terms to serve as more than a suggestion of the manner in which such affairs should be managed; but Governor van Grovestins, after laying them before the Council of Policy, was induced to consult the unofficial members of that Council and the College of Kiezers with a view to making some arrangements which might be satisfactory to them. His proposals did not meet their wishes. The matter was therefore again referred for the decision of the States-General; and, pending the result of that reference, the colonial members of the Council of Policy refused to concur in the imposition of any new taxes. No answer came from the States-General till 1794, when the Governor received despatches, dated the 15th August in that year, ordering him to ascertain, in conference with the College of Kiezers, what charges ought to be borne upon the Colony fund; whether the taxes necessary to meet them should not be imposed by the Governor and Council, with a certain limitation of amount; whether the administration of the fund should not be entrusted to some college in the Colony, as, for example, the College of Kiezers; and whether, in case of any difference as to what did or did not belong to that fund, the question ought not to be provisionally decided by the Governor and Council, who should at the same time transmit their opinion to the States-General. Tentative instructions such as these could obviously do little for the decision of the questions in dispute; and the local authorities determined to wait for something more definite, the financial business of the Colony being conducted in the meantime on the old footing. But,

before any further orders were received, the revolution of
1795 took place in Holland; news arrived that British troops
were about to occupy the Two Rivers; Baron van Grovestins
threw up the government; there was an interregnum without
any Governor; and at the same time there happened an
insurrection of slaves.

In this general confusion, funds being urgently needed to
put down the slave insurrection, the members of the Council
of Policy called the College of Kiezers to a con-
The Colonial Finance Department. ference with them; and, on the 3rd June, 1795, it
was resolved that the Colony fund should be under
the care of the colonial Councillors (*i.e.*, the unofficial section of
the Council of Policy), joined to four Kiezers, two from the
Demerara College and two from the Essequebo College, and
that this Combined Council should superintend the raising of
that fund and regulate its expenditure.   When the interregnum
ended, Beaujon, who became Governor, consented to preside
in the Combined Council as established in June, 1795, by the
provisional government.   He observed, however, that he did
not choose to discuss the sufficiency of the authority by which
this Combined Council had been established, and that he only
gave his sanction until the pleasure of the sovereign authority
in the Netherlands should be made known, and on the understanding that this provisional arrangement should not affect
such orders and resolutions as in the meantime might come
from the mother-country.   This novel form of Combined
Council appears to have been designated " the Colonial Finance
Department "; and at a later period it developed into the
so-called Financial College.

The British Government had hoped to induce the Dutch
colonies in the West Indies to espouse the cause of the Stadt-
Second Brit-ish Occupa-tion of the Two Rivers. holder and range themselves on the side of Great
Britain in the war with France.   When, however,
these expectations were disappointed, a British
squadron was sent to capture the Two Rivers, and anchored
off the mouth of the Demerara on the 20th April, 1796.   The
ships were under the command of Captain Parr, and convoyed
a force of 1,200 men commanded by Major-General Whyte.
These officers called upon the Colony to surrender, promising
that the inhabitants should

" enjoy full security in their persons, and free exercise of their religion, with the full and immediate enjoyment of all private property, whether on shore or afloat, excepting such as may belong to the subjects of the French Republic, according to their ancient laws and usages, or such other as may be determined upon previous to the Colony being placed under His Majesty's Government, upon the most liberal and beneficial terms."

In the event of the Colony remaining under British government at the conclusion of peace, it was stipulated that the colonists should enjoy the same commercial rights and privileges as the British colonies in the West Indies. If the officers and men of the Dutch military forces were willing to enter His Britannic Majesty's service, they would be allowed to do so, with leave to return to the service of the Stadtholder on his restoration. The Governor and all civil officers, after the oath of allegiance to the British Sovereign, might remain, if they chose, in their respective positions (excepting those who had shown a decided partiality to the French), the Governor resigning only the military command. Governor Beaujon and his Council had no option but to accept these terms; and, on the 22nd April, 1796, the Two Rivers passed for the second time under the British flag.

A special meeting of the Council of Policy was convened on the 25th April, at which Major-General Whyte formally

Agitation as to Method of conducting Financial Business. took his seat as President, with Governor Beaujon on his right; and next day the Governor and the Councillors took the oath of allegiance to His Britannic Majesty. It was resolved on the 26th April, 1796,[1] that the Plan of Redress should be strictly followed in future; that accordingly the Council of Policy should consist of the Governor, the Commandeur of Essequebo, the two Fiscals, and two Colonial Councillors from each river; and that the Colonial Finance Department should no longer be recognized as an integral part of the constitution. However, within a month of the capitulation, the manner in which financial business should be conducted began to be agitated between Beaujon, who continued to administer the civil government, and three out of the four colonial members of the Council of

[1] B. G. Laws (1870), vol. i, p. 23.

Policy, who, in a memorial dated the 5th May, 1796, submitted an elaborate retrospect of the circumstances which led to the first formation of a Combined Council.   From this document it may be gathered that the complaints of the colonists, after the adoption of the Plan of Redress, were in no sense directed against the exercise of the powers of the Sovereign for the purpose of taxation, but were entirely by way of an appeal to the Sovereign against the local authorities—namely, the Governor and his official majority in the Council of Policy. It was represented that these authorities had not fulfilled what was assumed to have been the intention of the States-General, inasmuch as they had placed upon the revenue of the colonial chest charges not properly payable therefrom ; and further, that it was not the intention of the States-General that the four public servants in the Council of Policy, with the Governor's casting vote, should dispose of the taxes arbitrarily and against the advice of the four colonial members of the Council. Moreover, the memorial contended for the maintenance of the system adopted under the provisional government, and insisted upon the terms of the capitulation as guaranteeing the Colonial Finance Department until abolished by orders from a higher quarter.

Governor Beaujon, in his reply to this memorial, showed that the Colonial Finance Department, whether lawfully con-

Views of Governor Beaujon. stituted or not, could not be considered to be one of the ancient laws or usages which, under the capitulation, were to remain in force; that it was merely a provisional measure awaiting the pleasure of the Sovereign; and that the private instructions to Baron van Grovestins, quoted in the memorial as appearing to direct some such measure, had been annulled by a positive resolution of the States-General of the 11th April, 1795, which ordered that everything should remain upon the former footing.   The Governor then proceeded to discuss the system of financial representation upon its own merits; and, after reciting the argument that some such system was not alien to British law and had probably been contemplated by the States-General, he proposed

"that the Council should adjoin to the college of the government and the Council of Policy (in lieu of the

Kiezers, who have received no mandate from the inhabitants for representing them in financial affairs), an additional number of six inhabitants entitled to vote on questions relative to the raising of colonial taxes, and for no other purpose, and that each River should delegate three of these representatives to be elected every two years by such inhabitants as are qualified for that effect by the provisional Plan of Redress, and in such manner as is thereby directed; the whole measure, however, to be only provisional until the pleasure of His Majesty, or of his representative, shall be made known."

The majority of the Council of Policy agreed with the Governor; and it was accordingly decided, on the 11th June, 1796, that the resolution passed by the provisional government on the 3rd June, 1795, should be repealed, and that the Colonial Finance Department set up by that resolution should be abolished. Then follows in the minutes of that day's proceedings the resolution in which the system of Financial Representation, as it eventually existed, is first adumbrated.[1] This resolution provided that six Financial Representatives—three from each river—should be adjoined to the Governor and Councillors of Policy with the right of voting " on all matters relative to the raising of taxes and examination of accounts, without any other power whatever"; that the Kiezers should no more be present at the sittings of the Council : " that the Council of Policy shall again finally dispose of the Colony fund, and that in urgent occurrences, during this Council's recess, the immediate disposition of the fund shall be entrusted to the Governor." The six Financial Representatives were to be elected by those inhabitants of the Two Rivers who possessed twenty-five or more slaves, and they were to serve for two years. The electors were admonished " to observe in the election of such representatives that they invest their interest in the hands of those who, from their connexions, will take the real welfare of the Colony in general, and that of the inhabitants in particular, to heart." It was added " that a resolution shall hereafter be determined upon, if necessary, under gracious approbation from a higher quarter, tending, as

Resolution to appoint Six Financial Representatives.

[1] See Appendix B.

far as possible, to ascertain what articles of expenditure are, or are not, payable out of the Colony fund, in order to establish some fixed regulations on that head, to be invariably attended to in the common course of affairs. The whole of these resolutions to be determined upon until His Britannic Majesty's pleasure, or that of his representatives, shall be made known."

Pursuant to this resolution, the first Financial Representatives were elected on the 25th July, 1796; and the first meeting of the new Combined Council, consisting of the Governor, the Councillors of Policy and the six Financial Representatives, was held on the 2nd November, 1796, when the financial situation was taken into consideration. The Colony chest was found to be in debt to the amount of over 95,000 guilders ($47,000 or £9,791 12s. 8d.), while it was estimated that another 59,000 guilders ($23,600 or £4,916 13s. 4d.) were required, besides some other expenses which had not yet been exactly ascertained. The Combined Council thereupon agreed that the head-tax should be fixed at 4.10 guilders ($1.64 or 6s. 10d.) on all plantation slaves, including even sucking infants, and at 9 guilders ($3.60 or 15s.) for domestic servants. On account of the scarcity of coin, the Receiver of Taxes was permitted to take payment in ready money, bills of exchange, claims on the Colony chest, or promissory notes. These last were payable in produce, could only be received from owners of plantations, and were to be negotiated as paper money at full value, every one being bound to accept them as legal tender. From now onwards, until the capitulation of the 19th September, 1803, the minutes of the Combined Council show that the regular course of business was for the Governor to lay before that Council an estimate, which had been previously prepared, of the expenses of the ensuing year, and for the Combined Council to appoint the taxes required in order to provide the estimated sum. The Combined Council had, however, no say in matters of expenditure.

Combined Council constituted.

Meanwhile, in Essequebo, all interest in the constitution had been languishing. The Commandeur reported on the 8th June, 1796, that at the election of Kiezers only four votes were found in the box, and that, even when elected, the Kiezers often refused to sit. It was therefore resolved that a proclamation should be issued in

Interest in Constitution languishes in Essequebo.

Essequebo, earnestly exhorting the people not to neglect this part of their lawful constitution. On the 31st July in the following year, Governor Beaujon informed the Council that persons elected to seats in the Colleges of Kiezers and the Councils were continually refusing to accept office on various pretexts, so that it became more and more difficult to fill vacancies; and he drew attention to a proclamation, issued on the 20th May, 1778, in the name of the Commandeur and Council of Demerara, for preventing the persons elected to hold a seat in the Councils of Policy and Justice from refusing to accept these places. There was also the more recent precedent of the year 1785. Accordingly it was on that day resolved that any person nominated by the Kiezers should be bound to discharge the duties of his office during the full term, on pain of a fine of 3,000 guilders, unless he should have lawful and statutory excuse in the judgment of that body to which he was elected. Next day a memorial from the Essequebo College of Kiezers was read, complaining of the great inconvenience caused by the want of accommodation on Fort Island both for them and for the Council of Justice during the sessions; and the Commandeur was directed to purchase a house and make suitable provision for the sessions of those bodies in the same manner as in Demerara. The establishment on Fort Island had by this time almost gone to ruin.

With the British occupation, trade in the Two Rivers received considerable impetus from the merchant shipping of the West India Islands; while many planters came over to settle in Demerara, bringing their slaves and other effects with them. Much progress was made both in improving the town of Stabroek and in developing the plantations. Thus it was a blow to the inhabitants when by the Treaty of Amiens, signed on the 25th March, 1802, His Britannic Majesty agreed to restore the Two Rivers to the Batavian Republic. The treaty stipulated that the conquered territory must be evacuated within three months, but that the British inhabitants should be allowed three years to dispose of their possessions, during which time they were not to be molested, or in any way disturbed, in person or property, on account of political conduct, opinion, or attachment to either party. On the 2nd December, 1802,

Treaty of Amiens: British Evacuation of the Two Rivers.

Antony Meertens, formerly Fiscal of Demerara, arrived to take over the Colony as Governor on behalf of the Batavian Republic. Proclamation to that effect was duly made next day, and those who intended to remain in the Two Rivers were required to take the oath of allegiance to the Republic. With the Governor arrived a new official, styled Vice-President of the Courts, who was to act, in the absence of the Governor, as President of the Courts of Justice.

The new *régime* was very transient ; for the Peace of Amiens proved to be little more than a truce. War broke out again *Final Capitu-* in May, 1803, between Great Britain and Bonaparte. *lation of the* England offered to respect the neutrality of Holland, *Two Rivers* *to Great* if France would do the same. The offer was not *Britain.* accepted ; and on the 17th June, 1803, Parliament was informed that the King had been compelled, with regret, to issue Letters of Marque against the Dutch. Commodore Hood and General Grinfield, then in command of the British naval and military forces in the West Indies, at once set about recapturing the Two Rivers ; and, on the evening of the 17th September, 1803, a squadron of His Majesty's ships arrived off the mouth of the Demerara. The immediate surrender of the Colony was demanded. Governor Meertens convened the Council of Policy, which framed terms of capitulation and deputed a committee to wait on the commanders of the British squadron with full authority to conclude the surrender. The deputation having gone on board H.M.S. *Heureux*, the terms of capitulation, then agreed to, were formally published on the 19th September, 1803.[1] Thus Demerara and Essequebo came finally into His Britannic Majesty's possession. There was no further retrocession, nor has a hostile attack ever since been made on the Two Rivers.

The terms of capitulation provided that

> " the laws and usages of the Colony shall remain in force and be respected, the mode of taxation now in use be adhered to, and the inhabitants shall enjoy the public exercise of their religion in the same manner as before the capitulation " : that " no new establishments shall be introduced without the consent of the Court of Policy and the legislature of the Colony " : that " the constituted

[1] See Appendix C.

Authorities and Public Officers, whether in the Civil Law or Church establishments, as well as the members of the respective Courts (except the Governor) shall be continued in their respective offices and situations, until His Majesty's pleasure shall be known " : that " the inhabitants, those who at present are in the Colony, as well as those who may be abroad, shall be protected in their persons, and have the free enjoyment of their properties, without being troubled or molested for any acts whatsoever other than such as they might commit subsequent to the capitulation and in violation of the oath of fidelity they shall be required to take " : that, until the conclusion of the war, " the inhabitants shall on no account whatever be obliged to take up arms against the external enemy, but their services shall only be required for quelling internal commotions or disturbances, according to the regulations of the Burghers, and for maintaining the internal tranquillity of the Colony, in conformity to what has always taken place to this day " : and that " the debts contracted by the Government for the building of new barracks, the erection of batteries, the purchase of provisions for the garrison, the salaries of civil officers due, shall, on the first demand, be paid out of the Sovereign's or Government chest, as well as other demands that would have been paid or reimbursed by Government had the Colony not been taken." Finally, it was laid down that, " should any difficulties arise in consequence of any dubious expressions occurring in the present capitulation, the same shall be explained or construed in the sense most favourable to the Colony."

(c) *From the Cession to the Union with Berbice* (1803–31)

The first meeting of the Court of Policy after the capitulation was held on the 22nd September, 1803, when Lieut.-General Grinfield took his seat as President. Governor Meertens sent in his resignation, as did also the Fiscal of Essequebo. But the other Councillors, including G. H. Trotz, the Commandeur of Essequebo, took the oath of allegiance to the British Sovereign. Before leaving Demerara, Lieut.-General Grinfield, on the 1st October, 1803, provisionally appointed Lieut.-Colonel Robert Nicholson of the 1st battalion of the First, or Royal, Regiment of Foot to be Lieut.-Governor of the Colony until His Majesty's pleasure should be known : and ultimately, on the 18th August, 1804,

British Government inaugurated.

Antony Beaujon, who had administered the government from 1795 to 1802 both under Dutch and under British rule, was reappointed Governor of the Two Rivers, much to the satisfaction of the whole Colony. When he died, on the 17th October, 1805, he was provisionally succeeded by Brig.-General James Montgomery; and, on the 8th May, 1806, H. W. Bentinck, who was a relative of the Duke of Portland, and who, though born in Holland, had spent a considerable portion of his life in the United Kingdom, became Governor of the Two Rivers.

No change was made in the constitution as it had existed since the resolution of the 11th June, 1796, and the business *No Change in the Constitution.* both of the Court of Policy and of the Combined Court, as these bodies were now called, proceeded on the same lines as before. The first meeting of Combined Court after the capitulation took place on the 17th October, 1803, when the financial position was considered. On account of the Colony chest being exhausted, 12,000 guilders ($4,800 or £1,000) had been borrowed from the Government chest; and it was proposed that an income-tax be introduced, commencing with 40 guilders ($16 or £3 6s. 8d.) on incomes ranging from 2,000 to 3,500 guilders ($800 or £166 13s. 4d. to $1,400 or £291 13s. 4d.). This proposal was objected to as a new impost, contrary to the laws and usages of the Colony; but it was nevertheless adopted by the Court and remained in force for many years. Next day it was resolved to levy the arrears of head-tax for the years 1796 to 1802, which had not been collected on account of the events of that period.

There was no hitch in the proceedings of Combined Court for the next seven years; but, on the 4th December, 1810, the *Financial Representatives desire an Increase of their Powers.* Financial Representatives urged that their powers were insufficient, claimed to have a control over the expenditure as well as over the taxation, and stated their intention of resigning office unless their claims were admitted. Thereupon the Combined Court resolved that, as the constitutional changes desired could not be made without the sanction of the Sovereign, the Financial Representatives should be requested to specify them in a memorial and obtain the sense of the majority of the inhabitants upon them; and that, if a majority were in their favour, the Governor should be requested to submit them for the approbation of His Majesty's Government. It was further resolved that, " should in the meantime any necessity arise for incurring heavy extraordinary expenses, and that necessity should admit of a sufficient delay for the purpose, the Financial Representatives shall be consulted on the expediency thereof." Nothing more was heard of the matter until at a meeting, not of the Combined Court, but of the Court of Policy, held on the 1st May, 1811, two Financial Representatives were admitted to present a memorial from a number of inhabitants, in which it was stated that by the then existing constitution the Financial Representatives were " compelled to confine their deliberations solely to the mode of taxation and to checking the accounts of the Receiver of Taxes "; and the memorial prayed that the sanction of His Majesty's Government might be obtained to the addition of a certain number of colonial members to the Court of Policy and the abolition of the Combined Court. Again some months elapsed; and on the 15th November, 1811, at a meeting of the Combined Court, one of the Financial Representatives inquired of the Governor concerning the fate of the memorial. The Governor's answer was, that the Court of Policy had examined the memorial, and, not finding it to be subscribed by a majority of the tax-paying inhabitants, as had been required, had not submitted it to His Majesty's Government; but that, whenever the prescribed condition should be fulfilled, it would be so submitted. Thereafter the matter remained in abeyance.

An important change was, however, made by Governor Bentinck in one of his last proclamations, dated the 1st April, 1812. The Courts of Justice for Demerara and *Courts of Justice for Demerara and Essequebo united.* Essequebo were united, and it was ordered that in future they should be held in Demerara. The Court of Justice on Fort Island was thus abolished; and from this time the amalgamation of the administrative system in the Two Rivers was made complete. The Commandeur and several other officials of Essequebo necessarily lost their posts as the result of these changes, while the archives were brought from Fort Island to Georgetown, as Stabroek was in this year renamed in honour of His Majesty King George III. The office of President of the Court of Justice was now made separate from that of Governor; and the English language was substituted for the Dutch in legal pleadings.

A few days later Bentinck was recalled, and Major-General Hugh Lyle Carmichael—then commanding the garrison—provisionally took over the civil administration of the Colony for little more than a year. In that time, however, he changed the constitution considerably. His attention was drawn to the fact that the Kiezers, who, having been appointed for life, were nearly all Dutchmen, persisted in nominating, both for the Court of Policy and the Court of Justice, only men of their own race, so that the British colonists, who were really the more numerous as well as the more important element in the community, had no voice in the administration. Carmichael, as he told the Court of Policy, held the view that " in every country where the British flag flies, the ascendancy must be with it; and, as long as Holland is in its present state of subjugation—however its ancient laws may be respected by capitulation—the executive government must be English." Accordingly at an extraordinary meeting of the Court of Policy, held on the 7th September, 1812, at which only four persons were present, namely, Carmichael himself and three of the electives—Joseph Beete, Peter Grant and James Johnstone—certain resolutions were passed and embodied in a proclamation, issued on the same day " by and with the advice and consent of the Honourable Court of Policy," making important alterations in the constitution. This proclamation appears to have been drawn up by someone neither conversant with the style of legislative enactments, nor, indeed, competent to express distinctly the purposes designed to be carried into effect. The principal changes are declared in the preamble without being afterwards included in the enactments; but the effect was " to combine the Board of Electors (College of Kiezers) with that of Financial Representatives, and to extend the right of suffrage to all such persons that pay the income-tax on 10,000 guilders *per annum*, who shall have an equal right to vote in all elections in the same manner as those who are possessed of twenty-five negroes." The members of this " Combined Board of Kiezers and Financial Representatives " were to serve for two years, the eldest retiring at the end of two years and their places being supplied

Combined Board of Kiezers and Financial Representatives established.

by a new election. At this same meeting, on the 7th September, 1812, the Court of Policy further resolved that " the office of Kiezer, or elector, and Financial Representative shall be combined, and form in future one Court, and that the members so elected shall serve two years."

The result of these measures was doubtless to purge the obnoxious College of Kiezers, which would elect only Dutchmen as members of the Court of Policy and the Court of *Effect of this* Justice; but Carmichael's action had another far-*Measure.* reaching effect, never contemplated by him, for the six colonists elected to form the Combined Board of Kiezers and Financial Representatives, and adjoined to the Court of Policy so as to form the Combined Court, became themselves the electors of the colonial members of the Court of Policy, thereby obtaining great influence over those members. The result was a silent and unresisted usurpation by the Combined Court of that control over expenditure which had hitherto been steadily withheld from it. The first meeting of the reconstituted Combined Court took place on the 18th November, 1812; and from that time until the Three Rivers were united to form British Guiana in 1831, the minutes show that the Combined Court was allowed to vote upon items of the estimates of expenditure. Accordingly, as the elective section in the Combined Court outnumbered the official section, the control, not only of taxation, but also of expenditure passed out of the hands of the executive government.

In making these changes Carmichael had acted without previously consulting His Majesty's Government; and in a despatch, dated the 25th November, 1812, Lord *His Majesty's* Bathurst rebuked him for so doing, and wrote that *Government* *displeased* the Prince Regent could not " view without surprise *with Car-* *michael's* the strong measure of dissolving the existing College *Action.* of Kiezers without authority or previous communication," adding—" I am to signify the commands of His Royal Highness that you should on no further occasion proceed to any fundamental change in the constitution without previous communication and receiving the opinion and direction of His Majesty's Government." It is, indeed, evident that the measures taken by the Administrator and the Court of Policy were unconstitutional. The essential preliminary to a change in the constitution, as it existed at the date of the capitulation, was that both the parties to the obligation contracted by the first article of the capitulation should unite, in order to effect a dissolution of it.   But Carmichael's action does not appear to have been founded upon the expressed desire of a majority of the inhabitants; and it did not meet with the approbation of the Sovereign.   Nevertheless His Majesty's Government did not at the time annul the measures which had been taken, but remained content with the remonstrance addressed by Lord Bathurst to Major-General Carmichael, who in May of the following year was succeeded by Major-General John Murray as administrator of the Colony.   Murray was substantively appointed Governor on the 18th December, 1813; and, with intervals of absence on leave, held that office for upwards of ten years, being in turn succeeded on the 26th April, 1824, by Major-General Sir Benjamin D'Urban, the Governor under whom the Three Rivers were united.

When the Napoleonic wars ended in 1814, it became necessary to decide, in terms of the answer to the third article of the *Convention* capitulation of 1803, to what government the Two *between Great* Rivers should be subjected.   This matter was *Britain and Netherlands,* settled by a Convention between Great Britain and *1814.* the Netherlands, signed in London on the 13th August, 1814,[1] which provided that all Dutch colonies occupied by British forces during the war should be restored, except the Cape of Good Hope, Demerara, Essequebo and Berbice; and for these cessions it was agreed that Great Britain should pay £1,000,000 to Sweden on account of Swedish claims on Holland, and £2,000,000 towards augmenting and improving the defences of the Low Countries.   Thus the Three Rivers were finally ceded to Great Britain.   Traders to the last, the Dutch in ceding the colonies secured a condition that any of the Guiana proprietors, who were subjects of the Netherlands, should enjoy the right of free trade with their mother-country, and this condition was regulated by a supplementary convention, dated the 12th August, 1815.[2]   It was, however, a matter of little real importance; for, at the beginning of the year 1840, there were in the Three Rivers no more than sixteen plantations belonging to Dutch proprietors resident in Holland, and eleven

[1] See Appendix E.   [2] See Appendix F.

which were subject to the interests of Dutch mortgagees; while not long afterwards the Dutch proprietary interest in British Guiana became quite extinct.

The system of financial administration in the Two Rivers again attracted the attention of His Majesty's Government in *Reform of* 1823, when the Combined Court refused to liquidate *Financial* a debt due to His Majesty's Treasury; and Governor *System in* *Two Rivers* Murray, in explaining to Lord Bathurst the effects *postponed.* which had followed from the changes in the constitution, made by Carmichael in 1812, and the usurpation by the elective section of control over expenditure resulting therefrom, stated that, these alterations having been made known to His Majesty's Government at the time they took place and not having been annulled, he had continued to administer the government in that form, which the total absence of party feeling upon the general affairs of the Colony had enabled him to do. As, however, the union of the Three Rivers into one Colony was now in contemplation, Murray recommended that any interference with the system of 1812 should be postponed until that union should have been accomplished. His Majesty's Government accepted this recommendation; and accordingly no further change was made in the constitution until, in 1831, the United Colony of Demerary and Essequebo was amalgamated with the Colony of Berbice as one colony thereafter to be called " The Colony of British Guiana."

CHAPTER IV

DEVELOPMENT OF THE COLONY OF BERBICE FROM THE TREATY OF MÜNSTER TO THE UNION WITH DEMERARA AND ESSE-QUEBO (1648–1831)

WHEN by the Treaty of Münster, signed on the 30th January, 1648, the Berbice river with Fort Nassau was definitely ac-

Partnership of Van Pere and Van Rhee in Berbice Settlement. knowledged by Spain to be a Dutch possession, that settlement was but a trading-post, of which Abraham van Pere was recognized as patroon by the Dutch West India Company. Subsequently Abraham van Pere seems to have taken Abraham van Rhee into partnership, and these two merchants became joint patroons of the settlement. The trading-post itself was managed by Commandeurs, who were skippers and traders, and who relieved each other at frequent intervals as had originally been the case in Essequebo.

The settlement prospered; and in 1666, when Essequebo and Pomeroon were attacked and captured by a British force, Berbice escaped unscathed. Indeed, it was a Commandeur of Berbice, Matthijs Bergenaar, who recaptured Fort Kijk-over-al and restored Essequebo to the Dutch West India Company. That Company, however, was wound up in 1674, and the concession in Berbice granted by it to Abraham van Pere and Abraham van Rhee necessarily lapsed. Accordingly Van Pere asked for a renewal of the concession from the reconstituted West India Company, to which the States-General granted a

Reconstituted Dutch West India Company renews Concession to Van Pere, 1678. charter on the 20th September, 1674; and, after prolonged disputes, the Ten signed on the 14th September, 1678, "Articles and Conditions under which the Lords Committee of Directors from the respective Chambers of the General Chartered West India Company of the United Netherlands, under the authority of the High Mighty Lords States General of the same territories, have given over as a fief the Colony situated on the river named

F

Berbice, on the great coast of America, in latitude six degrees north of the equinoctial line, to Heer Abraham van Pere." [1] Under this agreement the Colony of Berbice, " with all its belongings on the surface, minerals, forests, rivers, fountains, and whatever else shall be found there," became the property of Van Pere, his heirs and successors, during the period of the Company's charter until the year 1700 inclusive, to be held " with all its royalties and appurtenances, high, middle and low jurisdiction, tithes, fisheries and water privileges, on payment, as often as the fief shall be transferred to another person, of a manorial fee of forty Flemish pounds [$96 or £20], which tax, being the right of the aforesaid General Company, shall be paid to the Chamber of Zeeland at Middelburg."   Van Pere, his heirs and successors, under the title of Patroons of the Colony of Berbice, were authorized to " conduct and execute everything for the preservation of the Colony, including the maintenance of good order, police and justice, according to the laws and customs of these territories," and were enjoined to " take particular care that the Reformed Christian Religion be professed and taught."   They were permitted, " in the name and by the authority of Their High Mightinesses and the Company, to make binding contracts and alliances with the natives of the country, as well as to erect fortresses and other works for protection and defence."   The Company agreed to supply the Colony at reasonable prices with such " negroes or black slaves " as should be required ; while in commutation of the taxes and recognitions, to which the Company would otherwise have had pretensions, Van Pere, his heirs and successors, were bound to pay for each vessel, great or small without distinction, trading to Berbice the sum of 575 Carolus guilders, and no more, " as a tax to and on behalf of the aforesaid Company."

It will be noticed that this agreement ignored the rights of Abraham van Rhee, who had died.   Accordingly his widow, *Cornelis Demetris takes Van Rhee's place as Patroon.* who was re-married to Cornelis Demetris, a predicant of Middelburg, applied to the States-General for redress ; and, on the 24th January, 1681, the matter was decided in her favour.   Berbice thus became the " lordship in fee " of two patroons, Abraham van Pere and Cornelis Demetris, who appear to have kept up the system of

<hr>

[1] Rodway, vol. i, pp. 29–31.

annual, or at least frequent, changes in their Commandeurs; for mention is made of Gideon Bourse as Commandeur in 1683, of Lucas Coudrie in 1684, and of Matthijs de Feer in 1687 : but from that time to 1712 the record is entirely lost.[1]

During the War of the League of Augsburg, which, while destroying Pomeroon, left Essequebo unharmed, Berbice suf-

Du Casse attacks Berbice in 1689.

fered severely : for in 1689 Du Casse, one of the most famous privateer leaders, sent two of his ships up the Berbice river to pillage and destroy the plantations, thereby compelling Commandeur De Feer to promise 20,000 guilders ($8,000 or £1,666 13s. 4d.) as ransom for the Colony. In payment of this sum De Feer gave a draft on the patroons, with the customary hostages; but, fortunately for Berbice, the matter was compounded by the Governor of Surinam. Du Casse had bombarded the fort at Paramaribo in May, 1689, without success; and in retiring from the attack one of his vessels got aground and was captured by the Dutch with all on board, to the number of 184 men. By holding these prisoners the Governor of Surinam was able to obtain better terms for Berbice; and the matter was ultimately settled by a payment of 6,000 guilders ($2,400 or £500) and by handing over a few hogsheads of sugar.

Twenty-three uneventful years then elapsed until, towards the close of the War of the Spanish Succession, Berbice was

Berbice again held up to ransom by French Privateers in 1712.

again ravaged in October, 1712, by a French privateer leader, Baron de Mouans. At that time the administration of Berbice was in the hands of a Governing Council, which consisted of the Commandeur and the six managers of the patroons' plantations. This Council decided that resistance was hopeless, and Fort Nassau surrendered. The privateers exacted a ransom of 10,000 guilders ($4,000 or £833 6s. 8d.) in cash for the estates and goods of the private planters, while as ransom for the fort and the six plantations of the patroons a sum of 300,000 guilders ($120,000 or £25,000) was demanded, of which 118,024 guilders ($47,209.60 or £9,835 6s.) were paid locally in sugar, slaves, stores, etc. It was stipulated that the balance should be paid by a bill of exchange drawn by the Commandeur and his Council on the house of Van Pere to the order of Baron de

---

[1] Rodway, vol. i, p. 43.

Mouans. The patroons, however, absolutely refused to accept this bill of exchange, but agreed to compound the matter by ceding the Colony of Berbice to the French privateers. Thus we have the extraordinary spectacle of a Dutch mercantile firm offering to commute a bill of exchange drawn upon it by surrendering Dutch territory, held by the firm as a fief from a Company chartered by the States-General, without reference either to the Company or to the States-General; while, to add to the difficulties, before any decision was reached, the Peace of Utrecht, which purported to settle all disputes, was signed on the 14th April, 1713, and made no mention of Berbice.

The French ambassador at the Hague brought the matter before the States-General, who, however, would have nothing *Berbice trans-* to do with it, regarding it as no more than a mer- *ferred to the* cantile transaction. Thereupon Joseph Maillet, one *Van Hoorns* *and their* of five merchants who had equipped the privateering *Associates.* squadron to which Berbice surrendered, went himself to Amsterdam, where he offered to sell either the bill of exchange or the Colony. After some delay he entered into negotiations with Nicolaas van Hoorn and Pieter Schuurman. These merchants appear to have been backed by Cornelis van Pere, although his name was kept out of the transaction, and to have been promised by him that he would facilitate the transfer to them of the rights of the old proprietors, whose heir he was. They accordingly approached the West India Company, and, being influential shareholders, obtained the support of the Company, which agreed to supply them with the slave-labour necessary for developing the Colony of Berbice. This agreement was sanctioned by the States-General on the 10th September, 1714; and, all preliminaries being satisfactorily settled, Van Hoorn and Schuurman offered Maillet 108,000 guilders ($43,200 or £9,000) for the bill of exchange, which, it will be remembered, was for 181,976 guilders ($72,790.40 or £15,164 14s.). Maillet accepted the offer; and on the 24th October he executed, on behalf of the five French merchants who had equipped the squadron of Baron de Mouans, an " act of cession," whereby Berbice was transferred to Messrs. Nicolaas van Hoorn, Hendrick van Hoorn, Arnold Dix and Pieter Schuurman, who upon payment of the sum of 108,000 guilders became entitled to all the privateers' rights, hypothecations and preferences upon Berbice, and were authorized to take possession of the Colony.   In order to complete the transaction, an " acte van abandon " was passed on the 28th November, 1714, by which Johan and Cornelis van Pere, Maria van Pere (widow of Cornelis Kien) and Thomas Alexander Koninck, the late patroons of the Colony, ceded all their rights to the Van Hoorns and their associates.   Thus, after eighty-seven years, the control of the mercantile house of Van Pere over the Colony of Berbice came to an end ; and in its place there succeeded as patroons a new mercantile association, deriving title from the West India Company, which in turn derived its authority from the charter given to it by the States-General.

During the next six years Berbice continued to be under the control of the Van Hoorns and their associates.   Commandeurs were now no longer changed at frequent intervals. *Formation of the Berbice* Attempts were made to open up new plantations ; *Association.* but the want of labour and capital was much felt ; and, the profits being small and unsatisfactory to the shareholders, it was decided in 1720 to raise more capital by forming a new joint-stock company.   A prospectus [1] was issued, which stated that

> " for the proper administration of all the business of the Colony, an office shall be opened in the town of Amsterdam, and seven Directors shall be elected by majority of votes to decide what shall, or shall not, be done, of which number shall be Messrs. Nicolaas van Hoorn and Pieter Schuurman.   It shall also be permitted to Mr. Hendrick van Hoorn to attend all meetings, and, in the absence of his brother, to sit as a Director ; but, when both attend together, only one vote will be counted.   In case of death the surviving brother will succeed."

The other five Directors were to be experienced merchants elected by a majority of votes from shareholders owning not less than ten shares.   The Directors were to hold office for life, unless they became disqualified by no longer possessing the requisite ten shares or by absenting themselves from all the meetings during a whole year ; and they were to appoint

---

[1] Rodway, vol. i, pp. 85–9.

" all the necessary servants " including, of course, the Commandeur, who was their attorney in the Colony.

There was some difficulty in floating the Berbice Association (Societat), as the new Company was called : and of 1,200 *Inauguration* shares open to the public only 941 were taken up. *of New* Nevertheless directors were duly elected, and met *Régime in* *Berbice.* for the first time on the 4th October, 1720, when certain regulations were adopted. It was decided that the President should be changed every two months, and that the duties of Secretary should be performed in rotation by each Director; while, on the 14th December, 1720, the Directors wrote to the Commandeur of Berbice informing him of the change of ownership and instructing him to open up eight or ten new sugar plantations, for which purpose 1,200 slaves would shortly be sent to the Colony, to increase the cultivation of cocoa, and to begin planting indigo, cotton and coffee. At this time there were in Berbice six sugar and two cocoa estates owned by the Association, and 895 slaves were employed on these plantations. There existed also a principal fort (Fort Nassau) with a redoubt opposite it, a guard-house (Redoubt Sampson) about half-way between the fort and the river-mouth, and four outlying trading-posts in the interior.

The change in the ownership of the Colony of Berbice did not escape the notice of the West India Company, which, on *Dispute be-* the 23rd March, 1721, informed the Association that *tween Berbice* *Association* it still considered the Colony as under its supremacy, *and West* *India* and demanded payment of the commuted " taxes *Company.* and recognitions " previously paid to the Company by the patroons. Against this the Association protested, stating that, when Berbice was seized by French privateers, all the rights of the Company lapsed; and that, when bought by the Van Hoorns, the Colony was entirely free and independent. The dispute would probably have remained unsettled but for the necessity of getting slaves, in order to make a profit out of the Colony. This being urgent, the Association waived their point, in 1730, and agreed to pay the Company 300 guilders for the voyage of each vessel trading to Berbice, on condition that the Company supplied slaves at reasonable prices. Next year, however, the Association petitioned the States-General for a charter, with a view to securing their rights against a possible refusal of the Company to abide by the agreement just made. This did not please the Ten, who strenuously opposed the grant of a charter as being an infringement of their rights and privileges. After much discussion it was agreed between the Company and the Association, on the 27th September, 1732, that all claims of the former on the latter should be compounded for an annual payment of 600 guilders ($240 or £50). Finally, on the 6th December, 1732, the States-General issued a charter to the Directors of the Berbice Association, providing, however, that under certain conditions the trade and navigation to the Colony might be open to all inhabitants of the United Provinces.[1]

This charter permitted

> *Charter granted by States-General to Berbice Association, 1732.* " the Directors of Berbice, under the sovereignty of their High Mightinesses and their patronage and protection, to grant lands to particular persons on such conditions as may be arranged between the contracting parties " : " to collect an annual head-tax of fifty pounds of sugar for each inhabitant living in the Colony, white as well as black, also a customs duty of $2\frac{1}{2}\%$ of the value of all goods imported to, or exported from, the Colony, and a tonnage duty on all vessels, entering or clearing, of three guilders per *last*[2] to be paid at the place where the ship enters or clears."

The Directors were further declared to be entitled, in compensation for the cost of maintaining forts and a garrison, " to receive an extraordinary head-tax of such an amount yearly as shall be agreed upon with the planters and inhabitants, or otherwise by their High Mightinesses, on the information of the colonists of what shall have been found just." It was, however, added that the Directors should " not be allowed to impose any other taxes during the first ten years, nor even afterwards, without the consent of their High Mightinesses and on application of the Governor and Council." The Governor was to be appointed by the Directors, but his commission was to be given him by the States-General, before whom he had to take the oath of office. The Council of Government (Raad van Regeering) was provisionally to consist of the Governor as

---

[1] See Appendix G.   [2] A *last* is equivalent to 4,000 lb.

President and of six other persons " chosen by the Governor from a double number of names submitted to him, for the first time by all the colonists, and afterwards by the other Councillors." The Governor and Council of Government were charged with the executive administration as well as with the dispensation of criminal justice; but civil justice was to be dispensed by a Council of Justice consisting of the Governor as President and of six other persons chosen by the Governor and the Council of Government from a double number both of Councillors and of colonists. Where votes were equal, the Governor had a casting vote. In all matters, civil or military, the Governor had supreme control; but the Governor and his Councillors were bound to obey and carry out whatever might be ordered by the Directors, it being well understood that neither the Governor nor the Council, together or separately, could make or introduce, much less execute, anything contrary to the tenour of the charter, but that there would " be no objection to a few small moderate taxes being fixed by the Governor and Council, with the approval of the Directors, so as to provide certain necessary expenses of the respective Councils of Government and Justice, the schoolmaster and suchlike." The Council of Justice was bound by oath to decide in accordance with (i) the colonial ordinances or *placaats*, which dealt with municipal, rather than civil or criminal, matters, (ii) the laws and customs of the United Provinces, and (iii) the Roman law. In civil matters an appeal lay to the States General.

The Charter expressly provided that the trade and navigation of the Colony generally should not be permitted otherwise than to and from the United Provinces, " and that direct, without calling at other places "; that all produce grown in the Colony, such as sugar, coffee, cocoa, indigo, etc., should not be delivered or exported otherwise than to the United Provinces; but that, subject to the conditions of the charter, the trade and navigation of the Colony should be opened to all inhabitants of the United Provinces. The colonists, however, were not allowed " to import or buy slaves from anyone, whosoever he may be, except from the West India Company, and through the medium of the Directors of the Colony." Thus, from 1732 onwards, the only connexion of the West India Company with the Colony was to receive an annual payment of 600 guilders from the Directors of the Berbice Association and to supply the colonists with slaves.

The first Governor of Berbice, under the new Charter, was Bernard Waterham, whom the Directors appointed on the 24th March, 1733. A month passed before the *Instructions to Governor of Berbice.* written instructions issued to him were ready. He then took the oath before Their High Mightinesses, from whom he duly received his commission, and a few days later he left Holland for Berbice. His instructions required him to inspect the Association's estates twice a year; to see if cattle-farms could be established so as to lessen the expense of salt provisions, if the plough could be used, if the Surinam method of drying coffee could be introduced, if Toucoux's process could be established in the sugar factories, and if the Indians could be induced to grow coffee, cocoa, vanilla, etc. He was to keep registers of the births and deaths of slaves, to inquire into the condition of Fort Nassau and, if necessary, build another fort, to appoint a weigh-officer and sugar-valuer, and to establish an orphan chamber. As long as there was no predicant, he must see that the psalms were sung, the scriptures read, and other religious services performed ; while, at the same time, he might inquire of the free planters what they would be willing to pay towards the support of a predicant, schoolmaster, and clerk or choir-leader. With the Governor went a Land Surveyor, to superintend the laying out of new concessions, and nine settlers, to whom free grants of land in Berbice had been given.

On Waterham's arrival in the Colony, the Councils of Government and Justice were established without delay, the former *New Adminis- trative System established.* being apparently composed of the Governor and the master-planters of the six estates owned by the Association, with a Secretary as Clerk of the Council. Two years later, in 1735, the Association's estates had become twelve in number, nine being sugar plantations, and the other three coffee, cocoa and cotton plantations. Each estate was under the management of a master-planter appointed by the Governor or by the Directors ; while the supervision of the Association's estates as a whole was entrusted to a General Superintendent, who held the most important office in the

Colony after that of the Governor and took second place in the Council of Government, his duties being similar to those of an estate's attorney of to-day.   The private plantations at this time numbered ninety-three in the Berbice River and twenty in the Canje Creek; but few of these estates were of much importance, having been but lately established.   From the Association's master-planters, as well as from the private planters, Burgher Officers were chosen to command the Burgher militia, which was organized in Berbice on the same lines as in Essequebo and Demerara.   The seat of government was still at Fort Nassau.

It would seem that the inquiries made by Waterham in accordance with his instructions proved that the planters were willing to pay towards the support of a predicant, schoolmaster and choir-leader; for, on the 21st February, 1735, the Association resolved to impose a tax of 25 guilders ($10 or £2 1s. 8d.) *per annum* on each planter to provide a Church fund; and, on the 7th June, 1735, Johannes Christian Frauendorff was appointed Predicant of Berbice; while, on his recommendation, a choir-leader was appointed who acted as sexton and school-master as well.

The inhabitants of Berbice made repeated demands, during the next five years, that a fort should be built near the mouth of the river in accordance with the fourth article of the Charter; but want of funds prevented Water-ham from carrying out this part of his instructions.

Fort St. Andries Built.

He was succeeded as Governor, on the 6th April, 1740, by Andries Lossner, who had been General Superintendent and had given great satisfaction while holding that office.   During Lossner's government, a fort near the mouth of the river was at last erected and named Fort St. Andries; but, on account of want of money, it was poorly built and proved to be of little use as a protection to the Colony.

In 1748, the Directors, owing to the amount of petty litigation, appointed Justices of the Peace (Vrederechters) to adjudicate suits in which the amount in dispute was less than a hundred guilders, thus making the work of the Governor and Council of Justice less onerous.   As yet no Fiscal had been appointed; and the Governor had, therefore, to act as Fiscal in addition to his other duties.   But, in 1755,

Staff of Civil Servants increased.

on the appointment of a new Secretary, that officer was given a Commission both as Secretary and Fiscal. In the same year, on the 5th December, Hendrick Jan van Ryswick became Governor of Berbice and set about the revision of the Colony's taxes, which had hitherto consisted of head-money, church-money, weigh-money, tonnage duties and flag-money. To these, in 1758, he added stamp-duties, customs duties on imports, licences for butchers and bakers, and a tax on liquor.

The population of Berbice, according to the official returns for the year 1762, numbered 346 whites, 244 Indian slaves and *Slave In-* 3,833 negro slaves; a total of 4,423 excluding the *surrection,* free Indians. But, in the following year, the *1763.* Colony suffered severely from a slave insurrection. Fort Nassau was unable to resist attack and was abandoned; and, notwithstanding help from St. Eustatius and Surinam, it was eleven months before the insurrection was finally subdued by the arrival of a squadron from the Netherlands. The census of the population of Berbice, on the 15th June, 1764, after order had been restored, gave a total of 3,486 souls, only 116 being whites. Thus the insurrection reduced the population as a whole by 21% and the white population by 66%; while financially the Directors of the Berbice Association were so embarrassed that they doubted whether the Colony was *Consequent* worth keeping. No produce had been received *Financial* from Berbice since the insurrection broke out; *Embarrass-* *ment.* but heavy liabilities had been incurred on account of the expeditions sent from Surinam and St. Eustatius as well as on account of the vessels and troops sent by the States-General. A call on the shareholders for 8%, namely 160 guilders per share, was paid, but only setted a few of the most pressing demands; while the free planters petitioned against paying any part of the expenditure incurred in connexion with the slave insurrection, pointing out that, if such a burden were placed upon them, they would have to leave the Colony. In these circumstances the Directors appealed to the States-General, who made them a grant of 12,000 guilders ($4,800 or £1,000) and promised an annual contribution for twelve years towards the support of the troops in Berbice: moreover, the States of Holland and West Vriesland agreed to advance 500,000 guilders ($200,000 or £41,666 13s. 4d.) to the Berbice

Association, in half-yearly instalments of 50,000 guilders ($20,000 or £4,166 13s. 4d.) at interest of 2½% *per annum*, on condition that no dividend should be declared by the Association until the debt was paid off, and that the Directors should give a proper account of their affairs, whenever called upon.

Even this financial assistance was by no means sufficient; and the Directors imposed an extraordinary head-tax of one *Planters'* guilder (40 cents or 1s. 8d.) and deducted a tax of *Society* 5% from the salaries of their officials. They also *formed in* 5% from the salaries of their officials. They also *Opposition to* endeavoured to abolish " the ten years' freedom *Berbice* *Association.* from taxes on land already granted but not transported." Against these measures the planters protested; and it appears that the estate owners and other persons interested in Berbice formed a society in Amsterdam to protect their interests. There were thirty-nine original members of this Planters' Society, which held its first meeting on the 4th April, 1769, and organized itself in opposition to the Berbice Association. A crisis came, in 1772, when the last half-yearly instalment of the advance of 500,000 guilders was paid by the States of Holland and West Vriesland. Interest became due in the following year : it had hitherto been paid out of the advances received; but the Directors had now no funds from which to meet it. The Association's estates were not paying : sums aggregating 786,354 guilders ($314,541.60 or £65,529 8s. 10d.) had been contributed to re-establish the Colony, and only 134,815 guilders ($53,926 or £11,234 11s. 8d.) had been received in taxes. Even current expenses could not be paid. Ultimately, however, the States concerned gave the Berbice Association an unlimited time in which to pay. This settled the matter, as thereafter no attempt was made to provide for either capital or interest. Moreover, consequent on a long struggle by petition and counter-petition between the Berbice Association and the Planters' Society, the States-General at last decided, on the 1st April, 1774, that the *Dispute as to* Directors should be permitted for three years to *Taxation* double the existing taxes and impose another tax *settled.* of 125 guilders ($50 or £10 8s. 4d.) on each plantation, provided the total amount did not exceed 12,500 guilders ($5,000 or £1,041 13s. 4d.). In consideration for this, the Directors were bound to make adequate provision for the security of the Colony and always maintain there at least 200 soldiers properly equipped, and further to furnish the Planters' Society with a muster-roll of the troops in Berbice every six months.

This decision put an end to the prolonged dispute as to taxation, and the whole affair clearly showed that in Berbice *Slow Recovery of Berbice ; its Surrender in 1781.* the final decision of such matters vested in the States-General. But the Colony took a long time to recover; and the ground lost had not been made up when, early in March, 1781, came the news of the capture of Demerara by British privateers. A few days later two British privateers made their way into the Berbice river, attacked, captured and burnt Fort St. Andries, and proceeded towards Fort Nassau. Berbice was as helpless as Demerara and Essequebo; and, when the King's officers had arranged for the surrender of the Two Rivers, an emissary was sent to Berbice, which capitulated on similar terms. For the next three years Berbice followed the fortunes of Demerara and Essequebo, being under the same Governors—first British and then French—but nominally retaining her constitution, her Council of Government and her laws : while the estates owned by the Berbice Association were, during the French occupation, treated as private estates and administered by the Directors as private planters. It was at this time that the project of removing the establishment at Fort Nassau to the mouth of the river and of building a town where New Amsterdam now stands was first mooted.

On the 20th February, 1784, Pieter H. Koppiers, the Governor who, in 1781, had surrendered Berbice to the British officers, *Berbice restored to Dutch in 1784 : Seat of Government moved to New Amsterdam.* received back the government from the hands of the French commander; and the government and defence of the Colony were again entrusted to the Directors of the Berbice Association. Application was at once made to the States-General for a subsidy to restore the Colony to its old position and to put its defences in proper order; and a grant of 200,000 guilders ($80,000 or £16,666 13s. 4d.) was given by their High Mightinesses, on condition that the trade to Berbice should be quite free. Next year, it was finally resolved to abandon Fort Nassau and remove the seat of government to the neighbour-

hood of Fort St. Andries, the site of what is now New Amsterdam. But, although this resolution was adopted in 1785, it
was not until five years later that the construction of the
town was actually taken in hand, the engineer being meanwhile engaged in the improvement of Fort St. Andries.

The end of the Dutch West India Company, on the 31st
December, 1791, did not in any way affect Berbice, which had
severed practically all connexion with that Company
Colonial Council of Batavian Republic takes over Administration of Berbice. for about sixty years. But when, in 1795, the
so-called Batavian Republic was established in the
Netherlands, all the powers of the Berbice Association
in respect of the government and defence of the
Colony were assumed by the Colonial Council of the
Republic, the Association retaining only its proprietary rights
and being placed on the same footing as all other owners of
estates in Berbice. The Governor, Abraham van Batenburg,
whom the Directors of the Berbice Association had appointed
in 1793, was continued in office ; and, as the local administration
under the Charter of 1732 was not changed and no alteration was
made in the local officials, the slight modification in the method
of exercising the supreme control from the mother-country was
hardly noticed.

Very slow progress had been made since the slave insurrection,
the return of slaves for the year 1790 showing that the number
Slow Progress. was only 5,862—little more than before the year
1763. But the transfer of the seat of government
from Fort Nassau to the mouth of the river gave an impetus to
development. The number of slaves increased from 6,709
in 1792 to 8,232 in 1795 ; and in the latter year the population
of Berbice may be estimated at about 10,000 souls, as against
some 60,000 in the Two Rivers. In the white population
the Dutch element preponderated. French settlers were few
and English fewer still. This was due largely to the injudicious
action taken by the Berbice Association in expropriating by
a notice, issued on the 15th June, 1785, most of the lands given
out during the British and French occupation, " as having been
illegally granted." Such a breach of faith deterred immigrants
from settling in Berbice as readily as they did in Demerara and
Essequebo.

In 1796, as in 1781, Berbice followed the fortunes of the

Two Rivers, being compelled to surrender in May to a British detachment.   By the articles of capitulation private property *Surrender to* was to be respected, and Governor Van Batenburg, *Great Britain in 1796 and* who was retained as Administrator, interpreted *1803.* this in favour of the estates of the Berbice Association, as having been, since 1795, nothing more than a private company.   The fact that Berbice was now for some years in British occupation made it important that the boundary between that Colony and the adjoining Dutch colony of Surinam should be properly delimited.   Accordingly " the adjustment of the differences with respect to the correct boundary between the two Colonies " was during 1799 discussed by Governor Van Batenburg with Governor Frederici of Surinam and an arrangement, which lasts to this day, was made and published on the 7th February, 1800, whereby the Corentyne river became the boundary between their respective colonies.[1]

The prosperity of Berbice was now much increased by the arrival of planters from Barbados ; and, in the seven years 1796 to 1802, the number of slaves in the Colony was more than doubled, increasing from 8,232 to 17,885.   Great fears were naturally entertained by these new settlers when Berbice was given back to the Batavian Republic, in 1802, by the Treaty of Amiens.   Van Batenburg at once sailed for the Netherlands, leaving the administration in the hands of two Councillors, Herlin and Hobus.   But, on the 23rd September, 1803, the Colony was called upon by Captain L. O. Bland and Lieut.-Colonel R. Nicholson to surrender once more to Great Britain on terms similar to those of 1796 ; and the provisional government, knowing resistance to be hopeless, capitulated next day.[2]

Berbice having again become a British colony, Van Batenburg was reinstated as Governor on the 25th June, 1804, *Berbice as a* just as Antony Beaujon was reinstated as Governor *Separate Colony under* of the Two Rivers ; and the two colonies, which had *British Rule.* been temporarily united since the 1st October, 1803, under the governorship of Lieut.-Colonel R. Nicholson, were again separated, although the military command both of Berbice and of the Two Rivers might sometimes devolve on the same officer, as in the case of Brig.-General John Murray, who, while acting as Governor of Berbice, was called upon to ad-

---

[1] B. G. Laws, vol. i, pp. 5–6.   [2] See Appendix D.

minister the government of the neighbouring Colony as well. Most of the early British Governors, who succeeded Van Batenburg, were military commanders; and there was no interference with the constitution as laid down by the Charter of 1732. Steady progress continued; and, in 1811, the population of Berbice numbered 550 whites, 240 free coloured people, and 25,169 slaves, while the Government's expenditure for that year amounted to 207,980 guilders ($83,192 or £17,231 13s. 4d.). Meanwhile, however, the Berbice Association was languishing. In 1812, the number of its estates had been reduced to four, with a total of 791 slaves, the whole property being valued at £110,625; and, in 1818, these four estates with the slaves, whose numbers had decreased to 683, were finally sold for £66,000 to Messrs D. C. Cameron, Henry Davidson and Aeneas Barkly. Thus, after ninety-eight years, the connexion of the Association with Berbice came to an end; and in 1848 its affairs were finally wound up and it ceased to exist.

PART II

THE COLONY OF BRITISH GUIANA

CHAPTER I

CHANGES IN THE CONSTITUTION DUE TO THE UNION OF THE THREE RIVERS

MAJOR-GENERAL SIR BENJAMIN D'URBAN became Governor of the Two Rivers on the 24th April, 1824; and from March, *Creation of* 1825, to July, 1826, during the absence of Mr. Henry *the Colony of British* Beard, the last Governor of Berbice, he administered *Guiana.* the affairs of all three rivers, thus foreshadowing the union which was to come a few years later. Ever since the events of 1781, when Berbice was for the first time temporarily united to the Two Rivers, the former colony had become more and more secondary to Demerara, whose prosperity threw into the shade both Essequebo on the west and Berbice on the east, and made the inhabitants of the latter river anxious to unite with the more flourishing sister-colony, with which they were already connected by community of origin, language and rural economy. Moreover, several temporary experiments had satisfied His Majesty's Government that there was no difficulty in governing all three rivers from Georgetown; and Sir Benjamin himself had during sixteen months administered the affairs of both colonies, while Mr. Beard was not altogether liked by the residents in Berbice, who appear to have been glad to be rid of him. In these circumstances, on the 4th March, 1831, a Commission [1] was issued to Sir Benjamin D'Urban by King William IV, under the Royal Signet and Sign Manual, reciting that,

"whereas for divers good causes to Us appearing, We have deemed it right that Our settlements and factories on the northern coast of the continent of South America, comprising the United Colony of Demerary and Essequebo and the Colony of Berbice, should henceforth be united together, . . . We . . . do constitute and appoint you, the said Sir Benjamin D'Urban, to be, during Our will and pleasure, Our Governor and Commander-in-Chief in and over all Our settlements on the northern coast of the

[1] B. G. Laws, vol. i, pp. 11–14; see Appendix H.

continent of South America, comprising all such territories and jurisdictions as have hitherto been comprised in the said United Colony of Demerary and Essequebo and the said Colony of Berbice respectively, with their respective dependencies, and all forts and garrisons erected and established, or which shall be erected and established within the same, and which such settlements shall henceforth collectively constitute and be one Colony, and shall be called ' The Colony of British Guiana.' "

It will be remembered that hitherto the Colony of Berbice had been under the control of a Council of Government comprising six members, presided over by a Governor, in whom, as representing the Crown, was vested the right of appointing to all vacancies in the Council. The power of the Crown in that Colony had been absolute, there being no representative institutions of any kind. On the other hand, the Two Rivers had since 1812 been governed by a Court of Policy, presided over by the Governor, and composed of three official members, two colonial Councillors from Demerara and two from Essequebo : thus the number of official and unofficial members was equal; but, as the Governor had a casting vote, the power of the Crown in the Court of Policy was almost as absolute as in the Berbice Council of Government. In Berbice, however, the Councillors were all nominated by the Governor, whereas in the Two Rivers the four unofficial members of the Court of Policy were nominated by a Combined Board of Kiezers and Financial Representatives, consisting of six members elected by the suffrages of all colonists who paid tax on an income of 10,000 guilders *per annum*, or were possessed of twenty-five slaves. Moreover, since 1812, in the Two Rivers, when matters of taxation and expenditure were under consideration, the six members of the Combined Board of Kiezers and Financial Representatives sat in Combined Court with the members of the Court of Policy, thus giving the elective section, if unanimous, a preponderating vote in such matters.

Constitution of the Two Rivers extended to all Three Rivers.

The Royal Commission to Sir Benjamin D'Urban now directed

" that the form of civil government heretofore by law established in the said United Colony of Demerary and Essequebo shall be, and the same is hereby, established in and throughout the said Colony of British Guiana; and that all such bodies politic and corporate as have heretofore

lawfully existed in the said United Colony of Demerary and Essequebo shall in like manner exist in and throughout the said Colony of British Guiana, and shall in and throughout the Colony have, exercise and enjoy all such powers and authority as have heretofore been lawfully had, exercised and enjoyed by them respectively in the United Colony of Demerary and Essequebo : provided nevertheless, and We do hereby declare Our will to be, that the number of the members of certain of the said bodies politic and corporate heretofore existing in the said United Colony of Demerary and Essequebo shall in the said Colony of British Guiana be augmented and enlarged in such manner as by your said instructions [1] is directed in that behalf; provided also, and We do further declare Our pleasure to be, that nothing herein contained shall extend, revoke or abrogate any law or lawful usage or custom, now in force in the said United Colony of Demerary and Essequebo, or in the said Colony of Berbice respectively, save only in so far as relates to the separate constitution and form of civil government heretofore established and in use in the said Colony of Berbice, which said constitution or form of civil government We do hereby abrogate and dissolve and do declare that the same hath become and shall henceforth be extinct and merged in the government of the Colony of British Guiana."

The Royal Instructions above referred to were dated the 5th March, 1831, and declared the King's pleasure to be

" that the Court of Policy heretofore existing in the United Colony of Demerary and Essequebo shall be augmented and increased by the addition of two members, that is to say, of the Protector of Slaves for the time being and of one unofficial member to be chosen in such and the same manner as the said unofficial members of the said Court have heretofore been chosen."

Thus the constitution which had previously obtained in the Two Rivers was now extended to all three rivers. But His *Combined Board of Kiezers and Financial Representatives abolished.* Majesty's Government took advantage of the opportunity for carrying into effect the decision, arrived at in Governor Murray's time, to annul the unconstitutional changes made by Major-General Carmichael in 1812. Accordingly the Royal Instructions of the 5th March, 1831, directed that,

[1] See Appendix I.

" whereas on the 7th day of September, 1812, Major-
General Carmichael, then administering the government
of the said United Colony of Demerary and Essequebo,
did, by a proclamation [1] by him for that purpose issued,
declare the College of Kiezers of the said United Colony
to be no longer a distinct and separate institution, and did
direct in substance that the said College of Kiezers and the
College of Financial Representatives should thenceforth
be combined into and constitute one single College, and
that the elections thereof should be by other persons than
those who had theretofore elected the said two Colleges :
and whereas the said Major-General Carmichael was not
authorized by the Commission under which he administered
the government of the said United Settlements, or by any
instructions issued to him in pursuance of that Commission,
so to alter the constitution and system of government of
the said Settlements, or to promulgate any such proclamation as aforesaid ; and the same was not transmitted by
him to be laid before His late Majesty King George the
Third for confirmation, and hath not in fact been confirmed
or allowed by His said late Majesty, or by His late Majesty
King George the Fourth, or by Us : Now, We do hereby
annul, rescind and disallow the said proclamation, and do
declare Our pleasure to be that the College of Kiezers and
the College of Financial Representatives of the said United
Colony shall henceforth be two distinct and separate bodies,
and shall have such powers and duties as such Colleges
respectively had, and shall be elected by such persons and
in such manner as such Colleges were respectively eligible
by law before the said proclamation was so issued, save only
that the right of voting upon the election of the members
of the said Colleges shall henceforth be extended to, and
enjoyed by, Our subjects in every part of Our said Colony
of British Guiana."

Upon receipt of these Royal Instructions, Sir Benjamin
D'Urban published them in a proclamation,[2] dated the 21st
July, 1831, whereby in His Majesty's name he constituted "a
College of Kiezers of the Colony of British Guiana, for the purpose of electing members to fill vacancies in the Court of Policy
of the said Colony " : the said College to consist of seven
Kiezers, the term of whose service therein was to be respectively
for their lives, or until they resigned their office therein, or
ceased to be inhabitants of the Colony. By the same proclamation Sir Benjamin, in His Majesty's name, constituted " a

---

[1] *Vide supra*, pp. 61, 62.   [2] B. G. Laws (1870), vol. i, pp. 75–8.

Body of Financial Representatives of the Colony of British Guiana, for the purpose only of raising, in conjunction with the Governor and Court of Policy of the said Colony, the colonial taxes to supply the sums required by the annual estimate previously prepared by the said Governor and Court of Policy, and of examining, in conjunction with the Court of Policy, the accounts of the colonial Receiver-General for the preceding year "; the said Body of Financial Representatives to consist of six members, the term of whose service therein was to be for two years respectively. Moreover, as the King had dissolved the Combined Board of Kiezers and Financial Representatives, it was necessary to proceed at once to the election both of a College of Kiezers and of a Body of Financial Representatives. Accordingly, Sir Benjamin called upon all inhabitants of the Colony of British Guiana, possessed of twenty-five slaves or upwards, to vote for the election of seven Kiezers and of six Financial Representatives.

On the same day, the 21st July, 1831, a special meeting of the Court of Policy took place, being attended by those persons *Special Meeting of Court of Policy.* who had hitherto formed the Court of Policy of the United Colony of Demerary and Essequebo—namely, Mr. Charles Wray (President of the Court of Civil and Criminal Justice of Demerara and Essequebo), Mr. Charles Herbert (First Fiscal), Mr. George Bagot (Second Fiscal), and the four colonial members : C. A. Baron van Grovestins, James Johnstone, John Croal, and F. P. van Berckel. At this meeting Sir Benjamin D'Urban exhibited to the Court the Royal Commission appointing him to be Governor and Commander-in-Chief in and over British Guiana; and, the Commission having been read and proclaimed with due solemnity, His Excellency took the prescribed oaths and assumed the civil government of British Guiana, while all the members present, having taken and signed the oaths prescribed by His Majesty's Commission and Instructions, became " members of the Court of Policy of British Guiana." At a subsequent meeting, held *Election of a College of Kiezers and of a College of Financial Representatives.* on the 29th August, 1831, the Secretary opened the two boxes containing the votes for Kiezers, as sent in by the inhabitants from Demerara and Essequebo and from Berbice; and, the votes having been counted, the majority appeared in favour of the following inhabitants, viz., C. Bean, A Jackson, G. Rainy,

T. Barry, T. Blake, C. Spenser, and W. Fraser, who were thereupon " declared duly elected and to be henceforth collectively
the College of Kiezers of British Guiana." Next day the
Governor drew the attention of the Court of Policy to the
fact that two colonial members, Baron van Grovestins and
Mr. John Croal, having resigned their seats during the previous
month, it would now be necessary to fill these vacancies by
means of the College of Kiezers just elected; and he expressed
the desire that this should be done in strict accordance with the
ancient practice, extending the spirit of that practice to the
newly added District of Berbice.   Thereupon F. P. van Berckel
suggested that the Kiezers, when called to make nominations
for filling the two vacancies,

> " should be desired to send in two nominations, each of
> two persons, being colonists of Essequebo (the District of
> Demerary being already fully represented), and one other
> nomination of two persons being colonists of the District
> of Berbice, out of which nominations persons are to be
> selected by this Court in the usual manner, by which means
> every one of these three Districts will be sure of a fair
> representation in this Court."

The other members present having concurred in this suggestion, Sir Benjamin accepted their advice and stated that he
would act upon it.   The Court then resolved to proceed with
the examination of the votes sent in by the inhabitants of the
Colony of British Guiana for filling up the College of Financial
Representatives.   The Secretary produced the boxes containing the votes; and, upon a count being taken, the majority of
the votes was found to be in favour of H. Bruce, P. Rose, J.
Downer, D. Melville, J. Croal, and A. Glen, who were thereupon
declared to be duly elected to constitute collectively the College
of Financial Representatives of British Guiana.

The newly elected College of Kiezers met for the first time
on the 20th September, 1831, in consequence of a summons
Membership from the Governor to make nominations for filling
of Court of three vacancies in the Court of Policy, two for the
Policy
increased. District of Essequebo being due to the resignations
above mentioned, and one for the District of Berbice owing to
the addition of a fifth colonial member by the Royal Instructions.
After mature deliberation the College agreed to make the
following nominations :   (*a*) J. Croal and P. Rose for the first

vacancy; (*b*) T. Barry and T. Frankland for the second vacancy; and (*c*) W. Ross of Plantation Skeldon and J. Cameron of Plantation Lochaber for the third vacancy. These nominations were duly considered by the Court of Policy on the 27th September, 1831, when a majority voted in favour of John Croal for the first vacancy and of John Cameron for the third vacancy, and these gentlemen were declared duly elected to be members of the Court of Policy for the Districts of Essequebo and of Berbice respectively. The nomination for the second vacancy was unanimously resolved by the Court of Policy to be void on the ground that T. Barry, one of the nominees, was not a proprietor in the District of Essequebo. Accordingly the College of Kiezers met again on the 6th October, 1831, to reconsider the matter; and, although equally unanimous in the opinion that the Court of Policy was mistaken in thinking that the representative members of that Court should necessarily be selected from specific districts of the Colony, and while refusing to recognize the right of that Court to prescribe any such restriction on the exercise of the privilege of the College in the selection of the individuals, whom its members under the oath they had taken deemed the best qualified for the situation to be filled, nevertheless the College withdrew, under protest, its previous nomination and substituted the names of T. Frankland and P. Ross. This nomination was considered by the Court of Policy on the 19th October, 1831; and, the votes of the members being in favour of T. Frankland, that gentleman was declared to be duly elected. In virtue of the Royal Instructions, C. Elliott, the Protector of Slaves, became an official member of the Court of Policy, which thus, when fully constituted in the autumn of the year, consisted of :

The Governor, Sir Benjamin D'Urban.	
Charles Wray, the President of the Court of Justice.	Official Members.
Charles Herbert, First Fiscal.	
George Bagot, Second Fiscal.	
Charles Elliott, Protector of Slaves.	
James Johnstone } Members for Demerara. F. P. van Berckel	Unofficial Members.
John Croal } Members for Essequebo. Thomas Frankland	
John Cameron, Member for Berbice.	

The King's Commission gave the Governor full power and authority, with the advice and consent of the Court of Policy, *Royal Instructions as to Legislation.* " to make, enact, ordain and establish laws for the order, peace and good government " of the Colony, subject nevertheless to rules and regulations set out in the Royal Instructions, which enjoined upon the Governor—

(*a*) that no ordinance should be enacted for any purpose, which had not been by him first proposed so to be enacted :

(*b*) that he should not propose, or assent to, any ordinance whatever respecting the constitution of the Court of Policy, or of any other body politic or corporate within the Colony, its proceedings, numbers, or the mode of appointing or electing any of its members, if in any way inconsistent with the Royal Commission and the Royal Instructions, or repugnant to any Act of Parliament, or to any Royal Order-in-Council made, or to be made :

(*c*) that he should not propose, or assent to, any ordinance whatever, whereby the King's revenue might be lessened or impaired, or whereby the royal prerogative might be diminished or in any way infringed, or whereby any increase or diminution might be made in the number, salary or allowances of public officers, without the King's special leave or command therein first received :

(*d*) that he should not, without the King's special permission in that behalf first obtained, propose or assent to any ordinance whatever, whereby bills of credit, or other negotiable securities of whatever nature, might be issued in lieu of money on the credit of the Colony, or whereby any government paper currency might be established therein, or whereby any such bills, or other paper currency, or any coin, save only the legal coin of the realm, might be made or declared to be a legal tender :

(*e*) that he should not propose, or assent to, any ordinance whatever, by which any tax or duty might be imposed upon the trade or shipping of the United Kingdom, or whereby any tax might be imposed upon transient traders or upon persons residing, or carrying on business, for a short time within the Colony, from which other traders or persons carrying on the like business would be exempt :

(*f*) that he should not propose, or assent to, any ordinance whatever, whereby any grant of money or land or other donation or gratuity might be made by the Court of Policy to himself or to any of its members.

Furthermore the Royal Instructions authorized and required the Governor to frame and propose to the Court of Policy for *Standing* adoption, and from time to time as occasion might *Rules and* require to revoke, alter or renew, Standing Rules *Orders of the* *Court of* and Orders " for the sake of orderly despatch and the *Policy.* prevention of undue precipitation in the enactment of ordinances," and for " insuring, previously to the passing of any ordinance intended to affect or benefit private persons, that due notice be given to all parties concerned of the provisions thereof, with ample opportunity for opposing the same, and that a full and impartial examination may take place of the grounds upon which the same may be proposed or resisted." Accordingly, at a meeting of the Court of Policy on the 5th November, 1831, F. P. van Berckel moved that a committee of the Court should be appointed to carry this instruction into effect. The motion being agreed to, Sir Benjamin requested Van Berckel himself with the assistance of the Secretary to undertake the preparation of such Standing Rules and Orders. Van Berckel consented, and his draft was laid before the Court at its next meeting on the 11th November and was, after discussion and some amendment, adopted by the Court and published the same day.[1]

But, although the Governor was given power to legislate, with the advice of the Court of Policy, for the order, peace and *Power of* good government of the Colony, the King's Com- *Crown to dis-* mission expressly reserved to His Majesty, his heirs *allow Laws* *and to legis-* and successors, his and their " undoubted right *late for* and authority to disallow any such laws, and to make *British* *Guiana by Act* and establish from time to time with the advice and *of Parliament* *or by Order-* consent of Parliament," or with the advice of the *in-Council.* Privy Council, all such laws as to him and them appeared necessary for the order, peace and good government of the Colony.

[1] B.G. Laws (1870), vol. i, pp. 79–81. See also Appendix K.

The Governor was authorized by his Commission to make grants of Crown land; to remit fines, penalties or forfeitures *Powers given* payable to the Crown up to a limit of £50, or, if *to Governor by Royal* exceeding that sum, to suspend payment until the *Commission.* Royal pleasure was known; to grant to offenders convicted of any crime in any Court, or before any Judge, Justice or Magistrate within the Colony, a free and unconditional pardon, provided that in cases of treason or murder no such pardon should be granted until the King's pleasure was known.   Finally, in case of the Governor's death or absence, the senior officer for the time being in command of the land forces within the Colony was to assume the administration of the government.

At the same time steps were taken to improve the judicial system.   Before the union of the Three Rivers, the Supreme *Reform of the* Court for the trial of criminal and civil cases had *Judicial System.* consisted in the Two Rivers of a President (Mr. C. Wray) and eight members elected by the College of Kiezers from the merchants or planters of the Colony; while in Berbice the Governor had been the Chief Justice, assisted by six gentlemen drawn from the ranks of the mercantile and planting community.   Lord Goderich, in a despatch dated the 1st June, 1831, willingly admitted that in criminal matters " this mixture of persons unlearned in the law is not destitute of important advantages."

" In the absence of trial by jury," he wrote, " it probably infuses into criminal trials some of that popular feeling, with the ready appeal to common sense and ordinary habits of mankind, which in a great measure constitute the advantage of juries wherever that institution has been established.   In the present state of West India society, where the number of competent jurymen is so small, and where the indelible distinctions of African and European birth or descent, with the distinctions of freedom and slavery, have introduced such barriers between the different classes, I have no reason to suppose that trial by jury could be engrafted on the present law without producing mischiefs which must much more than compensate for any benefit which could be expected from it.   Dismissing, therefore, for the present the further consideration of any measure of that nature, it remains for me to state that,

although in civil cases and in the adjudication of questions
of law arising in criminal trials none but professional judges
will be employed hereafter, yet that upon the trial of
criminals in the Supreme Court, assessors will be appointed
from the principal merchants and planters of the Colony,
whose votes upon the question of ' guilty ' or ' not guilty '
will be of equal value with the votes of the regular
judges.''

The retirement of the unprofessional judges involved, of
course, the appointment of new judges, regularly educated as
lawyers; and Lord Goderich explained that three judges would
be nominated, '' as being the smallest number which will yield
a majority, and as being perhaps the smallest number to which
it would be right to confide interests of such magnitude and
questions of such variety.''

There was not, however, in British Guiana work enough for
three judges, nor could the revenue of that Colony afford to pay
their salaries; and, as similar circumstances prevailed in the
neighbouring colonies of Trinidad and St. Lucia, it was decided
to constitute the same three persons judges of the Supreme
Court in each of the three colonies of British Guiana, Trinidad
and St. Lucia, and to arrange that they should hold sessions
twice in each year in Demerara, Berbice, Trinidad and St.
Lucia, the times of holding such sessions being regulated by
agreement between the Governors of the three colonies concerned. When not employed on circuit, each of the three
judges would reside in the Colony to which he might more
peculiarly belong, and would there perform such acts as it was
competent for a single judge to do; while, in the absence of the
judge from his fixed place of abode, it was intended to establish
in each colony a second judge, bearing the title of Vice-President
of the Court of Justice. In British Guiana the Vice-President
would discharge the duties of his office alternately in Demerara
and in Berbice, attending in each district for that purpose
according to such arrangements as the Judges of the Supreme
Court might make. The Vice-President would be charged with
the despatch of that description of judicial business known
as '' interlocutory,'' the effect being that, on the arrival of
the judges in any colony, all preliminary questions arising in
any suit, whether civil or criminal, would have been disposed

of, and all causes would be ready for the final adjudication of the Court.

The judicial system so outlined was embodied in a Royal Order-in-Council made on the 23rd April, 1831,[1] which directed that

Royal Order-in-Council, 23rd April, 1831. " henceforth the Court of Criminal and Civil Justice of Demerary and Essequebo, and the Court of Civil Justice and the Court of Criminal Justice of Berbice, and the Court for the Trial of Criminal Prosecutions and the Court of First Instance of Civil Jurisdiction in the Island of Trinidad, and the Royal Court of St. Lucia shall be respectively holden by and before three Judges and no more—that is to say, each of the said Courts shall be holden by and before the President for the time being of the Court of Criminal and Civil Justice of Demerary and Essequebo, and the Chief Judge for the time being of Trinidad, and the First President for the time being of the Royal Court of St. Lucia or by and before the persons who, during the vacancy of any of such offices, or during the absence or temporary incapacity of any of the said Judges, may have received a provisional or temporary appointment to act as and in place and stead of, any such Judges or Judge."

At the time when this Order was made and for some nine years prior to 1831, the President in the United Colony of Demerary and Essequebo had been Charles Wray, who became the first Chief Justice of the Colony of British Guiana. Among the Counsellor Commissaries, who formed the Court over which he presided, there appear during the years 1829 to 1831, the following names : N. M. Manget, W. Wilkinson, G. Goppy, Henry Halket, James Douglas, C. Grant, W. Wheeler, Alexander Glen, Gavin Fullerton, Peter Rose, and J. A. D. Koolhaas. They were not legal men. The members of the Court of Civil Justice for the Colony of Berbice, who last sat during the year 1831, were D. Fraser, William Campbell, Charles Kyte, William Scott, F. Maurenbrocher, and Thomas Williams, two of whom together with the Lieut.-Governor, Henry Beard, formed a quorum.

It would appear that the Royal Order-in-Council of the 23rd

---

[1] See *Royal Gazette*, 11th August, 1831.

April, 1831, never came into force, because, contrary to expectation, the volume of work in British Guiana made it
This Order- impossible for a judge to be spared to leave the Colony.
in-Council
never came Entries on the minutes of the Courts are not want-
into force. ing as to the delay which had arisen both from
continuous and heavy work in Court and from illness; while
the record of the number of days occupied in sessions of the
Supreme Court of Criminal and Civil Justice in the Colony of
British Guiana with the number of suits brought before that
Court, and the number of witnesses from January, 1832, to
August, 1833, was as follows :

(i) *District of Demerary.*
 Supreme Court of Criminal and Civil
  Justice . . . . . 80 days; 657 suits.
 Roll Court . . . . . 100 days; 2,662 suits; 349
             witnesses.
 Inferior Court . . . . 3 days; 621 suits; 4 witnesses.
 Transports. 151
 Mortgages 29
 Cancelments 18
 Willing Condemnations . . 2

(ii) *District of Berbice.*
 Inferior Court . . . . 23 days.
 Roll Court. . . . . 37 days; 572 suits; 56 wit-
             nesses.
 Transports and Mortgages . . 80

The Order-in-Council of the 23rd April, 1831, was in fact
suspended a few months later by another Royal Order-in-
Royal Order- Council, dated the 20th June, 1831,[1] and published
in-Council,
20th June, in British Guiana on the 22nd of November in the
1831. same year, which directed that

 " the Court of Criminal and Civil Justice of Demerary and
 Essequebo, and the Court of Civil Justice and the Court of
 Criminal Justice of Berbice, shall henceforth be holden by
 and before three Judges, and no more; and that the first
 or presiding Judge of the said Court shall be called and
 bear the style and title of Chief Justice of British Guiana;
 and that the second and third of such Judges shall be called
 and bear the respective styles and titles of First Puisne
 Judge and Second Puisne Judge of British Guiana."

The three judges constituted " the Supreme Court "; and it
was ordered that no Court other than the Supreme Court
  [1] B.G. Laws (1870), vol. i, pp. 82–91.

should be competent to hold jurisdiction (*a*) in any civil case in which the sum or matter in dispute exceeded the value of £20, or in which the right of any slave to his or her freedom, or the title of lands or tenements, or any fee, duty, or office, or His Majesty's Royal Prerogative were in question, or whereby rights in future might be bound; or (*b*) in any criminal case wherein any person was accused of any crime punishable by death, transportation or banishment. Further, no Court other than the Supreme Court was authorized " to inflict any greater or other punishment than imprisonment, with or without hard labour, for a term not exceeding three months, or fine not exceeding £20, or whipping not exceeding 39 stripes, or any two or more of such kind of punishment together within the limits aforesaid." It was, however, ordered that the Governor of British Guiana, with the advice and consent of the Court of Policy, might establish " Inferior Courts," having jurisdiction in civil and criminal cases which were not expressly reserved, under the above limitations, for the jurisdiction of the Supreme Court. Thus the Order-in-Council laid the foundation not only of the Supreme Court, but also of the Magisterial Courts of the Colony. Moreover, it laid down the conditions under which leave might be given to appeal to His Majesty, his heirs and successors, in his or their Privy Council, against any judgment, decree or sentence, or against any rule or order made in any civil suit or action and having the effect of a final or definite sentence.

From April to December, 1831, there is a break in the minutes of the Supreme Court, but in November of that year the Court was constituted as follows :

Supreme Court constituted.

Charles Wray, Chief Justice.
John Walpole Willis, First Puisne Judge.
Samuel Firebrace, Second Puisne Judge.

The first and last were men conversant with local law and local requirements, but the First Puisne Judge was apparently an English barrister newly arrived in the Colony, somewhat impatient of colonial ways, and apparently not desirous at his time of life of acquiring any legal knowledge beyond that of the English law which he brought with him.

The manner of proceeding in civil cases for Demerara and

Essequebo then in use was that which had been framed on the 4th October, 1774, by the Ten, and approved by *Old Procedure* Their High Mightinesses the Lords States-General *(a) in Civil* of the United Netherlands, and is set out in the *Cases :* Second Report of the Commissioners of Enquiry into the Administration of Criminal and Civil Justice in the West Indies and South American Colonies, dated the 14th April, 1828, and ordered by the House of Commons to be printed on the 25th July, 1828.[1] The procedure in the Colony of Berbice was very similar, but with respect to accounting parties had received some later improvements.[2]

The manner of proceeding in criminal cases was the same in all three Rivers, and was according to the Ordinance of Philip *(b) in Crimi-* II of Spain, dated the 9th July, 1570.[3] This had been *nal Cases.* reported by the Commissioner, Fortunatus Dwarris, to be no longer adapted to the existing state of society in these Colonies; and accordingly an Order had been issued by His Majesty in Council on the 15th December, 1828, pre-scribing, among other provisions, that upon the trial of any criminal action or prosecution in the Supreme Court the *Revised* evidence of all witnesses either for or against the *Procedure.* person accused should be delivered *viva voce* in open Court. Rules made under this Order required that the indict-ment should contain such a description of the offence that the accused might clearly understand the crime he was called upon to answer; and further it was provided that under the plea of " Not Guilty " all matters of fact or law could be argued in favour of the accused. In any question of form in any criminal trial not otherwise provided for, the Court was to follow as nearly as possible the practice that would be adopted in Eng-land under similar circumstances. In addition to these rules an ordinance dated the 12th May, 1829, was passed by the Court of Policy enacting that the same principles and laws of evidence which were then or should be thereafter in use in criminal trials in England, and no other, should be thereafter in force and be used in criminal trials in Demerary and Essequebo.

Mr. Justice Willis, the newly appointed First Puisne Judge

[1] See Appendix B of this Parliamentary Report, pp. 203–11.
[2] See Appendix C of the Report, pp. 212–22.
[3] See Appendix J of the Report, pp. 141–51.

H

of British Guiana, who arrived in the Colony in the latter half of 1831, began as early as the 25th November of that year to advocate the introduction of English law, but without success. Even the moderate changes brought into force by the Royal Order-in-Council of the 28th June, 1831, led to some excitement in the Colony, so much so that in or about July, 1831, an attempt was made by two of the then leading lawyers in the Colony to impugn the validity of Royal Orders-in-Council as law in British Guiana. This excitement happily subsided; but the Order-in-Council was very unfavourably received, the colonists demanding their former Courts, and their ancient laws and practice. However, after consideration amongst themselves, and with the two practitioners who had questioned the validity of the Royal Orders-in-Council, the Judges of the Colony, on the 30th March, 1832, settled on the new manner of proceeding in civil matters, retaining to a very great extent the old procedure, use being still made of the Commissaries—" gentlemen unlearned in the law," as Mr. Justice Willis called them—in the Roll Court.

On the 13th September, 1832, an ordinance was passed instituting the Inferior Court of Civil Justice to be presided over by the Chief Justice or one of the Puisne Judges, *Inferior Courts established.* and by despatch dated the 16th October, 1832, the Secretary of State for the Colonies confirmed the new manner of proceeding settled by the Judges of the Supreme Court of British Guiana.

CHAPTER II

CHANGES IN THE CONSTITUTION DUE TO THE ABOLITION OF SLAVERY

Meanwhile another change of far-reaching importance had for some years past been impending. In 1806, Lord Grenville

Beginnings of Imperial Anti-Slavery Legislation, 1806–8.

and Mr. Fox having come into power, a Bill was passed in both Houses of Parliament to put an end to the British slave-trade for foreign supply, and to forbid the importation of slaves into colonies won by the British arms in the course of the Napoleonic wars. On the 10th June in the same year Mr. Fox brought forward a resolution, which was carried in the House of Commons by a large majority, requiring " that effectual measures should be taken for the abolition of the African slave-trade in such a manner and at such a period as should be deemed advisable." A similar resolution was successful in the House of Lords. A Bill was then passed through both Houses forbidding the employment of any new vessel in the trade. Finally a Bill was presented by Lord Grenville in the House of Lords providing for the abolition of the trade, was passed by a large majority, was then sent to the Commons, was there amended and passed, and received the royal assent on the 25th March, 1807. This Bill enacted that no vessel should clear out for slaves from any port within the British dominions after the 1st May, 1807, and that no slave should be landed in any British colony after the 1st March, 1808.

It was found, however, that the abolition of the British slave-trade did not lead to an improved treatment of the negroes in

Recommendations made by His Majesty's Government to British Colonies in 1823.

the West Indies. The slaves were overworked now that fresh supplies were stopped, and their numbers rapidly decreased. In 1807, there were in the West Indies 800,000 negro slaves; in 1830, the number was only 700,000. It became more and more evident that the evil could be stopped only by abolishing slavery alto-

99

gether: and, in 1821, an appeal was made by William Wilberforce to Thomas Fowell Buxton to undertake the conduct of this new question in Parliament.   An anti-slavery society was established in 1823, the principal members of which, besides Wilberforce and Buxton, were Zachary Macaulay, Dr. Lushington, and Lord Suffield.   Early in 1823, Buxton moved that the House of Commons should take into consideration the state of slavery in the British colonies.   The object, which he and his associates then had in view, was gradual abolition by establishing something like a system of serfdom for existing slaves and by passing at the same time a measure emancipating all their children born after a certain day.   Canning, however, carried, against Buxton and his friends, a resolution to the effect that the desired ameliorations in the condition and treatment of the slaves should be recommended by the home Government to the colonial legislatures and be enforced only in case of resistance.   Accordingly a despatch, dated the 24th May, 1823, was addressed by Lord Bathurst to all British colonies in the West Indies on the subject.   In Demerara a special meeting of the Court of Policy was summoned on the 21st July to consider this despatch; and after prolonged discussion and several adjournments, it was decided on the 6th August that an ordinance should be passed to prohibit the flogging of female slaves, to discontinue carrying the whip in the field, and to take some measures for the control of female slaves; but, no order for publication of this decision having been made, the matter was left over and the Court adjourned.   Meanwhile the news of the debate in Parliament had spread rapidly through the Two Rivers, and the negroes became impressed with the idea that they had all been set free.   When, however, no overt action was taken by the Governor and the Court of Policy, it was rumoured among the slaves that the King had ordered their emancipation and that the planters had refused to give it them.   Accordingly the negroes refused to work, and, compulsion being resorted to, they offered resistance.   Martial law was proclaimed, and the disturbances were repressed with great severity.

After the events of 1823, the question of abolishing slavery made little progress in Parliament for some years, action being suspended to allow the colonial legislatures time to carry into effect the measures expected of them.   Brougham, however, moved in Parliament a vote of censure on the Government and Court of Policy of Demerara, which was lost by 193 votes to 146, while a general outcry was raised *Court of Policy legislates in 1825 for meliorating the Condition of Slaves.* by the planters at the acquiescence of His Majesty's Government in the principles of the anti-slavery party. At last, after great delays and strenuous resistance, the Court of Policy was persuaded to pass an ordinance in general conformity with Canning's resolution, bearing the title " an Ordinance for the religious instruction of slaves and for meliorating their condition." It was dated the 7th September, 1825, published on the 15th October, and was to take effect from the 1st January, 1826. It provided for the appointment of a Protector of Slaves; secured the slaves an immunity from labour (except in certain specified cases) from sunset on Saturday to sunrise on Monday; limited field work from 6 a.m. to 6 p.m., with two hours' intermission; prohibited the whip from being carried in the field; abolished the whipping of women; limited the number of lashes to 25; required a record-book of punishments to be kept; and secured to the slaves the privileges of marriage, of acquiring and holding property, and of purchasing their freedom. Subsequently, in April, 1830, an Order by His Majesty in Council, made in the previous February, was *Royal Order-in-Council of 1830 amends this Legislation.* published in the Colony amending this ordinance and making additional provision for the benefit of the slaves by appointing Assistant Protectors of Slaves; by prohibiting the separation of relations; by making slaves good witnesses in the law courts, and by requiring a specified allowance of food and clothing to be given them. The colonial members of the Court of Justice in Demerara attempted to prevent this Order-in-Council from coming into operation, on the ground that it was an unconstitutional violation of the rights of the colonists as contained in the Plan of Redress and guaranteed by the Articles of Capitulation. But Lord Goderich, the Secretary of State for the Colonies, utterly refused to recognize these doctrines; and, as we have seen, the Court of Justice itself was remodelled in the following year by another Order-in-Council.

A further step was taken in an ordinance, passed by the Court of Policy on the 21st December, 1831, and brought into operation next day, which repealed all laws, ordinances and enactments existing in the Colony, or any part thereof, to

Further Legislation by Court of Policy in 1831.

which persons of European birth or descent were not also subjected and made liable. Free people of colour were thus placed on a footing of legal equality with their fellow-citizens.

In the following month, on the 12th January, 1832, His Majesty's Order-in-Council of the previous November, commonly known as the " Consolidated Slave Ordin-

Royal Order-in-Council known as the " Consolidated Slave Ordinance."

ance," was published in the Colony. It provided for the appointment of paid Assistant Protectors of Slaves; reduced the hours of labour to nine, and for children under fourteen years of age and pregnant women to six hours; increased the food and clothing allowances; and limited the number of lashes to fifteen. The colonial members of the Court of Policy made the most strenuous efforts to prevent the publication of this Order-in-Council, and their opposition led Sir Benjamin D'Urban to issue a notification,[1] in which, so as to dissipate erroneous opinions denying the right of His Majesty in Council to make laws binding on the Colony, he published for general information some extracts from a despatch, dated the 1st October, 1830, written by Lord Goderich, the Secretary of State for the Colonies. This despatch stated that His Majesty's Government had received with serious concern the intelligence of the efforts made in the Colony to resist the execution of the Order-in-Council of February, 1830, and of the contention by certain members of the Court of Justice that the Capitulation of 1803 invested the Court of Policy with exclusive legislative power within the Colony, subject to no control except the ultimate veto of the Sovereign. His Majesty's Government maintained, on the contrary, that under the Dutch Government the Court of Policy had neither enjoyed as a matter of right, nor exerted as a matter of fact, any such exclusive power, for the authority of the States-General and of the Stadtholder had been habitually exercised as occasion required. It even seemed questionable whether the Court of Policy had, under the Dutch *régime*, any right to legislate at all, except on matters of revenue and taxation and on minor local affairs, which were

[1] See *Royal Gazette of British Guiana*, 9th February, 1832.

too petty to engage the attention of the parent State. The Capitulation had not invested the Court of Policy with any new powers; and, as a matter of fact, a few years after the Capitulation and before the final Cession, while the state of war still continued, His Majesty had by Order-in-Council abolished the slave-trade.[1] Since the final Cession, numerous Orders by His Majesty in Council had been promulgated in Demerara. The King was now advised that his Privy Council had power to make laws binding on the Colony, and His Majesty's Government was fully prepared, if necessary, to enforce obedience to the Royal Order-in-Council by the most decisive measures consistent with law.

This authoritative pronouncement by His Majesty's Government appears to have checked further opposition at the moment. Now, however, the mother-country began *Slavery abolished by Act of Parliament in 1833.* to be aroused to a serious prosecution of the anti-slavery campaign. It was becoming plain that the planters would take no steps tending to the future liberation of the slaves. Therefore, the leaders of the anti-slavery movement determined to urge the entire abolition of slavery at the earliest practicable period. The home Government had for many years hesitated and contented itself with pressing for mitigations of the existing system : but, in 1833, the Ministry of Earl Grey took the question in hand and carried the abolition with little difficulty. The " Act for the abolition of slavery throughout the British Colonies, for promoting the industry of manumitted slaves, and for compensating the persons hitherto entitled to the services of such slaves," passed the House of Commons on the 7th August, 1833, and received the royal assent on the 28th of the same month. A sum of £20,000,000 was voted as compensation to the planters, and of this sum British Guiana was awarded £4,297,117 10s. 6½d. for 84,915 slaves, being an average of £50 12s. 1d. *per caput.*[2] A system of apprenticeship for seven years was established as a transitional

[1] The slave-trade in Demerara was abolished by Royal Order in Council of 15th August, 1805.

[2] Report, dated 7th July, 1835, by Office of Commissioners of Compensation on inter-colonial apportionment of the compensation fund of £20,000,000, provided by the Act 3 & 4 Will. 4, cap. 73. See *Royal Gazette of British Guiana*, 18th August, 1835. In this report the average value of a slave in British Guiana from 1822 to 1830 is given as £114 11s. 5¾d.

preparation for liberty. The slaves were bound to serve their masters during this period for three-fourths of the day, and were liable to corporal punishment if they did not give the due amount of labour. The master was, in return, to supply them with food and clothing. All children under six years of age were to be free at once, and provision was to be made for their religious and moral education.

The task of giving effect to these measures in British Guiana was entrusted by His Majesty's Government to Major-General

System of "Apprenticed Labourers" introduced in British Guiana, 1834. Sir James Carmichael Smyth, who arrived in the Colony as Governor on the 22nd June, 1833, and issued next day a proclamation to the slaves respecting the measures in progress for their benefit. The Abolition Act passed by the British Parliament was published in the Colony on the 19th October, 1833; and on the 11th February, 1834, the Court of Policy passed " an Ordinance for the classification and registration of slaves, hereafter to become and be apprenticed labourers," while a further " Ordinance for the government and regulation of apprenticed labourers " was passed by the Court of Policy on the 22nd July, 1834. The effect was that on and after the 1st August in that year all slaves became " apprenticed labourers "; that their hours of labour were reduced from nine to seven; and that they were no longer punishable by their masters, but by Justices of the Peace. The Governor explained the intention of His Majesty's Government to be that in August, 1840, the " apprenticed labourers " should become as free as any white men, while domestic servants, having to give more of their time to their masters, would be set at liberty two years earlier. He trusted, therefore, that they would in the meanwhile work quietly, happily and contentedly.

Unfortunately the commencement of the apprenticeship system brought on another collision between the slaves and

Initial Troubles due to Misunderstanding of Apprenticeship System. their masters. The former did not well understand the new system; and, as they naturally enough expected that, slavery being at an end, freedom had begun, a strike occurred on several estates. The trouble was most acute on the Essequebo coast, where seven or eight hundred labourers collected in Trinity churchyard, hoisted a flag, insisted that the King had made them free, and, when ordered to disperse, refused to do so. They were unarmed and offered no violence except hustling a man, whom they mistook for a constable, out of the church-yard. The colonists insisted that the Governor should proclaim martial law and compel the people to work at the point of the bayonet. This he refused; and, having sent a few soldiers to the Essequebo coast, he proceeded thither himself, admonished the people, and requested them to disperse, which they instantly did. There is no doubt that the judicious action of Sir James Carmichael Smyth on this occasion prevented a repe-tition of the scenes of 1823.

It had been arranged that domestic servants, or "non-prædial apprenticed labourers," as the law described them, *Liberation of* should be set entirely free and be discharged from *" Appren-* their apprenticeship on the 1st August, 1838; but, as *ticed* that date approached, it was felt that to keep the *Labourers"* *in 1838.* prædial labourers in apprenticeship for two years after many of their friends and relations had been set free would give rise to much trouble, while the difficulties and complaints connected with the classification of apprenticed labourers as prædial and non-prædial brought the matter to a head. On the 20th June, 1838, Mr. (afterwards Sir) Michael McTurk moved in the Court of Policy to abolish the apprenticeship of prædial, as well as of non-prædial, labourers; and, on the 12th July, the Court of Policy passed " an Ordinance to terminate the apprenticeship of the prædial labourers of British Guiana on the first day of August next." Thus, on the 1st August, 1838, slavery became a thing of the past in British Guiana; but the signature on the ordinance which finally abolished it was that of Governor Henry Light, for Sir James Carmichael Smyth had died at his post on the 4th March, 1838.

The emancipation necessitated considerable changes in the constitution, the administrative organization and the financial *Changes in* system of British Guiana. In 1834, the free popula-*Constitution* tion was estimated at about 10,000 souls; and *of British* compensation was paid upon 84,915 slaves. Thus, *Guiana due* *to Abolition* in round numbers, the total population of the Colony *of Slavery.* in that year may be estimated at 95,000 souls. But hitherto the elective franchise both for the College of

Kiezers and for the College of Financial Representatives had been limited to inhabitants " possessed of twenty-five slaves or upwards." Again, from the earliest days of the Colony the main income of the Company's chest, which was now the King's chest, had been a head-tax on slaves. Evidently in both these matters a change was now necessary. Moreover, the slave system had made administration economical. Under it there had been no poverty, very little crime, no magistrates and no police. Its abolition, however, necessitated a considerable increase in the civil establishments of the Colony at the very time when the established methods of taxation had been swept away; while the planters, sullen and sore at their treatment over the slavery question and at the campaign of calumny which had been conducted against them in the mother-country, were in no mood to facilitate the work of reform.

As from the 1st August, 1834, no head-tax could be levied, for there were no slaves upon whom to levy it, all slaves having *Negotiation* on that day become " apprenticed labourers." It *of the First* was, therefore, necessary to consider ways and *Civil List,* means of replacing the revenue thus lost to the *1835.* King's chest. The Secretary of State desired to compromise the matter by merging the King's chest and the Colony's chest into one, and by placing the whole fund under the control of the Combined Court, upon condition that a " Civil List," virtually equivalent to the amount of the King's taxes, which had never before been under the control of the Court, should be guaranteed for seven years. The Court, however, objected to saddle the Colony with a permanent impost; and the Financial Representatives, who had, since the reorganization of 1831, been restrained from exercising that control over the expenditure which they had usurped after Brig.-General Carmichael's proclamation of 1812, refused to exercise any functions whatsoever. Thus all supplies were stopped. Moreover, relations between Sir James Carmichael Smyth and the unofficial members of the Combined Court became so strained that the Secretary of State appointed Sir Lionel Smith, then Governor-General of the Southern Division of the West Indies, to reconcile the differences. Sir Lionel reached Georgetown on the 27th May, 1835; and, having been sworn in next day as Governor-in-Chief of British Guiana, he succeeded in negotiating a Civil List of £20,980, being virtually the amount of the King's taxes as previously collected. This Civil List was guaranteed for seven years, expiring on the 31st December, 1840, and included among other officials the Governor, the Chief Justice and two Puisne Judges, the Government Secretary and the Attorney-General.[1] Under the Civil List arrangement the two chests were merged into one. The revenue of the King's chest, over which neither the Court of Policy nor the Combined Court had ever exercised any control, was surrendered to the Combined Court as a part of the " ways and means " in return for a guarantee of the Civil List and during its term. Moreover, the powers of the Combined Court were enlarged conditionally, the Crown expressly conceding to the Court, during the term of the Civil List, certain rights of free and unreserved discussion over the annual estimates prepared by the Court of Policy. His mission being thus successfully accomplished, Sir Lionel Smith left the Colony on the 17th June, 1835; and the arrangements negotiated by him were embodied in " an Ordinance for settling upon His Majesty a certain and competent revenue for defraying the expenses of the Civil Government of British Guiana, until the 31st day of December, 1840, under certain provisions and qualifications." This law was enacted on the 16th February, 1836.

The change in the elective franchise, consequent on the abolition of slavery, was made by " an Ordinance to establish a new qualification for the exercise of the elective franchise " (No. 57 of 1835), enacted by the Governor and Court of Policy on the 2nd May, 1835, which provided that

Change in the Elective Franchise.

> " every inhabitant of this Colony of full age, and not subject to any legal disability, who shall have paid direct taxes to the colonial revenue to the amount of seventy guilders (£5) or upwards, in the year of, or in the year preceding, any new election of a member of the College of Electors [2] or of the College of Financial Representatives

---

[1] The office of Attorney-General, so called, was established by Ordinance No. 39 of 1834, B. G. Laws (1870), vol. i, p. 104.

[2] Ordinance No. 39 of 1834, section 4, enacted " that the College of Kiezers of British Guiana shall, in future, be called the College of Electors of British Guiana, and the Members thereof Electors." B. G. Laws (1870), vol. i, p. 104.

of this Colony, or who, after the publication of this ordinance, shall be assessed and liable to pay to the colonial
revenue of the said Colony direct taxes to the amount
of seventy guilders, or upwards, and not being in arrear
with the payment of such taxes for more than six months
from the date of such taxes becoming payable, shall be
entitled to vote upon the election of any such member
of the respective Colleges aforesaid."

This qualification was slightly modified by a further ordinance
(No. 86 of 1836), passed by the Court of Policy on the 2nd
December, 1836, extending the elective franchise to inhabitants "assessed to pay direct taxes to the colonial revenue
upon an income of not less than 2,001 guilders" (£143), as
well as those who paid direct taxes amounting to 70 guilders
(£5). Elections, however, were conducted in a manner which
gave little or no influence to the great body of the inhabitants
of the Colony. Absentees had the privilege of voting by proxy;
and this fact, together with the high franchise, placed the control
of elections completely in the hands of a very small number of
persons. Both the College of Financial Representatives and
the College of Electors were chosen by the same body of constituents, the former for two years only, but the Electors for
life. Moreover, the unofficial members of the Court of Policy
were chosen, not by the inhabitants possessed of the elective
franchise, but by the seven Electors, who nominated two
candidates for each unofficial seat vacant in the Court of Policy,
one such seat being vacated every second year by the retirement of the senior unofficial member. The Governor and Court
of Policy made choice in each case between the two nominees
Proceedings of Court of Policy and Combined Court thrown open to the Public. of the College of Electors. Such a constitution
obviously did not partake at all of a popular char-
acter, in spite of an important innovation, made on
the 30th March, 1837, when the doors of the Court
of Policy and of the Combined Court were for the
first time opened to the public. Thenceforth the proceedings
of these two bodies always took place in public, unless there
were special reasons for excluding strangers.

CHAPTER III

HISTORY OF THE CIVIL LIST AFTER 1840

THE approach of the 31st December, 1840, on which day the first Civil List was due to expire, made it necessary to enter *Negotiations* upon negotiations for the renewal of a similar engage-*for Renewal* ment.[1] At the time when the first Civil List was *of the Civil* *List*, 1840. negotiated in 1835, the revenues of the King's chest had been much reduced by the loss of the head-tax on slaves. But, in 1840, this loss had been made up to a great extent by an increase which had taken place in the yield of the customs' duties;[2] and the revenues which were to revert to the Crown were considerably larger than those which had been conditionally surrendered in 1835.[3] Moreover, during the intervening years the question of immigration had, owing to the emancipation of slaves, become very important. The planters were anxious to be allowed to introduce negroes from the coast of Africa and coolies from India, and to spend for that purpose, not only a large amount of surplus annual revenue, but also money to be raised on loan by the Colony. Serious objections to these schemes were entertained in Parliament by missionaries and others, who contended that the taxes to which the labourers contributed ought not to be expended in bringing competitors into the labour market to reduce their wages.[4] Also, a large mortality having taken place amongst gangs of immigrants imported into British Guiana by private enterprise, the Government of India was opposed to the emigration of Indian coolies to the West Indies. It was under these circumstances that the Combined Court made on the 24th April, 1840, an offer of a Civil List of £42,893 9s. upon the following terms and conditions, amongst others :[5]

[1] Parl. Paper 404 of 1840, pp. 47 *sqq.*   [2] *Ibidem*, pp. 56, 58.
[3] Governor Light's despatch of 30th July, 1839.
[4] Lord J. Russell's despatch to Governor Light, of 15th February, 1840. *Papers Relative to the West Indies, Presented to Parliament by Command in 1841*, pp. 70 *sqq.*   [5] Parl. Paper 404 of 1840, p. 64.

"That, under such rules and regulations for their due care, protection, and comfort, as may be deemed reasonable, all restraints upon immigration of free labourers into this Colony from all parts of the world, unfettered by indentures, be removed.

"That, simultaneously with the allowance by Her Majesty of such Civil List, an order of Her Majesty in Council be published, securing to this Court the free and uncontrolled power of raising such sums as this Court may deem necessary and of appropriating the same to such purpose as this Court may judge requisite for the advantage of the Colony; and also during the continuance of the Civil List and after due provision for the same, of pledging the revenues of the Colony for the redemption of, and payment of interest on, any loan which this Court may deem it right to contract for the promotion of immigration or otherwise."

These conditions were not accepted by Her Majesty's Government; and the result was that the Combined Court *Combined* stopped supplies for the last half of the year 1840. *Court stops* Thereupon two ordinances were passed by Governor *Supplies.* Light and the Court of Policy on the 5th and 6th May, 1840, the former entitled " an Ordinance for the support of the Civil Government of British Guiana," and the latter intituled " an Ordinance to apply the surplus duties of Her Majesty's Customs in aid of the Civil List Establishment of British Guiana, on and after the 1st January, 1841," the Governor's object being to impose a duty by the Court of Policy, with the concurrence of the Crown, on British goods imported into the Colony, and thus to override the recalcitrant Combined Court. Both these ordinances were referred by Lord John Russell, *Constitutional* the Secretary of State for the Colonies, to the Law *Questions re-* Officers of the Crown with an inquiry (*a*) whether *ferred to the* *Law Officers* it was competent for Her Majesty in Council to *of the Crown.* allow and confirm the first-mentioned ordinance; (*b*) whether it was within the power of Her Majesty in Council to raise a revenue in British Guiana and to determine its appropriation; (*c*) if not, by what other authority and under what limitations that power might lawfully be exercised; (*d*) whether it was competent for Her Majesty to allow and confirm the second-mentioned ordinance, and if not, by what authority the surplus customs duties in British Guiana could be lawfully appropriated.[1]

The Law Officers of the Crown who grappled with these questions, were J. Dodson, the Queen's Advocate, J. Campbell, *Reply of the* the Attorney-General, and T. Wilde, the Solicitor-*Law Officers.* General; and they returned a joint answer over their signatures, dated the 21st October 1840, as follows:[2]

" (a) In our opinion it is competent to Her Majesty in Council to allow and confirm the first-mentioned ordinance, if Her Majesty should be advised; but it appears to us that such allowance and confirmation would be nugatory, for the main enactments in this ordinance are conditional, being made to depend upon the civil list thereby established being adopted and provided for by the Combined Court, and the Combined Court having rejected the civil list and stopped the supplies. With the concurrence of the Combined Court, there can be no doubt that this ordinance might have been carried into effect; but, as matters now stand in the Colony, the finances must be conducted as if this ordinance had not passed.

" (b) We are of opinion that such a power cannot be legally and constitutionally exercised by Her Majesty. British Guiana does not appear to us to be in the situation of a conquered colony, in which the Crown has supreme legislative authority. By the capitulation of the 19th September 1803 it was stipulated ' that the laws and usages of the Colony should remain in force and be respected; that the mode of taxation then in use should be adhered to; and that no new establishment should be introduced without the consent of the Court of Policy, as the legislature of the Colony.' This capitulation is binding in good faith upon the Crown; and even in strict law we conceive that the sanction of the Crown, since the cession of the Colony, to the political institutions in existence has given the same force to these institutions as if they had been established by an express grant from the Crown, like the legislatures in colonies settled by British subjects. The researches which have been made show that the Dutch colonies in Guiana were subject to the supreme authority of the States-General. But we do not think

---

[1] Parl. Paper 297 of 1849, pp. 209–19.
[2] *Ibidem*, pp. 220–1. Enclosure in despatch from Lord John Russell to Governor Light, dated 28th October, 1840.

that the Crown can be considered as now coming in the place of Their High Mightinesses, even if they could have imposed taxes and appropriated them in Demerara and Essequebo. Looking to the laws and usages and mode of taxation prevailing in the Colony in 1803, and since sanctioned by the Crown, we are clearly of opinion that no tax can lawfully be imposed there except by the Combined Court. Notwithstanding the recent origin of the representatives for taxation, they were fully established in 1803, and have been uniformly recognized since that time, while they confined themselves to their proper functions of providing ways and means for the supplies voted by the Court of Policy. The King's chest was certainly provided for by taxes over which neither the Court of Policy nor the Combined Court had any control; but we do not find any provision in the constitution of the Colony for adding to these taxes, or substituting others for them, in case they should be extinguished or become unproductive. We give no weight to Governor Carmichael's proclamation of 1812, or the usage under it; and we consider the Order-in-Council of 1831, rescinding it, as placing things in the same state in which they had been before this proclamation was issued. But, whatever doubts there might be as to the power of the Combined Court to interfere with the estimates, its exclusive power to raise a revenue by internal taxation had been uniformly admitted and acted upon. Therefore, however much the members of Combined Court may misconduct themselves, we apprehend that their power of taxation cannot be considered as transferred to the Crown.

" (c) We are of opinion that, if the Combined Court refuses to act, there is no mode in which a tax can lawfully be imposed in British Guiana without the interposition of the Imperial Parliament. . . . We are of opinion that, in a case of extremity like that which has arisen, this power may both legally and constitutionally be exercised to raise the necessary revenue in British Guiana and to determine its appropriation. The representative members of Combined Court having broken their contract and abdicated their functions, the safety of the State requires that the supreme power of the mother-country should be called in to supply the deficiency. Under these circumstances we conceive that Parliament might, without any just objection, remodel the constitution of the Colony, and confer the power of imposing taxes in British Guiana, for the benefit of the inhabitants, upon some new body that might be expected to exercise it with discrimination, loyalty and disinterestedness.

"(d) We are of opinion that the second ordinance, for applying the surplus of the customs, is valid; and, being confirmed by Her Majesty, may be carried into complete effect. The statute of the Imperial Parliament, 3 & 4 Will. 4, c. 59, s. 13, makes this fund disposable by the colonial legislature, and we think that the Court of Policy is the body in whom the power of disposition is reposed in British Guiana; the Court of Policy having legislative power, subject to the control of the Crown and of Parliament except with respect to the imposition of taxes. We conceive that the Combined Court can, neither by grant nor usage, make any just pretension to direct the disposition of the fund."

A further question was propounded to the Law Officers of the Crown by Lord Stanley on the 4th November, 1841—

Power of Sovereign in Council to legislate in Matters not Fiscal. namely, "whether, in cases in which it is not intended to impose any tax or duty, the legislative powers of the Sovereign in Council, which have hitherto been asserted and exercised over British Guiana, can or cannot be lawfully asserted and exercised by Her Majesty in Council." To this, J. Dodson, the Queen's Advocate, Fred. Pollock, the Attorney-General, and W. Follett, the Solicitor-General, replied in a letter, signed by them jointly and dated the 23rd February, 1842, as follows:

"We are of opinion that, in those cases in which it is not intended to impose any tax or duty, the legislative power of the Sovereign in Council, which has hitherto been asserted and exercised over British Guiana, may be lawfully exercised by Her Majesty in Council. We do not consider that the Crown has parted with its supreme legislative authority over the Colony, which was vested in it by right of conquest (in matters not fiscal), either by the terms of the capitulation and treaty, or by the sanction which it has given to the legislative acts of the Court of Policy, the Crown having continued at all times to assert and exercise this power in every matter of internal legislature not connected with the raising of taxes within the Colony." [1]

These very important legal opinions governed the attitude

[1] Parl. Paper 297 of 1849, pp. 221-3.

I

of the Imperial Government toward the constitution of British Guiana from that day onwards, the effect of the advice given by the Law Officers being that it was competent for the Crown to allow and confirm both the ordinances passed by Governor Light and the Court of Policy on the 5th and 6th May, 1840, but not to impose taxes; and that, therefore, the only funds which could be disposed of by the Crown and the Court of Policy without the help of the Combined Court or of Parliament were (a) the Surplus Customs' Duties and (b) the King's Chest Revenues, which would revive at the expiration of the Civil List on the 31st December, 1840.[1] Accordingly Lord John Russell determined to repeat the experiment, which had proved successful in 1835, of temporarily appointing the Governor of a neighbouring colony to compose the dispute between the Government and the Combined Court of British Guiana. For this purpose Sir Henry MacLeod, the Governor of Trinidad, was directed to proceed to Georgetown, where he was sworn in as Governor-in-Chief of British Guiana on the 7th December, 1840. He was instructed that there was no difference of opinion between the Secretary of State and the Combined Court as to the Civil List that was required; but that the conditions with which the Combined Court had coupled their grant of a Civil List were such as it was beyond the power and authority of the Queen's Government to fulfil, since it was not possible to hold the British Parliament and the Government of India to the obligations which the Combined Court of British Guiana wished to impose upon them. " You will, therefore," wrote Lord John Russell, " represent to the Combined Court the obvious impossibility of assenting to these conditions, and you will propose to them that they should pass their own Civil List without the conditions."[2]

Sir Henry MacLeod was successful in effecting a speedy settlement of the dispute. An ordinance was passed on the 7th January, 1841, by which a Civil List of £39,072 17s. 4d. was granted for seven years from the 1st of that month, the Crown revenues being

Governor of Trinidad instructed to negotiate with Combined Court as to Civil List.

Civil List renewed, 1841.

[1] Despatch from Lord John Russell to Governor Light, dated the 28th October, 1840.

[2] Despatch from Lord John Russell to Sir H. MacLeod, dated the 30th September, 1840; Parl. Paper 297 of 1849, pp. 223–4.

again surrendered for that term; while, in compliance with the wishes of the Combined Court, a Royal Order-in-Council was made on the 3rd June, 1842, directing that, during the continuance of the Civil List Ordinance, but no longer,

> " the Court of Policy, with the Financial Representatives of the inhabitants of British Guiana in Combined Court assembled, shall be, as they are hereby declared to be, entitled and shall have and possess full power and authority to discuss in detail, freely and without reserve, the several items of the Annual Estimate of the Colonial Expenditure, subject always to the terms and conditions of the said Civil List Ordinance." [1]

This Order-in-Council was renewed on the passing of every subsequent Civil List Ordinance.

At the same time as the Civil List Ordinance, Sir Henry MacLeod had, with the concurrence of Her Majesty's Govern-

Immigration authorized, but Loan negatived. ment, introduced " an Ordinance to regulate and encourage immigration into British Guiana," which was passed on the 18th January, 1841, and enabled the Combined Court to apply a large surplus revenue to the importation of immigrants.[2] The result was the introduction of no less than 8,144 immigrants—namely, 2,745 from the West India Islands, 4,297 from Madeira, and 1,102 from Africa, but none from India, during the year 1841. Thus the first condition which the Combined Court had tacked on to its offer of a Civil List of £42,893 9s. in 1840, was in effect complied with. But as regards the second of these conditions—namely, a loan ordinance—Sir H. MacLeod, having instructions from home not to assent to such a law, declined to introduce it. A draft ordinance for that purpose was, however, introduced by an elective member of the Court of Policy and, without being passed by the Court or sanctioned by the Governor, was sent home by Sir Henry for the opinion of Her Majesty's Government, who continued to disapprove of such a law, and it was rejected.[3] Having thus completed his mission, Sir Henry left British Guiana on the 28th January, 1841, and Governor Light resumed his administration.

[1] B. G. Laws (1870), vol. i, pp. 279–81. See Appendix L.
[2] Governor Light's despatch, 1st January, 1848; *Guiana Civil List Papers*, p. 4.
[3] Parl. Paper 297 of 1849, pp. 111–14.

But the trouble was not yet at an end. The planters clung to their wish that immigration should be largely increased and its expenses met by means of a loan on the credit of the colonial revenues; and, during the proceedings connected with the passing of the estimates and the tax ordinance for 1842, the Combined Court adopted the following resolutions :

Resolutions of Combined Court concerning the Civil List, 1842.

" Resolved, that this Court, taking into consideration the depressed state of the Colony, and referring to its re-peated declarations that the Civil List was only granted in perfect reliance upon a scheme of extensive immigration being promoted by Her Majesty's Government, and that it would be impossible for the Colony without such relief to bear the burthen of taxation imposed upon it, finds that the result justifies these declarations, and that the country is now unable to bear the burthen of the present Civil List, as well as other heavy charges for religious [1] and charitable institutions."

" Resolved, that, notwithstanding the distressed finan-cial state of the Colony, this Court, in order to keep faith as far as possible, and to show its earnest desire to main-tain the dignity of the officers of Her Majesty's civil government here, and its anxiety to avoid any act tending to embarrass the Secretary of State for the Colonies, will proceed with the estimate for 1842; but that, unless a large and comprehensive measure of relief be afforded to the Colony in the course of the current year by immigration or otherwise, it will be utterly out of the power of this Court, consistently with a due regard to the interests of the Colony thereafter, to vote the Civil List on its present scale."

Lord Stanley, to whom Governor Light forwarded these resolutions, replied in a despatch, dated the 12th October, 1842,[2] that as regards the finances of British Guiana, notwithstanding the very serious falling off in the exports, the revenue sustained itself, and would in all probability be adequate to meet every necessary expenditure : that Her Majesty's Government were exempted, during the term of the Civil List, from any responsibility for the support of the services

Lord Stan-ley's Reply : Annual Vote of Combined Court not required for Maintenance of Civil List from Year to Year.

[1] The Civil List voted as from the 1st January, 1841, included a sum of £9,429 19s. 6d. on account of the ecclesiastical establishments, which sum was placed on the Civil List at the instance of the elective members of the Combined Court.　　[2] Parl. Paper 297 of 1849, pp. 261–4.

outside the scope of the Civil List, which were left by
that arrangement to be provided for, or not, according to
the pleasure of the Combined Court; and that the only duty
which devolved upon Her Majesty's Government in respect of
those services, during that arrangement, was to recommend
what they thought right to be done, and to observe carefully
the course taken by the Combined Court, and the manner in
which it exercised its powers, with a view to forming a just
judgment when the time should arrive for making future
arrangements : but that, if the Combined Court were under
the impression that their vote was required by law for the
maintenance of the Civil List from year to year, after the Civil
List Ordinance had already been passed and confirmed, that
impression was erroneous.

> " The power of stopping the general supplies," he con-
> tinued, " may render it impossible to carry on business
> with the Combined Court on the peculiar system of repre-
> sentative legislation which has been temporarily adopted ;
> but, if it be so, and the public money and the affairs of the
> Colony cannot be properly administered upon this system,
> it will be necessary that Her Majesty's Government should
> consider whether a system cannot be established by which
> the interests of the Colony would be better secured and
> permanently provided for. There can be no doubt that
> the possession of so much power as has been temporarily
> transferred to the Combined Court tends to the usurpation
> by that body of every other power, and also that the pos-
> session of unlimited power by a representative body resting
> upon so limited a constituency would be pregnant with
> abuse. But this is a reason rather for resisting encroach-
> ments in detail, than for yielding to them."

In the same despatch Lord Stanley animadverted severely
on the proceedings by which the Combined Court during this
session had voted a sum of $20,000 of public money
as a loan to the British Guiana Steam Navigation
Company, a private trading firm, which appears
to have been unable to meet its liabilities, and of
which several members of the Combined Court were
shareholders. A petition from the directors of that
Company, signed by their Chairman, who was also a
member of the Combined Court, was addressed to that Court,

Proposal of Money-Votes in Combined Court not permissible except on Responsibility of Government.

and by it referred to the Court of Policy with a recommendation
that the loan of \$20,000 should be put on the estimates.   This
reference Governor Light was induced to allow the Court of
Policy to receive, because he thought that the Combined Court,
if not gratified in this particular, might stop the supplies.
The item was put upon the estimate by the unofficial members
of the Court of Policy, assisted by the single official vote of the
Collector of Customs; and, of course, the vote was carried in
the Combined Court.

> " The process by which this vote was originated,"
> wrote Lord Stanley, " was extremely irregular, and a mere
> evasion of the regulations by which the practice as to
> initiation of money-votes is governed.   Those regulations
> are founded upon the same principles which govern the
> proceedings of the House of Commons in this country.
> The well-known tendency of every representative body to
> be betrayed into abusive grants of the public money is
> guarded against in the House of Commons by requiring
> that no proposal involving a vote of money shall be
> entertained by the House unless made on the part of the
> Crown by one of its responsible advisers, or with the
> consent of the Crown previously signified through the same
> channel.   In the Crown Colonies Her Majesty's Govern-
> ment have established it as an invariable rule that no
> vote or estimate shall be proposed except on the responsi-
> bility of the local government; and, as a further safeguard,
> they have required that the Estimates shall be sent home
> for revision by the Secretary of State and the Lords of the
> Treasury before they are submitted to the local bodies by
> which they are to be voted."

Lord Stanley added that he could easily appreciate the difficulties of the situation in which Governor Light might have
been placed by a stoppage of the supplies; but His Lordship
did not think that this was a sufficient ground for departing
from an essential principle in the conduct of financial business
in the Court of Policy; and the Collector of Customs,[1] being
the only official member of the body implicated in the transaction, was removed from his seat in the Court of Policy by
Her Majesty's Government " to mark their sense of the irregu-

[1] Mr. Robinson; he was, however, reinstated upon representations
made by Governor Light in a despatch dated the 2nd December, 1842,
explaining that Mr. Robinson had no self-interested motive and that
his services in the Court of Policy were valuable.

larity committed in thus misapplying the money of the Colony."

The resolute stand made by Lord Stanley was effective, and eventually the supplies for 1843 were voted by the Com-

Loan for Immigration Purposes sanctioned and Civil List renewed, 1844.

bined Court;[1] while, later in the same year, the objections of Parliament and of the Indian Government to the importation of Indian labour into British Guiana having been overcome, the wish of the planters to raise a loan for immigration purposes was granted. The principle, which the Government was at first inclined to adopt, was that charges on the revenue for interest and sinking fund of a loan should not be created without co-extension of the Civil List as a prior lien, so that no charges should at a future period fall to be provided for out of revenue precedently to those which were most essential to the good government of the Colony.[2] This principle was not, however, rigorously adhered to; and the royal assent was given to an ordinance authorizing the creation of annual charges for a loan for twenty years, whilst the extension given to the Civil List was only for seven years beyond its termination in the year 1847—that is, until the 31st December, 1854.[3]

The Civil List was thus renewed for the second time; but, as in 1834 the abolition of slavery had incidentally deprived

Effect of Reduction in Protection given to Sugar by Imperial Tariff.

the Crown of the greater part of the ancient revenue of the King's chest, so now another large measure of imperial policy had as one of its side-issues the dislocation of the finances of British Guiana. The Sugar Duties Act of 1846 (9 & 10 Vict., cap. 63) arranged, as from the 5th July, 1847, for a progressive reduction in the protection given by the British customs' tariff to sugar or molasses the growth and produce of British colonies, until from and after the 5th July, 1851, sugar or molasses the growth and produce of any " foreign country " should pay the same customs duties as sugar or molasses the growth and produce of British colonies. This Act, by admitting the slave-labour sugar of Brazil and the Spanish colonies to competition in the

[1] Parl. Paper 342 of 1846.
[2] Governor Light's despatch, 29th April, 1844; Lord Stanley's despatch, 31st July, 1844.
[3] Lord Stanley's despatch, 30th November, 1844; B. G. Ordinances Nos. 13 and 14 of 1844.

markets of the United Kingdom with the free-labour sugar of British colonies, dealt the planters of British Guiana a heavy blow, and led the Combined Court on the 30th December, 1847, to pass resolutions in favour of reducing all salaries guaranteed by the Civil List to the extent of 25% of their amount, upon the grounds (1) of the fall in the price of sugar, rendering it " impracticable to continue the cultivation of the staple commodities at a remunerative price "; [1] (2) of the consequent inability of the Colony to afford payment of the Civil List in full; (3) that the Civil List was granted in 1841, and renewed in 1844, under the conviction that the faith of the British nation was pledged to the exclusion of slave-labour sugar.[2]

Her Majesty's Government, however, would not consent to the proposed general reduction of salaries included in the Civil List,[3] because the honour of the Crown was *Combined Court's Proposal to make 25% Reduction in Civil List Rejected by Her Majesty's Government.* regarded as pledged to the holders of the offices, to which these salaries were assigned, that they should continue unaltered at least until the expiration of the period for which the Civil List had been granted; and the reduction was further objected to on the ground that, if it were allowed to take place in the manner proposed, the arrangement made for providing a Civil List for a fixed term of years would be virtually set aside. It was also pointed out that there was no pressing necessity for the proposed reduction, inasmuch as there was no falling off in the revenue, which, on the contrary, rather showed a tendency to improve,[4] and that this measure would do little or nothing for the relief of that class of colonists who were chiefly suffering from the depressed state of the sugar trade,

[1] Resolution of Court of Policy, 21st March, 1848.

[2] *Guiana Civil List Papers*, laid before Parliamentary Committee in 1849, pp. 4, 6.

[3] Despatches from Earl Grey to Governor Light and Lieut.-Governor Walker, dated 15th February, 17th June, 15th August, and 1st September, 1848 : *Guiana Civil List Papers*, pp. 180 *sqq.*

[4] Revenue of British Guiana : see page 72 of *Blue Book Report* for 1846 :

Year	$	Year	$
1842	838,970	1845	825,198
1843	829,868	1846	900,849
1844	832,479	1847	1,135,507 (estimated)

See also Parl. Paper 297 of 1849, pp. 66, 105, 155.

since the existing taxes fell almost exclusively upon the labouring classes, who, far from being unable to pay them, were in
such easy circumstances that it had always been represented
by the planters to be one of their chief difficulties that labourers
could earn enough to satisfy all their wants by two or three
days' labour in the week and could not, therefore, be induced
to perform such an amount of regular labour as was required
for the successful cultivation of sugar.[1] Nevertheless Earl
Grey expressed his willingness to permit a reasonable reduction
of salaries in case of a vacancy, and the Combined Court was
informed by his direction that Her Majesty's Government
had no wish to oppose any obstacle to the retrenchment of
all unnecessary expenditure provided due regard were shown
to existing interests, and provided also that the reductions
were made in such a manner as not to involve the principle of
making the Civil List liable to annual revision by the Combined
Court.   On this latter point Earl Grey, in a despatch dated
the 1st January, 1849, repeated and reinforced the principle
laid down in Lord Stanley's despatch of the 12th October
1842.

" It appears," he wrote, " that misapprehension as to
the right of the Combined Court to interfere with the
Civil List has been occasioned by the fact that the sum
required to defray the Civil List, and some partial specifica-
tion of the items borne upon it, has been annually placed
as a sort of prefix to the Estimate, and in one year at least,
that of 1847, is stated in the Minutes to have been
' passed,' as if it had been made the subject of a vote.   It
is clearly inexpedient that any documentary form should
be adopted which tends to confound a permanent appropriation with the Annual Estimates, and it will be proper
in future that the account of the expenditure of the
Civil List, which is necessary for the information and
guidance of Combined Court in imposing the taxes, should
be laid before the Court in a separate document, in accordance with the practice in this country."

In view of these instructions, the Civil List was withdrawn
from the Estimates, and presented in the form of a statement
showing the total amount to be provided, which was brought
forward on the Estimates being closed, and furnished to the

[1] Parl. Paper 297 of 1849, p. viii.

Committe of Ways and Means as a sum to be provided for as a matter of course. This continued to be the practice up to the year 1869. After that, the items comprised in the Civil List were inserted *pro forma* in the body of the Estimates in varying arrangements for convenience of record only, no vote being ever taken upon these items except when the Civil List was due for renewal.

Governor Light finally left the Colony on the 20th May, 1848, and Mr. W. Walker, the Government Secretary, became *Combined Court stops Supplies, 1848.* Administrator in the interval before the arrival of a new Governor. The crisis now came. The elective section of the Court of Policy, on learning of the declaration made in Parliament early in 1848 that Her Majesty's Government had determined to propose no change in the Sugar Duties Act of 1846, refused to vote the Estimates for 1848, and these had to be forced through the Court by the casting vote of the Administrator. Thereafter, when the Estimates came up for consideration in the Combined Court on the 20th July, 1848, a motion was adopted by a majority reducing the Civil List from £39,072 17s. 4d. to £26,072, almost every item being subjected to reduction varying between 25% and 50%. The Administrator thereupon adjourned the Combined Court *sine die*, and the supplies were in consequence stopped. On the 30th September, 1848, the Tax Ordinance of 1847, which had been extended to that date in the hope of a solution of the controversy being achieved in the interim, expired, and the Colony was left without a revenue.

This position of affairs continued until April, 1849, in spite of two attempts made during that time to proceed with business, *Parliamentary Committee appointed to inquire into the Colony's Grievances, 1849.* both of which ended in the adjournment of the Court *sine die*. Meanwhile, on the 14th February, 1849, Mr. H. Barkly [1] assumed the government of the Colony, and on the 20th of the same month the House of Commons appointed a Select Committee [2] to inquire into the grievances complained of in British Guiana

[1] Mr. Barkly at the time of his appointment was Member of Parliament for Leominster, and was specially selected for the appointment because he owned property in British Guiana.

[2] The members of the Committee were Messrs. Gladstone, Disraeli, Hume, Charles Villiers, Hawes, Adderly, Wilson, Stuart Wortley, Baillie, McCullagh, Sir Robert Peel, Sir James Hogg, Sir Joshua Walmsley, Lord Hotham, and Major Backall.

in connexion with the administration and government of that Colony, and to report their opinion whether any measures could be adopted for the redress of any grievances, of which there might be just reason to complain, and also whether any measures could be adopted for the better administration and government of the Colony.

In April the Combined Court met again; and, after lengthy and stormy discussion, a motion was carried by the Governor's *Failure of* casting vote to proceed with the Estimates, leaving *Governor* the question of the Civil List to be decided by *Barkly to* *induce Com-* Parliament. But, before the completion of the *bined Court to* Estimates, further interruptions of a serious nature *vote* *Supplies.* occurred when a resolution by one of the unofficial members, that salaries be paid as from the 30th June in the preceding year in accordance with the reduced estimate then being voted, was vetoed by the Governor, who regarded the proposal as calculated to disturb the arrangement respecting the abeyance of the vote on the Civil List. The exercise of the veto raised a storm of protest from the electives, who vehemently opposed it, declaring it to be unconstitutional and illegal. But Governor Barkly stood firm. Failing to induce the Court to proceed with the Estimates, he appealed to the members to provide the funds immediately necessary for the maintenance of the gaols, hospitals and other public institutions by imposing duties on tobacco, wine, malt and other spirituous liquors imported since the expiration of the Tax Ordinance in September, 1848. But the electives were obdurate and subsequently rejected an alternative proposal, made by one of their own party and accepted by the Governor, to proceed with the Estimates " under solemn protest " that their rights in regard to the Civil List should not be prejudiced thereby. Finally, on the 30th April, after ten days of acrimonious debate, the Governor, for the eighth time during its session, adjourned the Combined Court *sine die*.

It was probably anticipated by the elected members of Combined Court that the embarrassment in which the local *Policy of* government was thus placed, would compel Her *Lord John* Majesty's Government to apply to Parliament for *Russell's* *Cabinet.* power to continue to levy the usual taxes without the sanction of the Combined Court, or to have recourse to some other expedient involving a departure from the regular and established mode of conducting the Government of the Colony. Indeed, Mr. Gordon, one of the principal planters of the Colony, in his correspondence with the Colonial Reform Association, distinctly asserted that the attempt to cut down the Civil List " was in the first instance suggested by the Protectionists, as a part of a general system for embarrassing Government with a view of regaining lost protection "; [1] and, as regards the above-mentioned expedients, Earl Grey wrote to Lord John Russell that " in the then state of parties in the House of Commons, we should in either case have been exposed to a defeat, which would have greatly promoted the success of those who were struggling to recover for the British sugar-grower the monopoly of the home-market, of which he had been deprived." [2]   The course, however, which after much consideration was decided upon by Lord John Russell's Cabinet, differed greatly from that which seems to have been expected.

The Governor was informed that the adoption by the Combined Court of the unreasonable course of withholding *Instructions* the pecuniary means required for carrying on *to Governor.* the public service would have no effect in inducing Her Majesty's Government to recommend to Parliament, or Parliament to sanction, the change in commercial policy which the planters believed would relieve them. He was instructed that he must strictly confine himself to the exercise of his legal powers, and that those public services for which he was refused the means of providing must be discontinued, even if this involved disbanding the police and shutting up the hospitals and an interruption of the regular administration of justice; and that, if the usual Colonial allowances were not paid to the officers of Her Majesty's troops serving in the Colony, the troops would be withdrawn. The Governor was further told that no more liberated Africans could be sent to the Colony so long as no provision was made for the maintenance of the public establishments required for taking care of them. [3]

The settlement of this harassing affair was at length facili-

[1] House of Commons Sessional Papers of 1851, No. 624, p. 486.

[2] *The Colonial Policy of Lord John Russell's Administration*, by Earl Grey (1853), vol. i, p. 150.

[3] House of Commons Sessional Papers of 1849, No. 594.

tated by the publication of the report of the Parliamentary
Committee which had been appointed to inquire into the
Report of matters in dispute. This report [1] was presented to
Parlia- the House of Commons and ordered to be printed,
mentary
Committee. on the 18th May, 1849, and it reached the Colony
early in July. It declared in explicit terms in favour of the
claim of the Crown and against that advanced by the elective
section of the Combined Court, stating that the Crown was
" entitled (if considerations of good faith or of public policy
require it) to insist upon an adherence to the Civil List arrangement made in 1844, for the full period for which the Civil
List was granted; and that no attempt to set aside that
arrangement, either by direct or indirect means, could be
justified." The Committee added that at no remote period
the whole Civil List would be open to review, and strongly
recommended that " in the interim, whenever there may be
vacancies in offices included in the Civil List, no permanent
appointment should take place until the circumstances of the
vacant office have been fully considered, in friendly concert
with the colonial authorities, for the purpose of ascertaining
whether the maintenance of such office be necessary; and, if
necessary, whether the office require regulation and whether
its emoluments can properly be reduced." In conclusion the
Committee stated that their attention had been drawn to
the general feeling prevalent in the Colony that it was desirable
to alter the existing form of the government, as being one
" liable to serious interruptions, and occasionally productive
of grave inconvenience and injury "; and they suggested that
any changes which it might be deemed necessary to make in
the constitution of British Guiana should be decided in friendly
concert with the colonial authorities, and that " such changes
should proceed upon the basis of extending the elective franchise
as far as may be deemed practicable and prudent, and at the
same time conceding to the legislature of British Guiana a
greater control over the conduct of public affairs than they have
hitherto enjoyed."

The Court met on the 13th July, 1849, to take this report
into consideration. It then appeared that all difficulties were
not yet ended; for the elective members repudiated the Parlia-

[1] Parl. Paper 297 of 1849.

mentary Committee's decision on the ground that it had not yet been confirmed by Parliament and might be reversed; and *Civil List Dispute ends in 1850.* on this and other pleas they made further attempts to reopen the Civil List question. Eventually, however, in deference to the wishes of the public, who petitioned the Court deprecating any further opposition and praying that the business of the Colony might be proceeded with, the Estimates for 1848 were passed on the 7th August, 1849, and on the same day the Tax Ordinance for 1847 was revived for a further period. Throughout these proceedings the most strenuous opposition had been shown by certain of the elective section, six of whom resigned their seats on the following day. After further delays occasioned by the refusal to sit of those elected to fill the vacancies, a Tax Ordinance for 1848 was belatedly passed on the 27th November, 1849, on which day the eventful session of 1848 was closed. With the meeting of the new Court opposition came to an end; and on the 4th February, 1850, the Estimates and a Tax Ordinance for 1849 were passed. Thus ended a series of disputes which had resulted in grave financial loss to the Colony, the loss on abandoned import duties alone being estimated at $705,426.

From this time onwards the Civil List was regularly renewed for septennial periods [1] expiring on the last day of the years *Varying Periods for which Civil List has been renewed since 31st December, 1854.* 1861, 1868, 1875, 1882 and 1889. In 1889, however, proposals for the reform of the constitution of British Guiana were under consideration; and, pending such reform, it was considered inadvisable to renew the Civil List for a longer period than one year,[2] to expire on the 31st December, 1890. But, when the reform movement was about to culminate in Ordinance No. 1 of 1891, and the measure of constitutional change authorized by Her Majesty's Government was known, the Civil List was again renewed, without hesitation, for seven years to expire at the end of 1897.[3] That year coincided with a great wave of depression which passed over the Colony. The sugar industry was threatened with extinction. A Royal

---

[1] Ordinances No. 5 of 1853; 15 of 1860; 17 of 1868; 10 of 1875; 8 of 1882.

[2] Ordinance No. 15 of 1889.   [3] Ordinance No. 28 of 1890.

Commission had been appointed to visit the West Indies and make recommendations with the object of saving the planters from ruin. The report of this Commission, although issued, had not been fully considered. Moreover, the report of local Commissioners on the civil service of British Guiana, although sufficiently advanced to permit of recommendations being made by the Commissioners to the Governor in regard to the salaries of the public servants on the Civil List, had not been published. In these circumstances it was the earnest desire of the elective section of the Combined Court not to pass the Civil List for more than one year, and it was resolved on the 1st October, 1897, to extend it to the end of 1898 only.[1] During 1898, however, confidence in the future of the Colony revived sufficiently to encourage the electives to vote the Civil List for a further period of three years—that is, to the end of 1901;[2] and it was continued by further triennial periods to the 31st December, 1907.[3] Thereafter, with increasing optimism, the periods were made quinquennial, the last Civil Lists expiring at the end of 1912,[4] 1917,[5] 1922,[6] and 1927.[7]

[1] Ordinance No. 21 of 1897.
[2] Ordinance No. 24 of 1898.
[3] Ordinances Nos. 1 of 1902; 18 of 1904.
[4] Ordinance No. 32 of 1907.
[5] Ordinance No. 19 of 1912.
[6] Ordinance No. 26 of 1917.
[7] See p. 267, *infra*.

CHAPTER IV

THE MUNICIPALITY OF GEORGETOWN

WE have seen that the town of Stabroek, at the mouth of the Demerara River, was founded in 1782, became the seat of *Georgetown* government for the two Rivers (Demerara and Esse-*superin-* quebo) soon afterwards, and was renamed George-*tended* (a) *by* *Commissaries* town in 1812. In early days the different districts *prior to 1812;* of the town were superintended by Commissaries, who were appointed by the proprietors of urban lots, and who, it appears, maintained in proper order the canals, dams, bridges, etc., within the town limits and assessed the proprietary body of the town for the expenses thus incurred. Powers were also vested in Commissaries, appointed by proclamation dated the 2nd May, 1811, for the control of the public markets of the town. But, on the 29th April, 1812, the Governor and Court *(b) by Board* of Policy passed an ordinance confiding the care and *of Police,* superintendence of the town to a committee of six *1812–1837;* persons, known as the Board of Police of Georgetown and appointed by the Court from the most respectable inhabitants of the several urban districts. This Board had the right of levying the town taxes according to the appraisements; and, in 1815, the Government appointed a Receiver of Town Taxes, who with the Inspector-General, an officer appointed to superintend the public works of the town, was placed under the orders of the Board. In the same year the supervision of the public markets of Georgetown was also transferred to the Board of Police, and the officer known as the Clerk of Markets was placed under its orders. This system continued until by an ordinance, passed on the 1st March, 1837 (No. 2 *(c) by a Mayor* of 1837), Governor Sir James Carmichael Smyth *and Town* *Council since* and the Court of Policy established " a Board of *1837.* Superintendence of Georgetown to be called and styled the Mayor and Town Council of Georgetown," consisting of eleven Town Councillors representing the eleven wards into which the town was then divided, one Councillor being elected each year by his colleagues to be their President and " to be styled the Mayor of Georgetown." The Mayor and Town Council were by this ordinance declared to be vested with

> " all the powers, authorities, and immunities hitherto vested in and exercised by the Board of Police, and more especially to superintend and direct the collection and appropriation of the town taxes; to direct, order, and enforce the cleanliness and repairing of the public streets, dams, sluices, kokers,[1] roads, stellings [2] and bridges of Georgetown; to superintend the public markets, and to cause the regulations for the government thereof to be enforced; to have the direction of the public fire engines; to cause the same to be exercised from time to time; to have all necessary repairs made so as to keep them at all times in efficient working order, and fit for service on the most sudden emergency; and for the aforesaid purposes to frame such regulations and by-laws as they may deem fit and necessary "; [3]

and the further privilege was conferred on the Town Council of appointing its own officers and fixing the emoluments of their offices.

The Town Council of Georgetown was originally entirely elective; and " every inhabitant of Georgetown within his *Qualification* respective ward, being of full age and not subject *of Voters for* to any legal disability, being the proprietor or repre- *Town Councillors.* sentative of any house or tenement in Georgetown, rated in the books of the Receiver of Town Taxes at the value of 3,500 guilders," [4] was entitled to vote in the election of a Town Councillor for the ward in which such house or tenement was situated. This qualification was reduced by section 12 of Ordinance No. 25 of 1860 to the " possession by the voter or his wife, under a title by grant from the Crown, transport, letters of decree, inheritance *ab intestato vel ex testamento*, devise, or lease for a term of years exceeding three, or assignment thereof duly deposited or recorded in the Registrar's office, of premises within the City of Georgetown of the appraised value of $250 or upwards, on the books of the Receiver of Town Taxes." A further concession was made by section 10

---

[1] Sluice-gates.
[2] Wharves.
[3] Section 12 of Ordinance No. 2 of 1837.
[4] 70 guilders equal £5.

K

of Ordinance No. 25 of 1898, which provided that the property qualification for a voter should be :

> " (1) Possession by the voter individually, or as father or natural guardian of his minor children, or by his wife under a title by grant from the Crown, transport, letters of decree, or inheritance *ab intestato vel ex testamento* or devise, of premises within the City of the appraised value of $250 or upwards; or
> " (2) Occupation of premises within the City the rental whereof is not less than $40 a month : provided that the occupant has resided in the same premises during the six months immediately preceding his being registered as a voter."

This latter qualification was amended by section 3 of Ordinance No. 13 of 1909, which substituted a rental of $15 a month for $40 a month; and so amended the qualification remained in force, it being further stipulated that

> " no person shall be entitled to be registered as a voter who (*a*) cannot read or write the English language; or (*b*) has, within three months previous to registration, received any relief from public or parochial funds; or (*c*) has been sentenced in any part of His Majesty's Dominions to death, or penal servitude, or imprisonment with hard labour for any term exceeding twelve months, and has not either suffered the punishment to which he was sentenced or such other punishment as by competent authority may have been substituted for the same, or received a free pardon from His Majesty." [1]

It is also provided that " no person liable to pay town taxes shall be entitled to vote at the election of a member of the Council for a Ward, who, at the time of tendering his vote, has been for more than three months, and still is, in arrear in the payment of the town taxes, if any, payable by him." [2]

The original qualification for a Town Councillor, as prescribed by Ordinance No. 2 of 1837, was to be " proprietor or
Qualification of Town Councillors. representative of any house or tenement within the town of Georgetown of the value of 8,000 guilders or upwards, on the books of the Receiver of Town Taxes." This qualification was reduced by section 8 of Ordinance No. 25 of 1860, which read :

---

[1] Ordinance No. 25 of 1898, section 11 (1).
[2] Ordinance No. 25 of 1898, section 11 (2).

" Every male inhabitant of the Colony, of full age, and not subjected to any legal disability, residing in British Guiana, born in the allegiance of Her Majesty, or, if born out of such allegiance, actually resident in the Colony for the space of three years next before his election, shall be eligible to be elected a Town Councillor, provided that at the time of his election and during the whole time of his sitting as such Councillor, he or his wife shall be possessed under a title by grant from the Crown, transport, letters of decree, inheritance *ab intestato vel ex testamento*, decree, or lease for a term of years exceeding three, or assignment thereof duly deposited or recorded in the Registrar's office, of premises within the City of Georgetown of the appraised value of $1,500 or upwards, on the books of the Receiver of Town Taxes."

Ordinance No. 25 of 1898, while leaving the property qualification of Town Councillors substantially unchanged, provided that no person should sit and vote in the Council, who :

(1) is not entitled to vote at the election of a member of the Council for any Ward ; or

(2) is a minister of religion ; or

(3) is the holder of any place of profit in the gift or disposal of the Council or has, directly or indirectly, by himself or his partner, either as principal or surety, any share or interest in any contract or employment with, by, or on behalf of the Council : provided always that no person shall be disqualified from being a member of the Council—

(i) by reason of his being a proprietor or shareholder in or of any banking or insurance company, or any public company or association not trading in or for supply of goods, wares and merchandise, which contracts with the Council ; or

(ii) by reason that he himself, or his partner, has directly or indirectly any share or interest in any contract with the Council, where the whole amount payable or receivable under such contract does not exceed in any period of twelve consecutive months the sum of $500.

Finally, by Ordinance No. 17 of 1914 the property qualification for election as a Town Councillor was defined as either (a) possession by himself or his wife, under a title by grant from the Crown, transport, letters of decree, inheritance *ab intestato vel ex testamento,* or devise, of premises within the city of the appraised value of $1,500 or upwards, over and above the amount of any mortgage; or (b) occupation of premises within the city, the rental whereof is not less than $30 a month, provided that the occupant has resided in the same premises during the six months immediately preceding his being elected as a Councillor. And it was further enacted that the attorney or chairman of the board of directors of any limited liability company should be qualified for election as a member of the Town Council if such company possessed or occupied premises within the city which would have given the necessary qualification to any owner thereof not being a company.

As a result of the growth of Georgetown in size, the original number of eleven wards was gradually increased to fourteen; *Town Council* and, as each ward had one representative in the *reorganized* Council, the number of Town Councillors also rose *in 1914.* to fourteen; but the table on the next page, prepared in January, 1914, from information supplied by the Town Clerk, shows how inadequately the citizens of Georgetown were represented by the Town Council.

Several interesting facts were disclosed by these statistics. For example, Queenstown Ward, with a population of 1,892 and a valuation of $140,250, had in it only one person qualified for election as a Town Councillor.   North Cumingsburg, West, with a population of 1,298 and a valuation of $492,600, contained only eleven registered voters.   In fact, of the whole population of Georgetown only 0·98% were registered as entitled to vote for the election of Town Councillors; while only 0·32% of the residents in Georgetown, or 33·1% of the registered voters, were qualified to serve as Town Councillors. But although, as the law then stood, only an insignificant number of the citizens of Georgetown were qualified to sit in the Town Council, and although the mass of the citizens were not even entitled to vote at the municipal elections, it was evident that the few registered voters prized their vote and exercised it readily at contested elections; for at the general municipal elections of December, 1912, when there were contests in five out of the fourteen wards, the electorate consisting of 186

Ward.	Population.	Appraised Valuation.	Number of Voters on Register.	Number Qualified for Election.	Number who Voted at General Election held in December, 1912.	Number of Persons Represented by each Voter.	Valuation Represented by each Voter.
		$					$
Kingston	2,691	374,250	38	19	28	71	9,849
North Cumingsburg, West	1,298	492,600	11	7	Uncontested	118	44,782
Do. East	3,224	342,150	27	14	22	119	12,672
South Cumingsburg, West	1,359	784,850	17	6	13	79	46,168
Do. East	4,118	507,500	41	25	Uncontested	100	12,378
Robb's Town	211	614,150	12	2	Do.	17	51,179
Lacytown	6,159	606,150	67	26	56	91	9,047
New Town	286	361,500	18	2	Uncontested	16	20,083
Stabroek	2,613	359,900	53	27	Do.	49	6,790
Werk-en-Rust (including Wortmanville	10,682	1,002,295	69	20	Do.	155	14,526
Charlestown (including Albuoystown	9,889	783,120	35	6	Do.	282	22,374
Bourda	4,726	467,995	64	12	Do.	74	7,312
Albert Town	3,773	210,525	37	5	27	101	5,690
Queenstown	1,892	140,250	30	1	Uncontested-	63	4,675
Total	52,921	7,047,235	519	172	146	102 (mean)	13,578 (mean)

voters, 146 persons (or 79·5%) recorded their votes. Another anomaly, disclosed by the above table, was the wide difference in the value of votes in the several wards. Thus in Charlestown the number of citizens represented by each voter was 282, while in New Town it was no more than 16. Again, the valuation represented by each voter in Robb's Town was $51,179, while in Queenstown it was only $4,675. These were the extreme fluctuations; for, taking the total figures for the whole city,

the average number of citizens represented by each vote was
102, and the mean value of each vote was $13,578.   Moreover,

Government not repre- sented in the Town Council before 1914. it had long been anomalous that the Government,
although the largest rate-payer in the city of George-
town, and the only possible representative of such
general tax-payers resident in Georgetown as were
not qualified to vote at the municipal elections, had no voice
in the Town Council.   Prior to the year 1895–6, the Government
made an annual contribution of $20,000 to the Municipality.
In the year 1895–6 this contribution was increased by $10,000.
But the increase was withdrawn in the following year; and the
present arrangement whereby the Government pays taxes
on the same basis as private property-holders, the amount
of the taxes payable being determined by a rate levied on the
appraised valuation of the several properties, was agreed upon
by a joint-committee of the Government and the Town Council
in the year 1897.   The Government, moreover, paid half the
cost of the Fire Brigade and made further miscellaneous
payments to the Town Council for scavenging and other
services.   The whole can be tabulated thus for the three years
1911, 1912, and 1913:

	1911.	1912.	1913.
	$	$	$
Rates	24,632	23,409	27,533
Half cost of Fire Brigade. . .	12,417	12,537	12,496
Other payments . . .	16,525	16,525	17,000
Total	53,574	52,471	57,029
Total receipts of the Town Council from all sources	273,499	270,139	283,923
Percentage of Town Council's income derived from Government . .	19%	19%	20%

In the autumn of 1913, the Georgetown Chamber of Commerce made proposals to the Government to remedy what they

Recommenda- tions of Georgetown Chamber of Commerce. described in a letter, dated the 25th November,
1913, as " the existing highly unsatisfactory state
of affairs " in the municipality of Georgetown.
These proposals the Chamber summarized as follows:

" 1. That Limited Liability Companies should have the

privilege to vote for the election of a Town Councillor in the same way as private individuals.

2. That the voting power of every property holder should be in proportion to the value of the property owned.

3. That the mercantile community should be allowed to nominate at least two of its members to seats at the Council Board, provided its contribution to the taxes of the city amounted to 20% of the whole : *or* that the wards of the city should be rearranged or the number increased, so as to allow of property holders in Water Street, or such portions of the city as may be regarded as the business portion, electing their own members to the Council Chamber of the Town.

4. That the Government should have the right to nominate certain members to the Council Chamber of Georgetown, which the Council of the Chamber of Commerce regards as a very necessary step in the interests of the community."

" Legislation on the above lines," concluded the letter from the Chamber's Secretary, " would, my Council believes, meet with the cordial approval of the majority of the tax-payers and would result in a healthier and better administration of the affairs of the Municipality."

It was in these circumstances that Governor Sir Walter Egerton and Court of Policy passed on the 4th July, 1914, the " Ordinance to amend the Georgetown Town Council Ordinance " (No. 17 of 1914), already mentioned. This law provided that from and after the 1st January, 1915, the number of wards in the city of Georgetown should be reduced from fourteen to nine by the amalgamation (*a*) of North Cumingsburg West Ward with North Cumingsburg East Ward; (*b*) of South Cumingsburg West Ward with South Cumingsburg East Ward; (*c*) of the three wards Robb's Town, Lacy Town, and New Town; (*d*) of Albert Town Ward with Queenstown Ward. Each of the nine wards was to be represented as formerly by one Councillor elected by the registered voters, whose qualification was not changed : but power was given to the Governor-in-Council, after any general election of Town Councillors, to " nominate in writing a number of persons, not exceeding three, to serve on the Town Council until the date of the next general election," and under this provision the Director of Public Works, the Surgeon-General, and the Commissioner of Lands

Ordinance No. 17 of 1914.

and Mines were nominated Town Councillors with effect from the 1st January, 1915. The qualification of Town Councillors was altered in the manner already described; and the control and management of the Fire Brigade were transferred from the Town Council to the Governor-in-Council.

This ordinance was strenuously opposed by the Town Council, who, on the 16th July, 1914, petitioned His Majesty the King to disallow the new law. The petition of the Mayor and Town Council was laid before the King; and by His Majesty's command Mr. L. Harcourt, then Secretary of State for the Colonies, gave careful consideration to it. "I have, however," wrote Mr. Harcourt to Governor Sir W. Egerton on the 14th September, 1914, "been unable to advise His Majesty to comply with the prayer which it contains, and His Majesty has not been pleased to give any directions in the matter. . . . The Ordinance has been passed by the Court of Policy and is supported by the local press, and it appears to me to be calculated to improve the administration of the municipal affairs of Georgetown." Accordingly the royal power of disallowance was not exercised, and the Town Council was reconstituted on the 1st January, 1915.

A general election of Town Councillors for all the wards of the city is required by section 27 of Ordinance No. 25 of 1898 to be held every two years, during the first ten days of December, such elections taking effect from the 1st January in the ensuing year; and by-elections are held as necessary for filling vacancies in the Town Council, from whatever cause, between the general elections. It was, however, provided by the new law that, in case of the death, resignation, illness, incapacity or absence from the Colony of a nominated Councillor, the Governor-in-Council might nominate in writing any other person to serve in his place until the date of the next general election. Finally it was enacted that the appointment by the Town Council of the Town Superintendent, the Managing Engineer of Waterworks and the Medical Officer of Health should be subject to previous consultation with, and approval by, the Governor-in-Council; and that the Governor-in-Council might, after consultation with the Town Council, direct the Town Council to suspend, dismiss, or, on giving three months' notice, to terminate the employment of any of these officers.

CHAPTER V

ABORTIVE PROPOSALS TO REFORM THE CONSTITUTION, 1838–42

In 1838, only three months prior to the termination of the apprenticeship of the prædial labourers,[1] a movement for the *Reform of* reform of the constitution was set on foot in the *Constitution* *petitioned for* Colony. A memorial, signed by " a numerous and *in 1838.* highly respectable class of inhabitants of Berbice," [2] was forwarded to Governor Henry Light and by him transmitted to Lord Glenelg on the 30th June, 1838. The memorialists complained that their interests were not represented owing to the mode in which the Electoral College was formed. Meanwhile at Georgetown a public meeting, over which the High Sheriff, Mr. George Bagot, presided, was held in the hall of the Court of Justice on the 23rd May, 1838; and a petition was drawn up by the inhabitants of British Guiana generally, praying that Her Majesty the Queen would be graciously pleased to abolish the College of Electors (Kiezers), to allow the elective franchise to be direct in the selection of colonial members for the Court of Policy, and to grant inhabitants of the three counties—Demerara, Essequebo, and Berbice—the right of choosing their own members, in the proportion due to their respective importance. The signatures appended to this petition also were " of the highest respectability "; [3] and, in forwarding it to Lord Glenelg on the 16th July, 1838, Governor Light wrote : " The general wish seems to be to give two members to Demerara (55,000 inhabitants), two to Berbice (22,000 inhabitants), and one to Essequebo (33,000 inhabitants), unless it may be thought right to add another member for Essequebo and balance by some other official member." Lord Glenelg replied [4] that he would be prepared to take both these

---

[1] The apprenticeship terminated on the 1st August, 1838.
[2] Governor Light's despatch, 30th June, 1838.
[3] Governor Light's despatch, 16th July, 1838.
[4] Lord Glenelg's despatches, dated 22nd August and 14th September, 1838.

petitions into consideration and commended " the very calm and dispassionate tone," in which the petitioners sought redress; but he desired in the first instance to have a report from the Court of Policy and the College of Electors, as well as from the Governor, on the subject of the proposed reforms.

Governor Light lost no time in communicating Lord Glenelg's request to the Court of Policy, the colonial section of which declined to make any reply till that of the College of Electors was obtained. Various excuses were made by the latter body prior to meeting; and, when after some delay they did meet on the 26th January, 1839, they declined to express any view on the subject, although two members of the College had signed the petition from the inhabitants of British Guiana. The vacation between the last session of the year and the meeting of the Combined Court prevented the Governor from recurring to the subject until the second session of 1839, when, finding that it would be vain to expect any voluntary expression of opinion from the unofficial members, he directed the Government Secretary (Mr. H. E. F. Young) to move " that the College of Electors be abolished and the inhabitants possessed of the elective franchise be allowed to vote for the election of the unofficial members of the Court of Policy in the same manner as they are now entitled to vote for the election of Financial Representatives." This brought matters to a head, and on the 7th June, 1839, the whole unofficial section [1] voted for the continuance of the College, while the whole official section voted against it. The Governor refrained from using his casting vote and contented himself with reporting what had occurred to the Secretary of State in a despatch dated the 13th June, 1839. In this despatch he stated that the number of persons owning or representing estates in Demerara and Essequebo who had votes for the Electoral College and for the Financial Representatives was 113, while the number not owning or representing estates, but having votes, was 460; that in Berbice the number of those owning or representing estates and having votes was 78, while those who did not own or represent estates, but had votes, was 154; that the elective

[1] The unofficials were Messrs. Croal, Bach, Cameron, Rose, and McTurk.

franchise was conferred by law upon such persons as had an income of £150 *per annum* or made direct payment to the Receiver-General of taxes amounting to £5; but that these qualifications did not include more substantial ones, and that, for example, the possessor of a house or land, which, if sold, would produce seven or eight thousand pounds sterling, had no franchise, unless he kept some object of luxury, on which tax was imposed by ordinance; that membership of the College of Electors (Kiezers) did not require the possession of any property; that the Financial Representatives might be either merchants or landed proprietors, but that the former had little chance against the latter; and that the colonial section of the Court of Policy must be possessed of landed property, this being " the wrong construction put on their selection by the College of Kiezers—the law says ' good and honest men,' or words to that purpose."

" Hitherto," wrote Governor Light, " the College of Kiezers, the Financial Representatives and the colonial section of the Court of Policy have been the *Governor Light's Views and Recommendations.* nominees of a few wealthy merchants and proprietors, or attorneys, of estates. . . . They uniformly oppose the executive, and now represent a very small section of the population : the mass may be considered supported by the watchfulness of the official section. . . . On a vacancy in the Court of Policy, the College of Kiezers, assembled by proclamation, take an oath in the presence of the Governor to be uninfluenced in their selection of two persons to be presented for election by the Court of Policy. The oath does not prevent the public from being pretty well assured beforehand who will be named ; and, of the two, one is generally so objectionable as to secure the choice of the other. The Financial Representatives, though assumed as elected by the free votes of the community, yet are virtually the nominees of the same parties. The form ' I vote for —— ' is written by two or three clerks in the ruling Houses, on slips of paper equal to the number of votes, and sent off by the town agents to their dependents in the country for signature, who circulate them at the bidding of their employers. They are returned to the Secretary's Office, produced in Court of Policy and counted. I have seen three or four hundred in the same handwriting."

With regard to the working of this constitution in practice, Governor Light observed :

> " My first session in Combined Court has shown how powerless the Governor and official members are. They are forced to sit spectators, whilst the business is in the hands of the colonial section and the Financial Representatives. In consequence of this influence, I have been more than once threatened in Court of Policy, on some trifling difference of opinion with the colonial section, with refusal of supplies. . . . Nothing can be more irregular than the mode in which the estimates, framed by the Court of Policy, are examined. The official members are excluded from the Committee composed of the colonial section and the Financial Representatives. The resolutions are secret. The estimates are thus reframed at the will of this secret conclave, and the ways and means devised. The mockery of discussing the estimates and voting the supplies in open Court, after an interval of three or four weeks, is then adopted. As the items are read over, those rejected by previous arrangement are put to the vote and struck out. No argument can prevail against the ruling party. The Governor has no choice between acceptance or refusal. With him would then rest the onus of the stoppage of supplies for the year."

Whilst the population consisted of a comparatively small number of free persons, the rest being slaves or apprentices, the existence of the College of Electors could not interfere much with the privileges of the mass; and even in 1839, after the complete abolition of slavery, society in British Guiana was not, in the Governor's opinion, sufficiently advanced to justify any great diminution in the qualification for the elective franchise. He was, however, in favour of the abolition of the Electoral College, and he thought that

> " a considerable addition might be made to the number of electors, were the elective franchise extended to the Assessors, established by Order-in-Council of the 15th August, 1832,[1] the qualification for which being a £10 freehold or £20 household would, particularly in the towns, gradually bring forward the mass into strength and knowledge of their rights. The list of Assessors, taken in 1836, gave 705 Assessors for Demerara and Essequebo, 240 for Berbice."

[1] See p. 158, *infra*.

Governor Light further suggested that, with a view to a less arbitrary election of colonial members, the prayer of the petitioners for a local representation should be granted.

> " It would be advantageous," he wrote, " to increase the number of the Court of Policy, adding two colonial members and two officials, arranging the elections for the colonial section in the following manner : Georgetown, one member; Demerara County, two members; Essequebo, one member; New Amsterdam, one member; Berbice County, two members : total, seven members. The election to be local, each county and town choosing by their respective electors, not limiting their choice to an inhabitant of the town or county. . . . The number of Financial Representatives need not be increased; but they should be chosen by the local franchise, two for each county."

Finally, Governor Light urged that

> " the system of examining the estimates and fixing the supplies in secret committee, excluding the official section of the Court of Policy, should be changed into a committee of all, excepting the Governor, until the arrangements are made and public business resumed.   The present mode renders it a useless prelude for the Court of Policy to fix the estimates, as the Financial Representatives strike out what they please, fix what taxes they please, and can make public good subservient to private interests."

Governor Light concluded that the changes recommended by him would give the merchants representation in the towns, would result in the respectable part of the coloured people having their just influence, would give the county of Berbice its proper weight in the Colony, would be a boon to the mass and be gratefully received, while His Majesty's Government would find less difficulty in the future financial arrangements of the Colony.

The Marquess of Normanby replied on the 16th August, 1839, that the ill-success of the attempt made by Lord Glenelg

Marquess of Normanby's Reply. to obtain the advice of the Court of Policy and College of Electors rendered it necessary to proceed without the benefit of their previous opinion; that there could be " no doubt whatever respecting the necessity of requiring for the Governor an initiative of all money-votes, nor for insisting that the estimates, when proposed by the Governor should be discussed and voted *seriatim* in the full Court "; that the constitution of British Guiana seemed to have " gradually, but widely, departed in practice from the constitution of Demerara as it existed on the cession of that Colony to the Crown "; and that the habits now introduced were " open to many well-founded objections "; but that Her Majesty's decision on the two petitions, which had been presented, would not be announced until a later date, in order that a further opportunity might be afforded to any persons, or bodies in the Colony, to address through the Governor to the Crown any representations which they might think necessary for the assistance of Her Majesty's councils on this subject.

No further step was, however, taken until fifty-eight of the leading residents in British Guiana, " being deeply impressed
Public Meet- with the conviction that a strong necessity exists for
ings at the introduction of several important changes in the
Georgetown, Constitution of this Colony," requested the High
1842. Sheriff,[1] in a letter dated the 3rd August, 1842,[2] to convene a public meeting of the inhabitants " to consider this most serious and interesting subject; and, if so decided on by the meeting, to adopt a petition to Her Majesty's Secretary of State for the Colonies embodying the wishes and views of the colonists." The High Sheriff, with the Governor's sanction, convened such a meeting in the Guiana Public Buildings at Georgetown on the 12th of that month, and presided over it as chairman. After much debate, opinions being in strong conflict, the following motions were carried :

(1) " That it is the opinion of this meeting that one Chamber, possessing legislative functions and powers, should be substituted for the present constitution of the Colony " : (2) " that, in the opinion of this meeting, the Chamber should consist of 24 members, 8 official and 16 elective—say, 3 for Georgetown, one for New Amsterdam, 5 for the County of Demerary, 4 for the County of Essequebo, and 3 for the County of Berbice—and that the Colony be divided into 14 districts, 2 urban and 12 rural " : (3) " that the qualification for electors for the rural districts be the proprietorship of 5 acres of freehold land in cultivation, or 10 acres of leasehold or rented land in cultivation,

[1] George Bagot.   [2] See *Royal Gazette*, 11th August, 1842.

within the district, or the payment of $15 *per annum* direct taxes, by persons being of the age of 21 years; and that the qualification for electors of the urban districts be the proprietorship of a freehold or leasehold tenement within the district, assessed at the value of $1,200, or the payment of rent to the amount of $250 *per annum*, or of direct taxes to the amount of $15, by persons being of the age of 21 years." [1]

Five hours having been spent in debating these resolutions, the meeting adjourned, and met again on the 19th August, 1842, when a fourth resolution was moved and seconded to the effect " that the qualification for the members of the Legislature should be the following : For the rural districts 80 acres of freehold, or the occupancy of 100 acres leasehold or rented land, or an annual income of $2,000, by persons of the age of 21 years; and for the urban districts an income of $2,000 or a rental of $1,000." Thereupon Mr. G. McFarlane moved as an amendment " that the resolutions passed at the last meeting be cancelled, and that a petition be presented to Her Majesty, through the Secretary of State for the Colonies, pointing out the defects of the present political constitution of the Colony, and praying her Majesty to alter and amend it, or to grant a new constitution." This amendment was seconded by Mr. N. Belgrave and was carried by a very large majority. It was then further resolved " that the following gentlemen be appointed to draw up the petition to Her Majesty : His Honour the High Sheriff, and Messrs. Edward Carbery, N. Belgrave, Alexander Macrae, George McFarlane, Hugh Grant, Bruce Ferguson, Henry Montaroux, John Emery, W. Furlonge (Attorney-General), James Glen, and Sir Michael McTurk." [2] The meeting thereafter dispersed, its proceedings having throughout been characterized by great propriety and orderliness. Neither the Attorney-General nor Sir M. McTurk had attended either meeting or been associated with the movement, and both declined to take part in drawing up the proposed petition, as also did the High Sheriff. Moreover, in the end the whole affair proved abortive, as no petition was framed for submission to the Queen.

[1] See *Royal Gazette*, 13th August, 1842.
[2] See *Royal Gazette*, 20th August, 1842.

Commenting on this episode in a despatch to Lord Stanley,
dated the 7th October, 1842, Governor Light observed that

*Governor
Light's Com-
ments on the
Public
Meetings.*
the signatories of the requisition to the High Sheriff
to convene the public meeting were the principal
planters and merchants, who had hitherto directed
public opinion; but that the final resolution of the
meeting on the 19th August, although it prayed Her Majesty
to alter the constitution, was not such as these gentlemen
anticipated or wished, when they decided on obtaining the
meeting. A committee of their number had, prior to the
first meeting, agreed upon certain resolutions, which embodied
their opinion of the constitutional changes necessary; and it
was intended that these resolutions should be submitted
seriatim to the meeting for adoption. Three of these resolutions were in fact, after considerable opposition, adopted on the
12th August; but, as they did not embrace a sufficient extension
of the franchise, and as the further resolutions, which were to
be subsequently put to the meeting, contemplated a very high
qualification for members of the Legislature, a considerable
increase took place in the number of persons who attended
the meeting of the 19th August. These persons consisted
chiefly of agricultural freeholders from the East coast of
Demerara County; and it was plain that the majority preferred the constitution to be amended for their protection by
Her Majesty rather than that a few educated and wealthy
colonists should suggest a constitution for the comparatively
vast remainder.

" The inconveniences of the present constitution,"
continued Governor Light, " have never been so marked as

*He describes
Inconveni-
ences of the
Constitution.*
at the present moment. There happened at the
same period, by the departure of two members of
the College of Kiezers and of two in the Court of
Policy, vacancies in both. The vacancies in the
Kiezers must be filled up before the body can act. The
elections last for a month, boxes being kept open in the
Government Secretary's office at New Amsterdam and
Georgetown to receive votes, in writing and sealed, during
that period. These boxes are opened in the Court of
Policy, the votes are taken, and the majority declared.
Till very lately the College of Electors has been filled by
nominees of the influential men in the Colony; but latterly

there have been some attempts at popular election.   There have been two candidates for one of the vacancies in the College of Electors, the votes pretty well equal, giving a small majority to one of the candidates.   By a resolution of the Court of Policy, either party may demand a scrutiny. Lists of voters on each side are given and fourteen days allowed for both candidates to write the objections to each other's votes.   The registry of votes is so irregular that objections are readily made.   The Court of Policy has now under scrutiny upwards of 400 names on the part of one candidate for the Financial body, and upwards of 200 on the part of the opponent, to each of which in many instances half a dozen or more objections are appended. It may be a month of useless and tiresome investigation; and the same may result from the scrutiny in the case of the electors.   In the meantime some important business is delayed in the Court of Policy; and, if by any unforeseen casualty, or by a member of the College of Electors choosing to quit the Colony, another vacancy should occur in their body, another month would be lost, besides the chance of scrutiny to cause additional delay."

These considerations confirmed Governor Light in his opinion that the College of Electors ought to be abolished; *His Further Recommendations.* and further experience had taught him that, when the Court of Policy, as then constituted, met the Financial Representatives in Combined Court for the purpose of raising the taxes, the local government was confronted with an assembly, not only omnipotent in all financial questions, which alone were proper subjects for their decision, but one which constantly encroached on the legislative functions that were by law exclusively within the province of the Court of Policy.

" The only remedy for this inconvenience and often misused power," he thought, " would be to give the nomination of the unofficial members of the Court of Policy to the Crown, restricting the selection to persons not holding office. Thus its members would be more disposed than they now are to limit the Combined Court to its proper sphere, taxation, and perhaps with more equity than of late years."

He believed that there would be few opponents to the less popular order of legislation by such a " Council of Government,"

L

for the mass knew that the officials, being themselves servants of the Crown, were their surest protectors. The Governor also considered that, for the purpose of electing the Financial Representatives,

> " the franchise should be extended to all freeholders possessed of land and tenement valued at \$400; to leaseholders of land and tenement of an annual rent of \$100; to all persons assessed to pay any amount of tax on income; to all persons paying direct tax of \$15 in any one year, and not being six months in arrear of payment."

Lord Stanley replied on the 3rd January, 1843, that, if the constitution of the Colony were to be amended, it would be necessary to proceed upon much more ample in-*Lord Stanley decides to* formation, " and, if possible, at the instance, or with *postpone any* the concurrence or active participation, of some *Constitutional Reform.* numerous and influential body of colonists "; that, if a change were then to be attempted, it did not appear that any large body of the inhabitants would be of one opinion as to what the change should be; while, considering the rapid progress which the lower classes were making, it was probable that any change, made at the time, would soon become very unsatisfactory.

> " Under these circumstances," he concluded, " I am not disposed to undertake the reform of the British Guiana Constitution at the present moment, unless the conduct of the Combined Court should force it upon me; and I trust that the course which matters took at the second of the public meetings which you have reported, will induce the opponents of your government to pause before they hazard the consequences which might ensue from rendering it impracticable to carry on the government upon the present plan."

CHAPTER VI

THE EMERY INCIDENT, 1843

REFORM questions, then, for a time fell into abeyance; but an incident of some constitutional significance occurred in Com-

Annual Session of Combined Court opened in April, 1843. bined Court a few months later. Governor Light opened the session by delivering an address to the Court on the 25th April, 1843. Mr. John Emery, part-proprietor and editor of the *Guiana Times* newspaper, who had been elected Financial Representative in the preceding year by a large majority, which a close scrutiny did not much diminish, but whose political views were obnoxious to the planting interest, then gave notice of the following motions :

> " That any address which may be brought up in this Court in answer to the speech of His Excellency the Governor, shall be read, considered, and, if need be, debated and put paragraph by paragraph in full Court, with open doors, and that, when so disposed of, it shall be held to be the address of the whole Combined Court :
> " That the Minutes of this Court be resumed and signed with open doors."

The result was that, when the Court met again, on the 22nd May, the usual reply by the electives to the Governor's speech

Petition alleging Mr. Emery to be outlawed from Scotland for Felony. was not made ; but Mr. G. H. Loxdale, a Financial Representative, handed in a petition from Mr. R. G. Butts alleging that John Emery's real name was John Imray ; that John Imray had been indicted by the Lord Advocate of Scotland for felony, " which, if it had been substantiated, might have issued in his transportation " ; and that John Imray did not appear for trial, but forfeited his bail-bond, and, being outlawed, was a fugitive from justice. The petition prayed that the Combined Court would elicit the truth of the foregoing averments and adopt such further course as would " effectually protect the interests of the constituency and, at the same time, vindicate the honour and dignity of the Combined Court."

It was then moved by Mr. J. L. Smith and seconded by Mr. Loxdale that the petition should be referred to Mr. *Petition referred by Combined Court to Mr. Emery.* Emery, in order that he might answer the charges therein made against him. But Mr. Emery, who was present in Court, rose in his place and said :

"It may save the Court some trouble and me great pain, if I candidly inform the Court that, if you, by order of this Court, or the Government Secretary by order of this Court, refer this petition to me for report, I will make no report on it, but will send it back to the Secretary with as much of contempt and insult against him, as Officer of this Court, as is consistent with perfect abstinence from outrage to him as a private gentleman."

Mr. Smith at once moved that Mr. Emery, having declared in open Court that he would treat the orders of the Court with contempt and insult, should be expelled from the Court. Thereupon Mr. Emery apologized for using those expressions and retracted all that followed the words "no report on it." Mr. Smith observed that Mr. Emery had better retract the whole. He did so; and the motion was then carried, there being only two dissentients, namely, Mr. John Noble, a Financial Representative, and Mr. H. E. F. Young, the Government Secretary.

Next day, Mr. Emery being present in Court, a letter from him was read acknowledging the receipt of the petition and replying to the Government Secretary in the *Mr. Emery declines to enter on the Subject-matter of the Petition.* following terms :

"Without power to enforce the production of documents, or the attendance of witnesses; without power to imprison for contempt; with functions marked out by very clear and narrow limits; with even less authority than almost any other deliberative body in the West Indies—I cannot for a moment imagine that the Combined Court intends to erect itself into a tribunal for trying the moral character of its members. I must, therefore, infer that the reference of the petition to me was dictated by kindness and consideration, in order that I might have an opportunity, if I thought fit, of denying so injurious accusations. Under that impression

I have to request that you will convey my sincere and hearty thanks to the Governor and Combined Court, for the courtesy with which they have treated me in this respect, and which I can readily discriminate from the insolence of the petition itself.   I have further to request you, however, to inform His Excellency and the Court that I respectfully decline to avail myself of the permission which they give me.   To enter on the subject-matter of the petition and its accompaniments, would involve me in a most unpleasant and indecorous contention with individuals out of the Court, if not with some members of it—a contention which would only aggravate the irritation and excitement now abroad in the community, and impede the public business, or rather render men's minds totally unfit to discuss it, without at the same time leading to any impartial or satisfactory solution of the question which the petition starts."

After hearing this letter read, Mr. Smith gave notice that he would move, next day, that Mr. Emery, having returned the petition without answering it, had been guilty of contempt of the Court and breach of its privileges, and that he be, therefore, expelled from the Court. The whole of the 24th May was spent in debating this motion and an amendment moved by Mr. W. Furlonge, the Attorney-General, and supported by the Government, " that this Court do now proceed with the other order of the day." On the 25th May a numerously and respectably signed petition from inhabitants of British Guiana, possessed of the elective franchise, some of whom had voted for, and some against, Mr. Emery at his election in 1842, while some had not voted at all, was presented and read to the Combined Court. The petitioners contemplated " with the utmost alarm " the possibility of any member whatsoever, returned as Financial Representative by a majority of the constituency, being turned out by a majority of the Combined Court, to whom he had made himself personally obnoxious. They, therefore, prayed the Court not to sanction any vote of expulsion, but by proceeding with the ordinary agenda to relieve the public mind of anxiety and to save the public business from further injurious interruption. The Court then, all members being present, continued the debate on the Attorney-General's amendment, which on

Attempt to expel Mr. Emery from the Combined Court.

division was lost by two votes, Messrs. Noble and Emery with the official section voting for, and all the other elective members voting against, the amendment. Thereupon the Governor stated that it was necessary there should be an adjournment, in order that he might consider what measures were necessary to be taken " to prevent an act of gross injustice."

On the following day various amendments, having for their object the reference of the matter to the Secretary of State for the Colonies and the Law Officers of the Crown, were rejected by the electives; while an amendment, moved by Mr. Noble and seconded by Mr. E. Bishop, a member of the Court of Policy, recommending Mr. Emery to vacate his seat, in order that he might be thrown back on the constituency, was opposed by the official, as well as by the other unofficial, members. An amendment that the petition, laid on the table on the 25th May, should be entertained was also lost; and, after long and fruitless debate, the Court again adjourned.

On the 27th May, a further petition from certain prominent inhabitants of the Colony, possessed of the elective franchise, *Governor Light vetoes the Motion for Mr. Emery's Expulsion.* was laid on the table of Combined Court. It prayed the Governor to " put a decisive veto " on the motion to expel Mr. Emery and to proceed with the long-interrupted ordinary business of the Court. After this petition had been read, Governor Light made the following statement with reference to Mr. Smith's original resolution :

" My legal advisers inform me that there is not a particle of evidence to show that Mr. Emery labours under a sentence of outlawry, alleged to have been pronounced in Scotland, his native country, in the year 1834 ; and indeed the resolution, although it mentions the charge of outlawry, does not make that charge the reason for the proposed expulsion. The resolution is one of expulsion for an alleged contempt in not answering, it is said, a petition which was referred to him. The fact, however, is that a respectful answer from Mr. Emery to the petition is on the records of your proceedings. My legal advisers further inform me, and I learn also from the speech of the Chief Justice in this Court,[1] that the power of expelling

[1] Mr. J. H. Bent. The Chief Justice was at this time, and continued until the 9th May, 1865, to be, an official member of the Court of Policy.

from the Combined Court a member of the College of Financial Representatives, is not a power which legally can be exercised by this Court, owing to the very anomalous composition of the Court itself. If, therefore, the resolution be put and carried, I should be unable, according to the advice of my law advisers, to aid or assist in giving practical effect to the decision of the majority of the Court. I am advised that even a proclamation declaring the office of a Financial Representative to be vacant, by reason of a resolution from this anomalously composed Court, would not be legal. Under these peculiar circumstances, I have deemed it best for the dignity of the Court itself, for the peace of the country, and for the due carrying on of the public service, to resort to a measure which, although precedents may be found on your minutes, I hope and believe will never be adopted except under some similar emergency to that which at present exists. I respect the motives and the judgment of all who think the proposed expulsion lawful, equitable, and necessary, and who differ with me in my opinion of its gross injustice; with that opinion, however, unshaken by all the arguments that have been used to the contrary, I trust the Court will reciprocally respect my conscientious scruples, and uniting them with the legal advice which I have received, acquiesce in the veto which I now put on Mr. Smith's resolution, and proceed with the other business of the session."

At the next meeting of the Court, on the 31st May, a protest against the Governor's veto was made by Messrs. W. Ranken, *Electives protest against Use of Governor's Veto.* U. J. F. Bach, J. L. Smith, and J. T. White, members of the Court of Policy, and by Messrs. G. H. Loxdale, W. Davison, G. Laing and A. R. Hollingsworth, Financial Representatives, for the following reasons :

" 1st, Because we deny the right of His Excellency to put a veto on any motion not initiating a money-vote.

" 2nd, Because, if His Excellency possessed any such power with regard to other motions, we deny that he has any such power with regard to motions arising out of a breach of the privileges of this Court; nor can any such power be allowed without virtually denying the existence of any rights or privileges of the Court, beyond such as the Governor for the time being may think fit to accord.

" 3rd, Because, if any such power as that claimed by His Excellency exists, it can be exercised only for the purpose of preventing the motion from being entertained at all, but can never be exercised for the purpose of, in effect, reversing the decision of the Court to which the question had once been submitted by His Excellency.

" 4th, That in the present case, not only was the motion entertained after due notice thereof, but amendment after amendment was moved on it, with His Excellency's sanction; and one of these amendments His Excellency declared himself willing personally to move; and it was only after a debate of three days, and when the motion was about to be carried, that His Excellency interposed his veto.

" 5th, Because, if His Excellency can, at any stage of the proceedings, put a veto on a motion, it is, in effect taking away all power from this Court and reducing it below the level of a deliberative assembly."

On the same day Mr. Smith, seconded by Mr. Ranken moved

"that His Excellency be requested to adopt the necessary measures for eliciting the truth of the charges contained in the petition of R. G. Butts to this Court against John Emery, Esquire, lately elected a Financial Representative; and that until this matter be settled, the Court do not proceed to any other business, save only that, to prevent loss to the public revenue, the Court do now proceed to continue in force, for the space of three months from the 30th June next, the existing Tax Ordinance, and that the Attorney-General be requested to prepare an Ordinance re-enacting such clauses of the Tax Ordinance of 1842 as relate to the duties on rum, spirits and wine, and to a duty on imports, to continue in full force for three months from and after the 30th June next, unless the Combined Court make other provision in the meantime. The revival of the Tax Ordinance to be subject, as regards the levying duty on imports or other articles, to such modification, if any, as may be rendered necessary by the Act of the Imperial Parliament of the 5 and 6 of Her present Majesty Victoria, chap. 49; and also that the Court do authorize for the same period, the payment of all salaries fixed by the Civil List or otherwise, and of all contracts in progress as voted and sanctioned by the last Combined Court."

This resolution was, in effect, an attempt to coerce the Governor by a threatened stoppage of supplies, which would *Attempt to coerce the Governor by Stoppage of Supplies.* take place at the end of September, unless in the meantime some solution of the deadlock had been attained; and, on its being carried by seven votes to four, the Governor declared the Court to be prorogued until the 10th June.   Subsequently he issued a proclamation dissolving the College of Financial Representatives and calling for a new election.   As a result both Mr. Emery and his supporter, Mr. Noble, lost their seats, and were replaced by Mr. A. Macrae and Mr. P. Rose.   Political excitement subsided and the Combined Court resumed ordinary business on the 24th July, 1843, two months having been wasted over this *Mr. Emery unseated at a New Election.* sordid squabble.   The loss, which might have been caused to the revenue by this delay, was obviated by the passage of an ordinance requiring the importers of all goods and the purchasers of rum for local consumption, subsequent to the date of the ordinance, to give bond for the payment of such duties as might be imposed by the Combined Court.   The ordinance of 1842 was afterwards revived until the passing of the next Annual Tax Ordinance, which took place on the 16th August, 1843.

CHAPTER VII

THE ROYAL ORDER-IN-COUNCIL OF THE 3RD JUNE, 1842

THE session of Combined Court in 1843 is also of interest because it was the first held under the provisions of the Royal *Constitution* Order-in-Council of the 3rd June, 1842, which author-*of Committee* ized free discussion of the several items of the annual *of Ways and* *Means.* estimate of colonial expenditure, subject always to the terms and conditions of the Civil List Ordinance then in force. This Order-in-Council further directed that

> " it shall not be necessary for the Governor to attend the meetings of the Combined Court, when assembled for the purpose of framing the Ways and Means to meet the amount of the annual estimate, but that the said Court shall at such times consist of all the remaining members of of the Court of Policy, with the Financial Representatives, or a majority of them, and that all discussions touching and concerning the framing and raising of the said Ways and Means shall take place in such Court, and not elsewhere."

Previously it had been the duty and privilege of the Financial Representatives, in consultation with the elective members only of the Court of Policy, to frame the Ways and Means to meet the estimate of expenditure passed by the Combined Court for each year. The attempt had frequently been made to alter this procedure, and to introduce the official members of the Court of Policy into the Committee of Ways and Means; but it was always successfully resisted by the elective section. Now, however, the condition that the Committee of Ways and Means should consist of the official, as well as of the unofficial, members of the Combined Court became an integral part of the Civil List compromise.

There were not, and never were, any standing rules and orders for the guidance of the Committee of Ways and Means,

and this Committee always had full control over its own procedure.   Its first step every year was to choose its own chair-

Procedure of
this Com-
mittee.

man ; and as, in view of the large majority of electives, it was by no means certain that the Governor,
if he attended the Committee, would be voted into
the chair, and as it would have been derogatory to the dignity
of his office for him to attend the Committee's deliberations in
any capacity other than that of chairman, the Royal Order-in-
Council recited that it should " not be necessary for the
Governor to attend the meetings."   Accordingly, on the 29th
July, 1843, Governor Light, at the end of the day's agenda,
addressed the Combined Court as follows :

> " The estimate having been agreed to and closed, I have
> to acquaint you that the Court, in pursuance of Her
> Majesty's Royal Order-in-Council of the 3rd June, 1842,
> becomes a Committee of the whole Court, with the excep-
> tion of the Governor, and that it is now your privilege to
> appoint a chairman, and to proceed to frame the Ways and
> Means, and thereafter to report the same to the full Court
> for adoption, for the purpose of receiving which report I
> will again attend on any day the Committee may hereafter
> think it convenient to appoint."

He then retired from the Court ; and Mr. J. T. White,
seconded by the Government Secretary, moved that Mr.
J. Croal, elective member of the Court of Policy, should take
the chair.   But Mr. Croal himself, seconded by Sir Michael
McTurk, moved as an amendment that the Vice-President of
the College of Financial Representatives, Mr. A. Macrae, should
be chairman of the Committee ; and, this amendment being
carried, the Committee proceeded to prepare a scheme of Ways
and Means, which was embodied in a report dated the 4th
August, 1843, and presented to the Combined Court next day,
when the Governor again presided and the Attorney-General
was requested to frame the Annual Tax Ordinance upon this
scheme.   He did so, and presented the draft of such an
ordinance to the Combined Court on the 7th August, when it
was read a first time.   On the 15th August, this bill was
read a second time, debated, and several amendments were
made in it.   Next day further considerable amendments were
made in the bill, after which it was read a third time, passed,

and its title settled as " Colonial Taxes Publication, No. 11 of 1843." The Governor then declared the session of Combined Court to be closed.

Another clause in the Royal Order-in-Council of the 3rd June, 1842, which needs some commentary, is that directing *All Public* all money-votes, passed by the Combined Court, *Moneys paid* to " be paid out under the authority of a warrant, *under* *Governor's* or warrants, under the hand of the Governor, *Warrant.* and not otherwise." [1] Prior to the Civil List compromise, the " King's Chest " had been under the exclusive control of the Governor; but the " Colony Chest " had been in charge of the Governor and Court of Policy, aided by a so-called " Finance Committee," chosen from the College of Financial Representatives, who examined the several accounts against the Colony. If this scrutiny showed the accounts to be in order, payment issued under authority of the Court. The effect of the Royal Order-in-Council was, however, to abolish the Finance Committee, and to make the whole revenue of the Colony subject to the Governor's control in the same manner as the " King's Chest " had been, the Governor being, of course, responsible for insuring that the appropriations voted by the Combined Court should not be exceeded without the authority of the Court. Herein lies the origin and explanation of section 134 of the British Guiana Constitution Ordinance No. 1 of 1891, which recites : " All moneys paid from the Treasury shall be paid on a warrant under the hand of the Governor."

[1] See Appendix L.

CHAPTER VIII

INTRODUCTION OF TRIAL BY JURY, 1844–6

I⊤ will be remembered that Lord Goderich, when outlining in his despatch of the 1st June, 1831, the contemplated reform *Royal Order-* of the judicial system in British Guiana, wrote that, *in-Council of* while trial by jury could not be engrafted on the *20th June,* colonial laws " without producing mischiefs which *1831.* must much more than compensate for any benefit which could be expected from it," yet that, upon the trial of criminals in the Supreme Court, assessors would be appointed " from the principal merchants and planters of the Colony," whose votes upon the question of " guilty " or " not guilty " would be of equal value with the votes of the regular judges. A few days later, a Royal Order-in-Council, made on the 20th June, 1831, directed that, upon the trial of any person for any crime or offence, three Assessors should be associated with the three Judges of the Supreme Court ; that these three Assessors should be entitled to deliberate and vote with such Judges upon the final judgment to be pronounced in every criminal case ; that no person should be convicted of any crime or offence, or be adjudged to suffer any punishment by any judgment, unless a majority of the total number of such Judges and Assessors should, in open Court, vote in favour of such judgment ; and that the decision of such majority should in all criminal cases be recorded as the judgment of the whole Court. It was further ordered that the Assessors in Demerary and Berbice should " be chosen and appointed in such and the same manner as the members of the Court of Civil and Criminal Justice of Demerary " had theretofore been chosen and appointed.

This judicial system was formulated and brought into operation by an ordinance, enacted by Governor D'Urban *Ordinance* and the Court of Policy on the 5th December, 1831, *No. 6 of 1831.* " to provide a sufficient number of Assessors to be associated with the Judges of the Supreme Court of Criminal

Justice of British Guiana " (No. 6 of 1831), wherein it was laid down that there should be " for the Supreme Criminal Court of Demerary and Essequebo a number of twelve Assessors, and for the Supreme Criminal Court of Berbice a like number of twelve Assessors "; that the right to elect Assessors should be vested in the College of Electors (Kiezers) of British Guiana; that, in the exercise of this right, the College should " be bound to make a double nomination of persons for the office of Assessor, to be transmitted through the hands of His Excellency the Governor to the Judges of the Supreme Court "; that these Judges should then select one of the persons nominated to serve as an Assessor; and that the like form should be observed on each and every occasion of a vacancy occurring in the full complement of Assessors. It was also enacted that each Assessor should be liable to serve two years; and that, after having served for such period of two years, he should not be compellable to serve again, until after the expiration of two years from the date on which he relinquished office as Assessor. It was further laid down that, before any person was brought up for trial, the names of all the Assessors in office for the time being, in the jurisdiction concerned, should be written on similar pieces of paper, placed in a box by the Secretary of the Supreme Court, and be drawn therefrom in succession by the second Puisne Judge; and that, after three Assessors had been found, to whom there was no legal ground of challenge or objection, the trial should proceed.

Next year, a further Royal Order-in-Council, made on the 15th August, 1832, directed that, with certain specified *Royal Order-* exceptions, every free man, between the age of *in-Council of* twenty-one years and sixty years, resident in British *15th August,* *1832.* Guiana, should be liable to serve as Assessor, provided he was possessed of one of the following qualifications, namely,

(*a*) ownership, or beneficial use, within the Colony of £10 a year, above reprizes, in any immovable property, or in rents, or other annual proceeds issuing out of such immovable property, either in perpetuity or for life :

(*b*) beneficial use in the Colony of £20 a year, above reprizes, in immovable property held by lease or leases for the absolute term of twenty-one years, or for any term of years determinable on any life or lives :

(c) household rated to any direct tax on a value of not less than £20 *per annum* :

(d) occupation of " a house of the annual value of £20."

For the purpose of this Ordinance, all slaves, whether præential or personal, were considered as " immovable property." The persons exempted from service as Assessors were all members of the Legislative Bodies, Judges of the Supreme Court, clergymen, lawyers in practice, officers of the Supreme Court, jailers, medical practitioners, officers in the army or navy on full pay, licensed pilots, and customs' officers. It was further ordered that, " after deducting six from the whole number of persons summoned, and actually appearing to act, as Assessors on any criminal prosecution, the Public Prosecutor and the person or persons against whom the prosecution " was brought should each have as many peremptory challenges as were equal to one-half of the remaining number, or, should the remainder not be an even number, then the defendant should have one peremptory challenge more than the Public Prosecutor. Thereafter the procedure for selecting three Assessors from among those unchallenged followed the provisions contained in the law of 1831.

Subsequently, by a Royal Order-in-Council, made on the 3rd April, 1843, power was given to the Governor and Court *Royal Order-* of Policy of British Guiana, notwithstanding the *in-Council of* Orders-in-Council of 1831 and 1832, " to make, *3rd April,* *1843.* ordain, and establish all such laws, statutes or ordinances as to them should seem meet for regulating the constitution of the Courts of Civil and Criminal Justice in the said Colony, or for regulating the form and manner of proceeding to be observed in those Courts or any of them "; but it was not until 1844 that a movement was initiated which resulted within the next three years in the establishment of trial by jury.

On the 12th October, 1844, Governor Light and the Court of Policy passed an " Ordinance to introduce into the Colony of *Ordinance* British Guiana trial by jury in certain cases " (No. 22 *No. 22 of* of 1844). The 1st *section* of this law was as follows : *1844.*

" Whenever any action shall be brought or instituted in the Supreme Court of Civil Justice of British Guiana to procure reparation by pecuniary damages, for any breach of promise of marriage, or for criminal conversation with any wife, or for seduction of any daughter or servant, or for any malicious prosecution, or for false imprisonment, or for assault and battery, or for slander, verbal, written, or printed, or for any trespass to any person or property not involving title, or for any injury occasioned by the negligence or folly of any person, and in any such action the plaintiff and defendant shall join issue in any matter of fact, or the defendant shall suffer judgment by default, it shall be lawful for the plaintiff or defendant in every such action to apply to any one of the Judges of the said Supreme Court for an order directing such issues to be tried, or such damages to be assessed by a jury; and, upon such order being obtained, the trial of every such issue, and the assessment of all such damages on any judgment by default, shall be before the said Court and a Jury of twelve men."

The *2nd section* recited :

" Every male person, except as hereinafter excepted, between the ages of 21 years and 60 years, residing in the Colony of British Guiana, who shall be the proprietor, attorney, agent, representative, or manager of any plantation, or who shall be a merchant or banker, or principal clerk to a merchant or banker, or who shall be a manager of any chartered or incorporated bank, or who shall be a householder occupying a house and tenements to the value of $3,000 and upwards *per annum*, shall be qualified and liable to serve on juries for the trial of all such issues and assessment of all such damages as aforesaid : Provided always, that no member of the Court of Policy, nor any clergyman, nor any practising barrister, advocate, attorney-at-law, nor practitioner before the said Supreme Court, nor any clerk to any practising barrister, advocate, attorney-at-law, or practitioner aforesaid, nor any schoolmaster, nor any medical practitioner, nor any public officer, whose daily attendance is required at his office, shall be returned or summoned to serve on juries."

These two sections were, however, repealed by an " Ordinance to extend the provisions of Ordinance No. 22 of the year *Ordinance No. 19 of 1846.* 1844 . . . to actions and suits for other causes than therein mentioned, and to make provision for the striking of special juries " (No. 19 of 1846), which was passed on the 10th July, 1846, and which re-enacted the 1st section of the law of 1844 with the addition that power was given to the Supreme Court of Civil Justice in any such actions or suits to insist upon trial by jury, " any dissent thereto of the plaintiff and defendant or either of them to the contrary in any wise notwithstanding " : while for the jurors' qualifications set out in the 2nd section were substituted the qualifications and exemptions prescribed for Assessors by the Royal Order-in-Council of the 15th August, 1832. This law also made provision for the striking of special jurors, when necessary; and the 4th section recited :

> " It shall be lawful for the said Supreme Court of Civil Justice, upon motion made on behalf of Her Majesty, Her Heirs, or Successors, or on the motion of any plaintiff or defendant, in any action, cause, or suit whatsoever depending, or to be brought and carried on in the said Court, and the said Court is hereby authorized and required upon motion as aforesaid in any of the cases before mentioned, which would form or be the subject of a trial at bar in any of Her Majesty's Supreme Courts of Common Law at Westminster, to order the trial by jury to be had, heard, and determined at bar, that is to say before and by the said Court, composed of all the three Judges thereof."

The final step was taken in an ordinance enacted by Governor Light and the Court of Policy and published on the 8th August, *Ordinance No. 26 of 1846.* 1846, but not brought into full effect until the 2nd January, 1847, " to introduce into the Colony of British Guiana trial by jury in criminal cases " (No. 26 of 1846). This law did away with the system of trial before a Court composed of three Judges and three Assessors and enacted that, " on the trial of any person or persons, upon any indictment or information before any Supreme Court of Criminal Justice in British Guiana," such trial should be had " by any one or more Judge or Judges of the said Court and a jury of twelve men, according to the course of the law in England." The jurors' qualifications for the purpose of this ordinance were the same as those embodied in Ordinance No. 19 of 1846; and the first criminal trial by jury in British Guiana took place under the new law on the 26th January, 1847, Chief Justice J. H. Bent presiding.

M

CHAPTER IX

FURTHER ABORTIVE PROPOSALS FOR CONSTITUTIONAL REFORM :
1845–49

MEANWHILE the agitation for constitutional reform had been renewed; and, on the 17th September, 1845, a requisition similar to that of the 3rd August, 1842, was addressed *Public* to Mr. G. Bagot, the High Sheriff, by thirteen *Meeting at Georgetown,* prominent residents in British Guiana, desiring him *20th October,* to convene a public meeting of the inhabitants for *1845.* the purpose of adopting a petition to Her Majesty, or to Her Majesty's Principal Secretary of State for the Colonies, embodying the views of the colonists as to the changes necessary to be made in the constitution. Governor Light, however, did not on this occasion sanction either the use of the name of the High Sheriff as convener of the meeting or his official presence thereat; but he addressed to the thirteen subscribers of the requisition an " admonition " to the effect that the local Legislature for the time being was " the legitimately appointed tribunal for taking cognizance, in the first instance, of the political wants and wishes of the people of this Colony," and that representations from the colonists, when considered and matured by the local Legislature, were more likely to meet with favour from Her Majesty's Government than if presented through any other channel. Nevertheless the subscribers of the requisition, who pointed out not only that the conduct of the College of Electors and of the elective section of the Court of Policy with respect to the reform petition of 1839 had been obstructive, but also that Lord Normanby, in a despatch dated the 16th August, 1839, had forbidden the re-introduction into the Court of Policy of the proposal for abolishing the College of Electors, " because any constitutional changes which may be necessary should originate with the Sovereign, and not with the local Legislature," persisted in their determination to hold a public meeting, which accordingly took place in the

British Theatre, High Street, Georgetown, on the 20th October, 1845.   About 1,100 persons attended; and Mr. Richard Haynes who in the following year was Mayor of Georgetown, took *Petition to* the chair.   The meeting unanimously adopted a *the Queen.* petition to the Queen, praying Her Majesty " to abolish the whole of the existing legislative institutions of this province, and to substitute, in lieu of them, a form of government based on direct popular representation, comprehending a Council and House of Assembly, to legislate under the authority of the Crown, and similar to what has long prevailed, and now prevails, in the chartered colonies of Jamaica, Barbados, Antigua, and St. Christopher's, with such modifications as local circumstances may require."   This petition was signed by upwards of 2,000 persons, but " had very few signatures of persons in a respectable condition of life "; [1] and it was forwarded to Mr. W. E. Gladstone, then Secretary of State for the Colonies, by Messrs. R. Haynes and J. Spooner, under cover of a joint letter dated the 17th March, 1846.

A copy of the petition was supplied to Governor Light, who communicated it to the Court of Policy on the 25th March, *Minute of* 1846, whereupon the Court recorded the following *Court of* minute for communication to the Secretary of *Policy on this* *Petition.* State :

> " That in their opinion the petition in question has no claim to be considered as the expression of the wants and wishes either of the majority of the respectable, intelligent and independent portion of the Colony, or even of a numerical majority of its inhabitants.   Numerous persons of weight and influence, who were favourable in 1842 to a reform of the political constitution of British Guiana, have on this occasion deliberately withheld their signatures and support from the present petition.   Suitable persons to be elective members of the College of Electors, Court of Policy and Financial Representatives are at present found with great difficulty, although the aggregate number required is only 18; there being but comparatively few residents of suitable qualifications and acquirements in the Colony, and of these few the greater number are so occupied in private pursuits that their acceptance of gratuitous and arduous offices is very reluctantly given and then only from a sense of public duty.   The Court

---

[1] Governor Light's despatch, 11th November, 1847.

are unanimously and decidedly averse to the establishment of a House of Assembly and Legislative Council
such as exist in other West India colonies. Moreover,
the Court is confident that those persons, connected either
with agriculture or with commerce in British Guiana, best
entitled from their stake in it to pronounce an opinion
on the subject, would concur with the Court in considering
the introduction of such institutions, at the present time
and in the present state of society, altogether premature.
The preparatory training, which the prevalence of English
law and custom, trial by jury, and a system of parochial
assessments has imparted to the inhabitants of other
colonies, and thus fitted them for an English political
constitution, is not only non-existent or as yet but im-
perfectly developed in British Guiana, but there is also
in this Colony a greater diversity of races and religious
tenets than in Jamaica and Barbados. The Court, when
either authorized by Her Majesty, or invited by their
fellow-colonists, or moved thereto by stronger induce-
ments to originate changes than at present exist, will be
found not unwilling or unable to prepare for Her Majesty's
gracious confirmation and allowance an enactment to
modify and improve the political constitution of British
Guiana in such particulars as would probably render the
exercise of the franchise and the attendance on legislative
and financial duties more acceptable to the constituency
and more convenient to the members of the Legislature
than is the existing system. Until honoured with Her
Majesty's instructions, the Court refrain from doing more
in the meantime than to indicate in general terms the
improvements which the existing system is capable of
receiving without such organic and premature changes
as would render necessary an entire reconstruction of the
legislative and financial constitution of British Guiana :

" 1st, that Her Majesty's Government authorize His
Excellency the Governor to replace the College of Electors
on the footing as to term of service on which it stood
previous to 1831, namely, limiting the period of service
for each member of the College to two years, instead of
for life as at present. This would throw back the members
of the College of Electors on the constituency every two
years.

" 2nd, that at a future fitting time there be an abolition
of the College of seven Electors, who now nominate the
members of the Court of Policy.

" 3rd, that the elective members of the Court of Policy

and the Financial Representatives be then chosen by local constituencies in the towns and counties in appropriate numbers.

" The Court are, however, of opinion that, as there is nothing in the actual circumstances of the Colony to render necessary at this time even the above modifications of the present constitution, it would be wise and politic to postpone all political changes, except the first, until the public mind shall be more disposed than at present to regard them with favour."

This minute was signed by Governor Light, by Mr. C. Robinson (Collector of Customs), and by Messrs. J. Stuart, P. Rose, and J. Croal, elective members of the Court; while Mr. J. T. White, another elective member, who was absent from the meeting of the 25th March, 1846, added the following note at the foot of the minute : " I concur entirely in the views above stated with reference to a gradual reform of the present constitution of the Colony."

This decided expression of opinion by the Court of Policy rendered the petition abortive. However, the political agitation persisted; and, at a meeting of the Court of Policy on the 29th October, 1847, two more petitions praying for constitutional reform were laid on the table and read. The first petition was dated the 17th August, 1847, and signed by the Mayor of Georgetown, the leading merchants and professional men, few in number, but " capable of giving unbiassed opinions." [1]   It prayed for

Further Petitions in 1847.

> " an extension of the franchise and an increase of the number of members, elective and official, of the Court of Policy and of the Financial College, who shall be elected for each county, the city of Georgetown, and the town of New Amsterdam by *viva voce* voting at the polling booths, the qualification for a seat in the Court of Policy being a certain income derived from real property, and for a seat in the Financial College being also a certain income derived from real property; any qualified resident of the Colony being eligible to represent any part of it."

An immediate opposition was raised to these moderate proposals; and a second petition, dated the 18th October, 1847, was signed by 1,470 persons, and forwarded by Mr. R. Haynes,

---

[1] Governor Light's despatch, 11th November, 1847.

chairman of the so-called " Reform Committee." It prayed the Governor and Court of Policy " to recommend Her Majesty's Government to abolish the whole of the existing legislative institutions of this province, and to substitute in lieu of them a form of government based on direct popular representation, comprehending a Council and House of Assembly." Of the signatories 706 males and 74 females were able to write their names, but the penmanship of at least one-half among these was most questionable; while the remaining petitioners, 440 males and 250 females, had only been able to express their wishes by marks.[1]

Governor Light asked for the views of the elective members on these two petitions; and it then appeared that a great *Debate in Court of Policy.* change had taken place in their opinions during the past nineteen months. This was the year in which there supervened on a terrible famine in Ireland a grave commercial crisis in England; and, in the autumn of 1847, a series of failures in the great mercantile centres created a panic in the city of London, which forced consols down to 78, and induced Her Majesty's Government to suspend the Bank Charter Act. This step, enabling the Directors of the Bank of England to issue notes unsecured by bullion, had the effect of gradually restoring confidence. But British Guiana was hard hit in this year by the Sugar Duties Act of 1846 (9 & 10 Vict., cap, 63), which arranged as from the 5th July, 1847, for a progressive reduction in the protection given by the British customs' tariff to sugar and molasses produced in British colonies; and already the shadow of the great Civil List dispute was impending over the Colony. It is not, then, surprising to find that the members of the Court of Policy adhered to the view, expressed by them in the previous year, that the time was inopportune for constitutional reform. It was, said Mr. J. T. White,

> " a moment when the bonds of society were nearly loosened asunder, when by the most recent advices from England men's minds were filled with the gloomiest prospects of the future; and we know not how long our interests will even continue to exist, or whether the prosperity of the country is capable of being recalled."

[1] Governor Light's despatch, 11th November, 1847.

In the same strain Mr. P. Rose remarked :

"We find already great difficulty in taking off the crop
of the present year—perhaps the last we shall ever take
off—and, I say, to encourage an agitation of political
reform at this moment will be to risk the loss of those
crops and our ruin. This has been a year of almost
unparalleled disaster. Not even the mother-country
has been exempt from misfortune. Look at the failures
which have taken place within the last three months—
houses, whose names twelve months ago could raise a
million of money, ruined and swept away ; three Directors
of the Bank of England bankrupts ! There has not been
such a crisis in the commercial world within my lifetime."

However, as to the reform which should be attempted, when
times became less unfavourable, Messrs. Rose, White, Stuart,
Elective and Croal, who had all signed the minute of the
Members 25th March, 1846, as well as Mr. J. Jones, who had
favour in the meantime been elected to the Court, now
Radical Re- expressed themselves against any measure of partial
form when reform. They contended that no advantage what-
Time is
opportune. ever could be derived from an enlargement of the Court of
Policy by adding equal numbers of official and elective members.
Such a change would, they argued, give more power to the
executive, both by increasing the probability of the absence of
one or more elective members from any given meeting, and by
making division of opinion in the elective section more likely.
They objected to any increase in the power of the Crown at
the expense of the constituency ; and they contended that a
Council and House of Assembly would constitute a legitimate
representative form of government, much more in accordance
with British institutions and more likely to be productive of
permanent advantage to the community. When twitted by
the Attorney-General (Mr. R. R. Craig) as inconsistent, Mr.
Croal retorted that the petition of 1846 did not contain more
than four or five hundred signatures, whereas the petitions
then being discussed contained upwards of two thousand
signatures in all. Upon this the Collector of Customs (Mr. C.
Robinson) observed that the wishes of a Colony containing
130,000 inhabitants could not be considered to be adequately
expressed by no more than 1,581 signatures, some of which
carried no weight whatsoever ; and that he would have looked

for a petition signed by at least 15,000 or 50,000 persons.   Mr.
Croal rejoined that the Court of Policy did not possess the
confidence of the people.   " It has become unpleasant to
serve here," he said, " I feel it myself; for, notwithstanding
that we do all in our power to serve the public faithfully, we
are taunted and told that we are not the representatives of the
people."   Mr. Rose, seconded by Mr. Stuart, then moved
" that this Court, having duly considered the petitions for
reform, are of opinion that it is not expedient at the present
moment to agitate any change in the present constitution of the
Colony.   The Court, however, will, when the proper time
arrives, support the introduction of a House of Assembly and
Council, as the only reform that would be satisfactory or beneficial to the Colony at large."   The Court divided; and there
voted for the motion Messrs. Rose, Stuart, Jones, White, and
the Chief Justice (Mr. W. Arrindell); against it, the Government
Secretary (Mr. W. Walker), the Attorney-General, the Collector
of Customs, and also Mr. Croal, who gave the following reason
for his vote : " I consider that the time has already arrived
for granting to this Colony a Council and Assembly, in lieu of
the present legislative institutions; and, although I vote
against the appointment on the petition, I do so for the reason
that it postpones the object of the petition."

Both petitions were, then, in the language of the minutes,
" taken for notification," a phrase which disrespectful critics
of the Court of Policy averred to be a synonym for " consigned
to oblivion."   Governor Light, however, reported the matter
to Earl Grey in a despatch dated the 11th November, 1847,
Governor Light's Views. adding with respect to the sweeping change proposed by those who petitioned for a Council and
House of Assembly, " my conviction is that it is
impracticable; and the upholders of the change may well say
they will support it when ' the proper time arrives ' : the
present generation will not see its arrival."   But he was " disposed to believe that direct representation for the counties
and towns in the existing legislative and financial bodies would
be a useful change "; and he suggested that the Mayor of
Georgetown should be given a seat in the Court of Policy and
that this additional unofficial vote should be balanced by
placing the Solicitor-General also in the Court.

" No alteration," he wrote, " need at present be made in the elective franchise. The city of Georgetown has at this moment a total number of voters for the eleven wards into which it is divided of 1,020; and the number of persons qualified to serve as town councillors amount to 141. The number of voters for the College of Kiezers and Financial Representatives is 612 for Demerara and Essequebo, and 155 for Berbice, more or less."

Governor Light was also in favour of allowing the city of Georgetown to send two members to the College of Financial Representatives, the numbers in which would thus be increased from six to eight. He argued that the election of two Financial Representatives for the city would

" secure the continuance of its affairs to the management of men of substance, which is now the case, and would, with the aid of the Mayor in the Court of Policy, give due weight on financial subjects connected with the expenditure of the city. I am disposed to think," he concluded, " these concessions to the city would prevent any desire to ask for privileges which it would be dangerous to grant, particularly that one of independent taxation at the will of the corporation. Were the members of the Town Council allowed to select two of their body to sit as Financial Representatives, annually, without a general election, it might save the agitation which such mode of introducing new members into the financial body would naturally produce; and I see no objection to this privilege being granted to the Town Council, the members whereof have already stood as candidates to the public."

Earl Grey replied in a despatch, dated the 23rd January, 1848, that, the Civil List arrangement for British Guiana being *Earl Grey's* based upon a compact on the part of the Government *Reply.* to maintain, during the term for which it was voted, the form of constitution then in existence, he could do no more in the meantime than express his readiness to give his best attention to any constitutional changes desired by the colonists and recommended by the Governor with the concurrence of the Court of Policy and the Combined Court. However, the crisis in the Civil List dispute, which came a few months later, compelled Her Majesty's Government to consider seriously whether the constitution of British Guiana was not inconsistent with the Colony's welfare, and even with its safety; and on the

Views of Her Majesty's Government. 1st September, 1848, Earl Grey wrote to Mr. W. Walker, who administered the government of British Guiana from the 20th May, 1848, to the 13th February, 1849, that the stoppage of supplies, by putting an end to the Civil List, involved the termination of the political arrangement which was coincident with it; and that, by law, the Colony thus reverted to its old constitution, under which the functions of the Combined Court were limited to fixing the particular taxes to provide for an amount of expenditure previously estimated by the Court of Policy.

" But," continued Earl Grey, " Her Majesty's Government have no desire or intention to re-establish this form of government without essential modifications. It is, no doubt, the form in which the power of the Crown would be the least under local restraint; but it is far indeed from the desire, and it is equally far from the interest, of Her Majesty's Government to exercise in British Guiana, or any other colony, any power which they can properly avoid to exercise. In these times it is for the interest of every Government, and especially conducive to their ease and relief, to devolve responsibility upon local legislatures, wheresoever there can be found any considerable body of the colonists capable of forming a constituency and controlling the conduct of their representatives. If Her Majesty's Government forbears in any case to delegate the uncontrolled management of the affairs of a colony to local bodies, it is from the fear that it might thereby fail to acquit itself of the duty which it owes to the colonial community at large, and especially to those classes of its inhabitants which, from want of instruction, are incapable of securing for themselves, by the intelligent exercise of political franchises, a real representation of their interests in the colonial Legislature. When persons possessing education and intelligence, sufficient for the due exercise of political power, form only a very small minority of the whole population, if the uninstructed classes are not permitted to exercise the franchise, and if their interests are at the same time deprived of the guardianship of the Crown, there must be great danger of the malversations, oppressions and abuses, which are notoriously incident to the exercise of supreme power by irresponsible and oligarchial bodies. If they *are* permitted to exercise the franchise, from their numbers they must obtain a predominating power, and there is a possibility, from their ignorance and want of appreciation of the objects and institutions of civilized life, that those objects, and property and life itself, may be endangered. To avoid these risks on both sides, and at the same time secure to an uninstructed population some of the benefits of representative government, it might seem peculiarly fitting that the ministers of the Crown, responsible to Parliament, and having no partial interests, should intervene as umpires between the represented classes and those which are incapable of being represented, and for this purpose should exercise a controlling authority. Such has practically been the system of government which has for some years existed in Guiana, I believe with advantage to the community. . . . It would be with regret that I should see a necessity created for altering this system in its general structure, although I am aware that it is susceptible of some material improvements in detail. But, looking to our experience of its results on the less favourable side, I find that, whilst working well under ordinary circumstances, it has more than once exposed the public interests to serious injury and danger from the adoption by the Combined Court of the same extreme proceeding to which they now threaten to resort—a proceeding which in well-constituted representative governments is always regarded as a resource not to be thought of except in some extremity of danger to popular rights. On the former occasions on which the Combined Court has stopped the supplies, or indicated an intention of doing so, my predecessors, Lord Aberdeen and Lord Stanley, had under their consideration the changes which it might become necessary to make in the constitution of that body ; and it has appeared formerly, as now, that at those conjunctures the Combined Court represented the sentiments of the very inconsiderable number of the inhabitants (not much exceeding 800) who possess the franchise, and that these were not in harmony with the sentiments of any large portion of the colonists. The remedy to which this state of things pointed was a change in the electoral system, which should bring the elected members of the Combined Court into more direct and extensive connexion with the inhabitants at large. For the reasons to which I have already adverted, I should regard such a change as not unattended with hazard, nor to be adopted except in a case of necessity ; but a necessity will undoubtedly arise for adopting some essential alteration in the existing system of government, if that system should once more involve the best interests and the safety of the Colony in the dangers with which they are now again so seriously threatened."

In conclusion, Earl Grey expressed a wish to be favoured with the opinions of Lieut.-Governor Walker and of " the *Earl Grey* more intelligent, moderate and prudent of the *asks for* colonists " as to the nature of the change to be *Views of* effected, adding that he was led to believe that *Lieut.-* *Governor* the modification most required was " the admission *Walker as to* *Constitutional* of the population of Georgetown to the influence *Reform.* in the Legislature to which the great increase of its population and property would seem to entitle it."

By this time it had become sufficiently evident that there were only three possible methods of constitutional reform, *Three Possible* namely : (1) to abolish the Court of Policy, the *Methods of* College of Financial Representatives, and the College *Reform :* of Electors, and to substitute Crown Colony government by an Executive and a Legislative Council ; (2) to bestow upon British Guiana a House of Assembly and a Council, similar to those in Jamaica, Barbados, and other old colonies ; or (3) to modify or remodel the existing Court of Policy and Combined Court in such manner as to remedy the worst defects of those bodies. Under these heads the various suggestions now made can conveniently be grouped.

It will be remembered that Governor Light, in his despatch of the 7th October, 1842, had declared in favour of Crown *(a) Crown* Colony Government ; and in this view Lieut.-*Colony* Governor Walker now concurred. *Government ;*

" Unpopular as the proposition would undoubtedly be," he wrote on the 19th October, 1848, " I do not hesitate to say that I believe the appointment of a Governor, to be aided by the advice of a Council nominated by the Crown, would be at present the most eligible mode of administering this Government, since it would afford the opportunity and means not only of framing such a form of constitution as might be more acceptable to the great body of the colonists hereafter, but also of perfecting such measures as are imperatively required to facilitate the adaptation of such a constitution to the peculiarly composed population of this country."

Indeed, it was difficult to resist the argument that society in British Guiana was composed of elements too discordant, and that slavery had been abolished too recently, to justify the Crown, as the exponent of the wishes of the people of Great Britain, in parting with any share of its paramount authority. Mr. W. B. Wolseley, the acting Government Secretary, in a memorandum dated the 13th October, 1848, also advocated a Council of Government with an official majority in lieu of the existing bodies politic. Similarly Mr. Whinfield, Sheriff of Berbice, considered that a Governor and four persons selected by the Crown, on the same principle as the Government of British India, would be the most suitable arrangement.[1]

Representative government naturally suggested itself as the system under which men, born and bred in Great Britain, were entitled to be governed, when they settled in a British colony. But a " colony " involves the idea of a body of people drawn from the mother-country to inhabit some distant place; and, in that sense of the word, British Guiana was not a " colony," but rather a plantation, formed by a foreign Power, and ceded to the British Crown in right of conquest. Not one-fiftieth of the population of British Guiana was drawn from Great Britain; and even of that small portion few could be said to " inhabit." The majority came to sojourn for a few years, to make a fortune, and to carry it home to spend. Such men could hardly be called " colonists." An Englishman in the plantations, said Lord Mansfield, " has no distinct right from the natives while he continues there." [2] These natives in the case of British Guiana were at this time for the most part emancipated negroes; and the real question in granting representative institutions was : Shall the benefit of such institutions be extended to uneducated men, who little more than ten years ago were slaves; or are these benefits to be conferred exclusively upon their former masters? Either course was fraught with grave danger.

(b) Representative Government;

Moreover, the supposed analogy of constitutional systems in the British West India Islands was really inapplicable; for, at the emancipation, the whites were in Barbados to the rest of the population as one to six, and in Jamaica as one to

---

[1] Lieut.-Governor Walker's despatch, 2nd November, 1848.
[2] See Appendix S : the judgment delivered by Lord Mansfield, as Chief Justice, in 1775, in the case Campbell *v.* Hall.

thirteen; while in British Guiana they were only as one to thirty, the mixed race being probably in even smaller proportion than that indicated by this comparison.[1]   Again there was, as the Court of Policy had pointed out in its minute of the 25th March, 1846, a greater diversity of races and religious tenets in British Guiana than in Jamaica or Barbados, an absence of preparatory training for self-government by parochial and other similar institutions, as well as a comparative lack of education among the inhabitants.   There was also in the respective colonies an enormous discrepancy in the social conditions of the emancipated negroes, occasioned by the high wages and low price of land which had prevailed in British Guiana.

" Immense tracts of land," wrote Governor Barkly on the 20th April, 1849, " are every day purchased by associations of labourers.   The number of such freeholders is probably under-estimated by the stipendiary magistrates at 10,000, or about one in four of the adult male population of the Colony; but I have little doubt that, if political privileges were attached to the possession of land, it would become universal.   Indeed it would in that case be desirable that it should extend to all classes; for hitherto the acquisition of a plot of ground has not been so much the sign of superior intelligence or manly independence, as of unfounded suspicions or a love of uncivilized ease; the freeholders being, I am inclined to think, as a body far less industrious than the older and steadier negroes, who from confidence in their employers and a desire to work continuously have remained on the plantations."

Well might Governor Barkly exclaim that to mould a miniature model of the British Constitution out of materials as rude as these was a task far above the power of man !

[1] See R. Montgomery Martin, *History of the British Colonies*, vol. ii (1835), pp. 29–33, where detailed statistics are given for British Guiana. The same author, in his work *The British Colonies* (1851–7), part 43, book i, *West India Islands*, gives the following statistics :

(a) on p. 179, for British Guiana, " at the period of emancipation (1834)," whites 2,883; free coloured 7,236; blacks or slaves 83,824 (of whom 9,893 were children under six years of age and 3,852 aged, diseased or otherwise non-effective); total 92,943 :

(b) on p. 118, for Barbados, also in the year 1834, whites 12,797; free coloured 6,584; slaves 82,850; total 102,231 : and

(c) on p. 93, for Jamaica in the same year, free coloured 35,000; slaves 310,368; but no figure for whites.   The Jamaica statistics are defective. Its white population is given by Martin as 30,000 in the year 1800 and as 15,776 in the year 1844.   Martin gives no figures for the white population between those years.   But, if there were 16,000 whites in Jamaica at the time of the emancipation, the ratio 1 : 13 results.

Nevertheless, several schemes for such a constitution were drafted, though with very indifferent success. Mr. James Spooner, a merchant in Georgetown, long notable for active participation in local political agitation, proposed in a letter to Lieut.-Governor Walker, dated the 12th October, 1848, to substitute for the existing bodies politic a House of Assembly, adopting " a reasonable franchise, enacting that writing be a part of the qualification." Mr. Carbery, the acting Sheriff of Essequebo, also proposed, in a memorandum dated the 18th October, 1848, government by a single chamber, to be called " the Colonial Parliament of British Guiana," consisting of seven official and nine elective members, but without a change in the elective franchise. The propaganda of radical reform was, however, carried on most zealously by the " Constitutional Reform Committee "; and its members intimated a wish to send Governor Barkly a deputation on the subject within a few weeks of his arrival in the Colony. But, after various communications with Mr. P. Rose, an elective member of the Court of Policy, they abandoned their design; and in their stead, on the 17th March, 1849, Mr. Rose submitted to Governor Barkly a scheme which had, he said, not only met with the approval of ten-elevenths of the unofficial members of the Combined Court, but was also assented to by the leading members of the reform party. The scheme proceeded on the basis of a Council and a House of Assembly. Of the constitution of the former nothing was said; but the latter was to consist of thirty-nine members, five to be returned by the towns, five by the villages, and twenty-nine by the rural districts, thus :

	Number of Representatives in House of Assembly.
i. *County of Demerary :*	
(*a*) Villages—	
The villages extending from Georgetown to Abary Creek	1 ⎫
The villages from Georgetown, on the east and west banks of the River Demerary, and the west coast of Demerary to Boraseree Creek	1 ⎬ 2
(*b*) City of Georgetown	4
(*c*) Rural Districts—	
Parish of St. Paul's, including the estates from Georgetown to Nooten's Ziul	4 ⎫
Parish of St. Mary's	2
,, ,, St. Matthew's	2 ⎬ 13
,, ,, St. Mark's and St. Swithen's . . .	3
,, ,, St. Luke's	2 ⎭

(Total: 19)

	Number of Representatives in House of Assembly.
ii. *County of Essequebo :*	
(a) Villages	1 ⎫
(b) Rural Districts—	⎪ 10
Parish of St. James's	2 ⎫
,, ,, St. Peter's	1 ⎪ 9
,, ,, St. John's	2 ⎬
,, ,, Trinity	4 ⎭
iii. *County of Berbice :*	
(a) Villages—	
West coast and west bank of River Berbice . .	1 ⎫ 2
East bank of river and east coast of Corantyne river .	1 ⎭
(b) Town of New Amsterdam	1
(c) Rural Districts—	⎫ 10
Parish of St. Saviour's	1 ⎫
,, ,, St. Patrick's	2 ⎪
,, ,, St. Catherine's	1 ⎬ 7
,, ,, St. Clement's	2 ⎪
,, ,, St. Michael's	1 ⎭

The franchise in the rural districts was to be the same as that established for voters for Kiezers and Financial Representatives; in other words, a few leading attorneys of absentee proprietors of sugar estates were to continue to elect three-fourths of the Legislature. The qualification in Georgetown and New Amsterdam was likewise to be maintained at its then limits, leaseholders of whatever extent being excluded from the franchise. The same qualification as in the towns— namely, a house in fee worth $500—was to be required from villagers, who were in addition to be able to read and write English. The constituency of the twenty-nine members for the rural districts would thus be limited to about five or six hundred electors. The constituency of the towns would amount to about 1,500; while there might perhaps have been found two or three persons in each village, the doctor and one or two storekeepers, to elect the members for the villages.

Remembering the wide gulf which had previously separated the advocates of radical reform from the conservative party, Governor Barkly carefully examined this scheme framed under the joint auspices of the opposing factions; and it was with some disappointment that he perceived in it " rather a studious compromise of party differences than a satisfactory adjustment of popular pretensions." [1]   Practically the very same persons who already formed the electorate would continue to choose

[1] Despatch, dated 26th March, 1849.

the elective portion of the proposed Legislature. But there would have been this important difference, that the Crown, instead of being invested with positive legislative authority by means of the preponderance of its officers in the Court of Policy, would have retained only the negative power in legislation, which it had in finance, of rejecting a measure by means of the Governor's veto. The absolute power of the Crown in the colonial Legislature had hitherto been exercised with a view of protecting the interests of the labouring classes, who were confessedly unrepresented except through such a medium; and Governor Barkly was decidedly of opinion that it would be imprudent " to do more than slightly qualify the power of the executive in matters of legislation, and that it would be most unjust to do even that without at the same time giving those of the labourers who had acquired a certain degree of education and property a voice in the making of the laws." [1] On the other hand, he was far from wishing to exclude the planters from that fair share in the representation to which they were entitled as the landed aristocracy of the country.

> " I do not believe," he wrote to Earl Grey,[1] " that they would be a bit more inclined to abuse power than any other aristocracy; but on the same ground that I should regret to see Your Lordship's House the paramount legislative authority at home, should I consider it a fatal error to establish in British Guiana a House of Assembly, three-fourths elected by proprietors of sugar estates, and uncontrolled either by popular responsibility, or by the power of the Crown."

Such a change would, moreover, at that time have been attended with peculiar danger, for the imperative necessity of reducing wages, to meet the competition of slave countries, had involved the planter in a struggle with the labourer, calculated to revive feelings of antagonism, which had almost been effaced by the establishment of a settled rate of profuse remuneration.

> " The labour question," said Governor Barkly in the same despatch, " is still, and must long continue to be, that which will principally occupy the attention of the Legislature of British Guiana and, faulty as the constitution at present may be, I doubt whether such branches of

[1] Despatch, dated 26th March, 1849.

N

that question as the relations of masters and servants, and the regulation of immigration, are not discussed in the present Court of Policy with more justice to their real merits, than they would be if encountered in the proposed Assembly by the hostility of a small minority, necessarily driven to strengthen itself out of doors by agitating for popular support."

There remained the conservative proposal that the existing Court of Policy and Combined Court should be modified or *(c) Modifica-* remodelled in such manner as to remedy the worst *tion of the* defects of those bodies. Of the schemes to that end *Existing* the one involving least change was a " draft project " *Bodies* *Politic.* by Sir Michael McTurk, who recommended that the College of Electors should be abolished ; that the elective section of the Court of Policy and of the College of Financial Representatives should be composed as follows :

Members for :		In Court of Policy.	In College of Financial Representatives.
County of	Demerara . . .	2 ⎫	2 ⎫
	Essequebo . .	1 ⎪	1 ⎪
	Berbice . . .	1 ⎬ 6	1 ⎬ 6
City of Georgetown . . .		1 ⎪	1 ⎪
Town of New Amsterdam .		1 ⎭	1 ⎭

that the elective franchise should be extended to all adult male inhabitants who paid colonial taxes to the amount of $25 or more annually ; that no estate, however numerously owned, should be entitled to more than one vote ; and that the qualification of all elective members should be the possession of a clear annual income of $2,000 or ownership of an estate valued at $10,000.[1]

Mr. William Arrindell, the Attorney-General, at this time acting as Chief Justice, and formerly an elective member of the Court of Policy, had no hesitation in declaring that there was not in the Colony a sufficient number of persons, duly qualified, who could or would spare the time necessary to be devoted in attendances on the Assembly and Council, and in a letter to Lieut.-Governor Walker, dated the 18th October, 1848, he

[1] See Parl. Papers, " Correspondence Relative to the British Guiana Civil List " (1848), pp. 132-4.

suggested that the College of Electors should be abolished;
that the elective franchise should be altered, the qualification
to vote for a member of the Town Council being made sufficient
to vote for an elective member of the Court of Policy; that
votes by proxy, agents, and representatives of every description, in right of the party represented, should be abolished;
that votes be given in person *viva voce*, and not in writing;
and that the Court of Policy and the Combined Court should
be reorganized as shown in the following table :

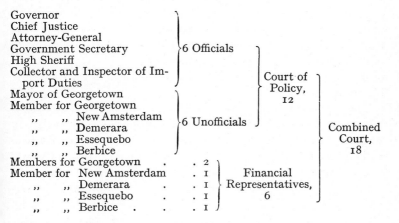

```
Governor                      ⎫
Chief Justice                 ⎪
Attorney-General              ⎪
Government Secretary          ⎬ 6 Officials   ⎫
High Sheriff                  ⎪                ⎪
Collector and Inspector of Im-⎪                ⎪
    port Duties               ⎭                ⎬ Court of  ⎫
Mayor of Georgetown           ⎫                ⎪  Policy,   ⎪
Member for Georgetown         ⎪                ⎪   12       ⎪
   ,,     ,,  New Amsterdam    ⎪                ⎪            ⎪
   ,,     ,,  Demerara        ⎬ 6 Unofficials ⎭            ⎬ Combined
   ,,     ,,  Essequebo        ⎪                            ⎪  Court,
   ,,     ,,  Berbice          ⎭                            ⎪   18
Members for Georgetown    .  . 2  ⎫                         ⎪
Member for New Amsterdam  .  . 1  ⎪ Financial               ⎪
   ,,     ,,  Demerara    .  . 1  ⎬ Representatives,        ⎭
   ,,     ,,  Essequebo   .  . 1  ⎪      6
   ,,     ,,  Berbice  .  .  . 1  ⎭
```

But the most interesting of the proposals to remodel the
existing bodies politic was that put forward in a despatch to
Lord John Russell, dated the 20th April, 1849, by Governor
Barkly, who saw in his own office, in the Court of Policy
and in the Combined Court a tripartite legislature in embryo,
and argued somewhat fancifully that the Colony's history for
sixty years past recorded successive efforts to effect that balance
of power between the three estates, which constituted the
liberty of the mother-country. On a humble scale its society,
he thought, had passed rapidly through all the political phases,
which had been the work of centuries in England. It had its
Magna Charta in the " Plan of Redress "; its abolition of
villenage in emancipation; while its struggles between the
Crown and Parliament were then being fought out in the Civil
List dispute; and he hoped that the day was not far distant
when the respective rights of the Sovereign and the People

would be as amicably defined as they had been in the United Kingdom since the revolution.

Influenced by this far-fetched analogy, Governor Barkly considered that the first step towards restoring due equilibrium to the machinery of the local government would be " to curtail the power of the Governor in the Court of Policy so far as to deprive him of his ' double vote,' and confine his voting at all to cases where the Court was equally divided." Instead, moreover, of leaving to the Governor the initiation of all legislative measures, and the power of withdrawing at any stage of their progress those he might have permitted to be introduced, Mr. Barkly proposed to give every member permission to bring in and carry through any bill, subject to the pleasure of the Court alone ; imposing on the Governor the responsibility of preventing its passing into an ordinance by withholding his signature.

The Court of Policy, presided over by the Governor thus restricted in authority, Mr. Barkly proposed to increase in number from ten members to twelve, " in order to secure a sufficient attendance in a climate like this " ; but he would have retained the proportion of half official and half elective members, turning by this means the scale as much in favour of the latter as it had previously been turned against them by the Governor's double vote. The elective members were to be chosen as theretofore " upon the principle of compound election," and not, as most reformers suggested, by the direct vote of the inhabitants of different electoral districts.

" I am aware," wrote Governor Barkly, " that the mode of election now practised has been universally reprobated ; nor have I much to urge in defence of the College of Kiezers, admitting, as all must do, that the idea of seven gentlemen appointed for life to return representatives for an entire community is not only ' un-English,' as it is called, but absurd. The fault, however, lies, not in the principle of the institution, but in the provision which thus exempts the Kiezers from responsibility to their constituents. The principle of election by an elected body, though applied but in a limited degree to political affairs in Great Britain, is one which has stood the test of experience in many countries, as witness the Senate of the United States, an assembly second to none in the efficient discharge of the most important functions, yet elected by the respective State Legislatures. Indeed, wherever an hereditary aristocracy does not exist, I doubt if a fitter substitute for it can be found. Whilst, therefore, the College of Kiezers, with its outlandish name and irresponsible powers, might very well be abolished, I know no better plan for electing the non-official section of the Court of Policy than to leave it to be chosen on the former principle, popularly, yet at the same time indirectly, by the people through their Financial Representatives."

Governor Barkly was, indeed, aware of the objectionable preponderance formerly given to the College of Financial Representatives by empowering it to elect the unofficial members of the Court of Policy, as it had done for nearly twenty years (1812–31) under General Carmichael's proclamation amalgamating the Colleges of Kiezers and of Financial Representatives; but he proposed to obviate that danger by abolishing altogether the meetings of the Court of Policy with the Financial Representatives in Combined Court, and by completely separating the legislative and the financial chambers. He desired that the Court of Policy should continue to conduct the entire business of legislation, but that it should be denuded of the power of framing the annual estimates and of joining in the discussion of ways and means. All bills involving the expenditure of money would be sent down blank by the Court of Policy to a Financial Chamber, acting as a distinct and independent body and entrusted with the sole guardianship of the Public Purse. In order to qualify the Financial Chamber to fulfil its part without the five elective members of the Court of Policy, Governor Barkly proposed to increase the number of Financial Representatives from six to thirteen, adding to them, six official members, and thus making the proportion of elective to official members as nineteen to six in the new Financial Chamber as against the proportion of sixteen to five in the existing Combined Court.

The elective members of the Financial Chamber, instead of being chosen as the Financial Representatives had been by the united constituency, were, according to Governor Barkly's scheme, to be returned by the different counties and towns in the following manner :

i. *County of Demerara :*
  (a) East coast district . . . . 1 ⎫
  (b) Villages on east coast . . . 1 ⎬ 4
  (c) River district and villages . . 1 ⎪
  (d) West coast district . . . . 1 ⎭

ii. *City of Georgetown* 2

iii. *County of Essequebo :*
  (a) Aroabisce coast . . . . 1 ⎫
  (b) Queenstown, and villages on the Aroa-
      bisce coast . . . . . 1 ⎬ 3
  (c) Islands in the Essequebo, and banks
      of that river . . . . 1 ⎭

iv. *County of Berbice :*
  (a) East coast, and east bank of Canje
      Creek . . . . . 1 ⎫
  (b) East bank of river and west bank of
      Canje Creek . . . . 1 ⎬ 3
  (c) West coast, and west bank of river . 1 ⎭

v. *Town of New Amsterdam* . . . 1

13 Members

The qualification of members for towns was to be that required for a Town Councillor; that of members for villages and counties to be half the amount of that proposed below for elective members of the Court of Policy. The official seats in this Chamber were to be reserved for a set of government officers distinct from those in the Court of Policy, and selected as far as possible from those more immediately connected with the finances of the Colony. As, however, it might be expedient to have from time to time some authoritative spokesman of the Government in the Financial Chamber, Governor Barkly suggested that the Government Secretary should form an exception to the rule excluding from that Chamber the official members of the Court of Policy, and should act as President whenever present. In the Government Secretary's absence from the Financial Chamber, the Assistant Government Secretary would preside, supported by the Receiver-General, Financial Accountant, Comptroller of Customs, and the Registrar. The presence of these functionaries, Governor Barkly thought, would go far to check the irregular proceedings of the elective members of the Combined Court, who met in private, elected committees, sent for account-books, and attempted to control officers immediately responsible to the Government alone; and it would tend to introduce instead the parliamentary custom of public statements by the Heads of Departments and of returns ordered in open Court and furnished by competent authority.

The Financial Chamber, so reconstituted, would elect the six unofficial members of the Court of Policy, whose qualification would be an income of £300 *per annum* derived from real property in the Colony, or the ownership of an estate making one hundred hogsheads of sugar; the latter alternative being suggested by Governor Barkly, not to give undue weight to the planting interest, but because unfortunately, as things then stood, almost all the planters would have been disqualified under the former alternative. Elective members of the Court were to serve for a term of five years and be re-eligible. The official members would be the Governor, Chief Justice, Government Secretary, Attorney-General, High Sheriff, and either the Solicitor-General or the Inspector-General of Police. Thus it would be possible for the Court of Policy to sit at the same time as the Financial Chamber, and, therefore, to proceed without those frequent interruptions of its work which had, especially during the Civil List disputes, retarded legislation as well as the Court's administrative business.

With regard to " the most important question of all, namely, the franchise," Governor Barkly considered that the safest course would be to substitute, in the counties and villages, the qualification established by Ordinance No. 26 of 1846 for persons liable to be summoned on juries—namely, possession of immovable property worth $96 *per annum*, or of a house rated to direct taxes of any kind on a value of $192, or receipt of $192 *per annum* from lease of immovable property, or of an annual salary of $720; and to substitute in the towns the qualification fixed by Ordinance No. 11 of 1839 for persons qualified to vote at the election of a Town Councillor in Georgetown—namely, the possession of a house rated on the books at a value of $500; this right of voting to be extended in both cases to leaseholders; and absentee proprietors to continue to vote through their attorneys.

Meanwhile, however, there had been forwarded to the House of Commons from British Guiana a very numerously and respectably signed petition, dated the 29th December, 1848, praying, *inter alia*, for " the abolition of the legislative and financial institutions of the Colony, and the substitution in their place of a Council and House of Assembly similar to those of the island of Barbados, and based on a franchise *Her Majesty's* suitable to the existing state of society in the *Government express no* Colony." This petition, together with other griev-*Opinion on* ances of the Colony, was referred by the House of *the Suggested Methods of* Commons on the 20th February, 1849, to a Select *Reform.* Committee of its members; and, pending the report of that Committee, Her Majesty's Government were unwilling to express any opinion on the various proposals for constitutional reform which had been formulated in British Guiana.

CHAPTER X

NEVERTHELESS a reform of the Colony's elective franchise became urgently necessary during the year 1849 owing to *Reason for extending the Elective Franchise.* the prolonged Civil List dispute, which, having begun in December, 1847, left British Guiana without a revenue as from the 30th September, 1848. Governor Barkly, who assumed office on the 14th February, 1849, was naturally " desirous of referring to the judgment of those by whom the Financial Representatives were elected," [1] the important controversy then at issue. But at this time the exercise of the franchise was still governed by Ordinance No. 86 of 1836, under which the persons qualified to vote for the election of members of the College of Electors and of the College of Financial Representatives respectively were :

1st, Any inhabitant assessed to pay direct taxes to the colonial revenue upon an income of not less than 2,001 guilders (£143) in the year of, or in the year preceding, any new election of a member of the College of Electors or of the College of Financial Representatives ; or

2nd, Any inhabitant who had paid direct taxes to the amount of 70 guilders (£5) or upwards in the year of, or in the year preceding, any new election of a member of the College of Electors or of the College of Financial Representatives ; or

3rd, Any inhabitant assessed, after the publication of Ordinance No. 86 of 1836, upon an income of not less than 2,001 guilders, and not being in arrear in payment for more than six months from the date when income-tax became payable ; or

4th, Any inhabitant, assessed and liable to pay to the

[1] Speech in Court of Policy, 11th June, 1849.

'colonial revenue direct taxes to the amount of 70 guilders or upwards, and not being in arrear in the payment of such taxes for more than six months from the date of such taxes becoming payable.[1]

Thus the elective franchise of the Colony rested upon payment of taxes and, therefore, upon the existence of a Tax Ordinance; and, such being the qualifications to vote, the Annual Tax Ordinance No. 12 of 1847, as extended by Ordinance No. 7 of 1848, was by reason of the Civil List dispute allowed to expire on the 30th September, 1848. Accordingly, persons who had formerly voted in right of their being assessed to pay income-tax or other direct taxes, could not be so assessed and were disfranchised. They formed the large majority of the voters; nor would there have been any constituency at all but for the fact that Ordinance No. 9 of 1845, being brought into operation by Ordinance No. 10 of 1845, raised up, or rather preserved, a class of voters in right of assessment to pay direct taxes to the colonial revenue upon agricultural produce; but even this tax had been paid up, for 1848, by very few of the planters. The result was that no annual register of voters, either for 1848 or 1849, could be published; and that, in the

[1] This was the interpretation placed by the Attorney-General, Mr. William Arrindell, in a memorandum dated the 3rd October, 1849, upon the first section of Ordinance No. 86 of 1836, which reads: "Every inhabitant of this Colony, of full age and not subject to any legal disability, who, for himself, or as curator, administrator, sequestrator, guardian, or in any other capacity, shall have been assessed to pay direct taxes to the colonial revenue upon an income of not less than 2,001 guiders, or who shall have paid direct taxes to the amount of 70 guilders or upwards, in the year of, or in the year preceding, any new election of a member of the College of Electors or of the College of Financial Representatives of this Colony, or who, after the publication of this Ordinance, shall be assessed upon an income of the amount as aforesaid, or who shall be assessed and liable to pay to the colonial revenue of the said Colony direct taxes to the amount of 70 guilders or upwards, and not being in arrear in the payment of such taxes for more than six months from the date of such taxes becoming payable, shall be entitled to vote upon and for the election of any such member of the respective Colleges aforesaid." Mr. Roney, the legal adviser of the elective section in the Legislature, made, in May, 1849, a tender to the Colonial Receiver-General of income-tax for 1848, with the object of establishing his qualification as a voter (which he thereby admitted to depend on its payment). This tender was rejected on the joint advice of the acting Attorney-General (Mr. R. R. Craig) and the acting Solicitor-General (Mr. S. N. Harvey) that, as no income-tax had been assessed by the Combined Court, none could be received.

event of an election, the persons qualified to vote would have been a few attorneys of absentee proprietors.   In fact, Governor Barkly reported on the 30th April, 1849, that the only claims to vote sent in at that date were as follows :

Peter Rose, for Messrs. Cavan Brothers & Company.
John Croal, for the owners of Plantation Vreed-en-hoop.
Peter Watson, for Messrs. Ewing & Company.
Charles Conyers, for his mercantile firm.
Alexander Duff, for the owners of Plantation William.
William Brand, for his mercantile firm.
W. O. Canzius, for certain Dutch proprietors.

These gentlemen, with the exception of the last, being every one of them members of the then Combined Court, it was obvious that an appeal to the electorate would be no more than an appeal from the Combined Court to the Combined Court, and that, therefore, it was necessary to renovate the constituency prior to a dissolution of the College of Financial Representatives.

The necessity for an extension of the franchise was further demonstrated by the proceedings at the election of a member of the College of Electors, which took place on the 8th May, 1849.   It was a contested election to fill a vacancy caused by the departure from the Colony of Mr. A. Macrae, the rival candidates being Messrs. A. McLaren and T. Clarke.   When the boxes of votes for Demerara, Essequebo and Berbice were opened in Court of Policy, it was found that the Berbice box was empty, and that in the other two counties a total of 122 votes had been cast for Mr. McLaren and 47 for Mr. Clarke.   Thus, in a Colony containing 130,000 inhabitants, the aggregate number of votes was only 169.   But, upon scrutiny by the Court of Policy, after the elimination of voters who had been disenfranchised by the cessation of the Tax Ordinance, it resulted that, the test of the voters being payment of produce tax, the joint poll consisted of only 75 good votes, namely, 60 for Mr. McLaren and 15 for Mr. Clarke.   Moreover in August, 1849, at the last election held before the franchise was extended, when five candidates contested two vacancies, thus showing some popular interest in the result, the voters in the Colony were only 88, those absent from the Colony 181, while of the latter number no fewer than 134 were repre-

sented by five gentlemen, who, therefore, with their own
votes alone carried the day by a sheer majority.[1]

The case for extending the franchise could hardly have been
stronger; and Governor Barkly, knowing that all local parties
anticipated a change of one kind or another in the
political institutions of the Colony, decided to turn
the exigencies of the situation to account by pro-
posing " a basis for the elective franchise more in
conformity with that usually prevailing in free countries." [2]
He accordingly framed a measure " in some degree upon the
model of the English Reform Bill," but copying the nature of
the qualification for electors in the rural districts from that
fixed by Ordinance No. 26 of 1846 for the jury lists, while in
the town districts the right to vote at municipal elections served
as the criterion; for, said the Governor, " this at least seems to
me indisputable, that neither the man who is intelligent enough
to vote for a Town Councillor, nor he who is liable to be summoned as a juror to decide questions involving the life or property
of his neighbour, can be deemed incapable of forming a sound
opinion on matters affecting his own pecuniary interests "; [2]
while the danger of resting the electorate of the Colony upon
the chance of the annual Tax Ordinance being passed had
demonstrated the necessity of establishing the franchise upon
a solid basis.

Governor Barkly intro-duces Bill to extend the Franchise.

Accordingly, at a meting of the Court of Policy on the
8th May, 1849, a bill " to repeal Ordinance No. 86 of the year
1836, and to regulate the qualification for the exercise of the
elective franchise in British Guiana " was introduced by the
acting Attorney-General (Mr. R. R. Craig), read a first time and
ordered to be published.[3] As originally drafted this bill had
two objects only—namely, the extension of the franchise
and the introduction of improved machinery for conducting
elections. The second reading was deferred for a fortnight
at the instance of Mr. W. B. Ferguson, in order that the inhabitants of the Colony might have time to express their
repugnance to the measure. However, when on the 11th June,
1849, the bill was brought up for a second reading, there were

---

[1] Governor Barkly's despatch, 23rd September, 1850.
[2] Governor Barkly's speech in Court of Policy, 11th June, 1849.
[3] *Royal Gazette*, 24th May, 1849.

laid upon the table three petitions in its favour, signed by 723 persons in all, and only one petition against it, signed by 234 persons; while of those who petitioned in favour of the general principles of the bill, 422 objected strongly to the retention of the power of voting by proxy, then enjoyed by absentees, although this was the only part of the bill which met with the concurrence of the whole unofficial section of the Court. Mr. Ferguson's expectations were thus disappointed; and an amendment moved by Mr. P. Rose, to the effect that the bill should be read a second time that day six months, resulted in an animated debate, in which opposition was, in greater or less degree, threatened by all the unofficials. Mr. Gordon, however, offered to support the bill, if a clause were introduced dividing the Colony into electoral districts.

The electives maintained, in spite of the plain wording of Ordinance No. 86 of 1836, that the existing basis of elective *Elective Members of Court of Policy object to Bill.* franchise in the Colony was *liability* to assessment for taxation, and not *actual* assessment or payment of taxes; that consequently the non-existence of a Tax Ordinance did not in any degree affect the right of the inhabitants to exercise the franchise; and that, even if by the temporary lapse of the Tax Ordinance any portion of the community had been disfranchised, the proper remedy was to introduce a declaratory bill, making the elective franchise depend on the Tax Ordinance of the previous year until another Tax Ordinance should be passed; but that any alteration of the franchise was both unwise and unnecessary. They pointed out that a Committee of the House of Commons was then sitting to consider how the grievances of British Guiana could be redressed; and that radical changes, if any, were required; whereas Governor Barkly's bill, being partial in its operation and likely soon to be superseded by a general and comprehensive measure of reform, would create excitement and confusion throughout the Colony. It was unwise, they argued, to make any change in the elective franchise unless the Colony was divided into electoral districts for the proper representation of local interests. Moreover, the bill did not require that the voter should possess " any, the smallest amount of, intelligence and education "; and they contended that there would be great danger to the community if political power should be unaccompanied by a moderate amount of educational knowledge, and that such educational knowledge should, therefore, be made an integral and essential condition for an exercise of the franchise. They also objected that the bill placed the machinery of election in the hands of the Government, and that this might result in the officials becoming "little better than electioneering agents, to carry out party objects, or to promote the success of the government candidate." Finally they stated it to be "essentially necessary for the protection of the rights of the inhabitants" that, whenever a change should take place, a House of Assembly and Council of Government should be instituted instead of the existing political institutions; and they expressed the belief that "any measure of partial and imperfect reform would delay to an indefinite period this object of vital and permanent importance." A document embodying all these objections was laid on the table of the Court. It was signed by Messrs. J. Stuart, P. Rose, J. Gordon, W. Bruce Ferguson, and J. T. White, all of whom voted against the second reading, which was, however, carried by the Governor's casting vote.

The committee stage of the bill began on the 9th July, 1849, and provoked long debates. During its progress Governor

Progress of Bill in Committee. Barkly received two despatches from Earl Grey, dated the 30th June and 31st July, 1849, approving of the course he had taken and adding that the bill was entirely in accordance with the recommendations made in the report, just issued, of the Committee of the House of Commons and with the views of Her Majesty's Government. Moreover, in spite of the opposition of the unofficial members of the Court of Policy to the two original objects of the bill, Governor Barkly was successful in obtaining the benefit of their local experience and advice in arranging its enactments, when in committee on the bill; and it was at their instance that the scope of the measure was enlarged to embrace two additional objects—namely, the division of the Colony into electoral districts and the establishment of a qualification for Kiezers and Financial Representatives.

Under the old Dutch constitution, Demerara and Essequebo had returned separate members both to the Electoral and to the Financial Colleges, and this practice had never been authoritatively abrogated. But, upon the union with Berbice in 1831, the old system was necessarily discontinued, because no pro-

Colony divided into Electoral Districts. vision was made for any increase in the number of Kiezers and Financial Representatives. This formed the subject of an annual protest for several years afterwards by the College of Kiezers, whenever a member was returned to it for the united Colony. The feeling of the Court was now decidedly in favour of reverting to the Dutch method; and, there being only six Financial Representatives and seven Kiezers to be allotted in the whole, no fairer distribution seemed attainable than to divide them equally between the three counties in the first case, and, as this was undoubtedly to the disadvantage of the metropolitan county of Demerara, to give the seventh Kiezer to Georgetown, its capital city.

The second of the additional objects effected by the Bill—namely, the establishment of a qualification for Financial

Qualification for Financial Representatives and Kiezers. Representatives and for Kiezers—originated, like the first, in a recommendation by the unofficial section, to which the Governor gave cordial support " not for the purpose of circumscribing the choice of the electors, but in order to secure as high a standard of independence and mental cultivation in the political colleges of British Guiana as is insisted on in the legislatures of other West India Colonies." [1] Any regulation on this point had been superfluous so long as the franchise was vested solely in the higher classes, who, of course, confined their selection to their own body; but it was clearly natural for the Court of Policy to stipulate for some precaution when placing a vote within the reach of every industrious labourer. The qualification decided upon, and set out below, was a liberal one, embracing not only real and personal property, but an income of £300 *per annum*, derived from commercial or professional pursuits. One class alone, the ministers of religion, were excluded, however qualified in other respects, from a seat in the Legislature—an exception justified by its proposers from the analogy of the British House of Commons, and acceded to by the Governor, " not from any jealousy of the influence exercised over the emancipated peasantry by their spiritual guides, but from a

[1] Governor Barkly's despatch, 5th October, 1849.

conviction, on the contrary, that that influence would be diminished by their interference in secular affairs." [1]

The importance of this bill justifies its description in detail. The *1st section* repealed Ordinance No. 86 of 1836. The *Detailed Description of the Bill.* *2nd and 3rd sections*, which were introduced into the bill by desire of the elective members, divided the Colony for the purpose of distributing members of the Colleges of Electors (Kiezers) and of Financial Representatives into five electoral districts and provided for their representation as follows :

Electoral Districts.	Number of Representatives in College of :	
	Kiezers.	Financial Representatives.
County of Demerara, exclusive of city of Georgetown　.　　.　　.　　.	1	1
City of Georgetown, according to its municipal boundaries　.　　.　　.	2	1
County of Essequebo .　　.　　.　　.	2	2
County of Berbice, exclusive of town of New Amsterdam　.　　.　　.　　.	1	1
Town of New Amsterdam, according to its municipal boundaries .　　.　　.	1	1

The *4th section* prescribed the order in which vacancies in the two Colleges should be filled up. *Section 5*, which set out the qualifications of members of the two Colleges, was as follows :

" No person shall be qualified to be elected a member of either of the Colleges aforesaid, nor shall be eligible to sit as a member in either of said Colleges, unless at the time of his being elected, and during the whole time of his sitting as any such member, he shall be possessed, under a title by grant from the Crown, transport, letters of decree, inheritance *ab intestato vel ex testamento*, devise, or marriage, of not less than 80 acres of land within this Colony, 40 acres whereof shall be actually and *bona fide* under cultivation, or unless he shall be possessed of any house, or house and land, under any such title as aforesaid, or held on lease for 21 years or upwards, in any part of said Colony, the rental or value of which *per annum* shall be at least

[1] Governor Barkly's despatch, 5th October, 1849.

$1,200 or unless he shall be possessed of a clear annual income of $1,440, derived from any other kind of property in the Colony than hereinbefore mentioned, or from the profits of any trade or profession carried on within the said Colony : Provided always, that no clergyman or minister of the Established Church of England and Ireland, nor of the Established Church of Scotland, nor of the Roman Catholic Church, nor of the London Missionary Society, nor of the Wesleyan Society, nor of any other church or religious society whatsoever, nor any person engaged in the ministration of any religion, or any particular tenets of any religion, or in any spiritual instruction of any kind or description whatsoever, nor any person who shall gain his living, wholly or in part, by, or shall practise, preaching in any manner whatsoever, nor any school-master or catechist shall be eligible to be returned or to sit as a member of either of said Colleges."

The *6th section* enacted that joint-owners of property should be qualified for election, and the *7th section* recited the oaths which the members of two Colleges were required to take. The next four sections set out the qualifications of voters and read as follows :

8. " Every male inhabitant of this Colony, of full age, not subject to any legal disability, residing in British Guiana, born in the allegiance of Her Majesty, or who, being born out of such allegiance, has resided in British Guiana for the space of three years before any election, possessing any of the qualifications hereinafter mentioned, and who at the time of tendering his vote shall not be in arrear in the payment of taxes, whether general or local, for more than three months from the day on which such taxes severally became payable, shall be entitled to vote upon and for the election of any and every member of the College of Electors and of the College of Financial Representatives of this Colony respectively, to be returned for the electoral division in which such voter's property qualification is situated, or, in the event of such voter's qualification being other than one of those mentioned in the 9th and 10th sections of this Ordinance, then for the electoral division in which such voter shall reside."

9. " The qualifications to vote for the election of a member for a county as aforesaid shall be—

" *Firstly.*—The possession, under a title by grant from the Crown, transport, letters of decree, inheritance *ab*

o

intestato vel ex testamento, devise, or marriage, of not less than three acres of land actually and *bona fide* under cultivation, and situated in the electoral division for which any such member as aforesaid is to be returned.

" *Secondly*.—The possession, under any title as aforesaid, of a house, or of a house and any portion of land, of the rental or value of not less than $96 *per annum*, and situated in the electoral division for which any such member as aforesaid is to be returned.

" *Thirdly*.—The occupation or tenancy of six acres of land actually and *bona fide* under cultivation, secured by lease, or any document in writing, for three years or upwards, and which lease or document in writing shall be deposited or recorded in the Registrar's office of the county in which such land is situate, such land being situate in the electoral division for which any such member as aforesaid is to be returned.

" *Fourthly*.—The occupation or tenancy of any house, or of a house and any portion of land, of the rental or value of $192 *per annum*, secured by lease or document in writing for one year or upwards, deposited or recorded as aforesaid, such house and land being situated in the electoral division for which any such member as aforesaid is to be returned."

10. " The qualifications to vote for the election of any member for the city of Georgetown or town of New Amsterdam shall be—

" *Firstly*.—The possession under a title by grant from the Crown, transport, letters of decree, inheritance *ab intestato vel ex testamento*, devise, or marriage, of a house, or of a house and premises of the value of $500, as appraised for local taxation, situated in the city or town for which any such member as aforesaid is to be returned.

" *Secondly*.—The occupation or tenancy of a house, or of a house and premises, of the rental or value of not less than $120 *per annum*, secured by lease or any document in writing for one year or upwards, and which lease or document in writing shall be deposited or recorded in the Registrar's office of the county in which such city or town is situate, such house, or house and premises, being situate in the city or town for which any member as aforesaid is to be returned."

11. " The qualification of any person to vote not specified as aforesaid, shall be, in the electoral division in which he shall reside—

" *Firstly*.—The possession or enjoyment of an income

or salary of not less than $600 *per annum* the amount of
which to be proved by the oath of the party, if required,
or in any other manner which may be prescribed by law.

"*Secondly.*—The assessment in the year of, or in the
year preceding, any new election to pay direct taxes to the
colonial revenue of the amount of $20 and upwards;
provided that no sum of money paid for any licence of any
kind or description shall be included in, or shall be considered to be within the meaning of, the words 'direct
taxes.'"

During the debate in committee the qualification was at one
time, on the motion of Mr. Rose, placed higher than it finally
stood; for, after that gentleman resigned his seat, the qualification was without a division restored to the basis originally
proposed by Governor Barkly, which had for some time past
served, on the one hand in the selection of jurors at the Supreme
Court of Justice, and on the other hand for the municipal
elections in Georgetown and New Amsterdam. To those
unacquainted with the social condition of British Guiana, some
of the various qualifications, particularly in the rural districts,
might still, the Governor thought, "seem preposterously
high"; [1] but upon consideration that, out of a population not
exceeding (exclusive of transient immigrants) 110,000 persons
of all ages and sexes, there were no less than 11,000 proprietors
of small lots of land with houses on them, he decided that a
freehold qualification of the annual value of £20, or a leasehold of £40 *per annum*, could not be deemed to be beyond what
was calculated to prevent the undue preponderance of the
democratic element.

The 12*th clause*, which a large section of the community
considered most obnoxious, but which the elective members
in the Court of Policy unanimously supported, gave absentees
the right of voting by proxy. It enacted

"that, if any person, who, if resident in the Colony,
would be entitled to vote as aforesaid, in virtue of any
plantation or property in said Colony, shall be absent
therefrom, he shall be entitled to vote by his agent or
attorney, thereto specially authorized by letter or other
document in writing, for the election of any member for the

[1] Governor Barkly's despatch, 5th October, 1849.

electoral division in which such plantation or property is situate."

Governor Barkly believed that in a country where the greater proportion of the landowners were non-resident, the mercantile portion of them necessarily so, where direct taxation on agricultural produce still formed one branch of the revenue, and where, above all, education had made little progress among the lower orders, to abolish absentee votes altogether, because they had given rise to abuses, would be " a suicidal policy." [1] He therefore rested content with simply destroying that monopoly of political power in the hands of a few leading agents, which constituted the true objection to proxy votes, while limiting the privilege to those whose principals would have been duly qualified, if on the spot, and not, as theretofore, extending it to females and infants.

Section 13 permitted joint-owners or joint-occupiers to vote, when their property divided by the number of joint-owners or joint-occupiers, as the case might be, gave a qualification for each and every such owner or occupant.

The remaining sections dealt with the registration of voters, the method of ascertaining the value of property qualifications, the machinery for conducting elections and for adjudicating on disputed elections, as well as the penalties for fraud or contravention of the law. The principal alteration consisted in substituting *viva voce* voting for the ballot, which, as practised in British Guiana, had been not a democratic, but a most aristocratic engine of political warfare, the votes, though given in secret, being opened and examined, likewise in secret, by the members of the Court of Policy, who thus became alone cognizant of the manner in which any voter had exercised the franchise. The danger of popular commotion, which was urged as a reason against adopting the British system, was obviated, as far as practicable, by confining elections to a single day, and by fixing several polling-places in each district, in accordance, as far as possible, with the provisions of the English Reform Act. Similarly the rest of the machinery, introduced for the first time by this ordinance, for making up and revising the register of voters,

The Machinery for Elections.

---

[1] Governor Barkly's despatch, 5th October, 1849.

for deciding contested elections, etc., had been borrowed either
from that Act, or from the laws in force in Jamaica or Barbados
on the subject of the franchise, the whole being harmonized
and adjusted to the institutions of British Guiana.

The committee stage of the Bill was concluded on the 21st
September, 1849.   Meanwhile, early in July, the report of the
Ordinance Parliamentary Committee had reached the Colony,
No. 15 of and the Civil List dispute had been adjusted by an
1849 passed ordinance passed on the 7th August, 1849, reviving
and for a further period the Tax Ordinance of 1847, and by
confirmed.
the consequent resignation of Messrs. Rose, Stuart, and White.
Mr. White's place in the Court of Policy was filled by Mr. E. L.
Christiani, who took his seat on the 5th September; and
during the concluding stages of the debate on the Franchise
Bill, the elective section consisted of three members only,
namely, Messrs. Gordon, Ferguson, and Christiani.   Finally,
on the 26th September, 1849, the bill was read a third time,
passed without dissent, and the following title given to it :
" an Ordinance to extend the exercise of the elective franchise
in British Guiana; to establish a qualification for members of
the College of Electors and the College of Financial Representatives respectively; to divide the Colony into electoral divisions;
and to repeal Ordinance No. 86 of the year 1836 " (No. 15 of
1849).   The ordinance was transmitted by Governor Barkly
to Earl Grey in a despatch dated the 5th October, 1849, and it
was " ratified, confirmed, and finally enacted " by a Royal
Order-in-Council made on the 8th January, 1850, which also
gave the Governor and the Court of Policy full authority to
enact " any Ordinance or Ordinances in amendment of the
said Ordinance or in furtherance of the objects thereof."

A more important measure concerning British Guiana had
not received the sanction of the Crown since the abolition of
First slavery; and the ordinance remained in force for
Elections upwards of forty years, until repealed by the
under the
Ordinance. Political Constitution Ordinance of 1891.   The first
election of Financial Representatives under its provisions took
place in November, 1849, and passed off without occasioning the
slightest excitement in any part of the Colony.   Indeed it is
surprising to find that, after the prolonged and bitter struggles
over the Civil List, no candidate anywhere, excepting in the

city of Georgetown, declared himself before the day of nomination, and no opposition was in any case offered to the candidates
nominated, who were, therefore, declared duly elected, in two
instances, as it afterwards appeared, without their knowledge or
consent.   In Georgetown, Mr. W. Brand, who, in his address
to the electors, grounded his claim for support upon the success
of his exertions for the settlement of the Civil List controversy,
carried on a canvass, until his election was secured, against the
opposition with which it was at first threatened.   The other
elections presented negative, rather than positive, political
indications, the members nominated being all new to public
life and having given no clue to their opinions on the questions
of the day.   They were, however, gentlemen of as high standing
and as extensive property as those returned under the old
system.   Mr. O'Donoghue took the seat for the county of
Berbice; Mr. Hicks that for the town of New Amsterdam.
Mr. Sandbach, a Liverpool merchant, who was elected without
his knowledge or consent for the county of Demerara, pleaded
the shortness of his stay in the Colony as an excuse for refusing
to accept the post; and Mr. W. O. Canzius, who was returned in
the same way for Essequebo, likewise declined to sit, on the
score of not being able to take the oath as to qualification.
Further elections were, therefore, necessary; and on the 3rd
December, 1849, Mr. J. Croal, who had taken a decided part
in putting an end to the stoppage of supplies, was elected without opposition for the county of Demerara in the room of Mr.
Sandbach.   There remained two vacant seats for the county
of Essequebo, which were filled also without contest, on the 7th
idem, by the election of Mr. J. Daly, Superintendent or Chief
Municipal Officer of the town of New Amsterdam, and of
Mr. R. R. Craig, the Solicitor-General of the Colony.   The
unopposed election of Mr. Craig, who, as acting Attorney-
General, bore the brunt of the Civil List struggle in the Combined
Court of 1848, was a significant fact, for it proved that the
feelings of antagonism to the Government, in which that
struggle originated, no longer existed in the minds of the
majority of the colonists.   Meanwhile the vacancies in the
Court of Policy had been filled by the selection of Messrs. A. D.
Vander Gon Netscher and W. B. Pollard from the names sent
in by the College of Electors; and thus the elective section of

the Combined Court was fully reconstituted, when the annual session opened on the 18th December, 1849.

The first registration of voters under the new franchise law resulted, according to a report made by Mr. A. Schrack, the Registrar, on the 3rd December, 1849, as follows :

Voters registered for the	County of Demerara	.	.	.	.	181
	City of Georgetown	.	.	.	.	186
	County of Berbice .	.	.	.	.	64
	Town of New Amsterdam	.	.	.	94
	County of Essequebo	.	.	.	.	96

Total, 621

These constituencies were far more limited in numbers than Governor Barkly had anticipated. His calculation had *Registration of Voters under the New Franchise Law.* been founded upon the fact that the jury list embraced 900 names, and that the list of municipal voters for Georgetown and New Amsterdam contained respectively 1,071 and 448 names, in all 2,419 ; for, though it was taken into account that many persons were entitled both to act as jurors and to vote at municipal elections, it was believed that this would be more than counterbalanced by the addition, first, of the large number exempted from serving on juries ; second, of the new class of voters under lease ; and third, of the absentee proprietors, whose political rights were continued to them. But the Governor's forecast was falsified owing partly to the short time allowed for making up the lists of voters, and partly to the suspicion entertained by the more ignorant among the freeholders of the real objects of registration, which, being based upon a declaration of the possession of a certain amount of property, they fancied to be preparatory to the levy of direct taxes. Moreover, few proxy voters could be registered within the time prescribed, as the ordinance required a written delegation of authority from the absentee principal. Much allowance must also be made for the novelty of the whole proceeding in the case of the great majority of the community, and for the political apathy which generally prevails in a tropical climate, except when some exciting question of personal interest temporarily arouses the passions of the inhabitants.

The second annual registration of voters showed a distinct improvement, Mr. Schrack's return, dated the 23rd September, 1850, being as follows :

Electoral Divisions.	Voters Registered in 1849.*	Additional Voters Registered in 1850.	Total Con-stituency.
County of Demerara . . .	166	160	326
City of Georgetown . . .	180	83	263
County of Berbice . . .	60	20	80
Town of New Amsterdam . .	92	17	109
County of Essequebo . .	89	49	138

* These figures are in each case less than those given in Mr. Schrack's report of the 3rd December, 1849, several names having been struck off in consequence of the death of the parties or for other causes.

Thus the total number of registered voters was 916, an increase of 295 or 47·8% during the year. The numbers in the town constituencies were still disappointing, the voters registered in Georgetown being only 263, and in New Amsterdam only 109, in both cases but one-fourth of the number of municipal electors. This, no doubt, arose in a great degree from the circumstance that a very large proportion of females possessed houses in their own right, which entitled them to vote in municipal elections, whereas the franchise was restricted to adult males. It was also in part due to the want of success which had attended the extension of the franchise to tenants under lease, only fifteen voters having claimed to be registered under this qualification, out of the hundreds who might be expected to possess it, a fact attributable to the uncertain tenure prevalent in British Guiana, not excepting even the wealthiest classes, who often occupied their private residences, and their stores also, under agreements by the week or month, and very seldom thought of entering into or recording leases, such as the Franchise Ordinance required. In the rural districts, indeed, the difficulty of securing greater permanency of tenure was still more strongly exemplified, only fifteen leases of farms, and seven of houses, appearing among the claimants to a vote. But, despite impediments of this kind, the new ordinance was successful in creating a resident constituency of between 800 and 900 voters, representing every class in the community, from the labourer upwards; and the measure of the improvement effected may be judged from the fact that at the end of 1847, on the eve of the Civil List struggle, the legally qualified voters had numbered only 561 ; while under the old system, as Governor Barkly wrote,[1] on the occasion of a contest with Government

> " votes in the name of non-resident proprietors, minors, females, etc., were manufactured by the dozen, and thrust into the ballot-boxes, by attorneys or *soi-disant* attorneys, or agents of attorneys, who, perhaps, not liking their constituents at home to know the use made of their names, never registered them publicly ; the large number of illegal votes occasionally polled thus serving but to show how powerless in reality the resident voters were to resist this oligarchy."

In fact, the importance of the reform must be judged, not positively in relation to abstract theories of representation, but comparatively by contrast with the vicious system which had been rooted out in the Colony.

[1] Governor Barkly's despatch, 23rd September, 1850.

CHAPTER XI

ORDINANCE NO. 2 OF 1850

ON the 19th December, 1849, Mr. S. Firebrace, Second Puisne Judge of British Guiana, died suddenly of apoplexy at his residence in Werk-en-Rust. Mr. Downie, the First Puisne Judge, was at that time absent from the Colony on leave, but was expected to return from Europe in the course of two or three weeks. Nevertheless it was necessary to fill the vacant judgeship at once, because, unless this was done, the Supreme Court, which was in session when Mr. Firebrace died, could not even be adjourned; and upon the advice of the Chief Justice, Mr. J. H. Bent, Governor Barkly appointed Mr. E. L. Christiani, a gentleman of mature years and considerable legal experience, who had on a former occasion occupied temporarily a seat on the bench, to act as First Puisne Judge pending Mr. Downie's return. Mr. Christiani accordingly took his seat on the bench on the 22nd December, 1849.

Mr. Christiani, Elective Member of Court of Policy, appointed to act as Puisne Judge.

But at this time Mr. Christiani was also an elective member of the Court of Policy, which was then in session from day to day with the Financial Representatives in Combined Court: and on the 28th December, 1849, Mr. J. Gordon, seconded by Mr. A. D. Vander Gon Netscher, moved in Court of Policy that Mr. Christiani, having accepted an office of profit under the Crown, had thereby ceased to be an elective member of the Court, and that the Governor be, therefore, requested to issue the usual proclamation for a new nomination by the College of Electors in the room of Mr. Christiani. However Mr. Arrindell, the Attorney-General, not being able to discover any law on the point, advised that, in the absence of all law, Mr. Christiani had not *de facto* or *de jure* vacated his seat in the Court of Policy by his acceptance of the office of acting Puisne Judge; but he added the opinion that a law should be passed to prevent in future elective members of the Court of Policy or Combined

Court, who accepted offices of emolument under the Crown, from retaining their seat. Mr. W. B. Pollard, seconded by Mr. W. B. Ferguson, then moved as an amendment to Mr. Gordon's resolution that His Excellency be requested to instruct the Attorney-General to frame such an ordinance. This amendment was supported by Mr. A. D. V. Gon Netscher; and, when Mr. Gordon challenged a division, he found himself in a minority of one, whereupon he next day resigned his seat, stating that it would be derogatory to his public character to sit in the Court as then constituted. But, on the 28th December, immediately after the discussion in Court of Policy, Mr. Christiani had also resigned his seat, feeling that, " as a good citizen and loyal subject," it was his " duty to surrender a point of no importance whatever in itself." Both resignations were accepted; and the vacancies were filled, on the 5th January, 1850, by the appointment of Mr. S. Bean of plantation " Domburg " and Mr. R. Haynes of plantation " Broomhall."

Meanwhile, on the 31st December, 1849, the Attorney-General brought in a bill " to prevent elective members of the *Ordinance* Court of Policy, and members of the College of *No. 2 of* Financial Representatives, continuing such after *1850.* accepting of any office of profit from the Crown." This bill was passed into law on the 10th January as Ordinance No. 2 of 1850; and its confirmation and allowance by Her Majesty were conveyed to Governor Barkly by Earl Grey in a despatch dated the 11th March, 1850. The ordinance was a transcript from clause 26 of the Imperial Act 6 Anne, cap. 7, and read :

> " If any person being chosen an elective member of this Honourable Court, or a member of the College of Financial Representatives of this Colony, shall accept of any office of profit from the Crown during such time as he shall continue a member as aforesaid, his seat shall be and is hereby declared to be vacant, and a proclamation shall issue for a new election, as if such person, so accepting was naturally dead : provided nevertheless that any such person shall be capable of being again elected, as if his place had not become vacant as aforesaid."

These provisions were subsequently embodied in sections 15 and 35 of the Political Constitution Ordinance, 1891.

CHAPTER XII

(a) *Ordinance No. 8 of 1852.*

ON the 11th January, 1850, a deputation consisting of a number of gentlemen of various political parties, headed by Mr.

Petition for Council and House of Assembly. P. Rose, waited upon Governor Barkly with a petition which prayed that the Court of Policy would adopt resolutions " recommending that the present legislative and financial institutions of the Colony should cease; that they be replaced by a ' Council ' and ' House of Assembly,' as in Barbados and other chartered colonies; and that such resolutions be transmitted for the sanction of the Queen's Most Excellent Majesty." The petition included among its 812 signatures, the names of many of the most respectable planters and merchants throughout British Guiana; but it was dated the 31st August, 1849, a period when the Civil List controversy had not yet been composed, and when the ordinance extending the elective franchise was still in committee. Governor Barkly, therefore, doubted whether some of those who then signed the petition would have done so at the close of the year. Moreover, there were names of consideration withheld from the petition, which led him to believe that a counter-petition limited in its prayer to the abolition of the College of Electors and to more direct representation in the Court of Policy would obtain at least equal support, and that a large and influential class of the community would look with alarm at any sudden accession of popular impulse in the then state of society in British Guiana.[1] Accordingly he replied to the deputation that he would place the proposed resolutions before the Court of Policy; but that, if the Court adopted them, the advice he would tender to Her Majesty would be " to accede in substance to them, but to

---

[1] Governor Barkly's despatch, 12th January, 1850.

authorize the introduction of the necessary alterations only by slow and cautious degrees "; adding that, if he were required to adduce proof of the wisdom of such a mode of proceeding, he need only refer to the unanimity alleged to prevail regarding the attainment of an object to which not long ago some of the most influential members of the community, including Mr. Rose himself, were so decidedly opposed.

The petition was brought up for consideration in the Court of Policy on the 3rd April, 1850, and the debate had no other *Debate in* result than a resolution that " the petition should *Court of* lie on the table," the variance of opinion among the *Policy,* *April,* 1850. five elective members—Messrs. W. B. Ferguson, A. D. Vander Gon Netscher, W. B. Pollard, R. Haynes, and S. Bean—being so irreconcilable that, though all were agreed that some change or other was expedient, they could not be brought to unite in recommending any particular course for adoption. Messrs. Pollard and Haynes moved " that the petition from the inhabitants praying for a Council and House of Assembly be forwarded to the Queen's Most Excellent Majesty, with the earnest solicitations of this Court that Her Majesty may be graciously pleased to grant the prayer thereof." But they were outvoted by their three elective colleagues, and received no support from the official section. Mr. Ferguson then moved for the introduction of an ordinance to abolish the College of Electors and to provide for the direct election of members of the Court of Policy by the voters in the several electoral districts. But Messrs. Bean and Vander Gon Netscher refused to go further than a reform of that College by increasing its numbers and limiting the term of each Kiezer's service to three years—a minimum of change to which, in his turn, Mr. Ferguson would not agree, while Messrs. Pollard and Haynes were so desirous of immediate radical reform that they would support no proposition for a gradual improvement of the constitution. A motion that the petition be referred to a committee of the elective members was lost; and finally four of the elective members agreed to a motion by Mr. Vander Gon Netscher, seconded by Mr. Bean, that the petition should lie on the table, Mr. Pollard declining to vote.

Governor Barkly believed that the elective section of the Court of Policy exhibited on this occasion no very inaccurate

representation of the divided feelings of the colonists generally
with respect to this question.[1]   A public meeting was, however, convened by the Mayor of Georgetown, Mr.

*Public
Meeting at
Georgetown.*

Obermuller, and took place at Mrs. Parnell's Assembly
Rooms on the 15th April, 1850, when strong resolutions were passed, amounting in effect to a vote of censure on
those members of the Court of Policy who disagreed with
Messrs. Pollard and Haynes ; but, as Governor Barkly remarked,
those who read the account of the proceedings on this occasion [2]
will find " some reason to doubt whether that meeting really
tended either to swell the importance or to display the unanimty
of those who called it." [3]   An address to Her Majesty was,
however, adopted on this occasion praying for the establishment
of an Elective Council and House of Assembly in lieu of the
existing political institutions.

Governor Barkly reported to Earl Grey, in a despatch
dated the 2nd May, 1850, what had occurred both in Court

*Views of
Governor
Barkly.*

of Policy and at the public meeting.   It was
easy, he wrote, for speakers at public meetings
to

" lay claim to the ' birthright of Britons ' ; but in sober
earnest it would be difficult, out of the 130,000 inhabitants
of this Colony, to find 1,000 natives of the United Kingdom
of the requisite age and sex ; and, though I do not mean to
deny that there are thousands of others equally fit as these
to be entrusted with political power, it is impossible to
overlook the fact that but a small proportion of the emancipated peasantry, and fewer still of the Portuguese, African
or Cooly [4] immigrants, could be, with any show of reason,
comprehended in that number.   Yet to exclude the great
majority from all share of power, under a system claiming
to embody the principle of popular representation in
contradistinction to the protection of classes by the Crown,
is contrary to the professed object of all parties, and may
safely be pronounced to be as unjust as it is impracticable,
whether numbers or property be made the basis of qualification, in such a state of society as exists in this country,
where I can venture to affirm, without the least danger of

[1] Governor Barkly's despatch, 2nd May, 1850.
[2] Parl. Papers No. 154 of 1851, pp. 23–39.
[3] Governor Barkly's despatch, 2nd May, 1850.
[4] *I.e.*, East Indian labourers.

exaggeration, that the exchangeable value of the property, real and personal, acquired by the labouring population since emancipation, considerably exceeds the sum which at the present moment could be obtained for the fee-simple of all the plantations and cultivated lands in the Colony. A few years may make an important difference in this respect by restoring landed property to its true level, and they cannot fail to develop, under judicious treatment, the political capacity of these numerous small proprietors, in which latter expectation I am encouraged by what has taken place in the few months since the Franchise Bill has put a vote within the reach of many of them; for, though they very generally at first neglected to register themselves, no sooner did the first contested election occur, last month, than numbers who were unregistered presented themselves at the polling-booths to claim the privilege, and, while disappointed at not being allowed to do so, exhibited the most perfect order and good humour. . . . As the Court of Policy, from causes already explained, has not availed itself of the opportunity of expressing any opinion upon the subject, it rests with Your Lordship alone to decide what shall be the next step towards that gradual reform of the present institutions of the Colony, in the necessity of which all parties so cordially concur.   My own judgment would certainly have counselled such delay as would at any rate have afforded experience of the effects of this Franchise Bill, when sufficient time had elapsed to allow of its coming fairly into play; but, as a systematic agitation is threatened, which may become dangerous if altogether disregarded, it may now be more prudent to remove at once those anomalies in the constitution which are most likely to be dwelt upon by the agitators : and, as Your Lordship is aware, none stands higher in this category than the old Dutch custom of returning the representatives of the people to the Court of Policy through the medium of seven individuals, styled Kiezers, or ' choosers,' to whom such power is delegated for life.   I would, therefore, solicit permission to introduce a bill into the Court of Policy for reforming this College, by enlarging the number of its members to at least twelve, and limiting their period of service to three or five years at furthest, a measure which would probably meet the support of a majority of the elective members, while it could, on principle, be opposed by none. . . . I am quite aware that it will be contended by many, whose opinions are well entitled to respect, that instead of thus attempting, as they would call it, ' to patch up a rotten institution,' it would be far preferable immediately to abolish the College of Kiezers, and to fill up the non-official seats in the Court of Policy by means of direct election through the new constituencies. In my humble opinion, however, new political institutions generally work more successfully when they are but developments of those which pre-existed; and looking upon the Court of Policy as the germ of a future Legislative Council, whilst the Financial College may hereafter expand into a House of Assembly, I cannot but think that it would be imprudent to extend the principle of direct popular representation to the former body also. How best to reproduce that balance of power which constitutes the excellence of the British constitution, in these colonies, where two out of its three elements, the splendour of majesty and the influence of an aristocracy, are almost imperceptible, is a problem which perhaps still remains to be solved; but it is evident that if, in such a state of society, two branches of the legislature be made dependent on the popular will, the only check to pure democracy will consist in a vain struggle on the part of the representative of the Crown, to interpose an authority which will prove as ineffectual as it will be odious."

Earl Grey replied on the 15th June, 1850, that the division of opinion in the Court of Policy and in the Colony at large on the subject of constitutional reform placed Her Majesty's Government in a position of much difficulty. Understanding, however, that all parties were agreed on the propriety of enlarging the number of Kiezers and limiting their tenure of office, he authorized Governor Barkly to introduce a measure for that purpose, but not to press for it unless with the support of a majority of the elective section.

Earl Grey authorizes Reform of the College of Kiezers.

"I am of opinion," he concluded, "that it will not be advisable to alter the present constitution by the establishment of a Council and Assembly, until the great body of the population shall have made such an advance in civilization and capacity for the exercise of political power, as to render it safe to base the representation upon a franchise which shall make the Assembly a really popular body; a representative government resting upon a narrow basis, I should regard as most objectionable."

In the meantime Mr. Ferguson had left the Colony, and Mr. P. Rose, who took the vacant seat in the Court of Policy, *Further* moved on the 13th June, 1850, for reconsideration *Debate in* of the petition from the inhabitants of British *Court of* *Policy, June,* Guiana, which, on the 3rd April, had been ordered *1850.* to lie on the table. To this end he brought forward three resolutions :

> 1st, " That it is the opinion of this Court, that the legislative institutions of British Guiana are unsuited to the existing state of society, and it is desirable that they should be abolished, and a House of Assembly and an Elective Legislative Council be established in their stead."
>
> 2nd, " That it is the opinion of this Court, that the electoral districts for the House of Assembly shall consist of the towns, and such subdivisions as may be found convenient of the counties of the Colony ; that the elective franchise should be so extended, as thoroughly to carry out the principle of a full, free and popular representation, and that the districts for the election of the Council should be more extensive, while the qualification of the electors should be different from, and higher than, that of the electors of the House of Assembly."
>
> 3rd, " That His Excellency the Governor be respectfully requested to transmit a copy of these resolutions and a copy of the petition of the inhabitants of British Guiana to the Right Honourable the Secretary of State for the Colonies, with the earnest solicitation of this Court, that he will be pleased to lay the same before Her Majesty the Queen."

It will be observed that, whereas the petition had asked for a Council similar to that of " Barbados and other chartered colonies," Mr. Rose now advocated a purely elective Council, to be returned by constituents possessing a higher qualification than that of electors of the House of Assembly. He justified this change by stating that, since the petition was drawn up, he had received the draft of the new constitution granted by the Queen to the Cape of Good Hope, which included both an elective Assembly and an elective Legislative Council ; and he read a passage from the report of the Committee of the Privy Council, presented on the 30th January, 1850, and confirmed by Her Majesty, explaining the grounds on which this

P

principle had been adopted.[1] The fact was that a Legislative
Council, elected by the higher classes only, precisely met the

[1] The passage reads as follows : " The question as to how the
Legislative Council ought to be constituted, which we will now proceed
to consider, is one of much greater difficulty. It is on all hands
admitted that it is highly desirable that there should be a second
branch of the Legislature less easily swayed by the popular feeling
of the moment than the Representative Assembly, and capable of
acting as a check and counterpoise to that body, in order to guard
against hasty legislation without requiring the too frequent interference of the Governor or the Crown. But, in order to perform these
functions with effect, it is necessary that the Legislative Council should
be a body of real weight and influence, commanding the respect and
confidence of the public. To create such a body is obviously a problem
of no easy solution. If the ordinary colonial constitution be taken as
the example to be followed, the Council ought to be composed of a
moderate number of persons (including some holding offices in the public
service) nominated by the Crown, and holding their seats (practically
at least) for life; this is the description of Legislative Council of which
the majority of Sir Harry Smith's advisers have recommended the
adoption; but, after very careful consideration of the subject and of
the arguments they have advanced in favour of the conclusion to which
they have come, we have not been able to concur in it. In stating
their reasons for advising that a representative legislature should be
established in the Colony of the Cape of Good Hope, the very able
and experienced servants of the Crown, who were consulted by the
Governor, have unanimously expressed the strongest opinion that
the existing Legislative Council does not command the confidence
of the Colony, and has little influence on public opinion. But the
composition of the Legislative Council is practically the same with
that which is recommended for the body, which, under some designation, is proposed to be joined with the Representative Assembly in
the work of legislation; it consists of official members, and of members
not holding any office in the public service, who owe their seats to the
nomination of the Crown. We cannot believe that the character of
this body would be essentially altered by increasing the proportion
of the unofficial to official members, or by making the life tenure of
their seats to depend, not on a usage which is practically almost invariably followed, but on the law; nor have we any reason to believe
that it would be in the power of the Governor of the Colony in time to
come to make a more careful and judicious selection of members to be
appointed to the Council than that which has been made by their
predecessors. On the contrary, we are persuaded that, after the
establishment of a Representative Assembly, that body will have so
much more real authority than a Council nominated by the Crown,
that seats in the former will be a greater object of ambition than those
in the latter; and it will thus become impossible to obtain the services
in the Legislative Council of gentlemen of as much weight and influence
with their fellow-citizens as those who have been heretofore appointed.
The inference, we think, is irresistible, that a body, which even while
it exercised the whole power of legislation had little hold over public
opinion, will cease to have any real weight or influence when it comes
to be overshadowed by so substantial a power as that of an Assembly
elected by the people. Hence we concur with the Chief Justice of the
Colony in believing that, if it is desired to give to the Legislative Council

danger to planting interests in British Guiana, which the plantocracy had apprehended ever since the agitation for constitutional reform began—namely, the danger of being out-voted in a representative Assembly; for such a Council would have given them every assurance of ability to make terms with the popular party in the House of Assembly by means of the legislative power which they would themselves possess. Thus the publication of the proposals concerning the Cape of Good Hope reconciled to the reform movement in British Guiana many who before either stood aloof from it altogether or gave it their adherence with suspicion and alarm.

Mr. Rose's first resolution was seconded by Mr. Haynes, but was opposed by Mr. Vander Gon Netscher, who pointed out that, while it was true that the total population in the Cape of Good Hope was but slightly larger than that of British Guiana, the inhabitants of the former colony numbering some 150,000 and of the latter some 130,000, nevertheless an analysis of those figures showed a profound difference in the state of society in the two colonies. There were at the Cape about 80,000 white inhabitants, the descendants of Europeans, men who had always been free, farmers and proprietors of land, while there were not more than 50,000 blacks, Hottentots and other races. But in British Guiana there were 90,000 recently emancipated slaves and 30,000 immigrants, utterly unfit to enjoy the political privileges claimed for them; and only 10,000 persons—some 2,000 being whites and the remainder being of the free coloured classes—who could by any stretch of imagina-

---

strength to act in any degree as a balance to the Assembly, the elective principle must enter into its composition.   We are fully aware of the importance of such a departure from all former precedents; but the considerations by which the innovation is recommended are, in our judgment, of too much weight to be disregarded.   We recommend, therefore, that the members of the Legislative Council should be elected, but by a different body of electors from those by whom the members of the Assembly are to be chosen, and for a longer term; we would propose that the Council, unless sooner dissolved, should be chosen for ten years; that is to say, for a term equal to twice that for which we have proposed that the Assembly should be elected; and that it should be renewed, not all at once, but by half of the members being subject to re-election at the end of every five years.   In the first instance, the members who had been elected by the smallest number of votes should be those to go out of the Council at the end of five years. At the subsequent periodical renewals of the Council, the members to go out would, of course, be those who had served their full time."

tion be compared with the Cape colonists. It would, he thought, be the ruin of British Guiana to endeavour to make it " a free republic."

Mr. Rose then intimated that, if his first resolution were carried, he would withdraw the second; and, upon a division being taken, there voted for the first resolution four elective members—Messrs. Rose, Haynes, Pollard, and Bean, the last-named thus reversing the vote which he gave on the 3rd April—and against the resolution Mr. Vander Gon Netscher, the High Sheriff (Mr. G. Bagot) and the Attorney-General (Mr. W. Arrindell), both of the latter being old colonists and pro-prietors of estates in British Guiana. The Chief Justice (Mr. J. H. Bent) and the acting Government Secretary (Mr. W. B. Wolseley) declined to vote, while Governor Barkly refrained from influencing in any way the decision of the Court. The first resolution was thus carried by four votes to three. There-after the second resolution was withdrawn, and the third resolution was adopted without opposition. Pursuant thereto Governor Barkly, in a despatch dated the 14th July, reported *Earl Grey's Views.* what had taken place to Earl Grey, who replied on the 1st August, that the withdrawal of the second resolution left him " to infer that those who voted in the Court of Policy for the institution of a House of Assembly were not prepared to vote for a full, free and popular representation," and that he could, therefore, only repeat what he had written on the 15th June, that a representative government, resting upon a narrow basis, would be most objectionable, whilst at the same time concurring " in what would appear to be the opinion of the Court of Policy as to the present incapacity of the body of the people for the exercise of political power," and adding that he regarded the political state and capabilities of British Guiana as bearing no resemblance to those of the Cape of Good Hope.

Governor Barkly laid Earl Grey's despatches of the 15th June and 1st August before the Court of Policy at a meeting *Political Agitation in the Colony continues.* on the 18th September, together with a minute by himself, in which he stated that he was prepared " to introduce a bill for the reform of the Electoral College by enlarging the number of its members and limiting their tenure of their seats "; and that, if called on by a unanimous vote of the Court of Policy to go further, with a

view to a more permanent settlement of the question, he
" would not refuse to submit to Her Majesty's Government
the expediency of readjusting the balance of the legislative
power in this Court by the addition of the Mayor of Georgetown to the elective members, thereby constituting that section
henceforth a majority of the Court of Policy, and of extending
at the same time the number of Financial Representatives in
the Combined Court from six to ten."   The Governor's object
was to allay, as far as possible, the excitement occasioned by
the recent proceedings of the Reform Association, which had
convened two public meetings in Georgetown and five others
in different parts of the county of Demerara since the commencement of the agitation in April.   But his overtures,
though in unison with the wishes of a majority of the elective
members of the Court of Policy, failed because the more
violent party out of doors was preponderant.   A memorial,
praying the Court of Policy to reject any measure which did
not go the full length of " substituting for the existing legislative institutions an Elective Council and House of Assembly,
based on a system of full, free and direct popular representation," was sent to all parts of the Colony for signature, and was
presented to the Court on the 30th September by Mr. Haynes.
Of this memorial Governor Barkly remarked [1] that, although
the names of some highly intelligent and respectable persons
might be recognized among the eleven hundred *signatures* said
to be attached, those of the great bulk of the resident proprietors of plantations were certainly absent, and their places
ill-supplied by the clerks and overseers of the former; while
the fourteen hundred *marks* annexed, principally by London
missionary congregations, could, on a question so abstruse as
that of the form of government best suited for a country
emerging from serfdom, be reckoned as no more than the
single opinion of each pastor by whom the marks were witnessed.

Mr. Haynes, seconded by Mr. Rose, moved that the prayer
of the memorial be endorsed by the Court of Policy and sub-

*Renewed
Debate in
Court of
Policy,
September,
1850.*

mitted to Earl Grey for Her Majesty's most
favourable consideration.   But this motion was
opposed by Mr. G. Booker, who moved as an
amendment

[1] Governor Barkly's despatch, 9th October, 1850.

"that this Court, recognizing the propriety of not altering the constitution for the present without the full assent of all classes of the inhabitants, will abstain from legislation on the subject until sufficient opportunity has been afforded to the memorialists for explaining in detail their plan of an elective Council and House of Assembly, and defining what would, in their opinion, constitute a full, free and direct popular representation."

The amendment was seconded by Mr. Bean, who thus reverted to the moderate party; it was supported by Mr. Vander Gon Netscher and by the High Sheriff; and, upon a division, the only opponents of the amendment proved to be Messrs. Haynes and Rose, whose original motion was thus defeated. Governor Barkly then stated that, in consequence of the resolution adopted by the Court, which he considered a very wise one, he would for the present abstain from taking any steps with reference to the constitutional changes suggested in the minute which he had addressed to the Court on the 18th September.

The resolution, thus adopted by the Court of Policy, pointed clearly to the difficulties which beset the immediate intro-

Dilemma of the Reform Association. duction of a Council and Assembly and put forward a reasonable challenge to those who, influenced by love of change, ambition, revenge or self-interest, would have run the risk of plunging the Colony into confusion by undue precipitancy. If the challenge was not promptly accepted, and the views of the Reform Association as to the elective franchise explicitly avowed, the inference would be plain that the Association was a mere temporary coalition of hostile factions to overturn the existing constitution, each hoping to secure power to itself in the struggle which must thereafter ensue; and the argument against the abrogation of the authority vested in the Crown would thus gain immensely in strength. On the other hand, the mystification previously attempted by the Association in regard to the franchise had been so remarkable, that there was little prospect of its members concurring as a body in any definition whatsoever, especially as, notwithstanding the withdrawal on the 13th June of Mr. Rose's second resolution on this subject—a withdrawal which was now confessed to have been made for the purpose of catching votes—the attempt was again made to take refuge in the

same vague generalities about " full, free and direct representation," words which in the mouth of Mr. Rose, who had,
as will be remembered, on the 17th March, 1849, gravely proposed as the sole franchise for villagers " a house in fee of the
value of $500," might mean anything or nothing, when this
object was attained.

In this dilemma, the extreme party, instead of answering
the Court of Policy's challenge, attempted further demonstra-
Its Threaten- tions with a view of intimidating those who differed
ing Attitude. from them in opinion. A threatening attitude
had, indeed, been assumed by Mr. Haynes, when speaking
in the Court of Policy on the 8th October, for he very im-
properly alluded to the negro insurrection of 1823 as a political
" revolution " and hinted at the possibility of recourse to
physical force as a means of coercing either the Home Government or the local Legislature. Similarly the *Colonist* newspaper, both in leading articles and in letters, used very violent
language. The paramount authority of the Crown was protested against as " a usurpation." " Free self-government "
was spoken of as a thing to be " achieved." The elective
members, who voted contrary to the wishes of the Association,
were to be " forced " to resign, whilst Messrs. Rose and Haynes,
who supported the memorial for a new constitution, were
reproached for their lukewarm speeches. The consequences of
the agitation, " for good or for bad," were to be on the heads
of the Government. Language such as this was interspersed
with frequent allusions to " fighting battles," " gaining vic-
tories," " striking terror into the Government," " overpowering
and disarming enemies," all meant, no doubt, to be taken
figuratively, but very likely to be understood in their literal
sense by those to whom they were addressed. Finally, on the
16th October, the Committee of the British Guiana Reform
Association decided that " a great general meeting " of the
inhabitants of the Colony should be held in Georgetown on
Saturday, the 9th November, at noon ; and, on the 28th
October, the Association announced that this meeting would
take place on the Parade Ground and that " the question of
constitutional reform, and petitions to Her Majesty the Queen
and both Houses of Parliament in favour of a change from our
present legislative and financial institutions to an elective

Council and House of Assembly," would be summitted for consideration. Considerable alarm was felt by many colonists at the impending demonstration; and, as it was impossible to say what the result of the first open-air meeting ever held in the Colony would be, the Governor took every precaution to be ready to quell promptly any disturbance which might arise, by withdrawing beforehand as many police as could be safely spared from the counties of Berbice and Essequebo, and concentrating the force in Georgetown, as well as by arranging that the officer commanding the troops should keep his men under arms in their quarters on the day in question. The promoters of the agitation themselves, when the 9th November, the day appointed for the meeting, drew near, became as apprehensive as others of its possible effects, and not only applied for twelve policemen—a considerable portion of the Governor's small reserve—to keep order on the hustings, but distributed a printed circular, signed by the Rev. E. A. Wallbridge of the London Missionary Society, a leading member of the Reform Association, exhorting the people to abstain from violence.

Fortunately these precautions proved altogether superfluous. The attempt to assemble the labouring population in any considerable number, to discuss constitutional reform, *Open-air Meeting in Georgetown, 9th November, 1850.* failed signally, notwithstanding the efforts made by the Association in despatching messengers through the villages to put the subject in the captivating light of " no taxes and high wages," and in the dissemination of placards ending with the usual style of Government notices, " God save the Queen ! ", and resembling Government proclamations sufficiently to have, in some cases, persuaded the peasantry that the Queen, whose name they reverenced, commanded the meeting. Of the number actually present on the Parade Ground on the 9th November, no precise estimate could be made. It was stated in the newspapers to be upwards of 2,000; but two separate attempts to count the people as they moved off, the one made from the windows of Government House, the other from a neighbouring residence, gave only 1,200 to 1,400 persons, the great majority consisting of boys, who pursued their usual amusements, unmindful of the orators on the hustings, or of women selling cakes and ginger-beer, or promenading in smart dresses as on a gala day.

" In fact it would be difficult," wrote Governor Barkly, when reporting the affair to Earl Grey on the 11th November, " to conceive any event coming off in the centre of a town, now numbering not far short of 30,000 inhabitants, and connected by railway and steamboat with villages containing at least as many more, and on a Saturday too, which is a general holiday among the labouring classes, which would not have occasioned a far larger attendance, and no one was more astonished than myself at the result."

At noon precisely Mr. Rose took the chair on a platform erected and covered for the speakers. Mr. G. Quayle officiated as secretary ; and there were on the platform some 200 persons. The proceedings began with three cheers for the Queen. The meeting was then addressed by the following gentlemen : Mr. Rose, Mr. Obermuller (the Mayor of Georgetown), Messrs. J. Stuart, R. Haynes, C. Simson, J. T. Gilbert, J. E. Roney, C. Smith, J. C. Rodmaker, R. Hick, and the Reverends Wallbridge, Rattray, and McFarlane. Four resolutions were adopted : the first, declaring the unsuitableness of the existing political institutions to the condition of the Colony; the second, indicating an elective Council and a House of Assembly as the proper substitute for them; the third, affirming the petitions to Her Majesty and both Houses of Parliament, which had been prepared and were laid before the meeting; and the fourth appointing Lord Stanley to present the petition to the Lords, and Mr. Joseph Hume to present that to the Commons. The proceedings, from beginning to end, were conducted in a very orderly manner; and, at about 2.15 p.m., the business closed and the meeting quietly separated.

The petition adopted by this meeting was signed in due course by about 5,000 persons, of whom some 1,400 were *Petitions* " marksmen." It prayed " for the abolition of the *presented to* Court of Policy and the Combined Court of this *Parliament.* Colony, and of all the offices and institutions necessarily connected with these Courts, and for the introduction in lieu thereof of a Representative Constitution, comprising an Elective Council and House of Assembly, with an elective franchise so extensive as thoroughly to carry out the principle of a full, free and direct popular representation "; but no attempt was made to define these generalities. The copy of the petition entrusted to Mr. Hume was presented by him to the House of Commons on the 27th March, 1851; and, about the same time, Lord Stanley gave notice in the House of Lords that, on the 16th April, he would present the petition from British Guiana and, in doing so, call the attention of their Lordships to the statements which it contained.

But in the meantime the very clear proof, which had been afforded, that the dissatisfaction with the existing institutions of the Colony did not extend to the labourers, although they might suffer their marks to be affixed by the dozen to petitions praying for reform, when called on by their pastors or employers, led the more moderate members of the Reform Association, and particularly those with a stake in the Colony, to consider whether it would be prudent to admit such an extension of popular influence in British Guiana as would entitle the inhabitants to solicit from Her Majesty a countervailing modification of the powers vested in the Crown. It was evident that the emancipated labourers had very little idea of the abstract merits or demerits of different forms of government.

Moderate Views gain strength.

> " They are perfectly contented," wrote Governor Barkly,[1] " so long as they preserve their freedom untrammelled, and get as high wages as they can for as little labour. But they are, at the same time, not inattentive observers of the dissensions among their former masters, and a sense of injury may be created in their minds by the reiteration of the alleged oppression inflicted on them, which may lead to consequences widely different from those contemplated by the planters who have joined in the Reform agitation."

Moreover, the opposition of the radical party to immigration tended to alienate the planting interest.

Earl Grey was convinced that the true interest of all classes of the inhabitants of British Guiana required that great caution should be observed in introducing political changes until the population at large was better fitted for the exercise of the franchise by the more general diffusion of education, and also by the establishment of municipal institutions, under which they might be trained

Earl Grey urges Caution.

---

[1] Governor Barkly's despatch, 11th November, 1850.

with advantage to take a more extensive share in the government of the Colony.   Entertaining these views, although he did not positively object to Governor Barkly's suggestion that the casting vote of the Governor in the Court of Policy should be surrendered, he expressed much doubt as to the expediency of so diminishing the power of the Crown, and doubted even more whether it would be advisable that such a change should be effected by giving a seat in the Court to the Mayor of Georgetown *ex officio*.   " My belief is," he wrote,[1] " that, in such a state of society as now exists in Guiana, it generally happens that the capital town is apt to exercise too much, rather than too little, influence as compared with the rural districts, even without the addition which such a change would make to its power."

It was in these circumstances that on the 4th April, 1851, certain proprietors of estates, and others beneficially interested in property in British Guiana, held a meeting at the London Tavern, under the chairmanship of Mr. Charles Cave, to consider the petition which had been presented to the House of Commons by Mr. Hume on the 27th March. This meeting unanimously resolved that the principle of representation already enjoyed by the inhabitants of British Guiana, might " be advantageously extended—

Resolutions of Meeting at the London Tavern, on 4th April, 1851.

> " 1st, by increasing the number of the College of Electors from seven to eleven, and fixing their term of services at three years, instead of appointing them for life, not to vacate their office except by continued absence from the Colony of more than three months :
> " 2nd, by the addition of another elected member to the Court of Policy, thereby increasing the number of unofficial members from five to six :
> " 3rd, by increasing the number of Financial Representatives from six to ten " ;

that, considering the new Franchise Ordinance had been little more than a year in operation, any further alteration at the time was inadvisable ; but that it was desirable

> " to abrogate the power which may be assumed by the Governor to veto the introduction of any measure into

[1] Earl Grey's despatch, 30th December, 1850.

the Court of Policy, or to interrupt the progress of the proceedings at any stage; and that, on the contrary, it should be competent for any member of the Court to introduce a measure for consideration, and to have full and free discussion thereon; that, with these amendments the existing institutions of the Colony will be well calculated to secure good government, whereas, in the present state of its population, the substitution of a Council and House of Assembly would be unsuitable and highly inexpedient."

The 48 gentlemen [1] who signed these resolutions were largely interested in British Guiana, and their opinions on any subject connected with its affairs naturally carried great weight. Earl Grey, to whom Mr. Cave forwarded the resolutions, regarded them as "generally judicious," and instructed Governor Barkly, in a despatch dated the 15th April, to lay them before the Court of Policy, adding that "the weight to which they are entitled as bearing the signatures of so large a proportion of those most deeply interested" would without doubt be duly recognized by the Court. Next day, when Lord Stanley brought forward in the House of Lords the petition entrusted to him, he was met by Earl Grey, who produced these resolutions and urged that the matter should be allowed to remain in the hands of the Government, a course to which in the circumstances of the case Lord Stanley agreed.

The resolutions of the London meeting and Earl Grey's covering despatch were laid before the Court of Policy on the 26th May, 1851; and, on the 6th June, Mr. S. Bean moved " that this Court is now prepared and willing to adopt, and to legislate upon the basis of, the resolutions now on the table, and requests His Excellency to instruct the Attorney-General to intro-

Court of Policy accepts the London Resolutions as Basis for Legislation.

[1] The resolutions were signed by Charles Cave (chairman), Jno. Crosthwaite, Thos. Porter, junr., Robt. Gardner, Henry M. Numshead, G. Anderson, Richard Davis, A. Denoon, Thos. Naghten, James Campbell, Colin Campbell, Alex. Crum, W. H. Stopford Blair, Charles S. Parker, Geo. Rainy, Geo. H. Loxdale, J. Shand, John Daniel, James Cavan, Henry Davidson, Thos. D. Hill, William Davidson, A. Colville, Mic. McChlery, Jas. Ewing, Chas. Marryat, N. S. Chancy, H. D. Baillie, H. E. Crum, W. R. Sandbach, A. G. Milne, Jno. Torrance, Jonathan Hopkinson, J. E. Baillie, John Semple, M. S. Higgins, John Moss, Adam S. Gladstone, Jas. H. Alboury, Jno. Stewart, Charles McGarel, C. Davison Kerr, Wm. King, Stephen Cave, John Kingston, Gavin Fullarton, J. B. Smith, and Thomas Bouch.

duce the necessary Ordinances accordingly." Mr. G. Booker
seconded. An amendment was then moved by Mr. P. Rose,
seconded by Mr. R. Haynes, and supported by Mr. G. Quayle,
to the following effect :

> " Whereas on the 13th June, 1850, this Court adopted
> the following resolution—' That it is the opinion of this
> Court that the legislative institutions of British Guiana
> are unsuited to the existing state of society, and it is
> desirable that they should be abolished and a House of
> Assembly and an Elective Legislative Council be estab-
> lished in their stead '; *resolved*, that this Court is now
> prepared to legislate on the basis of the above resolution,
> being the only change that would be satisfactory to the
> great majority of the inhabitants of this Colony."

This amendment was, upon division, rejected by five votes
to three; and thereafter the original motion was carried
without dissent.

Accordingly, on the 25th August, 1851, Governor Barkly
laid before the Court of Policy the draft of two measures
intended to give effect to the resolutions of the
First Attempt at Legislation fails. London meeting, namely, a bill to increase the
number of members of the College of Electors and
of the College of Financial Representatives, and draft instructions proposed to be issued by the Sovereign. The latter were
necessary because the Royal Instructions to Governor Barkly,
dated the 9th January, 1849, directed that he should " not
propose nor assent to any ordinance whatever respecting the
constitution, proceedings, numbers or mode of appointing or
electing any of the members of the Court of Policy, or of any
other body, politic or corporate, within the Colony "; and the
Governor, therefore, proposed that, in so far as the contemplated reforms affected the Court of Policy, they should be
carried out by new Royal Instructions, but that the changes
in the Colleges of Electors and of Financial Representatives
should be effected by an ordinance to be passed by the Court
of Policy itself. On the 30th September, 1851, the bill came
up for a second reading; and Mr. Rose, seconded by Mr.
Haynes, then moved " that His Excellency the Governor be
requested to withdraw the draft of Royal Instructions and the
bill submitted to the Court, and introduce a bill embracing all
the measures recommended in the resolutions " of the London

meeting. This motion was lost; and the second reading was passed by four votes to three, Mr. Booker, the acting Government Secretary (J. G. Austin), the Attorney-General (W. Arrindell), and the High Sheriff (G. Bagot) supporting the bill, and Messrs. Rose, Haynes and G. Quayle opposing it, while the Chief Justice (J. H. Bent) and Mr. S. Bean declined to vote. Subsequently, on the 1st October, Mr. Bean recorded in the minutes of the Court of Policy that his reason for declining to vote was the doubt, which he entertained, whether, if it was not competent for the Governor, in view of the Royal Instructions, to introduce a bill enlarging the membership of the Court of Policy, he was not equally prevented by the selfsame instructions from introducing a bill enlarging the numbers of " any other body, corporate or politic " within the Colony. Moreover, at a meeting of the Court of Policy on the 13th October, the three dissentient members recorded the following reasons for having voted against the second reading of the bill :

" 1st, Because the bill before the Court does not embrace the whole of the changes suggested by the resolutions of a meeting of proprietors held in London, 4th April last, and subsequently forwarded by the Right Honourable the Secretary of State for the Colonies to His Excellency the Governor :

" 2nd, Because a draft of Royal Instructions has been submitted to this Court for discussion and approval, which we conceive to be unconstitutional, to be derogatory to Her Majesty's dignity and prerogative, to be framed by this Court, and contrary to all precedent and practice.

" 3rd, Because the constitutional mode of effecting the changes in the Court of Policy, the Colleges of Electors and Financial Representatives, is by bill :

" 4th, Because the Capitulation in 1803 secured to the Court of Policy, as the Legislature of the Colony, certain rights which have been acknowledged by the Crown in various instances, and more particularly by the Commission under the Great Seal, granted 4th March, 1831, to Governor Sir Benjamin D'Urban by His late Majesty William the Fourth :

" 5th, Because we cannot recognize the right of the Crown to legislate for this Colony by Royal Instructions, as such would in effect endanger the rights and privileges possessed by, and secured to, this Court :

" 6th, Because the bill before the Court alters the mode

of electing the members of the Court of Policy; consequently the doctrine held by the Attorney-General that His Excellency is precluded by his instructions, under Signet and Sign Manual, from introducing a bill to increase the number of members of the same Court is unsound and untenable.   If His Excellency has the power to introduce a bill to alter the manner of electing a member of the Court of Policy, it is manifest he is not precluded from bringing in a bill to increase the number of its members :

" 7th, Because the amendment, moved and supported by four of the elective members of this Court, points out, as we conceive, the regular and constitutional manner of making the alterations in the constitution as suggested by the resolutions of 4th April last, forwarded by the Right Honourable the Secretary of State for the Colonies :

" 8th, Because we are ready to give our assistance in passing a bill which shall embrace all the alterations proposed in the resolutions of 4th April last, but we cannot be consenting parties to any legislation under Royal Instructions :

" 9th, Because the proposed alterations cannot become law until they first receive the sanction of Her Majesty; consequently the argument that the Royal Instructions preclude the introduction of a bill to increase the number of members of the Court of Policy appears to us to be untenable."

In view of this opposition, the Governor withdrew both the draft instructions and the bill, stating that, while he had no wish to force constitutional changes of such importance through the Court by a slender majority, chiefly composed of official members, he could not, either directly or indirectly, countenance the attempt made to impugn the prerogative, which the Crown had exercised ever since the Capitulation, of legislating for the Colony.   On the next day, the 14th October, Messrs. Rose, Haynes, Bean, and Quayle requested Governor Barkly " to address Her Majesty's Government by the earliest mail for leave to introduce a bill comprehending, in general, the alterations in the Court of Policy and the Colleges of Electors and Financial Representatives, on the basis of the resolutions of the meetings of proprietors in London on 4th April last."   The Governor accordingly reported the whole proceedings to Earl Grey in a despatch dated the 30th October.

Earl Grey's opinion was that, looking to precedent and to

the fact that so large a portion of the political and judicial institutions of the Colony rested upon the authority of Royal Orders-in-Council, and of Instructions under the Signet and Sign Manual, there could be no doubt that Governor Barkly's view of the constitutional powers of the Crown and of the Court of Policy was correct. He was, however, willing to admit that " some inconvenience would result from having the proposed changes introduced, partly by legislation in the Colony, and partly by an alteration in the Royal Instructions "; and that " it would certainly be more desirable that the whole of the new regulations as to the constitution of the Court of Policy and the Combined Court and the College of Kiezers should be contained in one instrument." He, therefore, advised the Queen expressly to invest the Court of Policy by an Order-in-Council with power to make the proposed arrangements, subject to the condition that no ordinance passed for that purpose should come into force until confirmed by Her Majesty. A Royal Order-in-Council to this effect was issued on the 26th December, 1851, granting Governor Barkly and the Court of Policy " power and authority to enact an Ordinance or Ordinances respecting the constitution, proceedings, numbers, and mode of appointing or selecting any of the members of the said Court of Policy, or of any other body politic or corporate " within the Colony, any provisions contained in the Royal Instructions of the 9th January, 1849, or in any previous Order-in-Council, notwithstanding : " provided always that every Ordinance so enacted by the said Henry Barkly and the said Court of Policy shall, for any of the purposes aforesaid, contain a clause suspending the operation thereof until Her Majesty's pleasure thereon shall be signified through one of her Principal Secretaries of State."

Earl Grey transmitted this Order-in-Council by a despatch, dated the 19th January, 1852 ; and it was laid upon the table of the Court of Policy on the 9th March, on which day a bill " to increase the number of members of the Court of Policy, of the College of Electors, and of the College of Financial Representatives " was read a first time. In moving the first reading Governor Barkly stated that, if it should be thought fit to take this opportunity for the revision of the Civil List about to expire at the end

Royal Order-in-Council of 26th December, 1851, empowers Governor Barkly and the Court of Policy to amend the Constitution.

Proposal of Permanent Civil List left in abeyance.

of the year 1854, he had reason to believe " that Her Majesty's Government would not merely be prepared to consider the question with every desire to meet the views of the colonists, but further to advise Her Majesty, concurrently with any extension that might be determined on, to confirm and vest absolutely in the Combined Court the entire functions now exercised by that body." No response was made to this suggestion, owing (as Governor Barkly wrote on the 25th March, 1852) to " a very general conviction that it would be unbecoming in the members of an expiring body to bind the Colony by conditions to this effect, and that the duty would devolve upon the newly constituted Combined Court at its first session of marking its sense of the confidence, which they thus asked Her Majesty's advisers to repose in them." Accordingly Governor Barkly suggested that the point should be met by inserting in the Royal Order-in-Council, by which the bill, when passed, would have to be confirmed, a general proviso limiting its operation to the duration of such provision for the support of the Civil Government of the Colony as might from time to time be made by the Combined Court with Her Majesty's sanction and approval.

The bill passed its second reading without opposition on the 24th March, 1852, being moved by Mr. Booker and seconded by Mr. Bean; but, on endeavouring to make further *Second Attempt at Legislation opposed during Committee Stage.* progress, Governor Barkly was met by every possible obstruction, and was at last compelled, after consenting to repeated adjournments, to go into committee upon it with only two elective members out of five, one of the number, Mr. J. Croal, a supporter of the bill, being absent in Barbados for his health's sake, and the other two, Messrs. Haynes and Quayle, purposely absenting themselves from the sittings of the Court as suggested to them by the opponents of the bill.

The first step taken by the opposition was to urge that Mr. Bean, the senior elective member, ought to vacate his *Opposition endeavour to secure Retirement from Court of Policy (a) of Mr. Bean,* seat. The point was tested in Court of Policy on the 13th April, 1852, when the Attorney-General moved: " That there is no law nor authority regulating the retirement of the elective members of this Court, except the Plan of Redress, provisionally adopted for the government of the Colony of Demerary and Essequebo in the year 1789, which enacts that ' after

Q

a lapse of two years, and afterwards yearly, during the course of the present charter, one of the Members of Policy, chosen from the colonists, shall retire; the first year the senior in rank in Essequebo, and the second year the senior in rank in Demerary, and so on, successively.'

" That the period of the year at which this retirement should take place, being in the Plan of Redress undefined, has, from time to time, been declared by various resolutions of the Court of Policy itself, according to the convenience of the public service :

" That the Court, having sanctioned the retirement of the Honourable Richard Haynes, its then senior member, in the month of January last, and having unanimously concurred with the College of Kiezers in their re-election, or return, of that Honourable Member to this Court, now declares that the provision of the Plan of Redress, already alluded to, has been satisfied, and that no other member of this Court is bound to retire during the present year."

Mr. Booker seconded this resolution, which was passed, Messrs. Haynes and Quayle alone dissenting. On the following *and* (b) *of* day Mr. Haynes, seconded by Mr. Quayle, moved *Mr. Croal.* " that it is undesirable to proceed with so important a measure as a change in the Constitution, while the chair of one of the elective members is vacant, and that this Court now requests His Excellency the Governor to issue his proclamation summoning the College of Electors to make a nomination in place of the Honourable John Croal, absent from the Colony." This motion was rejected, only the mover and seconder voting for it; and thereafter both these members left the Court. They resumed their seats, however, on *Three Peti-* the 28th April, when Mr. Haynes presented a petition *tions against* against the bill from 510 inhabitants, of whom some *the Bill re-* *jected by Court* 50 or 60 were electors, and Mr. Quayle presented a *of Policy.* petition from the Reform Association to the same effect, while a petition from the Mayor and Town Council of Georgetown was laid on the table praying the Court either to abstain from legislation upon the subject of constitutional reform until the vacant seat in the elective section had been filled, or " to recommend the adoption of the Cape Constitution." Mr. Haynes, seconded by Mr. Quayle, then moved " that the petitions be entertained and a favourable answer returned to their prayer." But all the other members voted against this motion, which was, therefore, lost.

Messrs. Haynes and Quayle now finally withdrew from the Court during the further discussion of the bill; and their *Failure of* partisans called a public meeting in the Georgetown *Public Meet-* market-place, on the 8th May, with a view of *ing to protest* openly repudiating the contemplated reforms and *against the* of appointing delegates in London, in imitation of *Bill.* the Cape Colonists, to demand full political rights. This attempt to stir up agitation on the subject failed utterly.

> " There were," wrote Governor Barkly,[1] " some twenty persons on the platform of the meeting and some two or three hundred more in the surrounding area. Of the former, a small sprinkling were respectable merchants or storekeepers, scarce any, however, possessing an acre of land in the Colony—one alone of the whole number being the owner of half a small sugar estate, purchased last year for £1,500, I believe, by himself and a brother reformer, with singular inconsistency, one would think, considering how misgoverned and ruined they consider the Colony to be. Of those in the crowd some, no doubt, were members of the congregations of the three or four London missionaries, who stood on the platform, and, as such, taught to believe themselves entitled to every political privilege; the majority, idlers, in all probability attracted by mere curiosity, or a vague expectation of better wages for less work, as formerly promised by agitators."

The *Colonist*, a newspaper which was the organ of the opposition, attributed the non-attendance of the expected multitudes to the state of the weather—a lame excuse, so far as the 30,000 inhabitants of Georgetown were concerned, because no rain fell for at least two hours before the meeting, which, moreover, was advertised to be held under cover of a new iron roof ! Subsequently a more probable cause of the failure was found in the schism, which was said to exist in the ranks of the reform party on the subject of an extension of the franchise.

This attempt to obstruct the bill having made it quite clear that the general feeling was in favour of its passing, the *Ordinance* Governor was urged by several influential parties to *No. 8 of 1852* stop further efforts at agitation by reading the bill *passed.* a third time and submitting it for Her Majesty's confirmation. About this time Mr. Croal returned to the

[1] In a despatch, dated 22nd May, 1852.

Colony and resumed his seat in the Court of Policy; and the Governor, having ascertained that Mr. Croal would support the bill, decided to pass the measure through its final stages without further delay. Accordingly the bill was read a third time on the 19th May, passed without a division being challenged, and its title settled as " an Ordinance to alter and amend the political institutions of the Colony of British Guiana " (No. 8 of 1852). Mr. Quayle absented himself on this occasion, while Mr. Haynes, who was present, contented himself with intimating his dissent and claiming his right to record his reasons therefor. At a later meeting of the Court, on the 1st June, these two members recorded in the minutes the following reasons for their dissent :

> " 1st, Because it is essential to have seven elective members in the Court of Policy to secure to the popular element its just influence, and without such addition the elective section will not possess any real power so long as His Excellency the Governor can exercise the double vote :
> " 2nd, Because it is essential to have periodical general elections of members of the Colleges of Electors and Financial Representatives, which is calculated to develop more freely the action of public opinion than elections in detail as in the bill :
> " 3rd, Because proxy voting, as intended to be practised by the College of Electors, is unwise in its principle and susceptible of being viewed with great doubt and suspicion in its operation :
> " 4th, Because the bill makes no provision for the withdrawal of His Excellency the Governor from the Combined Court, after opening the annual financial session, and the subsequent election of one of the members to act as Speaker for each session."

The ordinance itself, although it never came into operation, merits careful study. Its *1st section* was designed to carry *Description of* into effect the resolution of the 4th April, 1851, " to *its Twenty-* extend the representative principle " by the addition *seven Sections.* of a sixth elected member to the Court of Policy, thereby making the votes of the unofficial section and of the official section (when the Governor exercised his casting vote) exactly equal, but giving the unofficials a majority of one, whenever the Governor refrained from exercising his casting vote. This concession did not go far enough to please the extreme party in British Guiana, who demanded at least two additional members, " to secure to the popular element," as stated in the protest of Messrs. Haynes and Quayle, " its just influence "—a singular misapprehension of the true position of the elective section of the Court of Policy, which, apart from the concessions made for appearance sake during the reform agitation, never had represented, and never could without a radical alteration in the franchise represent, aught else than the aristocratic class, known as " the planting interest."   Mr. Croal, with a clearer perception of the real state of the case, declared his support of a seventh elective member to be conditional upon express enactment that five out of the seven members should be *bona fide* owners of sugar estates, situated within the districts they were to represent—an unnecessary precaution, under the circumstances then existing, from the point of view of the planting interest, and one by no means chiming in with the tone of the dissentient members' " protest."   Governor Barkly strongly resisted the addition of more than one elected member on the ground that, with so decided an unofficial majority against him, the Governor might be forced to become a mere puppet in the hands of the plantocracy, although all business would continue to be conducted in his name and on his responsibility.   He was willing that a fair trial should be given to the experiment of counterbalancing by an additional elective vote the Governor's preponderating authority, wielded through the exercise of the casting vote ; but he believed that to add two elected members would render the whole scheme " an impracticable absurdity, and that the immediate introduction of a Council and House of Assembly, based on a low franchise, would be a less evil than thus throwing the balance so decidedly on the other scale." [1]   He thought that the change, as projected in the ordinance, would " provide a safe mode of transition from the present system of legislation by ordinance to one in which the Representative of the Crown will simply be called upon for his formal assent to the legislative acts of the People."

Besides equalizing the power of the official and unofficial halves of the Court of Policy, the 1st section also fixed a period for the retirement of the senior elected member in each year, thus obviating the frequent controversies arising out of the

[1] Despatch, dated 8th June, 1852.

vague language of the " Plan of Redress," which provided that
the senior member should retire " yearly," a phrase to which
had been given every interpretation that party ingenuity
could from time to time suggest.   In the bill as introduced the
Governor had tried to meet the difficulty by making each
unofficial member serve three years precisely from the date of
his election; but for many reasons it was decided to be preferable to adhere to the old plan of the senior elected member
retiring in annual rotation, merely fixing the period of that
retirement for the 30th June, so as to avoid any delay for
re-election during the session of the Combined Court, which
in the usual course would have terminated before that time,
as the Tax Ordinance of each year came into operation on the
1st July.

The *2nd and 3rd sections* required the presence of five members of the College of Electors at any election of members of
the Court of Policy, and permitted the privilege of voting
without personal attendance to Electors representing the
counties of Essequebo and Berbice.   This privilege, erroneously
termed " proxy voting " in the protest of the dissentient members, was granted because, as Governor Barkly explained,
" without it the choice of members for the Court of Policy
would devolve as heretofore on the Electors living in Georgetown and its vicinity—the county of Essequebo having for
years past sent only one gentleman at irregular intervals to
represent it, whilst the county of Berbice has had no resident
representative at all."   Moreover, far from the transmission
of written votes being an innovation, as might be supposed
from the " protest," the Colleges, both of Electors and of
Financial Representatives, were elected in that manner exclusively, until *viva voce* voting at the hustings was introduced
by Governor Barkly in the year 1849.

The 3rd section also took away the power, until then enjoyed
by the Court of Policy itself, of selecting its members from a
double return made by the Electoral College; and it conceded
to the College under all circumstances the absolute right of
choice.

" This concession," wrote Governor Barkly, " was not
stipulated for; but I thought it better to proffer it,
knowing full well that the opportunity of rejecting an
obnoxious candidate, thus practically vested in the

Government, was a source of great jealousy, and generally served to convert the rejected into an open foe, even when the matter was left, as it has been invariably by myself, to the elective members; whilst the power was after all of little real value, as the College of Electors were nearly sure, when limited, of carrying their own man into the Court by coupling his name with that of somebody else so utterly unfit or objectionable, on some score or other, as to render it almost impossible for any Governor, having the good of the Colony at heart, to prefer him."

The 4th *section* enacted, in nearly the words of the London meeting's resolution, the abrogation of the Governor's right to use the veto or to interrupt at any stage the progress of proceedings in Court of Policy and in Combined Court; and it gave permission to the elective members to introduce into Court of Policy whatever measures they might consider necessary.

" The withdrawal of this veto," Governor Barkly observed, " is beyond compare the most important concession which the Crown is called upon to make in the whole Ordinance; but it must nevertheless be borne in mind that its direct interference by Order-in-Council is still contemplated, and that the exercise by its representative of this minor right of obstruction has not infrequently led to disputes with the Colonial Legislature, which, if not healed by timely concessions, could eventuate in but one result, the stoppage of the supplies, the consequences of which have generally proved almost as embarrassing to the Secretary of State as injurious to the interests of the colonists themselves. The right, on the other hand, to introduce bills will make little difference, as permission was never (so far as I am aware) refused, though rarely indeed requested."

It was provided, moreover, that the Governor should retain the right to withdraw any government measure, if he so wished, and to withhold his signature from any bill which he might consider objectionable, such bill nevertheless to be transmitted by the earliest opportunity for the consideration of Her Majesty's Government.

The 5th *section* provided for the dissolution of the existing Colleges of Electors and Financial Representatives. The 6th *section* increased the number of members of the College of

Electors from seven to eleven, and reduced their term of service from life to three years at the most, in accordance with the proposal of the London meeting. The *7th section* in like manner enlarged the College of Financial Representatives from six to ten, leaving their term of service unaltered. In both the 6th and 7th sections the Governor's right to dissolve the Colleges at pleasure was recognized. The "protest" of the dissentient members demanded in addition periodical general elections, in order to " develop more freely the action of public opinion "; but Governor Barkly was confident that in British Guiana " many years must elapse before systematic agitation of the masses on political questions will become either safe or useful."

The electoral divisions prescribed in the *8th section* were adopted from those established by Ordinance No. 15 of 1849, as also were the qualifications to vote at the election of members of either of the two Colleges. In the next sections the following representation of the electoral divisions was laid down :

| | Representatives in : | |
Description of Electoral Divisions.	College of Electors.	College of Financial Representatives.
1. The part of the County of Demerary east of the Demerary river, exclusive of the City of Georgetown .	2	2
2. The part of the County of Demerary west of the Demerary river . .	1	1
3. The City of Georgetown according to its municipal boundaries . . .	2	2
4. The part of the County of Essequebo west of the Essequebo river . .	2	1
5. The islands of the Essequebo river and the part of the County of Essequebo east of the Essequebo river .	1	1
6. The part of the County of Berbice east of the Berbice river, exclusive of the town of New Amsterdam .	1	1
7. The part of the County of Berbice west of the Berbice river . .	1	1
8. The town of New Amsterdam according to its municipal boundaries .	1	1
Total	11	10

" *Section* 13 providing a qualification for elective members of the Court of Policy is," remarked Governor Barkly,
" one of extreme importance; for the word in the Plan of
Redress translated ' colonist,' though long most strictly
construed to mean, as the Dutch Government doubtless
intended it, ' planter ' (*i.e.*, *colonus*), ' one holding a grant
of land from the Sovereign on the usual conditions of
cultivation and employment of slaves,' has of late years
lost all peculiar significance, and practically no qualification has existed save the will and pleasure of the College
of Electors. The anomaly became more glaring, when
Ordinance 15 of 1849 defined the qualification to be
possessed by members of the two Colleges, in lieu of the
exploded one of the possession of 25 slaves; and, though
the point was not mooted at the London meeting, I felt
it my duty to avail myself of the earliest opportunity to
extend the operation of that clause to the elective section
of the Court of Policy. The conservative party out here
were, however, of opinion that the possession of mere
income ought not to suffice in a Colony like this, where
so many persons—especially of the professional and mercantile class—are mere birds of passage, transferring their
allegiance as easily as their portmanteaux, or returning
to Europe directly they have realized a competency without investing a farthing in the soil; but that, on the
contrary, a high qualification, consisting of real property,
was indispensable for those entrusted with the duty of
making the laws and guiding the destinies of the
country."

Mr. Booker accordingly gave notice, during the committee
stage, of an amendment raising the qualification to " 100 acres
of land in cultivation or an income of £500 *per annum* from real
property in the Colony," and, though Governor Barkly did not
approve of so restrictive a qualification, he was obliged, as
neither Mr. Haynes nor Mr. Quayle attended to oppose the
amendment, to accept a compromise of 80 acres in cultivation or
an income of £300 *per annum* from real property in the Colony.
Even this he feared would confine the choice by the Electoral
College to but few candidates; and he believed that this part
of the law would be the first of which a modification would be
demanded.

The 14*th section* re-enacted the qualification, prescribed by
Ordinance No. 15 of 1849, for the two Colleges, with some trifling

amendments, which would admit of members being qualified by holding property of one or more descriptions in different localities, if it made up together the requisite value—a point on which some doubt had existed. *Section* 15 prevented persons from attempting to be at one and the same time electors and elected, or electors associated with the elected in Combined Court as Financial Representatives—an inconsistency which had prevailed for years under General Carmichael's proclamation of the 7th September, 1812, converting the two Colleges into one, and which was so difficult of eradication that even during Governor Barkly's tenure of office the same individual sat and voted both as a member of the College of Electors and a Financial Representative.

Sections 16 *to* 18 were adaptations of clauses in Ordinance No. 15 of 1849; and the 19*th section*, which enacted a penalty for refusing, after election, to sit or act as member of the Court of Policy or either of the Colleges, was borrowed from a " publication " by Governor Anthony Beaujon and the Court of Policy dated the 31st July, 1797.[1]

Sections 20 *and* 21 laid down rules on the subject of leave of absence to elective members and the vacating of seats, much required, as the facilities for quitting the Colony for short periods were greater than formerly, and designed to obviate the disputes which had frequently arisen on such points. The 22*nd section* formed a preface to *section* 23, by which it was proposed to change the name of " Court of Policy " into that of " Legislative Council," and the name of " Combined Court " into that of " Financial Assembly." Governor Barkly attached very considerable importance to this change, " believing with a profound writer on legislature that ' a mere change in the name of a thing is sometimes enough to change the sentiments of a nation,' " and that the change would deprive agitators of their stock invective against " the Dutch Slavish Constitution," and force them to define a little more distinctly what was meant by agitating for " a Council and House of Assembly " in the abstract and without reference to the awkward question of the elective franchise. The 24*th and* 25*th sections* were required for accommodating the unrepealed portions of Ordinance No. 15 of 1849 to the new law. *Section* 26 was the interpretation

---

[1] B. G. Laws (1870), pp. 25-6. See pp. 55-6, *supra*.

clause; and *section* 27, which was the last, suspended the operation of the whole Ordinance until allowed by Her Majesty.

It remains to notice a proposal, referred to in the " protest,"
and made while the bill was in committee, for excluding the
Governor from the Combined Court during the debate on the
annual estimates, in the same manner as he was already excused
from attendance during the framing of the Ways and Means
by the Royal Order-in-Council of the 3rd June, 1842. This
proposal was not among the recommendations of the London
meeting; but was pressed from both sides of the Court, by Mr.
Bean on the one hand and by Mr. Quayle on the other, upon
Governor Barkly, who successfully resisted it as rendering the
Combined Court virtually independent of the Governor and
enabling it to postpone its adjournments for an indefinite period,
or even to render its sessions permanent except when dissolved
by proclamation.

Meanwhile, in the United Kingdom, there had been a change
of Ministry; and it devolved upon Sir John S. Packing-
Ordinance not ton, who succeeded Earl Grey as Secretary of State
confirmed by for the Colonies, to advise Her Majesty upon the
the Crown. " Ordinance to alter and amend the political constitution of British Guiana." Her Majesty's Government, on
examining the ordinance, found in it two provisions which
they considered inadmissible; the one, that for excluding all
but planters from seats in the Legislature, as unduly favouring
that portion to the injury of other portions of the community;
the other, that for constituting the elective section a majority
in the Legislature, as unduly depriving the Crown of the
authority essential for the welfare and protection of the unrepresented classes.

" I find," wrote Sir John Packington in a despatch
dated the 13th November, 1852, " that the represented
Objections of classes, so far as they can be estimated by the
Her Majesty's number of voters, are but about 916 out of a
Government population of about 127,695. The rest of the
to the
Ordinance. population are not entitled to the franchise even
under the Ordinance of 1849, or, if some few possess the
right, they are too ignorant and indifferent to exercise it.
Thus the great bulk of the people of British Guiana are
dependent on the Crown for their political well-being, and
the Crown is their only representative in the Legislature.

To place the Crown in a minority in that body would be to deprive the people of all effective protection of their interests there, and in effect to place those interests and the Government of the Colony in the hands of a very limited body, whose interests are not always identical with those of the population at large. Her Majesty's Government cannot consent to this innovation. . . . I wish to continue in the Crown, to be cautiously exercised, and chiefly where the interests of the unrepresented classes are involved, that control over the proceedings of the Legislature which is vested in it by the constitution of the Colony. This control by the Crown, instead of being inconsistent with free representative institutions, is in reality the only means by which it is possible to impart the benefit of them to a community of which the population at large is ignorant or barbarous. The representative institutions of the mother-country become a substitute for local representative institutions; and the Crown, whilst exercising this control, is, in its turn, controlled by Parliament."

Sir John also remarked with reference to the proposed abolition of the Governor's power to forbid the introduction or stop the progress of bills :

" I think it indispensable that the same rule should prevail in the Court of Policy as in the House of Commons, and that no vote of money should be proposed except by a responsible servant of the Crown. Without this rule and this responsibility, there can be no security for rectitude and economy in financial administration."

Holding these views, Her Majesty's Government decided that the ordinance, as it stood, should not be confirmed, especially as the Civil List was due to expire on the 31st December, 1854; but Sir John stated that, if the local authorities desired " to anticipate that period and make a permanent settlement at once," and if the two objectionable provisions of the ordinance were amended, he would be ready to meet them on that ground.

"I am certainly of opinion," he ended, " that such a settlement cannot be too soon concluded, since it is far from being a fitting or an economical arrangement for the Colony that the salaries of its principal officers should rest upon an uncertain foundation; and nothing would contribute more to efficiency and frugality in the public service than a permanent Civil List based upon a permanent provision of revenue."

Ordinance No. 8 of 1852 was, in these circumstances, not confirmed by Her Majesty, and, therefore, never came into operation.

Governor Barkly laid Sir John Packington's despatch before the Court of Policy on the 7th January, 1853, when he was asked by Mr. A. D. V. Gon Netscher what action, if any, the Government proposed to take. The Governor replied that, if it was the wish of the Court, he would re-introduce the bill, omitting the points objected to by Her Majesty's Government. After some conversation, Mr. Haynes suggested that the despatch should be printed for the use of members and taken into consideration on a future day. This course was agreed to, and thereafter the question of constitutional reform fell into abeyance. Neither did anything come of the suggestion that the Civil List should be permanently secured; for by Ordinance No. 5 of 1853 the Civil List was renewed for a term of seven years only, the period for which it had been voted on the two previous occasions. In forwarding this Ordinance to the Secretary of State, Governor Barkly explained [1] that, knowing how averse the colonists were from parting irrevocably with what they believed to be one of their dearest privileges, and perceiving himself not only no objection to, but a positive advantage to be derived—in the transitional state of the Colony—from extending the provisional arrangement both as to the Civil List and as to the powers of Combined Court, he did not deem it prudent to stand out for a permanent Civil List at the risk of getting none at all.

Sir John Packington's Suggestion that the Civil List should be made Permanent not entertained.

(b) *Ordinance No. 19 of 1855.*

No further steps were taken in the matter by Governor Barkly during the remainder of his term of office. Mr. W. Walker, the Government Secretary, who was Administrator from the 11th May, 1853, until the government was assumed by Mr. P. E. Wodehouse on the 23rd March, 1854, did not take it up; and so completely had all interest in reform of the constitution died

Question of Constitutional Reform revived in 1854.

[1] Despatch, dated 4th May, 1853.

away that the new Governor was scarcely aware that any such problem was still unsolved, when at a meeting of the Court of Policy on the 17th November, 1854, Mr. J. E. Roney, an elected member, gave notice of his intention to ask the following questions:

> " 1st, Whether His Excellency has received from either Her Majesty's present or late Secretary of State for the Colonies any instructions on the subject of an alteration in the Constitution of this Court and of the Colleges of Electors and Financial Representatives?
>
> " 2nd, If His Excellency can inform this Court whether it is the intention of Her Majesty's present Government to confirm Ordinance No. 8 of the year 1852, entitled ' An Ordinance to alter and amend the political institutions of the Colony of British Guiana,' as passed by this Court on the 19th May, 1852?
>
> " 3rd, Whether, in the event of Her Majesty's present Government being determined not to confirm Ordinance No. 8 of the year 1852, His Excellency is in a position to hold out to the inhabitants of this Colony any hope that some modification of the said Ordinance, or that some other Ordinance of a similar character and description, is likely to be favourably considered by Her Majesty's Government; and whether in such case, His Excellency is in a position to point out or suggest in what particular Ordinance No. 8 of 1852 may be considered to require alteration and amendment? "

Governor Wodehouse forwarded a copy of these questions to Sir George Grey,[1] the Secretary of State for the Colonies, and pointed out that the clause in Sir Henry Barkly's instructions, revoked by the Royal Order-in-Council of the 26th November, 1851, had been inserted *verbatim* in his own instructions, and that he was, therefore, peremptorily restrained from introducing any measure relative to the constitution of the Colony.

> " I have not the slightest desire," he wrote, " needlessly to revive discussions upon a subject of this character; but it is very possible that some useful modifications might be effected with advantage at a time when there is an entire absence of political excitement or irritation, and I would, therefore, venture to recommend that the per-

[1] Despatch, dated 24th November, 1854.

mission given to Sir Henry Barkly should without delay be
conceded to myself."

Governor Wodehouse at the same time asked to be favoured
with an expression of the views of Her Majesty's Government
upon some of the most important questions raised in the
previous correspondence, and drew special attention to four
points—namely, (a) the proposal, assented to by Earl Grey
but rejected by Sir John Packington, that one more elected
member should be added to the Court of Policy, where thus
in addition to the abolition of the Governor's veto, there would
be established a majority of elective members over the officials
including the Governor; (b) the proposal that only persons
possessing certain immovable property, or in other words the
planters, should be qualified to sit in the Court of Policy;
(c) whether the members of the Court of Policy should not,
like the Financial Representatives, be returned by the direct
votes of the electoral body, and the College of Electors be
abolished ? (d) whether, in view of the fact that, since Sir John
Packington's despatch was written, a Civil List for a limited
period, expiring on the 31st December, 1861, had been granted
by the Combined Court and accepted by Her Majesty, it would
still be the wish of the Queen's Government to make their
assent to a reform of the Colony's constitution conditional upon
the establishment of a permanent revenue ?

Pending Sir George Grey's reply, Governor Wodehouse
stated in answer to Mr. Roney's questions, at a meeting of the
Discussion in Court of Policy on the 4th December, 1854, that he
Court of had received no instructions from Her Majesty's
Policy. Government and could not, therefore, say whether
Her Majesty would be prepared to confirm Ordinance No. 8
of 1852, or not ; and that, in any case, as the prohibition to deal
with the constitution of the Colony, contained in Governor
Barkly's instructions and repealed by the Order-in-Council of
the 26th November, 1851, had been revived to its full extent
in the instructions furnished to himself, he was not in a position,
even if it were desirable, to introduce into the Court of Policy
any bill relating to this matter.   He added that he had referred
to the Secretary of State for instructions.   Mr. Roney replied
that he certainly would not press for any action in the matter
until an expression of opinion came from the public, or the

views of Her Majesty's Government were known; and he acknowledged that he believed himself to stand alone in this matter.   Mr. T. Porter and Mr. R. Smith, two elective members, expressed regret that the questions had been put, and deprecated any political agitation.   The discussion then dropped; and Governor Wodehouse, in reporting to Sir George Grey what had taken place, observed [1] that the Court of Policy was by no means disposed to encourage a revival of the question of constitutional reform, in which the inhabitants generally seemed to take very little interest.

There were no less than six Secretaries of State for the Colonies [2] during the year 1855; and Mr. Sidney Herbert, who took Sir George Grey's place for about a month,

Royal Order-in-Council of 28th February, 1855, empowers Governor Wodehouse and Court of Policy to amend the Constitution.
replied in a despatch dated the 16th February that, looking to the entire absence of popular excitement on the subject of the Colony's constitution, he saw no necessity for taking the matter into consideration. A Royal Order-in-Council was, however, made on the 28th February, 1855, in terms similar to that of the 26th December, 1851, empowering Governor Wodehouse and the Court of Policy to make such changes in the constitution of British Guiana as might be desirable, provided that every ordinance passed for this purpose should contain a clause suspending its operation until Her Majesty's pleasure was made known.   Sir George Grey [2] forwarded this Order-in-Council, in a despatch dated the 7th March, 1855, to Governor Wodehouse, who laid it before the Court of Policy on the 16th August, 1855, on which day the Attorney-General (Mr. R. R. Craig), by direction of the Governor, introduced and moved the first reading of a bill " to amend

Reasons prompting Governor Wodehouse to introduce a Bill into Court of Policy amending the Constitution:
the constitution of the Legislature of British Guiana."   Nothing had occurred in the meanwhile to disturb the political tranquillity of the Colony, nor had Governor Wodehouse obtained the Secretary of State's approval for the introduction of this bill.   But, as he explained to the Court of Policy

[1] Despatch, dated 16th December, 1854.

[2] Their dates of appointment were as follows : (a) 1854, June 10, Sir George Grey, Bart.; (b) 1855, February, Mr. Sidney Herbert; (c) 1855, March, Sir George Grey, Bart.; (d) 1855, May 15, Lord John Russell; (e) 1855, July 21, Sir William Molesworth, Bart.; (f) 1855, November 17, Mr. Henry Labouchere.

on the occasion of the first reading of the bill, as well as to Sir William Molesworth in a subsequent despatch,[1] he was actuated by three principal reasons—namely, the increasing difficulty of filling vacancies in the Court of Policy, the uncertainty of the relations subsisting between the fiscal and executive authorities, and the inconvenient limitation by which the Combined Court was precluded from providing supplies for more than one year at a time.

Owing to the gradual diminution in the number of estates' proprietors resident in the Colony, and to the fact that many of

(a) Difficulty of Filling Vacancies in Court of Policy;

those who remained were compelled by the pressure of the times to superintend in person the management of their properties, it had become increasingly difficult, under the exclusive qualification of landed property, to find gentlemen able and willing to devote any considerable portion of their time to the transaction of public business in the Court of Policy.   Moreover, a very genuine impression existed that the mode of election in itself had a tendency to deter eligible persons from serving, and that men would feel a greater pride in being members of the Court of Policy if elected by the direct vote of their fellow-colonists instead of being nominated by seven Kiezers.   Many nominees had endeavoured to get themselves excused; and by a curious coincidence, on the very day on which the new bill to amend the constitution was introduced, an incident of this kind occurred.   The College of Electors had returned Mr. John Gordon and Mr. Richard Haynes as fit and proper persons to be appointed members of the Court of Policy in the room of Mr. Mungo Campbell, who had left the Colony; and, on the 15th August, 1855, Mr. Gordon was unanimously elected by the Court of Policy. Next day, however, a letter from him was read to the Court, in which he wrote that recent inundations had thrown so much loss and labour upon him that he begged to be excused from accepting the position.   The Court, nevertheless, ordered that the excuse could not be accepted, " as it would inevitably lead to great public inconvenience "; and, much against his will, Mr. Gordon was obliged to take his seat in the Court.

Next, as to the uncertainty of the relations subsisting between

---

[1] Despatch, dated 19th September, 1855.

R

the fiscal and executive authorities, Governor Wodehouse

(b) *Uncertainty of relations between Fiscal and Executive Authorities;* explained that, during the past session of Combined Court, the first at which he had been present, he made it his business to watch the course of proceedings narrowly, and became convinced that it was impossible to define with any degree of certainty the rights of the Court. At any moment, he believed, the Court might have been involved, either by accident or by design, in a question of privilege of the most embarrassing nature; and the Governor was at all times liable to be put in the position either of inadvertently restraining the Court from the exercise of a power, to which it might be held to have a fair claim, or of incurring the displeasure of Her Majesty's Government for making undue concessions. Lord John Russell had well described the real condition of affairs in a recent despatch.[1]

" The history of the Colony," he wrote, " since its conquest, shows the effect of its constitution is to produce compromises between the Governor for the time being and the two legislative, and partially representative, bodies, by which the Governor gains the object of the moment and the two bodies make permanent encroachments on the powers of the Crown. So often as it has become a duty or a necessity on the part of the Crown to withstand the wishes of the colonists on some important question—that of slave melioration, for instance, or that of immigration (which may now again lead to difficulties), or the sugar duty question—the result of the encroachments of the preceding years has been felt in an assertion by the colonists of rights, not recognized by the Crown or by law, and in a stoppage of supplies, with great loss to the Colony and injury to agriculture and commerce. This has in each instance been terminated in an arrangement for a term of years, by which the extreme constitutional powers of the Crown have been placed in abeyance, whilst the Crown has secured to itself, in terms at least, as much power as it is perhaps expedient it should exercise. But then again has recommenced the same process of encroachment and local compromise, by which the Governor for the time being and the representative bodies work together with advantage, as I believe, to the current administration of affairs, but with a tendency to the renewal of

[1] Despatch, dated 31st May, 1855.

great public mischief on the next occasion on which the Crown shall be compelled to come into collision with its colonists."

Lastly, it had been held that any act or resolution of the Combined Court was valid for one year only, and that only once in each year could the Combined Court provide Ways and Means for the public service.   The effect was to throw doubt upon all their financial proceedings; for arrangements entered into with the assent of the Combined Court at one annual session had been liable to be reversed or modified by the succeeding Court. Furthermore, the taxes had, under such a system, necessarily been imposed from year to year, to the great detriment of trade as well as of the public revenue.

(c) Inconvenience of Voting Supplies for One Year only.

" Each year," wrote Governor Wodehouse,[1] " it becomes necessary to have recourse to expedients for postponing to the latest day any alteration of duties, with a view to preventing speculation; and yet, as might be expected, the contemplated changes ooze out by degrees. This perpetual fluctuation is, moreover, a great bar to the maintenance of a fair and reasonable scheme of taxation."

Upon these three reasons Governor Wodehouse relied to justify the propriety of making an attempt to bring about a more satisfactory arrangement; and he further considered that the time for making the attempt was very favourable.   The Civil List had recently been settled for seven years ending on the 31st December, 1861.[2] There was no active ill-feeling in the Colony upon any subject. There was no organized party in the Legislature or out of it. The Governor, therefore, thought " that it would be a positive neglect of duty to omit to take advantage of such a state of affairs, in order that, if at any future day troubles should again arise, we might in dealing with them be freed from the additional embarrassment of uncertain relations between the different bodies composing the government of the Colony." [3]

Moment Opportune for Constitutional Legislation.

There was no opposition to the first reading of Governor

---

[1] Despatch, dated 19th September, 1855.
[2] Ordinance No. 5 of 1853.
[3] Governor's despatch, dated 19th September, 1855.

Wodehouse's bill on the 16th August, 1855, nor to the second reading on the 3rd September, 1855. The considera-

Description of Chief Provisions of Ordinance No. 19 of 1855. tion of the bill in committee began on the following day, the unofficial members of the Court being Messrs. J. E. Roney, R. Smith, T. Porter, G. L. Luckie, and J. Gordon; and it is interesting to examine in detail this second abortive attempt at constitutional reform.

The *1st and 2nd sections* show that there was, this time, no intention of altering either the designation of the existing bodies politic or the composition and equipoise of numbers in the official and unofficial sections of the Court of Policy.

By the *3rd section*, which reconstituted the Combined Court, the number of Financial Representatives was increased from six to ten. This change was one of those contemplated in Ordinance No. 8 of 1852, and not then objected to by Sir John Packington. It was, in Governor Wodehouse's opinion, " of little real consequence "; and the impression was that it would give additional strength to the popular party.

The *4th section* provided that, in the Court of Policy, the Governor with any five members should form a quorum for the despatch of business; and that, in the Combined Court, the Governor with any ten members should be a quorum. The concluding paragraph of the 4th section was of considerable importance, as it virtually abolished the Governor's privilege of voting twice in the event of an equality of votes. In the Ordinance of 1852 there had been a provision for adding one elective member to the Court of Policy and thus giving a majority to the elective section of that body. This was, however, objected to by Sir John Packington, who held the view that, the number of voters in the whole population being exceedingly small, the great bulk of the people were dependent for their political well-being upon the Crown, as their only representative in the legislature, and that to place the Crown in a minority in the Court of Policy would be to deprive the people of all effective protection of their interests by that body. Accordingly in the reform bill, as introduced by Governor Wodehouse,[1] the privilege of the Governor's casting vote was retained; but during the committee stage, on the 6th September, Mr. Luckie urged that this privilege should be surrendered, as

[1] *Royal Gazette*, 18th August, 1855.

the exercise of the Governor's double vote was much disliked and conferred, in his opinion, no real power on the executive government.   Several elective members having expressed their concurrence with Mr. Luckie, Governor Wodehouse stated that he did not consider the possession of the double vote to be of any practical value, but that Her Majesty's Government might take a different view.   He, however, agreed to add to section 4 the following words : " The Governor and each member of the said Courts [1] shall be entitled to a vote upon any motion made in the said Courts respectively ; and, in the event of the votes being equal, the motion shall be declared lost."   The effect of this amendment was that in the Court of Policy the Governor could not coerce the elective members, nor could he be coerced by them ; while in the Combined Court the elective section so far outnumbered the official members that the Governor's vote seldom affected a division.

The *5th section* provided that the Governor, whenever it appeared to him necessary, might by proclamation convene sessions of the Court of Policy and of the Combined Court, and prorogue or adjourn either of the Courts ; that either of the Courts might also be adjourned on motion by any member, if carried ; and that at least one session of the Court of Policy should be held in each quarter, and at least one session of the Combined Court in each year.

The *6th section* gave to all members of the Court of Policy the right of introducing bills and having a discussion upon them, without the previous consent of the Governor ; and it provided that " all laws for the management and good government of the Colony " should be enacted by the Governor and Court of Policy ; while *section 7* declared that the Court of Policy should also form a Council of Advice for the Governor in the administration of the affairs of the Colony.   The *8th section* required that " all laws for authorizing the expenditure of public money " should be enacted by the Combined Court : and it carried out to the fullest extent the provision which Sir John Packington had stated to be indispensable—namely, that all expenditure of public money should originate with the executive government.[2]   No opposition whatever was offered

---

[1] *I.e.*, the Court of Policy and the Combined Court.
[2] Sir J. Packington's despatch, dated 13th November, 1852.

to this proposal, which the elective members recognized to be for the real benefit of the Colony. They even rendered the section more strict than in the bill as introduced, by prohibiting motions for the increase of any money-vote without the Governor's consent.[1]

The *9th section* granted freedom of debate to the members of the Combined Court in respect of ordinances for raising taxes; and the *10th section* put an end to the Governor's right of veto, as had previously been proposed by section 4 of the 1852 Ordinance.

Sections 11 to 15 laid down the rules under which the annual expenditure was in future to be voted and the Ways and Means provided.[2] When the elective members gave their attention to the proposals for getting rid of the annual Tax Ordinance

[1] Section 8, as passed, read: "All Ordinances for authorizing the expenditure of public money shall be enacted by the Combined Court, and shall be introduced by or by direction of the Governor; and no member of the said Combined Court may introduce any bill for any such purpose, or propose any item, *or the increase of any item*, of expenditure, except by direction or with the consent of the Governor." The words in italics were inserted in the bill during committee stage, on the 4th September, 1855, on the motion of Mr. J. Gordon seconded by Mr. R. Smith.

[2] Section 14, to which strong objection was afterwards taken by Her Majesty's Government, was proposed by Mr. J. E. Roney during committee stage, on the 17th September, 1855, and agreed to without division. It read: "If, on or before the 30th day of June in each and every year, the Combined Court shall not have passed any resolutions of supply or any bill introduced under the provisions of the preceding section, or if the Governor shall not, at said date, have signified his assent to any ordinance which may have been passed during the same session for imposing, abolishing, altering, reducing or increasing any duty or tax which may be leviable under any law or ordinance to be enacted after the taking effect hereof, then and in any such case all duties and taxes leviable under any ordinance to be enacted after the taking effect hereof, shall, as from and after the said 30th day of June in such year, cease to be levied and collected; but such duties and taxes shall again become payable if, at any time during the continuance of the ordinance imposing the same, a bill shall be introduced into and passed by the Combined Court in manner hereinbefore provided; and if at any time any ordinance for imposing, abolishing, altering, reducing or increasing any duty or tax, which may be leviable under any law or ordinance to be enacted after the taking effect hereof, after having been duly assented to by the Governor, shall be disallowed by Her Majesty, then and in such case all duties and taxes, leviable as aforesaid under any ordinance to be enacted after the taking effect hereof, shall, from and after the expiration of thirty days from the date of the proclamation in the Colony of such disallowance, cease to be levied and collected until satisfactory arrangements shall be made for the general taxation of the Colony."

and substituting more permanent arrangements, they became alarmed at the idea of parting with the means of coercing the Government year by year. They were not satisfied with the system of annually voting the supplies; but they held that, if the Tax Ordinance were made permanent, the Governor would find means of making use of the revenue at his own will. The ordinance of 1855, therefore, prescribed the following course. The Governor was to submit annually the estimate of expenditure and obtain the necessary resolutions of supply. He was then to submit a scheme of Ways and Means; and, if it was founded upon existing Tax Ordinances, and the Court did not think it necessary to alter them, the Ways and Means would be granted accordingly, and a bill would be introduced for giving the form of law to the resolutions of supply. If, however, no bill of supply was passed, or if the Governor refused his assent to any alteration of the Tax Ordinance carried by the Combined Court, then the taxes in force were after a certain time to cease to be levied, until the dispute could be adjusted. Similarly, if the Sovereign should disallow any ordinance for altering a Tax Ordinance, the taxes leviable under the unaltered Tax Ordinance would after a given time cease to be levied. In short, the Combined Court would retain the power, which the electives so highly prized, of stopping supplies. It is, however, interesting to note that the task of providing a scheme of Ways and Means, which had previously been left altogether in the hands of the elective members of the Combined Court, would, at the suggestion of the electives themselves, have been devolved by the new law upon the Governor.

The 16th *section* enacted that ordinances should remain in force until disallowed by the Sovereign. This was not in accord with the Royal Instructions, which declared that, in the absence of the signification of Her Majesty's pleasure within two years, an ordinance should be null and void. But it was preferable, Governor Wodehouse urged, that the Sovereign's pleasure with respect to colonial ordinances should in each case be openly expressed, and that disapproval should not merely be inferred from prolonged silence.

The 17th *section* required that all sums authorized by law to be paid out of the public revenue should be paid out by the authority of the Governor, and not otherwise.

Section 18 abolished the College of Electors. Upon the propriety of this change there was the greatest unanimity of opinion, one member only, Mr. Gordon, expressing dissent; and Governor Wodehouse wrote that he was not aware of any other dissentient in the Colony.

> " There is nothing rash," he observed, " in the character of the change. It is not proposed to transfer the right of electing members of the Court of Policy to a new body of electors to be created for the purpose, but to give that right to the electoral body, which has existed since 1849, by which the College of Electors themselves as well as the Financial Representatives have been elected, and who have in no manner whatever shown themselves unworthy of the trust."

The 19*th and* 20*th sections* set out the procedure for constituting the new Court of Policy and Combined Court, in the event of the ordinance being confirmed; while *sections* 21 *and* 22 governed the qualifications of members of the Court of Policy and of Financial Representatives. In the ordinance of 1852 it had been proposed that landed proprietors only should, as before, be eligible for the Court of Policy; but Sir John Packington had held that such a proposal favoured the planters unduly, to the injury of other portions of the community. In the new law, therefore, the qualification for elected members of the Court of Policy was made the same as that which had, since 1849, been required for Financial Representatives, and under which persons possessing a prescribed amount of property of any description were eligible. Governor Wodehouse was satisfied that there was no necessity for different qualifications.

> " In the Court of Policy," he wrote, " there are now one barrister, one merchant, and three planters. There is not, nor is there likely to be, any difference in the social status of the two sets of members; but I ought perhaps to explain that those members of the Court of Policy who are not by their calling planters, are at present obliged to acquire a landed qualification."

Section 23 made clergymen, schoolmasters and catechists ineligible for membership of the Court of Policy or as Financial Representatives. *Sections* 24 *to* 26 prescribed the apportionment of representation between the different parts of the

Colony and followed as far as possible the lines of Ordinances No. 15 of 1849 and No. 8 of 1852.

The *27th section* enacted that the Financial Representatives should vacate their seats at the end of two years and the elective members of the Court of Policy at the end of three years.   It also empowered the Governor at any time to declare all elective seats both in Court of Policy and in Combined Court vacant, with a view to a general election.   Previously there had been no dissolution, but individual members had vacated their seats periodically.   This course of proceeding was retained in the original draft of Governor Wodehouse's bill; but, as the members of the Court expressed a wish for establishing a system of general elections, he did not resist the alteration.

The remaining clauses call for no special comment, save that by *section* 36 " the Plan of Redress, the Publication of the 21st day of June in the year 1796, the Publication of the 31st day of July in the year 1797, the Proclamation of the 31st day of July in the year 1831, the Order-in-Council of the 3rd day of June in the year 1842, the 3rd, 4th, 5th, 6th, and 7th sections of the Ordinance No. 15 of the year 1849, and the Ordinance No. 2 of 1850 " were to be repealed.   The *38th section*, which was the last, suspended the operation of the new law pending the signification of Her Majesty's pleasure.

The bill was read a third time on the 18th September, 1855, passed without opposition, and its title settled to be " an *Governor* Ordinance to alter and amend the Political In-*Wodehouse* stitutions of British Guiana " (No. 19 of 1855). *considers the* *Ordinance* On the following day it was transmitted for the *satisfactory.* signification of Her Majesty's pleasure.   In the covering despatch [1] Governor Wodehouse wrote that the ordinance had been conceived in the spirit of the recommendation of the Parliamentary Committee of 1849,[2] but with a due regard to the practical efficiency and independence of the executive government; that it had been discussed freely and fully, but without the slightest exhibition of animosity; that it had been passed as a whole without one dissentient voice and gave " satisfaction generally out of doors "; and that he believed it to be calculated, if confirmed, to save the Colony in future from trouble and confusion.

[1] Despatch, dated 19th September, 1855.   [2] Parl. Paper 297 of 1849.

Her Majesty's Government, however, saw two insuperable objections to the confirmation of this ordinance—namely, the abolition of the Governor's casting vote in the Court of Policy, and the fact that the proposed financial arrangements left nearly all the supplies in any year liable to a sudden cessation on the occurrence of a momentary difficulty in the Combined Court. Mr. Wodehouse had endeavoured to draw a distinction between abrogating the Governor's casting vote and the measure, formerly objected to by Sir John Packington, of adding one to the number of elective members in the Court of Policy. But Mr. Labouchere, to whom as Secretary of State for the Colonies it fell to advise Her Majesty upon the subject, did not regard this distinction as having any practical significance, because the Governor, so long as he had the power of disallowing laws, would on either plan have a power tantamount to that of preventing their enactment.

Her Majesty's Government object to the Ordinance : (a) because it abolished Governor's Casting Vote in Court of Policy ;

"It may be," wrote Mr. Labouchere,[1] "that the Governor rarely, if ever, exercises his power of carrying a law against the opinion of the whole of the elective members; and it may not be easy to foresee any circumstances in which he is likely to exercise it; but I have no hesitation in avowing my opinion that in a Colony, where the constituencies amount only to one thousand persons and the population to 130,000, the power of the Crown is to be guarded with jealousy, as being itself the guardian of popular rights and interests. The Crown is the only representative of the people at large and is bound to maintain its own rights as involving theirs. With these views, I do not hold myself to be at liberty to part with any portion of the acknowledged powers of the Crown in British Guiana, unless there should be some plain and strong reason for deeming the power in question to be injurious to the public interest, and in the present case I can see no reason for parting with the Governor's double vote, since if, as alleged, it is never used, it can be no grievance to any class of the colonists."

If, however, it was the wish of the colonists, not so much to abate the power of the Crown in the Court of Policy, as to prevent its being used by local factions, which might happen at

[1] Despatch, dated 16th February, 1856.

one time or another to prevail with the local government, Mr. Labouchere professed himself to be willing to promote such an object; and he thought that it would be fully accomplished by providing in the Governor's instructions that, in any case in which an ordinance was carried by the Governor's double vote, such ordinance (unless of a very pressing character) should be reserved so as not to take effect until her Majesty's pleasure upon it had been signified. The decision would thus be removed from all local influence of a partial nature, and the elective members of the Court of Policy would have an opportunity of appealing to Her Majesty's Government against the confirmation of any law of which they might not approve.

To the 14th section of the ordinance Mr. Labouchere had a still stronger objection.

(b) because its Financial Arrangements left Supplies in any Year Liable to Sudden Cessation.

" There is," he observed,[1] " no doubt, an actual power in the Combined Court to refuse to perform the functions entrusted to it by the constitution of the Colony; and it has been found that the constitution has provided no method of compelling it to vote the supplies or of securing the performance of that function by any other authority. There exists, therefore, a power of stopping the supplies, and a possibility that they *may be* stopped, and that either prolonged confusion may ensue, or that the intervention of Parliament may be required to remedy the existing defects in the constitution. It is, however, one thing to acknowledge this power and this possibility to exist, and another and quite a different thing to prepare and make legal provision for a neglect of duty so unconstitutional, and for so extravagant an exercise of privilege. Though I am quite willing to believe that the provisions of the 14th section of this ordinance were not designed for that purpose, they do in reality prepare the way by legal enactment for arriving at a state of anarchy such as under a constitutional system of government is only contemplated as the last result of extreme collisions. But there is, in addition, this insuperable objection to the proposed enactment, that it is so framed as to expose the public interests to a disastrous condition of anarchy and confusion, even under circumstances in which no deliberate intention to produce such a result might exist in any quarter. This danger arises from the provision which is made that

[1] Despatch, dated 16th February, 1856.

the levy of taxes should cease from a particular date, the 30th June, in each year, unless the Combined Court should by that time have passed resolutions of supply or a bill founded on such resolutions, and unless the Governor should have assented to any ordinance which might have been passed during the same session for imposing, abolishing, altering, reducing or increasing any duty or tax leviable under future ordinances. Not only would this enactment make every question of taxation, however small, produce a suspension of the whole levy of revenue in the Colony so long as a difference of opinion should last, but it might enable any party, which could throw delay in the way of the resolutions or the bill, to bring about a lapse of the duties, even contrary to the deliberate intention of the Combined Court. If a large proportion of the present taxes of the Colony be, as possibly they may be, subject to some such contingencies by mere omission of the Combined Court to impose them before a certain day in each year, this is a state of things much to be deprecated; and the enactment, which is required, is an enactment, not to declare and confirm this practice, but to amend it. If the notion exists, founded on general practice, that the Combined Court cannot impose taxes for a longer period than one year, it would be very desirable to invest the Combined Court with that power, which, of course, it would be at liberty to exercise or not as it pleased; but this ordinance, as it stands, appears to me to give no stability to the existing system of taxation, but rather to aggravate the present amount of uncertainty and instability."

In point of form, Mr. Labouchere noted that there was objection to the 36th section, which assumed to repeal the *Objections in* Royal Order-in-Council of the 3rd June, 1842, and *Point of Form to Sections 16* to the 16th section, which, contrary to the Royal *and 36.* Instructions under the Signet and Sign Manual, provided that laws passed thereafter by the Court of Policy or the Combined Court should remain in force unless disallowed. No doubt the power to enact these sections had been assumed by the Court of Policy as derived from the Royal Order-in-Council of the 28th February, 1855, granting to the Governor and Court of Policy the necessary powers to make such changes in the constitution of the Colony as the Governor might think desirable, provided that the ordinances passed for the purpose should contain a suspending clause. But it was material, said

Mr. Labouchere, that the authority under which such provisions were enacted by the Governor and Court of Policy should appear upon the face of the ordinance, and that such ordinances should not wear the appearance of proceeding from an authority inherent in the Governor and Court of Policy. The Royal Order-in-Council of the 28th February, 1855, should, therefore, have been recited in the ordinance as conveying the authority thus exercised.

Mr. Labouchere further remarked that, as Ordinance No. 19 of 1855 was not accompanied by any provision of per-

Mr. Labouchere outlines the Permanent Fiscal Arrangements acceptable to Her Majesty's Government. manent salaries for the Governor, the Judges, the Government Secretary, the Attorney-General, and the Stipendiary Magistrates, it would (if sanctioned) satisfy only a temporary purpose, leaving, as before, the ultimate adjustment of the respective powers of the Crown and of the local bodies politic to be

effected, at the end of the subsisting period of the Civil List, by the authority of Parliament or otherwise as might be found practicable.

" Her Majesty's Government have no disposition," he wrote, " to prolong a system of compromises and of Civil Lists for terms of years. On the contrary, they think it very desirable that such a system should be brought to an end as soon as conveniently may be, and that the powers which it is for the welfare of the people that the Crown should possess, and those which it is proper that (in a Colony affording such very limited constituencies) the representative bodies should exercise, should be definitively ascertained and prescribed by competent authority. I will proceed, therefore, to point out to you what Her Majesty's Government consider to be the substantial bases on which such an arrangement ought to rest. They do not consider that the Crown is in any way bound to maintain at a particular amount the salaries of government functionaries, excepting that of the Governor, and those appropriated to certain services peculiarly connected with the interests of the great unrepresented mass of the population. With regard to salaries in general, they are satisfied that the local authorities ought to be entrusted with the duty of fixing their amount and reducing them, when thought proper, prospectively on condition that the existing interests of parties who have accepted office on the present footing are equitably preserved.   It appears to them that the power of the Governor is quite sufficient to prevent any sudden or rash reduction of salaries, without pledging the Colony or the Crown to their maintenance as matter of compact.   But they consider that the Crown is bound to preserve that essential principle of good government, that the most important classes of public services, at whatever amount the salaries belonging to them may be fixed, should be permanently secured by enactment, and not left to be placed on the annual estimates.   Upon this principle the Crown and Parliament have acted of late years, in fixing what are commonly, but rather loosely, termed ' Civil Lists ' in colonies, when their form of constitution has been modified. They have not generally insisted on the maintenance of particular amounts, but on making such amounts unalterable except by act of the Legislature.   The outlines of the arrangement which I have to propose would, therefore, be as follows :

" That, instead of the present renewable Civil List, an ordinance or ordinances should be passed, fixing permanently the salaries and necessary establishments of the Governor, Judges, Attorney-General, Secretary to Government, and Stipendiary Magistrates.   These ordinances, like other laws, would, of course, be subject to alteration by the Legislature which passed them.   But it should be established by the Governor's instructions that any ordinance diminishing the salaries of existing incumbents of office, provided for by a former ordinance, or diminishing prospectively the salary of the Governor or of the Stipendiary Magistrates (officers whose duties peculiarly concern the unrepresented classes of the people) shall contain a suspending clause or be otherwise reserved for the sanction of the Crown. Ordinances altering in any other manner the provisions of the Civil List, to be dealt with by the Governor, like other ordinances at his discretion.

" A small proportion of the colonial revenue would be required to meet the expenditure for the permanent salaries : but to render the officers really independent, and the salaries more than nominally secure, it would be further necessary that this small portion of revenue should accrue from sources permanently established by law.   All the other establishments and the expenditure of the Colony (not including, of course, the disbursements in liquidation of the interest and principal of the public debt, which are already regulated by law) I should be quite willing to leave to the discretion of the Combined Court."

Mr. Labouchere accordingly instructed Governor Wodehouse to ascertain whether the Court of Policy would be prepared to *"Portuguese* co-operate in the enactment of a measure of con-*Riots" of* stitutional reform, free from the serious objections *1856 prevent* *Reconsidera-* which Her Majesty's Government had to Ordinance *tion of Con-* No. 19 of 1855; and to consider whether those *stitutional* *Questions.* alterations in the constitution to which Her Majesty's Government had no objection, and on some of which they placed a high value, could not be combined with a permanent arrangement of the Civil List question.   However, in February, 1856, serious riots broke out in British Guiana as the result of a strong feeling of hostility, which had long existed on the part of the Creole labouring population, towards the Portuguese generally and the Portuguese shopkeepers in particular.   This feeling vented itself in active violence owing to the excitement occasioned by the fanatical ravings of a man named John Sayers Orr, who had previously, both in Scotland and in the United States of America, under the soubriquet of the " Angel Gabriel," caused riots attended with loss of life.   At first he confined himself to reproaching the Creole population with idleness, and to emphasizing the industry and success of the Portuguese; but he soon launched out into bitter invectives against all Roman Catholics, and still further excited the people by denouncing the Portuguese as foreigners who had come to the Colony to take the bread out of their mouths.   He was at length arrested; but the evil had been already done; and, on the very day of his arrest, disturbances broke out which rapidly spread to nearly every part of the Colony.   Property to the value of about $270,000 was destroyed and several lives were lost.   Energetic measures were taken to suppress the riots, and order was soon restored; but Governor Wodehouse considered the moment inopportune for the further discussion of constitutional questions, and he saw no hope that the Court of Policy would be induced to meet the views of Her Majesty's Government by amending Ordinance No. 19 of 1855.   He reported in this sense, on the 15th March, 1856, to Mr. Labouchere, *Ordinance* who replied, on the 31st July, that Her Majesty's *No. 19 of 1855* Government, after giving the matter most serious *disallowed.* consideration, continued to entertain strong objections to Ordinance No. 19 of 1855 :

" 1st, Because, for the permanency of the arrangement, it would be necessary that a permanent provision should be made for the independent support of certain judicial and other officers of the government :

" 2nd, Because, to effect a substantial amendment of the fiscal system, it would be necessary to make other provision for the levy of taxes than that which leaves nearly all the supplies in any year liable to a sudden cessation on the occurrence of a momentary difficulty in the Combined Court :

" 3rd, Because the relinquishment of the Governor's double vote, though that vote represents rather a latent than an active power in the Crown, is yet the relinquishment of a power which is acknowledged to constitute no present grievance, whilst to part with it would imply an avowal on the part of Her Majesty's Government, inconsistent with their real opinion, that the power of the Crown in British Guiana is greater than it is necessary for the interests of the people that it should be."

In these circumstances Mr. Labouchere announced Her Majesty's disallowance of the ordinance, whilst expressing regret that his views and those of the local authorities should be so much at variance as to defeat the desire by which they and Her Majesty's Government were equally animated to improve the institutions of the Colony. Governor Wodehouse informed the Court of Policy, at a meeting held on the 1st September, 1856, of the decision of the Crown to disallow the ordinance; and thereafter proposals for constitutional reform remained in abeyance for more than thirty years.

CHAPTER XIII

PROPOSALS TO MAKE THE CIVIL LIST PERMANENT : 1874-1928

IT will be remembered that the first proposal to make the Civil List a " permanent settlement " came from Sir John Packington in his despatch dated the 13th November, 1852, and that this very natural recommendation had been repeated and pressed in Mr. Labouchere's despatches, dated the 16th February and the 31st July, 1856. The question was not, however, put to the vote in the Court of Policy or in the Combined Court until, in 1874, Lord Carnarvon revived the proposal in the following circumstances.

Prior to the year 1873 the general revenue of British Guiana contributed one-third of the expenses of immigration, the remaining two-thirds being paid by the planters in the form of indenture fees. The cost of immigration at that time included bounty on re-indentures, but did not include the cost of the medical establishment, which was entirely paid by the employers of labour.

Proposal to make the Civil List Permanent revived in 1874.

However, as the result of recommendations made by a Royal Commission appointed to examine into alleged abuses in the immigration system, certain alterations in the immigration laws were made by Ordinance No. 7 of 1873. The operation of the fiscal clauses of the new law appears to have been such that, in any year in which the number of immigrants introduced did not exceed 2,500, one-third of the cost of immigration, including the medical establishment, but excluding bounty on re-indentures, was payable from the general revenue ; but that, when this number was exceeded, the proportion was diminished. Now, the average annual number of immigrants introduced between the years 1857 and 1872 inclusive having been 4,364, as many as 8,000 Indian immigrants were introduced in 1873. Thus the proportion of the cost of immigration payable from the general revenue under the new ordinance fell to one-fifth.[1] The employers complained that this reduction, coupled with increased freights and increased expenses of recruiting in India, pressed very heavily upon them, and they requested that the proportion of the cost of immigration payable from the general revenue might be restored to one-third. Lord Carnarvon replied in a despatch, dated the 8th April, 1874 :

> " I am prepared to accede to this request, though I must annex the condition that the general revenue shall not be thus chargeable in respect of more than 5,000 Indian and Chinese immigrants in any one year, and that the Combined Court shall undertake to give the Government full control over all expenses connected with immigration and to pass a permanent Civil List Ordinance, the present system of septennial ordinances being unusual and unsuited to the circumstances of a Colony importing Indian labourers, in which it is specially important that the Government should be under no uncertainty whatever as to the due payment of the salaries of public officers."

The Secretary of State's despatch was laid before the Combined Court ; and on the 13th June, 1874, it was resolved, *Conditional Consent by Combined Court.* without division, upon the motion of two elected members, Mr. R. Smith and Mr. Josias Booker, " to grant a permanent Civil List, provided that no additions to the present Civil List be proposed, either as to the amount of salaries or number of officers," and provided further that a series of suggestions made by the electives with respect to the financing of immigration were adopted, and a continuous stream of immigrants at the rate of about 6,000 *per annum* was assured. These resolutions were forwarded by Governor J. R. Longden in a despatch, dated the 17th June, 1874, to Lord Carnarvon, whose answer was long delayed, because the Secretary of State for India entered upon a careful

---

[1] See Governor Longden's despatch, 2nd November, 1875. The following was the result of the change made in the adjustment of immigration charges by Ordinance No. 7 of 1873 during the year after it came into operation. The whole expenditure, exclusive of bounties, was $958,182.96. Towards this under the old system the Colony would have contributed a sum equal to one-third, or $319,394.23 ; and the planters would have paid the remainder, $638,788.64. According to the new ordinance, however, the contribution from the Colony was only $208,235.37, showing a difference against the planters of $111,158.95 on the first year's working of the new system.

consideration of various questions relating to East Indian emigration. The Governor was, however, authorized [1] to allow the alteration of the fiscal provisions of Ordinance No. 7 of 1873 for one year only.

It was under these circumstances that the annual session of Combined Court opened on the 11th May, 1875, and the *Decision on* question of the renewal of the Civil List, which was *Proposal* due to expire on the 31st December, 1875,[2] came *postponed in* up for consideration. Therefore, in view of the value *1875.* attached to the ancient customs and privileges of the Combined Court by its elective members, it is not surprising to find that they were reluctant to pass a permanent Civil List at a time when the Government was not prepared to bring forward any measure for permanently distributing the cost of immigration. Governor Longden, on learning that opposition was likely to be offered to proposals for a permanent Civil List, determined to avoid a division which would have placed the whole of the Combined Court, except the four official members, in an attitude of opposition to Her Majesty's Government, and so have raised an obstacle to the future settlement of the question at a more favourable time. Accordingly, on the 12th June, 1875, he proposed to the Court that the Civil List should be renewed for the usual septennial period; and this motion, being passed unanimously, was carried into effect by Ordinance No. 10 of 1875. In explaining to the Secretary of State what had taken place, Governor Longden wrote : [3]

> " Although there was undoubtedly very great reluctance felt to the passing of a permanent Civil List, I feel bound to say that there was an absence of anything like factious opposition to the Government; and I believe that, had I been able to propose a permanent settlement of the whole question, the Civil List might have been passed without restriction of time. Nor will the action now taken interfere with such a settlement being made at a future time."

But these expectations were not realized and, as time went on, opposition to the enactment of a permanent Civil List *Opposition to* increased. On the 2nd November, 1875, Governor *making Civil* Longden informed Lord Carnarvon that there had *List Perma-* *nent increases.* arisen among the mercantile and planting class,

---

[1] Lord Carnarvon's despatch, 1st February, 1875.
[2] Ordinance No. 17 of 1868.   [3] Despatch, dated 18th June, 1875

from whom elective members both of the Court of Policy and of the Financial College were commonly chosen, a strong feeling against the measure. The passing of a permanent Civil List was, it appears, viewed by many as almost equivalent to a surrender of the ancient constitution of the Colony. Others, with more reason, urged that the social state of the Colony, and the maintenance of its institutions, depended entirely upon sugar; that, if any great disaster should happen to that interest, it would be necessary to revise the whole public expenditure; and that it would be inexpedient for this reason to make the Civil List permanent. It was also felt that for many years past the Civil List had been regularly voted without trouble; and it was looked upon as a reproach to the Combined Court to require it to make the change. Moreover, Her Majesty's Government found it impossible to adopt the whole series of suggestions with respect to immigration put forward by the Combined Court on the 13th June, 1874; and, although several concessions were made, and Lord Carnarvon agreed that the maximum number of immigrants to be introduced in any one year should be 6,000 (instead of 5,000), provided that in any three years the number introduced did not exceed a total of 15,000, nevertheless a return to the old adjustment of immigration charges was made contingent on the grant of a permanent Civil List by the Combined Court.

The matter was at last put to the test on the 8th June, 1876, when the Attorney-General (W. F. Haynes Smith) moved that

Proposal negatived by Combined Court in 1876. there should be granted to Her Majesty the Queen, Her Heirs and Successors, a permanent Civil List at the rate of £26,333 6s. 8d., that being the amount of the Civil List for the septennial period then current. After considerable debate this motion was rejected on division by a majority of ten to five, all the six Financial Representatives voting in the majority with four elective members of the Court of Policy, while the fifth elective member of the Court of Policy (R. Smith) voted with the Government. In that debate no argument was adduced by the unofficial section in any way affecting the wisdom or justice of making the Civil List permanent; but the feeling seems to have been, wrote Governor Longden,[1] " that to pass a permanent Civil List

[1] Despatch, dated 24th June, 1876.

would be, in some definite way, to surrender a valuable part of the old privileges of the Court," and contingent on this sentiment was another, which also found expression, " that under existing circumstances the Court might be accused of surrendering its privileges in the interests of a single class alone." The Attorney-General believed that this last feeling had considerable weight; and he thought that a more successful effort would be made to pass a permanent Civil List, if the matter were treated quite apart from the question of reapportionment of immigration charges. Moreover, Governor Longden remarked that the moment had been a very unfavourable one for such a proposal, as there was depression in almost every branch of colonial industry.   Lord Carnarvon replied in a despatch, dated the 25th October, 1876 :

> " Whilst I feel great regret that the Combined Court has not concurred in the proposal of a permanent Civil List Ordinance, which I made with the strongest desire to promote the true interest of the Colony, and the principle of which is, of course, unquestionable, I shall not on this occasion renew my recommendation of it, but I approve of the estimates for 1876 and of the new apportionment of the immigration charges, which they contain."

The proposal to make the Civil List permanent was thereafter held in abeyance, until Mr. W. A. G. Young, who was present *Proposal* as Government Secretary at all the discussions of *again re-* the years 1874 to 1876, and who at the beginning *vived in 1882.* of 1882 was administering the government of the Colony, pointed out to Lord Kimberley, in a despatch dated the 31st of January in that year, that the Civil List granted under Ordinance No. 10 of 1875, would expire on the 31st December, 1882, and inquired whether the question of making the Civil List permanent should again be brought before the Combined Court, adding that he was not able to say how the elective section would view the matter, as no discussion had of late been raised upon it.   Lord Kimberley answered on the 16th March, 1882 :

> " Her Majesty's Government think it especially important that the salaries of the judges should be permanently secured ; and it would be satisfactory to them, if the Combined Court should now be disposed to place the

other salaries provided in the Civil List on a permanent footing. I should not, however, desire to press that the whole Civil List should be made permanent in opposition to any strong feeling on the subject which the Combined Court may entertain in favour of a Civil List limited to a term of years; and, if you find that such a feeling still exists, the Combined Court should be invited to make the judicial salaries permanent and to provide for the others for a term of ten years, instead of seven years as at present."

But, when the Combined Court met in June, 1882, a resolution that the Civil List be made permanent was rejected by the unanimous vote of the elective members; and, *Proposal again re- jected by Combined Court.* in view of the feeling of the Court, Governor Sir Henry T. Irving thought it useless to propose as an amendment that the salaries of the judges should be permanently secured, believing that this object was more likely to be attained by bringing the matter forward on some future occasion as a substantive proposal, apart from the passing of the Civil List. The suggestion that the Civil List should be renewed for ten years was also dropped; and the list was renewed for the usual septennial period, to expire on the 31st December, 1889.[1] Lord Kimberley did not question the prudence of the Governor's decision, but observed :

" Her Majesty's Government view with much dissatisfaction the continuance of the objectionable practice of not voting permanently the salaries of the judges. In well-governed countries it has long been a settled principle that, in order to secure the complete independence of the judges, their salaries should be permanently assured to them." [2]

Accordingly, on the 21st June, 1883, Governor Irving brought before Combined Court a resolution providing for the salaries of the Chief Justice and the two Puisne *Salaries of Judges made Permanent.* Judges of British Guiana being permanently determined and secured by ordinance. This resolution was carried by the Governor's vote, the numbers on division being six to six, one member not voting. Mr. De Jonge, the Financial Representative for Georgetown, protested against the resolution on the ground that two elective members—Messrs. Howell Jones and Mulligan—were absent; but he

[1] Governor Irving's despatch, 14th July, 1882.
[2] Lord Kimberley's despatch, 22nd August, 1882.

failed to find any countenance or support from the other elective members who had voted with him against the resolution; while, on the presentation of his protest to the Court, several of those members, as well as Mr. Howell Jones, deprecated the course which Mr. De Jonge had adopted and expressed their dissent from it.   The resolution of Combined Court was formally carried into effect by Ordinance No. 10 passed on the 29th August, 1883, entitled " an Ordinance to determine and secure the salaries attached to the offices of the Chief Justice and of the Puisne Judges of British Guiana." This ordinance granted to Her Majesty the Queen, Her Heirs and Successors, from the 1st January, 1884, an annual sum of £5,500, out of which the salaries of the Chief Justice and the two Puisne Judges should be defrayed; and provided that the annual salary of the former should be £2,500 and of the latter £1,500 each.   However, a report dated the 20th January, 1898, by a local commission on the civil service of the Colony, recommended that the annual salary of the Chief Justice should be reduced to £1,800, that of the Junior Puisne Judge to £1,250, while that of the Senior Puisne Judge should be continued at £1,500.   This recommendation was accepted by Her Majesty's Government; and, in point of fact, the officers who held these three posts in 1898 had been appointed by the Secretary of State on the condition that their respective salaries should be paid at these rates.   Accordingly, upon the motion of the acting Government Secretary (Mr. H. A. Bovell), the Combined Court resolved on the 29th November, 1898, that there should be granted to Her Majesty, Her Heirs and Successors, the annual sum of £4,550 in substitution for the sum of £5,500 granted with the consent of Combined Court by the Judges (Salaries) Ordinance, 1883.   This resolution was made law by Ordinance No. 7 of 1899, which further enacted that any part of the sum of £4,550 which may not be applied in payment of the salaries of the said judges shall lapse to the Colony.

The subsequent position with respect to the Civil List may conveniently be illustrated by taking as an example the years

Subsequent Position as to Civil List. immediately preceding the Great War.   Permanent provision at the rate of £4,550 *per annum* had been made for payment of the salaries of the Chief Justice and the two Puisne Judges, and provision for a period of five years, ending on the 31st December, 1917, had been made by the Civil List then current at the rate of £24,000 *per annum*.[1] The total annual grant was, therefore, £28,550, or actually £10,522 17s. 4d. a year less than was granted by the second Civil List of 1841 [2] and calculated in that year to be equivalent to the revenues of the King's Chest.

One further point in connexion with the Civil List requires explanation. By Ordinance No. 3 of 1841 an *ad valorem* customs duty of not less than 2%, and not more than 2½%, was made payable upon all imports into British Guiana during the continuance of the Civil List Ordinance No. 2 of 1841. The purpose of imposing these customs duties was to supplement the permanent revenues forming the King's Chest in such manner that, in the event of Combined Court stopping supplies altogether or voting supplies insufficient to pay the Civil List then in force, a fund would at once be available from which salaries secured by the Civil List could be defrayed. For this reason

Funds provided by Law to ensure Payment of Civil List.

---

[1] The Civil List Establishment under Ordinance No. 19 of 1912 was as follows (compare schedule on p. 312 *infra*) :

	£
The Governor (in addition to a residence) . . .	5,000
The Governor: Contingencies, to include the salaries of Private Secretary and Aide-de-Camp and the lighting of Government House	1,000
The Governor: Allowance in lieu of exemption from Customs Duty	250
The Government Secretary (£1,350 rising to £1,500 by annual increments of £50)	1,500
The Assistant Government Secretary and Clerk to the Court Policy and Combined Court	600
The Attorney-General (£1,350 rising to £1,500 by annual increments of £50)	1,500
The Solicitor-General (not allowed private practice or fees) .	750
The Auditor-General	800
The Colonial Treasurer	800
The Comptroller of Customs	800
The Inspector-General of Police and Inspector of Prisons .	750
The Director of Public Works	800
The Surgeon-General	900
The Commissioner of Crown Lands and Mines . .	800
The Postmaster-General	700
Stipendiary Magistrates	6,300
The Registrar	750
Total . . £ . . .	£24,000

[2] Ordinance No. 2 of 1841.

these customs duties were made non-leviable whenever Combined Court voted other adequate provision for payment of the Civil List. The Civil List granted by Ordinance No. 2 of 1841 was afterwards extended by Ordinance No. 14 of 1844 to the 31st December, 1854; and presumably this extension had the effect of keeping Ordinance No. 3 of 1841 also in force to the same date, as during the stoppage of supplies in 1848 and 1849 these *ad valorem* duties were collected and formed a portion of the funds for carrying on the government. In 1850 an ordinance was passed (No. 8 of 1850), subsequently slightly amended by Ordinance No. 6 of 1851, declaring that the *ad valorem* duties should be payable during the continuance of the then existing Civil List—that is, to the 31st December, 1854—but that they should not be levied so long as adequate provision was made to meet the Civil List; and in the Tax Ordinance of the same year (No. 11 of 1850) it was also declared that the *ad valorem* customs duties should during the continuance in force of that ordinance, and no longer, cease to be leviable and payable. This suspending clause, in precisely the same terms as contained in Ordinance No. 11 of 1850, was inserted in all the annual Tax Ordinances down to the year 1870, when the clause was omitted from Ordinance No. 8 of 1870 by the advice of the Attorney-General on the ground that it was of no effect as the *ad valorem* customs duties, to which it referred, had ceased to be leviable after the close of the year 1854, when the Civil List provided by Ordinance No. 2 of 1841 and continued by Ordinance No. 14 of 1844 expired. How the mistake occurred cannot be traced; but, as Governor Wodehouse assumed the government of the Colony in 1854, and as nothing occurred to call his attention to these *ad valorem* customs duties, he may have been unaware that, if they were to be continued, re-enactment was necessary. Governor J. Scott, to whose notice the matter was brought, suggested to the Secretary of State on the 11th July, 1870, that, while it was sincerely to be hoped that no necessity for the use of these duties would arise, nevertheless it was " desirable that there should exist the means of raising a revenue, independent of the Combined Court, sufficient to provide for Her Majesty's Civil List, should any political crisis occur calling for a resort to such an extreme measure on the part of the executive

government." He added that he believed the Combined
Court would not object to make this contingent provision to
defray, if not otherwise provided for, the annual amount
granted to Her Majesty by the Civil List.

In reply [1] Lord Kimberley authorized the Governor to
propose to Combined Court, if he had reason to think the Court

Ordinance No. 6 of 1871. would not object to pass it, " an ordinance levying
permanently for the maintenance of the Civil List
the *ad valorem* duties which were temporarily levied
for that purpose in the years 1841, 1850, and 1851," on the
understanding that these duties would not be enforced during
any period for which other provision was made by the Civil
List. Accordingly a bill, entitled " an Ordinance to provide
for the levying of certain *ad valorem* duties during the existence
of a Civil List Establishment in this Colony," was introduced
and passed in Combined Court on the 29th May, 1871.[2] It
recited :

> " Whenever, during the existence of the present or any
> future Civil List Establishment in this Colony, no pro-
> vision other than the present is made by the Colony for
> the payment of the amount payable in support thereof,
> there shall be raised, levied and collected a tax or duty of
> four dollars on every one hundred dollars of the value of
> all goods, wares and merchandize whatever imported into
> this Colony, and not entered for exportation; and the
> proceeds of such tax shall be applicable, first to the
> payment of such amount, and afterwards to any other
> purposes to which the colonial revenues are properly
> applicable; provided that, whenever and so long as other
> sufficient provision is made by the Colony for such pay-
> ment, the operation of this ordinance shall remain and
> be suspended."

There was no opposition in Combined Court to the principle
of this law. A motion was, however, made to strike out the
words " or any future " near the beginning of the section, and
thereby limit the time of the ordinance to the period over
which the then Civil List extended—that is, to the 31st De-

[1] Despatch, 5th September, 1870.
[2] Ordinance No. 6 of 1871 : but re-numbered as Ordinance No. 1
of 1871 in Sir T. C. Rayner's revised edition of the *Laws of British
Guiana*.

cember, 1875; [1] but it was lost. A second amendment was proposed to reduce the duty from 4% to 2½% *ad valorem*, but this was not supported by the majority of the members. The ordinance was " confirmed, ratified and finally enacted " by a Royal Order-in-Council, dated the 28th July, 1871; [2] and thus provision for the Civil List during its currency was insured by a permanent statute.

The last of the quinquennial Civil Lists expired on the 31st December, 1927, when a drastic reform of the constitution of British Guiana was impending. It was, therefore, resolved by the Combined Court, on the 19th December, 1927, that the next Civil List should only be for a period of one year from the 1st January to the 31st December, 1928, " or for such less period as might thereafter be decided," and the sum voted was £24,985—only £985 more than in the years immediately preceding the Great War. The reform of the constitution actually took effect in July, 1928; and it was then at long last decided to make the Civil List permanent. For this purpose the Colony's newly constituted Legislative Council passed an Ordinance (No. 33 of 1928) " to secure a Civil List for His Majesty," and to this law the then Governor, Sir F. G. Guggisberg, gave his assent on the last day of that year. The ordinance provided that there should be payable to His Majesty, His Heirs and Successors, in each and every year beginning on the 1st January, 1929, the sum of £28,185 ; that this sum should be " charged upon and made payable from and out of the Revenues of the Colony, with preference over and above all other payments whatsoever which have heretofore been or which may hereafter be charged or become chargeable to or payable from or out of the said Revenues " ; and that, during the continuance of the ordinance, the entire revenues of the Colony of whatever nature and howsoever arising should be " payable to the use of the Colony." The details of the establishment payable from the total allocation of £28,185 were set out in schedule as had previously been done; and the permanent arrangement already made with respect to the payment of the judges was not disturbed.

Ordinance No. 33 of 1928.

---

[1] Ordinance No. 17 of 1868.
[2] Enclosed in Lord Kimberley's despatch of 10th August, 1871.

CHAPTER XIV

STANDING RULES AND ORDERS OF THE COMBINED COURT, 1837–1911

THE Royal Instructions,which directed Sir Benjamin D'Urban to frame Standing Rules and Orders for the Court of Policy,

Rules drafted by a Committee of Combined Court in 1838. were silent as to the necessity of framing such rules for the Combined Court; but at a meeting of the Combined Court, held on the 7th March, 1837, it was resolved upon the motion of Mr. William Arrindell, seconded by Mr. John Croal—both at that time elective members of the Court of Policy—that a Committee should be appointed to frame rules for regulating the proceedings of the Combined Court. The Committee appointed consisted of the Attorney-General (Mr. W. Furlonge), two members of the Court of Policy (Mr. W. Arrindell and Mr. J. Croal), and two Financial Representatives (Mr. H. O. Seward and Mr. J. Matthews). Its deliberations were very prolonged; and not until the 23rd April, 1838, were draft rules, signed by Messrs. Furlonge, Arrindell, and Croal, laid before the Combined Court. In the meantime the two last-named gentlemen had ceased to be members of the Combined Court, as also had Mr. Seward; while Mr. Matthews, although still a Financial Representative, did not sign the draft, for what reason does not appear. At a meeting of the Court three days later the draft rules were read and certain amendments made in them; and on the 27th April, 1838, the draft as amended was adopted by the Court, under the title " Rules and Regulations for the Combined Court of British Guiana." The only rules which call for special comment are the first three :

" 1. The Court being assembled, the Secretary shall read over the Estimate, item by item.
" 2. Each item shall be considered an original motion; and any Member desirous of increasing or decreasing an

item, or of having it struck off the Estimate, shall be
bound to move an amendment to that effect.

" 3. Should the amendments not be seconded, they will,
of course, fall to the ground; otherwise, being seconded,
they shall be put to the vote; and, if lost, the original
motion shall then be put."

It will be observed that in these rules the Court made an
attempt to enlarge its powers to the extent of *increasing* items
These Rules on the annual estimate : and further that the rules
disapproved were " framed and agreed to " by the Court itself
of by Her
Majesty's and were signed, not only by the Governor, but also
Government. by all the members, official and unofficial, of the Combined Court.   In both these respects the rules were *ultra vires*;
for Her Majesty's Government maintained, on the one hand,
that the Combined Court, deriving its powers from the Civil
List compromise arrived at in 1835, and holding such powers
conditionally only, had no inherent authority to make standing
rules and orders for its guidance, but that such authority
vested in the Governor alone, as representative of the Crown;
and, on the other hand, that the right of Combined Court to
discuss " fully and without reserve the items of the annual
estimate " of expenditure, framed by the Court of Policy, did
not give the elective members the right of increasing any item,
for such an innovation would undermine the great constitutional
principle, recognized in the Standing Orders of the House of
Commons, that the Government is responsible for expenditure.
Accordingly these rules never received the approval or recognition of Her Majesty's Government.   Governor Light, however, in 1842, split the second rule into two separate rules
which read as follows :

" 2. No member (His Excellency the Governor excepted) shall be permitted to move the increase of an
Rules made item upon the Estimate.
by Governor   " 3. Each item shall be considered an original
Light in 1842. motion; any member desirous of decreasing an
item, or of having it struck off the Estimate, shall be
bound to move an amendment to that effect."

The subsequent rules were then re-numbered, and the rules so
amended and made by the Governor, not by the Court, were
submitted to the Secretary of State for the Colonies and

approved by Lord Stanley in a despatch dated the 8th June, 1842. A copy of these rules was then printed for the use of the members.[1]

However, at a meeting of Combined Court on the 26th July, 1849, a Financial Representative, Mr. W. Davison, moved *Rules changed by Resolution of Combined Court in 1849.* " that the rules and regulations for governing the proceedings of this Court, adopted on the 27th April, 1838, be printed for the use of the Court, and that the rules and regulations now in print [2] be destroyed." These latter rules, he said, were quite at variance with the practice of the Court, and he did not know how they had come to be in use. The former rules, on the other hand, were framed by a Committee of the Court, discussed and approved of, and they bore the signature of every member of the Court. Governor Henry Barkly requested that the motion might be postponed. The fact was, he said, that some objection to the rules of 1838 had been taken by the Secretary of State for the Colonies; but, as he was not master of the subject, he would prefer that discussion should be deferred. Mr. Davison, while agreeing to the postponement of his motion, replied that he was not aware any objection had been taken to the rules by the Secretary of State.

The deferred motion came up for decision at a meeting of Combined Court on the 1st August, 1849, being duly moved by Mr. Davison and seconded by Mr. J. T. White, an unofficial member of the Court of Policy. Governor Barkly then said that he had looked into the matter, and that it struck him there was very little difference between the two sets of rules. The only difference was that one of the rules, the second, of the set passed in 1838 was not to be found in the other set. This second rule conferred the power on the Court to increase or reduce an item on the annual estimates; and, so far as he was concerned, he had not the slightest objection to the Court's enjoying that power. Mr. Davison stated that he did not know why the other set of rules should be used in Court at all; and that the Court had always possessed the power of increasing or reducing an item. The motion was thereupon agreed to without a division, in the following form :

[1] See Appendix J.
[2] *I.e.*, those made by Governor Light in 1842.

" *Resolved*—that the only rules for regulating the
proceedings of this Court are the Rules and Regulations
framed and agreed to at an Annual Adjourned Assembly
of this Court, held on the 27th April, 1838, and inserted
in the minutes of the Court of that date, bearing the
signatures of the Members of this Court at that time,
and that such rules are hereby adopted, and confirmed
by this Court."

It does not appear that any report of this resolution of the
Combined Court was ever transmitted to the Secretary of
Endeavour of State for the Colonies; and, as a result of the action
Combined then taken, the Court appears for several years to
Court to
usurp Power have exercised the right of suggesting new items to
of Increasing the Government and of increasing the amount of some
Money-
Votes. of those proposed by the Government.   But, in 1855,
the attention of Mr. Sidney Herbert, then Secretary of State
for the Colonies, being drawn to a money-vote which had
Opposed by originated in the Combined Court, he wrote in a
(a) Mr.
Sidney despatch dated the 15th February:
Herbert

" The irregularity which has occurred in this and
perhaps in other cases seems to be owing to a miscon-
ception of the proper limits of the functions of the Combined Court, to which body it properly belongs to control,
and, if they see fit, to negative expenditure by rejecting
items on the Estimate, but not to originate expenditure
nor, consequently, to originate measures and arrangements
which cannot be carried out without money.   If this
function were conceded to the Combined Court, the result
would be the creation of that irresponsible power of
initiating money votes by others than the representatives
of the Government which more than any other course
has led to the ruin of the finances in Jamaica and
elsewhere."

(b) Lord John Lord John Russell added, in a despatch dated the
Russell; 31st May, 1855:

" It is unquestionably the strong desire of His Majesty's
Government to do nothing unnecessary which would disturb the harmony now existing between the Colony and
the Crown.   But with regard to the virtual initiation of
money-votes in the Combined Court, the practice which
you describe is of a much more dangerous tendency.   It

is certainly not justified by the terms of the Order-in-Council defining the function of that Court, and it is of great importance that it should not be acknowledged as a legitimate practice. The British House of Commons, which is not reluctant to claim whatever privileges are really conducive to the due exercise of its functions, does not pretend to the exercise of the privilege which has been assumed by the Combined Court, and I look for the introduction of sounder principles more in conformity with constitutional precedent."

The Governor was requested "to regard these observations as for your general guidance, but not as meant to fetter your discretion when you can satisfy the Secretary of State that it is necessary to take a different course from that prescribed."

Nevertheless many attempts were made by unofficial members to assert the power of the Court to initiate expenditure (c) *and Mr.* and to increase money votes; and two years later *Labouchere.* the question again engaged the attention of the Secretary of State, Mr. Henry Labouchere, who, on the 27th July, 1857, wrote to the Governor :

> " I have been led to examine the reports of the proceedings of the Combined Court with reference to this question of the initiation of money-votes in that Court, and by unofficial members, and I regret to perceive that the legal and proper practice has been very frequently departed from notwithstanding the observations made upon the subject by Lord John Russell in his despatch of 31st May, 1855. . . . I have to request that you will furnish me with a return of the number of money-votes which have been initiated in the Combined Court, or to which additions have been initiated, since the date of Lord John Russell's despatch of 31st May, 1855, distinguishing those which have been initiated by unofficial members."

In acknowledging, on 1st January, 1858, the receipt of a return of 81 instances of such money-votes, Mr. Labouchere wrote :

> " It does not seem to be made out that, in any one of the 81 instances in which votes of money have been initiated in the Combined Court, there would have been any difficulty in taking the regular and lawful course of placing an item on the Estimate or on a Supplementary Estimate in the Court of Policy, and then sending it to the Combined Court for concurrence or rejection. The

proper function of the Combined Court, as constituted under the Civil List arrangement, is to check and control the public expenditure and this function will be destroyed, if money votes shall be originated in the Combined Court instead of the Court of Policy, on the sole responsibility of the Governor with the consciousness that he will have to carry them through the Combined Court also, and that that Court has not been in any way committed to acquiescence. I must add that, unless Her Majesty's Government can rely upon the Governor for adopting the principle of the Court of Policy on this point, they will be under the necessity of withdrawing the discretion which has been accorded to meet exceptional cases."

The matter was finally settled on the 3rd June, 1858, when a motion by Mr. J. E. Roney, seconded by Mr. Peter Rose, both unofficial members of the Combined Court,

Claim to initiate Money-votes or increase them abandoned by Combined Court, 1858.

" that it is the undoubted privilege of this Court to increase, diminish, or strike off any item on the Estimate annually submitted to it as prepared by the Court of Policy, and that in the event of the Court's seeing fit to suggest a totally new item for Estimate, it is likewise their undoubted and long-established privilege to request His Excellency the Governor and Court of Policy to place such item on the Estimate for the purpose of having the same brought under the consideration of this Court,"

was negatived by a majority of 9 to 3 votes, after the Governor had addressed the Court in conformity with instructions from the Secretary of State not to permit the initiation of money-votes in the Combined Court. It appears, however, that during these discussions the question of amending the Rules and Regulations for the Combined Court was never touched upon, save that on the 22nd May, 1855, it was resolved, upon the motion of Mr. G. J. Luckie, seconded by Mr. Robert Smith, that a tenth rule should be added to the Rules and Regulations of 1838 as follows :

Rules for Combined Court amended in 1855.

" The Court will not in future receive any petition for an increase of salary from any person officially employed, unless such petition be approved of, and sent in to the Court by, the Executive Government."

T

No mention of Standing Rules and Orders of Combined Court was made in the Royal Orders-in-Council from time to *Royal Order-* time renewing the privilege of Combined Court to *in-Council of* discuss the annual estimates of colonial expenditure *1891.* until the Order made by Her Majesty Queen Victoria in Council on the 23rd February, 1891, expressly stated :

> " It is hereby further ordered that the Governor for the time being of British Guiana may from time to time make such standing Rules and Orders as may be necessary to ensure punctuality of attendance of members of the said Combined Court, and to prevent meetings of the said Combined Court being holden without convenient notice to the several Members thereof, and to maintain order and method in the despatch of business, and in the conduct of debates in the said Combined Court, and that all such Rules and Orders, not being repugnant to this Order, shall at all times be followed and observed, and shall be binding on the said Combined Court, unless the same shall be disallowed by Her Majesty." [1]

A similar clause was included in all Royal Orders-in-Council on the subject from that time forward ; and, in accordance with *Standing* the authority so conferred, Governor the Viscount *Rules and* Gormanston made on the 9th February, 1892, a *Orders made* revised set of Standing Rules and Orders for the *by Lord* *Gormanston,* Combined Court. In laying these before the Court, *1892.* at its meeting on the 16th February of that year, he said that they had been framed in the spirit, and as far as possible in the terms, of the Standing Rules and Orders of the Court of Policy. However, on the 2nd March, 1892, Financial Representative Mr. N. R. McKinnon, on behalf of the elective members of Combined Court, presented a protest against these rules on the ground that they had not been submitted to the Court for discussion and adoption, and requested that the protest should be transmitted to the Secretary of State for the Colonies " with a view to Her Majesty disallowing the said rules in the present form, and until they have been submitted to and adopted by this Court." Lord Gormanston forwarded the protest to Lord Knutsford in a despatch dated the 8th March, 1892, remarking that, as he had acted strictly in accordance with the provisions of the Order-in-Council of the 23rd February, 1891,

[1] See Appendix L (ii).

there appeared to be no reason why Her Majesty should be advised to disallow the Standing Rules and Orders. Lord Knutsford replied on the 5th April, 1892 :

> "You will be good enough to inform the protesting members that the Order-in-Council of the 23rd February, 1891, does not require that the Standing Rules and Orders to be made under its authority should be submitted to and adopted by the Combined Court, and that I do not perceive that there is anything in the Standing Rules and Orders which you have made repugnant to the spirit of the Order-in-Council. I shall not, therefore, advise Her Majesty to disallow them."

The Governor communicated this reply to the Combined Court at its meeting on the 28th February, 1893; and thereafter the elective members, at a meeting of Combined *Protest against these Standing Rules and Orders.* Court held on the 14th March, 1893, handed in a

> "most solemn protest against the regulation which empowered His Excellency the Governor to make rules for the conduct of the business of this Court without laying them before it for discussion, modification, if necessary, and subsequent sanction, for the following reasons :
>
> "*First*. It is degrading to the Court, the implication plainly being that its members are wanting in the intelligence necessary to frame such rules.
>
> "*Second*. It is a restriction of the rights which this Court possessed prior to the introduction of the Reformed Constitution in 1892.
>
> "*Third*. It is an arbitrary and unconstitutional act, Elective Assemblies having the inherent right to frame and pass the rules necessary for the proper conduct of their business."

Beyond recording this protest in the minutes, no further action was taken : and the question then dropped until at a Special Session of Combined Court on the 30th October, 1896, the elective members moved that

Proposal for Revision of the Standing Rules and Orders, 1896.

> "whereas the Standing Rules and Orders of this Court, which were not framed by this Court, have been found to be defective in many respects, and a new set should be framed, and whereas it is advisable that the said Rules and Orders should be framed

by this Court, *Be it Resolved*,—that His Excellency the Governor be respectfully asked to obtain the consent of Her Majesty in Council to allow this Court to frame a set of Rules and Orders for its own guidance."

This Resolution was accepted by the Officer Administering the Government, Mr. C. Boyle, as an expression of opinion from the elective members and forwarded by him to the Secretary of State in a despatch, dated the 9th November, 1896, in which he wrote :

"The existing Rules and Orders require revision; and I think that perhaps two or three of the elective members of the Court might be asked to confer with the Government Secretary and Attorney-General and to submit to the Governor their recommendations on such revision : but I am not prepared to recommend that the Court itself should make the rules, or that the Order-in-Council should be altered."

Mr. Joseph Chamberlain replied in a despatch dated the 15th December, 1896 : " I request that you will inform the elected members of the Combined Court that the question of the Standing Orders will be considered when the question of renewing the Civil List, and issuing a new Order-in-Council, comes up for consideration in 1897 "; and he concurred in Mr. Boyle's proposal that the Governor should consult a few members of the Combined Court after the coming election as to any amendments of the Standing Orders which might be desirable.

The matter was, however, postponed until on the 5th May, 1902, Governor Sir J. A. Swettenham appointed a Commission, *Commission for their Revision appointed, 1902.* consisting of the Attorney-General (Sir T. C. Rayner), the Auditor-General (Mr. N. Darnell Davis), Mr. P. Dargan, and Mr. H. H. Laurence, unofficial members of Combined Court, " to inquire into and report upon the best means of amending the Standing Rules and Orders of Procedure at present in force for the guidance of the Combined Court of this Colony." The Commissioners submitted on the 18th November, 1902, a re-draft of the Standing Rules and Orders containing, as they said, little that was really new, and taken largely from those already in force with the addition of a few of the Standing Rules and Orders of the Court of Policy.

"Those which in form are new," wrote the Commissioners, "are for the most part declaratory of what has long been the mode of procedure in the Combined Court and merely put into formal shape the unwritten rules which at present govern the proceedings of the Court."

The draft submitted by the Commissioners was carefully *Commis-* considered by Governor Sir J. A. Swettenham and *sioners' Draft* Mr. Joseph Chamberlain, then Secretary of State *Amended by* *Secretary of* for the Colonies, with the result that the following *State.* amendments in it were made :

Commissioners' Draft.	Amendments made by Governor with sanction of Secretary of State for the Colonies.
§ 4 (2) A (*b*)—Motions by Official Members *to increase the Estimate*.	§ 4 (2) A (*b*)—Motions by Official Members *to increase or decrease items in the Estimate*.
§ 4 (2) A (*c*)—Motions by Elected Members *recommending an increase of the Estimate*.	§ 4 (2) A (*c*)—Motions by Elected Members *for decreasing or omitting items in the Estimate*.
§ 8—When a question concerning any business before the Court, or any matter which the Court is competent to deal with, has been asked of any Member of the Court, the reply shall be conclusive, and no speech or debate on the reply shall be allowed.	§ 8—When a question concerning any business before the Court, or any matter which the Court is competent to deal with, has been asked of any Member of the Court, the reply shall be conclusive, and no speech or debate on the reply shall *then* be allowed.
§ 9—Except as provided by rules 7 and 10 no Motion or Question shall be moved or asked unless two clear days' notice in writing, stating the terms thereof, shall have been given by delivering the same to the Clerk of the Court. Every such notice shall be headed "Combined Court," and shall be dated and signed, and copies shall be *at once* forwarded to Members of the Court.	§ 9—Except as provided by rules 7 and 10 no Motion or Question shall be moved or asked unless two clear days' notice in writing, stating the terms thereof, shall have been given by delivering the same to the Clerk of the Court. Every such notice shall be headed "Combined Court," and shall be dated and signed, and copies shall be forwarded to Members of the Court *by the Clerk as soon as printed*.
§ 13—There shall be no debate or discussion on Reports, Petitions or other Documents laid on the table, *unless relevant to a Motion before the Court*.	§ 13—There shall be no debate or discussion on Reports, Petitions or other Documents laid on the table, *but they may be referred to and discussed in debate on a Motion before the Court*.
§ 15—Each item shall be considered an original Motion, and	§ 15—Each item shall be considered an original Motion, and

Commissioners' Draft.	Amendments made by Governor with sanction of Secretary of State for the Colonies.
any Member desirous of decreasing any item or striking it off, *or of recommending an increase of the Estimate*, may move an amendment to that effect. If the amendment be seconded, it shall be put to the vote, and if lost the original item shall stand part of the Estimate.	any Member desirous of decreasing any item or striking it off may move and amendment to that effect. If the amendment be seconded, it shall be put to the vote, and if lost the original item shall stand part of the Estimate.
§ 24 (*a*)—The mover of an original Motion shall have the right of reply after *each* Member who desires to speak shall have spoken, but the mover of an amendment, *except as is next hereinafter provided for*, shall not have any right of reply.	§ 24 (*a*)—The mover of an original Motion shall have the right of reply after *every* Member who desires to speak shall have spoken, but the mover of an amendment shall not have any right of reply.
(*b*)—The mover of an amendment to decrease or strike off or recommending an increase of an item on the Estimate shall have the right of reply after each Member who desires to speak shall have spoken.	(*b*)—Deleted.

The draft so amended was finally approved by Governor Sir J. A. Swettenham on the 19th May, 1903, under the authority of the Royal Order-in-Council, dated at *Standing* Windsor, the 23rd February, 1891; and the Standing *Rules and* *Orders made* Rules and Orders so made [1] are those which governed *on 19th May,* the procedure of the Combined Court during the rest *1903.* of its existence. But two additional Standing Rules and Orders were made on the 15th September, 1911, modelled upon the 20th Standing Order of the House of Commons and prescribing methods of procedure against "any member or m embers whose conduct is grossly disorderly."

[1] See Appendix J.

CHAPTER XV

PRIOR to the year 1808, it appears to have been customary for the negroes, or Congoes as they used to be called, in various parts of British Guiana to form themselves into "Companies" and to choose head-men, or "Kings," under whom were several subaltern officers, such as "Governors," "General Drummers," "Doctors," and "Lawyers." The duties of the "Kings" were to take care of the sick, to purchase rice, sugar and other necessaries for them, and to conduct burials, arranging that the corpse should be properly enclosed in a cloth and that the customary rites and dances were duly performed. The breakdown of this system among the Congoes began with a quarrel between one of the "Companies" and their "King," who at a certain burial declared that he had no money for the rites, although the people believed him to have enough for the purpose, as it was impossible that their contributions could have been exhausted in a proper manner.[2] Accordingly the "Company" in question broke up; and, possibly as the result of similar malversation of funds becoming frequent, the West

Negro Communal Institutions disappear in British Guiana prior to Emancipation.

---

[1] Based on (a) *The Handbook of Village Law*, being an attempt to explain the provisions of the new Village Ordinance, No. 10 of 1873, as affecting the rights and liabilities of the owners and occupiers of village property, with some account of the origin and progress of the village communities of British Guiana; by J. Brumell, Sheriff of Demerara and Member of the Central Board of Villages; printed at the *Royal Gazette* office, Main Street, Georgetown, 1873; (b) Memorandum by the Honourable A. M. Ashmore, C.M.G., Government Secretary, on the subject of Village Administration from the time of the abolition of slavery to the present day; with an economic census of the villages of British Guiana for 1902; Georgetown, Demerara; C. K. Jardine, printer to the Government of British Guiana, 1903; (c) Village Administration and Local Government in British Guiana, by Dr. J. E. Godfrey, M.B., C.M., Surgeon-General; printed in *Timehri*, the Journal of the Royal Agricultural and Commercial Society of British Guiana, 1912.

[2] Rodway, vol. ii, pp. 297–8.

African village organization under " Kings " or " Captains of Companies " had disappeared in British Guiana before the emancipation. Moreover, during slavery the negroes had no lands of their own, but lived on the front lands of estates and in the negro yards, the property of their masters; while, during the " apprenticeship," which preceded complete emancipation, the blacks were still *adscripti glebæ*, bound to the soil, and occupied cottages and provision grounds, rent free, on the estates to which they were " apprenticed."

It was not until 1838, when the relations between master and servant became entirely changed, and the labourer was as free *Effect of the* to leave his employer's service as the employer was *Emancipa-* *tion: Villages* to discharge his labourer, that the latter became fully *formed.* aware of the uncertain tenure under which he then lived and tilled his plot of land on the plantations. He had become a tenant at will, liable to be evicted on fourteen days' notice, and sometimes without any notice at all. Hence arose a movement among the negroes to purchase properties of their own, on which they might live as they liked and work when they pleased. Among the first of the properties so purchased were those which now constitute the large villages of Victoria, Buxton, Friendship, and Plaisance on the east coast of Demerara. These were all cotton estates without any buildings of much value upon them, and the prices paid for them were $10,000 for Victoria, then called Northbrook, containing 600 acres of land; $80,000 for Friendship with 750 acres; $50,000 for Buxton, then known as New Orange Nassau, with 580 acres; and $39,000 for Plaisance with 300 acres. So rapid was the acquisition of landed property by the peasantry that, according to an official return, they owned in 1842 upwards of 15,000 acres, for which they had paid not less than $250,000, and on which 3,355 families consisting of 15,906 persons had already settled.

The way in which these purchases were conducted showed great union among the people and great confidence in each *Difficulties as* other. The negotiations were usually carried on by *to Village* two or three head-men, selected in some instances *Titles.* from two or three hundred shareholders or persons who had subscribed money towards the general undertaking. When the terms were concluded, no credit was asked, but the money was paid down at once, sometimes in bags of silver, conveyed in wheelbarrows to the office of the seller. The transport of the property was then passed in the names of these head-men, making them legally the sole owners of the estate, and leaving the subscribers, some of whose names were not even on record, without the slightest legal claim to the property they had paid for. This system of purchasing in community soon gave rise to considerable difficulties of title.

But a more pressing difficulty was that of drainage, drainage being in British Guiana the condition of existence. The

Difficulties of Village Drainage. estates which the peasants had bought were laid out in parallelograms on the sea-coast and for a short distance up the tidal rivers; and the surface of the land being perfectly flat and lying from three to four feet below high-water mark of spring tides, it was, and still is, necessary to secure each estate against inundation from the sea by a strong sea-dyke in front, while similar drains at the back or inland boundary, as well as on each side, are essential, in order to keep off the immense body of water accumulated in the wet savannahs during the rainy seasons. Inside, and at the foot of these dams, are large trenches twelve to eighteen feet wide, running round the whole estate, into which smaller trenches and open drains convey the water which falls on the land. The large trenches discharge their contents into the sea through one or more sluices, or " kokers " as they are called, the doors of which are opened day and night as the tide ebbs, and shut against the returning flood. The natural outfall at extreme low water of spring tides is only between five and six feet, and at neaps much less; and this fall, trifling as it is, can only be obtained in many parts of the Colony by considerable labour in keeping the channel outside the sluices free from mud and other obstruction. The whole of this drainage system admits of no neglect. Constant attention must be paid to every point, and immediate action taken on the first sign of danger, otherwise, especially in wet weather, the fields become flooded, the crops are destroyed, the houses stand as it were in a lake, and the roads are impassable. No individual villager could cultivate his plot with success unless the whole system of main drainage throughout the estate was kept in order. So long, therefore, as the drainage system, with which the plantation was provided at the time of purchase, remained in good order, it was not impossible that the new village situated in the plantation should prosper. But want of unanimity and of combined action on the part of the villagers, who found themselves without any communal institutions or organization for managing their affairs, soon led to disastrous consequences.

A third difficulty which the villagers had to meet, was that of fulfilling the obligation, which rested on all owners of planta-

Difficulties of Road Maintenance. tions, to maintain the public road through their properties. The question of title might wait. The neglect of drainage would injure chiefly, if not exclusively, the negligent villagers themselves. But the difficulty of the roads came home early. The remedy open to Government in the case of an omission to repair roads was against the estate (*in solidum*) liable for maintenance, and was in the case of a village obviously impracticable. It was with this difficulty that the Government first endeavoured to grapple; and the earliest legislation passed affecting the newly formed villages was Ordinance No. 18 of 1845 " to make provision for keeping in repair the line of public road and bridges passing through and over the front lands of plantations *Dageraad and Mocha* and Westfield, respectively, which front lands now form Queenstown," a village in Essequebo. This was followed by Ordinance No. 10 of 1849, which authorized the " Commissioners of Queenstown " to levy and recover a rate of 2% on the value of all lots and buildings in the village, for the purpose of meeting the expenses of repairing and maintaining the roads and bridges. The election of these Commissioners was the first legislative attempt to provide a village organization. A similar remedy was by subsequent ordinances applied to the like difficulty in other cases, and was more or less effectually put into operation; but, even up to a late date, complaints of the state of the main roads through the villages were very common.

In 1850, the Government made an attempt to establish a general administration for sanitary purposes throughout the

Central Board of Health. Colony. By an Ordinance, No. 32 of 1850, two Central Boards of Health were established—one for Demerara and Essequebo, and one for Berbice—and Local Boards of Health, composed of the vestries of the parishes and the medical gentlemen residing therein, were set up in every rural parish of the Colony, the towns of Georgetown and New Amsterdam being separately provided for. This ordinance probably never had any effect. It was repealed two years later, and replaced by Ordinance No. 5 of 1852, a more elaborate measure, by which a single Central Board at Georgetown was substituted for the two Boards of the earlier law, and the parish vestries were formed into Local Boards of Health for the rural districts with authority to establish general systems of drainage for their districts, and to make and enforce sanitary regulations within villages, power being taken to declare new villages, and so to bring them under the operation of these regulations. The Local Boards of the Sanitary Districts were to be entitled to levy rates so soon as " provision shall have been made by ordinance for the election of the members of the vestries of the several parishes," which had previously been nominated bodies. But no such provision was ever made and, therefore, no rates were ever struck, with the result that, so far as the rural districts, including villages, were concerned, the machinery of administration never came into general operation.

Meanwhile, in 1851, the Government had dealt with the difficulty as to titles by passing an ordinance (No. 4 of 1851

Attempt to regularize Village Titles. amended by No. 1 of 1852) for partitioning plantation *New Orange Nassau*, a part of which forms the village of Buxton, among its joint proprietors, and for partitioning other lands and villages similarly circumstanced. Under these laws Commissioners were appointed to divide the lands of villages among the individual proprietors, to whom in due course transport was passed.

But the germ out of which the existing more elaborate system of village administration has grown was Ordinance No. 33 of

Ordinance No. 33 of 1856. 1856, passed by Governor Wodehouse and the Court of Policy, " for the better management and regulation of villages and estates held in undivided shares in this Colony." This was the first general law dealing with all the villages. It provided :

(*a*) that the Governor and Court of Policy might by resolution bring under its provisions all estates which, having been purchased in community, had been divided, or should in future be divided, in severalty among the proprietors, and enacted the means of division for the future :

(*b*) for the electon and payment of an overseer;

(*c*) for the election of two Commissioners for each village :

(*d*) for the assessing of rates :

(*e*) that all moneys received were to be deposited in the local banks, and drawn out by cheque signed by the overseer and the Commissioners.

(*f*) that the overseer might require the shareholders to perform what work was necessary to be done, and in default cause the work to be done at the expense of the shareholders.

This ordinance remained in force for seventeen years, but was not very effectual, owing on the one hand to the lack of any central administration by means of which the Government could supervise its working and influence the people to co-operate for their own good, and on the other hand to the reluctance of the authorities to compel the recalcitrant minority, always to be found in every community, to discharge their share of the common obligations.

Governor Hincks took up the village question very earnestly soon after his arrival in the Colony. His first ordinance on *Special Laws for Particular Villages.* the subject was No. 10 of 1862, " to levy special improvement rates in the villages of Buxton, Friendship, and Beterverwagting, and for other purposes." The preamble of this law insists that " it is necessary that measures should be immediately adopted to afford the means of drainage to the villages of Buxton, Friendship and Beterverwagting, and also that proper roads and streets should be established therein; and that special improvement rates should be levied in the said villages to defray the required expenditure." This law was amended by Ordinance No. 1 of 1863, which also provided " for the better management of villages generally and for the more effectual recovery of village rates." These ordinances created Commissioners with Boards of Advice to manage the three villages named and other villages, if any, brought under their operation. But the collection of rates, when initiated under these laws, led to some sales of villagers' property; and a good deal of friction ensued between the peasantry and the authorities, which, in the village of Friendship, culminated in a forcible levy by police supported by a military force. In these circumstances the Combined Court voted, on

the 15th May, 1862, as a loan from borrowed money the sum of
$60,000 for the purpose of improving village drainage and works of
a like nature, intended to ameliorate the deplorable condition of
many of the villages. This loan was never repaid by the villagers.

It had now become evident that the whole subject needed
careful and comprehensive reconsideration and, pursuant to a
Report of resolution adopted by the Court of Policy on the
Committee on 2nd February, 1864, a Committee was appointed to
Villages,
1864–5. report upon the condition and deficiencies of existing
villages, and to inquire whether their position could be amelior-
ated by any improvement in their legal constitution, regulation
or management. This Committee consisted of Mr. W. Walker
(Government Secretary), Mr. L. Porter (elective member of
the Court of Policy), Mr. J. Brumell (Sheriff of Demerara), Mr.
N. Cox (Inspector-General of Police), and Mr. W. J. Jeffrey
(Stipendiary Magistrate) ; and, after visiting a number of
villages in all parts of the Colony, they reported them to be
" generally in a most unsatisfactory state, and in some instances
in a deplorable condition : the houses in the latter case in ruin
and disrepair, and the lands attached to them undrained,
uncultivated and neglected ; the means of internal communication most defective, and the most utter disregard for all sanitary
considerations." They advised that a central board of management should be formed ; that provision should be made for
inspection by a government officer ; that aid should be provided
in the shape of loans ; and that there should be village boards
of advice, with overseers to collect rates and transact local
business. They also proposed the survey of the villages, and
arrangements for giving the several owners good titles.[1]

This report resulted in the passing of an ordinance,
No. 1 of 1866, " to provide for the better mangement
Ordinance and sanitary superintendence of villages," which
No. 1 of
1866. created :

(*a*) one Central Board of Villages composed of the
Governor and Court of Policy and such other persons as
might be appointed from time to time by the Governor :
and

[1] Messrs. Walker and Porter left the Colony before the work of the
Committee was completed. Mr. Brumell submitted a report, signed
by himself only, dated the 20th April, 1865 ; and Messrs. Cox and
Jeffrey submitted a separate joint-report dated the 8th May, 1865.

(b) Local Boards of Superintendence appointed by the Governor, one for each village, or one for a number of villages combined.

The new law vested in the Central Board of Villages power to declare places to be villages and to divide villages into incorporated and unincorporated. In the former the cost of work done by the Local Board was recoverable from rates; but in unincorporated villages work might be set out by the overseer and done by the villagers under a threat, in case of failure, to sell the village as a whole, or in the alternative to levy a rate. Eighteen incorporated villages [1] were duly created, for each of which a Board of Superintendence was appointed, consisting for the most part of the local clergy and some of the gentry: while almost every property in the Colony not in European hands was declared an unincorporated village. Overseers were appointed, and rates levied for local improvement, in very many villages. The law also gave the Central Board power to borrow money on behalf of any village and to recoup itself out of the rates; and, under its borrowing powers, the Board raised and lent considerable sums of money to the villages, very large loans being made to provide Buxton, Plaisance and Beterverwagting with drainage by steam machinery.

As the Commissaries elected under Ordinance No. 33 of 1856 were not swept away, but might be continued by order *Effect of* of the Central Board of Villages, the effect of all *Legislation* the legislation passed up to the year 1866 had *up to 1866.* been to create a number of different kinds of local government for villages. Four—Queenstown, Buxton, Friendship and Beterverwagting—had special constitutions under laws peculiar to themselves. Ordinance No. 1 of 1866 had established two more kinds of villages, incorporated and unincorporated, with differing forms of government; and, under Ordinance No. 33 of 1856, there were villages with yet another kind of administration; while, side by side with the Central Board of Villages, there still

[1] Ann's Grove, Two Friends, Nabaclis, Golden Grove, Friendship, Buxton, Beterverwagting, Plaisance, Den Amstel, Fellowship, Sisters, Good Intent, Bagotville, Stanleytown, Craig, Queenstown, Danielstown, Agricola.

existed the Central Board of Health. But, apart from this confusion of control, the system of management under the new law broke down beneath its own weight. The smaller villages could not bear the cost of overseers, whose salaries swallowed up nearly the whole of the rates. The unpaid Boards of Superintendence failed to recruit suitable volunteer members who would face the petty squabbles and disagreeable details of village politics. The clergy found themselves involved in chronic disagreement with their parishioners; while not the smallest detail of village administration could be finally settled until submitted to the Central Board of Villages, which included all the principal officers of the Colony, from the Governor downwards.

In 1871, the failure was apparent. On the 20th May in that year the Court of Policy, on the motion of Mr. H. Watson, resolved

Commission on Villages in 1871-2.

> " that, looking at the deplorable state of many of the villages throughout the Colony, and the great sickness and mortality in many of them from the want of proper drainage and efficient sanitary arrangements; and looking further at the failure of the laws heretofore enacted with the view of promoting these objects and the proper management and control of these villages : His Excellency the Governor be requested to appoint a Commission to inquire into the whole matter, and to suggest some scheme whereby they may be placed under efficient control and management, and also to report on the most practicable way of providing medical attendance to the poor in the villages situate in the more remote districts of the Colony."

Accordingly, on the 24th June, 1871, Governor Scott, who had meanwhile succeeded Sir Francis Hincks, appointed a Commission for this purpose consisting of Mr. J. Brumell (Sheriff of Demerara) ; the Revs. F. J. Wyatt, W. J. Webber, J. Kinnison, W. G. G. Austin (Inspector of Schools), J. Dalgleish, and E. A. Wallbridge; Messrs. H. C. Huggins and B. Maxwell (Stipendiary Magistrates) ; Mr. N. Cox (Inspector-General of Police) ; and Messrs. J. Craigen, J. G. Gray, P. C. Barlow, A. Hunter, and R. J. Kelly (Justices of the Peace). Before this Commission brought its duties to a close, some of the members had died and others left the Colony. Those who remained—namely, Messrs. Brumell, Barlow, Kelly, Wall-bridge, Maxwell, and Dalgleish—submitted a joint-report, dated the 21st March, 1872. They found that, according to the last Census, there were upwards of 200 villages and small settlements in the Colony, containing a population of 80,000, of whom 30,000 were under fifteen years of age. Some of these villages were very populous; for example, Plaisance on the east coast of Demerara with 3,169 inhabitants; Buxton and Friendship, immediately adjoining each other, in the same district, with 4,600 and Victoria with 2,047. In the County of Essequebo, Queenstown and Henrietta had populations of 1,726 and 1,067 respectively; and in Berbice were numerous villages and settlements containing in all not far short of 20,000 inhabitants. The Commission recommended that government officers should be appointed to manage the villages, assisted in each case by an elected council of advice, and that proper accounts should be kept and duly audited. The report makes reference to financial mismanagement and disorganization, but not to the same causes of complaint—want of drainage and breakdown of village works—as the former report; and it may perhaps be assumed that in these last respects there was less to complain of in 1872 than there had been in 1864.

There followed on this report the enactment of an elaborate Ordinance (No. 10 of 1873) " to consolidate and amend the *Ordinance* law relating to villages and to provide for the *No. 10 of* management, regulation and sanitary superintendence *1873.* of villages." This ordinance consolidated the village laws of 1856 and 1866, and provided for:

(*a*) a Central Board of Villages:
(*b*) Village Councils, composed of three persons elected in each village by the inhabitants.
(*c*) the District Commissary, or some person appointed in his stead, as superintendent of all villages in his district, and chairman of each village Council:
(*d*) the appointment of an Inspector of Villages:
(*e*) the borrowing of money by the Central Board on behalf of the villages.

All endeavour to work the unincorporated villages appears now to have been abandoned; and only the eighteen in-corporated villages were administered under the new law.

But village business was still carried on at excessive expense. In the two villages, Buxton and Friendship, the rates ran up to 4% on the valuation; and in Plaisance to $3\frac{1}{2}$%. Several villages on the east coast of Demerara petitioned against the continuance of the new ordinance, which suffered the fate of its predecessors, proving unworkable owing to want of money for village administration. It was repealed in 1883.

Meanwhile Ordinance No. 8 of 1878 had been passed " to consolidate and amend the law relating to the public health in *Ordinance* British Guiana." It divided the whole colony for *No.8 of 1878.* purposes of sanitary administration and regulation into (a) Town Sanitary Districts, *i.e.*, Georgetown and New Amsterdam; (b) Village Sanitary Districts, *i.e.*, the incorporated villages; and (c) Country Sanitary Districts, *i.e.*, the rest of the Colony. It left the two former in charge of the authorities already provided for them, and arranged for the local government of the third by Sanitary Authorities, to whom were given certain powers of administration and of levying rates. This ordinance was administered by means of the Central Board of Health, which continued to exist under it and which was re-named the Local Government Board by Ordinance No. 13 of 1907. There were thus two superior authorities, dealing with village government, in existence side by side—namely, the Central Board of Villages governing eighteen villages, all control of which was expressly vested in it to the exclusion of the Central Board of Health, and the Central Board of Health, to which the local authorities of the rest of the Colony were subject. The former had the assistance of an Inspector of Villages; the latter had no effective supervisory staff at all, and it is not very clear how it was expected to put its powers into operation. It appears to have contented itself, whenever complaint was made that any inhabited place was in bad order, with declaring such locality to be a Sanitary District and appointing a Local Sanitary Board, which was then left to act or not as it chose.

In 1881 and 1882, the condition of most of the incorporated villages was described as lamentable owing partly to the *Ordinance* restricted powers given to the chairmen of the Village *No.4 of 1883.* Councils, which precluded their getting any real work done, and partly to the heavy burdens for road maintenance,

U

as well as to several other minor causes, all of which tended to dishearten the industrious villager and to make the idlers even more thriftless. The crisis came in 1883, when, because of the general discontent and dissatisfaction with the village administration and in view of the deplorable conditions then existing, the whole system was changed by Governor Irving. Ordinance No. 4 of that year, "to amend the law relating to villages," swept away the whole of the previous machinery for managing incorporated villages, and placed their administration under the Public Works Department and the Inspector of Villages, the latter being appointed the Sanitary Authority under Ordinance No. 8 of 1878, and so made subject to the Central Board of Health. All village property of a communal character, which had been vested in the Central Board of Villages, was now placed under the control of the Public Works Department. Funds were provided by the levy of a 2% rate, which was collected by the Inspector of Villages, the chronic deficiencies being made up from public funds voted by the Combined Court. Under this ordinance the affairs of fifteen incorporated villages (fourteen in Demerara and one in Essequebo) passed into the hands of the Public Works Department, the number next year being increased to nineteen by the addition of five newly incorporated villages, one in Demerara, three in Berbice, and one in Essequebo. Moreover, in 1883, the maintenance of the trunk roads, other than those passing through sugar plantations or through Georgetown and New Amsterdam, was assumed by the Government, and the villages were thus finally relieved of one burden on their slender resources.

On the 27th September, 1890, the Board of Superintendence of the Town of New Amsterdam forwarded to the Government *Mayor and* Secretary the draft of a proposed New Amsterdam *Town Council* Town Council Ordinance, which was passed into law *created for* *New Amster-* in the following year as Ordinance No. 15 of 1891. *dam, 1891.* It provided that the municipal affairs of New Amsterdam should be administered by a Town Council consisting of seven members, one of whom should annually be elected by his fellow Councillors to be Mayor. Every inhabitant of the town who was of full age and not subject to any legal disability, and who was proprietor of any house or tenement in the town rated in the books of the Town Clerk at the value of $400 or more, was entitled to vote at the election of a member of the Town Council; and every person of full age and not subject to any legal disability, who was proprietor of any household property in the town, rated in the books of the Town Clerk at the value of $1,000 or more, was qualified to be elected a member of the Town Council. It was provided that on the 1st July in each year the two senior members of the Council for the time being should go out of office, and a new election be held. The Town Council was vested with full power and authority:

(1) to assess, levy, and raise town taxes for the uses and purposes of the corporation, and to superintend and direct the collection and appropriation of the same:

(2) to direct and enforce the cleanliness, good order, and repair of the public streets, roads, thoroughfares, dams, trenches, drains, ways, places, sluices, kokers, stellings, bridges, and canals of the town:

(3) to exercise sanitary superintendence over the town:

(4) to superintend the public market, slaughter-house, tanks, pound, and burial ground, and to cause the regulations for the good government thereof respectively to be enforced; and

(5) to have the direction of the public fire-engines, to cause the same to be exercised from time to time, to have all necessary repairs made thereto, and to keep them in efficient working order and fit for immediate service.

Thus a municipality was created in New Amsterdam, the chief town of the county of Berbice, similar to that in Georgetown. Ordinance No. 15 of 1891 continued in force until the reform of the Georgetown Town Council, in 1914,[1] suggested the propriety of similarly reforming the New Amsterdam Town

Reform of New Amsterdam Town Council in 1916. Council. Accordingly by Ordinance No. 10 of 1916, passed by the Court of Policy and assented to by Governor Sir Walter Egerton on the 26th May, 1916, the original New Amsterdam Town Council Ordinance was repealed, and a new law substituted. This

[1] Ordinance No. 17 of 1914. (See Chapter IV above.)

measure provides that the New Amsterdam Town Council
" shall consist of not more than nine Councillors, of whom
six are elected by the inhabitants of New Amsterdam, and
three are nominated by the Governor-in-Council." The
qualification for a Town Councillor is ownership of any
household property in the Town of New Amsterdam, rated
in the books of the Town Clerk at the value of $1,000 or more,
over and above the amount of any mortgage, or occupation
of premises in the town, the rental of which is not less than
$20 a month. Every inhabitant of the town, being of full age
and not subject to any legal disability, and being a British
subject or a resident in the Colony for not less than three
years, and being a proprietor of any house or tenement in the
town rated in the books of the Town Clerk at the value of
$250 or more, over and above the amount of any mortgage,
or occupying premises in the town the rental value of which
is not less than $15 a month, is entitled to vote at the election
of a Councillor. The Mayor is elected by the Town Councillors
from among their own number, on the second Friday in the
month of January every year, or on the first convenient day
thereafter, and continues in office until the election of his
successor. Any five Councillors form a sufficient quorum for
the despatch of business of all kinds, and in the absence of the
Mayor, the senior elected member presides. If the votes on
any matter under discussion are equal, the Mayor or any other
presiding member has a casting vote. The executive officers
of the Town Council are the Town Clerk, the Town Superintendent, an Engineer of electric works and waterworks, a Clerk of
the Market, a Health Officer, and Sanitary Inspectors. The
Powers of the New Amsterdam Town Council. Town Council has full power and authority to assess,
levy and raise town taxes, and to superintend and
direct the collection and appropriation thereof for
all or any of the following purposes, viz :

(1) The maintenance of the public streets, roads,
thoroughfares, dams, trenches, drains, ways, places,
sluices, kokers, stellings, bridges, and canals of the Town
which are vested in or under the control of the Council.

(2) The exercise or discharge of any authority or
obligation, for the benefit of public health, within the

Town vested in or imposed on the Council by the Local Government Ordinance, 1907,[1] or any other Ordinance.

(3) The supply of water for the use of the Town.

(4) The provision and maintenance of any burial ground, public garden, pound, market or slaughter-house.

(5) The lighting of all public buildings, streets, roads, thoroughfares, stellings, and bridges of the Town, and the manufacture and supply of gas or electric light for all purposes, public or private, within the limits of the Town, and within a radius of five miles of the Town Hall.

(6) The acquisition of land subject to the provisions of Ordinance No. 10 of 1916.

(7) The equipment and upkeep of a Fire Brigade and the payment of any necessary staff.

(8) The repayment of any moneys raised on loan, and the payment of interest on any part of such moneys for the time being not repayable.

(9) The payment of the salaries and wages of all officers and servants duly employed by the Council.

(10) The payment of any expenditure which the Council is by ordinance authorized to incur.

(11) Any other purpose for which by ordinance the Council is authorized to levy and raise taxes.

(12) To appropriate out of the Town Funds such sum, not exceeding the sum of $250, as it may think fit to be placed at the personal disposal of the Mayor.

(13) To award such pensions or gratuities to any of its officers or servants as may seem to it just, to be paid out of the general revenue of the Town Council.

As regards the raising of money on loan, the ordinance gives power to the Town Council to do this with the approval of the Governor-in-Council from time to time by the issue of bonds not exceeding $30,000 in any one year or $160,000 in the whole.

Municipalities have thus been established both in Demerara and in Berbice; but the county of Essequebo remains to this day without any township of sufficient importance to warrant its management by a Mayor and Town Council.

[1] See *infra*, p. 295.

In 1892, the whole system of village administration was again changed by an ordinance " to consolidate and amend the laws relating to villages " (No. 11 of 1892). This law removed the villages from the control of the Public Works Department, placed them under the control of the Central Board of Health, and made the Inspector of Villages an officer of that Board. The main object of the enactment was to give the villages a large measure of local self-government by the formation of elected Village Councils acting under the Central Board of Health at Georgetown. It gave the Village Councils the power of voting funds and taxes, of appointing village officers, and constructing village works; and it re-invested in the Village Councils all the village property which by Ordinance No. 4 of 1883 had been transferred to the Public Works Department. The Central Board of Health was, however, given very large powers, for it was entrusted with " the superintendence of all villages in the Colony," and with the " supervision, inspection and control over the several Village Councils and the officers and servants thereof." Nineteen incorporated villages now passed from the administration of the Public Works Department to that of the Village Councils and of the Central Board of Health, which in May, 1893, recommended to the Governor-in-Council, under section 4 of the ordinance, the appointment of a Committee from among its members to be styled the Villages Committee of the Central Board of Health. This recommendation was approved, and the following members of the Board were appointed in July, 1893, to form the first Committee, namely, Mr. H. Kirke, the then Chairman of the Board, Messrs. A. Weber and W. Craigen, members of the Court of Policy, the Director of Public Works, and the Mayor of Georgetown. Out of this Committee has grown what is now known as the Districts Committee.

Ordinance No. 11 of 1892.

Thus it will be observed that, outside Georgetown and New Amsterdam there were two systems : (*a*) the " incorporated villages " working under the Village Ordinance of 1892 and the Public Health Ordinance of 1878; and (*b*) the " country districts " working under the latter ordinance only. The Central Authority, however, found that to deal with the administration of the incorporated villages under one ordinance and their

Local Government Board created : Ordinance No. 13 of 1907.

sanitation under another was cumbersome and hampered progress. Moreover, the country districts developed considerably between the years 1892 and 1907, and the need of a more liberal administrative machinery than that provided for them by the Public Health Ordinance of 1878 was being felt almost daily. Accordingly a law to incorporate Ordinance No. 8 of 1878 with Ordinance No. 11 of 1892, and to deal comprehensively with both sanitation and village administration, became an absolute necessity; and the task of amalgamating the two ordinances was undertaken by Mr. A. G. Bell (the Director of Public Works) and Dr. J. E. Godfrey (the Surgeon-General), whose draft, after revision by the Attorney-General, was passed by Governor Sir F. M. Hodgson and the Court of Policy in 1907, and entitled " an Ordinance to consolidate and amend the law relating to Local Government and to Public Health and for other purposes connected therewith (No. 13 of 1907)." By this ordinance the Local Government Board was created in substitution for the Central Board of Health and the Central Board of Villages.

The new law, which is still in force, divides the whole Colony into districts of four kinds :

(a) " urban sanitary districts," of which there are only two, namely, the City of Georgetown and the Town of New Amsterdam :

(b) " village districts," comprising all villages hitherto declared as such under any ordinance for the time being in force :

(c) " country districts," corresponding to the " country sanitary districts " of Ordinance No. 8 of 1878 :

(d) " rural sanitary districts," including all plantations which do not form part of an urban, village or country district.

In the " urban sanitary districts " of Georgetown and New Amsterdam the respective Mayors and Town Councils are the *Urban Sanitary Districts.* " urban authority." But the Local Government Board has certain powers of supervision, inspection and control over the work done, or to be done, and acts performed, or to be performed, by the respective Town Councils in matters affecting the general sanitation of these towns and in some matters of local administration. In the other three kinds of districts the Board has much more extensive powers, and in fact directly superintends all their works and actions.

The Local Government Board consists of not less than eight members appointed by the Governor, and each member holds *Composition of Local Government Board.* office during the Governor's pleasure. The Governor also appoints one of the members to be Chairman and another to be Deputy-Chairman of the Board. At all meetings four members form a quorum, and in case of an equality of votes the Chairman has a casting vote. The chief executive officers of the Board are its Secretary and the Inspector of Districts, who were provided with an office and with clerks paid for out of funds voted by the Combined Court. The Board may appoint one or more Committees of its own body for the transaction of business, the Chairman and Deputy Chairman being *ex officio* members of all Committees. At present there is one such Committee, called the Districts Committee, which deals with questions relating to Village, Country and Rural Districts.

Village Districts are administered locally by Village Councils. These consist of such number of members, not less than four, *Village Districts and Country Districts.* as the Local Government Board may from time to time determine. The Village Councillors may all be elected by the villagers, or all be appointed by the Board, or some be elected and others appointed, as the Board may decide. The general rule is that the Village Councils consist of both elected and appointed Councillors. Country Districts are administered by Country Authorities, consisting of not less than three members, all of whom are appointed by the Board, which may add to or diminish the number of the members. The Board appoints the Chairmen of all Village Councils and Country Authorities; and may for good cause remove from office any Chairman of such Council or Authority. It may also review and declare invalid the order or decision of a Village Council or Country Authority, and substitute any order or decision which the Board may deem proper. It is in fact the paramount authority in the Villages and Country Districts, and insists on the regard of strict business principles by the local authorities, while training them to manage their own affairs.

In addition to these powers the Local Government Board, with respect to each Rural Sanitary District, (*a*) possesses all

Rural Sanitary Districts. powers conferred on the local authority of any Village or Country District, including the power of levying a rate and enforcing its payment; but the Board, exercising the powers of such authority, is not bound to perform any act required by the ordinance to be performed by such authority, which it appears inexpedient to the Board to perform; (*b*) has and may exercise in any Village or Country District any or all of the powers of a local authority whenever it appears to the Board expedient to do so, and may exercise any or all of such powers in any district, whether there is, or is not, a local authority of such district.

The annual report of the Local Government Board for the year 1913–14 shows that, on the 31st March, 1914, there were under its administration (*a*) in the County of Demerara, fourteen Village Districts and twenty-four Country Districts; (*b*) in the County of Essequebo, three Village Districts and twenty-seven Country Districts; and (*c*) in the County of Berbice, two Village Districts and twenty-nine Country Districts; and that in the whole Colony there were only two Rural Sanitary Districts—namely, Beterverwagting on the East Coast of Demerara, and La Grange on the West Bank of Demerara river.

CHAPTER XVI

EVENTS RESULTING IN THE REFORM OF THE POLITICAL CONSTITUTION : 1887–1892

A REPORT written by Dr. Williams, the Medical Inspector of the Colony, on his work for the year 1886, and published in
Court of 1887, became the object of much angry criticism by
Policy resent the planters, being in effect a description of insanitary
Medical
Inspector's conditions found to exist among labourers on the
Report on his
Work for the sugar estates. The *raison d'être* of the report was
Year 1886. the fact that, in 1886, the Medical Department took
over from the Immigration Department the control of the estates' hospitals and the medical and sanitary care of immigrants on the plantations. But Mr. Alexander, the Immigration Agent-General, who resented this transfer of control, maintained an attitude of hostility towards the Medical Department; and at a meeting of the Court of Policy, on the 11th October, 1887, the elective members, all of whom were planters, declined to discuss any business whatsoever, unless the Governor, Sir Henry T. Irving, publicly withdrew this report, which they regarded as slanderous and without foundation. The Governor declined to withdraw the report, and in this decision he was supported by the Secretary of State for the Colonies, Sir H. T. Holland. He was, however, willing to recommend that there should be a commission of inquiry "into the working of the Government Medical Service as regards the public institutions and the medical and sanitary care of immigrants on estates." This did not satisfy the electives, who withdrew in a body from a meeting of the Court of Policy, on the 25th October, at which the Governor announced his decision. They also wrote to the Secretary of State for the Colonies giving warning of possible difficulty, which would arise at the approaching session of Combined Court, in connexion with the estimates for 1888.

The Court of Policy at this time consisted of the Governor, four official members and five elective members.   No quorum

Deadlock in Court of Policy due to Withdrawal of Elective Section. was prescribed by any ordinance or by the Standing Rules and Orders of the Court; but by long usage the custom had been established of transacting no business in Court of Policy unless at least one elective member was present.[1]   Moreover, the Governor had no power to dissolve the Court, or in any other way to compel an appeal to the electorate.   Consequently the elective members by refusing either to attend the Court or to resign their seats were able to produce a deadlock.   In these circumstances, at the meeting of the Court on the 25th October, the Attorney-General (Mr. W. F. Haynes Smith) by direction of the Governor gave notice of a motion that the Court should " co-operate with the Governor in considering the question of an amendment of the political constitution of the Colony, with a view to secure wider representation of the inhabitants."

" It has long been obvious," Governor Irving remarked,[2] " that some change in the existing constitution of the Colony is inevitable, and these recent occurrences cannot fail to bring home to the minds of all persons interested in the Colony that the time has come when such a change must be effected.   A constitution, in which one interest only is represented, and in which that interest can, when it may deem proper to do so, bring about a deadlock in public affairs from which there is no constitutional mode of escape, is politically indefensible and necessarily breaks down the moment the elective members come into collision with the Government, acting on behalf of the unrepresented classes.   This is what has occurred now, has occurred in the past, and will recur with growing frequency in the future as other interests than those of the sugar planter increase in importance. . . . I do not think that any more convincing illustration of the necessity for such reform could be afforded than by the action of the elective members of the Court of Policy in refusing to do business on personal grounds, arising out of a matter in which none but themselves, and the class to which they belong, have any interest or concern."

[1] Governor's despatch, 26th October, 1887.
[2] *Ibid.*, 22nd October, 1887.

The conflict between the Government and the Electives caused no excitement in the Colony, where the Government was supported by a preponderance of public opinion and the necessity for reform in the constitution was generally recognized. A public meeting was convened at Georgetown by the Political Reform Club on the 2nd November, 1887, at which a memorial from the inhabitants of British Guiana to Her Majesty the Queen was read and unanimously adopted. The memorialists represented that, under the Royal Order-in-Council of 1864, no person was qualified to sit as an elective member of the Court of Policy unless he owned not less than 80 acres of land within the Colony, whereof not less than 40 acres must be " actually and *bona fide* under cultivation "; that this form of qualification excluded colonists who were not connected with the planting interest, and operated hardly on inhabitants who were exclusively members of the commercial, professional, and other interests, and who were fit and proper persons to represent those interests and were otherwise " fully qualified, in a monetary point of view, to share in the administration of the legislation of the Colony "; that, sugar being the staple product of British Guiana, the planting element was dominant in the legislature of the Colony; but that, owing to the depreciation in the value of sugar and the advanced condition of other products, known as " minor industries," principally belonging to the middle class which had grown up in the Colony, a form of government more representative in its character, " and more in touch and harmony with the present requirements " of British Guiana, was necessary; and that, unless the political constitution was remodelled, there would be " no guarantee against another political deadlock such as that of October, 1887, it being quite natural for the minds of persons to be biassed during the consideration of a subject affecting the particular interest to which they belong—and the legislature of the Colony being composed of persons who are all members of one interest, other interests not directly represented would not influence their minds against a suspension of political business." Accordingly the memorialists prayed the Queen to adopt such measures as Her Majesty might deem most advisable and best to afford relief

Public Meeting in Georgetown adopts Memorial to the Crown praying for Reform of the Constitution.

by granting the Colony a representative government similar to that recently granted to Jamaica and Trinidad.

This memorial, signed by 4,675 inhabitants of British Guiana, was forwarded to the Governor on the 7th December, 1887, and *Her Majesty's Government agree that Constitutional Reform is desirable.* by him transmitted to Sir H. T. Holland, who replied on the 8th February, 1888, that the memorial had been laid before the Queen, who was pleased to receive it very graciously; that Her Majesty's Government were prepared to advise that some amendment of the constitution of British Guiana was desirable; and that the nature and extent of such amendment would receive careful consideration.

Meanwhile Sir H. Irving had written to the Colonial Office on the 11th November, 1887, submitting his views as to the reforms to be proposed.

Views of Governor Sir H. Irving. " In the first place," he said, " the College of Electors should be abolished. This institution is indefensible; and its retention is not advocated, I believe, by any section of the community. The non-official members of the Court of Policy should be elected direct by the constituencies. Their number should be increased from five to six—giving four members for the county divisions and two for the city of Georgetown. The number of the official members should be similarly increased by one, *i.e.,* from four to five. For the elective members of the county divisions the present qualification might, if deemed proper, be maintained, namely, ownership of at least 80 acres, of which 40 are in cultivation, so as to secure adequate representation of the landed interest. For the city of Georgetown the qualification should be that of a Financial Representative. There does not appear to be occasion to alter the number or qualification of the Financial Representatives in the Combined Court. The Governor should have power to dissolve either the Court of Policy or the Combined Court. Some moderate improvement of the franchise might be effected. I am of opinion that these reforms will be sufficient to secure the object which the Government have in view, namely, the adequate representation of all classes and interests in the Legislature; and I believe that, if the question of these reforms be approached without delay and in a spirit of moderation, they may be disposed of by amicable arrangement, and without the creation of class feeling or political excitement in the Colony."

On the 22nd November, 1887, the Court of Policy resumed ordinary business, the elective members having in the mean-

Viscount Gormanston succeeds Sir H. Irving as Governor. time reconsidered their attitude; and the resolution, of which the Attorney-General had given notice on the 25th October, concerning the amendment of the political constitution of the Colony was adopted without a division, all the elective section being present.[1] However, at the close of the year, Sir H. Irving retired from the government of the Colony, and Viscount Gormanston, who succeeded him as Governor on the 13th January, 1888, not unnaturally desired to make himself familiar with local conditions before taking up so serious a question as that of constitutional reform. In these circumstances the reform proposals remained in abeyance until revived by the fact that the Civil List was due to expire on the 31st December, 1889.[2]

It will be remembered that, in 1882, the question of substituting a permanent Civil List for the septennial system had been

Reform Proposals and Increase of Civil List regarded as interdependent. debated, but that the only measure of reform then achieved was to make permanent provision for the judicial salaries. Subsequently, at a meeting of Combined Court on the 13th December, 1887, the salary of Mr. Hutchens, the Colonial Civil Engineer,[3] who was an object of dislike to the electives, was by them reduced from £1,000 to £600 *per annum*, as an amendment to a motion, made by one Financial Representative and seconded by another, that the item be struck off the estimate entirely. Two days later the annual salary of the Medical Inspector was reduced by the electives to one cent, with the object of wreaking vengeance upon Dr. Williams, who held the post, for his obnoxious report on the insanitary conditions which he had found to exist among labourers on the sugar estates. These incidents caused Lord Knutsford [4] to express to Lord Gormanston the opinion that recent proceedings in the Combined Court had demonstrated the necessity of " very considerably modifying the Civil List by making the salaries of the principal Heads of Departments independent of the annual vote of the Combined Court," and further that the enactment of the Civil

[1] The elective members were C. L. Bascom, B. Howell Jones, J. J. Dare, Thos. Mulligan, and W. A. Wolseley.

[2] Ordinance No. 10 of 1883.

[3] Title changed to " Director of Public Works " by Ordinance No. 23 of 1914.　　　　[4] Despatch, dated 1st May, 1889.

List Ordinance was " closely connected with the question of a reform of the constitution of the Colony, now under consideration "; and he desired to be furnished with the Governor's views as to the salaries which should be secured by ordinance either permanently, or for a term of years, and as to the nature and extent of the reform of the constitution which it was desirable to effect.

Lord Gormanston replied, on the 24th May, 1889, that the Civil List " should include, in addition to the Government *Lord Gorman-* Secretary, and Attorney-General, all the principal *ston recom-* Heads of Department, namely, the Auditor-General, *mends that* *Civil List* the Colonial Receiver-General,[1] the Comptroller of *should in-* *clude all the* Customs, the Chief Commissary, the Colonial Civil *Principal* Engineer, the Crown Surveyor,[2] the Postmaster- *Heads of De-* *partments.* General, the Surgeon-General, the Inspector-General of Police "; and that it might be considered later on " whether the salary of the Immigration Agent-General and the Medical Inspector should not be included."

> " I do not consider," added Lord Gormanston, " that it is desirable at present to make any change in the constitution of the Colony. Should such a modification of the Civil List as Your Lordship seems to suggest, and which I have detailed, be decided on, Your Lordship, I presume, anticipates that it will be strenuously opposed in the Combined Court, as it no doubt will be; and I infer from the terms of your despatch that, if these modifications were rejected, Your Lordship would insist on a reform of the constitution of this Colony being made. But such reform could not, in my opinion, be carried out—the present constitution being guaranteed by the treaties, which were made at the time of the cession of the Colony, between the Dutch and English Governments—without the intervention and consent of the Imperial Parliament."

Lord Knutsford, however, remarked [3] that the opinion of Her Majesty's Government as to the desirability of some amendment *Civil List* of the constitution had already been made known to *renewed for* the Colony, and had been more than once stated in *One Year* *only pending* Parliament; and he considered that the time had *Decision on* *the Reform* come for giving effect to it. Nor could he agree that *Proposals.* the intervention of Parliament was necessary.

[1] Title changed to " Colonial Treasurer " by Ordinance No. 23 of 1914.
[2] Title since changed to " Commissioner of Lands and Mines."
[3] Despatch, dated 27th July, 1889.

" It is quite possible," he explained, " to reform the constitution without infringing any condition made at the time of the cession of the Colony to the British Government. I must, therefore, request you to reconsider the question, and, after consulting the members of the Court of Policy, to furnish me with the heads of such a measure of reform as would, in your opinion, secure an adequate representation to the inhabitants of the Colony in the elective branch of the Court of Policy and the Combined Court."

In a further despatch,[1] Lord Knutsford added that, pending the settlement of the reform questions, it was not desirable that the Civil List Ordinance should be renewed for a period of seven years, and that the best course would be to re-enact the ordinance for the period of one year only. This was accordingly done by Ordinance No. 15 of 1889, which continued the existing Civil List until the 31st December, 1890.

Meanwhile, in yet another despatch,[2] Lord Knutsford informed Lord Gormanston that Her Majesty's Government, *Views of Her Majesty's Government as to Reforms required.* as then advised, did not desire to abolish the system of a Court of Policy for general legislation and of a Combined Court for fiscal legislation; that it was the wish of Her Majesty's Government that the Crown should retain the control of legislation in the Court of Policy by means of the Governor's casting vote, and that the elective section of the Legislature " should represent not, as at present, exclusively, or nearly exclusively, a single class, but all classes who are capable of intelligently exercising the franchise. There will still remain, even so," he remarked, " a large numerical majority of the inhabitants, who will not be directly represented, and whose interests must be guarded by the Government through the official members of the Legislature." As to the method of enacting the reform, Lord Knutsford observed, in a despatch dated the 18th November, 1889, " that, as the Colony was added to the British dominions by conquest, and the conquest confirmed by the cession contained in the Treaty of 1814, the power of making laws was, from the first, exercisable by the King-in-Council"; that " this power was expressly reserved, in 1831, by a clause in Sir Benjamin D'Urban's com-

---

[1] Despatch, dated 4th September, 1889.
[2] Despatch, dated 27th September, 1889.

mission as first Governor of the combined Colony "; that a
similar clause would be found in the existing Letters Patent
constituting the office of Governor; that, having regard to the
stipulations of the Capitulation of 1803, doubt had been
expressed " whether any such change in the constitution of the
Colony could be effected, otherwise than by an Act of Parliament, as would enable the Crown to impose taxes without the
authority of the Combined Court "; but that, subject to this
doubt, he was advised " that either the Queen-in-Council, or
the Governor and the Court of Policy, are competent to enact
any law requisite for altering the constitution." Lord Knutsford apprehended that it would probably be preferred by the
Colony that, looking to the importance of the matter, any
change should be made by Order of Her Majesty-in-Council,
but he desired to learn Lord Gormanston's views on this
point.

Lord Gormanston, after consulting informally the members
of the Court of Policy, submitted to the Secretary of State, in
a despatch dated the 3rd January, 1890, the heads
Petition of the British Guiana Constitutional Reform Association. of a scheme of reform prepared by him; and, on
the 17th *idem*, he forwarded a numerously signed
petition, which had been presented to him two days
previously by the British Guiana Constitutional
Reform Association, praying :

> " 1st, That the Court of Policy, College of Electors and
> Combined Court may be abolished, and an Executive
> Council and Legislative Assembly substituted therefor.
>
> " 2nd, That the Executive Council may consist of the
> Governor, as President, and six members to be nomi-
> nated by the Crown—not more than three to be officials
> —to discharge the executive functions of the Court of
> Policy.
>
> " 3rd, That the Legislative Assembly may consist of
> five members, nominated by the Crown, the Governor not
> being one, and sixteen members elected by ballot by the
> registered voters, and upon the same qualification as our
> present Financial Representatives, namely, ' possession of
> any house, or land, under title, or held on lease for 21 years,
> or upwards, the rental or value of which *per annum* shall
> be at least $1,200 (£250), or to be possessed of a clear
> annual income of $1,440 (£300), derived from any other
> kind of property in the Colony, or from the profits of

x

any other trade or profession carried on within the Colony.'

" 4th, That the franchise be altered on the following basis:

" (*a*) In a County—possession of three acres of land under cultivation, or land of $96 (£20) annual rental; or occupancy for three years of six acres of land under cultivation, or for one year of a house or land of $192 (£40) rental, or of an income amounting to $300 (£62 10s.) *per annum*, or payment of $20 (£4 3s. 4d.) direct taxes.

" (*b*) In a Town—possession of a house, or house and premises, of the value of $500 (£104 3s. 4d.), or occupancy of same for one year at a rental of $120 (£25), or of an income amounting to $300 (£62 10s.) *per annum*, or payment of $20 (£4 3s. 4d.) direct taxes.

" (*c*) Aliens, after three years' residence, and in possession of any of these qualifications, to be entitled to vote at elections.

" 5th, That the mode of voting be by ballot on the principle adopted in the United Kingdom.

" 6th, That the Legislative Assembly may have power to appoint from among its members one to preside over their deliberations, who shall be vested with the authority of the Speaker of such an Assembly.

" 7th, That the Representatives of the Government be responsible for the introduction of all government measures and money votes; but that the other members may introduce legislative measures with the permission of the Legislative Assembly.

" 8th, That Bills introduced into the Legislative Assembly, having been read a first time, if passed for second reading, may then be published in one or more newspapers of the Colony for general information—thereafter be committed for discussion and revision; passing through committee may be read a third time, passed and sent to the Governor, who shall have power to refuse his assent until Her Majesty's pleasure be known; and, when Her Majesty's assent shall have been obtained, Bills shall become Law on publication in the *Official Gazette* of the Colony.

" 9th, That the Governor may summon an Annual Session of the Legislature for the despatch of business: that a general election shall take place every third year, but the Governor may have the right of proroguing or dissolving the Legislative Assembly at any time and calling for a new election, such election to take place within three months from date of dissolution.

" 10th, That the Colony may be divided into Electoral Districts, represented thus :

Georgetown	4 members
County of Demerara . .	6 do.
County of Essequebo . .	3 do.
County of Berbice . .	2 do.
New Amsterdam . . .	1 member
Total .	16 members."

The Governor's view was that the Court of Policy, which had hitherto exercised administrative as well as legislative functions, was " a slow and cumbrous machine for executive purposes, while the many and rapid changes which take place in the *personnel* of the elective members have made it impossible to bring before it business of a confidential nature with perfect freedom and without risk of detriment to the public service." He was therefore, in favour of transferring the administrative functions of the Court of Policy to an Executive Council. He attached importance to the exclusion from the Legislature of all but natural-born or naturalized British subjects. " The admission of aliens," he wrote, " probably originated in a desire to place the old Dutch colonists on an equal footing with the English ; but this class has disappeared." For the franchise he proposed to fix the income qualification at $480 (£100) *per annum,* while extending the qualifications of the elective members by admitting the possession or lease of immovable property, in order to open the Court to members of the mercantile community and others not connected with the planting interest. It was advisable, he thought, to adhere to the system of open voting, which was in force in the municipal elections in the Colony, as well as in elections to the Colleges of Electors and of Financial Representatives. On the Civil List question he stated : " I have come to the conclusion that there is no section of influential men in the Colony, either on the side of the planting interest, or on the side of those who have been

Views of Lord Gor-manston.

prominent in supporting the movement in favour of reform, who would support either a permanent or an extended Civil List." The other matters of principle had already been determined by Her Majesty's Government; and Lord Gormanston believed that a reform on these lines would secure the adhesion of the moderate men, who were fortunately also the most influential, representing interests for which it was the design of the scheme to obtain adequate representation and protection.

After careful consideration of these opinions, Her Majesty's Government decided [1] that the College of Electors should be abolished; that the unofficial members of the Court

Decision of Her Majesty's Government as to the Reforms to be authorized.

of Policy should be chosen by direct election in the several constituencies, and should be eight in number —namely, two for the County of Demerara (excluding Georgetown), two for the County of Essequebo, one for the County of Berbice (excluding the town of New Amsterdam), two for the City of Georgetown, and one for the town of New Amsterdam; that there should be seven official members in addition to the Governor; that the executive functions of the Court should be transferred to an Executive Council, to include the Government Secretary, the Attorney-General and such other persons as the Crown might from time to time appoint; and that measures should be proposed to the Court of Policy for altering the qualifications for election to the Court of Policy and for election as a Financial Representative, as well as the qualifications for voters in elections both of members of the Court of Policy and of Financial Representatives. In a despatch dated the 11th June, 1890, Lord Knutsford added that it would not be necessary to frame a Royal Order-in-Council empowering the Governor and Court of Policy to enact a law altering the constitution, as was done in 1855, because the existing Letters Patent constituting the office of Governor, and the accompanying Royal Instructions, did not restrict the Colonial Legislature from enacting such a law, or the Governor from assenting to it, provided that it contained a suspending clause. Lord Gormanston was, however, instructed to submit to the Secretary of State for the Colonies the draft of an Ordinance embodying the authorized scheme of reform, prior to its first reading in Court of Policy; and Lord Knutsford

---

[1] Lord Knutsford's despatch, 30th April, 1890.

directed that the draft Ordinance should not deal with the Executive Council, nor define the powers and functions of the Combined Court. " The former," he wrote, " will be dealt with by Letters Patent; the latter by an Order-in-Council to be made after the enactment of a Civil List Ordinance, and conferring powers as heretofore limited in duration to the existence of that Ordinance."

The draft Ordinance to amend the constitution was forwarded by Lord Gormanston, on the 20th June, 1890, to Lord Knuts-

Heads of Reform Bill approved by Her Majesty's Government. ford, who returned it under cover of a despatch, dated the 14th October, 1890, as revised and altered by his directions. So amended, the bill comprised the following material reforms :

(1) The Court of Policy was enlarged by the addition of three official members, to be appointed by the Crown, or provisionally appointed by the Governor, and of three elected members.

(2) The College of Electors was abolished, and the unofficial members of the Court of Policy were to be elected directly in the same manner as the Financial Representatives, five by country constituencies, two by Georgetown, and one by New Amsterdam.

(3) The property qualification of an elected member of the Court of Policy was assimilated to that of a Financial Representative; and for both an additional property qualification—namely, possession of immovable property in the Colony to the value of not less than \$10,000 was provided. This sum was, however, reduced in section 12(4) of the ordinance, as passed, to \$7,500.

(4) Aliens were, as in other parts of Her Majesty's dominions, excluded from the franchise, and were disqualified for election as members of the Court of Policy or as Financial Representatives.

(5) The income qualification for the franchise was reduced to \$480.

(6) The Court of Policy might be dissolved at any time by the Governor, and must be dissolved at the end of five years from a general election; and, upon a dissolution of the Court of Policy, the seats of the Financial Representatives were vacated, so that general elections of members

of the Court of Policy and Financial Representatives would be held simultaneously, and the latter would no longer hold their seats for two years only.

(7) The quorum of the Court of Policy was to be ten, and of the Combined Court twelve, members; but in each case business might be carried on with a quorum of eight members only, that is to say, by the Governor and the official section, if the full quorum failed to attend after an adjournment of one day.

(8) Election petitions were to be addressed to the Supreme Court and to be tried by one of the Judges, sitting without a jury.

(9) Revising barristers were to be appointed for the revision of the lists of voters.

(10) Power was to be given to the Court of Policy and the Combined Court to expel contumacious members, and to punish by committal to prison persons who were guilty of contempt of Court.

(11) The executive and administrative functions of the Court of Policy were transferred to an Executive Council to be constituted under Letters Patent.

" This bill, as now revised by me," Lord Knutsford concluded, " embodies those changes in the constitution of British Guiana, which, after careful consideration, Her Majesty's Government are of opinion that, having regard to the peculiar circumstances of the Colony and its population, they can safely permit to be introduced; and, if it should become law, though it may not altogether give effect to the views of those who have petitioned Her Majesty on the subject, it will constitute a considerable and, I trust, beneficial measure of reform."

The bill was read a first time in Court of Policy on the 27th November, 1890. It was brought up for a second reading on *Ordinance* the 11th December, when a petition was laid on the *No. 1 of 1891* table, signed by the President and Secretary of the *passed by* *Court of* British Guiana Constitutional Reform Association, *Policy and* *confirmed by* praying for certain alterations in it; and another *the Crown.* petition, signed by the Reverend Mr. Crookall and certain inhabitants of Berbice, praying for the postponement of

the second reading of the bill.   At this meeting Lord Gormanston, in accordance with the unanimous wish of the elective
members, agreed to the deletion of the proviso that the business
of the Court of Policy and the Combined Court might be carried
on with a quorum of eight members, if the full quorum should
fail to attend after an adjournment of one day.   One elective
member only, Mr. Mulligan, voted against the second reading
because he objected to the 2nd subsection of clauses 24 and
42 of the bill, which provided that no member of the Court
of Policy or Combined Court should be entitled, after having
taken his seat at any meeting, to withdraw without the
leave of the Governor or other presiding member, and that, if
any member withdrew without leave, the remaining members,
not being less than seven in number beside the Governor or other
presiding member, might proceed with and transact business
in the same manner as if a quorum had been present.   The
committee stage of the bill was taken on the 3rd February,
1891; and on that day the bill was also read a third time,
passed, and its title settled as Ordinance No. 1 of 1891, " an
Ordinance to alter and amend the Political Constitution of
the Colony." [1]   The royal assent to the Ordinance was communicated to the Governor in a despatch from the Secretary of
State, dated the 30th of the following month.

Meanwhile the Combined Court had, on the 12th December,
1890, passed a resolution to make provision for the establishment of a Civil List for the term of seven years, com-

Civil List enlarged to include the Principal Heads of Departments.
mencing from the 1st January, 1891. This resolution
provided in the Civil List for all the additional Heads
of Departments proposed in Lord Gormanston's
despatch of the 24th May, 1889, but it did not include
the Immigration Agent-General [2] and the Medical Inspector. [3]
It was formally confirmed by Ordinance No. 28 passed on the
20th December, 1890; and the total sum thus allocated for

---

[1] See Appendix P.

[2] Subsequently, by section 6 (2) of the Immigration Ordinance No. 18
of 1891, it was enacted that " the Immigration Agent-General shall
receive a salary at the rate of not more than £1,500 *per annum.*"   This
office is, therefore, permanently provided for by statute in the same
manner as are the offices of the Chief Justice and of the two Puisne
Judges (see Chapter XIII, *supra*).

[3] This post no longer exists.

payment of the Civil List was at the rate of £27,683 6s. 8d. *per annum*.[1]

Letters Patent constituting the Executive Council[2] were passed under the Great Seal of the United Kingdom on the 5th *Executive* March, 1891, and published in the Colony by pro- *Council* clamation dated the 2nd January, 1892; and the *constituted.* original members appointed to the Council were the Governor (Viscount Gormanston), the Government Secretary (Sir Charles Bruce), and the Attorney-General (Mr. A. Kingdon) *ex officio*; two other officials—namely, Mr. F. Villiers (Auditor-General) and Mr. A. H. Alexander (Immigration Agent-General) —nominated by the Crown; and three unofficial members, Messrs. W. H. Sherlock,[3] J. J. Dare,[4] and W. A. Wolseley,[5] also nominated by the Crown. The first meeting of the Executive Council was held on the 25th January, 1892. Its chief function, as defined by the Letters Patent, was " to advise and assist the Governor for the time being in the administration of the Government." The Council was also given certain statutory powers by the Political Constitution Ordinance (No. 1 of 1891),

[1] The details of the Civil List provided by Ordinance No. 28 of 1890 were as follows (compare schedule on p. 264 *supra*) :

	£	s.	d.
The Governor	5,000	0	0
,, ,, Contingencies	1,000	0	0
The Government Secretary	1,500	0	0
The Assistant Government Secretary and Clerk to the Court of Policy and Combined Court . . .	700	0	0
Clerks and expenses of the Offices of the Court of Policy and the Government Secretary . . .	833	6	8
The Attorney-General	1,500	0	0
The Solicitor-General	500	0	0
The Auditor-General	1,000	0	0
The Receiver-General	1,000	0	0
The Comptroller of Customs	1,000	0	0
The Chief Commissary	800	0	0
The Inspector-General of Police	750	0	0
The Colonial Civil Engineer	1,000	0	0
The Surgeon-General	1,200	0	0
The Crown Surveyor	800	0	0
The Postmaster-General	700	0	0
The Stipendiary Magistrates	8,400	0	0
Total	£27,683	6	8

[2] See Appendix M.
[3] Attorney of Messrs. Sandbach, Parker & Co.
[4] Attorney of Messrs. Booker Brothers & Co.
[5] Part proprietor of Plantation " Lusignan," East Coast, Demerara.

which enacted in sections 30 and 31 that " if and so soon as Her Majesty shall constitute an Executive Council for this Colony, all the executive and administrative functions, which at present belong by law or usage to the Governor and Court of Policy, or the Court of Policy, shall be transferred to, and vested in, the Governor and the Executive Council"; and that " where in any enactment or any document reference is made to the Governor and Court of Policy, or to the Court of Policy, or the like, in relation to such executive or administrative functions as aforesaid, the Governor in Executive Council shall, if such Council is constituted, be intended and taken in lieu thereof"; while the expression " Governor-in-Council " was defined by the Interpretation Ordinance (No. 14 of 1891, section 5) to mean " the Governor acting with, but not necessarily in accordance with, the advice of the Executive Council."

The first general election under the reformed constitution was held in January, 1892; and the first meeting of the reorganized Combined Court was held on the 16th February, 1892. It is interesting to observe how inappreciable was the change which the reform of the constitution at first made in the *personnel* of the elective section of the Colony's legislature.   Prior to the general election of 1892, there had been in the Court of Policy and the two Colleges combined eighteen colonial representatives.[1]   Of these, as regards race, thirteen were white, four were men of colour, and one was a negro; while, as regards occupation, five were proprietors of sugar estates, three were attorneys of firms largely interested in sugar, one was a planter, two were bank-managers, one was manager of the Demerara Railway, three were merchants, and three were barristers.   The reform of the constitution reduced the number of colonial representatives to fourteen; and of these, as regards race, twelve were white, and two were men of colour; while, as regards occupation, two were proprietors of sugar estates, two were attorneys of firms largely interested in sugar, three were planters, five were merchants, and two were barristers.   It is also noteworthy that one-half of the fourteen new colonial representatives were the same persons who had, prior to the general election, occupied seats in one or other of the three bodies politic.   Ten of the original eighteen

First General Election.

[1] See Appendix Q.

representatives had not offered themselves for re-election; six were returned unopposed to seats either in the Court of Policy or the College of Financial Representatives; and one (Mr. W. H. Sherlock) was appointed to be a member of the Executive Council. There were only three contested elections. Mr. A. Barr, attorney of Messrs. Hogg, Curtis Campbell & Company, and a member of the unreformed Court of Policy, contested the seat for West Demerara in the Court of Policy with Mr. J. A. Murdoch, a barrister of negro race, who, however, polled only sixty-eight votes as against eighty-one votes cast for Mr. Barr, and was, therefore, defeated by a majority of thirteen. The other two contests were between candidates none of whom had seats in any body politic prior to the reform law. For the East Demerara seat in the Court of Policy there was a triangular fight between Mr. J. P. Farnum, a coloured storekeeper, who polled 171 votes; Mr. E. C. Luard, a white planter, who polled 165 votes, and Mr. W. E. Lewis, a negro barrister, who polled eighteen votes. Mr. Farnum, who headed the poll, was, however, unseated on election petition because his name was not in the list of voters; and the seat, therefore, went to Mr. Luard. The third contest was for the financial representation of Demerara, and took place between Mr. G. Garnett, a white merchant, and Mr. P. Dargan, a coloured barrister. The former won the seat with 245 votes against 230. It is somewhat striking that there was no contested election in Georgetown or New Amsterdam; and, in fact, that the only contests were in respect of the representation of the county of Demerara.

Not long afterwards, at a meeting of the Court of Policy, on the 24th March, 1892, an interesting constitutional question was raised by Mr. D. M. Hutson, who asked whether, *Privileges of Combined Court not repealed by Ordinance No. 1 of 1891.* under the new Political Constitution Ordinance, the rights and privileges of the Combined Court had not been repealed and taken away. The cause of this question was the fact that the new law had repealed Governor Beaujon's publication of the 21st June, 1796, as well as Governor D'Urban's proclamation of the 21st July, 1831. The acting Attorney-General (Mr. A. Kingdon) gave a reply, which had been previously approved by Lord Knutsford, to the effect that (a) Governor Beaujon in submitting to the Court of Policy his scheme for a system of financial representation, which was subsequently embodied in his publication of 1796, himself stated that the whole measure was only provisional until the pleasure of His Majesty should be known; and that, as a matter of fact, it was not confirmed by His Majesty's Government; (b) that " the system of June, 1796, was placed by the Capitulation of September, 1803, upon a different footing from that on which it stood previously; a validity, which did not belong to it in virtue of the authority by which it was established, was imparted to it in 1803 by the first article of the Capitulation, which stipulated that the mode of taxation then in use should be continued "; [1] (c) that the minutes of Combined Court, from its first meeting on the 2nd August, 1797, until the restitution of the Colony to the Dutch on the 2nd December, 1802, and from that period to the second capture by the British on the 19th September, 1803, show what was the mode of taxation then in use and the regular course of business transacted by that body; (d) that Governor Carmichael's proclamation of 1812 was rescinded by the Royal Order-in-Council of 1831, pursuant to which Governor D'Urban's proclamation of that year was issued; and that, therefore, Governor D'Urban's proclamation merely replaced things in the same state in which they had been before Governor Carmichael's proclamation was made, but gave no additional validity to the publication of 1796; (e) that the existing powers of the Combined Court were dependent on two distinct terms; the power to raise revenue being an absolute right conferred by the terms of the Articles of Capitulation, which were the real charter of the Combined Court; whilst the right to discuss the estimates fully and freely depended upon the Royal Orders-in-Council, issued from time to time, in consideration of the grant of a Civil List to the Sovereign. But the non-renewal of the Civil List would not affect the right of the Combined Court to raise revenue, a right which could only be taken away by an Act of the Imperial Parliament.

It was thus shown that the Political Constitution Ordinance of 1891 had not in any way affected the rights and privileges of the Combined Court.

[1] Letter of Law Officers of the Crown, J. Dodson, J. Campbell, and T. Wilde, dated 21st October, 1840 : Parl.   Papers 297 of 1849.

CHAPTER XVII

SUBSEQUENT CONSTITUTIONAL LEGISLATION PRIOR TO THE YEAR 1928

THE general elections of 1906 brought into prominence several defects in the machinery for elections provided by the British Guiana Constitution Ordinance No. 1 of 1891; and, with a view to remedying them, a bill was drafted by the Law Officers of the Colony under the direction of Governor Sir F. M. Hodgson, was approved by Lord Elgin in a despatch dated the 2nd December, 1907, and was read a first time in the Court of Policy on the 27th April, 1908. The second reading was passed without debate on the 17th December, 1908, and on the same day the Court went into Committee to consider the bill clause by clause.

Ordinance No. 24 of 1909.

One of the most important sections of the bill was the fourth, which dealt with the qualification of elected members of the Court of Policy and disqualified any person who had " failed for the space of three months to comply with any order of the Supreme Court, made after the commencement of this Ordinance, directing him to pay any money held or received by him in a fiduciary capacity." Similarly another section of the bill provided that, if any elected member of the Court of Policy or any Financial Representative failed to comply with such an order of the Supreme Court, his seat should thereupon *ipso facto* become vacant. Mr. P. N. Browne, a negro barrister, seconded by Mr. F. Dias, a Portuguese solicitor, moved that these provisions should be deleted, on the ground that the parties directly concerned could take legal proceedings against a defaulting trustee, levy on his property by means of execution sale, and thus remove his property qualification and render his seat vacant. But the Attorney-General, Sir T. C. Rayner, pointed out that, where trust moneys were not forthcoming upon order of the Supreme Court, there must be a certain amount of moral delinquency; while Mr. J. P. Santos, a

Portuguese merchant, added that members of the Legislature should be free from debt, as otherwise they could not express an independent opinion on matters brought before them. A division was called for, and Mr. Browne's motion was rejected by ten votes to five.

The 4th section, as originally drafted, also amended the property qualification of elected members of the Court of

Property Qualification for Membership of Court of Policy modified.

Policy by requiring it to be unencumbered by mortgage. The effect would, therefore, have been to increase the qualification. But discussion in Committee elicited the fact that, in the opinion of the elective section, the time had come for reducing the value of the property qualification. It was suggested by Mr. P. N. Browne, with whom the other elected members concurred, that the qualification should be reduced from $7,500 to $5,000 for the reason that the value of immovable property had undoubtedly declined, and that the number of persons possessing a property qualification of the value of $7,500 was very much less than formerly. The principal cause had been the decadence of the sugar industry, which resulted in the dispersion of property into more hands; and it was maintained that an unencumbered qualification of the value of $5,000 would probably be quite the equivalent of an encumbered one of $7,500. Governor Hodgson concurred in these views; but he could not, in view of the Royal Instructions, adopt the amendment without the sanction of the Crown. The clause was, therefore, left over.

Again, the bill as drafted, while leaving unchanged the qualification of Financial Representative, aimed at making it clearer than in the principal Ordinance that the property qualifications must be either:

Property Qualification of Financial Representatives elucidated.

(a) $1,440 a year arising from property, over and above any interest payable under any mortgage thereon; or

(b) an annual income of $1,440 from a trade or profession,

and not an income arising partly from property and partly from a trade or profession. The bill also made it clear that the above qualifications were in lieu of the property qualifications prescribed for members of the Court of Policy, and that a Financial Representative would not have to be possessed of the qualifications of a member of the Court of Policy in addition to one or other of those now required.   There was no opposition to these amendments.

It was, however, the unanimous wish of the elective section that the income qualification for the elective franchise should *Elective* be reduced from $480 a year to $300 a year.   Here *Franchise* again there was no doubt that the salaries paid to *reduced.* clerks were less than formerly; and the Governor was assured that in consequence several individuals, otherwise qualified to exercise the franchise, were without a voice in the selection of their representatives.   This point, therefore, was left over for reference to the Secretary of State for the Colonies, since the bill as drafted had done no more than amend the principal Ordinance by making the ownership or occupation of land alone a qualification for city or town voters.   Under the law as it then stood, only land with a house upon it gave the right to vote for the members of Court of Policy and for the Financial Representatives of Georgetown and New Amsterdam, while the amendment proposed that a land lot with no building upon it should, if of the requisite value, give a right to such a vote.

The remaining provisions of the bill aimed at effecting improvement in the machinery for elections, and met with no opposition.

Governor Hodgson, in a despatch dated the 7th January, 1909, reported what had taken place in Committee to Lord *Lord Crewe's* Crewe, the Secretary of State for the Colonies, who *Approval.* replied on the 25th March, 1909, that he approved the reduction of the property qualification of elected members of the Court of Policy from $7,500 to $5,000, provided that the reduced qualification was an unencumbered one.   Lord Crewe also acceded to the wish of the elective section that the income qualification for a vote should be reduced from $480 to $300 a year.   But he decided that the sections relating to disqualification and unseating of a member of the Court of Policy or a Financial Representative, who had failed to comply with any order of the Supreme Court directing him to pay any money held by him in a fiduciary capacity, must be maintained as they stood.

The bill was accordingly recommitted on the 28th June, 1909; and, as amended, was read a third time and passed *Royal* on the 30th November, 1909, as Ordinance No. 24 *Assent.* of that year,[1] the royal assent being conveyed by Lord Crewe in a despatch dated the 8th February, 1910.

The only constitutional legislation subsequently enacted, before the radical reforms of 1928, was that contained in two *Ordinances* Ordinances, namely, (*a*) No. 14 of 1914,[1] which, apart *of 1914* from substituting the Colonial Treasurer for the *and 1927.* Auditor-General as an *ex officio* member of the Court of Policy, aimed solely at further improvement in the machinery for conducting elections; and (*b*) the Register of Voters (Electoral District No. 1) Ordinance of 1927. All this constitutional legislation was eventually repealed by the British Guiana (Constitution) Order-in-Council, made by King George V at the Court at Buckingham Palace on the 13th July, 1928.

[1] See Appendix P.

PART III

CRITICAL ANALYSIS OF THE CONSTITUTION OF BRITISH
GUIANA PRIOR TO THE YEAR 1928

CHAPTER I

REFERENDA IN 1914 ON CONSTITUTIONAL REFORM

DURING the autumn of the year 1913, Sir Walter Egerton, Governor of British Guiana, made a memorable journey to the *Financing of* Rupununi savannahs with the object of acquiring *Trunk-rail-* such accurate knowledge of the country between *way through* the Atlantic coast, at the mouth of the Demerara *British* *Guiana* river, and the Amazon watershed, at the point *dependent on* *Change in the* where the Takutu river forms the boundary between *Constitution.* British Guiana and Brazil, as would enable an estimate to be framed of the probable cost of a railway connecting Georgetown, the capital of the Colony, with the State of Amazonas. The scheme was one which might well fire the imagination. It was, in effect, that through British Guiana, our only colony in South America, should pass the first section of a great trunk-line, traversing the whole continent from north to south, and that the port of Georgetown should be the northern terminus.[1]

The results obtained by the journey were eminently satisfactory;[2] and in a despatch to the Secretary of State for the Colonies, dated the 5th January, 1914, Sir Walter invited His Majesty's Government to assist the Colony in financing the construction of the British section of the contemplated transcontinental railway. But an initial objection to the grant of an Imperial loan for this purpose was the fact that the Colony possessed very complete local control, by means of the large elective majority in the Combined Court, over both its revenue and its expenditure.

" It is," wrote the Governor, " an axiom of the Imperial Treasury that, without control of the finances of a dependency, no advances can be made from Imperial funds. This is a very reasonable rule; but I believe I am right in

[1] B. G. Combined Court, Sessional Paper No. 746 of 1914, pp. 8–9.
[2] *Ibidem*, enclosure II, p. i.

saying that, although the people cherish greatly their present constitution, yet they would willingly, in order to secure the much longed-for railway to the interior, assent to such a reduction in the numbers of the elective section, or increase to the official members, as to give the Home Government, through the Governor and his officers, the same power and control over the administration and finances as now exist in, say, Trinidad; if not indefinitely, at any rate until the Colony is in a position to assume full responsibility for the financial obligations which the construction and working of the proposed railway must entail." [1]

Mr. L. Harcourt, in his answering despatch dated the 21st April, 1914, said :

" You have rightly assumed that, without full Imperial control over the finances of the Colony, there could be no question of advances being made from the Imperial Treasury; and you have mentioned as an illustration the present constitution of the neighbouring colony of Trinidad, under which that island has made remarkable progress. I entirely agree with what you say on this subject. The Secretary of State must be in a position to exercise in the last resort complete control over the raising and the spending of the colonial revenues, as well as over all legislation, before he could take the responsibility of submitting to the Lords Commissioners of the Treasury any proposal for a loan to the Colony. This preliminary condition is the basis on which any further discussion of the possibility of Imperial assistance must proceed." [2]

These despatches were published; and for some months the question of modifying the constitution of the Colony was *Referenda in Colony on the Subject.* actively discussed. A referendum taken in Georgetown by the elective members showed that 1,005 electors were for, and 96 against, the proposed alteration.[3] A similar referendum in New Amsterdam resulted in 100 electors voting for, and 66 against, the change; [4] while Mr. W. Whyte, who interviewed the majority of his constituents of South-East Essequebo, reported them to be unanimously agreed that the development of the interior of the

[1] B. G. Combined Court Sessional Paper No. 746 of 1914, pp. 6–7.
[2] B. G. Combined Court Sessional Paper No. 779 of 1914, p. 7.
[3] *Ibidem*, pp. 9–10.   [4] *Ibidem*, p. 11.

Colony could only be effected by the construction of a railway, and to be prepared to accept such modification of the constitution as the Secretary of State for the Colonies might deem advisable.[1] No final decision had, however, been reached when, in August, 1914, the great European war broke out, and the hope of obtaining an Imperial loan was indefinitely deferred.

At this point, therefore, when the force of circumstances imposed upon the inhabitants of British Guiana a pause for reflection, I venture to interrupt the story of the events which led in 1928 to the reform of the Colony's constitution, in order to analyse the nature of that constitution, as it then existed, and to consider whether it made for or against prosperity, progress and good government.

[1] B. G. Combined Court Sessional Paper No. 779 of 1914, p. 9.

CHAPTER II

ANALYSIS OF THE CONSTITUTION

(a) *Powers of the Crown, the Privy Council, and Parliament.*

THE foundation upon which the constitution of the Colony of British Guiana had been built was the Capitulation of 1803; and it is, therefore, necessary, as a preliminary to *Construction placed by His Majesty's Government on the Capitulation of 1803 and the Treaty of 1814.* analysis and criticism of the constitution, to consider the effect of that Capitulation. The view of this subject taken by the Ministers of the Crown was fully stated by Lord Goderich in a despatch, dated the 1st October, 1830,[1] at a time when efforts had been made, notably by certain colonial members of the Court of Justice, to resist the execution of the Royal Orders-in-Council of February, 1830, upon the ground that the Capitulation of 1803 invested the Court of Policy with an exclusive legislative power within the Colony, subject to no control except the ultimate veto by the Crown.

" The capitulation," he wrote, " is originally a compact for the military occupation of the conquered territory—it supposes the possibility of the dominion reverting to the former Sovereign. The general habit of belligerent states has, therefore, been to promise to the parties making the surrender the continuance of their laws and institutions, because to innovate pending the war would, in the event of a restitution, produce much evil with very little corresponding good. The promise thus made to Demerary, was made in nearly equivalent terms to every other colony conquered by Great Britain during the revolutionary war. The same was the case with the colonial conquests made by France. Was it, however, in any single instance maintained that, from the date of the conquest, the laws of the colony became fixed and unalterable? The very reverse is the case. Wherever the British or the French arms prevailed, there immediately followed, as a necessary legal

[1] See *Royal Gazette of British Guiana*, 9th February, 1832.

consequence, the operation of those laws of which the authority is co-extensive with the domination of the conquering state; thus, for example, the British laws of trade and navigation attached immediately upon the new territory, and the Courts of Vice-Admiralty and Piracy, though ' new institutions,' were erected at once, as the legitimate consequence of the capture. . . . Moreover within the short space of two years from the conquest of Demerary, when the terms of the capitulation were still fresh in the memory of the inhabitants, and a large proportion of the ancient Dutch settlers were still living, the right of His Majesty-in-Council to legislate for its government was asserted on an occasion the most considerable and momentous which had ever occurred in the annals of the settlement. I allude to the abolition of the slave-trade, which in Demerary was effected by the Royal Order-in-Council of the 15th of August, 1805. To the authority by which this great change was accomplished no objection was raised. The capitulants understood too well the real constitution of Demerary, and the real effect and design of the articles, to raise such a pretension as has now, for the first time, been advanced. The Order, to which I have referred, was no obscure Act of Parliament. On the contrary, it received in the following year the most direct and solemn sanction of Parliament. The statute, 46 Geo. III, c. 52, recites the Order at length, recognizes its authority, and proceeds to make various provisions for carrying it into more complete effect, by imposing penalties on all persons who should engage in supplying Demerary, or the other conquered colonies, with slaves. It is impossible to suppose a more complete and decisive proof, from precedent and authority, in favour of the right claimed by His Majesty, than that which I have just cited. The unpopularity of the abolition of the slave-trade within the Colony itself, in the year 1805, is matter of known history. Whence, then, the silent acquiescence of the inhabitants in such a law, promulgated by the King-in-Council, if they supposed that His Majesty had no right to legislate? Whence the solemn recognition by Parliament of the Order, if, on general principles, His Majesty was not entitled to exercise such a power? The inference is irresistible.

" Thus, then, one great exception to the supposed permanency of all institutions of the conquered colony, by force of the capitulation, arises from the general and implied condition that the laws of the conquering state, which are not local but universal, must be superinduced on the conquered territory.

" It is not only, however, certain positive enactments of the victorious nation, but certain fixed principles of constitutional law, from which the capitulation cannot derogate. Amongst these principles it is one, that the conqueror has the right to legislate for the benefit of his new subjects, unless he shall be pleased to grant them a constitution of government by which that right is surrendered. Upon this subject it is sufficient for me to refer you to the most elaborate decision of the Court of King's Bench, in the case of Grenada, as delivered by Lord Mansfield.[1] I should not hesitate to declare that no military officer, nor indeed any authority below that of Parliament, could legally make a compact which would abridge the range of those statutes, or of those legal maxims, which the constitution of the kingdom has made co-extensive with the British domination. Do I, then, intend to maintain that a capitulation may be violated before the cession of the conquered country, or disregarded afterwards ? It is needless for my present purpose to answer or to agitate that question. Whatever may be the right interpretation of that part of the law of nations, it is at least evident that military capitulations must in every case be understood with the implied qualifications which I have already mentioned ; and that, when the conquered territory has by a solemn cession been incorporated into the permanent dominion of the Crown, the changes which its new character may require must not be impeded by the capitulation. Without any prejudice to the practical conclusion which I seek to establish, I might further allow that such changes must be made with a constant reference to the capitulation, and with the strictest adherence to its terms, which may be compatible with the new character which the conquest is to assume. Demerary is now as completely vested in the British Crown as are the European possessions of His Majesty.

" This is a state of things to which the capitulants did not and could not advert. To maintain permanently Dutch institutions within the British Empire would be an anomaly in favour of which the usages of no civilized state could be quoted. I look forward to the day when

---

[1] See also Part IV, p. 399 (Viscount Haldane's remarks and Lord Lovat's reply) : and Appendix S.

the Colony will enjoy every privilege which the King can legally confer on its inhabitants, or which any other British colony possesses. With the King's Government rests the right and the responsibility of deciding by what measures the most steady advance to that consummation can be made. With His Majesty also resides the power of making such laws as the transition from the Dutch to the English colonial system may require."

Lord Goderich further pointed out that the language of the Capitulation itself sustained the same conclusion; for " amongst the laws and customs of which the continuance was thus promised, there was none more clearly established than the right in point of law, and the custom in point of fact, of legislation by the Sovereign power in Europe."

Thus, in the opinion of the Ministers of the Crown, the effect of the Capitulation of 1803, and of the subsequent Cession in 1814, was to vest in the Sovereign-in-Council the *Opinions given by the Law Officers of the Crown in 1840 and 1842.* right to legislate for British Guiana in all matters of Imperial policy, and in particular to make such laws for the Colony as the transition from the Dutch to the British colonial system might require. This opinion was reaffirmed by the Law Officers of the Crown in 1842 with one important reservation.

" We are of opinion," they wrote,[1] " that, *in those cases in which it is not intended to impose any tax or duty*, the legislative power of the Sovereign-in-Council, which has hitherto been asserted and exercised over British Guiana, may be lawfully exercised by Her Majesty-in-Council. We do not consider that the Crown has parted with its supreme legislative authority over the Colony, which was vested in it by right of conquest, *in matters not fiscal*, either by the terms of the Capitulation and Treaty, or by the sanction which it has given to the legislative acts of the Court of Policy, the Crown having continued at all times to assert and exercise this power *in every matter of internal legislature not connected with the raising of taxes* within the Colony."

The Capitulation promised that " the mode of taxation " then in use should be adhered to; and the Law Officers of the Crown had, in 1840,[2] advised that, " looking to the laws and

---

[1] *Vide supra*, p. 113.　　　　[2] *Vide supra*, p. 112.

usages and mode of taxation prevailing in the Colony in 1803, and since sanctioned by the Crown . . . no tax can lawfully be imposed there except by the Combined Court." They further advised that, if the Combined Court refused to act, there was no mode in which a tax could lawfully be imposed in British Guiana without the interposition of the Imperial Parliament; but that, in such extreme cases as arose in connexion with the Civil List disputes, the representative members of Combined Court having broken their contract and abdicated their functions, the safety of the State required that the supreme power of the mother-country should be called in to supply the deficiency; and that, under these circumstances, " Parliament might, without any just objection, remodel the constitution of the Colony, and confer the power of imposing taxes in British Guiana, for the benefit of the inhabitants, upon some new body that might be expected to exercise it with discrimination, loyalty and disinterestedness."

The effect of these opinions is that, in the last resort, the sovereign power over British Guiana vests in the King, acting *Powers of Parliament and of Privy Council.* " by and with the advice and consent of the Lords Spiritual and Temporal and Commons in Parliament assembled, and by the authority of the same "; but that in practice the Imperial Parliament would not legislate for British Guiana :

(i) in fiscal matters, unless the Combined Court refused to levy the taxes necessary for the good government of the Colony, or levied them in a manner contrary to Imperial policy : or,

(ii) in matters not fiscal, except—

(a) to ratify by Act of Parliament a Royal Order-in-Council; as, for example, when the Royal Order-in-Council of the 15th August, 1805, abolishing the slave-trade, was sanctioned by the Statute 46 Geo. III, c. 52; or

(b) to remodel the constitution of the Colony by transferring the power of raising taxes in British Guiana, for the benefit of the inhabitants, from the Combined Court to some other body politic; as was done by Act of Parliament in 1928.

When, however, it is not intended to impose any tax or duty, the supreme legislative authority over the Colony vests in the King, acting " by and with the advice of His Privy Council," the necessary directions for carrying into effect the Royal Orders-in-Council being given by His Majesty's Principal Secretary of State for the Colonies. Such Orders by the Sovereign-in-Council were not infrequently promulgated : the most notable in the history of British Guiana being that of the 12th January, 1832, commonly known as the " Consolidated Slave Ordinance," [1] and that of the 3rd June, 1842, since repeatedly renewed, which conferred upon the Combined Court " full power and authority to discuss in detail, freely and without reserve, the several items of the Annual Estimate of Colonial Expenditure, subject always to the terms and conditions of the Civil List Ordinance." [2]   It should be added that the Royal Letters Patent constituting the office of Governor of British Guiana passed under the Great Seal of the United Kingdom on the 25th February, 1911, recite in article V :

> " We do hereby reserve to Ourselves, Our Heirs and Successors, Our and their undoubted right and authority . . . to make, enact and establish from time to time, with the advice and consent of Parliament, or with the advice of Our or their Privy Council, all such laws as may to Us or them appear necessary for the peace, order and good government of the Colony." [3]

It will thus be seen that British Guiana was not one of the colonies possessing responsible government, in which the Crown has only reserved the power of disallowing legislation, and in which the Secretary of State for the Colonies has no control over any public officer except the Governor. Neither was British Guiana one of the Crown Colonies, properly so called, in which the power of the Sovereign, exerted through the Secretary of State for the Colonies, is paramount in all matters. But it was a colony in which the Crown had supreme authority save only in matters of taxation.   This authority of the Crown was exercised, within the Colony itself, by means of the Governor; and it is now necessary to examine in detail the place held by the Governor in the Colony's constitution.

[1] *Vide supra*, p. 102.   [2] *Vide supra*, p. 115.   [3] See Appendix N.

(b) *The Governor.*

It may seem a far cry from Jan van der Goes, who was the first officer in charge of the settlement by the Dutch West *Origin of the* India Company in Essequebo, and who was given *Office of* the rank of " Commandeur " by the Zeeland Chamber *Governor.* on the 21st February, 1639, to His Excellency the Right Honourable Viscount Gormanston, who governed Essequebo, Demerara and Berbice in 1891, at the time when the constitution of the Colony took the form now under analysis; but it is nevertheless historically true that the office of Governor of British Guiana derives ultimately from the Dutch Commandeurs of Essequebo and Berbice; then from the post of Directeur-General of the Two Rivers, which existed for some years side by side with that of Commandeur of Berbice; thereafter from the Governors of " the United Colony of Demerary and Essequebo," and from the Governors of Berbice; and finally, upon the amalgamation of the government of the Three Rivers, from the Commission issued on the 4th March, 1831, by King William IV to Major-General Sir Benjamin D'Urban as Governor and Commander-in-Chief in and over the Colony of British Guiana.

Prior to the 1928 reforms this office was constituted by Letters Patent, passed under the Great Seal of the United *Letters Patent* Kingdom, and issued on the 25th February, 1911, *and Royal* by King George V, who on the same day passed *Instructions* under the Sign Manual and Signet the Royal In-*of 25th* structions to the Governor and Commander-in-Chief *February,* of the Colony. These two documents, together with *1911.* the Commission, issued under the Royal Sign Manual and Signet appointing each successive Governor, were the warrant whereunder that officer acted and they conferred upon him all such powers and authorities as he did not obtain from the laws in force in the Colony.

Appointments to the office of Governor were made by the Crown upon the recommendation of the Secretary of State for *Appointment* the Colonies; and every person appointed to be *and Oaths of* Governor had, before entering on any of the duties *Office.* of his office, to cause the Royal Commission appointing him to be read and published in the presence of the Chief

Justice for the time being, or other Judge of the Supreme Court
of the Colony, and of such members of the Court of Policy as
were able to attend; which being done, he then and there took
the oath of allegiance in the form provided by the Imperial
Act, 31 & 32 Vict., cap. 72, as well as the usual oath for the
due execution of the office of Governor and for the due and
impartial administration of justice. These oaths the Chief
Justice, or in his absence the senior Judge then present of the
Supreme Court of the Colony, was required to tender and
administer.[1]

Apart from the powers exercised by the Governor in conjunction with the Executive Council, the Court of Policy, or
Power of the Combined Court, he was authorized by the Crown
Governor to to keep and use the Public Seal of the Colony,[2] and
dispose of
Crown Land. to make and execute under such Public Seal grants
and dispositions of any lands which might be lawfully granted
and disposed of by the Crown within the Colony : provided
that every such grant or disposition was made in conformity
either with the laws of the Colony, or with some instruction
under the Royal Sign Manual and Signet or conveyed through
one of the Principal Secretaries of State, or with such regulations
as were then in force, or might be made by the Governor in
that behalf and publicly promulgated in the Colony.[3] Before
disposing of any vacant or waste Crown lands, the Governor
was required to " cause the same to be surveyed, and such
reservations made thereout as he may think necessary or
desirable to be reserved and set apart for public roads or other
internal communication by land or water, or for purposes of
military defence, or for any other purposes of public safety,
convenience, utility, health or enjoyment "; and the Governor
might not, directly or indirectly, purchase for himself any of
such lands without the King's special permission given through
one of the Principal Secretaries of State.[4]

Subject to the provisions of any law of the Colony, the
Governor constituted and appointed all such Judges, Commissioners, Justices of the Peace, and other necessary officers
in the Colony as might be lawfully constituted and appointed

[1] Letters Patent, § 2.   See Appendix N.
[2] Letters Patent, § 8.
[3] *Ibidem*, § 9.
[4] Royal Instructions, § 19.   See Appendix O.

by the Crown.[1]   But all commissions granted by the Governor
to any person or persons for exercising any office or employment could, unless otherwise provided by law, be
granted during pleasure only; and, whenever the
Governor appointed to any vacant office or employment, of which the initial emoluments exceeded
£100 *per annum*, any person not specially directed by
the Crown to be appointed thereto, he had at the same time
expressly to apprise such person that the appointment must
be considered only as temporary and provisional until the
King's allowance or disallowance thereof was signified.[2]   The
Governor could also, upon sufficient cause to him appearing,
dismiss any public officer, not appointed by virtue of a warrant
from the Crown, whose pensionable emoluments did not
exceed £100 a year, provided that in every such case the
grounds of intended dismissal were definitely stated in writing
and communicated to the officer, in order that he might have
full opportunity of exculpating himself, and provided also that
the matter was investigated by the Governor with the aid of
the head for the time being of the department in which the
officer was serving.[3]   Moreover, the Governor could, upon
sufficient cause to him appearing, suspend from the exercise
of his office any person holding office in the Colony, whether
appointed by virtue of any commission or warrant from the
Crown, or in the King's name, or by any other mode of appointment.[4]   But, before suspending any officer whose annual
pensionable emoluments exceeded £100, the Governor was
required to signify to such officer by a statement in writing
the grounds of the intended suspension, and to call upon him to
state in writing any grounds upon which he desired to exculpate
himself; and, if the officer did not furnish such a statement
within the time fixed by the Governor, or failed to exculpate
himself to the satisfaction of the Governor, the Governor was
required to appoint a Committee of the Executive Council to
investigate the charges made and to report fully to the Executive Council.   This report was then considered by the Council,
and a record was made in the minutes whether the Council,
or a majority thereof, did or did not assent to the suspension.

Power of Governor to appoint, suspend and dismiss Officers.

[1] Letters Patent, § 10.   [2] Royal Instructions, § 20.
[3] Letters Patent, § 12.   [4] *Ibidem*, § 12.

If the Governor thereupon suspended the officer, he had to transmit the report of the Committee and the evidence taken by it, together with the minutes of the proceedings of the Council, to the King through one of His Majesty's Principal Secretaries of State at the earliest opportunity;[1] and, if the suspension was confirmed by the King through one of the Principal Secretaries of State, the Governor forthwith caused the officer to be so informed, and thereupon the office in question became vacant.[2]   But, if in any case the interests of His Majesty's service appeared to the Governor to demand that a person should cease to exercise the powers and functions of his office instantly, or before there was time to take the proceedings above described, he might then and there interdict such person from the exercise of the powers and functions of his office.[3]

When any crime or offence had been committed within the Colony, or for which the offender might be tried therein, the *Grant of Pardons.* Governor could, as he saw occasion, grant in the King's name a pardon to any accomplice in such crime or offence, who gave such information and evidence as led to the conviction of the principal offender, or of any one of such offenders, if more than one; and further, he could grant to any offender convicted of any crime or offence in any Court, or before any Judge, Justice, or Magistrate within the Colony, a pardon, either free or subject to lawful conditions, or any remission of the sentence passed on such offender, or any respite of the execution of such sentence for such period as he thought fit, and could remit any fines, penalties or forfeitures which might become due and payable to the Crown : provided always that the Governor could in no case, except where the offence had been of a political nature unaccompanied by any other grave crime, make it a condition of any pardon or remission of sentence that the offender should be banished from, or should absent himself from, the Colony.[4]

The Governor was Commander-in-Chief of the Local Forces, which consisted of militia and police ; and all officers, civil and military, and all inhabitants of the Colony were by the Letters Patent required and commanded to be obedient, aiding and

---

[1] Royal Instructions, § 21.   [2] Letters Patent, § 12.
[3] Royal Instructions, § 21.   [4] Letters Patent, § 12.

assisting unto him.[1] All monies paid from the Treasury were paid on a warrant under the hand of the Governor.[2]

Governor is Commander-in-Chief of Local Forces. The Governor's fiat was necessary before any claim against the general government of the Colony could be prosecuted in the Supreme Court ; [3] and many other powers and authorities were conferred upon the Governor by the laws of the Colony then in force.

The Royal Instructions required the Governor not to quit the Colony, on any pretence whatever, without having first *Governor's Absence : Appointment of Governor's Deputy.* obtained leave for doing so from the King under His Majesty's Sign Manual and Signet or through one of the Principal Secretaries of State ; [4] but, in the event of the Governor having occasion to be temporarily absent for a short period from the seat of government, he could, by an instrument under the Public Seal of the Colony, constitute and appoint the Lieutenant-Governor, or if there were no such officer—at present there is none—then any other person, to be his Deputy within any part or parts of the Colony, during such temporary absence, and in that capacity to exercise, perform, and execute for and on behalf of the Governor all such powers and authorities vested in the Governor, as were specified and limited in and by such instrument, but no others. Every such Deputy was required to obey all such instructions as the Governor might from time to time address to him for his guidance : provided, nevertheless, that by the appointment of a Deputy the power and authority of the Governor was not abridged, altered, or in any way affected.[5]

Whenever the office of Governor was vacant, or if the Governor became incapable or was absent from the Colony, or was from any cause prevented from acting in the *Succession to Government.* duties of his office, the Lieutenant-Governor of the Colony, or if there were no such officer, then such person or persons as the King might appoint under the Royal Sign Manual and Signet, and in case no such person or persons within the Colony were so appointed, then the person for the time being lawfully exercising the office of Government Secre-

---

[1] Letters Patent, § 15.
[2] Ordinance No. 1 of 1891, section 134.   See p. 156, *supra*.
[3] Ordinance No. 9 of 1904, section 5.
[4] Royal Instructions, § 24.
[5] Letters Patent, § 14.

tary[1] administered the government of the Colony during His Majesty's pleasure, first taking the oaths directed to be taken by the Governor in the manner prescribed; which being done the Administrator was authorized, empowered and commanded to do and execute all things belonging to the office of Governor and Commander-in-Chief according to the tenour of the Letters Patent, the Royal Instructions and the laws of the Colony.[2] In point of fact it was always customary for the Government Secretary to administer the government during the absence of the Governor: and precedent for this may be found under Dutch rule as early as the year 1707.[3]

(c) *The Executive Council.*

The Executive Council is the youngest of the bodies politic in British Guiana. It was originally constituted by Letters *Constitution and Composition of the Executive Council.* Patent[4] passed under the Great Seal of the United Kingdom on the 5th March, 1891, and it met for the first time on the 25th January, 1892. The Letters Patent of the 5th March, 1891, were revoked by those dated the 25th February, 1911, to which reference has already been made,[5] and under which the Executive Council was constituted prior to the reforms of 1928. It was then composed of the Governor with two *ex officio* members—namely, the Government Secretary and the Attorney-General, or the persons for the time being lawfully discharging the functions of those offices; two other official members, usually the Colonial Treasurer and the Immigration Agent-General; and three nominated unofficial members;—eight persons in all. But the number was not limited by the Letters Patent, and might be increased or decreased according to the King's pleasure. The Governor was required to attend and preside at the meetings of Executive Council, unless prevented by illness or other grave cause, and in his absence the senior member of the Council actually present presided.[6] Unless duly summoned by authority of the Governor, and unless two members at least, exclusive of the Governor or of the member presiding, were present and assisting throughout the whole of the meeting, no

---

[1] Title changed to Colonial Secretary by Ordinance No. 23 of 1914.
[2] Letters Patent, § 13.   [3] See p. 25, *supra.*
[4] See Appendix M.   [5] See Appendix N.
[6] Royal Instructions, § 7. See Appendix O.

z

business could be despatched by the Council.[1] No periodical meetings or sessions of the Council were prescribed by the Letters Patent, the Royal Instructions, or the laws of the Colony; but it was customary for the Council to meet once a fortnight for the despatch of routine business, while emergency meetings were summoned in the interval whenever necessary. Members of the Council, other than the two *ex officio* members, were appointed provisionally by the Governor by an instrument under the Public Seal of the Colony; and such provisional appointments were forthwith reported to His Majesty for confirmation or disallowance through the Secretary of State for the Colonies. If disallowed by the Sovereign, the provisional appointment terminated so soon as notice of such disallowance was received by the Governor; if confirmed, the provisional appointment was made substantive by warrant under the Royal Sign Manual and Signet. All members of the Council, other than the two *ex officio* members, vacated their seats at the end of five years from the date of the instrument appointing them; but they might be re-appointed. Members also vacated their seats, if they left the Colony without written permission from the Governor, or outstayed any leave of absence granted them by the Governor or by the Secretary of State for the Colonies.[2]

In the execution of the powers and authorities granted him by the Crown, the Governor was required in all cases to consult with the Executive Council, excepting only in cases *Powers of Governor in relation to the Executive Council.* of such a nature that, in his judgment, His Majesty's service would sustain material prejudice by consulting the Council thereon, or when the matters to be decided were too unimportant to need their advice, or too urgent to admit of their advice being given by the time within which it was necessary for action to be taken. In all such urgent cases the Governor had, at the earliest practicable period, to inform the Council of the measures so adopted, with the reasons therefor.[3] The Governor was alone entitled to submit any question to the Executive Council for their advice or decision; but if the Governor declined to submit any question to the Council, when requested in writing by any member to do so, it was competent to such member to require that there be

[1] Royal Instructions, § 6.   [2] *Ibidem*, §§ 2–3.   [3] *Ibidem*, § 9.

recorded upon the minutes his written application, together with the answer returned by the Governor.[1] The Governor might act in opposition to the advice given to him by the members of the Executive Council, if in any case he deemed it right to do so; but in any such case he had fully to report the matter to His Majesty, by the first convenient opportunity, with the grounds and reasons of his action. In every such case it was competent to any member of the Council to require that there be recorded at length on the minutes the grounds of any advice or opinion he might give upon the question.[2] In view of this Royal Instruction the Interpretation Ordinance[3] defined the expression " Governor-in-Council " to mean " the Governor acting with, but not necessarily in accordance with, the advice of the Executive Council." Minutes were regularly kept of the proceedings of the Council; and at each meeting of the Council the minutes of the last preceding meeting were read over and confirmed or amended, as the case might require, before other business was transacted. Twice in each year a full and exact copy of the minutes for the preceding half-year were transmitted to His Majesty through the Secretary of State for the Colonies.[4] Meetings of the Executive Council always took place *in camera*, and the public was never admitted.

Whenever any offender was condemned by the sentence of any Court to suffer death, the Governor was instructed to *Procedure in Capital Cases.* call upon the Judge, who presided at the trial, to make to him a written report of the case of such offender, and to cause such report to be taken into consideration at the first meeting of the Executive Council which might be conveniently held thereafter, and he could require the Judge to be specially summoned to attend at such meeting and to produce his notes thereat. The Governor might not pardon or reprieve any such offender, unless, upon receiving the advice of the Executive Council thereon, it appeared to him expedient to do so; but in all such cases he had to decide either to extend or to withhold a pardon or reprieve, according to his own deliberate judgment, whether the members of the Executive Council concurred therein or otherwise; entering, nevertheless, on the minutes of the Council

---

[1] Royal Instructions, § 10. [2] *Ibidem*, § 11.
[3] Ordinance No. 14 of 1891, section 5. [4] Royal Instructions, § 8.

a full record of his reasons in case he should decide any such question in opposition to the judgment of the majority of the members.[1]

Apart from the duties imposed upon the Executive Council by the Letters Patent and the Royal Instructions, there had *Other Duties* been transfererd to the Council all the executive and *of Executive* administrative functions which formerly belonged to *Council.* the Court of Policy, among which the most important was the preparation of the annual estimates of the Colony's expenditure for consideration by the Combined Court. Moreover, multifarious duties had been imposed upon the Governor-in-Council by the laws of the Colony, particularly the power of making regulations under various ordinances: for example, under the Trade Marks Ordinance, 1914 (section 52), the Indian Hemp Ordinance, 1913 (section 29), the Patents Ordinance, 1902 (section 49), the Marriage Ordinance, 1901 (section 71), and many others.

(d) *The Court of Policy*

The Court of Policy was the oldest body politic in the Colony and had passed through many vicissitudes. In the last *Origin and* decade of the seventeenth century we first hear of a *History of the* *Raad* or managing council of the affairs of the Dutch *Court of* *Policy.* West India Company in Essequebo, its members being the Commandeur, the Secretary, and two managers of the Company's plantations, which then clustered round Fort Kijk-over-al. In 1718 this council was given the name of *Raad van Politie en Justitie* (Court of Policy and Justice); but its composition was not changed, and its membership was confined to servants of the Company, although, in addition to the management of the Company's affairs in Essequebo, it now acted as a court of justice. The first representative of the " free planters "—that is to say, of such Essequebo colonists as were not servants of the Company—was nominated on the 2nd January, 1739, to be a member of the *Raad van Politie en Justitie*, which thereafter consisted of five persons; and, in 1743, the membership of the Court was increased to seven, of whom five were servants of the Company and two were repre-

---

[1] Royal Instructions, § 22.

sentatives of the " free planters," nominated by the six officers of the burgher militia, who for that purpose formed a College of Kiezers (electors). In 1750, after the rise of Demerara, the *Raad van Justitie* was separated from the *Raad van Politie*, and the latter was again composed exclusively of servants of the Company—namely, the Directeur-General of the Two Rivers, the Commandeur of Demerara, the Captain of the Troops, and three managers of Company's plantations. The seat of the Court was now at Fort Island. In 1767 the Chamber of Zeeland decided that only the senior manager of the Company's plantations in Essequebo should have a seat in the *Raad van Politie*, the other two being replaced by burghers—one from Essequebo and one from Demerara—nominated by the respective Colleges of Kiezers. Thus the first representatives of the burghery were admitted into the *Raad van Politie*, which, instead of being exclusively concerned with the administrative control of the Company's affairs, now became a legislative and executive body for the whole of the Two Rivers. In 1772, the Ten instituted a separate *Raad van Politie* for each river and ordered that these Courts should consist :

> (*a*) in Essequebo, of the Directeur-General, the Fiscal, the Captain Commandant, and the Vendue-Master, who were all servants of the Company, and of " four other persons chosen from the most important, capable and pious of the inhabitants, members of the Reformed Church " ; and
>
> (*b*) in Demerara, of the same representatives of the Company, together with the Commandeur of Demerara, who presided in the absence of the Directeur-General, and of four elected members as in Essequebo.

The electives were nominated, both in Essequebo and in Demerara, by the College of Kiezers for their respective river ; and, although the number of Company's servants and of elected members was equal, the former had the dominant voice owing to the casting vote given to the Directeur-General in the Essequebo Court and to the Commandeur in the Demerara Court, where, however, if the Directeur-General attended, there were five Company's servants as against four elected members. The *Raad van Politie* for Essequebo continued to have its seat on Fort Island, while that for Demerara was established on Borsselen Island.

From the 27th February, 1781, to the 6th March, 1784, the Two Rivers were first under British and then under French domination; and, when the Colony was restored to Holland, the Dutch West India Company, in spite of great opposition on the part of the colonists, did away with the election of burgher representatives by the Colleges of Kiezers, and ordered that the *Raad van Politie* in each river should consist solely of servants and nominees of the Company, namely :

> (*a*) in Demerara, of the Directeur-General, who now resided near the *brandwagt* at the mouth of the river, where Georgetown was afterwards built; the President of the Court of Justice; the Fiscal; the Receiver of Taxes; the Commissary of Military Stores; and of three colonists nominated by the Directeur-General ;
>
> (*b*) at Fort Island, of the Commandeur of Essequebo; of the four servants of the Company next him in rank; and of three colonists also nominated by the Directeur-General.

These Courts were duly established in the spring of 1785, but were never recognized as constitutional by the great majority of the colonists, who appealed to the States-General and the Stadtholder. The result was the " Plan of Redress," which finally did away with the *Raad van Politie* in Essequebo, and established a single Court of Policy for both rivers, consisting of the Directeur-General, the Commandeur of Essequebo, the Fiscal of Essequebo, and the Fiscal of Demerara, together with two colonists of Essequebo and two of Demerara, elected by the College of Kiezers of their respective rivers. Thus the votes of the Company's servants on the one hand, and of the colonists on the other, were again made equal, and the principle of election was once more substituted for that of nomination; but the Directeur-General, as President of the *Raad van Politie*, was given a casting vote. The Court as reorganized under the Plan of Redress sat for the first time on the 29th May, 1789.

When the Company's control of the Two Rivers came to an end, on the 31st December, 1791, the constitution of the *Raad van Politie* was not changed, save that the office of Directeur-

General was replaced by that of Governor, while for the other three servants of the Company were substituted officials appointed by the Colonial Council of the Netherlands. Thus composed of the Governor of " the United Colony of Demerary and Essequebo," three official and four elected members, the *Raad van Politie* remained unaltered throughout the stormy period which intervened between the downfall of the Company and the Capitulation of 1803; and thereafter, under the appellation of Court of Policy, the anglicized form of the old Dutch name, it continued without change until the union of the Three Rivers in 1831, when its jurisdiction was extended to embrace Berbice, and a fifth elected member was added to represent the new county of " the Colony of British Guiana." At the same time another official member was added. Therefore, although the membership of the Court was increased, the balance of power in it was not affected, the official and unofficial sections remaining equal, and the Governor having a casting vote. Thenceforth the Court of Policy underwent no further change until it was reorganized by the British Guiana Constitution Ordinance (No. 1 of 1891).

As so reconstituted the Court of Policy was composed of :

(*a*) the Governor, who was its President;

Eventual Composition of Court of Policy. (*b*) four *ex officio* members—namely, the Colonial Secretary, the Attorney-General, the Colonial Treasurer, and the Immigration Agent-General;

(*c*) " such three other persons holding public offices in this Colony as His Majesty may from time to time appoint, or as the Governor may in the exercise of the power vested in him by this Ordinance from time to time provisionally appoint "; [1]

(*d*) eight unofficial, elected members, of whom two represented the city of Georgetown, one represented the town of New Amsterdam, and one each represented East Demerara, West Demerara, Berbice, North-West Essequebo, and South-East Essequebo.

The principle of equipoise between the official and unofficial sections was thus maintained; while the Governor, or other

[1] Ordinance No. 1 of 1891, section 3.

presiding member, was given a casting vote in addition to his original vote, if opinion was evenly divided.[1] The quorum for the transaction of business was " nine members besides the Governor or other presiding member." [2]

Upon the creation of an Executive Council, under the Royal Letters Patent of the 5th March, 1891, all executive and *Power to* administrative functions were withdrawn from the *Legislate de-* Court of Policy, which became thereafter a purely *rived from* *the Crown.* legislative body. The power to legislate was derived from the Crown and was conferred by article V of the Royal Letters Patent of the 25th February, 1911, which recited : " The Governor, with the advice and consent of the Court of Policy of the Colony, may make laws for the peace, order and good government of the Colony, subject to such rules and regulations as may from time to time be prescribed by Instructions under the Royal Sign Manual and Signet." Moreover, as the power to legislate was derived from the Crown, so also it was subject to veto by the Crown, which reserved by the same article of the Letters Patent the right and authority to confirm, disallow or, with advice of the Privy Council, to amend any laws made for British Guiana by the Governor and Court of Policy.

The Royal Instructions directed that no ordinance should be enacted for any purpose which had not been first proposed *Royal In-* to the Court of Policy by the Governor, or by some *structions as* member of the Court under his sanction previously *to Legislation.* obtained.[3] The Royal Instructions further directed [4] that the Governor should not assent in the King's name to any bill of the following classes :

(1) Any bill for the divorce of persons joined together in holy matrimony :

(2) Any bill whereby any grant of land or money, or other donation or gratuity, might be made to himself :

(3) Any bill affecting the currency of the Colony or relating to the issue of bank-notes :

(4) Any bill establishing any banking association or amending or altering the constitution, powers, or privileges of any banking association :

---

[1] Ordinance No. 1 of 1891, section 26.   [2] *Ibidem*, section 24.
[3] Royal Instructions, § 12 (2).   [4] *Ibidem*, § 13.

(5) Any bill imposing differential duties :

(6) Any bill the provisions of which appeared inconsistent with obligations imposed upon the Crown by treaty :

(7) Any bill interfering with the discipline or control of His Majesty's forces by land or sea :

(8) Any bill of an extraordinary nature and importance, whereby the royal prerogative, or the rights and property of His Majesty's subjects not residing in the Colony, or the trade and shipping of the United Kingdom and its Dependencies, might be prejudiced :

(9) Any bill whereby persons not of European birth or descent might be subjected or made liable to any disabilities or restrictions to which persons of European birth or descent were not also subjected or made liable :

(10) Any bill containing provisions to which the royal assent had been once refused, or which had been disallowed by the Crown :

(11) Any bill respecting the constitution, proceedings, numbers or mode of appointing or electing any of the members of the Court of Policy or of any other body politic or corporate within the Colony :

unless such bill contained a clause suspending its operation until the signification in the Colony of the King's pleasure thereupon ; or unless the Governor had satisfied himself that an urgent necessity existed requiring such bill to be brought into immediate operation, in which case he was authorized to assent in the King's name to such bill, unless repugnant to the laws of England, or inconsistent with any obligations imposed on the Crown by treaty. But the Governor was required to transmit to His Majesty by the earliest opportunity the bill so assented to, together with his reasons for assenting.

When a bill passed by the Legislature was presented to the Governor for his assent, he might, in his discretion, but subject to the Royal Instructions, declare that he assented thereto, or that he refused his assent, or that he reserved the bill for the signification of the King's pleasure.[1] A bill reserved for the signification of the King's pleasure took effect so soon as His Majesty gave assent by Order-in-Council, or through one of

[1] Letters Patent, § 6.

the Principal Secretaries of State, and the Governor had signified the royal assent by message to the Legislature, or by proclamation : provided that no such message or proclamation might be issued after two years from the day on which the bill was presented to the Governor for his assent.[1]

Every ordinance enacted by the Governor with the advice and consent of the Court of Policy was published in the *Official* *Gazette* and in a newspaper of the Colony as soon as *Publication* *and Com-* possible after it had received the assent of the *mencement of* *Ordinances.* Governor or of His Majesty, as the case might require; and, unless some other time was therein specified for its coming into force, it took effect on the date of publication in the *Official Gazette*.[2] If, however, the Crown disallowed an ordinance to which the Governor had given his assent, such ordinance ceased to operate from the date on which notification of its disallowance was published in the Colony.

The Governor was by the Royal Instructions authorized and required from time to time, as occasion might require, to frame *Standing* and propose to the Court of Policy for adoption, *Rules and* and, when adopted, from time to time with the con- *Orders.* sent of the Court to revoke, alter or renew, such Standing Rules and Forms of Proceeding as might be best adapted for orderly despatch of business and for preventing all undue precipitation in the enactment of ordinances, " and for ensuring, previously to the passing of an ordinance intended to affect or benefit private persons, that due notice be given to all parties concerned of the provisions thereof, with ample opportunity for opposing the same, and that a full and impartial examination may take place of the grounds upon which the same may be proposed or resisted." [3]   The Standing Rules and Orders finally in force were " framed and proposed by the Governor and adopted by the Court of Policy " on the 5th February, 1892, the 9th May, 1893, and the 18th December, 1902.[4] Under them the Governor, or other presiding member, was the sole judge of " order " at any meeting of the Court ; [5] and if any member of the Court, not being an *ex officio* member,

---

[1] Letters Patent, § 7.
[2] Ordinance No. 1 of 1891, section 28.
[3] Royal Instructions, § 17.
[4] B. G. Laws, vol. iv, pp. 555–8 and 563.   See Appendix K.
[5] Ordinance No. 1 of 1891, section 25.

obstinately refused to yield due obedience and conform himself
to the Standing Rules and Orders, it was lawful for the Court,
after affording such member a full opportunity of defending
himself, by resolution to expel him from the Court and to
declare his seat vacant.[1]

At least two sessions of the Court had to be held each year,
and there might not be an interval of more than eight months
Sessions and between the last sitting in one session and the first
Dissolution of sitting in the next session.[2] The Governor, or other
the Court. presiding member, could adjourn a meeting of the
Court at any time, but no motion for adjournment was in
order.[3] The Governor could also at any time by proclamation
prorogue or dissolve the Court; and in any case it was dissolved
at the end of five years from the date of the return of the first
writ at the preceding general election, and a general election
had to be held within two months of the date of dissolution.[4]

No person was capable of being elected a member of the
Court of Policy, who—

Qualification (1) was not entitled to vote at the election of
of Elected a member of the Court for any electoral district
Members. of division; or

(2) was a minister of religion; or

(3) was the holder of any office of emolument under
the Crown or under the Government of the Colony; or

(4) had failed for the space of three months to comply
with any order of the Supreme Court directing him to pay
any money held or received by him in a fiduciary capacity;
or

(5) did not possess one of the following property
qualifications, namely:

(*a*) ownership, under a title by grant from the Crown,
transport, letters of decree, inheritance *ab intestato
vel ex testamento*, devise, or marriage, or possession
under a licence of occupancy from the Crown, of
not less than 80 acres of land, unencumbered by
mortgage, situate in the Colony, of which not less

---

[1] Ordinance No. 1 of 1891, section 135.
[2] *Ibidem*, section 22.   [3] *Ibidem*, section 27.
[4] *Ibidem*, sections 19, 20 and 21.

than 40 acres were actually and *bona fide* under cultivation; or

(*b*) ownership of immovable property situate in the Colony, under any such title as aforesaid, of the value, over and above the amount of any mortgage, of not less than $5,000; or

(*c*) ownership, or possession under a lease for 21 years or upwards, of any house or house and land situate in the Colony, the annual rental or value whereof, over and above the interest payable under any mortgage, was not less than $1,200.[1]

Where any land, or immovable property, or house, or house and land, situate in the Colony was or were jointly owned or occupied by more persons than one as joint owners or tenants, each of such joint owners or tenants was deemed to have the property qualification for an elected member of the Court of Policy in case the total area of the land owned or occupied and the part thereof actually and *bona fide* under cultivation or the value of such land, or immovable property, or house, or house and land, were or was such as, when divided by the number of such owners or tenants, gave a qualification for each of such owners or tenants.[2]

Where any land, or immovable property, or house, or house and land, situate in the Colony, was or were owned or occupied by any Company, every shareholder in such Company was deemed to have the property qualification for an elected member of the Court of Policy in case—

(*a*) the total area of the land so owned or occupied and the part thereof actually and *bona fide* under cultivation unencumbered by any mortgage; or

(*b*) the value of such land or immovable property over and above the amount of any mortgage; or

(*c*) the annual rental or value of such house, or house and land, over and above the interest payable under any mortgage,

were or was such as when divided by the number of shares into which the capital of the said Company was divided and

[1] Ordinance No. 24 of 1909, section 4.
[2] Ordinance No. 1 of 1891, section 13 (1).

multiplied by the number of shares held by such shareholder gave a qualification for such shareholder.[1]

An elected member's seat in the Court of Policy became vacant, if he—

(1) by writing under his hand, addressed to the Governor, resigned his seat; or

(2) departed from the Colony without the leave of the Court or of the Governor; or

(3) having departed from the Colony with such leave, remained out of the Colony after such leave had expired; or

(4) failed without reasonable cause (the sufficiency whereof was determined by the Court) to attend any six consecutive sittings of the Court; or

(5) ceased to possess the prescribed property qualification; or

(6) made any declaration or acknowledgement of allegiance to any foreign state or power; or

(7) became a citizen or subject of any foreign state or power; or

(8) became a minister of religion; or

(9) accepted any office or emolument under the Crown or under the Government of the Colony; or

(10) was adjudicated a bankrupt in the United Kingdom or an insolvent in British Guiana; or

(11) was declared by any competent Court to be *non compos mentis*; or

(12) was sentenced in any part of His Majesty's Dominions to death, penal servitude, or imprisonment with hard labour for any term exceeding twelve months; or

(13) failed for the space of three months to comply with any order of the Supreme Court directing him to pay any money held or received by him in a fiduciary capacity.[2]

And, whenever it was shown to the satisfaction of the Governor that the seat of an elected member of the Court of Policy had become vacant, the Governor was required, within one month

---

[1] Ordinance No. 24 of 1909, section 5.
[2] Ordinance No. 1 of 1891, section 15; supplemented by Ordinance No. 24 of 1909, section 6.

thereafter, to issue a writ for the election of a new member; but, if any question arose as to the fact of such vacancy, it was referred to and decided by the Court of Policy.[1]

Every elected member had, before he sat or voted in the Court, to take and subscribe the oath of allegiance to His Majesty.[2]   The law also provided that the Court of Policy, or in non-session of the Court the Governor, might grant to any elected member leave of absence, not exceeding six months at any one time, from the service of the Court, whether such member did or did not remain in the Colony.[3]

Every person who, being returned as an elected member, but not qualified, or whose seat being vacant, sat or voted, was liable to a penalty of $250 for every day on which he sat or voted.[4]

(e) *The Combined Court*

The earliest form of the Combined Court in the history of the Colony was wholly unlike its final form.   It will be re-

Origin and History of the Combined Court. membered that the reorganization of administration in the Two Rivers, effected by the Ten in 1772, was objected to by the Zeeland Chamber on the ground that the management of Demerara had been separated from that of Essequebo.   To obviate this objection the States-General ordered that the Commandeur of Demerara with two members of the *Raad van Politie* for Demerara, which then sat on Borsselen Island, should go to Fort Island, once or twice a year, to meet the Councillors of Essequebo in Combined Court, and to consider such matters as affected both rivers. This Combined Court was called together by the Directeur-General, who had superintendence of the Two Rivers, at irregular intervals, whenever there was business to transact; and its first meeting was held at Fort Island on the 26th June, 1775.

The *raison d'être* of the Combined Court in this form ceased when, in 1789, the Plan of Redress did away with the *Raad van Politie* in Essequebo and established in Demerara a single Court for the Two Rivers; but the Combined Court was revived in a

[1] Ordinance No. 1 of 1891, section 16.
[2] *Ibidem*, section 17.
[3] Ordinance No. 24 of 1909, section 7.
[4] Ordinance No. 1 of 1891, section 14.

wholly different form when, during the confusion of the year 1795, the members of the *Raad van Politie* called the College of Kiezers to a conference and resolved, on the 3rd June, 1795, that the Colony's *ongeld* should be under the care of the four unofficial members of the *Raad van Politie* joined to four Kiezers, two from the Demerara College and two from the Essequebo College, and that this Combined Court should superintend the raising of the Colony's *ongeld* and regulate its expenditure. This novel form of Combined Court was designated " the Colonial Finance Department," and it was established to meet a local emergency without any authority from the States-General. It was merely a provisional expedient; and, while the pleasure of the sovereign power in the Netherlands with respect to it was still unknown, the Colony capitulated, on the 22nd April, 1796, to Great Britain. During the temporary British occupation, the resolution of the 3rd June, 1795, was repealed; and by a resolution dated the 11th June, 1796, the Court of Policy directed that six Financial Representatives—elected, three from each river—should be adjoined to the Governor and Court of Policy with the right of voting " on all matters relative to the raising of taxes and examination of accounts, without any other power whatever." The first meeting of the Combined Court in this altered form took place on the 2nd November, 1796; but in this form also the Combined Court had not been recognized by the Sovereign, when the Treaty of Amiens, signed on the 25th March, 1802, restored the Two Rivers to the Batavian Republic. No change seems to have been made in the short interval before the final capitulation to Great Britain on the 19th September, 1803. It was, therefore, from this capitulation that the Combined Court, which until then had never been recognized by sovereign authority, whether Dutch or British, derived its power of raising Colony taxes and of examining the colonial accounts; because a validity, which previously had not belonged to the system of the 11th June, 1796, was imparted to it in 1803 by the stipulation in the first article of the Capitulation that the mode of taxation then in use should be continued. The Capitulation of 1803 was, in fact, the charter of the Combined Court.

An unauthorized change was made, on the 7th September,

1812, at an extraordinary meeting of the Court of Policy, which was attended by four persons only—namely, Major-General H. L. Carmichael, then administering the government, and three elective members—the effect being to abolish the College of Kiezers, to combine the duties of Kiezer with those of Financial Representative, and to arrange that the six Financial Representatives should not only meet the Court of Policy in Combined Court, but should also be the electors (Kiezers) of the unofficial members of the Court of Policy. This change was never sanctioned by the Crown and was expressly annulled by the Royal Instructions, issued on the 5th March, 1831, to Governor Sir Benjamin D'Urban, which ordered that the College of Kiezers and the College of Financial Representatives should again be two separate and distinct bodies, thus restoring the system which had obtained at the date of the Capitulation of 1803.

During the rest of its existence, the College of six Financial Representatives remained unchanged; but the College of *Composition of the Combined Court.* Kiezers was abolished by Ordinance No. 1 of 1891, and thereafter the same electorate chose both the unofficial Councillors of Policy and the Financial Representatives; while Combined Court again meant—as it meant between the years 1796 and 1812, and had meant ever since the year 1831—the Governor and members of the Court of Policy with the Financial Representatives in Combined Court assembled. Thus there was a considerable unofficial majority in the Combined Court, a full attendance consisting of the Governor, seven official, and fourteen elected members. The quorum for transaction of business was eleven members besides the Governor or other presiding member.[1] The six Financial Representatives respectively represented the county of Demerara, the city of Georgetown, the county of Berbice, the town of New Amsterdam, the North-Western Division of Essequebo, and the South-Eastern Division of Essequebo.[2] The qualifications for election as a Financial Representative were the same as those prescribed for election as an unofficial member of the Court of Policy, provided, however, that either of the following property qualifications was accepted as

[1] Ordinance No. 1 of 1891, section 42.
[2] *Ibidem*, section 52.

sufficient in lieu of the three kinds of property qualification specified for elected members of the Court of Policy :

> (a) receipt of a clear annual income of not less than $1,440, arising from any kind of property in the Colony, not mentioned in the other property qualifications, over and above any interest payable under any mortgage thereon ; or
>
> (b) receipt of a clear annual income of not less than $1,440 from any profession, business, or trade carried on in the Colony.[1]

The Financial Representatives vacated their seats on the dissolution of the Court of Policy;[2] and the Combined Court was *ipso facto* dissolved by the dissolution of the Court of Policy.[3] Sessions of the Combined Court were held at such times and places as the Governor might from time to time by proclamation appoint.[4] There had to be at least one session in every year, and there might not be an interval of twelve months between the last sitting in one session and the first sitting in the next session.[5] The Governor, or other presiding member, could at any time adjourn any meeting of the Combined Court; but no motion for adjournment was in order.[6] The Governor could also at any time by proclamation prorogue the Combined Court.[7]

In addition to the power of raising taxes, derived from the first article of the Capitulation of 1803, the Combined Court *Powers granted to Combined Court (a) by Royal Order-in-Council;* derived from the Crown the right, first conceded by the Royal Order-in-Council of the 3rd June, 1842, during the continuance of the Civil List Ordinance No. 2 of 1841, but no longer, " to discuss, in detail, freely and without reserve, the several items of the annual estimate of the colonial expenditure subject always to the terms and conditions of the said Civil List Ordinance." In this respect the Combined Court was a creature of compromise; it being, in effect, stipulated that, so long as the Combined Court raised the revenue necessary to defray the salaries of the officials specified in the Civil List Ordinances, periodically passed by the Court, and so long as

---

[1] Ordinance No. 24 of 1909, section 8.
[2] Ordinance No. 1 of 1891, section 39.   [3] *Ibidem*, section 46.
[4] *Ibidem*, section 40 (1).   [5] *Ibidem*, section 40 (2).
[6] *Ibidem*, section 45.   [7] *Ibidem*, section 46.

A A

those salaries were duly paid, the Crown would allow the Court to exercise the privilege, which prior to 1842 it did not possess, of discussing the colonial expenditure. This privilege was renewed by successive Orders-in-Council on the passing of every subsequent Civil List Ordinance until in 1928 the Civil List was made permanent.

The vagueness of the phrase—" to discuss, in detail, freely and without reserve, the several items of the annual estimate of the colonial expenditure "—led to determined attempts by the elective section of the Combined Court, not only to exercise the privilege (which was never disputed) of moving the reduction or deletion of items of estimated expenditure, but also to assert *(b) by Standing Rules and Orders of Combined Court made thereunder.* the right of initiating money-votes and of moving an increase in items of estimated expenditure. " The Rules and Regulations for the Combined Court of British Guiana," irregularly made on the 27th April, 1838, conceded to members of the Court the right " of increasing or decreasing an item, or of having it struck off the estimate "; but these rules were amended, in 1842, by reserving to the Governor alone the privilege of moving the increase of an item of estimated expenditure, while allowing any member to move that an item be decreased or struck off the estimate. For many years, however, the elective section did not acquiesce in this decision, although it was pointed out that the British House of Commons itself did not pretend to the exercise of the privilege, to which the Combined Court laid claim. Finally, the matter was settled on the 3rd June, 1858, when the Combined Court itself negatived a resolution asserting it to be the Court's prerogative to initiate money-votes and to increase any item on the estimate. This question was subsequently governed by the Standing Rules and Orders of the Combined Court made by Governor Sir J. A. Swettenham on the 19th May, 1903, under the authority of the Royal Order-in-Council of the 23rd February, 1891.[1]

These Standing Rules and Orders allowed motions to be made:

(*a*) by official members to *increase or decrease* items in the estimate : and (*b*) by elected members to *decrease or omit* items in the estimate.[2]

---

[1] B. G. Laws, vol. iv, pp. 559–62. See Appendix J.
[2] Standing Rules and Orders, § 4 (2).

They provided further that each item should be considered
an original motion; and that any member desirous of decreasing any item, or striking it off, might move an
amendment to that effect.[1]   No money-vote could
be initiated except by the Governor, who framed
the annual estimate of colonial expenditure and
laid it before Combined Court.   When the estimate
had been discussed, " in detail, freely and without reserve,"
and the total expenditure for the ensuing year had been voted,
the Court resolved itself into a Committee of Ways and Means
to consider how the revenue requisite to meet this expenditure
should be raised.   The Royal Order-in-Council of the 3rd
June, 1842, and all those subsequently issued upon the passing
of successive Civil List Ordinances, recited that it should not
be necessary for the Governor to attend the meetings of the
Committee of Ways and Means, which, under the Standing
Rules and Orders, had power to elect any member to be its
chairman,[2] and was at liberty to discuss the budget without
motion.[3]   The invariable practice was for the Governor to
absent himself from these meetings; and thereafter the senior
unofficial member was usually voted into the chair.   The
Colonial Secretary then made the budget speech explaining
the means whereby the Government proposed that the revenue
necessary to meet the expenditure of the ensuing year should
be raised.   These proposals, and any others which members
of the Committee might make, were debated *seriatim* and put
to the vote, the chairman having both an original and a casting
vote; [4] and, when the " ways and means " were agreed upon,
the Committee embodied them in a report to the Combined
Court.   The Court then resumed, the Governor taking the
chair, and received the Committee's report, after which the
Governor directed some official member, usually the Attorney-
General, to frame and introduce the Customs and Tax Bills
for the ensuing year upon the lines recommended by the
Committee.[5]   Such member thereupon moved for leave to
bring in these two bills; and, upon such leave being given,
the Clerk of the Court read the marginal notes of the sections
and the headings of the schedules of the bills, the reading

*Mode of Pro-
cedure in
Combined
Court and in
Committee of
Ways and
Means.*

---

[1] Standing Rules and Orders, § 15.   [2] *Ibidem*, § 16.
[3] *Ibidem*, § 17.   [4] *Ibidem*, § 16.   [5] *Ibidem*, § 18.

of each note and heading operating as an original motion, and any member was at liberty to move any amendment. If the amendment was seconded, it was put to the vote; and, if lost, the section or schedule stood part of the bill.[1] After the marginal notes and the headings of the schedules had been read, the question " That this bill do pass " was immediately put;[2] and the bill thus passed, when assented to by the Governor, became law, subject to the Sovereign's disallowance or confirmation.

The annual Tax Ordinance and Customs Duties Ordinance, and any necessary amendments of them,[3] were the only laws " enacted by the Governor of British Guiana, with the advice and consent of the Combined Court thereof." In other legislation which needed the authority of Combined Court— the most important being the periodical Civil List Ordinances— the procedure was by way of resolution passed in Combined Court authorizing the Governor and Court of Policy to pass an ordinance giving effect to the resolution. Thus, on the 21st October, 1912, the Combined Court resolved that the Governor and Court of Policy be authorized to make provision by ordinance for the maintenance of the Civil List Establishment of the Colony for a term of five years commencing on the 1st January, 1913, and ending on the 31st December, 1917, in the amount and subject to certain conditions specified. Pursuant to this resolution, the Governor and Court of Policy passed the Civil List Ordinance, No. 19 of 1912. Similarly, at a meeting of the Combined Court on the 11th November, 1913, the following resolution was adopted :

" Whereas the Combined Court by resolution dated the 1st day of September, 1897, after the recital of certain previous resolutions of the 24th day of August, 1886, and the 10th day of March, 1897, sanctioned the conversion into stock inscribed in England in accordance with the provisions of the Inscribed Stock Ordinance, 1886, of all or any sums of money which the Combined Court had authorized or should thereafter authorize to be raised on loan, in addition to the powers already given of raising such moneys by the issue of bonds, debentures

[1] Standing Rules and Orders, § 19.   [2] *Ibidem*, § 20.
[3] Such an amendment of the Customs Duties Ordinance is Ordinance No. 24 of 1914, and of the Tax Ordinance is Ordinance No. 25 of 1914.

or otherwise, and pledged itself to provide the necessary funds for the repayment of all principal moneys and interest secured by any such stock created in pursuance of the said resolution and of all expenses of issuing and inscribing the same :

" And whereas the Inscribed Stock Ordinance, 1886, Amendment Ordinance, 1897, was thereafter passed by the Governor and Court of Policy to give effect to the said resolution and directed to be read as one with the Inscribed Stock Ordinance, 1886 :

" And whereas it is expedient to define in one Ordinance the terms and conditions applicable to loans hereafter authorized by the Combined Court :

" And whereas it is expedient to enable the Colony to take advantage of the provisions of the Act of the Imperial Parliament entitled ' The Colonial Stock Act, 1877,' and subsequent Acts on the same subject,

" *Be it Resolved,*—That this Court requests the Governor and Court of Policy to repeal the Inscribed Stock Ordinances, 1886 and 1897, while preserving the rights of any persons who hold stock or bonds under the authority of the same, and to pass such legislation as will give effect to this resolution."

Accordingly the Governor and Court of Policy, pursuant to this resolution, passed the General Loan and Inscribed Stock Ordinance. No. 31 of 1913, reciting the above resolution at full length in the preamble of the ordinance and declaring that it was expedient to give effect to it. Similar instances could easily be multiplied; but it is sufficient to say that, save in the matter of the Tax Ordinances and the Customs Duties Ordinances, the Combined Court always proceeded by way of resolutions, leaving the legislative action consequent on such resolutions to the Court of Policy, and their due execution to the Governor and his officers.

Ever since the year 1842, the " King's chest " had, in view of the Civil List compromise, been amalgamated with the " Colony chest," and the disbursement of all sums paid into the " Colony chest," a term now synonymous with " general revenue," had been controlled by the Combined Court. These two " chests " continued to be merged into one by virtue of the Civil List Ordinances from time to time in force. But this

Powers of Combined Court with respect to Raising Revenue.

did not mean that the Combined Court was ever given, or ever possessed, power to *raise* " King's taxes." It only meant that the Combined Court had been given, during the continuance of the Civil List compromise, a control, to which it had no inherent right, over the *expenditure* of revenue raised from " King's taxes." The one and only source from which the Combined Court derived the power to tax was the stipulation in the first article of the Capitulation of 1803 that the mode of taxation *then in use* should be adhered to. Now, what was the mode of taxation in use in 1803 ? It was two-fold. " King's taxes," payable by the inhabitants of the Colony into the " King's chest," were imposed by the Governor and Court of Policy; and " Colonial taxes," payable by the inhabitants of the Colony into the " Colony chest," were imposed by the Governor and Court of Policy together with the Financial Representatives in Combined Court assembled. Throughout its existence the revenue-raising power of the Combined Court was confined to " Colonial taxes," originally known in Dutch times as *ongeld*, and " King's taxes " did not come within the purview of that Court.[1]

An interesting illustration is the Registrar's " Fee Fund," which did not even form part of the Civil List compromise *Registrar's* until the year 1903, it being provided by section 18 *Fee Fund.* of Ordinance No. 6 of 1880 that the Fee Fund of the office of Registrar of the Supreme Court should " be subject to the appropriation and under the control of the Governor and Court of Policy for the purpose of carrying on the said office," and that " from and out of the said Fund the Receiver-General or the Assistant Receiver-General shall upon warrant of the Governor pay all salaries and expenses of the office." But by Ordinance No. 22 of 1903, in consideration of the office of Registrar being placed on the Civil List, the Fee Fund of the Registrar's office was abolished, and the matter was thereafter governed by section 7 of the Civil List Ordinance No. 19 of 1912, which recited : " The fees and revenues of the Registrar's Office, known as the Fee Fund of the Registrar's Office

---

[1] The phrases " King's chest " and " King's taxes " were substituted after the Capitulation, for the phrases " Government chest " and " Government taxes," which since the downfall of the Dutch West India Company had replaced the original phrases " Company's chest " and " Company's taxes."

of British Guiana . . . shall, during the continuance of this Ordinance, and no longer, be paid and payable into the Colony chest "—that is, into general revenue. Thus the Registrar's Fee Fund, instead of being earmarked to pay the expenses of the Registrar's Office, became part of the general revenue of the Colony, and its disbursement was under the control of the Combined Court. But this did not mean that the Combined Court had acquired the right of fixing the amount of these fees. On the contrary, the Combined Court never had any such authority, the fees being fixed by Rules of the Supreme Court, made by the Judges, or a majority of them, of whom the Chief Justice had to be one. This power was given to the Judges by the Governor and Court of Policy under section 58 (1) of Ordinance No. 7 of 1893; and prior to that year it was exercised by the Governor and Court of Policy direct. The Combined Court had no *locus standi* in the matter.

The position of the Registrar's Fee Fund was not singular in this respect; for the revenue from Crown Lands raised under the Crown Lands' Regulations was entirely in the discretion of the Governor and Court of Policy, who on the 25th January, 1915, increased the tariff under those regulations without any reference to the Combined Court. Similarly the fees for naturalization of aliens, under Ordinance No. 4 of 1891, were imposed by the Governor and Court of Policy, the reason being that naturalization is a prerogative of the Crown.

(f) *The Franchise*

The germ from which the elective franchise of the Colony developed, is to be found in the burgher militia system organized by the early Dutch settlers in Essequebo, which they divided for this purpose into two districts, the upper one centred at Kijk-over-al and the lower one at Fort Island. A burgher company was enrolled for each district, and every new settler was assigned to one or other of these companies. Each company was commanded by three burgher officers—a captain, a lieutenant, and an ensign—who at first were elected by the burgher companies, but afterwards were nominated by the Commandeur and his Council. In 1743, Commandeur Grave-

Burgher Officers formed into Colleges of Kiezers.

sande formed these six burgher officers into a College of Kiezers (electors) for the purpose of nominating the representatives of the free planters in the *Raad van Politie en Justitie*. Subsequently the burgher militia system was extended to Demerara, where in 1766 the settlements had become so numerous that they were divided into two districts—the East bank and the West bank—with one company of burgher militia for each district and three burgher officers in each company; while in the same year the six burgher officers in Demerara were formed into a College of Kiezers for that river, on the model of the one already existing in Essequebo, for the election of representatives of the free planters in the *Raad*. By the Plan of Redress, in 1789, the membership of both Colleges of Kiezers was increased from six to seven, " the said increase and further vacancy to be supplied by a plurality of voices of the inhabitants, who must possess five-and-twenty negroes, or upward." But no qualification was prescribed for the Kiezers themselves, whose term of office was for life, or until they resigned office in their College, or ceased to be inhabitants of the Colony. When Governor Bentinck, in 1812, completed the amalgamation of the administrative system in the Two Rivers, a single College of seven Kiezers at Georgetown was substituted for the Essequebo and Demerara Colleges; and later in the same year Major-General Carmichael replaced this College of Kiezers by a " Combined Board of Kiezers and Financial Representatives," the members of which served for two years only, and he extended the franchise to all persons paying income-tax on 10,000 guilders (£715) *per annum* as well as to those possessed of twenty-five negroes or upwards. However, upon the union of the Three Rivers, in 1831, the Combined Board of Kiezers and Financial Representatives was abolished, and there was substituted for it, on the one hand, a Board of Financial Representatives, and on the other hand a " College of Kiezers of the Colony of British Guiana " for the purpose of electing unofficial members to fill vacancies in the Court of Policy. This College consisted, as before, of seven Kiezers, whose term of office was for life, or until they resigned or left the Colony, and who were elected by all inhabitants of the Colony of British Guiana possessing twenty-five slaves or upwards, the income-tax qualification being annulled.

The abolition of slavery necessitated a change in the property qualification; and by Ordinances No. 57 of 1835 and No. 86

Changes in Franchise due to Abolition of Slavery and to Civil List Disputes.

of 1836 the franchise was extended to every inhabitant of the Colony who paid direct taxes to the colonial revenue to the amount of 70 guilders (£5), or upwards, in the year of, or in the year preceding, an election, as well as to all inhabitants assessed to pay direct taxes to the colonial revenue upon an income of not less than 2,001 guilders (£143). A further change was brought about by the Civil List disputes, which, by suspending all collection of Colony taxes, disfranchised the greater part of the electorate, as, in the absence of any Tax Ordinance, the inhabitants could neither pay, nor be assessed to pay, direct taxes. This dilemma led to the passing of Ordinance No. 15 of 1849, which divided the Colony into electoral districts and distinguished between three classes of voters, enacting that—

(*a*) a county voter must possess one or other of the following qualifications, namely :

   i. ownership of not less than 3 acres of land actually under cultivation : or

   ii. ownership of a house, or of house and land, of a rental or value of not less than $96 (£20) *per annum* : or

   iii. tenancy of 6 acres of land actually in cultivation under lease for 3 years or more : or

   iv. tenancy of a house, or of house and land, of a rental or value of $192 (£40) *per annum* under lease for one year or more.

(*b*) a town voter in the city of Georgetown or the town of New Amsterdam must either—

   i. own a house, or house and premises, of the appraised value of $500 (£104 3*s*. 4*d*.) : or

   ii. occupy as tenant a house, or house and premises, of a rental or value of not less than $120 (£25) *per annum* under lease for one year or more.

(*c*) the qualification of any person to vote, not above specified, should be residence in an electoral district during six months prior to registration, coupled with either—

   i. an income or salary of not less than $600 (£125) *per annum* : or

ii. assessment to pay direct taxes (other than licence duty of any kind) of not less than $20 (£4 3s. 4d.) to the colonial revenue in the year of, or the year preceding, any new election.

The same law also prescribed, for the first time, a qualification for members of the College of Kiezers, namely :

(a) possession of not less than 80 acres of land within the Colony, at least one-half being actually under cultivation : or

(b) tenancy on a lease for 21 years, or more, of a house, or house and land, of a rental or value of not less than $1,200 (£250) *per annum* : or

(c) a clear annual income of not less than $1,440 (£300) derived from any other kind of property in the Colony, or from the profits of any trade or profession carried on within the Colony.

Under this Ordinance, in 1850, the total number of registered voters was 916, the total population of British Guiana being 127,695, according to the census taken on the 31st March, 1851. Thereafter no change was made until by Ordinance No. 1 of 1891 the College of Kiezers was finally abolished, and the income qualification for the franchise reduced to $480 (£100) *per annum*.

Meanwhile, side by side with the process of electing Kiezers, whose function it was to nominate two qualified persons for *Franchise for* each vacancy in the elective section of the Court of *Electing* Policy, which itself made choice between the two *Kiezers same* *as for Elect-* nominees, there had existed since 1796 a system *ing Financial* of direct election of Financial Representatives by *Representa-* those qualified to exercise the franchise. Under the *tives.* resolution of the 11th June, 1796, the six Financial Representatives were elected by those inhabitants of the Two Rivers who owned twenty-five slaves, or more—the same qualification as that prescribed by the Plan of Redress, in 1789, for voting for Kiezers—and the franchise of voters for Financial Representatives in all its subsequent modifications remained coextensive with that of voters for Kiezers; while, after the abolition of the College of Kiezers in 1891, the unofficial members of the Court of Policy as well as the Financial Representatives were elected by the direct vote of the constituencies.

The electoral districts of the Colony and their representation
were, before the 1928 reforms, as follows :

Electoral Districts.

Electoral Districts.	Number of Representatives :	
	in Court of Policy.	among Financial Representatives.
Demerara County, exclusive of Georgetown :		
(a) Eastern Division . .	I	} I
(b) Western Division . .	I	
Essequebo County :		
(a) North-Western Division .	I	I
(b) South-Eastern Division .	I	I
Berbice County, exclusive of New Amsterdam . .	I	I
City of Georgetown. . .	2	I
Town of New Amsterdam . .	I	I

The franchise then in force was set out in sections 53–57
of Ordinance No. 1 of 1891, as amended by Ordinance No. 24
of 1909, and may be summarized thus. Every
Franchise now in force. male person, having attained the age of 21 years,
being under no legal incapacity, and being a British
subject by birth or naturalization, was entitled to be registered
as a voter, and, when registered, to vote at the election of the
member of Court of Policy (or members in the case of Georgetown) and of the Financial Representative for his electoral
district, provided that he possessed within such district one
of the property qualifications prescribed. The property
qualifications

(a) for a County voter were—

> i. ownership of not less than 3 acres of land actually
> under cultivation : or
> ii. ownership of a house, or house and land, of the
> annual rental or value of not less than $96 (£20) :
> or
> iii. tenancy of not less than 6 acres of land, actually
> in cultivation, under a lease for 3 years or more :
> or

    iv. tenancy of a house, or house and land, of the annual rental or value of not less than $192 (£40) under a lease for one year or more : or

    v. income or salary of not less than $300 (£62 10s.) *per annum*, coupled with at least 6 months' residence in the district : or

    vi. payment, during 12 months prior to registration, of direct taxes to the colonial revenue of $20 (£4 3s. 4d.) or upwards, coupled with at least six months' residence in the district.

(*b*) for a City or Town voter were—

    i. ownership of a house, or land, or of land with a house or other erections thereon, of the value of not less than $500 (£104 3s. 4d.) as appraised for local taxation : or

    ii. tenancy under lease for one year or more of a house, or land, or of land with a house or other erections thereon of the annual rental or value of not less than $120 (£25) : or

the fifth or the sixth qualification prescribed for a County voter. Where any land, or house, or house and land, or house and land or appurtenances in any electoral district was jointly owned or occupied by more persons than one as owners or tenants, each of such joint-owners or tenants was entitled to be registered as a voter for such district, if the area of the land actually under cultivation, or the value of the land, etc., was such as, when divided by the number of owners or tenants, gave a qualification for each and every such owner or tenant, but not otherwise. Similarly, where any land, or house, or house and land, or house and land or appurtenances in any electoral district was owned or occupied by any Company, every shareholder in such Company was entitled to be registered as a voter for such district, if the area of land actually under cultivation or the value of such land, etc., was such as, when divided by the number of shares into which the capital of the Company was divided and multiplied by the number of shares held by such shareholder gave a qualification for such shareholder. Finally it was provided that no person should be entitled to be registered as a voter, who—

(*a*) Could not read and write some language, provided always that any person, who knew how to read and write, but was incapacitated by blindness or other physical cause from reading or writing, should not be disqualified from being a voter; or

(*b*) had, within the twelve months previous to registration, received any relief from public or parochial funds : or

(*c*) had been sentenced in any part of His Majesty's dominions to death, or penal servitude, or imprisonment with hard labour, or for any term exceeding twelve months, and had not either suffered the punishment to which he was sentenced or such other punishment as by competent authority might have been substituted, or received a free pardon from His Majesty.

Such being the franchise, which, it should be noted, had undergone little essential change since 1849, save that the income qualification had been reduced by the half, it is important to ascertain how the voting power was distributed between the several races inhabiting British Guiana.

In 1850, the registered voters in a total population of some 127,695 souls were only 916, or 0·71% of the inhabitants of the Colony. Further analysis must be based, on *Composition of Electorate in 1850-1.* the one hand, upon Mr. A. Schrack's report,[1] dated the 23rd September, 1850, giving the statistics of voters registered to that date in the several electoral districts, then existing; and, on the other hand, upon Table I in the Appendix, which has been extracted from the report [2] on the Census taken on 31st March, 1851. The six months which elapsed between Mr. Schrack's report and the Census of the following year are not likely to have appreciably affected the statistics either of voters or of population; but, unfortunately, in the Census of 1851, the age-groups given are 1–15 years, 15–30 years, etc., whereas only the male population of 21 years and upwards could exercise the franchise. Still more unfortunate is the fact that Mr. Schrack has given no information as to the race of the registered voters. Therefore, the direct comparison made in the following table can only be between

---

[1] *Vide supra*, p. 199. [2] Table at p. 16 of the Census report for 1851.

the total registered voters and the total male population of 15 years and upwards in each of the five electoral divisions established by Ordinance No. 15 of 1849, while the racial distribution of the voting power at that time can only be a matter of inference.

Electoral Districts.	Registered Voters.	Total Male Population of 15 Years and Upwards.	Percentage of Male Population of 15 Years and Upwards Registered as Voters.	English, Scotch, Irish, Dutch and American.	Portuguese.	East Indian.	African.	Race not Stated.
County of Demerara . .	326	20,551	1·5%	404	2,145	2,480	15,522	—
County of Essequebo . .	138	9,356	1·4%	210	611	1,749	6,779	7
County of Berbice . .	80	7,936	1·0%	117	153	641	6,945	—
City of Georgetown . .	263	7,898	3·3%	686	894	520	5,798	—
Town of New Amsterdam .	109	1,515	7·1%	140	94	107	1,169	5
Total .	916	47,256	1·9%	1,557	3,897	5,497	36,293	12
Percentage of each race in male population of 15 years and upwards . . .				3%	8%	12%	77%	—

From the above table it appears to be highly probable that, in 1850–1, the electorate consisted almost exclusively of the adult male population of European race, which formed about 11% of the total adult male population of the Colony; and that only some 1·9% of the total adult male population of all races inhabiting British Guiana exercised the franchise. This is not at all surprising when we remember that the emancipation of slaves had taken place as recently as the 1st August, 1838; that the Portuguese immigration into British Guiana did not begin until the year 1841; and that regular East Indian immigration only dated from the year 1845.

More than sixty years later the position was very different, as may be readily ascertained from a study of Table II in the Appendix, which was compiled by Mr. G. D. Bayley from the report made by him on the Census taken on the 2nd April, 1911, and from the lists of registered voters as revised in 1915. This table shows that, since 1851,

Composition of Electorate in 1915.

the total adult male population of British Guiana had increased by about 98%—namely, from 47,256 to 93,377; that the total number of registered voters had been rather more than quadrupled, rising from 916 to 4,312; and that the percentage of the total adult male population exercising the franchise had increased from 1·9% to 4·6%. But the most striking change was in the relative numbers of the several races inhabiting the Colony, and in the distribution of the franchise among those races. The percentages in the electorate formed by the different races were then as follows : Africans 62·7%, British 17·0%, Portuguese 11·4%, East Indians 6·4%, Chinese 2·4%. Thus the voters of African descent, if of one mind at a general election, could outvote the whole of the rest of the electorate : for, in each of the seven constituencies, they numbered appreciably more than half of the total of registered voters. On the other hand, the percentage of adult males of each race resident in the Colony was in the following proportion : East Indians 51·8%, Africans 42·3%, Portuguese 2·9%, British 1·7%, Chinese 0·9%. Finally the percentages of the adult male population of each race registered as voters were : British 46·1%, Portuguese 17·7%, Chinese 12·3%, Africans 6·8%, East Indians 0·6%. The whole analysis may be shown compendiously in a single table, thus :

Race.	Percentage of each Race in the Adult Male Population.	Percentage of each Race in the Total Electorate.	Percentage of Adult Males of each Race Registered as Voters.
East Indian . .	51·8	6·4	0·6
African . .	42·3	62·7	6·8
Portuguese . .	2·9	11·4	17·7
British . . .	1·7	17·0	46·1
Chinese . . .	0·9	2·4	12·3

These figures are very instructive, for they show that, although 46·1% of the adult male inhabitants of British race had registered themselves as voters—a percentage far higher than in the case of any other race—yet the registered voters of British race formed only 17% of the whole electorate; whereas the registered voters of African descent formed

62·7% of the whole electorate, in spite of the fact that only 6·8% of their adult males exercised the franchise. Thus the electorate, which in 1851 consisted almost exclusively of the adult male population of European race, was now dominated by the African vote.

Another very striking fact was the insignificant position in the electorate of the East Indian immigrants, whose adult *Anomalous* males formed 51·8% of the whole adult male popu-*Position of* lation of the Colony. It appears that only 0·6% *East Indians* *in the* among them were registered as voters; and that *Electorate.* this race, although its adult males constituted rather more than half the whole adult male population of British Guiana, formed only 6·4% of the whole electorate. Attention was drawn to this matter, on the 19th August, 1908, by Mr. R. Duff, who had been connected with East Indians in British Guiana for 37 years, and had filled the post of Immigration Agent-General since 1905,[1] in his departmental report for the year 1907–8. He pointed out that, although the East Indians formed a larger proportion of the Colony's population than any other race, nevertheless

> " their attachment to the soil and their confidence in the ' Sircar ' render them disinclined to take part in politics—content, so long as they are not overburdened with direct taxation, or perplexed with regulations, to plod on in their rice-fields or provision-farms, and bring up their children in their footsteps. By this means," Mr. Duff continued, " the area under cultivation in this country has been hitherto slowly, but surely, extended. Under these circumstances, it is not a matter for surprise that but few East Indians have recorded their names as voters; and, as a consequence, the political power has passed into the hands of a section of the community, alien to themselves in race, religion, habits and interests, and, moreover, not superior to them in numbers, wealth, industry and thrift. This state of affairs is, I fear, causing an uneasy feeling of distrust to spring up in their minds; and, if efforts to induce these people to remain in the Colony are to be successful, the first step to be taken will be to find some means of reassuring them."

[1] Parl. Papers Cd. 5193 of 1910; questions 9916 and 10021.

In the following year, on the 23rd July, 1909, Mr. Duff was summoned to give evidence in London before the Committee on Emigration from India to the Crown Colonies and Protectorates; [1] and, in reply to a question by Lord Sanderson, the Chairman of the Committee, he observed :

> " At the present time the voting power is, as I said in my last annual report, almost entirely in the hands of the negroes. The Government, so far as making the laws is concerned, have a majority; but where the public purse is concerned the power is in the hands of those representatives of the black people."

Then followed these questions and answers :

> *Mr. S. H. Freemantle :* Why is that?
>
> *Mr. Duff :* Simply because they have the votes.
>
> *Mr. H. B. Cox :* That is the constitution?
>
> *Mr. Duff :* No, it is not the constitution. The Indians could take up the franchise, if they liked; but they do not care to interfere; they are quite content to abide by the responsible officers of the Government, otherwise the ' Sircar.'
>
> *Sir G. S. Robertson :* How would you propose to remedy that state of things?
>
> *Mr. Duff :* It would be a simple matter—by adding to the official members of the Combined Court.
>
> *Lord Sanderson :* You would practically make it an official majority?
>
> *Mr. Duff :* An official majority. I think British Guiana is the only colony, with the exception of Natal, importing East Indians, where the Government has not a majority. I do not know of any other colony where they have not.

Subsequently in the Court of Policy, on the 22nd August, 1910, Mr. C. P. Gaskin, an unofficial member, drew attention to the evidence given by Mr. Duff; and after much discussion, in which the members of the elective section then present— namely, Messrs. C. P. Gaskin, G. Garnett, A. B. Brown, and P. N. Browne—took exception to Mr. Duff's views, the electives resolved " that the unofficial section of this Court protests against many of the statements made by the Immigration

[1] Parl. Papers Cd. 5193 of 1910, pp. 320–3.

BB

Agent-General, and especially those having reference to the constitution of this Colony." The official members abstained from voting on this resolution, which, therefore, was taken as an expression of opinion by the elective section. It was not until 1928 that effect was given to Mr. Duff's advice that there should be an official majority in the Legislature of British Guiana.

CHAPTER III

CRITICISM OF THE CONSTITUTION

ARISTOTLE, in his treatise on *Politics*, drew a luminous and interesting distinction between constitutions which are normal

Constitution of British Guiana was a "Deviation-Form" of Crown Colony Government. (ὀρθαὶ πολίτειαι) [1] and those which deviate from the norm (διημαρτήκασι τῆς ὀρθοτάτης πολιτείας) ; [2] and, if the constitution of British Guiana is compared with other forms of government usual in the British dominions, we may well describe it in Aristotelian phraseology as " Crown Colony Government gone wrong." Why it went wrong has already been narrated in detail. Suffice it, then, to say, by way of recapitulation, that the constitution of Berbice, while that Colony had a separate existence, never deviated from the norm. It began as administration by a Dutch mercantile house; and, becoming eventually Crown Colony Government, pure and simple, it continued as such until, upon the union with Demerara and Essequebo, in 1831, the constitution of the Two Rivers was by act of the Sovereign applied also to Berbice. Similarly the government of Essequebo, and afterwards of Demerara as well, had at the outset been in the hands of the Dutch West India Company, which, although giving the free planters a voice in the legislature, had jealously maintained its paramount authority in the Two Rivers. In 1791, when the Company fell and the control of Demerara and Essequebo was vested in the Colonial Council of the Netherlands, the power of the Governor and his officials was preserved unimpaired, and for a short time the Two Rivers were under Crown Colony Government. But, during the stormy period of nine years from 1795 to 1803, while the Colony changed hands thrice, and

---

[1] Aristotle, *Politics*: 1279 a 7, ἀνάγκη δ'εἶναι κύριον ἢ ἕνα ἢ ὀλίγους ἢ τοὺς πολλούς· ὅταν μὲν ὁ εἷς ἢ οἱ ὀλίγοι ἢ οἱ πολλοὶ πρὸς τὸ κοινὸν συμφέρον ἄρχωσι, ταύτας μὲν ὀρθὰς ἀναγκαῖον εἶναι τὰς πολιτείας, τὰς δὲ πρὸς τὸ ἴδιον ἢ τοῦ ἑνὸς ἢ τῶν ὀλίγων ἢ τοῦ πλήθους παρεκβάσεις.

[2] Aristotle, *Politics*, 1293 b 8.

Europe was in the throes of revolutionary warfare, the financial exigencies of the local government induced it to make to the plantocracy those concessions which eventually formed the charter of the Combined Court. The action of the local government in this matter was never confirmed by sovereign authority, whether Dutch or British, but was validated inferentially by the military capitulation of the Two Rivers to Great Britain on the 19th September, 1803. The deviation from the norm was not, then, the result of mature deliberation between the Colony and the mother-country, but may be said to have been the accidental ratification of emergency methods.

Hard cases make bad law; and the expedients of turbulent times are not apt to form the basis of a sound constitution. It is not, therefore, surprising to find that the Combined Court of British Guiana was on more than one occasion in conflict with the Imperial Government, with the Governor and his officers, and with the people of the Colony itself. But, before criticizing the " deviation-form " (παρέκβασις) [1] of Crown Colony Government, which existed in British Guiana prior to 1928, it is desirable to consider why Crown Colony Government is the normal type of constitution in the tropical possessions of the British Empire.

The Anglo-Saxon race, being acclimatized to temperate regions of the earth's surface, suffers in health and tends to *Position of the Anglo-Saxon Element in Tropical Colonies such as British Guiana.* lose vigour and activity, if resident for long periods in tropical or sub-tropical countries. Hence the Anglo-Saxon colonist in the tropics is for the most part of a type wholly different from that which inhabits Canada, Australia, New Zealand and South Africa. He does not settle in a tropical colony with the idea of making it the permanent home of himself, his children and his children's children. He does not, if he can help it, rear and educate his children in such a colony. He ought for his health's sake to absent himself from it and take leave in a temperate climate at periodical intervals; and he nearly always looks forward to the day when he can afford to take his final departure from the tropics and spend the close of his life in his mother-country. Even more significant is the fact that the working classes of the white

[1] Aristotle, *Politics*, 1279 a 7.

race are physically incapable of earning a livelihood in tropical colonies by tilling the soil or by hard manual labour, whether indoors or out of doors. In the year 1851, some English ploughmen were, as an experiment introduced into British Guiana; but the experiment failed completely and was not repeated.[1] It follows that the white race in a tropical country— and especially in a tropical country which is mainly agricul- tural—must employ labour of other races than its own. This is a comparatively easy matter in countries such as Africa, India and China, where native labour is abundant. But the early Dutch settlers in British Guiana were confronted with a complete absence of any native population which could be made use of in the sugar estates. The Amerindians are, strictly speaking, the only " natives " of British Guiana; but they take no part in the agricultural, political or commercial life of the Colony, the more remote parts of which they inhabit.[2] Accordingly the Dutch solved the labour problem by importing African slaves; and their Anglo-Saxon successors, after the abolition of slavery, arranged for the introduction of im- migrant labourers from the West India islands, from Madeira, from China, and mainly from East India. A good idea of the sources from which the very mixed population of British Guiana has been drawn is given by the following table : [3]

Whence	1835 to 1840	1841 to 1850	1851 to 1860	1861 to 1870	1871 to 1880-1	1881-2 to 1890-1	1891-2 to 1900-1	1901-2 to 1910-1	Totals.
West India Islands	8,092	4,836	—	10,130	12,887	4,161	707	—	40,813
Madeira . .	429	16,744	9,587	1,533	2,170	182	—	—	30,645
East India .	406	11,841	23,381	38,715	53,327	38,851	39,473	23,769	229,763
Casuals .	—	—	—	800	878	918	1,027	788	4,411
Azores . .	—	—	164	—	—	—	—	—	16
Africa . .	91	9,893	1,968	1,403	—	—	—	—	13,355
England .	—	—	21	—	—	—	—	—	21
China . .	—	—	3,288	9,343	903	—	—	—	13,534
Cape de Verde .	—	—	819	—	—	—	—	—	819
Malta . .	208	—	—	—	—	—	—	—	208
United States .	70	—	—	—	—	—	—	—	70
Totals .	9,296	43,314	39,228	61,924	70,165	44,112	41,207	24,557	333,803

[1] *Handbook of British Guiana* (1909), p. 118.
[2] At the census of 1911 the aborigines within the settled portion of the Colony were enumerated as 6,901 souls, and those outside the settled limits were estimated at a total of 13,000 souls.
[3] *Handbook of British Guiana* (1913), p. 65.

The essential feature of Crown Colony Government is the fact that, under it, the sovereign power, which resides ultimately in the Crown acting through the Principal Secretary of State for the Colonies, is exercised locally by means of an official majority in the bodies politic of the Colony, consisting usually of an Executive Council and a Legislative Council. In point of detail there are many varieties. The Executive Councils sometimes consist exclusively of officials, sometimes of a majority of official members together with a minority of unofficial members, nominated by the Governor and appointed by the Crown. In the Legislative Councils, although there is always an official majority, so that, when division of opinion arises, the views of the Crown may prevail, there is considerable diversity in the methods of constituting the unofficial minority. In the purest type of Crown Colony Government all the unofficial members of the Legislative Council are nominated by the Governor and appointed by the Crown. In some colonies an elective element is introduced by substituting election or nomination by certain groups of colonists for nomination by the Governor, the right to appoint remaining vested in the Crown. For example, in the Hong Kong Legislative Council one of the unofficial members is elected by, and represents, the Justices of the Peace; another is nominated by, and represents, the Chamber of Commerce; and the remainder are nominated by the Governor. Again, in Mauritius, where the Legislative Council consists of twenty-seven members, eight hold their seats *ex officio* ; nine are nominated by the Governor, it being provided that not less than three of the Governor's nominees must be persons holding no public office; and ten are elected—two for the town of Port Louis, and one for each of the eight rural districts : the nominations, but not the elections, being subject to confirmation by the Crown. Representation in the Legislature is secured for non-European races by the constitution of some Crown Colonies. Thus, in Hong Kong three Chinese members of the Legislative Council are nominated by the Governor and appointed by the Crown.

Now, there were several points in which the pre-reform constitution of British Guiana deviated from that of a Crown

Marginal note: Essential Feature of Crown Colony Government.

Colony. One such deviation was the fact that all the unofficial members of the Court of Policy and the Combined
Points Court were elected by the constituencies and that
wherein
Constitution none were nominated by the Crown. With this
of British must be coupled the fact that the Colony's con-
Guiana
deviated stitution did not provide for the nomination of
from Crown
Colony representatives of the chief races, composing the
Government. population, to be members of the Court of Policy or
of the Combined Court. There was, moreover, the fact that
the Colony possessed very complete local control, by means of
a large elective majority in the Combined Court, over both
its revenue and its expenditure. The result was that there
existed in British Guiana neither Crown Colony Government
nor Representative Government, but a travesty of both these
types of government. It was not Crown Colony Government,
for the control of revenue and expenditure was vested in a
large unofficial majority. Nor could it be called Representative
Government, for, as has been shown, only 4·6% of the total
adult male population exercised the franchise. It is indeed
open to doubt whether the system of administration then in
vogue could properly be called a government at all; for an
executive which could not command a majority in the chief
body politic, and had neither the power of the purse nor the
power to tax, might reign but could not rule.

Representative Government naturally suggests itself as
the system under which men born and bred in Great Britain
Danger of are entitled to be governed. But, in granting
Representa-
tive Govern- representative institutions to such a colony as
ment resting British Guiana the real question was : Shall the
upon a
Narrow benefit of such institutions be extended to the great
Basis. body of the population before it has made such an
advance in civilization and education as would render it capable
of exercising political power ? or are these benefits to be
conferred exclusively on the colonists of Anglo-Saxon race ?
Either course was fraught with grave danger; for, as Earl
Grey wrote in 1848 :

" When persons possessing education and intelligence,
sufficient for the due exercise of political power, form
only a very small minority of the whole population, if
the uninstructed classes are *not* permitted to exercise

the franchise, and if their interests are at the same time deprived of the guardianship of the Crown, there must be great danger of malversations, oppressions and abuses, which are notoriously incident to the exercise of supreme power by irresponsible and oligarchical bodies. If they *are* permitted to exercise the franchise, from their numbers they must obtain a predominating power, and there is a possibility, from their ignorance and want of appreciation of the objects and institutions of civilized life, that those objects and property and life itself may be endangered. To avoid these risks on both sides, and at the same time secure to an uninstructed population some of the benefits of representative government, it might seem peculiarly fitting that the ministers of the Crown, responsible to Parliament, and having no partial interests, should intervene as umpires between the represented classes and those which are incapable of being represented, and for this purpose should exercise a controlling authority." [1]

Unfortunately the path of safety, thus indicated by Earl Grey, was not taken. On the contrary, when government by an unofficial majority was originally established in the Two Rivers, the power was wielded by an oligarchy of sugar planters, who, in the sole interest of their own industry, thrice came into serious conflict with the mother-country, first by opposing the abolition of slavery, next upon immigration matters, and finally over the Sugar Duties Act of 1846. On this last occasion the public petitioned Combined Court, deprecating any further opposition because the revenue of the Colony had been sacrificed by the plantocracy in their fruitless struggle and business was at a standstill; but peace was only achieved by the resignation of six members of the elective section. Indeed, the cleft between the oligarchy of planters and the community at large had become so wide, that Mr. J. Croal, speaking in the Court of Policy on the 29th October, 1847, remarked : " It has become unpleasant to serve here : I feel it myself ; for, notwithstanding that we do all in our power to serve the public faithfully, we are taunted and told that we are not the representatives of the people." The remedy was sought in an extension of the franchise; but the franchise so extended embraced, in 1850, only some 1·9% of the total adult male population of the Colony, while even in 1911 the electorate

[1] Despatch, 1st September, 1848.

consisted of no more than 4·6% of the adult males of all races inhabiting British Guiana. But representative government resting upon a narrow basis is, as Earl Grey observed in 1850, " most objectionable "; [1] and it became even more objectionable when the East Indian adult males, of whom only 0·6% were registered as voters, constituted 51·8% of the Colony's adult male population. Moreover, Earl Grey's prediction that the alternative to oligarchy would be government by mere numerical superiority was fulfilled; for the voters of African descent eventually formed 62·7% of the total electorate, although only 6·8% of their adult males were registered, and in each of the Colony's constituencies the black vote had a majority. This position was rendered still more hazardous by the fact that the adult males of African descent were only 42·3% of the total adult male population—that is to say, 9·5% less than the East Indian adult males, who, however, constituted no more than 6·4% of the total electorate. No East Indian had prior to 1912 been elected to a seat in the Court of Policy or the Combined Court, whereas the black element in those bodies politic became increasingly numerous. The condition was clearly one of unstable equilibrium; and it became more than ever desirable that, in Earl Grey's words, " the ministers of the Crown responsible to Parliament, and having no partial interests," should exercise a controlling authority in British Guiana; in other words, that there should be Crown Colony Government and nominated representation of the diverse racial elements in the population.

Another advantage which was lost to British Guiana before the introduction of Crown Colony Government was continuity in administrative policy. The effect upon the *Necessity for Strengthening the Executive Government.* Executive of finding itself in a permanent minority in Combined Court, and, therefore, unable to ensure the adoption of its measures and the steady pursuit of its undertakings, was undoubtedly to lame initiative; while the policy of successive Secretaries of State—although, as in the case of the Crown Colonies, guided by a desire to direct the general plan of government, applying to local problems the experience gained in a world-wide administration and shaping the course of the Colony in accordance with broad

[1] Despatch, 15th June, 1850.

Imperial aims—had always been to intervene as little as might be in the affairs of British Guiana, and thus to avoid such conflict with the elective section of the Combined Court as was almost incessant during the years 1832 to 1850. Consequently too much was left to the whim of an unofficial majority, responsible, if at all, only to that infinitesimal part of the population which composed the electorate, and not liable to be called to account, as are officers of the Crown, by loss of reputation and even of livelihood for errors in the conduct of public affairs. So there was lamentable vacillation over such vital questions as immigration, education, sea defence, irrigation, and development of the interior. Above all, there was deplorable want of continuity in matters of taxation, from the consideration of which—although surely one of the most important concerns of government—the Governor himself was excluded in Committee of Ways and Means. Taxation in British Guiana was the special plaything of the elective section, nor can any continuity of policy be traced in the multifarious vicissitudes through which it passed.

The Civil List compromise was a strange anomaly. Stated succinctly, the position was as follows. The salaries of the *Anomalies of* Chief Justice and of two Puisne Judges were per- *Civil List* menently secured by Ordinance No. 7 of 1899; *Compromise.* and, by section 6 (2) of the Immigration Ordinance No. 18 of 1891, it was enacted that "the Immigration Agent-General shall receive a salary at the rate of not more than £1,500 *per annum.*" Provision for a period of five years, ending on the 31st December, 1922, had been made at the rate of £22,800 *per annum* for a Civil List comprising the Governor, the Colonial Secretary and his Assistant, the Attorney-General, the Solicitor-General, the Auditor-General, the Colonial Treasurer, the Comptroller of Customs, the Inspector-General of Police, the Director of Public Works, the Surgeon-General, the Commissioner of Lands and Mines, the Postmaster-General, the Stipendiary Magistrates and the Registrar. No legislative provision, permanent or temporary, was made for payment of the salaries of any other government officers; and it was open to the Combined Court, when the annual estimates were under consideration, to strike off entirely, or to reduce, the salary of any officer not borne on the Civil List. A notable abuse of this privilege has been recorded [1] among the events which led to the constitutional reforms of 1891. It will be remembered that the elective section of the Combined Court on the 15th December, 1887, struck the salary of the Medical Inspector of the Colony clean out of the annual estimates, because the plantocracy, which then dominated the body politic, resented a report by Dr. Williams, the occupant of that post, describing the insanitary conditions prevalent in 1886 among labourers on sugar estates. The personal antipathies and business interests of the elected representatives of an oligarchy, thus empowered to wreak its spite upon any government officer, whom it disliked and whom the Civil List did not protect, inevitably exerted a detrimental influence upon public servants, encouraging disloyalty and backstairs' intrigue. Nor did the position in this respect improve, when political power was gradually transferred from a white plantocracy to negro demagogues. Several heads of departments were never included in the Civil List, as, for instance, the Chief Commissary, the Director of Science and Agriculture, the Harbour Master, the Official Receiver, the Director of Primary Education, and the Principal of Queen's College. Moreover, services of the greatest urgency were not borne upon the Civil List; and a threat to stop supplies, such as was made from time to time by the elective section to coerce the executive, might, if carried into effect, make it impossible to provide for the establishments most essential to the preservation of society. It would mean that the police force could not be maintained; that the prisoners could not be kept in the prisons, nor the convicts in the Penal Settlement; that the schools, the asylums for lepers and for lunatics, the almshouses and the hospitals must be broken up. " These are, no doubt," as Earl Grey said,[2] " fearful issues, if they should indeed be brought about "; and it is a matter of history that such issues were actually brought about by the elective section of the Combined Court during the last and most serious of the Civil List disputes, when the Colony was left without a revenue from the 30th September, 1847, until the 7th August, 1849. Nor did the constitution prior to 1928 furnish any safeguard, other than the good sense of the elective

[1] See p. 298, *supra*.   [2] Despatch, 1st September, 1848.

section, against " so extravagant an exercise of privilege " [1] by the unofficial majority.

Proposals for a permanent settlement were made by Sir John Packington in 1852, by Mr. Labouchere in 1856, by Lord Carnarvon in 1874, and by Lord Kimberley in 1882. But nothing came of these proposals, owing apparently to a feeling on the part of the elective section of the Combined Court " that to pass a permanent Civil List would be, in some indefinite way, to surrender a valuable part of the old privileges of the Court," [2] and to lose the power of coercing the executive by stoppage of supplies. Nevertheless it was, as Sir John Packington truly remarked, " far from being a fitting or an economical arrangement for the Colony that the salaries of its principal officers should rest upon an uncertain foundation; and nothing would contribute more to efficiency and frugality in the public service than a permanent Civil List based upon a permanent provision of revenue." [3] The system had, moreover, been stigmatized by Lord Carnarvon as " unusual and unsuited to the circumstances of a Colony importing Indian labourers, in which it is specially important that the Government should be under no uncertainty whatever as to the due payment of the salaries of public officers." [4] The views of the ministers of the Crown as to the nature of the reform which ought to be effected in this respect were clearly enunciated by Mr. Labouchere.

" Her Majesty's Government," he wrote on the 16th February, 1856, " have no disposition to prolong a system of compromises and of Civil Lists for terms of years. On the contrary, they think it very desirable that such a system should be brought to an end as soon as conveniently may be, and that the powers which it is for the welfare of the people that the Crown should possess, and those which it is proper that (in a Colony affording such very limited constituencies) the Representative Bodies should exercise, should be definitely ascertained and prescribed by competent authority. . . . The outlines of the arrangement which I have to propose would, therefore, be as follows : That, instead of the present renewable Civil List, an ordinance or ordinances should be passed,

---

[1] Mr. Labouchere's despatch, 16th February, 1856.
[2] Governor Longden's despatch, 24th June, 1876.
[3] Despatch, 13th November, 1852.
[4] Despatch, 8th April, 1874.

fixing permanently the salaries and necessary establishments of the Governor, Judges, Attorney-General, Secretary to Government and Stipendiary Magistrates. These
ordinances, like other laws, would, of course, be subject
to alteration by the Legislature which passed them.
But it should be established by the Governor's instructions that any ordinance diminishing the salaries of
existing incumbents of office, provided for by a former
ordinance, or diminishing prospectively the salary of
the Governor or of the Stipendiary Magistrates (officers
whose duties peculiarly concern the unrepresented classes
of the people) shall contain a suspending clause or be
otherwise reserved for the sanction of the Crown.
Ordinances altering in any other manner the provisions
of the Civil List, to be dealt with by the Governor, like
other ordinances, at his discretion. A small proportion
of the colonial revenue would be required to meet the
expenditure for the permanent salaries : but to render
the officers really independent, and the salaries more than
nominally secure, it would be further necessary that this
small portion of revenue should accrue from sources
permanently established by law." [1]

Reform on these lines was long overdue in 1928.

Finally, it was a serious matter that, as had been categorically
stated by Mr. L. Harcourt,[2] the Colony under its then constitu-
*Financial
Insecurity
of System.* tion could not obtain the financial help of the
Imperial Treasury in its project of building a railway to the interior. After the outbreak of war in
Europe, Mr. Harcourt wrote to the Colony in these terms :
" In the event, which I trust may be avoided, of its having
to apply to the Imperial Treasury for a grant-in-aid, I fear
that it will be necessary for it to accept, as the condition of
such a grant, financial control by the Lords Commissioners of
the Treasury in the same manner as other grant-in-aid
colonies." [3] Every thinking colonist could not but ask himself why it was that His Majesty's Government insisted upon
controlling the finances of British Guiana as a condition
precedent to giving that Colony any considerable financial
assistance, whether in times of peace or of war. It could
only be that, from long experience of the finances of British
Guiana, His Majesty's Government had concluded that the

[1] *Vide supra*, pp. 253–4. [2] *Vide supra*, p. 324.
[3] Despatch, 22nd February, 1915.

existing constitution afforded too insecure a financial control, too little certainty of liabilities being punctually met and taxation equitably distributed, to warrant the money of British tax-payers being risked for the benefit of this " magnificent province." [1]   But that fact in itself was a palpable condemnation of the Colony's constitution.

The truth is that, as Governor Barkly exclaimed, to mould a miniature model of the British Constitution out of materials as rude as those in British Guiana is a task far above the power of man; [2] and " how best to reproduce that balance of power, which constitutes the excellence of the British Constitution, in these colonies, where two out of its three elements, the splendour of majesty and the influence of an aristocracy, are almost imperceptible " [3] is a problem still remaining and likely to remain unsolved.   True citizenship makes a great demand on human nature and implies an intelligent comprehension of high ideals developed by suitable environment and by incessant training, not only from childhood upwards, but through long centuries of ancestors.   It implies also a steady purpose to live for these ideals oneself and to promote a similar life in others; and, above all, a capacity to rule and be ruled, as freemen should rule and be ruled, for the attainment of these ends.   But mere freedom will not make a citizen : while, although slavery is abolished, Aristotle's dictum still holds good that he who is the instrument (ὄργανον) of another, and fit for nothing better, and yet a man, is a slave.[4]   Mere " administrés " are not citizens : nor is citizenship connected essentially with social, or even with military functions, but with the right to share, and opportunities for sharing, in the political life of the State.   It is no easy thing to be in any sense a true member of the State.   Thus, in a colony such as British Guiana, there must inevitably be outside the citizen-body a multitude of inhabitants of all races—women, children, artisans, farmers, labourers for hire—necessary indeed to its existence, but not brought within its inner circle, and dependent

Political Education of a People takes many Centuries.

---

[1] Phrase used by Governor Sir James Carmichael Smyth to describe British Guiana.

[2] Despatch, 20th April, 1849.   [3] Despatch, 2nd May, 1850.

[4] Aristotle, *Politics*, 1254, a 14: ὁ γὰρ μὴ αὑτοῦ φύσει ἀλλ' ἄλλου, ἄνθρωπος δέ, οὗτος φύσει δοῦλός ἐστιν.

for their well-being upon the Crown and the officers of the Crown. Doubtless it is permissible to look forward, as Lord Goderich did, " to the day when the Colony will enjoy every privilege which the King can legally confer on its inhabitants, or which any other British colony possesses "; [1] but prudent men must recognize that this generation will not see that day. It is altogether fanciful to suggest, as Governor Barkly suggested,[2] that on a humble scale British Guiana had passed rapidly through all the political phases, which in England have been the work of centuries; that its Magna Charta was the Plan of Redress; its abolition of villenage, the emancipation; and its struggles between Crown and Parliament, the Civil List disputes. Political education cannot be " crammed "; and it is idle to suppose that the diverse racial elements which form the population of British Guiana will fit themselves for true citizenship more rapidly than was the case in the United Kingdom itself.

An answer can now be given to the question, implicit in the referendum of 1914—namely, whether the then con-*Anomalous Constitution retarded Development.* stitution of British Guiana made for or against the prosperity, progress and good government of the Colony.

Judged by past history, that constitution had retarded development. Before the close of the eighteenth century, the whole coastline from the Corentyne on the east to the Pomeroon on the west had been granted to colonists, while the banks of the rivers Essequebo, Demerara and Berbice had been settled in a manner of which to-day hardly a trace remains. All this was achieved under Crown Colony Government. But under the " deviation form " of that government, which had obtained in Essequebo and Demerara since 1796 and in Berbice since 1831, the area beneficially occupied along the sea-coast and the principal rivers with their islands tended to diminish rather than to increase, while the interior still remains for the most part entirely undeveloped. The reason is not far to seek. The coastal interests dominated the administration; and, not unnaturally, the sugar planters and others whose interests were exclusively on the coast disapproved of spending the colonial revenues or private capital on objects which could not be expected to bring any immediate benefit to that coastal

---

[1] Despatch, 1st October, 1830.   [2] *Vide supra*, p. 179.

C C

fringe, where all the sugar estates of the Colony are situated. Hence the roads and railways are coastal; and the chief works of the Colony, both public and private, have been drainage schemes and water-conservancy schemes for the benefit of the plantations and those who live on the coastal flats. Vast sums have been spent on defending the shore against the inroads of the sea. But any attempt to open up the interior has been looked at askance as likely to withdraw labour from the coast. There can, of course, be no doubt that the greatest asset of British Guiana at the present time is its sugar industry, and that a wise administration will safeguard that industry. Nevertheless it is also beyond doubt that, unless there is proper representation in the Colony's constitution for industries established in the interior, the back blocks of this " magnificent province " will remain an unpeopled wilderness.

But, even if undeveloped, was the Colony prosperous? Few would have ventured to give an affirmative answer to that *Lack of* question. Population is a sure index of prosperity; *Prosperity in British* and the population of Demerara, Essequebo and *Guiana.* Berbice at the time of their union in 1831 to form the Colony of British Guiana was estimated at 98,000 souls. Subsequently the population was returned as follows at each decennial census down to the time of the Great War :

Census Years.	1841.	1851.	1861.	1871.	1881.	1891.	1911.*
Total population . .	98,154	135,994	155,907	193,491	252,186	278,328	296,041
Increase .	154	37,840	19,913	37,584	58,695	26,142	17,713
Immigrants †	9,296	43,314	39,228	61,924	70,165	44,112	65,764
Immigration periods † .	1835–40	1841–50	1851–60	1861–70	1870 to 1880–1	1881–2 to 1890–1	1890–1 to 1910–1

* There was no census in 1901.   † Taken from the table on p. 373, *supra.*

This table shows a total increase in the population of 198,041 souls during 80 years, which gives an average yearly increase of 2,475 or 2·5% *per annum.* But the total number of immigrants landed in the Colony from 1855 to the 31st March, 1911, was 333,803. Therefore, apart from immigration, the population would have shown little or no increase; for, although the reckoning began with an estimated population of 98,000 souls, to which 333,803 immigrants were added, we are left at the close of 80 years with a total population actually less in number than the immigrants introduced. Clearly, then, the natural increase in the population has been negligible in comparison with the loss by mortality and by emigration, while the increase of 2·5% *per annum* appearing on the face of the census statistics is mainly artificial and due to immigration.

Again, the area of the Colony is calculated to be 90,277 square miles, which in extent is equal to the combined size of England, Scotland and Wales. The total population of the Colony at the census taken in 1911 was found to be 296,041 souls, or about that of Hertfordshire. Thus the average population to the square mile in British Guiana was 3·28. Compare this with the then population of two prosperous Crown Colonies—Ceylon, with an area of 25,332 square miles, somewhat smaller than Scotland, and a population of 4,110,367 souls, or 162 to the square mile; Hong Kong, with an area of 394 square miles, about half the size of Westmorland, and a population of 456,739 souls, or 1,159 to the square mile—and note that the area of the whole British Empire was computed to be 13,123,712 square miles, with an estimated population of 435,000,000 souls, or 32 to the square mile.[1] Clearly British Guiana fell far below the average.

Another indication of a country's prosperity can be found in its trade and in the shipping entering its ports. In this respect British Guiana lags a long way behind many British colonies of smaller size, as the following figures will show :

Colonies.	Estimated Area in Square Miles.	Total Imports in 1912. £	Total Exports in 1912. £	Shipping Entered and Cleared in 1912.	
				British Tonnage.	Total Tonnage.
British Guiana	90,277	1,703,355	1,798,597	600,473	934,745
Trinidad and Tobago .	1,860	4,682,325	4,472,577	2,499,623	2,657,695
Jamaica .	4,450	3,050,479	2,709,283	1,925,983	4,319,112
Ceylon .	25,332	12,133,332	13,263,660	10,114,584	15,420,142
Straits Settlements .	1,660	52,504,551	43,765,021	14,857,667	25,841,494
Hong Kong *	394	—	—	11,977,714	36,735,149
Gold Coast .	80,000	4,025,000	4,307,000	1,625,804	2,849,248

* Hong Kong is a free port, without a custom house, and kept no statistics of its imports and exports in 1912.

[1] *Whitaker's Almanack*, 1915, p. 106.

Finally, as regards good government, the former constitution was beset by the dangers inherent in representative institutions when they rest on a narrow basis, which cannot be broadened without even greater hazard : the executive was crippled by being in a permanent minority : and the financial system was unsound and exposed the Colony both to conflict with the mother-country and to the anarchy consequent upon stoppage of supplies by an elective majority, while directly discouraging His Majesty's Government from making any loan or grant-in-aid for the development of British Guiana. Under such circumstances, the old constitution could only be regarded as an incubus of which the Colony would be well rid ; and far from treating the constitution as something to bargain with, it should have been voluntarily surrendered not merely for the valuable consideration of an Imperial loan, had such a loan been forthcoming, but rather for the greater security and well-being of the community, which, as the history of British colonization in the tropics demonstrates, can be confidently expected from Crown Colony Government.

Conclusion.

PART IV

THE REFORMS OF 1928

PART IV

THE REFORMS OF 1928

SPEAKING at a dinner given in his honour by the West India Club in London on the 23rd September, 1925, Sir Graeme
Views of Sir Graeme Thomson. Thomson, then retiring from the post of Governor of British Guiana, said that he answered in the affirmative the question: " Is the present constitution a bar to progress and to the introduction of capital? " He explained that, when a man came to him, desirous of introducing a new industry into the Colony, and asked for an assurance that, until the new industry found its feet in five or ten years' time, he should be granted remission of customs duty, the only possible reply was: " The Governor's guarantee on such a point is worthless : for the only body competent to give a decision is the Combined Court and the matter will be reviewed by the Combined Court every year." The man then inquired whether the Secretary of State for the Colonies had overriding power and could give a guarantee. Sir Graeme was obliged to answer " No." Thereupon the man rejoined that " it was not good enough," tied up his purse-strings and went away. Dissatisfaction with the results obtained under such a system was, Sir Graeme said, shared by the electors, the officials and all thinking persons in the Colony. He wished to see the Combined Court and the Court of Policy abolished, one legislative body substituted, and the Secretary of State given the final " say." He believed the moment to be ripe for such a reform.[1]

Sharp financial stringency at this time also brought into glaring prominence the defects in the Colony's constitution.
Financial Situation in 1927. The Great War had made British Guiana prosperous temporarily; but this prosperity was of an unhealthy kind, being mainly due to enhanced prices realized owing to abnormal circumstances in the world's

[1] West India Committee's Circular for 1925, pp. 404–5.

markets by the staple produce of the Colony—sugar and rice—and not to any appreciably greater output. When peace was restored, the price of sugar and rice fell, and lean years followed the four years of plenty. Moreover, the shortage of labour consequent upon the cessation of all immigration from India in April, 1917, was acutely felt, and handicapped every effort to expand the resources of the Colony. In 1927 the crisis came. For seven years past the Colony's budgets had shown substantial deficits annually, except in 1923, when there was a surplus of £33,155. The deficit in the budget for 1926 was £119,364, and in the budget for 1927 it was £97,163.[1] The total assets and liabilities of British Guiana at the end of 1927 were £1,728,194 and £1,910,904 respectively, and the accumulated deficit was £182,170. The Colony's funded debt in July, 1927, was in round figures £3 millions, and about £1·3 millions were owing on short-term loans to the Crown Agents for the Colonies. This total sum of £4·3 millions meant that British Guiana's debt was equal to about £14 *per* head of its population—a very heavy load in comparison with that of other colonies. Moreover, 80% of the revenue of British Guiana was collected under the Customs Duties and Tax Ordinances, which were passed annually by Combined Court for a period of one year only. This was a disturbing factor to business men and no such system existed in other colonies.

The increasing gravity of the situation had decided Mr. L. S. Amery, Secretary of State for the Colonies, in October, *Report of Parliamentary Commission.* 1926, to appoint Mr. R. R. Wilson M.P. (Conservative), and Mr. H. Snell, M.P. (Labour), with Mr. R. A. Sedgwick, of the Colonial Office, as Secretary, to be a Parliamentary Commission, to visit British Guiana and to " report on the economic condition of the Colony, the causes which have hitherto retarded, and the measures which could be taken to promote, development and any facts which they may consider to have a bearing on the above matters." This Commission spent a month in British Guiana, from the 16th November to the 17th December, 1926, and issued a

[1] In 1923 revenue was £1,114,704 and expenditure £1,081,547 : in 1926 revenue was £1,054,127 and expenditure £1,173,491 : and in 1927 revenue was £1,068,865 and expenditure £1,148,028.

report dated the 5th April, 1927, which was laid before both
Houses of Parliament.[1] The Commissioners, although of
opposite political parties, were entirely agreed in their diagnosis
of the maladies afflicting the Colony and in the remedies they
recommended. " The Government in British Guiana," they
wrote, " have never been able to govern. This situation was
possible as long as the function of administration was confined
to attempting to prevent misgovernment. It is not possible
when the Government are expected to take a direct and active
part in the development of the country and the improvement
of the condition of the people." They pointed out that the
divorce of responsibility from power, which was so marked a
feature of the constitution, placed the elected members as well
as the Government in a false position : for the elected members
tended to be in permanent opposition, unrestrained by experience or prospect of office. The elected members were,
they said, " in the position of a minor who can overrule his
own trustee." One of the greatest impediments to the development of the Colony's undoubted resources was, in the opinion
of the Commissioners, its financial situation. Budgets were
not balanced ; there was no effective control by Government
over taxation, and there was no possibility of raising loans.
This state of affairs was attributable to " a thoroughly unsound financial system," caused by lack of ultimate control ;
it was prejudicial to trade, and the insecurity of salaries was
not an inducement for officials from elsewhere to enter the
British Guiana service. But it was hopeless to expect any
improvement, unless the Government had power to enforce
their own financial policy. " We are definitely of opinion,"
they reported, " that in the present stage of political, economic
and cultural development it is not merely desirable, but
essential, that the authorities finally responsible for the government of the Colony should have power in the last resort to
carry into effect measures which they consider essential for
its well-being." To secure this would involve an alteration
in the constitution, the precise nature of which, Messrs. Wilson
and Snell suggested, might be referred in the first instance to
a local commission convened by the Governor. They themselves, however, stated that much could be said for merging

[1] Cmd. Paper No. 2841.

the functions of the Court of Policy and the Combined Court into a single Legislative Council; that they were in favour of admitting to the Executive Council one or more of such elected members as the Governor might see fit to recommend to His Majesty the King, for appointment, for the usual period of five years, and they were agreed that the Colony would be wise to consider whether the time had not come for providing by means of a nominated element for the representation on the Legislature of classes and interests inadequately represented by the process of direct election.

Mr. Amery transmitted this report to Governor Sir Cecil Rodwell in a despatch, dated the 25th May, 1927. He pointed out that recent events had emphatically corroborated *Mr. Amery's Instructions.* the views of Messrs. Wilson and Snell; for the Crown Agents were advised that it would be impossible for the Colony to raise a loan on less than a 6% basis, that even on these terms it was uncertain whether the money could be obtained, and that such a loan would tend to depress permanently the level of the Colony's credit. Moreover, when the Combined Court took the budget for the financial year then current into consideration, " the Government's proposals were rejected *en bloc*, the substantial adverse balance was ignored, the abnormal arrears of revenue short-collected in 1926 were used to defray part of the anticipated shortage for 1927, and the budget was finally balanced, in spite of the warnings of the Government, by discriminatory export duties on the sugar and on the new bauxite industry." Also the truth of the Parliamentary Commission's remark that insecurity of salaries discouraged officials from entering the service of British Guiana had been " strikingly demonstrated by the decision of the Conservator of Forests (Mr. Wood) to take advantage of his option of reverting to the Indian Service in preference to accepting permanent employment in the Colony." Accordingly the Secretary of State directed the Governor to appoint a local commission of not more than five members, with the Colonial Secretary as chairman,

> " to advise upon the steps which should be taken to confer power upon the Governor to carry into effect measures which he and the Secretary of State consider essential for the well-being of the Colony, whether by an

alteration in the relative powers and in the composition of the Court of Policy and the Combined Court, or by the substitution of a new Legislative Council, in which the Crown would possess powers of effective control over financial as well as other matters; and generally upon any other improvements, such as those suggested by the British Guiana Commission, which might be effected in the constitution."

Pursuant to these instructions, Sir Cecil Rodwell appointed a local commission as follows: the Colonial Secretary (Mr. C. D. Douglas Jones), chairman; the Attorney-General (Mr. Hector Josephs), the Agent-General for Immigration (Mr. J. Hampden King), Mr. W. M. Shields (an unofficial member of the Executive Council), Messrs. E. G. Woolford and R. E. Brassington (elected members of the Court of Policy), the Commissioner of Education (Major W. Bain Gray), members; and Mr. G. C. Green, Secretary. This local commission held fifteen meetings and received evidence orally and in writing. The preponderance of the evidence was in favour of the abolition of the Court of Policy and Combined Court and the substitution therefor of a single legislative body. This the Commissioners recommended in their report, dated the 12th September, 1927, and laid before Parliament as " command paper " No. 2985. They expressed the view that the new Legislative Council should consist of fourteen elected members (the same number of electives as then sat in Combined Court) and, excluding the Governor, of at least fifteen *ex officio* and nominated members; that the *ex officio* members should be the Colonial Secretary and Attorney-General; that eight nominated members should be officials, and that the remaining five nominated members should be unofficial persons of standing in the community, but that no person in receipt of any emolument from the Crown or from the Government of the Colony should be a nominated unofficial member. The Governor should be President of the Legislative Council and should have a casting vote only. The total number of members being twenty-nine, the quorum should be the President with ten members. The sugar-planters and major commercial interests should receive special consideration when nominated unofficial members were being selected, particularly if they had not already secured adequate

Report of Local Commission.

representation among the elected members. With regard to the nominated official members, it might, the Commissioners thought, be an advantage to the public service, if it were possible to vary the personnel on occasions when the Governor considered it desirable to have a particular officer present in the Legislature for a specific purpose during a particular period. It should be a recognized practice for officials who were not members of Legislative Council to attend its meetings for the purpose of giving information. The life of the Legislature should be five years, and the nominated members should hold their seats until the next dissolution of the Legislature after their appointment. They recommended that all elections should be held on the same day, and they expressed the opinion that a woman who in her own right possessed the requisite qualifications should be entitled to exercise the franchise. " The extension of the franchise to qualified women would," they wrote, " have the important advantage of increasing considerably the number of electors in each constituency."

The local commission further reported that the Executive Council should (exclusive of the Governor, who would be its President) contain eleven members, the majority of whom should be officials, and that it should be constituted as follows :

> (*a*) two *ex officio* members—namely, the Colonial Secretary and the Attorney-General :
> (*b*) four nominated official members :
> (*c*) three nominated unofficial members : and
> (*d*) two elected members of the Legislative Council, nominated by the Governor.

Five members, apart from the President, would be a suitable quorum.

Having regard to the absolute necessity of safeguarding the credit and financial stability of the Colony, and in order to prevent any possibility of deadlock, when the Governor might find himself unable to carry some measure which he and the Secretary of State considered essential to the good government of the Colony, the local commission submitted the following recommendation :

> " Any matter requiring a vote or enactment of the Legislative Council may be decided by the Governor

according to his own deliberate judgment notwithstanding that such decision may be contrary to the vote of a majority of the Council; provided that he shall by writing under his hand declare such decision to be in his opinion necessary in the interests of public order, public faith, or other first essentials of good government including the responsibilities of the Colony as a component part of the British Empire; and provided further that effect shall not be given to any such decision until the Governor shall have reported fully to one of His Majesty's Principal Secretaries of State all the circumstances of every case in which he shall make any such declaration of opinion and the approval of a Secretary of State first obtained, save in cases of urgency where in the opinion of the Governor delay would be contrary to the public interests, in which cases such decision shall nevertheless be subject to review by a Secretary of State after considering the report of the Governor; and provided further that the Governor shall forward to the Secretary of State any statements or representations which any member or members of the Council may desire to make on the matter, if made within 14 days of the making of such declaration of opinion."

Mr. E. G. Woolford made certain reservations, stating that he could not conscientiously agree to any limitation or curtailment of any of the constitutional privileges which *Protest of Elected Members of Combined Court.* the Colony then enjoyed. But all the other members of the local commission signed the report; and, as Sir Cecil Rodwell said at a luncheon given by the Royal Colonial Institute at Cannon Street Hotel in the City of London on the 15th November, 1927, although some " politicians " in British Guiana seemed to think that the then existing constitution was a short-cut to responsible government, " that was wrong : they were really in a *cul de sac,* and it would be better to back out and enter the main road to responsible government through the various degrees of Crown Colony government." [1] However, many of the elected members of Combined Court were dissatisfied with the report of the local commission, and three " die-hards " left for London in January, 1928, to plead the cause of the existing constitution at the Colonial Office, and to present to Mr. Amery a memorandum prepared by the elected members of

[1] See West India Committee's Circular for 1927, p. 473.

the Combined Court in reply to the report of the local commission.

This memorandum, together with the comments on it made
by the local commission, by the Governor of British Guiana,
Reform Bill by the Crown Agents for the Colonies and others,
introduced in was presented to Parliament early in March, 1928,
House of
Commons. as " command paper " No. 3047; and the elected
members were given an interview by the Secretary of State.
But the case for reforming the constitution was overwhelming,
and Mr. Amery had on the 21st February, 1928, introduced
in the House of Commons a " Bill to make provision for the
Government of the Colony of British Guiana." [1] This bill,
which eventually passed through both Houses of Parliament
without amendment, makes it lawful for His Majesty in
Council

> " to create and constitute, in substitution for the
> existing legislature, a legislature for the Colony of British
> Guiana in such form and with such powers as His Majesty
> in Council may determine, and from time to time to alter
> and amend the constitution of the legislature and any
> powers thereof; and any such Order-in-Council may
> provide that, notwithstanding the powers conferred on
> the legislature thereby, there shall be reserved to or
> conferred upon His Majesty full power by Order-in-
> Council from time to time to make laws for the peace,
> order and good government of the Colony of British
> Guiana."

On the 6th March, Mr. Amery moved the second reading
of the bill, and he was supported by Mr. J. A. Tinne, who
Debates in described himself as " the only native-born British
Parliament. Guianian in the House," and who recalled the fact
that his great-great-grandfather, P. F. Tinne, as secretary
to Anthony Meertens, Directeur-General of Essequebo and
Demerary, had drawn the articles of the capitulation [2] of the
Two Rivers in 1803. The debate on the second reading fills
thirty-three pages of Hansard; but in spite of some opposition,
the bill was passed. No amendments were made in Committee. The bill was reported to the House on the 13th
March, and next day the third reading was carried by 178

---

[1] See Appendix R.   [2] *Vide infra*, p. 414.

votes to 70. Mr. Ormsby-Gore, the Under-Secretary of State for the Colonies, in winding up the debate on the third reading, said that the reason for the changes in the constitution was the badness of the existing system, and that the general type of the future administration would be " an advanced form of Crown Colony Government."

The bill was then sent to the House of Lords, where, on the 20th March, Lord Lovat, the Under-Secretary of State for the Dominions, moved its second reading. During the debate which ensued, Viscount Haldane (Labour) pointed out that, " if there was a substantial constitution which had been granted by the Crown, then, according to the law of this country, it could not be superseded without a statute, as was laid down by Lord Mansfield 150 years ago in Campbell *versus* Hall." [1] Lord Olivier (Labour), however, said that the constitution of British Guiana " according to his experience was the worst in the world," and that " they were doing away with what had been a scandal for a great part of his official life." Lord Lovat, in winding up the debate, stated that Lord Mansfield's decision had been considered most carefully, and that the bill had been introduced in order that the authority of Parliament might be behind the Order-in-Council.

On the 28th March the bill was finally approved by the House of Lords without amendment and, receiving *Act Passed* the royal assent, it became the Act of Parliament, known as 18 George V, chapter 5.

This Act requires that the draft of any Order by His Majesty in Council creating and constituting a legislature for the *Royal Order-* Colony of British Guiana or altering the constitu- *in-Council.* tion or powers thereof must be laid before each House of Parliament for a period of not less than 21 days on which that House has sat, and that, " if either House of Parliament before the expiration of that period presents an address to His Majesty against the Order or any part thereof, no further proceedings shall be taken on the draft, without prejudice to the making of a new draft Order." Accordingly the draft of a " British Guiana (Constitution) Order-in-Council " was placed before both Houses of Parliament. The statutory period during which addresses could be presented by either

[1] See Appendix S.

House against this draft expired on the 12th July, 1928, and, no such addresses having been presented, the draft was approved by His Majesty in Council on the following day. The third clause of this Royal Order-in-Council was as follows:

" From a date to be fixed by the Governor in Executive Council by Proclamation in the *Gazette*, the Court of Policy and the Combined Court of the Colony now subsisting and all and every the functions and privileges of those two bodies respectively shall cease and determine absolutely, and in place of the said Court of Policy and Combined Court there shall be in and for the Colony a Legislative Council, which shall be constituted and have such powers as is hereinafter provided."

The Court of Policy met for the last time on the 17th July, 1928; and next day, pursuant to clause 3 of the Royal Order-in-Council of the 13th July, 1928, there was published *Court of Policy and Combined Court abolished.* in the *Official Gazette* of British Guiana a proclamation by the Governor in Executive Council fixing the 18th July as the date on which the Court of Policy and the Combined Court should " cease and determine absolutely," and providing for the constitution of a Legislative Council in their place.

Legislative Council constituted. The new Legislative Council was composed as follows:

(a) the Governor (Sir Cecil Rodwell), President, with a casting vote only:

(b) the Colonial Secretary and the Attorney-General, *ex officio* members:

(c) eight nominated official members, viz. Dr. P. J. Kelly, Mr. T. Millard, Major W. Bain Gray, Professor J. S. Dash, Mr. S. H. Bayley, Major J. C. Craig, Mr. B. R. Wood, and Colonel W. E. H. Bradburn, all of them officers in the service of the Government of British Guiana.

(d) five nominated unofficial members, viz. Mr. A. P. G. Austin (bank manager), Mr. T. T. Smellie (merchant), Mr. F. Dias (solicitor, and in previous years an elected member of the Court of Policy and Mayor of Georgetown), Mr. James Smith (manager of Rose Hall sugar estate in Berbice), and Mr. S. H. Seymour (the proprietor of an estate in Essequebo and representative of secondary agricultural interests, including rice cultivation) :

(e) the fourteen elected members of the Combined Court, just abolished, who under the Royal Order-in-Council became *ipso facto* members of the new Legislative Council and retained their seats until the next general election, which, it was provided, should be held not later than two years after the Council had first been constituted, and which did in fact take place on the 18th September, 1930, the first Council having been dissolved on the 17th July of that year.

It was further provided in the Royal Order-in-Council that the President with ten members should form a quorum (clause 64) ; that the duration of the Legislative Council should be for periods of five years after its first dissolution (clause 69) ; that for the purpose of the first election of members to serve in the Council, and until the Council itself by ordinance otherwise provided, the Colony should be divided into such electoral districts as were constituted and defined by the Governor in Executive Council by proclamation in the *Gazette*, and that it should be lawful for the Governor in Executive Council by proclamation in the *Gazette* to declare what number of members should be elected to the Council for each electoral district (clause 20). Clause 21 prescribed the qualification for elected members and clause 25 the qualification for voters. Men only could be elected members; but the franchise (as recommended by the local commission) was extended to women upon the same terms as to men. The initiation of money-votes was permitted to the Governor only (clause 59), and the Governor's reserve power was provided for in clause 62, which followed exactly the wording of the draft clause proposed by the local commission in paragraph 24 of " command paper " No. 2985.[1] Moreover, full power was reserved to the Privy Council to revoke or amend any laws enacted by the Legislative Council and to " make, enact and establish " such laws as to His Majesty in Council appeared necessary for the peace, order and good government of the Colony (clause 54). Finally, by clause 75 His Majesty reserved " to Himself, His Heirs and

[1] See pp. 396–7, *supra*.

D D

Successors, full power and authority from time to time, with the advice of His or Their Privy Council, to revoke, alter or amend this Order as to Him or them shall seem fit."

Thus was British Guiana at last rescued from the constitutional quagmire in which it had floundered for more than *Mr. Amery's* a century. Undoubtedly a new chapter in the *Message.* Colony's history opened on the 18th July, 1928, and the *Gazette* of that day made public a message from Mr. Amery, the Secretary of State, to whose firm action the reforms were mainly due, expressing confident hope that a new era had dawned for British Guiana, that its problems could and would be solved by the continued and well-directed co-operation of all, and that the consolidation of a sound financial system would be the prelude to further and ordered advance for " this great, undeveloped member of the Empire, so rich in historic associations." Mr. Amery did not disguise from himself and from the people of the Colony the seriousness of the difficulties which still confronted them; but he believed these difficulties to be " symptomatic not of stagnation, but of progress."

The dross of a mischievous constitution has been taken from the silver of a land bounteously endowed by nature; now, therefore, we have good reason to expect that in due time " there shall come forth a vessel for the finer." British Guiana was called by one of its Governors a " magnificent province." Its colonists remember this phrase with pride, and they will do well to remember also Emerson's saying that " a creative economy is the fuel of magnificence."

APPENDICES

APPENDIX A

(See Part I, chapter iii, p. 44.)

CONCEPT PLAN OF REDRESS

For the Political and Judicial Government of the Colonies of
Essequebo and Demerara, determined by a Decree of the
Sovereign of 27th August, 1788, published in Demerary
26th May, 1789, and in Essequebo 4th June following,
and finally adopted by a Resolution of the Court of Policy,
26th April 1796.

THERE shall be one Court of Policy for both Rivers of the whole
Colony, and in each River provisionally one Court of Justice.

2. The Company, after taking the consideration of the Court of
Policy, shall serve their High Mightinesses of their answer, if the
administration of Justice in both Rivers could not in future be
recommended to one College, and hold their Sessions in the chief
Town of Demerary.

3. The Court of Policy shall consist in the Directeur-General
(Governor) of both Rivers, the Commandeur of Essequebo, the
Fiscal of Essequebo, and the Fiscal of Demerary, besides two Colonists from Essequebo, and two Colonists of Demerary; in case of
sickness or absence of the Governor, the Commandeur of Essequebo
shall occupy his place, and the place of Fiscal in both cases to be
supplied by one of the Advisers.

4. The Court of Justice in Essequebo shall consist in the Commandeur of that River and six Colonists, besides one Adviser.

5. The Court of Justice in Demerary shall consist in the Governor
of both Rivers and six Colonists, besides one Adviser.

6. The Councillors of Policy and Justice are to be elected from
among the principal, the most intelligent and religious inhabitants,
above five-and-twenty years of age, of the Protestant Religion, versed
in the Dutch Language, and at least to have resided three years
within the Colony : relative to family connections there, to observe
the 6th Article of the Instruction for the Government of the Colony
of the year 1773.

7. Those in employ of the Company, except the Fiscals, shall
also be admissible in the Court of Justice in both Rivers.

8. The College of Kiezers in Essequebo, consisting of five persons,
shall be augmented and continued to seven, the present augmenta-
tion and further supply, in case of vacancy, to be performed by the

majority of votes of the inhabitants, who have in possession five-and-twenty Negroes or thereabove in their employ, and such by signed Tender of Votes eight days after Advertisement, to be done by the Commandeur of Essequebo.

9. In Demerary there also shall be established a College of Kiezers, consisting of seven persons, upon the aforesaid footing, and by vacancies to be supplied; the College of Burgher Officers being exempted from forming the nomination of Counsellors.

10. The Kiezers, before they proceed to form a nomination, shall, either in the hands of the Directeur-General (Governor) or Commandeur, respectively, make Oath that they will nominate, to the best of their knowledge, such persons who are, according to the Regulations and Resolutions of their High Mightinesses, qualified to act as Magistrates, without regard to any inducement, persuasion or solicitation. Furthermore, the Kiezers shall, by new elections henceforward perform the Oath of Purge.

11. The Councillors of Policy, as well as those of Justice, shall, for the first time, be selected by the Governor by implicit drawing, in presence of the Kiezers, and in future by the Governor and Councillors in Council assembled, by a majority of votes, out of a double number, formed by the Kiezers in both Rivers respectively.

12. After the expiration of two years, and successively every year, the term of function of one of the Councillors of Policy, selected from the Colonists shall be expired, and in the first place the eldest Member in rank of Essequebo, and in the following year the eldest Member in rank in Demerary, and so subsequently.

13. From each Court of Justice a third shall remove every two years, to begin with the eldest in rank, nevertheless that such removed Members may again be nominated and selected. The vacancies which may occur in the meantime must be fulfilled within two months after the vacancy.

14. Whenever the votes are equal or standing in the Court of Policy, the Governor shall have a double or casting vote; and when such happen in the Court of Justice the advice, or vote of the Adviser, shall serve for a vote; and in case no majority therewith could be obtained in the Court of Policy, the eldest Member of the Court of Justice will be summoned; and when such happen in either Court of Justice, the eldest Member of the Court of Policy shall be summoned, and so successively.

15. All the Councillors of Policy and Justice, also the Advisers and Secretaries, before they enter into the functions of their respective Offices, shall take the Oath of Purge, as formerly. Further, the aforesaid Councillors of Policy shall take the following Oath:

> " I promise and swear, that I will be faithful to Their High Mightinesses the Lords States-General of the United Netherlands, my lawful Sovereign, likewise His Serene Highness the Prince of Orange and Nassau, &c., &c., &c.; that I will, to the best of my knowledge, observe, and cause to be

observed, the Laws, Ordinances, Regulations, and Resolutions of Their High Mightinesses in all their parts; that I will help to promote the interest of the Colony and connection with the Parent State; that, in all the Ordinary Sessions, or if properly summoned, I will appear in Court, and not absenting myself without proper reasons; that I will, with candour and sincerity, advise, to the best of my knowledge and abilities, without any hatred, favour, partiality, or respect to persons and capacity; and further do whatever a good and faithful Councillor of Policy is bound to do.　　　So true, &c., &c., &c." *

16. The Councillors of Justice will be obliged to make the following Oath :

" I promise and swear, that I will observe, and cause to be observed, the Laws, Ordinances, Regulations, and Resolutions of Their High Mightinesses the Lords States-General of the United Netherlands, likewise those of the West India Company, in all their parts, to the best of my knowledge; that in all Law Suits I will regulate myself by the Laws, Ordinances, Regulations, and Resolutions of the Netherlands, issued by Their High Mightinesses, or the Committee of Ten, with approbation of Their High Mightinesses; that in all the Ordinary Sessions, or if properly summoned, I will appear in Court, and not absenting myself without competent reason; that I will, with candour and sincerity, give a just sentence, to the best of my abilities and knowledge, without any hatred, favour, partiality or respect to persons or capacity; and further do whatever a good Councillor of Justice is bound to do.　　　So true, &c., &c., &c."

17. The Court of Policy shall at least assemble every three months in Demerary; and further, as often as the Governor shall summon the same, which Summons will not be refused to any of the Members, unless for sufficient reasons and to his responsibility to the Company.

18. The Secretary of Demerary shall act as Minister to this Court of Policy, as also to the Court of Justice, and be furnished with the necessary assistance.

19. The Secretary of Essequebo will act as Minister to the Court of Justice of that River, and be furnished with the necessary assistance.

20. By absence or sickness of the Adviser, the Adviser of the

* *Form of subsequent Oath* : I do solemnly promise and swear that I will under my allegiance to Her Most Sacred Majesty Queen Victoria, and to Her Heirs and Successors, faithfully perform, to the best of my knowledge, the duty of a Member of the Council of Policy of the Colony of British Guiana, observing with the interest of said Colony its connections with the Parent State—So help me God.

other River shall supply his place, provided then, that the days of meeting will be so regulated, that no inconvenience may arise.

21. Whereas, nothing can be more conducive for the good administration of Policy, and particularly that of Justice, nor more important to the interests of the inhabitants, we have reason to expect that the Members of the respective Courts will, for the benefit of the community, fulfil their places of honour, in the same manner as those of Surinam; although in case the said Members, and particularly the two Members from Essequebo in the Court of Policy to sit in Demerary, should feel themselves burthened, it is left to the Colonists to provide, or make good with mutual agreement for the necessary expenses, out of the Colony Chest, as they may judge reasonable.

22. The Adviser shall have a full knowledge of the Laws, of a good moral conduct, and be appointed by the Company on a suitable salary.

23. The Fiscal shall follow in rank to the Governor, and the Adviser after the Fiscal; it being well understood that the last mentioned never shall be allowed to act as Governor *ad interim*.

That the aforesaid Projected Plan of Redress of the Political and Judicial Government of Essequebo and Demerary is, by the Deputies, with due respect, submitted to the serious consideration of Their High Mightinesses, and flatter themselves, that in case it will meet their approbation, the form of Government of both Rivers will be restored and regulated on a good footing, to the satisfaction of the inhabitants and the welfare of the Colonies; that they, however, give into consideration, if Their High Mightinesses could not think proper that the aforesaid Plan merely be established provisionally, in expectation of the good effect that would result thereof in the Colonies; and at the same time to inform Directors of the West India Company that in case the inhabitants should, on the proposed Plan, or any part thereof, make any important remarks to the Committee of Ten, that Their High Mightinesses would willingly, after proper examination, take such notice thereof as Their High Mightinesses might judge proper, in order to attain the proposed object; provided, however, that in the meantime the already stated Redress should take place and be observed.

* * * * *

The Hague, 19th March, 1787.

(Signed) H. V. WYN.
N. C. LAMRECHTSEN.
H. L. WICHERS.

The foregoing is a faithful Translation from the Dutch.

C. T. RAPIN, Sworn Colonial Translator.

APPENDIX B

(See Part I, chapter iii, p. 54.)

PUBLICATION. Enacted 11th June, 1796, published 21st following.

ANTHONY BEAUJON, Governor.

KNOW YE !—That, on the 3rd of June last year, by the, at that time, existing Government, for reasons by the Publication proclaimed on the ensuing day, some arrangement and alterations had taken place concerning the administration of the Colony Funds, by which four Members, commissioned from the Colleges of Electors of both Rivers, were added to the Court of Policy, to have jointly the administration of said Funds, and which arrangements were made provisionally, under approbation of the Sovereign.

That since that time the situation of these Colonies relating to the Mother Country had undergone a total change by their being surrendered to the Commanders of His Great Britannic Majesty's Forces, from which the required approbation on the above arrangement relative to the administration of the Colony Funds can no longer be expected from our former Sovereign; and that, besides this, experience has learned that these provisional-made arrangements (although concluded on with good intention) are subject to many obstacles and retardation in the public administration, by which even the inhabitants who had legal pretensions against the Colony Funds remain, after a long time, deprived from obtaining their payments, as those could not be made then by General Assemblies of this Combined College.

That, moreover, it is true that the respective Electors have a power from the inhabitants to elect their Representatives in this Court, and that of Justice; but that they never have been authorized by them, in preference to other inhabitants, to hold for their lives the administration of the Colony Funds, as seems to have been the intention of the elected department of the said Funds; for which reasons we recall and annul the Resolution of the Extraordinary Assembly of the Court of Policy of these Rivers and Districts of Essequebo and Demerary, taken on the 3rd June, 1795, to this effect—the said Councillors of Policy combined with the Electors, as then constituted, is, and shall be, null and void. Moreover, as we have taken in consideration the reasonableness and equity that the inhabitants of these Colonies should be more amply represented at the raising of Taxes than by a number of four Colony Members fixed by the Constitutional Laws of these Colonies, and this being probably the intention and the motives of the former arrangements —at least, it having some connection with, or not foreign to, the nature of the British Laws in this case,—we have thought proper to adjoin to the College of Governor and Councillors of Policy, with a right of voting only for the raising of Colony Taxes, and not further, six inhabitants, viz., three from the River of Essequebo, and three from Demerary, elected to that purpose by the inhabitants, in whom the power or commission shall remain invested for a space of two ensuing years, at the expiration of which a Publication and Advertisement from Governor and Councillors shall be given to the inhabitants for the purpose of a new Election.

We have further fixed the same mode of electing such Members of the inhabitants entitled to vote as take place by the choosing of Electors; so that in consequence thereof, we have thought proper to advertise, as is done by these Presents, that they who confirm the Plan of Redress in the Politic and Judicial Government of the Colony, provisionally established by their High Mightinesses, are owners of a number of twenty-five slaves and thereabove, are competent and entitled to choose three representatives in their respective Colonies to represent them by the raising of Colony Taxes.

APPENDIX C

(See Part I, chapter iii, p. 57.)

ARTICLES OF CAPITULATION, 1803

Proposed by the Governor-General and the Court of Policy of the Colonies of Essequebo and Demerary, and the Commanding Officers of the Sea and Land Forces of the Batavian Republic, in the said Colony,

> To Their Excellencies the Commanders-in-Chief of His Britannic Majesty's Sea and Land Forces off Demerary.

ARTICLE 1. The Laws and Usages of the Colony shall remain in force and be respected, the mode of taxation now in use be adhered to, and the inhabitants shall enjoy the public exercise of their Religion in the same manner as before Capitulation; no new establishments shall be introduced without the consent of the Court of Policy, as the Legislature of the Colony. The constituted Authorities and Public Officers, whether in the Civil Law or Church Establishments, as well as the Members of the respective Courts (except the Governor-General), shall be continued in their respective Offices and Situations until His Majesty's pleasure shall be known.

> Answer—Granted.

ARTICLE 2. The inhabitants, those who are at present in the Colony, as well as those who may be abroad, shall be protected in their persons, and have the free enjoyment of their Properties, without being troubled or molested for any acts whatsoever, other than such as they might commit subsequently to the Capitulation, and in violation of the Oath of Fidelity they shall be required to take.

> Answer—Granted.

ARTICLE 3. The inhabitants shall, on no account whatever, be obliged to take up Arms against an external enemy; but their services shall only be required for quelling internal commotions or disturbances, according to the existing Regulations of the Burghers, and for maintaining the internal tranquillity of the Colony, in conformity to what has always taken place to this day.

> Answer—Granted, until, at the conclusion of the War, it shall be determined to what Government these Colonies shall be subjected.

ARTICLE 4. The Debts contracted by the Government for the building of new Barracks, the erection of Batteries, the purchase of Provisions for the Garrison, the Salaries of Civil Officers due, shall, on the first demand, be paid out of the Sovereign's or Government's Chest, as well as other demands that would have been paid or reimbursed by Government had the Colony not been taken.

Answer—Granted.

ARTICLE 5. The Sea and Land Forces of the Batavian Republic, stationed in the Colony, shall be allowed to depart freely. They shall retain their Arms and the whole of their Baggage, as well the Officers, non-commissioned Officers, as Privates. They shall be supplied by the Commandant of His Majesty's Forces with proper vessels to convey them, with the most convenient speed, to one of the Ports of the Batavian Republic, and during the passage thither they shall receive for account of His Majesty, each according to his rank, the same Rations, both as to quantity and quality, as are usually allowed to British Troops.

Answer—Granted; but the Troops and Seamen must be considered as Prisoners of War, and not to bear Arms against Great Britain or her Allies until regularly exchanged or released, and the Arms and Accoutrements of the Soldiers must be delivered up.

ARTICLE 6. The Corvette *Hippomenes* shall be given up unarmed for transporting her Officers and Crew to one of the Ports of the Batavian Republic; as many Troops of the Batavian Garrison shall embark and take their passage in the said Corvette as can be conveniently placed on board of her.

Answer—Cannot be granted; proper Vessels will be furnished at the expense of the British Government to carry the Troops and Seamen to Europe.

ARTICLE 7. The Governor-General, not having Military Rank, shall be at liberty to remain in the Colony until he shall have collected the necessary Documents, or Proofs, towards enabling him to lay before His Sovereign an account of his Administration; after which, every facility shall be afforded him to return to the Batavian Republic in a manner suitable to his rank. He shall be allowed to require such copies of Papers from the Government and Colonial Secretary's Offices as he may deem necessary for the purpose above expressed.

Answer—Granted.

ARTICLE 8. From the day of the Colony being taken possession of by the British Forces, the Batavian Troops shall be supplied with their usual Rations by the British Commanders until the day of their embarkation, and from that moment the Batavian Troops are to receive the same Rations as are usually allowed to British Troops when at sea, in the manner mentioned in the fifth Article.

Answer—Granted.

ARTICLE 9. The Batavian Troops shall continue, to all intents and purposes, under the command of their own Officers : every respect and honour shall be mutually shown by the Troops of both nations to one another; and care shall be taken, on both sides, to preserve peace and tranquillity until the departure of the Batavian Troops.

> Answer—Proper Quarters will be allowed for the Batavian Troops, and to which they must confine themselves until their embarkation.

ARTICLE 10. The Batavian Garrison shall be allowed freely, and without any hindrance, to take along with it all Accoutrements and Arms belonging to it; also the Effects of deceased Officers, non-commissioned Officers and Privates, that may yet be unsold, whether the same be deposited in the Public Magazines, or in any other place.

> Answer—That part of the Article relating to the Arms and Accoutrements is answered in Article 5; the remainder is granted.

ARTICLE 11. The sick of the Batavian Troops who may be left behind in the Hospital, shall be treated and taken care of in the same manner with the British Soldiers; they shall be entitled to the same terms of the Capitulation, and enjoy the same advantages as are stipulated for the rest of the Batavian Garrison; and, in like manner as the latter, they shall, after their complete recovery, be transported with the most convenient speed, to one of the Ports of the Batavian Republic.

> Answer—Granted.

ARTICLE 12. The Commanders of His Majesty's Forces shall, immediately on the Colony being taken possession of, furnish the Governor-General with a conveyance to transmit to the Batavian Government a copy of the Capitulation, with a statement of the reasons that induced him, as well as the Council of Policy, and the Commanding Officers of the Batavian Forces, to surrender the Colony to His Britannic Majesty.

> Answer—Granted; the Vessel which takes our Despatches to Europe will take those of the Governor of the Colonies.

ARTICLE 13. No Negroes shall be required from the Planters for the purpose of forming or recruiting any Black Corps.

> Answer—Granted.

ARTICLE 14. Should any difficulties arise in consequence of any dubious expressions occurring in the present Capitulation, the same shall be explained or construed in the sense most favourable to the Colony or the Batavian Garrison.

> Answer—Granted.

Government-House, 18th September, 1803.

(Signed)   A. MEERTENS, Governor-General of Essequebo and Demerary.

P. ROSMWINKEL, Major.

G. H. TROTZ, Commandeur of Essequebo.

D. J. C. LAMBERT, Captain of Artillery.

P. P. LUYKEN.

J. HOFFMAN, First Lieutenant.

Christ. D. MACK.

F. VAN DEN VELDEN.

F. KROLL.

By Command of the Court of Policy,

P. F. TINNE, Secretary.

(Signed)   WILLIAM GRINFIELD, Lieutenant-General.

SAMUEL HOOD.

By Order,

WILLIAM TATUM, Military Secretary.

H. TRACEY, Naval Secretary.

ADDITIONAL ARTICLES

ARTICLE 1. Possession of Fort William Frederick is to be given to a Detachment of British Troops, this evening, by seven o'clock; also, that of the Batavian Ship of War, the *Hippomenes*, to the British Seamen; and the *Hornet*, British Sloop of War, and the Schooner *Netley*, are to be allowed to pass into the Harbour of Demerary.

Answer—Acceded to.

ARTICLE 2. Possession of the Colonies of Demerary and Essequebo to be given to the British by twelve o'clock to-morrow noon.

Answer—Acceded to.

(Signed)   G. H. TROTZ, Commandeur of Essequebo.

F. KROLL.

J. HOFFMAN, First Lieutenant.

P. F. TINNE, Secretary.

R. PAAY HERKLOTS, Lieutenant Navy.

WILLIAM GRINFIELD.

SAMUEL HOOD.

Heureux, 19th September, 1803.

APPENDIX D

(See Part I, chapter iv, p. 79.)

By the Provisional Government and other Members of the Court of Policy and Criminal Justice in the Colony of Berbice, published 25th September, 1803,

A PROCLAMATION

WHEREAS the provisional Government (private intelligence having been received Thursday evening of the surrender of Essequebo and Demerary by Capitulation to the English on Monday), in an extraordinary assembly of all the Councillors to which were also convened Lieutenant-Colonel Carl Matthias, Commandant of the Troops, Lieutenant G. F. Hindt, of the Navy, Commander of the Republican Schooner *Serpent*, Capt. R. Stuivelaar, of the Artillery, and Captain J. R. Claessens, of the Rangers, held Friday, the 23rd instant, p.m., have laid upon the Table a letter delivered that morning, at 12 o'clock, by Brigade-Major Armstrong, of the British Land Forces, and Lieutenant Pardo, of the British Navy, who had arrived here with a Flag of truce:

The Contents of which Letter are as follows :

By Captain LOFTUS OTWAY BLAND, Commander of His Britannic Majesty's Ships, &c., &c., &c., and Lieutenant-Colonel ROBERT NICHOLSON, Commander of His Britannic Majesty's Land Forces, &c., &c., under the Orders of Their Excellencies Lieutenant-General WILLIAM GRINFIELD and Commodore SAMUEL HOOD, Commander-in-Chief of His Majesty's Land and Sea Forces in the Windward and Leeward Charibbe Islands, &c., &c.

SUMMONS

These are requiring you, the Governor, and Court of Policy and the Military and Naval Forces, of the Colony of Berbice, and its Dependencies, to surrender the said Colony to His Britannic Majesty's Forces, under our command, and to place the same under His Britannic Majesty's Government, in which case the Laws and Usages of the Colony shall remain in force and be respected, the mode of taxation now in use be adhered to, and the inhabitants shall enjoy the public exercise of their Religion in the same manner as heretofore ; no new Establishment shall be introduced without the consent of the Court of Policy as the Legislature of the Colony.

The Public Officers, whether in the Civil Law or Church Establishment, as well as the Members of the respective Courts (except the Governor), shall be continued in their respective offices and situations until His Majesty's pleasure shall be known, excepting those who may be attached to French principles. The inhabitants, those who are at present in the Colony, as well as those who may be abroad, shall be protected in their persons and have the free enjoyment of their properties, without being troubled or molested for any acts whatsoever, other than such as they might commit, subsequent to the Capitulation, and in violation of the Oath of Fidelity they shall be required to take.

The Sea and Land Forces of the Batavian Republic stationed in the Colony shall surrender themselves Prisoners of War, and proper vessels will be provided, at the expense of His Britannic Majesty, to convey them with the most convenient speed to one of the Ports of the Batavian Republic; but they are not to bear Arms against Great Britain, or her allies, until regularly exchanged and released.

The Officers shall retain their Arms and the whole of their Baggage, and the non-commissioned Officers and Privates their Baggage only.

With regard to the Military Forces, the Officers and non-commissioned Officers and Privates of the same, may, if agreeable to themselves, enter into the British Service, and receive pay and every advantage and emolument enjoyed by those of the same rank in His Britannic Majesty's Service.

Should these liberal terms, which in fact extend to the inhabitants of this Colony a free participation in the great advantages enjoyed by the Subjects of His Britannic Majesty, be refused, the Governor and Court of Policy, and all concerned, must be answerable for the consequences, as an immediate attack will be made by the Land and Sea Forces, which will render every resistance vain.

One hour and no more is given to the Governor from the delivery of this by Brigade-Major Armstrong and Lieutenant Pardo to accept or not.

LOFTUS OTWAY BLAND.
ROBT. NICHOLSON,
Lieutenant-Colonel.

On Board His Majesty's Ship *Heureux*, off Berbice, September 23rd, 1803.

To His Excellency the Governor and Court of Policy of the Colony of Berbice, &c., &c., &c.

AND WHEREAS, the said Letter being read, the Provisional Government have required the opinion of Lieutenant-Colonel Mathias and the other aforesaid Batavian Officers, severally, respecting the possibility or impossibility to defend with the present means the Colony against an attack of the considerable Land and Sea Forces of the enemy (as they appeared to be from information received, and from the Signals hoisted at the Signal Post, of the approaching number of Ships), so as to preserve the same unto the State:

AND WHEREAS, the said opinions insinuated, as was justly apprehended, that with the present means and general state of defence of this Colony, there was not the least ground for reasonable hope to resist with any success, and much less now, since the enemy's advantages had so considerable increased by the yielding of Essequebo and Demerara:

AND WHEREAS, these sentiments have naturally produced the serious conviction and consent, that thus circumstanced it became duty and honour rather to listen to a liberal Capitulation offered by the enemy to preserve the persons and property of the inhabitants and others interested in the Colony from violence, destruction and plunder, than by a vain resistance, certainly to expose the same to all those miseries:

The Provisional Government and other Members, Civil and Military, have felt impelled to resolve to surrender the Colony to His Britannic Majesty's Forces on the proffered Capitulation, with some additional Articles, which they would endeavour to get granted by the British Commanders, as tending to the advantage of this Colony, and all concerned; but the same Lieutenant-Colonel Mathias having —not, however, categorically—concurred in accepting the proffered terms, nor assisted in the framing of the additional Articles, but on being required to answer expressly on the subject, pretended that he could not positively express himself before consulting with the other Officers of the Garrison, leaving the Assembly for that purpose at half-past five o'clock, under promise to return before seven, the utmost period the bearers of the Summons would consent to tarry for an answer, but which he has not fulfilled, returning neither to the Assembly, nor sending in any reason for his not returning, and thus obliging the Assembly to frame the additional Articles without his assistance and concurrence:

And after the proposals on the part of the Assembly were committed to writing, it was resolved, that the same should be delivered to the British Commander by a Committee, composed of J. van den Broek, junior, of the Provisional Government, Councillor Fricke, Fiscal and Secretary Eggers, Captains Stuyvelaar and Claessens, and Lieutenant Gallas, of the Navy, with authorization finally to conclude with the said Commanders, and the said proposals having received the Signatures of the whole Assembly, the Committee departed with the Summons Bearers in the Flag of Truce for the *Heureux*, man-of-war (whence the Summons were dated), at ten o'clock at night:

AND WHEREAS, the Committee have returned to the Assembly next morning, at eleven o'clock, and reported the final conclusion of the Capitulation at nine o'clock, laying upon the table the Articles

E E

mutually signed, of which the counterpart remained with the British Commanders :

The Contents of which Articles are as follows :

By the Provisional Government and Court of Policy and the Commanders of the Batavian Land and Sea Forces in the Colony of Berbice and its Dependencies,

ANSWER TO THE SUMMONS

By Captain Loftus Otway Bland, Commander of His Britannic Majesty's Ships, &c., &c., &c., and Lieutenant-Colonel Robert Nicholson, Commander of His Britannic Majesty's Land Forces, &c., &c., &c., under the Orders of Their Excellencies Lieutenant-General William Grinfield and Commodore Samuel Hood, Commanders-in-Chief of His Britannic Majesty's Land and Sea Forces in the Windward and Leeward Charibbee Islands, &c., &c., &c.

The Sovereignty of the Colony, with its Forts, Posts, Artillery, and Ammunitions of War, will be surrendered to His Britannic Majesty's Forces on the Capitulation offered, with the following additional Articles, viz. :

ARTICLE 1. The inhabitants shall have the full and immediate enjoyment of all Property, whether on shore or afloat; absent persons shall, as far as regards their property in the Colony, be considered as inhabitants of Berbice. The Shipping now in the River, as either belonging to resident inhabitants of the Colony or to absent Proprietors of Plantations, shall be as sacred as other Property in the Colony, and be allowed to proceed to Europe or to any port of America, or disposed of in the Colony, at the option of the Owners or their agents.

With respect to absent inhabitants and their Property, this Colony will be on the same footing as Demerary. The Shipping and all belonging to them must be given up, but a particular case may be considered.

ARTICLE 2. The Plantations, Lands, Manufactories, Workshops, Slaves, Effects, and Possessions of the Berbice Association, of whatever nature, shall be considered as Private Property, in the same manner as is agreed to by the Capitulation with General Whyte in May, 1796.

All Private Property whatever of individuals to be respected.

ARTICLE 3. Provocations or Appeals of Sentences and Dispositions passed in the Colony shall be allowed as usual, and made unto such Court of Justice or Judges as shall be agreed upon; yet with this proviso, that such Court or Judges shall determine the case appealed of by the now existing Dutch Laws in the Colony.

> Granted, until decided which country the Colony belongs to, at the end of the War; in the meantime all Appeals to be made to His Majesty in Council.

ARTICLE 4. The Troops of His Britannic Majesty shall garrison all existing Inland Posts for the protection of the Colony against insurrections of the Negroes; and as many more Posts shall be created for that purpose as in future may be deemed necessary by the Court of Policy, on making application to the Commander of His Majesty's Troops at the time being.

> The Colony will be protected by British Troops. The Officer commanding and protecting the Colony is to judge where Posts are to be erected.

ARTICLE 5. The Colony Assignations and other Paper Currency of the Colony shall retain their present value and continue in circulation until such time as circumstances will permit a plan to be agreed upon for the withdrawing and cancelling of the same, founded on Justice and Equity, and without injury to individuals.

> Granted.

ARTICLE 6. All Salaries due by the Colony to the Provisional Government, Civil Officers, and other persons thereto belonging, shall be paid out of the ordinary Duties and Taxes.

> Granted out of the Colony Funds.

ARTICLE 7. All Debts contracted by the present Government, or by Governor van Batenburg, on account of the Colony, shall also be paid out of that Fund, or out of such other as might appear they belong to.

> Granted.

ARTICLE 8. The bartering of Provisions and other Commodities with the citizens of the United States of America for the Produce of this Colony shall continue on the same footing as at present.

> On the same footing as the British Colonies.

ARTICLE 9. The Grants of Land made by the Council of the American Colonies and Possessions of the Batavian Republic before this date shall be respected, and the Grantees admitted so and maintained in the peaceable possession of the same, except such Lands as might appear to be disposed of otherwise by the Government or Council here, and such as are reserved for public purposes; also, except certain part of a Grant the Governor and Council have, in their Assembly of the 4th October, 1802, judged to have been obtained surreptiously.

> All fair Grants to be respected; all others to be left for future investigation.

ARTICLE 10. The Grants of Land made by Governor and Council before this date shall be respected as conclusive, though the approvement and confirmation of the Council of the American Colonies and Possessions might not have arrived in the Colony, and Governor and Council shall have the power to issue Letters of Confirmation (Groudbrieven) to the Grantees, which shall be deemed a complete and indisputable title to them and their successors.

> Left for future investigation, and if found to have been fairly obtained, will be confirmed.

ARTICLE 11. The Grants of Lands on the West Coast and West Bank of the River Corentin, made by Governor Frederici, of Surinam, which territory was formerly held to make part of and belonging to that Colony, but since December, 1799, has been placed and considered as belonging to the Government of Berbice, shall, in the same manner as proposed by the preceding Article, be respected as conclusive, and Letters of Confirmation (Groudbrieven) issued by Governor and Council here to the same, complete and indisputable effect as aforesaid.

> Answered in Article 10.

ARTICLE 12. The Governor and Council shall have the power to dispose peremptorily of yet ungranted Lands in any part of the Colony for cultivation to persons that may petition for Grants, on customary conditions or otherwise, as may be deemed most adapted to promote agriculture, and of course the prosperity of the Colony.

> Cannot be granted.

ARTICLE 13. During two years from this date it shall be permitted to resident and other Proprietors who wish to quit the Colony, or to withdraw their interests from the same, to dispose of their Properties, and to transport and have remitted the proceeds of it wherever they shall think proper.

> Granted.

ARTICLE 14. A Detachment of His Britannic Majesty's Forces to take possession of the Gates of Fort St. Andrew and of the Battery below the Fort on Sunday morning, the 25th instant, at seven o'clock.

> The forces of His Britannic Majesty to take possession of Fort St. Andrew, and all other Posts of the Colony they may think proper to occupy, this day, at ten o'clock, or as soon after as possible, before two o'clock.

ARTICLE 15. The Garrison shall march out with the Honours of War, Horns blowing and Drums beating, and shall carry with them their Arms and Ammunition, and two Field Pieces.

> The Garrison to march out with the Honours of War, but no Arms, Ammunition, or Field Pieces, can be allowed to Prisoners of War, except the Officers, who are to retain their Arms.

ARTICLE 16. The Commandant of the Troops, all the Officers, Soldiers, and other persons belonging to the Military Department sent out from Holland to this Colony, and their Wives and Children, shall be embarked within one month from this date, and conveyed to the Batavian Republick, at the expense of His Britannic Majesty, and not be Prisoners of War; and the Surinam Detachment having been sent only from that Colony for the suppression of the Mutiny of the Garrison in this Colony, which took place some months ago, shall be conveyed back to Surinam, the Garrison they belong to, also within the same space of time and at His Majesty's expense, and not be Prisoners of War.

> Shall be conveyed to Europe as soon as possible, but must be considered as Prisoners, and not to serve against Great Britain, or her Allies, until regularly exchanged. The Surinam Detachment to be also Prisoners of War, and on the same footing as the other Troops, but the Officers of the said Detachment will be furnished with a conveyance to Surinam, if they wish it.

ARTICLE 17. A Vessel shall be furnished as soon as possible for the conveyance of the Commandant, his Family and Officers, and the baggage and effects to them belonging.

> Granted.

ARTICLE 18. The sick shall be attended at the Military Hospital at the expense of His Britannic Majesty, and when cured to be sent to Holland.

> Granted.

ARTICLE 19. It shall be permitted to such persons of the Military Department as should not wish to return to Europe to stay in the Colony and seek for employment in the Planter line, or any other business their capacities and inclinations may fit them for, or if they choose to quit this Colony for any other place.

> Such people as may be found useful to the Colony, on proof and proper representation, will be allowed to remain.

ARTICLE 20. The present Government of the Colony and the Commandant of the Troops shall despatch immediately the Republic Schooner *Serpent*, now in this River, to give advice to the Government of the Republic of the present Capitulation.

> Cannot be granted, but the same vessel that takes our despatches to Europe will take theirs. The Naval Officers, non-Commissioned Officers and Seamen, shall not be Prisoners of War, but depart with the *Serpent* for the Batavian Republic, and the necessary Passports shall be furnished by the Commander

of His Britannic Majesty's Naval Forces.   The Republican
Schooner *Serpent* to be given up to His Britannic Majesty's
Schooner *Netley* at 10 o'clock this day.

ARTICLE 21. The remainder of the Military Mutineers who, by
their insurrection from the 11th of April to the 10th of May last,
have put this Colony in danger of total destruction, and are now
in Prison, shall be received in custody of His Britannic Majesty's
Forces, and within one month from this date be embarked and sent
to the Batavian Republic, at His Britannic Majesty's expense, to
be tried for their high crimes and receive the merited punishment.

> The British do not protect Mutineers of any country, the dis-
> posal of them to be left to the Commanders-in-Chief of His
> Britannic Majesty's Forces in the West Indies.

ARTICLE 22. Should hereafter any differences arise concerning
the true meaning of any of the Articles of the present Capitulation,
the interpretation of the same shall always be given in favour of
the Colonists.

> Granted.

This Answer and additional Articles will be delivered by
Johannes van den Broek, junior, Member of the Provisional Govern-
ment, Z. J. C. Fricke, Member of the Court of Policy, Paul Eggers,
Fiscal and Secretary, Roelof Stuyvelaar, Captain of Artillery,
J. R. Claessens, Captain of the Rangers, and J. D. Gallas, Lieutenant
of the Navy, who are authorized finally to conclude.

Proposed at the Government House, New Amsterdam, on the
23rd September, 1803.

Finally concluded on Board His Majesty's Ship *Heureux* off
Berbice, at nine o'clock, a.m., the 24th September, 1803.

(Was Signed)   J. VAN DEN BROEKE, Jr.
               J. C. FRICKE.
               R. STUYVELAAR, Captn.
               J. R. CLAESSENS, Capt.
               D. J. GALLAS, Lieutenant.
               P. EGGERS, Secretary.
               LOFTUS OTWAY BLAND.
               ROBT. NICHOLSON, Lieut.-Colonel.
               JOHN HOCOMBE, Navy Secy.
               GEO. EDDINGTON, Mil. Secy.

ADDITIONAL ARTICLE

Possession of Fort St. Andrew's, York and Redoubt, and other
Posts are to be given to Detachments of the British Troops, this day
at 10 o'clock, a.m.; also, that of the Batavian Schooner *Serpent*

to the British Seamen, and the *Netley*, British Schooner, with other Boats, are to be allowed to pass into the Harbour of Berbice.

ACCORDED TO

On Board His Majesty's Ship *Heureux*, the 24th September, 1803.

(Was Signed)   LOFTUS OTWAY BLAND.
ROBT. NICHOLSON, Lieut.-Colonel
JOHN HOCOMBE, Naval Secretary
GEO. EDDINGTON, Military Secy.
J. VAN DEN BROEK, Jr.
J. C. FRICKE.
R. STUYVELAAR, Capt.
J. R. CLAESSENS, Capt.
D. J. GALLAS, Lieut.
P. EGGERS, Secretary.

AND WHEREAS, it thereby appeared that the Committee have laudably acquitted themselves of the trust to obtain favourable answers, indeed on more of the Articles, than by the local circumstances, and state of affairs, with any appearance of hope could be expected :

The Assembly have approved of the conduct of the Committee and ratified the Capitulation, and the provisional Government sent peremptory orders to Lieutenant-Colonel Matthias to behave conformably to the said Capitulation. In consequence, part of the British Forces passed into the River and came at anchor abreast of the Town yesterday afternoon, and have to-day taken possession of the Forts and Posts and hoisted the British Colours in this Colony.

And these Presents are to make known unto the inhabitants, the aforesaid recurrences and Capitulation, with serious recommendation to behave themselves conformably thereto, for the common benefit of this Colony, and all interested in the same.

And these Presents shall be Proclaimed, Posted up, and sent round as customary.

Enacted in an Extraordinary Assembly, New Amsterdam, 25th September, 1803.

PRESENT :

All the Members above named, except Lieut.-Col. Matthias.

(Signed)   J. C. W. Herlin, Vt.

By Command,

(Signed)   P. EGGERS, Secretary.

APPENDIX E

(See Part I, chapter iii, p. 63.)

CONVENTION between Great Britain and The Netherlands, relative to the Dutch Colonies; Trade with the East and West Indies; &c.—Signed at London, 13th August, 1814.

In the Name of the Most Holy and Undivided Trinity.

The United Provinces of the Netherlands, under the favour of Divine Providence, having been restored to their Independence, and having been placed by the loyalty of the Dutch People and the achievements of the Allied Powers, under the Government of the Illustrious House of Orange; and His Britannic Majesty being desirous of entering into such arrangements with the Prince Sovereign of the United Netherlands, concerning the Colonies of the said United Netherlands, which have been conquered by His Majesty's Arms during the late war, as may conduce to the prosperity of the said State, and may afford a lasting testimony of His Majesty's friendship and attachment to the Family of Orange, and to the Dutch Nation; the said High Contracting Parties, equally animated by those sentiments of cordial good will and attachment to each other, have nominated for their Plenipotentiaries, namely :

His Majesty the King of the United Kingdom of Great Britain and Ireland the Right Honourable Robert Stewart, Viscount Castlereagh, one of His said Majesty's Most Honourable Privy Council, a Member of Parliament, Colonel of the Londonderry Regiment of Militia, Knight of the Most Noble Order of the Garter, and his Principal Secretary of State for Foreign Affairs, &c;

And His Royal Highness the Prince of Orange-Nassau, Prince Sovereign of the United Netherlands, His Excellency Henry Fagel, His Ambassador Extraordinary and Plenipotentiary at the Court of His Britannic Majesty :

Who, after having exchanged their Full Powers, found in good and due form, have agreed to the following Articles :

Art. I. His Britannic Majesty engages to restore to the Prince Sovereign of the United Netherlands, within the term which shall be hereafter fixed, the Colonies, Factories, and Establishments, which were possessed by Holland at the commencement of the late war, viz., on the 1st of January 1803, in the Seas and on the Continent of America, Africa, and Asia; with the exception of the Cape of Good Hope and the Settlements of Demerara, Essequibo, and Berbice, of which Possessions the High Contracting Parties reserve to themselves the right to dispose by a Supplementary Convention, hereafter to be negotiated, according to their mutual interests, and especially with reference to the provisions contained in the VIth and IXth Articles of the Treaty of Peace, signed between His Britannic Majesty and His Most Christian Majesty, on the 30th of May, 1814.

II. His Britannic Majesty agrees to cede in full Sovereignty the Island of Banca, in the Eastern Seas, to the Prince Sovereign of the Netherlands, in exchange for the Settlement of Cochin and its Dependencies on the Coast of Malabar, which is to remain in full Sovereignty to His Britannic Majesty.

III. The Places and Forts in the Colonies and Settlements, which by virtue of the 2 preceding Articles are to be ceded and exchanged by the 2 High Contracting Parties, shall be given up in the state in which they may be at the moment of the signature of the present Convention.

IV. His Britannic Majesty guarantees to the Subjects of His Royal Highness the Prince Sovereign of the United Netherlands, the same facilities, privileges and protection, with respect to Commerce and the security of their property and persons within the limits of the British Sovereignty on the Continent of India, as are now or shall be granted to the most favoured Nations.

His Royal Highness the Prince Sovereign, on his part, having nothing more at heart than the perpetual duration of peace between the Crown of England and the United Netherlands, and wishing to do his utmost to avoid anything which might affect their mutual good understanding, engages not to erect any Fortifications in the Establishments which are to be restored to him within the limits of the British Sovereignty upon the Continent of India, and only to place in those Establishments the number of troops necessary for the maintenance of the Police.

V. Those Colonies, Factories, and Establishments, which are to be ceded to His Royal Highness the Sovereign Prince of the United Netherlands by His Britannic Majesty, in the Seas or on the Continent of America, shall be given up within 3 months, and those which are beyond the Cape of Good Hope within the 6 months, which follow the Ratification of the present Convention.

VI. The High Contracting Parties, desirous to bury in entire oblivion the dissensions which have agitated Europe, declare and promise, that no Individual, of whatever rank or condition he may be, in the Countries restored and ceded by the present Treaty, shall be prosecuted, disturbed or molested in his person or property, under any pretext whatever, either on account of his conduct or political opinions, his attachment either to any of the Contracting Parties, or to any Government which has ceased to exist, or for any other reason, except for debts contracted towards Individuals, or acts posterior to the date of the present Treaty.

VII. The Native Inhabitants and Aliens, of whatever Nation or condition they may be, in those Countries which are to change

Sovereigns, as well in virtue of the present Convention as of the subsequent arrangements to which it may give rise, shall be allowed a period of 6 years, reckoning from the exchange of the Ratifications, for the purpose of disposing of their property, if they think fit, whether it be acquired before or during the late War, and of retiring to whatever Country they may choose.

VIII.   The Prince Sovereign of the United Netherlands, anxious to co-operate in the most effectual manner with His Majesty the King of the United Kingdom of Great Britain and Ireland, so as to bring about the total abolition of the Trade in Slaves on the Coast of Africa, and having spontaneously issued a Decree dated the 15th of June 1814,* wherein it is enjoined, that no ships or vessels whatever, destined for the Trade in Slaves, be cleared out or equipped in any of the harbours or places of his Dominions, nor admitted to the Forts or Possessions on the Coast of Guinea, and that no inhabitants of that Country shall be sold or exported as Slaves,—does moreover hereby engage to prohibit all his Subjects in the most effectual manner and by the most solemn Laws, from taking any share whatsoever in such inhuman Traffic.

IX.   The present Convention shall be ratified, and the Ratifications shall be duly exchanged at London, within 3 weeks from the date hereof, or sooner if possible.

In witness whereof, we, the undersigned Plenipotentiaries, in virtue of our respective Full Powers, have signed the present Convention, and have affixed thereto the Seals of our Arms.

Done at London, this 13th day of August 1814.

(L.S.)   CASTLEREAGH.
(L.S.)   H. FAGEL.

ADDITIONAL ARTICLES

I.   In order the better to provide for the Defence and Incorporation of the Belgic Provinces with Holland, and also to provide, in conformity to the IXth Article of the Treaty of Paris, a suitable compensation for the Rights ceded by His Swedish Majesty under the said Article, which compensation, it is understood, in the event of the above Reunion, Holland, should be liable to furnish, in pursuance of the above stipulations; it is hereby agreed between the High Contracting Parties, that His Britannic Majesty shall take upon himself, and engage to defray the following charges :

1.   The payment of £1,000,000 to Sweden, in satisfaction of the Claims aforesaid, and in pursuance of a Convention this day executed with His Swedish Majesty's Plenipotentiary to that effect, a Copy of which Convention is annexed to these Additional Articles.

2.   The advance of £2,000,000, to be applied, in concert with the Prince Sovereign of the Netherlands and in aid of an equal sum to

* See Commercial Treaties, vol. 3, p. 270.

be furnished by him, towards augmenting and improving the defences of the Low Countries.

3.   To bear, equally with Holland, such further charges as may be agreed upon between the said High Contracting Parties and their Allies, towards the final and satisfactory settlement of the Low Countries in union with Holland, and under the dominion of the House of Orange, not exceeding, in the whole, the sum of £3,000,000, to be defrayed by Great Britain.

In consideration, and in satisfaction of the above engagements, as taken by His Britannic Majesty, the Prince Sovereign of The Netherlands agrees to cede in full Sovereignty to His Britannic Majesty, the Cape of Good Hope, and the Settlements of Demerara, Essequibo, and Berbice, upon the condition, nevertheless, that the Subjects of the said Sovereign Prince, being Proprietors in the said Colonies or Settlements, shall be at liberty (under such regulations as may hereafter be agreed upon in a Supplementary Convention) to carry on trade between the said Settlements and the Territories in Europe of the said Sovereign Prince.

It is also agreed between the 2 High Contracting Parties, that the Ships of every kind belonging to Holland, shall have permission to resort freely to the Cape of Good Hope for the purposes of refreshment and repairs, without being liable to other charges than such as British Subjects are required to pay.

II.   The small District of Bernagore, situated close to Calcutta, being requisite to the due preservation of the peace and Police of that City, the Prince of Orange agrees to cede the said District to His Britannic Majesty, upon a payment of such sum annually to His Royal Highness as may be considered, by Commissioners to be appointed by the respective Governments, to be just and reasonable, with reference to the profits or revenue usually derived by the Dutch Government from the same.

III.   The present Additional Articles shall have the same force and validity as if they were inserted word for word in the Convention signed this day.   They shall be ratified, and the Ratifications shall be exchanged at the same time and place.

In witness whereof, we, the Undersigned Plenipotentiaries, have signed and affixed to them the Seal of our Arms.

Done at London, this 13th day of August, 1814.

(L.S.)   CASTLEREAGH.
(L.S.)   H. FAGEL.

APPENDIX F

(See Part I, chapter iii, p. 63.)

CONVENTION between Great Britain and the Netherlands, relative to the Colonies of Demerara, Essequibo, and Berbice. Signed at London, 12th August, 1815.

In the Name of the Most Holy and Undivided Trinity.

His Majesty the King of the United Kingdom of Great Britain and Ireland, and His Majesty the King of the Netherlands, being equally desirous of promoting and cementing the harmony and good understanding so happily established between the 2 Countries, by carrying into immediate execution that part of the provisions of the 1st Additional Article of the Convention of the 13th of August 1814, which stipulates that the Subjects of His Majesty the King of the Netherlands, being Proprietors in the Colonies of Demerara, Essequibo, and Berbice, shall be at liberty (under certain regulations) to carry on trade between the said Settlements and the Territories in Europe of His said Majesty, have nominated for their Plenipotentiaries, viz.

His Majesty the King of the United Kingdom of Great Britain and Ireland, Henry Earl Bathurst, a Member of His Majesty's Most Honourable Privy Council, and one of His Principal Secretaries of State;

And His Majesty the King of the Netherlands, the Sieur Henry Baron Fagel, a Member of the Corps des Nobles of the Province of Holland, and His Ambassador Extraordinary and Plenipotentiary to His Britannic Majesty;

Who, after having communicated to each other their respective Full Powers, found in due and proper form, have agreed to the following Articles:

Art. I. It is hereby agreed that, for the space of 5 years from the 1st of January 1816, the aforesaid Trade may be carried on in any Ships, being the property of Subjects of His Majesty the King of the Netherlands, wheresoever built, and without any restriction or limitation as to the mariners navigating them; but at the expiration of the said five years, or as much sooner as His Majesty the King of the Netherlands shall think proper, such Trade shall be carried on only in such Ships as are Dutch-built, and whereof the Master and 3-4ths of the Crew are the Subjects of His Majesty the King of the Netherlands.

II. His Majesty the King of the Netherlands reserves to Himself the liberty of imposing such duties as He may think fit, upon the importation into the European Dominions of His said Majesty, of the produce of the Colonies in question; and vice-versa, with regard to exportation; but the duties to be paid within the Colonies shall be applicable to the Dutch, as well as to the British Trade.

III. The Subjects of His Majesty the King of the Netherlands, being Proprietors in the said Colonies, shall be at perfect liberty to go to the said Colonies, and to return, without being subjected in this respect to any delay or difficulty; or to appoint Persons to act for them in the management of the said intercourse, or of their properties in the said Colonies; subject, however, during their residence there, to the laws and regulations of the same.

They shall also have full liberty to dispose of their property in any manner in which they may think fit; but it is understood that in regard to Negroes, they are to be subject to the same restrictions as British Subjects.

IV. In order to protect the Proprietors of Estates in the said Colonies from the ruinous effects of the immediate foreclosure of mortgages due to the Subjects of His Majesty the King of the Netherlands, it is further agreed, that, in all cases in which the Proprietor of an Estate shall offer to the holder of any mortgage on the said Estate, made prior to the 1st of January, 1814, (such Mortgagee being a Subject of His Majesty the King of the Netherlands) the security hereinafter specified, such Mortgagee shall not be at liberty to proceed to the immediate or summary foreclosure of the said mortgage; it being, however, understood, that in all cases in which no such security shall be offered by the Proprietor, the Mortgagee shall retain all those rights as to foreclosure to which he is at present entitled.

The security in question must provide that the Mortgagee shall receive, at the expense of the Proprietor of the Estate, a new mortgage for the whole amount of the debt now due to him, including both that part of the original debt which has not been discharged, and the interest which may have accrued upon it up to the 31st December, 1814, inclusive.

That this security shall reserve to the Mortgagee that priority of claim over other Mortgagees and Creditors to which he is entitled under his original mortgage; that it shall bear an annual interest, beginning from the 1st of January, 1815, at the same rate, and payable in the same manner, as that which was payable under the original mortgage; and that the whole amount of the new debt shall be payable by 8 annual instalments, the first of which is to become payable on the 1st of January, 1820.

The new security shall also afford to the Mortgagee all those means of legal redress, in the event of non-payment of the interest, or omission to discharge the principal when due, and all those other privileges and advantages to which he would be entitled under his existing mortgage, and shall place him, with respect to

the debt for which the new security is given, in the same situation
as he stood with respect to his original claim upon the Estate,
excepting only in what relates to the period at which the payment
may be demanded, so that no later Creditor shall derive, from this
arrangement, any power to affect the rights of the original Creditor,
and that no further suspension of payment (surchéance) beyond
that herein agreed upon, shall take place without the original
Creditor's special consent.

It is further agreed, that in order to entitle the Mortgagee to receive
the security specified in this Article, he shall as soon as the said
security is duly recorded in the said Colony, and delivered to the
Mortgagee or his Agent in the Colony (the expenses of such record
being defrayed by the Proprietor), deliver up to be cancelled the
mortgages or bonds originally granted to him, or exhibit legal proof
that the said mortgages and bonds have been duly cancelled, and
are no longer of any value.

It is further expressly agreed, that, with the exception of the
modifications specified in this Article, the rights of Mortgagees and
Creditors shall remain intact.

V. It is agreed that all Dutch Proprietors, acknowledged to be
such by the present Convention, shall be entitled to supply their
Estates from the Netherlands with the usual articles of supply;
and in return, to export to the Netherlands the produce of the said
Estates. But that all other importation of goods from the Netherlands into the Colonies, or export of produce from the Colonies to
the Netherlands, shall be strictly prohibited; and it is further
agreed, that the exportation of all such articles as may be prohibited
to be exported to those Colonies from the British Dominions, shall
be also prohibited to be exported from the Netherlands.

VI. By Dutch Proprietors are to be understood :

First; all Subjects of His Majesty the King of the Netherlands
resident in His said Majesty's European Dominions, who are at
present Proprietors in the said Colonies.

Secondly; all Subjects of His said Majesty who may hereafter
become possessed of Estates now belonging to the Dutch Proprietors
therein.

Thirdly; all such Proprietors as, being now resident in the above
Colonies, and being natives of the Netherlands, may (by virtue of
Article VIII of the present Convention) declare that they wish to
continue to be considered as such; and

Fourthly; all Subjects of His said Majesty who may be the
holders of mortgages on Estates in the said Colonies, made prior to
the date of this Convention, and who may, under their mortgage-
deeds, have the right of exporting from the said Colonies to the
Netherlands, the produce of the said Estates; subject, nevertheless,
to the restrictions specified in Article IX.

VII. In all cases where the right of supplying the mortgaged
Estate with articles of supply, and exporting produce from it to
the Netherlands, is not actually secured to the Mortgagee by the

mortgage deed, the Mortgagee shall be allowed to export from the Colony, only such quantity of produce as will be sufficient, when estimated at the current prices of the Colony, to pay the amount of interest, or principal annually due to him and to import into the Colony articles of supply in the same proportion.

VIII. All Proprietors, Subjects of His Majesty the King of the Netherlands, now residing in the above Colonies, must, in order to entitle themselves to the benefits of this Convention, declare, within three months after the publication of this Convention in the said Colonies, whether they wish to continue to be considered as such.

IX. In all cases where both Dutch and British Subjects have mortgages upon the same property in the said Colonies, the quantity of produce to be consigned to the different Mortgagees, shall be in proportion to the amount of the debts respectively due to them.

X. In order more easily to carry into effect, and the better to insure the execution of the provisions of this Convention, it is agreed that exact and specific Lists shall be made out every year, by order of the King of the Netherlands, containing the names and places of abode of the Proprietors resident in the Netherlands, together with the name and description of the Estate belonging to them respectively, specifying whether the same be a sugar or other Plantation, and whether the whole or only part of the Estate belong to the Proprietor in question : similar Lists shall also be made out of the existing mortgages on Estates, in as far as these mortgages are held by Dutch Subjects, specifying the amount of the debt on mortgage, either actually existing, or to be made out by virtue of the provisions of Article IV.

These Lists shall be delivered over to the British Government, and shall be sent to the Colonies in question, in order to make out from them, in conjunction with a List of the Dutch Proprietors resident in the said Colonies, the whole amount of the Dutch population and property or interest in the said Colonies.

XI. His Majesty the King of the Netherlands, having represented to His Britannic Majesty that the Company of Dutch Merchants and others, (styling themselves the Berbice Association) have a just Claim to certain Estates formerly settled by them in the Colony of Berbice, of which they were dispossessed by the Revolutionary Government of Holland, and which, on the capture of the said Colony by His Britannic Majesty, were considered as Government property; His Britannic Majesty engages to restore to the said Berbice Association, within 6 months after the exchange of the Ratifications of the present Convention, the Estates of Dageraad, Dankbaarheid, Johanna, and Sandvoort, together with all the Negroes and stock now actually employed upon the same; such restoration to be in full compensation and satisfaction of all Claims which the said Association may have, or may pretend to have, against His Britannic Majesty or his Subjects, on account of any property heretofore belonging to them in the Colony of Berbice.

XII. All questions of a private nature relating to such property as comes within the operation of this Convention, shall be decided by the competent Judicial Authority, according to the laws in force in the said Colonies.

XIII. His Britannic Majesty engages that the utmost fairness and impartiality shall be shewn in all matters affecting the rights and interests of Dutch Proprietors.

XIV. The 2 High Contracting Parties reserve to themselves the power of making such future modifications in the present Convention as experience may point out to be desirable for the interest of both.

XV. Lastly, it is agreed that the provisions of this Convention shall be in force from the date of the exchange of the Ratifications.

XVI. The present Convention shall be ratified, and the Ratifications thereof shall be exchanged in London, within 3 weeks from the date thereof, or sooner if possible.

In witness whereof, the respective Plenipotentiaries have signed it, and affixed thereunto the seal of their arms.

Done at London, the 12th day of August, in the year of Our Lord 1815.

(L.S.) BATHURST.
(L.S.) FAGEL.

APPENDIX G

(See Part I, chapter iv, p. 71.)

CHARTER GRANTED BY THE STATES-GENERAL TO THE BERBICE ASSOCIATION : 6TH DECEMBER, 1732

Charter or Conditions whereby their High Mightinesses the States-General and the Directors of the Colony of Berbice have agreed to establish Free Trade and Navigation to that Colony, to be open to all the Inhabitants of these Territories, and also to grant land, either cultivated or not, on reasonable conditions.

The States-General of the United Netherlands to all those who shall see, hear or read this, greeting; be it known that we have received the petition presented to us in the name and on behalf of the Directors of the Colony of Berbice, asking us to grant them a Charter, so that, under certain conditions, the trade and navigation to the said Colony may be open to all the inhabitants of these territories, also to such as may apply, that as much land, cultivated or not, may be granted as they shall require, in accordance with certain projected regulations, supplied to us and here inserted.

PROJECTED REGULATIONS

1. It shall be permitted to the Directors of Berbice, under the Sovereignty of their High Mightinesses and their patronage and protection, to grant lands to particular persons on such conditions as may be arranged between the contracting parties.

2. The Directors shall be permitted to collect an annual head-tax of fifty pounds of sugar for each inhabitant living in the colony, white as well as black, also a customs duty of two and a half per cent. of the value of all goods, imported to, or exported from the colony, and a tonnage duty on all vessels entering or clearing, of three guilders *per last* (4,000 lb.) to be paid at the place where the ship enters or clears.

3. The Directors shall not be allowed to impose any other taxes during the first ten years, nor even afterwards, without the consent of their High Mightinesses and on application of the Governor and Council.

4. The Directors shall, besides the fort or forts already established, be bound to make, within a reasonable time, upon the so-called Crab

Island, or a little higher up the river, a suitable fort to guard the colony, and at their own cost to maintain the same, also to provide the guns and ammunition of war, as well as the pay and maintenance of the garrison and everything connected with the defence and protection of the aforementioned colony, they being entitled in compensation for this to receive an extraordinary head-tax of such an amount yearly as shall be agreed upon with the planters and inhabitants, or otherwise by their High Mightinesses on the information of the colonists, of what shall have been found just.

5. The Directors shall, being requested by the colonists, provide them with a qualified Minister, schoolmaster, choir-leader and the like, without being bound to furnish more than the free table of the Commandant for the minister, an anker of brandy, and half a hogshead of wine; everything beyond these being defrayed by the colonists.

6. The Colonists shall be bound to have one white man to every fifteen negroes, but they will only be required to pay for passage and board of each white person, whether introduced by themselves, or by the Directors at their request, the sum of thirty guilders; these persons will be forwarded from here by the first opportunity and be of such condition, profession or trade, as may be directed by the colonists.

7. All sugar or other produce, sold or exported, even that which may be damaged, will have to be passed through the customs, and will be valued by one or more assayers appointed by the Directors, and these assayers shall be bound to place on the sugars and other produce, the marks of the plantations from which they have been procured.

8. The Colonists shall not be allowed to import or buy slaves from any one, whosoever he may be, except from the West India Company, and through the medium of the Directors of this Colony, and they shall, from time to time, inform the Directors what number of negroes each will require.

The Directors have already arranged with the West India Company, that on the first requisition they will furnish them with such slaves as they require; these will be sold by public auction in the colony at such prices as would be realized in Surinam.

9. The Colonists shall, at all times, be allowed to sell their plantations, slaves, animals and other effects, or to leave the colony and take these with them to any other place they think desirable.

10. All produce grown in this colony, such as sugar, coffee, cacao, indigo or others, shall not be delivered or exported otherwise than to these territories.

11. Also, the trade and navigation of this colony generally shall not be permitted otherwise than to and from these territories, and that direct, without calling at other places.

12. Under the conditions aforesaid the trade and navigation of the aforementioned colony has by these been opened to all inhabitants of this state.

13. It must be well understood that all Captains wishing to go to the said Colony shall be bound to procure from the Directors a Commission or Pass, and to furnish security that they will return with their ships and cargoes to these territories, without calling, in either going or returning, at any other places, except in cases of very great necessity, or danger to the ship and goods, to be verified on their return by authenticated declarations from the place where, for the above reasons, they have been compelled to enter.

14. All Captains going to the Colony will be required on the order of the Directors, to each carry twelve persons as passengers, and convey them to the Colony, two children under twelve years being counted as one, at thirty guilders per head, no extra charge being allowed for either passage or board.

15. Otherwise than as aforesaid, the ships of the Directors, as well as those of the West India Company which have brought slaves, shall have no preference over the vessels of private parties, all being expedited without distinction, and not obliged to wait for the loading of either the ships of the Directors or those of the West India Company.

16. The Captains or Merchants having arrived in the colony with their ships and goods, will be allowed to lay at such places as may be most convenient to them, provided they do not cause an obstruction, or prejudice any one.

17. Until the tonnage dues are paid, that is the export duty on the clearing of the ships and the import duty on those coming from home, it shall not be permitted to discharge any goods, and further, nothing is to be discharged until permits are obtained, if for the outgoing ships, from the Governor and Councillors in the colony, and for the home-coming ships from the Directors, or those authorized by them.

18. For the above-mentioned ships and goods, in either going or coming, no territorial export or import duties will be payable.

19. The aforesaid colony shall be administered by a Governor and Council of Government (RAAD VAN REGEERING), together with a Council of Justice, under such regulations and form of oath as their High Mightinesses may think proper to publish.

20. The Governor shall be appointed by the Directors, but his Commission must be received from their High Mightinesses before whom also he must take the oath.

21. The Council of Government shall provisionally consist of, besides the Governor, six persons, to be chosen by the Governor from a double number of names submitted to him, for the first time by all the Colonists, and afterwards by the other Councillors.

22. The Governor, in all matters, civil or military, shall have the supreme control, and preside in the Council of Government, but the Governor and Councillors shall at all times be bound to obey and carry out whatever may be ordered or instructed by the Directors; in all other matters where the Governor and Councillors have received no special instructions or orders, the Governor, when this is of any importance, shall convene the Council, who shall deliberate upon it

and finally come to such a decision as may be considered desirable or necessary, by majority of votes.

23. It must be well understood on one side, that neither the Governor nor the Council, together or separately, can make or introduce, much less execute, anything contrary to the tenour of this Charter, or any article of it, but on the other side, under this prohibition, and not obstructing the course of affairs, there will be no objection to a few small moderate taxes being fixed by the Governor and Council, with the approval of the Directors, so as to provide certain necessary expenses of the respective Councils of Government and Justice, the schoolmaster, and such-like.

24. And, in regard to the Council of Justice, criminal justice shall be discharged by the Governor and Council, but Civil justice, by the Governor and six persons, chosen out of a double number from the Council of Government as well as the colonists, by the Governor and Council of Government, to be under the presidency of the Governor.

25. Of the aforesaid six Councillors of Justice, three shall retire every second year, being succeeded by three others, and so on every succeeding two years.

26. In the above-mentioned Council, the majority of votes shall decide all matters, and the Governor shall not have more than one vote, except in cases where the votes are equal, when the Governor shall settle the question.

27. All the forementioned Councillors of Government and Justice shall perform their duties willingly, without formulating excuses, and without claiming any salary or remuneration.

28. The Councillors of Government shall rank above those of Justice, and in both Colleges the eldest in years shall have priority during the first term, but afterwards he who has sat longest or who first took the oath.

29. To the sentence passed by the Council of Justice, appeals shall be allowed (so far as civil matters are concerned) to their High Mightinesses, in the same manner as is done in Surinam.

30. And, as provision cannot be made too soon for succession *ab intestato* of the colonists or others who have settled in the colony, freedom will be permitted to all going there to choose, but having chosen, to follow the Charter of the West India Company of these territories granted by their High Mightinesses on the 10th of January, 1661.*

* The remainder of the document comprises forms of Bond, Passport, and *Act of Visa*, which it is unnecessary to reproduce.

APPENDIX H

(See Part II, chapter i, p. 83.)

LETTERS PATENT constituting the Colony of British Guiana, and appointing Major-General Sir Benjamin D'Urban, K.C.B., Governor, dated 4th March, 1831.

WILLIAM R.

William the Fourth, by the Grace of God, of the United Kingdom of Great Britain and Ireland, King, Defender of the Faith, To our trusty and well-beloved Sir Benjamin D'Urban, Knight Commander of the Most Honourable Military Order of the Bath, Major-General of our Forces :

WHEREAS, for divers good causes to us appearing, we have deemed it right that our settlements and factories on the northern coast of the continent of South America, comprising the United Colony of Demerara and Essequebo and the Colony of Berbice, should henceforth be united together, and should constitute one Colony in the manner hereinafter provided : Now know that we, reposing especial trust and confidence in the prudence, courage, and loyalty of you, the said Sir Benjamin D'Urban, of our special grace, certain knowledge, and mere motion, have thought fit to constitute and appoint, and by these presents do constitute and appoint, you, the said Sir Benjamin D'Urban, to be during our will and pleasure, our Governor and Commander-in-Chief in and over all our settlements on the northern coast of the Continent of South America, comprising all such territories and jurisdictions as have hitherto been comprised in the said United Colony of Demerara and Essequebo and the said Colony of Berbice respectively, with their respective Dependencies, and all forts and garrisons erected and established, or which shall be erected and established, within the same, and which such settlements shall henceforth collectively constitute and be one Colony, and shall be called " THE COLONY OF BRITISH GUIANA " :

And we do hereby require and command you, our said Governor, to do and execute all things in due manner as shall belong to your said command, and the trust we have reposed in you, according to the several powers and directions granted to or appointed for you by this present Commission and the instructions herewith given to you, or according to such further powers, instructions, and authorities as shall at any future time be granted to or appointed for you under

our Signet and Sign Manual, or by our Order in our Privy Council
or by us through one of Our Principal Secretaries of State :

And we do further grant, direct and appoint that the form of civil
government heretofore by law established in the said United Colony
of Demerara and Essequebo shall be and the same is hereby established in and throughout the said Colony of British Guiana, and that
all such bodies politic and corporate as have heretofore lawfully
existed in the said United Colony of Demerara and Essequebo shall
in like manner exist in and throughout the said Colony of British
Guiana, and shall in and throughout the said Colony have, exercise,
and enjoy all such powers and authorities as have heretofore been
lawfully had, exercised, and enjoyed by them respectively in the
United Colony of Demerara and Essequebo : Provided, nevertheless,
and we do hereby declare our will to be, that the number of the
members of certain of the said bodies politic and corporate heretofore existing in the said United Colony of Demerara and Essequebo
shall in the said Colony of British Guiana be augmented and enlarged in such manner as by your said instructions is directed in
that behalf : Provided, also, and we do further declare our pleasure
to be that nothing herein contained shall extend, revoke, or abrogate
any law, or lawful usage or custom, now in force in the said United
Colony of Demerara and Essequebo or in the said Colony of Berbice
respectively, save only in so far as relates to the separate constitution
and form of civil government heretofore established and in use in
the said Colony of Berbice, which said constitution or form of civil
government we do hereby abrogate and dissolve, and do declare
that the same hath become and shall henceforth be extinct, and
merged in the government of the Colony of British Guiana : Provided,
also, and we do further declare our will and pleasure to be, that
nothing herein contained extends, or shall be construed to extend,
in any wise to alter or interfere with the provisions of a certain Act
of Parliament passed in the fifth year of the reign of our late royal
brother and predecessor King George the Fourth, intituled "An
Act to Consolidate and amend the Laws for the Abolition of the
Slave Trade," or to render legal any transfer or removal of any slave
which would have been illegal if these Presents had not been made,
it being our pleasure that, for the purposes and within the meaning
of the said Act of Parliament, the said United Colony of Demerara
and Essequebo and the said Colony of Berbice shall still continue
and be distinct and separate Colonies : And we do hereby give and
grant to you, the said Sir Benjamin D'Urban, full power and authority, with the advice and consent of the Court of Policy of our said
Colony of British Guiana, to make, enact, ordain, and establish laws
for the order, peace, and good government of our said Colony,
subject, nevertheless, to all such rules and regulations as by your
said general iustructions we have thought fit to prescribe in that
behalf : Provided, nevertheless, and we do hereby reserve to ourselves, our heirs and successors, our and their undoubted right and
authority to disallow any such laws, and to make and establish from

time to time, with the advice and consent of Parliament, or with the advice of our or their Privy Council, all such laws as may to us or them appear necessary for the order, peace, and good government of the said Colony as fully as if these presents had not been made : And we do hereby grant to you, the said Sir Benjamin D'Urban, the custody of the Public Seal appointed for the sealing of all things whatsoever that shall pass the Seal of our said Colony : And we do hereby give and grant unto you, the said Sir Benjamin D'Urban, full power and authority, in our name and in our behalf, but subject nevertheless to such provisions as are in that respect contained in your said general instructions, to make and execute, in our name and under the Public Seal of our said Colony, grants of our waste land to us belonging within the said Colony, to private persons for their own use and benefit, or to any persons, bodies politic or corporate in trust, for the public uses of our subjects, there resident, or any of them ; And we do hereby give and grant unto you full power and authority, as you shall see occasion, in our name and in our behalf, to remit any fines, penalties, or forfeitures which may accrue or become payable to us, so as the same do not exceed the sum of £50 sterling in any one case, and to respite and suspend the payment of any such fine, penalty, or forfeiture exceeding the said sum of £50, until our pleasure therein shall be known and signified to you : And we do hereby give and grant unto you full power and authority, as you shall see occasion, in our name and in our behalf, to grant to any offender convicted of any crime in any Court, or before any Judge, Justice, or Magistrate, within our said Colony, a free and unconditional pardon, or a pardon subject to such conditions as by any law in force in the said Colony may be thereunto annexed, or any respite of the execution of the sentence of any such offender, for such period as to you may seem fit : Provided always that, in cases of treason or murder no pardon, either absolute or conditional, be granted until the cases shall have been first reported to us by you for our information, and you shall have received the signification of our pleasure therein: And we do hereby give and grant unto you, the said Sir Benjamin D'Urban, as such Governor as aforesaid, full power and authority, upon sufficient cause to you appearing, to suspend from the exercise of his office within our said Colony any person exercising any such office under or by virtue of any commission or warrant granted or to be granted by us, or in our name and under our authority, which suspension shall continue and have effect only until our pleasure therein shall be signified to you : And we do hereby strictly require and enjoin you, in proceeding to any such suspension, to observe the directions in that behalf given to you in and by our said general instructions accompanying this our Commission : And in case of your death or absence from the said Colony, our will and pleasure is, that this our Commission and the several powers hereby vested in you, shall be exercised by such person as may by us be appointed to be our Lieutenant-Governor of our said Colony, or by such person as may be appointed by us, under

our Signet or Sign Manual, to administer the said government;
but if, at the time of such your death or absence, there shall be no
person within our said Colony commissioned to be such Lieutenant-
Governor or Administrator of the Government as aforesaid, then
our pleasure is, and we do hereby direct, that the senior officer for
the time being in the command of our land forces within our said
Colony shall take upon himself the administration of the government
thereof and shall execute this our Commission, and the several
powers herein and in the aforesaid instructions contained; and if
any such officer shall, during his administration of the government,
be superseded in the command of our said forces by any senior officer,
then our pleasure is that such senior officer shall assume the administration of the said government and the execution of this our
Commission and of the several powers aforesaid, and so from time
to time as often as any such case shall arise : And we do hereby
require and command all officers, civil and military, and all other our
subjects and persons inhabiting our said Colony of British Guiana,
to be obedient, aiding and assisting unto you, or to the officer administering the said government for the time being, in the execution
of this our Commission, and of the powers and authorities herein
contained : And we do further declare our pleasure to be that the
changes established in the constitution and form of civil government
in the said Colonies of Demerara and Essequebo and of Berbice
respectively, by this our Commission shall not take effect until this
our Commission shall actually have been by you received in our said
Colonies, or one of them : And we do hereby declare, ordain, and
appoint that you, the said Sir Benjamin D'Urban, shall and may hold,
execute and enjoy the office and place of our Governor and Commander-in-Chief in and over the Colony of British Guiana, together
with all and singular the powers and authorities hereby given unto
you for and during our will and pleasure.   In witness, &c.

Given at our Court at Brighton, the 4th day of March 1831, in the
first year of our reign.

By His Majesty's Command,

GODERICH.

APPENDIX I

(See Part II, chapter i, p. 85.)

WILLIAM R.

INSTRUCTIONS to Our Trusty and Well-beloved SIR BENJAMIN D'URBAN Knight Commander of the Most Honourable Military Order of the Bath Major-General of Our Forces; Our Governor and Commander-in-Chief in and over Our Colony of British Guiana in South America.

Given at Our Court at St. James's this Fifth day of March 1831 in the First Year of Our Reign.

First—With these Our Instructions you will receive Our Commission under Our Great Seal of Our United Kingdom of Great Britain and Ireland constituting you Our Governor and Commander-in-Chief in and over Our Colony of British Guiana. You are therefore with all conveneint speed to assume and enter upon the Administration of the said Government.

Second—And you are with all due solemnity to cause Our said Commission to be read and published in the presence of the President of the Court of Civil and Criminal Justice of Demerara and Esquebo and of the Members of the Court of Policy and you shall then and there yourself take the Oaths appointed to be taken by an Act passed in the first year of the Reign of King George the First intituled " An Act for the further security of His Majesty's Person and Government and the succession of the Crown in the Heirs of the late Princess Sophia being Protestants and for extinguishing the hopes of the pretended Prince of Wales and his open and concealed Abettors " as altered and explained by an Act passed in the sixth Year of His late Majesty King George the Third intituled " An Act for altering the Oath of Abjuration and the Assurance and for amending so much of an Act of the Seventh Year of Her late Majesty Queen Anne intituled An Act for the Improvement of the Union of the two Kingdoms as after the Time therein limited requires the Delivery of certain Lists and Copies therein mentioned to Persons, indicted of High Treason or Misprision of Treason " or in lieu thereof the Oath required to be taken by an Act passed in the Tenth Year of the Reign of His late Majesty King George the Fourth intituled " An Act for the relief of His Majesty's Roman Catholic Subjects " according as the said former Acts or the said last mentioned Acts shall be applicable

441

to your case And likewise that you take the usual Oath for the due
execution of the Office of Our Governor and Commander-in-Chief in
and over Our said Colony and for the due and impartial administration of Justice and further that you do take the Oath required to be
taken by the Governors of plantations to do their utmost that the
several Laws relating to Trade and the Plantations be duly observed
which said Oaths the President of the said Court of Civil and Criminal
Justice shall and he is hereby required to tender and administer unto
you all which being duly performed you shall administer to the said
President and to each of the Persons who at that time shall be
members of Our Court of Policy such of the Oaths mentioned in the
said several Acts as shall be applicable to the case of the individual
Member of Our said Court of Policy taking the same and you are
also to administer unto them the usual Oath for the due execution of
their places and trusts respectively all which Oaths shall also be
administered by the Governor or person administering the Government of Our said Colony for the time being to all such Persons as
shall hereafter be appointed to be Members of Our said Court of
Policy before they respectively enter upon the execution of the duties
of such their Office.

   Third—And We do further require you the said Sir Benjamin
D'Urban from time to time and at any time hereafter by yourself
or by any other to be authorized by you in that behalf to administer
and give to all and every such person or persons as you shall think
fit who shall hold any Office or Place of Trust or Profit or who shall
at any time or times pass into Our said Colony or be resident or
abiding there, such of the said Oaths in the said several Acts contained as shall be applicable to the case of the individual to whom
the same shall be administered.

   Fourth—And whereas We have in and by Our said Commission
declared Our Will to be that the number of the Members of certain
of the Bodies Politic or Corporate heretofore existing in the said
United Colony of Demerara and Esquebo shall in the said Colony of
British Guiana be augmented and enlarged in such manner as by
your Instructions is in that behalf directed Now We do hereby
declare Our Pleasure to be and do direct that the Court of Policy
heretofore existing in the United Colony of Demerara and Esquebo
shall be augmented and increased by the addition of two Members,
that is to say of the Protector of Slaves for the time being and of one
unofficial Member to be chosen in such and the same manner as the
said unofficial Members of the said Court have heretofore been
chosen.

   Fifth—And Whereas We have by Our said Commission declared
that nothing therein contained shall extend to sanction or to render
valid any change which may at any time heretofore have without
lawful authority been made and introduced in the Constitution and
former Government of the said United Colony of Demerara and
Esquebo And whereas on the seventh day of September 1812 Sir
James Carmichael then Administering the Government of the said

united Colony of Demerara and Esquebo did by a Proclamation by him for that purpose issued declare the college of Keysers of the said United Colony to be no longer a distinct and separate Institution and did direct in substance that the said College of Keysers and the College of Financial Representatives should henceforth be combined into and constitute one single College and that the Elections thereof should be by other persons than those who had theretofore Elected the said Two Colleges : And whereas the said Sir James Carmichael was not authorized by the Commission under which he administered the Government of the said United Settlements or by any Instructions issued to him in pursuance of that Commission so to alter the Constitution and system of Government of the said Settlements or to promulgate any such Proclamation as aforesaid and the same was not transmitted by him to be laid before His late Majesty King George the Third for confirmation and hath not in fact been confirmed or allowed by his said late Majesty or by His late Majesty King George the Fourth or by Us : Now We do hereby annul rescind and disallow the said Proclamation and do declare Our Pleasure to be that the College of Keysers and the College of Financial Representatives of the said United Colony shall henceforth be two distinct and separate Bodies and shall have such Powers and Duties as such Colleges respectively had, and shall be elected by such persons and in such manner as such Colleges were respectively eligible by Law, before the said Proclamation was so issued save only that the right of Voting upon the Election of the Members of the said Colleges shall henceforth be extended to and enjoyed by Our Subjects in every part of our said Colony of British Guiana.

Sixth—And Whereas We have by Our said Commission given and granted to you the said Sir Benjamin D'Urban full power and Authority with the advice and consent of the said Court of Policy of our said Colony of British Guiana to make enact ordain and establish laws for the order peace and good government of Our said Colony subject nevertheless to all such rules and regulations as by your said general Instructions we have prescribed in that behalf Now We do hereby direct that no Law or Ordinance shall be enacted for any purpose which shall not have been by you first proposed so to be enacted by the said Court of Policy.

Seventh—And it is Our further Pleasure that you do not propose nor assent to any Ordinance whatever respecting the Constitution proceedings numbers or mode of appointing or electing any of the Members of the said Court of Policy or of any other Body Politic or Corporate within Our said Colony or otherwise in relation to any of the matters mentioned or referred to in your said Commission and in these Our Instructions which shall be in any wise repugnant to or inconsistent with such Commission or Instructions or repugnant to any Act of Parliament or to any Order made or to be made by Us in Our Privy Council extending to or in force within our said Colony but that any such Ordinances or pretended Ordinances shall be absolutely null and void to all intents and purposes.

Eighth—And you are expressly enjoined not to propose or assent to any Ordinance whatever whereby any person may be impeded or hindered from celebrating or attending the Worship of Almighty God in a peaceable and orderly manner although such Worship may not be conducted according to the rites and ceremonies of the Church of England.

Ninth—And We do further enjoin you not to propose or assent to any Ordinance whatever whereby Our Revenue might be lessened or impaired or whereby Our Prerogative might be diminished or in any respect infringed or whereby any increase or diminution might be made in the number, Salary, or Allowances of any Public Officers which have or shall have received Our sanction without our especial leave or Command therein first received.

Tenth—And we do further direct that you do not propose or assent to any Ordinance whatever whereby Bills of Credit or other negotiable securities of whatever nature may be issued in lieu of Money on the credit of the said Colony or whereby any Government Paper Currency may be established therein or whereby any such Bills or any other Paper Currency or any Coin save only the legal coin of the Realm may be made or declared to be a legal tender without special permission from Us in that behalf first obtained.

Eleventh—And we do further enjoin and command you not to propose or assent to any Ordinance whatever by which Persons of African or Indian birth or descent might be subjected or made liable to any disabilities or restrictions to which persons of European birth or descent would not be also subjected and made liable.

Twelfth—And it is Our further Pleasure that you do not propose or assent to any Ordinance whatever for raising Money by the Institution of any Public or Private Lotteries.

Thirteenth—And it is Our Will and Pleasure that you do not propose or assent to any Ordinance whatever for the Naturalization of Aliens or for the divorce of persons joined together in Holy Matrimony or for establishing a Title in any person to Lands or other immovable property acquired by any Alien before his or her Naturalization.

Fourteenth—And we do further direct that you do not propose or assent to any Ordinance whatever by which any tax or duty might be imposed upon the Trade or Shipping of this United Kingdom or whereby any tax might be imposed upon transient Traders or upon persons residing and carrying on Business for a short time within Our said Colony from which other Traders or persons carrying on the like business would be exempt.

Fifteenth—And we do further direct that you do not propose or assent to any Ordinance whatever whereby any Grant of money or land or other donation or gratuity may be made by the said Court of Policy to you or to any Member of the said Court.

Sixteenth—And we do further direct that you do not propose or assent to any private Ordinance whatever whereby the property of any individual may be affected in which there is not a saving of the rights of Us Our Heirs and Successors and of all Bodies Politic and Corporate and of all other persons excepting those at whose instance or for whose especial benefit such Ordinance may be passed and those claiming by, from, through and under them.

Seventeenth—And it is Our Will and Pleasure that you do not propose or assent to any Ordinance whatever to which Our assent hath once been refused without express leave for that purpose first obtained from Us.

Eighteenth—And for the sake of orderly dispatch and the prevention of all undue precipitation in the enactment of Ordinances by the said Court We do hereby authorize and require you from time to time as occasion may require to frame and propose to the said Court of Policy for their adoption such standing Orders Rules and Forms of proceeding as may be best adapted for the purposes aforesaid and for insuring previously to the passing of any Ordinance intended to affect or benefit private persons that due notice be given to all parties concerned of the provisions thereof with ample opportunity for opposing the same and that a full and impartial examination may take place of the grounds upon which the same may be proposed or resisted and such Rules Orders and Forms from time to time with consent of the said Court of Policy to revoke alter or renew as there may be occasion and We do direct that the same when adopted by them shall be duly observed in all their proceedings.

Nineteenth—And it is Our further Will and Pleasure that all Laws to be Enacted by the said Court of Policy shall henceforth be styled Ordinances enacted by the Governor of British Guiana with the advice and consent of the Court of Policy thereof and that no other style or form shall ever henceforth be observed in any such enactments and that all such Ordinances be drawn in a simple and compendious form avoiding prolixity and tautology.

Twentieth—And we do further direct that when any Ordinance shall have been passed by you with the advice of the said Court of Policy the same shall forthwith be laid before Us for our final assent, disallowance or other direction thereupon to be signified through you for which purpose We do hereby require you with all convenient speed to transmit to Us through one of Our Principal Secretaries of State a transcript in Duplicate of every such Ordinance as aforesaid duly authenticated under the Public Seal of the said Colony and by your own Signature. And we do direct that every such transcript be so transmitted by the earliest occasion next after the enactment of the said Ordinance and that no such Ordinance be made to take effect until Our Pleasure thereupon be first made known and signified to you and by you to the said Colony unless in the case of Ordinances for raising the annual supplies for the service of such Colony and in any other cases in which it may appear to you that the delay incident to a previous communication with Us would be productive of serious injury or inconvenience in which case as often as any such case shall occur We hereby authorize you to determine by your Proclamation to be for that purpose issued the time at which the same shall take effect and have its operation within the said Colony which proceeding with the reasons thereof you shall on the earliest occasion report to Us through one of Our Principal Secretaries of State And We do hereby reserve to Us, Our Heirs and Successors full Power and Authority to confirm and finally enact or to disallow any such Ordinance as aforesaid either in whole or in part such confirmation or disallowance being from time to time signified to you through one of Our Principal Secretaries of State And we do further reserve to Ourselves, Our Heirs and Successors with the advice of Our and Their Privy Council, full power and authority to amend any such Ordinance as aforesaid in such manner as may be necessary or expedient and if on any occasion Our Pleasure should not be signified to you upon any such Ordinance as aforesaid within two years next after the date thereof, then and in every such case it is our pleasure that from and after the expiration of such term of two years such Ordinance shall be deemed to be disallowed and shall thenceforth cease to have any force or effect within Our said Colony.

Twenty-first—And We do require and enjoin you to transmit to the President of the Supreme Court or Courts of Civil and Criminal Justice of the said Colony to be enrolled in the said Court of Justice a transcript duly authenticated in the manner before mentioned of every Ordinance to be passed by you with the advice and consent of the said Court of Policy together with a Certificate under your Hand and Seal of the effect of every Order which you may receive from Us for confirming or disallowing in the whole or in part or for amending the provisions of any such Ordinance which Certificates shall in like manner be enrolled in the said Court of Justice and there remain on record to the intent that the Judges of the said Courts may without further or other proof take cognizance of all Ordinances to be made and promulgated for the peace, good order, and government of the said Colony.

Twenty-second—And we do further declare Our Pleasure to be that in the month of January or at the earliest practicable period in the commencement of each year you do cause a complete collection to be published for general information of all Ordinances enrolled during the preceding year. And We do particularly require and direct that Transcripts of all Minutes and Proceedings of the Court of Policy be regularly transmitted every Six Months without fail for Our information through one of Our Principal Secretaries of State.

Twenty-third—And We do further direct that all Ordinances to be made by you with the advice of the said Court of Policy be distinguished by Titles and that the Ordinances of each year be also distinguished by numerical marks commencing in each successive year with number One and proceeding in arithmetical progression to the number corresponding with the total number of Ordinances enacted during the year and that every such Ordinance be divided into successive Clauses or paragraphs distinguished in like manner by numerical marks and that to every such clause be annexed in the Margin a short summary of its contents and you are to observe that subjects which have no proper relation to each other be not comprised in one and the same Ordinance and that no enactments be introduced into any such Ordinance which may be foreign to its professed scope and object, and that no perpetual clause be part of any temporary Ordinance, and that no Ordinance or Law be suspended, altered, continued, revised or repealed by general words but that the title and date of every such Law or Ordinance be particularly mentioned and expressed in the Ordinance suspending, altering, continuing, revising or repealing the same.

Twenty-fourth—And whereas We have by Our said Commission given to you full power and Authority in Our name and on Our behalf but subject nevertheless to such provisions as are in that respect contained in these your general Instructions to make and execute in Our name and under the Public Seal of Our said Colony Grants of Waste Lands to Us belonging within the same to private Persons or for the public uses of Our Subjects there resident : Now we do hereby require and authorize you from time to time as occasion may require to cause all necessary surveys to be made of the vacant or Waste Lands to us belonging in Our said Colony and to cause the Persons making such survey to report to you what particular Lands it may be proper to reserve for Public Roads or other internal communications by Land or Water, or as the Sites of Towns Villages Churches Schoolhouses or Parsonage Houses, or as places for the Burial of the Dead or as places for the future extension of any existing Towns or Villages or as Places fit to be set apart for the recreation and amusement of the Inhabitants of any Town or Village or for promoting the health of such Inhabitants, or as the sites of Quays or Landing Places or Towing Paths which it may at any future time be expedient to erect, form or establish on the Sea Coast or in the Neighbourhood of Navigable Streams or as Places which it may be desirable to reserve for any other purpose of Public convenience, utility, health or enjoyment and you are specially to require persons making such survey to specify in their Reports and to distinguish in the Charts or Maps to be thereunto annexed such Tracts Pieces or Parcels of Land within Our said Colony as may appear to them best adapted to answer and promote the several purposes before mentioned And it is Our will and We do strictly enjoin and require you that you do not on any pretence whatsoever grant, convey, or demise to any Person or Persons any of the Lands which may be so specified as fit to be reserved as aforesaid nor permit or suffer any such lands to be occupied by any private Person for any private purposes.

Twenty-fifth—And we do further charge and require you not to make any Grant of Land to, or in trust for, or for the use of any private Persons, by any one Instrument or by successive Instruments exceeding 100 Acres in the whole without Our special permission for that purpose first obtained.

Twenty-sixth—And we do require and direct that in every Grant of Waste Land hereafter to be made by you in Our name and on Our behalf within the said Colony there be introduced a Provision or Condition to the effect that such lands or any part thereof shall not be cultivated by the labour of Slaves but shall be cultivated by the labour of Persons of Free Condition only, with a Proviso for the forfeiture of any such Lands and their immediate resumption by Us if any Slave or Slaves be employed in the cultivation of the same or of any part thereof whether by the Grantee or by His Heirs or Assigns.

Twenty-seventh—And We do further require that upon all Lands so to be granted there be reserved and made payable to Us Our Heirs and Successors such moderate and reasonable Quit Rents as can from time to time be obtained for the same unless in any case We should think proper by any Instructions to be by Us for that purpose issued through one of Our Principal Secretaries of State otherwise to direct.

Twenty-eighth—And Whereas in and by Your said Commission we have granted unto you power and authority in Our Name and on Our behalf to grant to any Person convicted of any Crime in any of the Tribunals in Our said Colony an absolute or conditional Pardon : Now we do enjoin and require you in every case where you shall be applied to for any such pardon and in every case whatever in which sentence of Death shall have been passed, to obtain from the Judge who presided at the trial of any such Offender a report in Writing of the proceedings upon any such Trial and of the Evidence then adduced and of the opinion of such Judge whether the conviction of any such Offender was obtained in due course of Law and whether any reason exists for the total or partial remission or commutation of any such sentence. And We do strictly command that you do not upon any occasion permit any punishment to be inflicted which can in no case be inflicted by the Law of England and that you do not remit any Fine or Forfeiture above the value of Fifty Pounds sterling without previously signifying to Us the nature of the Offence committed and the amount of the proposed remission and receiving Our directions thereupon but in the meanwhile it shall be lawful for you to suspend the payment of such Fine or Forfeiture.

Twenty-ninth—It being Our intention that all Persons inhabiting Our Colony under your Government should have full liberty of conscience and the free exercise of all such modes of Religious Worship as are not prohibited by Law We do hereby require you to permit all Persons within Our said Colony to have such liberty and to exercise such modes of Religious Worship as are not prohibited by Law Provided they be contented with a quiet and peaceable enjoyment of the same not giving offence or scandal to the Government.

Thirtieth—And whereas by Letters Patent under the Great Seal of Our United Kingdom of Great Britain and Ireland bearing date at Westminster the 11th day of May 1826 the Colonies and Settlements of Demerara Essequibo and Berbice were constituted and appointed to be respectively parts of the See of the Bishop of Barbados and the Leeward Islands and the said Bishop was thereby duly authorized to exercise Jurisdiction Spiritual and Ecclesiastical in the said Colonies, it is Our Will and Pleasure that in the Administration of the Government of Our Colony of British Guiana you should be aiding and assisting to the said Bishop and to his Commissary or Commissaries in the execution of their charge and the exercise of such Ecclesiastical Jurisdiction excepting only the granting licences for Marriages and Probates of Wills

Thirty-first—You shall be careful that all Orthodox Churches already built may be well and orderly kept and that in all cases where others shall be built, besides a competent maintenance to the Minister, a convenient House and a sufficient portion of Land for a Glebe be allotted to him.   And you are to take care that the Parishes be so limited and settled as you shall find most convenient for the accomplishing this good work.   And in all matters relating to the Celebration of Divine Worship, the Erection and Repair of Churches, the maintenance of Ministers, and the settlement of Parishes throughout your Government you are to advise with the Right Reverend Father in God the Bishop of Barbados and the Leeward Islands.

Thirty-second—Upon the vacancy of any Ecclesiastical Benefice in Our said Colony you will present to the said Bishop for the time being, for Institution to such vacant Benefice any Clerk in Holy Orders of the United Church of England and Ireland who shall have been actually resident within the said Diocese and officiating there as a Clerk in Holy Orders for Six Calendar Months at the least, next before such Benefice shall have become vacant, whom the said Bishop may certify to you to be a fit and proper person to fill such Vacancy, and to be a person of good life and conversation and conformable to the doctrine and discipline of the said United Church   But if at the time of any such Vacancy occurring there shall not be resident within the said Diocese any Clerk in Holy Orders of the said United Church who shall have been resident and officiating therein as aforesaid in whose favour the said Bishop shall think proper so to certify to you or if no such Certificate shall be received by you from the said Bishop within Three calendar months next after such Vacancy shall occur, then, and in either of such cases you shall forthwith report the circumstance to Us, through one of Our Principal Secretaries of State, to the intent that we may nominate some fit and proper person being a Clerk in Holy Orders as aforesaid to fill the said Vacancy.   And We do enjoin and command you to present to the said Bishop for Institution to any such vacant Ecclesiastical Benefice any Clerk who may be so nominated by Us through one of Our Principal Secretaries of State.

Thirty-third—You are to take especial care that a Table of Marriages established by the Canons of the Church of England be hung up in every Orthodox Church and duly observed.

Thirty-fourth—The Right Reverend Father in God Edmund then Lord Bishop of London having presented a Petition to His Majesty King George the First humbly beseeching him to send Instructions to the Governors of all the several Colonies and Plantations in America

G G

that they cause all Laws already made against Blasphemy, Profaneness, Adultery, Fornication, Polygamy, Incest, Profanation of the Lord's day, Swearing and Drunkenness in their respective Governments to be rigorously executed   And We thinking it highly just that all persons who shall offend in any of the particulars aforesaid should be prosecuted and punished for their said Offences   It is therefore Our Will and Pleasure that you take due care for the punishment of the aforementioned vices and that you earnestly recommend that effectual Laws be passed for the restraint and punishment of all such of the aforesaid vices against which no Laws are as yet provided and for the further discouragement of Vice and encouragement of Virtue and good living you are not to admit any person to public trusts or employments in the Colony under your Government whose ill fame and conversation may occasion scandal.

Thirty-fifth—It is Our further Will and Pleasure that you recommend proper measures for erecting and maintaining Schools in order to the training up of youth to reading and to a necessary knowledge of the Principles of Religion.   You are also to adopt the best means to facilitate and encourage the Instruction of Negroes and other Slaves in the Christian Religion.   You are not however to propose or assent to any Ordinance respecting Religion without a Clause suspending its operation until Our Pleasure shall have been signified thereupon unless a Draft thereof shall have been previously transmitted by you for Our consideration and approval.

Thirty-sixth—And we do further direct that in all matters arising within your Government connected with the Education of Youth in the Christian Religion according to the Doctrine of the said United Church of England and Ireland or connected with the prevention of Vice and Profaneness or the conversion of Negroes and other Slaves ; or connected with the Worship of Almighty God or the promotion of Religion and Virtue you be advising with the Bishop for the time being of the said Diocese of Barbados and the Leeward Islands and be aiding him in the execution of all such designs and undertakings as may be recommended by the said Bishop for the promotion of any of the objects before mentioned so far as such designs and undertakings may be consistent with the Law and with your Commission, and these Our Instructions.

Thirty-seventh—And Whereas We have by Our said Commission authorized you upon sufficient cause to you appearing to suspend from the exercise of his Office within Our said Colony any Person exercising the same under and by virtue of any Commission or Warrant granted or to be granted by Us in Our Name or under Our Authority and we have by the said Commission strictly required and enjoined you in proceeding to any such suspension to observe the directions in that behalf given to you in and by these your general Instructions :   Now we do charge and require you that before proceeding to any such suspension you do signify by a statement in writing to the Person so to be suspended the grounds of such your intended proceeding against him and that you do call upon such

Person to communicate to you in writing a statement of the grounds upon which and the Evidence by which he may be desirous to exculpate himself and that you transmit both of the said statements to Us, through one of Our Principal Secretaries of State by the earliest conveyance.

Thirty-eighth—And we do hereby direct and instruct you that all Commissions and Appointments to be granted by You to any Person or Persons for exercising any Office or Employment in, or concerning the said Colony be granted during pleasure only and that whenever you shall appoint to any vacant Office or Employment any Persons not by us especially directed to be appointed thereto you shall at the same time expressly apprize such Person that such appointment is to be considered only as temporary and provisional until Our allowance or disallowance thereof be signified.

Thirty-ninth—And Whereas great prejudice may happen to Our Service and to the Security of the said Colony by the absence of the Governor you shall not upon any pretence whatever come to Europe without having first obtained leave from Us for so doing under Our Sign Manual and Signet or through one of Our Principal Secretaries of State.

Renewed Commission on the Demise of the Crown the same as the preceding Commission, and dated the 10th March 1832.

APPENDIX J

(See Part II, chapter xiv.)

(i) RULES AND REGULATIONS

FOR THE

COMBINED COURT OF BRITISH GUIANA,

Framed and agreed to at their Annual Adjourned Assembly, on the 27th April, 1838.

No. 1. The Court being assembled, the Secretary shall read over the Estimate, item by item.

2. Each item shall be considered an original motion; and any Member desirous of increasing or decreasing an item, or of having it struck off the Estimate, shall be bound to move an Amendment to that effect.

3. Should the Amendments not be seconded, they will, of course, fall to the ground; otherwise being seconded, they shall be put to the vote, and if lost, the original motion shall then be put.

4. Any Member moving an Amendment, shall be at liberty to state his reasons for so doing; after which, each Member of the Court shall be at liberty to state his reasons in support of, or of opposition to, the Amendment.

5. After each Member shall have spoken, the mover of the Amendment shall be at liberty to reply, upon which the votes shall be taken, and the result entered on the Minutes accordingly.

6. No Member, the mover excepted, who shall have a right of reply, shall be allowed to speak on any motion or Amendment oftener than once, except by way of explanation.

7. Any Member desirous of having the doors closed, shall be allowed to demand the same being done, subject, nevertheless, to their being thrown open by the Court, should it think proper, after hearing the reasons of the Member wishing the exclusion of the public.

8. Any Member wishing to move an original motion shall give notice of the same in writing to the Court, and, having obtained leave, the same shall be entered in the Minutes, and shall not become a subject of discussion until twenty-four hours have elapsed after said entry.

9. If, in the course of a debate, or any other deliberation in this Court, a Member should be desirous to have his speech or observations inserted *verbatim* in the Minutes of the Court, he is to hand them, fairly written, to the Secretary, who is to embody the copy thereof in the Minutes of the Court; or, in case it should not be convenient

452

to do so immediately, the Member is then to give notice that he intends doing it on the next day of the Court's meeting, on which day (and not later), the same being in substance what he has stated the day before, he is to hand it in writing to the Secretary, who, after having obtained leave thereto, will read it to the Court, and in case no objection is made to any part thereof, the whole is to be copied and embodied in the Minutes of the Court, unless the document should be of some considerable length, when the original, signed by the Member himself, with the *Exhibitum* thereon under the Secretary's Signature, is to be annexed to the Minutes of that day. It being enjoined on the Secretary, as far as belongs to him, strictly to observe this Rule and to take care that no Documents of any kind be entered into the Minutes otherwise than by his own agency.

President—His Excellency Colonel Bunbury, K.H., &c., &c.

His Honour Jeffrey Hart Bent, Chief Justice.
The Honourable Henry Gloster, Attorney Gen'l.
„   Charles Stewart, Act'g Coll.
                                                    Customs.
„   Peter Rose.
„   George Warren,
„   Thomas Dougan,
„   Alexander Macrae,
„   Michael M'Turk,

Edward Bishop, Esq.   ⎫
Wm. Davison, Esq.   ⎪
James Matthews, Esq. ⎬   Financial
George Laing, Esq.   ⎪   Representatives.
Wm. Fraser, Esq.   ⎪
John Beete, Esq.   ⎭

W. B. WOLSELEY,
Acting Secretary.

(ii) STANDING RULES AND ORDERS OF THE COMBINED COURT MADE BY GOVERNOR LIGHT AND APPROVED BY THE SECRETARY OF STATE FOR THE COLONIES IN A DESPATCH DATED 8TH JUNE, 1842.

No. 1. The Court being assembled, the Secretary shall read over the Estimate Item by Item.

2. No member (His Excellency the Governor excepted) shall be permitted to move the increase of an Item upon the Estimate.

3. Each item shall be considered an Original Motion; and any Member desirous of decreasing an Item, or of having it struck off the Estimate, shall be bound to move an Amendment to that effect.

4. Should the Amendments not be seconded, they will, of course, fall to the ground; otherwise being seconded, they shall be put to the vote, and if lost, the Original Motion shall then be put.

5. Any Member moving an Amendment, shall be at liberty to state his reasons for so doing; after which each Member of the Court shall be at liberty to state his reasons in support of or in opposition to the Amendment.

6. After each Member shall have spoken, the Mover of the Amendment shall be at liberty to reply, upon which the votes shall be taken, and the result entered on the Minutes accordingly.

7. No Member (the Mover excepted) shall be allowed to speak on any Motion or Amendment oftener than once, except by way of explanation.

8. Any Member desirous of having the doors closed, shall be allowed to demand the same being done, subject, nevertheless, to their being thrown open by the Court, should it think proper, after hearing the reasons of the Member wishing the exclusion of the Public.

9. Any Member wishing to move an original motion, shall give notice of the same in writing to the Court, and having obtained leave, the same shall be entered in the Minutes, and shall not become a subject of discussion until twenty-four hours have elapsed after said entry.

10. If, in the course of a debate, or any other deliberation in this Court, a Member shall be desirous to have his speech or observations inserted *verbatim* in the Minutes of the Court, he is to hand them, fairly written, to the Secretary, who is to embody the copy thereof in the Minutes of the Court; or in case it should not be convenient to do so immediately, the Member is then to give notice, that he intends doing it on the next day of the Court's meeting, on which day (and not later), the same being in substance what he has stated the day before, he is to hand it in writing to the Secretary, who, after having obtained leave thereto, will read it to the Court, and in case no objection is made to any part thereof, the whole is to be copied and embodied in the Minutes of the Court, unless the document should be of some considerable length, when the original, signed by the Member himself, with the *Exhibitum* thereon under the Secretary's Signature, is to be annexed to the Minutes of that day. It being enjoined on the Secretary, as far as belongs to him, strictly to observe this Rule, and to take care that no Documents of any kind be entered on the Minutes otherwise than by his own agency.

(iii) STANDING RULES AND ORDERS OF THE COMBINED COURT MADE BY GOVERNOR THE RIGHT HONOURABLE VISCOUNT GORMANSTON, 9TH FEBRUARY, 1892.

Order of Business.

1. The following shall be the order in which the business of the Court shall be conducted :

   (1) The Governor's address to the Court; Reports, Petitions and other Documents intended for the consideration of

the Court during the Session to be laid on the table; Government Notices of motions; Unofficial Notices of Questions and of Motions;

(2) The Order of the Day, as follows :

A. At an Ordinary Session—

(*a*) The consideration of the Annual Estimate;
(*b*) The consideration of the Tax and Customs Ordinances in Committee of Ways and Means;
(*c*) The consideration of the Report of the Committee of Ways and Means;
(*d*) The enactment of the Tax and Customs Ordinances.

B. At a Special Session—

The business for which such Session is held.

2. At an adjourned meeting of the Court the first business shall be the reading and confirmation of the Minutes of the previous meeting.

Estimate, Questions on, &c.

3. Any petition or other document laid on the table may be referred to and discussed, and any motion or question, of which notice has been given, may be moved or asked when the item or head of the Estimate, or section of the Tax or Customs Ordinance to which it refers has been reached. Any petition, motion or question which does not refer to any head of the Estimate can only be dealt with after the enactment of the Ordinances mentioned above, unless leave be given by the Governor or President to bring it forward at any other stage of the business.

4. At the consideration of the Annual Estimate the Clerk of the Court shall read over the Estimate item by item.

5. Each item shall be considered an original motion and any member desirous of decreasing any item or striking it off the Estimate may move an amendment to that effect. If the amendment be seconded it shall be put to the vote, and if lost the original item shall stand part of the Estimate.

6. The mover of an amendment to decrease or strike off an item on the estimate shall have the right of reply, after each member who desires to speak shall have spoken, but the mover of an amendment to such an amendment or to any other motion before the Court shall not have any right of reply.

7. After the mover of the motion or amendment shall have spoken in reply, the Governor or President may address the Court by way of summing up in putting the question.

8. Whenever the Court divides and the names are taken down by the Clerk, they shall be entered on the minutes of the Court.

9. When a question concerning any business before the Court or any matter which the Court is competent to deal with has been

asked of any member of the Court, the reply shall be conclusive, and no speech or debate on the reply shall be allowed.

10. Any member wishing to move an original motion or to ask a question, other than a question relating to an item on the Estimate which is being considered at the time, or to a Resolution before the Court, shall give notice of the same in writing, and the same shall be entered upon the minutes and shall not become a subject of discussion until twenty-four hours shall have elapsed after such entry.

Rules of Debate.

11. Every Member shall speak standing and shall address himself to the Governor or President.

12. No Member shall interrupt another when speaking, except by rising to order. A member rising to order shall simply direct attention to the point he desires to bring to notice and submit it to the decision of the President.

13. If two Members rise to speak at the same time, the President shall call upon one of them to address the Court first.

14. No member shall speak twice to a motion except as hereinafter provided :—

> (*a*) The mover of an original motion shall have the right of reply after each member who desires to speak shall have spoken, but the mover of an amendment shall not have any right of reply.
>
> (*b*) After such reply the Governor or President may address the Court by way of summing up in putting the question.

Amendments.

> (*c*) Any Member who may second an original motion in the formal words " I second this motion " and no others, may reserve his speech until later in the debate.
>
> (*d*) When the Court is in Committee of Ways and Means.
>
> (*e*) A member may by permission of the Court be heard to explain himself in regard to some material part of his speech, but shall not introduce any new matter.

15. Every amendment must be relevant to the motion upon which it is moved and be so framed that the motion as amended would form an intelligible and consistent sentence.

16. No amendment can be proposed to that portion of a motion which is prior to a point where an amendment has been carried or has been moved and seconded, unless the previous amendment or proposed amendment be by leave of the Court withdrawn.

17. If an amendment be moved and seconded it shall be considered before the original motion.

18. If an amendment of a proposed amendment be moved and seconded it shall be considered as if such previous amendment were an original motion.

Procedure on Question being put.

19. Any member or number of members being in the minority on a division may require that a written protest, to be handed by them to the Clerk of the Court, be recorded on the minutes, provided that such written protest shall not be handed in at a date later than the next meeting after the meeting at which the division took place.

20. Any member who may alone dissent from any resolution or vote passed by the Court may require that his dissent be recorded on the minutes.

General.

21. Any member desirous of having the doors closed shall be allowed to move that this be done. No debate on such motion shall be held, but the Governor or President shall at once put the question. If it is decided in the affirmative, the doors shall be closed, and the member who made the motion shall then state, in form of a motion, the subject he wishes discussed, after which the question shall be put to the Court without debate whether the subject shall be discussed with closed doors or not. If the motion is carried, discussion shall take place under ordinary rules of debate ; if the motion is lost, the doors shall be opened.

22. No petition from any Public Officer asking for an increase of salary shall be received, unless it is submitted by the direction or with the sanction of the Governor.

23. Subject to the approval of the Governor or President, on motion made and seconded without notice, the Standing Rules and Orders may be suspended at any time by a vote of the majority of the members present.

Made by His Excellency the Governor, this 9th day of February, 1892, under the authority of the Order of Her Majesty in Council, dated at Windsor, the 23rd day of February, 1891.

By Command,

CHARLES BRUCE,
Government Secretary.

(iv) STANDING RULES AND ORDERS OF THE COMBINED COURT IN FORCE PRIOR TO 1928 REFORMS.

MEETINGS.

1. The meetings of the Combined Court shall be held on such days and at such hours as the Governor may appoint.

2. Notice of each meeting, other than a meeting fixed by adjournment, shall be given by the Clerk of the Court to each member, at least one week before the day of meeting; except in case of emergency, when as long notice as possible shall be given.

3. Where notice is given of a Special Session the notice shall state the business for which such meeting is summoned.

ORDER OF BUSINESS.

4. The following shall be the order in which the Business of the Court shall be conducted :—

(1) The Governor's Address to the Court; Reports, Petitions and other Documents intended for the consideration of the Court to be laid on the Table; Government Notices of Motions; Unofficial Notices of Questions and of Motions; Questions not relating to items on the Estimate.

(2)—*A.* At the Annual Session,—

(*a*) The consideration of the Annual Estimate;

(*b*) Motions by Official Members to increase or decrease items in the Estimate;

(*c*) Motions by Elected Members for decreasing or omitting items in the Estimate;

(*d*) Motion that Court go into Committee of Ways and Means;

In Committee of Ways and Means,—

(i) Appointment of Chairman;

(ii) Financial Statement of the Government and debate thereon;

(iii) Consideration of Customs and Tax Bills and preparation of Report;

(iv) Motion that Court do resume;

(*e*) Presentation of Report of Committee of Ways and Means;

(*f*) Passing of Customs and Tax Bills;

(*g*) Motions which do not refer to any head of the Estimate.

B. At a Special Session,—

(*a*) The Business for which such Session is held;

(*b*) Motions by (i.) Official Members;
(ii.) Elected Members.

5.—(1) At an adjourned Meeting of the Court the Minutes of the previous Meeting shall be read, and the question of their confirmation shall be put; but no debate shall be allowed thereon except as to the accuracy of the Minutes. The Minutes of the Meeting, when confirmed, shall be signed by the Governor or President.

(2) At the end of the last meeting of the Session, the Minutes of that meeting shall be read, confirmed and signed before the Session is closed.

Motions and Questions.

6. Any Motion or Question having reference to an item or head of the Estimate, or section of the Customs or Tax Ordinances, may be moved, or asked, when such item, head, or section is reached, provided that notice, as required by rule 9, shall have been given, stating that the Motion or Question will be then moved or asked.

7. Any Motion may be moved or Question asked, at any time, with the leave of the Governor or President, which may be applied for without notice.

8. When a question concerning any business before the Court, or any matter which the Court is competent to deal with, has been asked of any Member of the Court, the reply shall be conclusive, and no speech or debate on the reply shall then be allowed.

9. Except as provided by Rules 7 and 10, no Motion or Question shall be moved, or asked, unless two clear days' notice in writing, stating the terms thereof, shall have been given by delivering the same to the Clerk of the Court. Every such notice shall be headed " Combined Court," and shall be dated and signed, and copies shall be forwarded to members of the Court by the Clerk as soon as printed.

10. The following Motions may be made without notice :—

(a) Any Motion for the confirmation or amendment of the Minutes of the Court ;

(b) Any Motion for the adoption, modification or rejection of the Report of any Committee of the whole Court, or of any Committee appointed to consider the Annual or Supplementary Estimates ;

(c) Any Motion that any petition or paper be printed ;

(d) Any Motion for the suspension of the Standing Orders ;

(e) Any Motion for the reference of any matter to a Committee ;

(f) Any Motion for the closing of the doors ;

(g) Any Motion made when the Court is in Committee.

Petitions.

11. Every Petition intended to be presented to the Court shall be presented by a member of the Court, who shall afix his name at the beginning thereof.

12. Every member offering to present a petition to the Court, shall confine himself to a statement of the parties from whom it comes, of the number of signatures attached to it, and of the material allegations contained in it, and to the reading of the prayer of such petition.

13. There shall be no debate or discussion on Reports, Petitions, or other Documents laid on the table, but they may be referred to and discussed in debate on a motion before the Court.

Estimates.

14. At the consideration of the Annual, or any Supplementary Estimate, the Clerk of the Court shall read over the Estimate item by item.

15. Each item shall be considered an original motion, and any member, desirous of decreasing any item, or striking it off, may move an amendment to that effect.   If the amendment be seconded, it shall be put to the vote, and if lost the original item shall stand part of the Estimate.

Committee of Ways and Means.

16. The Committee shall have power to elect any member to be its Chairman, who shall have a casting vote as well as an original vote on all motions and amendments before the Committee.

17. The Committee shall be at liberty to discuss the Financial Statement of the Government, without motion.

Passing of Customs and Tax Bills.

18. The Governor may direct some official member to introduce the Customs and Tax Bills for the ensuing year : and such member shall thereupon move for leave to bring in the said Bills.

19. Upon such leave being given, the Clerk shall read the marginal notes of the sections and the headings of the schedules of the said Bills, and the reading of each of such notes and headings shall operate as an original motion, and any member shall be at liberty to move any amendment. If the amendment be seconded, it shall be put to the vote, and if lost the section or schedule shall stand part of the Bill.

20. After the marginal notes and headings of the schedules of the Bills have been read, the question " That this Bill do pass " shall immediately be put.

Rules of Debate.

21. Every Member shall speak standing, and shall address himself to the Governor or President.

22. No Member shall interrupt another when speaking, except by rising to order. A member rising to order shall simply direct attention to the point he desires to bring to notice, and submit it to the decision of the Governor or President.

23. If two Members rise to speak at the same time, the Governor or President shall call upon one of them to address the Court first.

24. No Member shall speak twice to a motion, except as hereinafter provided :—

(a) The mover of an original motion shall have the right of reply after every member who desires to speak shall have spoken, but the mover of an amendment shall not have any right of reply.

(b) After such reply the Governor or President may address the Court, by way of summing up, in putting the question.

(c) Any Member who may second an original motion in the formal words " I second this motion," and no others, may reserve his speech until later in the debate.

(d). A member may, by permission of the Court, be heard to explain himself in regard to some material part of his speech, but shall not introduce any new matter.

(e) When the Court is in Committee of Ways and Means.

25. Every amendment must be relevant to the motion upon which it is moved, and be so framed that the motion as amended would form an intelligible and consistent sentence.

26. No amendment can be proposed to that portion of a motion which is prior to a point where an amendment has been carried or has been moved and seconded, unless the previous amendment or proposed amendment be by leave of the Court withdrawn.

27. If an amendment be moved and seconded, it shall be considered before the original motion.

28. If an amendment of a proposed amendment be moved and seconded, it shall be considered as if such previous amendment were an original motion.

29. The Governor or President may require any motion or amendment, of which notice in writing has not been previously given, to be committed to writing by the mover and delivered to the Clerk of the Court.

30. The question having been put by the Governor, or President, he shall declare that the " Ayes " have it, or that the " Noes " have it, and thereupon any member shall be entitled to divide the Court.

31. Whenever the Court divides, the names shall be taken down by the Clerk and entered on the minutes of the Court.

Procedure on Question being put.

32. Any member or number of members being in the minority, on a division, may require that a written protest, to be handed by them to the Clerk of the Court, be recorded on the Minutes, provided that such written protest shall not be handed in at a date later than the next meeting after the meeting at which the division took place.

33. Any member who may alone dissent from any resolution or vote passed by the Court may require that his dissent be recorded on the minutes.

General.

34. Any member desirous of having the doors closed shall be allowed to move that this be done. No debate on such motion shall be held, but the Governor, or President, shall at once put the question.   If it is decided in the affirmative, the doors shall be closed, and the member who made the motion shall then state, in form of a motion, the subject he wishes discussed, and shall move that the discussion shall take place with closed doors : and, if such motion be carried, the substantive motion shall be proceeded with under ordinary rules of debate; if lost, the doors shall be opened.

35. No petition from any Public Officer asking for an increase of salary shall be received, unless it is submitted by the direction, or with the sanction, of the Governor.

36. Subject to the approval of the Governor, or President, on motion made and seconded without notice, the Standing Rules and

Orders may be suspended at any time by a vote of the majority of the members present.

Made by His Excellency the Governor, this 19th day of May, 1903, under the authority of the Order of Her late Majesty in Council, dated at Windsor, the 23rd day of February, 1891.

By Command,

N. DARNELL DAVIS,
Acting Government Secretary.

ADDITIONAL STANDING RULES AND ORDERS OF THE COMBINED COURT.

House of Commons Standing Order 20. **1.** The President may order any member or members whose conduct is grossly disorderly to withdraw immediately from the Court during the remainder of that day's sitting; and the Clerk of the Court shall act on such orders as he may receive from the chair in pursuance of this Standing Order. But if, on any occasion, the President deems that his powers under this Standing Order are inadequate, he may name such member or members or he may call upon the Court to adjudge upon the conduct of such member or members.

2.—(1) Whenever any member shall have been named by the President, or by the Chairman of a Committee of the whole Court, immediately after the commission of the offence of disregarding the authority of the chair, or of abusing the Rules of the Court by persistently and wilfully obstructing the business of the Court, or otherwise, then, if the offence has been committed by such member in the Court, the President shall forthwith put the question, on a motion being made, no amendment, adjournment or debate being allowed, "That such member be suspended from the service of the Court;" and, if the offence has been committed in a Committee of the whole Court, the Chairman shall forthwith suspend the proceedings of the Committee and report the circumstances to the Court; and the President shall, on a motion being made, thereupon, put the same question without amendment, adjournment, or debate, as if the offence had been committed in the Court itself.

(2) If any member be suspended under this Order, his suspension shall continue for the remainder of the session, or until the Court rescinds the resolution.

(3) Provided that not more than one member shall be named at the same time, unless several members, present together, have jointly disregarded the authority of the chair.

(4) Provided also that, if any member, or members acting jointly, who have been suspended under this Order from the service of the Court, shall refuse to obey the direction of the President, when severally summoned under the President's orders by the Inspector General of Police or any Inspector of Police to obey such direction, the President shall call the attention of the Court to the fact that recourse to force is necessary in order to compel obedience to his direction and the member or members named by him as having refused to obey his direction shall thereupon, and without further question put, be suspended from the service of the Court during the remainder of the Session.

(5) Provided always, that nothing in this Standing Order shall be taken to deprive the Court of the power of proceeding against any member according to ancient usages.

Made by His Excellency the Acting Governor, this 15*th day of September,* 1911, *under the authority of the Order of His late Majesty in Council, dated at the Court at Buckingham Palace, the* 29*th day of February,* 1908.

By Command,

J. HAMPDEN KING,
Acting Government Secretary.

APPENDIX K

(See Part II, chapter i, p. 91.)

STANDING RULES AND ORDERS OF THE COURT OF POLICY IN FORCE PRIOR TO 1928 REFORMS

Meetings.

1. The meetings of the Court of Policy during Session shall be held on such days and at such hours as the Governor may appoint.

2. Notice of each meeting other than a meeting fixed by Proclamation or by adjournment shall be given by the Clerk of the Court to each member (at least one week before the day of meeting) except in case of emergency, when as long notice as possible shall be given. The Clerk of the Court shall also send to each member of the Court, at least four clear days before the meeting, a copy of the *Orders of the Day.*

Order of Business.

AFTER PRAYERS.

3. When a quorum has been formed, the minutes of the previous meeting shall be read, and the question of their confirmation shall be put; but no debate shall be allowed thereon, except as to the accuracy of the minutes. The Minutes of the Meeting, when confirmed, shall be signed by the Governor or President.

4. The minutes having been confirmed and signed the order of business shall be as follows :—Reports, Petitions and other Documents for the consideration of the Court to be laid on the table; Government Notices of Motions; Unofficial Notices of Questions and Motions; Questions; The Order of the Day; Petitions.

5. Petitions and documents relative to matters before the Court may be read by the Clerk when presented, if the reading thereof be required by any member, with the sanction of the Court.

6. Petitions must bear the signatures of the Petitioners, or their marks attested by the signatures of two witnesses, as well as the signature of the person by whom they are drawn.

Questions and Motions.

7. Except as hereinafter provided, a member wishing to move a Resolution or to ask a Question not immediately connected with a Resolution or Bill under consideration shall deliver Notice in writing to the Clerk of the Court, mentioning the day on which it is intended to bring forward the Resolution or Question. Such Notice if not given at a Meeting of the Court must be delivered to the Clerk at least one clear day before the meeting at which it is intended to be brought forward.

8. The following Motions may be made without Notice :—

a. Any motion for the confirmation of the Minutes of the Court or for an amendment relating thereto; or, for the adoption, modification or rejection of the report of any Committee.

b. Any motion that a petition be taken for notification, granted or rejected; or that any petition or paper be printed.

c. Any motion for the suspension of the Standing Orders.

d. Any motion for the reference of any matter to a Committee.

e. Any motion for the closing of the doors.

f. Any motion made when the Court is in Committee.

9. When a question concerning any business before the Court or any public event has been asked of any member of the Court, the reply shall be conclusive and no speech or debate on the reply shall be allowed.

Rules of Debate.

10. Every member shall speak standing and shall address himself to the Governor or President.

11. No member shall interrupt another when speaking, except by *rising to order*. A member *rising to order* shall simply direct attention to the point he desires to bring to notice and submit it to the decision of the President.

12. If two members rise to speak at the same time, the President shall call upon one of them to address the Court first.

13. No member shall speak twice to a motion except as hereinafter provided :—

a. The mover of an original motion shall have the right of reply after each member who desires to speak shall have spoken; but the mover of an amendment shall not have any right of reply.

b. After such reply the Governor or President may address the the Court, by way of summing up, in putting the question.

c. Any member who may second an original motion in the formal words " I second this motion " and no others, may reserve his speech until later in the debate.

d. When the Court is in Committee.

e. A member may by permission of the Court be heard to explain himself in regard to some material part of his speech, but shall not introduce any new matter.

Amendments.

14. Every amendment must be relevant to the motion upon which it is moved, and be so framed that the motion as amended would form an intelligible and consistent sentence.

H H

15. No amendment can be proposed to that portion of a motion which is prior to a point where an amendment has been carried or has been moved and seconded, unless the previous amendment or proposed amendment be by leave of the Court withdrawn.

16. If an amendment be moved and seconded, it shall be considered before the original motion.

17. If an amendment of a proposed amendment be moved and seconded, it shall be considered as if such previous amendment were an original motion.

18. Any amendment moved and seconded may be required by the Governor or President to be committed to writing by the mover and delivered to the Clerk of the Court.

Procedure on Question being Put.

19. After the question has been put by the Governor or President no further discussion upon any motion shall be allowed.

20. Whenever the Court divides and the names are taken down by the Clerk, they shall be entered on the Minutes of the Court.

21. Any member or number of members being in the minority on a division, may require that a written protest, to be handed by him or them to the Clerk of the Court, be recorded on the minutes, provided that such written protest shall not be handed in at a date later than the next meeting after the meeting at which the division took place.

22. Any member who may alone dissent from any resolution or vote passed by the Court may require that his dissent be recorded on the minutes.

Bills.

23. The initiation of every Bill is vested in the Governor; nevertheless, leave for that purpose having been previously obtained from the Governor, a Bill may be introduced by any member.

24. Any Bill initiated by the Governor shall on introduction be read a first time without any previous debate.

25. A Bill proposed by a member may undergo debate as to whether it is to be read a first time, and for this purpose the member introducing the Bill shall be bound on introducing to state the substance of it.

26. Every Bill shall be published in the *Gazette* for general information.

27. No Bill shall be read a second time on the same day as the first reading, or before the expiration of fifteen days from the date of its publication; a copy of every Bill shall be sent to each member by the Clerk of the Court at least six clear days before it is read a second time.

28. When a Bill has been read a second time, the Governor or President shall at the same or any subsequent meeting put the question that the Bill be committed, which being carried, the Court shall resolve itself into Committee to consider it clause by clause and amend it as deemed necessary.

29. After the Bill has been read through in Committee, any member may with leave of the Court move an amendment of any clause already passed.

30. If no alteration be made in any Bill so committed, it may be read a third time and passed at the same meeting, if no member object; but if any alteration be made or if any member object to proceed immediately with the third reading, it shall be postponed to the next following meeting. If the Bill has been altered it may, if necessary, be ordered to be reprinted, and a copy sent to each member by the Clerk, at least one clear day before the motion for the third reading shall be made.

31. If on the third reading any member desire to omit or amend any provision contained in the Bill or to introduce any fresh provision relevant to the subject matter of the Bill, he may move that the Bill be recommitted; and if the motion be carried, the marginal notes of the Bill shall be read *seriatim* by the Clerk, and any alteration proposed shall be discussed in the proper place; after which the Court shall resume, and the third reading shall then be moved, unless the Court otherwise decides.

32. A Bill may be referred to a special Committee at any stage of its progress.

33. It shall be in the power of the Governor or President, at any stage of the progress of a public Bill, to order it to be withdrawn.

34. When the Bill has been read a third time, the question " That this Ordinance do pass " shall immediately be put.

Regulations.

35. Regulations shall be dealt with as Bills in Committee.

36. Regulations shall be published in the *Gazette* and shall not be passed within one week of the date of publication.

General.

37. The matter under discussion and any business not disposed of at the time of any adjournment, shall stand as *Orders of the Day* for the next meeting of the Court.

38. Any member desirous of having the doors closed shall be allowed to move that this be done. No debate on such motion shall be held, but the Governor or President shall at once put the question. If it is decided in the affirmative, the doors shall be closed and the member who made the motion shall then state, in form of a motion, the subject he wishes discussed, after which the question whether the subject shall be discussed with closed doors or not shall be put to the Court without debate. If the motion is carried, discussion shall take place under the ordinary rules of debate; if the motion is lost, the doors shall be opened.

39. Subject to the approval of the Governor or President, on motion made and seconded the Standing Rules and Orders may be suspended at any time by a vote of the majority of the members present.

Framed and proposed by the Governor and adopted by the Court of Policy this 3rd day of February, 1892.

By Command,

CHARLES T. COX,
Clerk of the Court.

ADDITIONAL STANDING RULES AND ORDERS OF THE COURT OF POLICY.

House of
Commons
Standing
Order 20.

1. The President may order any member or members whose conduct is grossly disorderly to withdraw immediately from the Court during the remainder of that day's sitting; and the Clerk of the Court shall act on such orders as he may receive from the chair in pursuance of this Standing Order. But if, on any occasion, the President deems that his powers under this Standing Order are inadequate, he may name such member or members or he may call upon the Court to adjudge upon the conduct of such member or members.

2.—(1) Whenever any member shall have been named by the President, or by the Chairman of a Committee of the whole Court, immediately after the commission of the offence of disregarding the authority of the chair, or of abusing the Rules of the Court by persistently and wilfully obstructing the business of the Court, or otherwise, then, if the offence has been committed by such member in the Court, the President shall forthwith put the question, on a motion being made, no amendment, adjournment or debate being allowed, " That such member be suspended from the service of the Court; " and, if the offence has been committed in a Committee of the whole Court, the Chairman shall forthwith suspend the proceedings of the Committee and report the circumstances to the Court; and the President shall, on a motion being made thereupon, put the same question without amendment, adjournment, or debate, as if the offence had been committed in the Court itself.

(2) If any member be suspended under this Order, his suspension shall continue for the remainder of the session, or until the Court rescinds the resolution.

(3) Provided that not more than one member shall be named at the same time, unless several members, present together, have jointly disregarded the authority of the chair.

(4) Provided also that, if any member, or members acting jointly, who have been suspended under this Order from the service of the Court, shall refuse to obey the

direction of the President, when severally summoned under the President's orders by the Inspector General of Police or any Inspector of Police to obey such direction, the President shall call the attention of the Court to the fact that recourse to force is necessary in order to compel obedience to his direction and the member or members named by him as having refused to obey his direction shall thereupon, and without further question put, be suspended from the service of the Court during the remainder of the Session.

(5) Provided always, that nothing in this Standing Order shall be taken to deprive the Court of the power of proceeding against any member according to ancient usages.

Framed and proposed by the Governor and adopted by the Court of Policy this twelfth day of July, 1911.

By Command,

JAS. DRYSDALE,
Acting Clerk of the Court.

APPENDIX L (i)

(See Part II, chapters iii, vii and xiii.)

ROYAL ORDER-IN-COUNCIL, 3RD JUNE, 1842.

Published 14th July, 1842.

At the Court at Buckingham Palace.

PRESENT:

THE QUEEN'S MOST EXCELLENT MAJESTY,

HIS ROYAL HIGHNESS PRINCE ALBERT	EARL OF ABERDEEN
ARCHBISHOP OF CANTERBURY	EARL OF HADDINGTON
	EARL OF RIPON
	SIR ROBERT PEEL, Bart.
LORD PRESIDENT	Mr. CHANCELLOR OF THE EXCHEQUER
LORD PRIVY SEAL	
DUKE OF WELLINGTON	SIR JAMES GRAHAM, Bart.
LORD STEWARD	
EARL OF JERSEY	

WHEREAS Her Majesty was graciously pleased to declare, that on the settlement of a Civil List Establishment for British Guiana, Her Majesty would be prepared to pass an Order in Council, whereby Her Majesty would continue to secure to the Combined Court the privilege of free and unreserved discussion of the Annual Estimate of Colonial Expenditure, which had been enjoyed by the Combined Court since the passing of the last Civil List in 1836, although not specially confirmed and ratified by His late Majesty:

AND WHEREAS, by an Ordinance passed in the year 1841, provision was made for a Civil List Establishment for a period of seven years, commencing from the 1st day of January, 1841, and the same has been duly confirmed by Her Majesty:

It is therefore ordered by Her Majesty, by and with the advice of Her Privy Council, that during the continuance of the said Civil List Ordinance, but no longer, the Court of Policy, with the Financial Representatives of the Inhabitants of British Guiana in Combined Court assembled, shall be, and they are hereby declared to be, entitled, and shall have and possess full power and authority, to discuss, in detail, freely and without reserve, the several items of the Annual

Estimate of the Colonial Expenditure, subject always to the terms and conditions of the said Civil List Ordinance.

And it is hereby further ordered, that it shall not be necessary for the Governor to attend the meetings of the Combined Court when assembled for the purpose of framing the ways and means to meet the amount of the Annual Estimate of Expenditure, but that the said Court shall at such times consist of all the remaining members of the Court of Policy, with the Financial Representatives, or a majority of them, and that all discussions touching and concerning the framing and raising the said ways and means shall take place in such Court, and not elsewhere.

And it is hereby further ordered, that all votes passed by the Combined Court for the payment of money, shall be paid out under the authority of a warrant, or warrants, under the hand of the Governor, and not otherwise.

And the Right Honourable Lord Stanley, one of Her Majesty's several Secretaries of State, is to give the necessary directions therein accordingly.

WM. L. BATHURST.

APPENDIX L (ii)

ROYAL ORDER-IN-COUNCIL of the 23rd February, 1891, AT THE COURT AT WINDSOR.

The 23rd day of February, 1891.

PRESENT:

THE QUEEN'S MOST EXCELLENT MAJESTY,

ARCHBISHOP OF YORK	LORD CHAMBERLAIN
LORD PRESIDENT	EARL OF LIMERICK
MARQUESS OF SALIS-BURY	LORD WINDSOR
	SIR C. BUTT

WHEREAS on the 3rd day of June, 1842, an Order was passed by Her Majesty, by and with the advice of Her Privy Council, in the following terms :

" Whereas Her Majesty was graciously pleased to declare that on the settlement of a Civil List Establishment for British Guiana Her Majesty would be prepared to pass an Order in Council whereby Her Majesty would continue to secure to the Combined Court the privilege of free and unreserved discussion of the Annual Estimate of Colonial Expenditure which had been enjoyed by the Combined Court since the passing of the last Civil List in 1836, although not specially confirmed and ratified by His late Majesty :

" And whereas by an Ordinance passed in the year 1841, provision was made for a Civil List Establishment for a period of seven years commencing from the 1st day of January, 1841, and the same has been duly confirmed by Her Majesty :

" It is therefore ordered by Her Majesty, by and with the advice of Her Privy Council, that during the continuance of the said Civil List Ordinance, but no longer, the Court of Policy, with the Financial Representatives of the Inhabitants of British Guiana in Combined Court assembled, shall be, and they are hereby declared to be, entitled, and shall have and possess full power and authority to discuss in detail, freely and without reserve, the several items of the Annual Estimate of the Colonial Expenditure, subject always to the terms and conditions of the said Civil List Ordinance.

" And it is hereby further ordered, that it shall not be necessary for the Governor to attend the meetings of the Combined Court when assembled for the purpose of framing the ways and means to meet the amount of Annual Estimate of Expenditure, but that the said Court shall at such times consist of all the remaining members of the Court of Policy, with the Financial Representatives, or a majority of them, and that all discussions touching and concerning the framing and raising the said ways and means shall take place in such Court and not elsewhere.

" And it is hereby further ordered, that all votes passed by the Combined Court for the payment of money shall be paid out under the authority of a warrant or warrants under the hand of the Governor, and not otherwise."

And whereas Ordinances have been enacted from time to time by the Governor and Court of Policy of British Guiana making provision for a Civil List Establishment during the successive periods therein respectively mentioned, and Orders have been made from time to time by Her Majesty by and with the advice of Her Privy Council continuing during successive periods, the last of which expired on the 31st day of December, 1890, the privileges accorded to the said Combined Court by the said Order in Council of the 3rd day of June, 1842 :

And whereas an Ordinance has been passed by the Governor and Court of Policy of British Guiana bearing the date of the 18th day of December, 1890, intituled " An Ordinance to provide for the maintenance during a certain term of years of the Civil List Establishment of this Colony," whereby the maintenance of the said Civil List Establishment is provided for for a period of seven years, commencing on the 1st day of January in the year 1891, which Ordinance has been duly confirmed by Her Majesty :

And whereas it is expedient that during the continuance of the said Ordinance, the privileges accorded to the Combined Court of British Guiana by the before-recited Order in Council should be continued :

It is therefore ordered by Her Majesty, by and with the advice of Her Privy Council, that the privileges accorded to the Combined Court by the said Order in Council of the 3rd day of June, 1842, shall be, and they are hereby continued until the 31st day of December, 1897.

And it is hereby further ordered that the Governor for the time being of British Guiana may from time to time make such standing Rules and Orders as may be necessary to ensure punctuality of attendance of Members of the said Combined Court, and to prevent meetings of the said Combined Court being holden without convenient notice to the several Members thereof, and to maintain order and method in the despatch of business, and in the conduct of debates in the said Combined Court, and that all such Rules and Orders not being repugnant to this Order shall at all times be followed and observed, and shall be binding on the said Combined Court unless the same shall be disallowed by Her Majesty.

And the Right Honourable Lord Knutsford, one of Her Majesty's Secretaries of State, is to give the necessary directions herein accordingly.

C. L. PEEL.

APPENDIX L (iii)

AT THE COURT AT BUCKINGHAM PALACE,
The 17th day of March, 1913.

PRESENT :

THE KING'S MOST EXCELLENT MAJESTY

LORD PRESIDENT	LORD STAMFORDHAM
VISCOUNT KNOLLYS	Mr. HERBERT SAMUEL.

WHEREAS on the 3rd day of June, 1842, an Order was passed by Her late Majesty Queen Victoria, by and with the advice of Her Privy Council, in the following terms :—

" Whereas Her Majesty was graciously pleased to declare that on the settlement of a Civil List Establishment for British Guiana, Her Majesty would be prepared to pass an Order in Council whereby Her Majesty would continue to secure to the Combined Court the privilege of free and unreserved discussion of the Annual Estimate of Colonial Expenditure which had been enjoyed by the Combined Court since the passing of the last Civil List in 1836, although not specially confirmed and ratified by His late Majesty :

" And whereas by an Ordinance passed in the year 1841, provision was made for a Civil List Establishment for a period of seven years, commencing from the 1st day of January, 1841, and the same has been duly confirmed by Her Majesty :

" It is therefore ordered by Her Majesty, by and with the advice of Her Privy Council that during the continuance of the said Civil List Ordinance, but no longer, the Court of Policy with the Financial Representatives of the Inhabitants of British Guiana in Combined Court assembled, shall be, and they are hereby declared to be, entitled, and shall have and possess full power and authority to discuss in detail freely and without reserve the several items of the Annual Estimate of the Colonial Expenditure, subject always to the terms and conditions of the said Civil List Ordinance.

" And it is hereby ordered, that it shall not be necessary for the Governor to attend the meetings of the Combined Court when assembled for the purpose of framing the ways and means to meet the amount of the Annual Estimate of Expenditure, but that the said Court shall at such times consist of all the remaining members of the Court of Policy with the Financial Representatives, or a majority of them, and that all discussions touching and concerning the framing and raising the said ways and means shall take place in such Court and not elsewhere :

"And it is hereby further ordered, that all votes passed by the Combined Court for the payment of money shall be paid out under the authority of a warrant or warrants under the hand of the Governor and not otherwise."

And whereas Ordinances have been enacted from time to time by the Governor and Court of Policy of British Guiana, making provision for a Civil List Establishment during the successive periods therein respectively mentioned, and further Orders have been made from time to time continuing during successive periods the privileges accorded to the said Combined Court by the said Order in Council of the 3rd day of June, 1842 :

And whereas an Ordinance has been passed by the Governor and Court of Policy of British Guiana, bearing the date of the 11th day of January, 1913, intituled " An Ordinance to provide for the maintenance during a certain term of years of the Civil List Establishment of this Colony," whereby the maintenance of the said Civil List Establishment, subject to certain modifications therein specified, is continued in force until the 31st day of December, 1917, which Ordinance has been duly confirmed by His Majesty :

And whereas it is expedient that during the continuance of the said Civil List Ordinance of 1912, the privileges accorded to the Combined Court of British Guiana by the before-recited Order in Council should be continued :

IT IS, THEREFORE, ordered by His Majesty, by and with the advice of His Privy Council, that the privileges accorded to the Combined Court by the said Order in Council of the 3rd day of June, 1842, shall be, and they are, hereby continued until the 31st day of December, 1917.

And it is hereby further ordered, that the Governor for the time being of British Guiana may from time to time make such standing Rules and Orders as may be necessary to ensure punctuality of attendance of members of the said Combined Court, and to prevent meetings of the said Combined Court being holden without convenient notice to the several Members thereof, and to maintain order and method in the despatch of business, and in the conduct of debates in the said Combined Court, and that all such Rules and Orders not being repugnant to this Order shall at all times be followed and observed, and shall be binding on the said Combined Court unless the same shall be disallowed by His Majesty.

And the Right Honourable Lewis Harcourt, one of His Majesty's Principal Secretaries of State, is to give the necessary directions herein accordingly.

ALMERIC FITZROY.

APPENDIX M

(See Part II, chapter xvi, p. 312, and Part III, chapter ii (c), p. 337.)

LETTERS PATENT providing for the Constitution of an Executive Council for the Colony of British Guiana, dated 5th March, 1891.

Victoria, by the Grace of God of the United Kingdom of Great Britain and Ireland Queen, Defender of the Faith, Empress of India : To all to whom these Presents shall come, Greeting.

Establishment of an Executive Council.

WHEREAS We are minded to constitute an Executive Council to advise and assist Our Governor for the time being of Our Colony of British Guiana in the administration of the Government thereof :

Now know ye that We do hereby declare and ordain that, for the purpose of aiding Our said Governor for the time being, there shall be in and for Our said Colony an Executive Council which shall be constituted in such manner and consist of such persons as We shall direct by the Instructions accompanying these Our Letters Patent or by any other instructions under Our Sign Manual and Signet, and that all such persons shall hold their places in the said Executive Council during Our pleasure.

Power reserved to revoke, alter, or amend present Letters Patent.

2. And We do hereby reserve to Ourselves, Our heirs and successors, full power and authority from time to time to revoke, alter, or amend these Our Letters Patent as to Us or them shall seem fit.

Publication of Letters Patent.

3. And We do direct and enjoin that these Our Letters Patent shall be read and proclaimed at such place or places within Our said Colony as Our said Governor shall think fit.

In witness whereof We have caused these Our Letters to be made Patent. Witness Ourself at Westminster, the Fifth day of March, in the Fifty-fourth year of Our reign.

By Warrant under the Queen's Sign Manual.

MUIR MACKENZIE.

476

APPENDIX N

(See Part III, chapter ii (b), p. 332.)

BRITISH GUIANA

LETTERS PATENT passed under the Great Seal of the United Kingdom, constituting the Office of Governor and Commander-in-Chief of the Colony of British Guiana.

Letters Patent,
Dated 25th February, 1911.

George the Fifth by the Grace of God of the United Kingdom of Great Britain and Ireland and of the British Dominions beyond the Seas King, Defender of the Faith, Emperor of India : To all to whom these Presents shall come, Greeting.

Recites Letters Patent of 12th September 1877, 5th March 1891, and 29th November 1902.

WHEREAS by certain Letters Patent under the Great Seal of Our United Kingdom of Great Britain and Ireland, bearing date at Westminster the Twelfth day of September, 1877, Her late Majesty Queen Victoria did constitute the Office of Governor and Commander-in-Chief in and over Our Colony of British Guiana, and did provide for the Government thereof :

And whereas by further Letters Patent under the Great Seal of Our United Kingdom of Great Britain and Ireland, bearing date at Westminster the Fifth day of March, 1891, and the Twenty-ninth day of November, 1902, respectively, further provision was made for the administration of the Government of Our said Colony :

And whereas We are minded to make other provision in lieu thereof :

Revokes Letters Patent of 12th September 1877, 5th March 1891, and 29th November 1902.

Now, therefore, We do hereby revoke the above-recited Letters Patent of the Twelfth day of September, 1877, the Fifth day of March, 1891, and the Twenty-ninth day of November, 1902, but without prejudice to anything lawfully done thereunder, and in lieu thereof We do ordain and declare Our Will and Pleasure as follows :—

477

Office of Governor constituted.

I. There shall be a Governor and Commander-in-Chief (herein-after called the Governor) in and over Our Colony of British Guiana (herein-after called the Colony), and appointments to the said Office shall be by Commission under Our Sign Manual and Signet.

Publication of Governor's Commission.

Oaths to be taken by Governor.

Imperial Act 31 & 32 Vict., cap. 72.

II. Every person appointed to fill the Office of Governor shall with all due solemnity, before entering on any of the duties of his Office, cause the Commission appointing him to be Governor to be read and published in the presence of the Chief Justice for the time being, or other Judge of the Supreme Court of the Colony, and of such Members of the Court of Policy as are able to attend, which being done, he shall then and there take the Oath of Allegiance in the form provided by an Act passed in the Session holden in the Thirty-first and Thirty-second years of the reign of Her late Majesty Queen Victoria, intituled "An Act to amend the law relating to Promissory Oaths"; and likewise the usual Oath for the due execution of the Office of Governor and for the due and impartial administration of justice; which Oaths the said Chief Justice for the time being of the Colony, or, in his absence, or in the event of his being otherwise incapacitated, the senior Judge then present of the Supreme Court of the Colony shall and he is hereby required to tender and administer unto him.

Governor's powers and authorities.

III. We do hereby authorize and command the Governor to do and execute in due manner all things that shall belong to his said Office according to the tenour of these Our Letters Patent and of such Commission as may be issued to him under the Royal Sign Manual and Signet, and according to such Instructions as may from time to time be given to him, under Our Sign Manual and Signet, or by Our Order in Our Privy Council, or by Us through one of Our Principal Secretaries of State, and to such laws as are, or shall hereafter be, in force in the Colony.

Executive Council. Constitution.

IV. For the purpose of advising the Governor, there shall be in and for the Colony an Executive Council which shall be constituted in such manner and consist of such persons as may be directed by any Instructions under Our Sign Manual and Signet, and all such persons shall hold their places in the said Executive Council during Our pleasure.

Laws to be enacted by Governor and Court of Policy.

V. The Governor, with the advice and consent of the Court of Policy of the Colony, may make laws for the peace, order, and good government of the Colony, subject to such rules and regulations as may from time to time be prescribed by Instructions under the Royal Sign Manual and Signet : Provided, nevertheless, and We do hereby reserve to Ourselves, Our heirs and successors, Our and their undoubted right and authority to confirm,

Confirmation, Disallowance, &c.

disallow, or with the advice of Our or their Privy Council to amend any such laws, and to make, enact, and establish, from time to time, with the advice and consent of Parliament, or with the advice of Our or their Privy Council, all such laws as may to Us or them appear necessary for the peace, order, and good government of the Colony, as fully and effectually as if these presents had not been made.

Assent to Bills.

VI. When a Bill passed by the Legislature is presented to the Governor for his assent, he shall, according to his discretion but subject to any Instructions addressed to him under Our Sign Manual and Signet or through one of Our Principal Secretaries of State, declare that he assents thereto, or that he refuses his assent to the same, or that he reserves the same for the signification of Our pleasure.

Reserved Bills.

VII. A Bill reserved for the signification of Our pleasure shall take effect so soon as We shall have given Our assent to the same by Order in Council, or through one of Our Principal Secretaries of State, and the Governor shall have signified such assent by message to the Legislature, or by proclamation : Provided that no such message or proclamation shall be issued after two years from the day on which the Bill was presented to the Governor for his assent.

Public Seal.

VIII. The Governor shall keep and use the Public Seal of the Colony, for sealing all things whatsover that shall pass the said Seal.

Grants of land.

IX. The Governor, in Our name and on Our behalf, may make and execute under the Public Seal of the Colony, grants and dispositions of any lands which may be lawfully granted and disposed of by Us within the Colony : Provided that every

To be made in conformity with the law.

such grant or disposition be made in conformity either with some law in force in the Colony, or with some Instructions addressed to the Governor under Our Sign Manual and Signet, or through one of Our Prncipal Secretaries of State, or with such regulations as are now in force or may be made by the Governor in that behalf and publicly promulgated in the Colony.

Governor empowered to appoint Judges and other Officers.

X. Subject to the provisions of any law of the Colony, the Governor may constitute and appoint all such Judges, Commissioners, Justices of the Peace, and other necessary Officers in the Colony, as may be lawfully constituted and appointed by Us, all of whom, unless otherwise provided by law, shall hold their offices during Our pleasure.

Grant of pardons.

XI. When any crime or offence has been committed within the Colony, or for which the offender may be tried therein, the Governor may, as he shall see occasion, in Our name and on Our behalf grant a pardon to any accomplice in such crime or offence, who shall give such information and evidence as shall lead to the conviction of the principal offender, or of any one of such offenders if more than one : and further, may grant to any offender convicted of any crime or offence in any Court, or before any Judge, Justice, or Magistrate within the Colony, a pardon, either free or subject to lawful conditions, or any remission of the sentence passed on such offender, or any respite of the execution of such sentence for such period as the Governor thinks fit,

Remission of fines.

and may remit any fines, penalties, or forfeitures which may become due and payable unto Us :

Proviso. Banishment from the Colony prohibited. Exception; Political offences.

Provided always that the Governor shall in no case, except where the offence has been of a political nature unaccompanied by any other grave crime, make it a condition of any pardon or remission of sentence that the offender shall be banished from or shall absent himself from the Colony.

Dismissal and suspension of Officers.

XII. The Governor may, upon sufficient cause to him appearing, dismiss any public officer not appointed by virtue of a Warrant from Us, whose pensionable emoluments do not exceed 100*l.* a year, provided that in every such case the grounds of intended dismissal are definitely stated in writing, and communicated to the officer in order that he may have full opportunity of exculpating himself, and that the matter is investigated by the Governor with the aid of the head for the time being of the department in which the officer is serving.

The Governor may, upon sufficient cause to him appearing, also suspend from the exercise of his office any person holding any office in the Colony whether appointed by virtue of any Commission or Warrant from Us, or in Our name, or by any other mode of appointment. Such suspension shall continue and have effect only until Our pleasure therein shall be signified to the Governor. If the suspension is confirmed by Us through one of Our Principal Secretaries of State, the Governor shall forthwith cause the officer to be so informed, and thereupon his office shall become vacant. In proceeding to any such suspension, the Governor is strictly to observe the directions in that behalf given to him by any such Instructions as aforesaid.

Succession to Government.

Lieutenant-Governor.

Administrator.

To take Oaths of Office before administering Government.

Powers and authorities.

XIII. Whenever the Office of Governor is vacant, or if the Governor becomes incapable or is absent from the Colony, or is from any cause prevented from acting in the duties of his Office, Our Lieutenant-Governor of the Colony, or if there be no such officer, or if such Officer be absent or unable to act, then such person or persons as We may appoint under Our Sign Manual and Signet, and in case there shall be no person or persons within the Colony so appointed, then the person for the time being lawfully exercising the Office of Government Secretary shall, during Our pleasure, administer the Government of the Colony, first taking the Oaths herein-before directed to be taken by the Governor, and in the manner herein prescribed; which being done, We do hereby authorize, empower and command Our Lieutenant-Governor, or any other such Administrator as aforesaid, to do and execute, during Our pleasure, all things that belong to the Office of Governor and Commander-in-Chief, according to the tenour of these Our Letters Patent, and according to Our Instructions as aforesaid and the laws of the Colony.

Governor may appoint a Deputy during his temporary absence from seat of Government.

XIV. In the event of the Governor having occasion to be temporarily absent for a short period from the seat of Government he may, in every such case, by an Instrument under the Public Seal of the Colony, constitute and appoint Our Lieutenant-Governor, or if there be no such Officer, or if such Officer be absent or unable to act, then any other person, to be his Deputy within any part or parts of the Colony, during such temporary absence, and in that capacity to exercise, perform, and execute for and on behalf of the Governor during such absence, but no longer, all such powers and authorities vested in the Governor, as shall in and by such Instrument be specified and limited, but no others. Every such Deputy shall conform to and observe all such Instructions as the Governor shall from time to time address to him for his guidance : Provided, nevertheless, that by the appointment of a Deputy as aforesaid, the power and authority of the Governor shall not be abridged, altered, or in any way affected, otherwise than We may at any time hereafter think proper to direct.

Officers and others to obey and assist the Governor.

XV. And We do hereby require and command all Officers and Ministers, Civil and Military, and all other the inhabitants of the Colony, to be obedient, aiding, and assisting unto the Governor, and such person or persons as may, from time to time, under the provisions of these Our Letters Patent, administer the Government of the Colony.

Term " the Governor " explained.

XVI. In the construction of these Our Letters Patent the term " the Governor " shall, unless inconsistent with the context, include every person for the time being administering the Government of the Colony.

Power reserved to His Majesty to revoke, alter, or amend the present Letters Patent.

XVII. And We do hereby reserve to Ourselves, Our heirs and successors, full power and authority, from time to time, to revoke, alter, or amend these Our Letters Patent as to Us or them shall seem meet.

Publication of Letters Patent.

XVIII. And We do further direct and enjoin that these Our Letters Patent shall be read and proclaimed at such place or places as the Governor shall think fit within the Colony.

In witness whereof We have caused these Our Letters to be made Patent. Witness Ourself at Westminster the Twenty-fifth day of February in the First year of Our Reign.

By Warrant under the King's Sign Manual.

MUIR MACKENZIE.

APPENDIX O

(See Part III, chapter ii, pp. 333, 337 and 344.)

BRITISH GUIANA

INSTRUCTIONS passed under the Royal Sign Manual and Signet to the Governor and Commander-in-Chief of the Colony of British Guiana.

Dated 25th February, 1911.

GEORGE R.I.

INSTRUCTIONS to Our Governor and Commander-in-Chief in and over Our Colony of British Guiana, or, in his absence, to Our Lieutenant-Governor or the Officer for the time being administering the Government of Our said Colony.

Preamble.
Recites Letters Patent of even date, constituting the Office of Governor.

WHEREAS by certain Letters Patent bearing even date herewith We have constituted, ordered, and declared that there shall be a Governor and Commander-in-Chief (hereinafter called the Governor) in and over Our Colony of British Guiana (hereinafter called the Colony) :

And whereas We have thereby authorized and commanded the Governor to do and execute in due manner all things that shall belong to his said Office, according to the tenour of Our said Letters Patent and of such Commission as may be issued to him under the Royal Sign Manual and Signet, and according to such Instructions as may from time to time be given to him, under Our Sign Manual and Signet, or by Our Order in Our Privy Council, or by Us through one of Our Principal Secretaries of State, and to such laws as are, or shall hereafter be, in force in the Colony :

Recites Instructions of 12th September 1877, and Additional Instructions of 5th March 1891, 22nd May 1896, and 10th November 1904.

And whereas Her late Majesty Queen Victoria did issue under Her Sign Manual and Signet certain Instructions bearing date the Twelfth day of September, 1877, and certain Additional Instructions bearing date respectively the Fifth day of March, 1891, and the Twenty-second day of May, 1896 :

And whereas His late Majesty King Edward the Seventh did issue under His Sign Manual and Signet certain Additional Instructions bearing date the Tenth day of November, 1904 :

And whereas We are minded to substitute fresh Instructions for the aforesaid Instructions and Additional Instructions :

Revokes Instructions of 12th September 1877, and Additional Instructions of 5th March 1891, 22nd May 1896, and 10th November 1904.

Now We do, by these Our Instructions under Our Sign Manual and Signet, revoke, as from the date of the coming into force of Our above-recited Letters Patent bearing even date herewith, the aforesaid Instructions and Additional Instructions, but without prejudice to anything lawfully done thereunder, and instead thereof We do direct and enjoin and declare Our Will and Pleasure, as follows :—

Oaths to be administered by the Governor.

I. The Governor may, whenever he thinks fit, require any person in the public service in the Colony to take the Oath of Allegiance, together with such other Oath or Oaths as may, from time to time, be prescribed by any laws in force in the Colony. The Governor is to administer such Oaths or cause them to be administered by some Public Officer in the Colony.

Executive Council. Constitution.

II. The executive Council of the Colony shall consist of Our Lieutenant-Governor, if any, for the time being of the Colony, and the persons for the time being lawfully discharging the functions of the respective offices of Government Secretary and Attorney-General of the Colony who shall be styled *ex-officio* Members of the said Council, and such persons as at the date of the coming into force of Our said Letters Patent are Members of the Executive Council, and such other persons as We may from time to time appoint by any Instruction or Warrant under Our Sign Manual and Signet, or as shall be provisionally appointed by the Governor as hereinafter provided. Every person so appointed by Us or provisionally appointed by the Governor shall vacate his seat at the end of five years from the date of the Instrument by which or in pursuance of which he is appointed, but may be re-appointed. He shall also vacate his seat if he shall leave the Colony without written permission from the Governor, or outstay any leave of absence granted him by the Governor, or by one of Our Principal Secretaries of State.

Vacation of Seats.

Provisional appointments.

III. In the event of the death, resignation, incapacity, suspension, or absence from the Colony of any Member of the Executive Council of the Colony other than the Lieutenant-Governor, and the persons for the time being lawfully discharging the functions of the respective offices of Government Secretary and Attorney-General of the Colony, or, if in the opinion of the Governor the number of such Members is insufficient, the Governor may by an Instrument under the Public Seal of the Colony appoint some fit person to be provisionally a Member of the said Council. The Governor shall forthwith report to Us for Our confirmation or disallowance through one of Our Principal Secretaries of State every such provisional appointment. If this appointment is disallowed by Us, any person so appointed shall forthwith cease to be a Member so soon as notice of such disallowance is received by the Governor. He shall also cease to be a Member if the Member in whose place he was appointed shall return to the Colony, or, as the case may be, shall be released from suspension, or shall be declared by the Governor capable of again discharging his functions in the said Council.

Precedence of Members.

IV. The seniority and precedence of the Members of the Executive Council shall be as follows : First, the *ex-officio* Members in the order in which their offices are above mentioned; and secondly, the other Members in the order of date of their appointments, or, if two or more are appointed by the same Instrument, according to the order in which they are named therein.

Governor to communicate Instructions to Executive Council.

V. The Governor shall forthwith communicate these Our Instructions to the said Executive Council, and likewise all such others, from time to time, as he shall find convenient for Our service to impart to them.

Executive Council not to proceed to business unless summoned by Governor's authority.

Quorum.

VI. The said Executive Council shall not proceed to the desptach of business unless duly summoned by authority of the Governor, nor unless two Members at the least (exclusive of himself or of the Member presiding) be present and assisting throughout the whole of the meeting at which any such business shall be despatched.

Governor to preside.

VII. The Governor shall attend and preside at the meetings of the Executive Council, unless prevented by illness or other grave cause, and in his absence the senior Member of the said Council actually present shall preside.

Journals or Minutes of Executive Council to be kept.

VIII. Minutes shall be regularly kept of the proceedings of the Executive Council; and at each meeting of the said Council the minutes of the last preceding meeting shall be read over and confirmed or amended, as the case may require, before proceeding to the despatch of any other business.

To be transmitted home twice a year.

Twice in each year a full and exact copy of the minutes for the preceding half year shall be transmitted to Us through one of Our Principal Secretaries of State.

Governor to consult Executive Council.

IX. In the execution of the powers, and authorities granted to the Governor by Us, he shall in all cases consult with the Executive Council, excepting only in cases which are of such a nature that, in his judgment, Our service would sustain material prejudice by consulting the said Council thereupon, or when the matters to be decided are too unimportant to require their advice, or too urgent to admit of their advice being given by the time within which it may be necessary for him to act in respect to any

Proviso : urgent cases.

such matters. In all such urgent cases he shall, at the earliest practicable period, communicate to the said Executive Council the measures which he may so have adopted, with the reasons thereof.

Governor alone entitled to submit questions.

X. The Governor shall be alone entitled to submit questions to the Executive Council for their advice or decision; but if the Governor decline to submit any question to the said Council when requested in writing by any Member so to do, it shall be competent to such Member to require that there be recorded upon the minutes his written application, together with the answer returned by the Governor to the same.

Governor may act in opposition to Executive Council.

Reporting grounds for so doing.

Members may require to be recorded on minutes their adverse opinions.

XI. The Governor may act in opposition to the advice given to him by the Members of the Executive Council, if he shall in any case deem it right to do so; but in any such case he shall fully report the matter to Us, by the first convenient opportunity, with the grounds and reasons of his action. In every such case it shall be competent to any Member of the said Council to require that there be recorded at length on the minutes the grounds of any advice or opinion he may give upon the question.

Rules as to the
making of laws.

XII. In the making of laws the Governor shall observe, as far as practicable, the following Rules :—

Style of laws.

(1) The style of enacting laws shall be " Ordin- " ances enacted by the Governor of British Guiana, " with the advice and consent of the Court of " Policy thereof," or " Ordinances enacted by the " Governor of British Guiana with the advice and " consent of the Combined Court thereof," as the case may be.

Governor to propose
Ordinances.

(2) No Ordinance shall be enacted for any purpose which shall not have been first proposed to the said Court of Policy or the said Combined Court by the Governor, or by some member of the Court under his sanction previously obtained.

Ordinances to be
numbered and
methodically
arranged.

(3) All Ordinances shall be distinguished by titles, and the Ordinances of each year shall also be distinguished by consecutive numbers, commencing in each successive year with the number one, and every such Ordinance shall be divided into successive clauses or paragraphs consecutively numbered, and to every such clause there shall be annexed in the margin a short summary of its contents.

All Ordinances passed in any one year shall, unless they require to be reserved for the signification of Our pleasure, be assented to by the Governor in that year, and shall be dated as of the day on which the assent of the Governor is given, and shall be numbered as of the year in which they are passed.　Ordinances not so assented to, but reserved by the Governor for the signification of Our pleasure, shall be dated as of the day, and numbered as of the year, on and in which they are brought into force.

Different subjects
not to be mixed
in the same
Ordinance.
No clause to be in-
troduced foreign to
what the title
imports.
Temporary
Ordinances.

(4) Each different matter is to be provided for by a different Ordinance, without intermixing in one and the same Ordinance such things as have no proper relation to each other; and no clause is to be inserted in or annexed to any Ordinance which shall be foreign to what the title of such Ordinance imports, and no perpetual clause is to be part of any temporary Ordinance.

Description of Bills
not to be assented to.

XIII. The Governor shall not assent in Our name to any Bill of the following classes :—

1. Any Bill for the divorce of persons joined together in holy matrimony :

2. Any Bill whereby any grant of land or money, or other donation or gratuity, may be made to himself :

3. Any Bill affecting the currency of the Colony or relating to the issue of Bank notes :

4. Any Bill establishing any banking association, or amending or altering the constitution, powers, or privileges of any banking association :

5. Any Bill imposing differential duties :

6. Any Bill the provisions of which shall appear inconsistent with obligations imposed upon Us by Treaty :

7. Any Bill interfering with the discipline or control of Our forces by land or sea :

8. Any Bill of an extraordinary nature and importance, whereby Our prerogative, or the rights and property of Our subjects not residing in the Colony, or the trade and shipping of the United Kingdom and its Dependencies, may be prejudiced :

9. Any Bill whereby persons not of European birth or descent may be subjected or made liable to any disabilities or restrictions to which persons of European birth or descent are not also subjected or made liable :

10. Any Bill containing provisions to which Our assent has been once refused, or which have been disallowed by Us :

11. Any Bill respecting the Constitution, proceedings, numbers or mode of appointing or electing any of the Members of the Court of Policy, or of any other Body Politic or Corporate within the Colony :

Proviso in cases of emergency for the immediate operation of a Bill.

Unless such Bill shall contain a clause suspending the operation of such Bill until the signification in the Colony of Our pleasure thereupon; or unless the Governor shall have satisfied himself that an urgent necessity exists requiring that such Bill be brought into immediate operation, in which case he is authorized to assent in Our name to such Bill, unless the same shall be repugnant to the law of England, or inconsistent with any obligations imposed on Us by Treaty. But he is to transmit to Us, by the earliest opportunity, the Bill so assented to, together with his reasons for assenting thereto.

XIV. When any Ordinance has been passed, or when any Bill has been reserved for the signification of Our pleasure, the Governor shall forthwith lay it before Us for Our final assent, disallowance, or other direction thereupon, and shall transmit to Us, through one of Our Principal Secretaries of State, a transcript in duplicate of the same, together with a marginal abstract thereof, duly authenticated under the public seal of the Colony, and by his own signature. Such transcript shall be accompanied with such explanatory observations as may be required to exhibit the reasons and occasion for passing such Ordinance or Bill.

Authenticated laws to be sent home in duplicate for approval or disallowance. Marginal notes.

XV. The Governor shall transmit to the Chief Justice of the Colony, to be enrolled in the Supreme Court, a transcript, duly authenticated in the manner before mentioned, of every Ordinance passed by him with the advice and consent of the said Court of Policy, or Combined Court (as the case may be), and of every Bill reserved by him for the signification of Our pleasure, together with a certificate, under his hand and seal, of the effect of every Order or other direction which he may receive from Us, or through one of Our Principal Secretaries of State, in regard to any such Bill or Ordinance, which certificate shall in like manner be enrolled in the said Supreme Court, and there remain on record, to the intent that the Judges of the said Court may without further or other proof take cognizance of all Ordinances made and promulgated for the peace, order, and good government of the Colony.

Enrolment of Ordinances in the Supreme Court.

XVI. At the earliest practicable period at the commencement of each year the Governor shall cause a complete collection to be published, for general information, of all Ordinances enrolled during the preceding year.

Annual collection of Ordinances to be published.

XVII. For the sake of orderly despatch, and the prevention of all undue precipitation in the enactment of Ordinances by the said Court of Policy, We do hereby authorize and require the Governor from time to time, as occasion may require, to frame and propose to the said Court, for their adoption, such Standing Rules and Forms of Proceeding as may be best adapted for the purpose aforesaid, and for insuring, previously to the passing of any Ordinance intended to affect or

Standing Rules, Orders, and Forms of proceeding.

Private Bills.

benefit private persons, that due notice be given to all parties concerned of the provisions thereof, with ample opportunity for opposing the same, and that a full and impartial examination may take place of the grounds upon which the same may be proposed or resisted; And We do further authorize and require him from time to time, with the consent of the said Court of Policy, to revoke, alter, or renew such Rules and Forms; and We do direct that the same, when so adopted, shall be duly observed in all the proceedings of the said Court of Policy : Provided that until varied or revoked, any such Standing Rules or Forms heretofore made shall continue in force.

Minutes of the Court of Policy to be sent home after every meeting.

XVIII. The Governor shall transmit to Us, through one of Our Principal Secretaries of State, as soon as possible after every meeting, fair copies of the minutes and proceedings of the said Court of Policy.

Surveys and reservations to be made of waste lands.

XIX. Before disposing of any vacant or waste lands to Us belonging in the Colony, the Governor shall cause the same to be surveyed, and such reservations made thereout as he may think necessary or desirable to be reserved and set apart for public roads or other internal communication by land or water, or for purposes of military defence, or for any other purposes of public safety, convenience, utility, health, or enjoyment. The

Governor not to purchase land without permission.

Governor shall not, directly or indirectly, purchase for himself any of such lands without Our special permission given through one of Our Principal Secretaries of State.

Appointments to be provisional and during pleasure.

XX. All Commissions to be granted by the Governor to any person or persons for exercising any office or employment shall, unless otherwise provided by law, be granted during pleasure only; and whenever the Governor shall appoint to any vacant office or employment, of which the initial emoluments exceed $100l.$ per annum, any person not by Us specially directed to be appointed thereto, he shall at the same time expressly apprise such person that such appointment is to be considered only as temporary and provisional until Our allowance or disallowance thereof be signified.

Suspension of Officers.

XXI. Before suspending from the exercise of his office any public Officer whose annual pensionable emoluments exceed $100l.$, the Governor shall signify to such Officer by a statement in writing the grounds of the intended suspension, and shall call upon him to state in writing any grounds upon which he desires to exculpate himself; and if the Officer does not furnish such a statement within the time fixed by the Governor, or fails to exculpate himself to the satisfaction of the Governor, the Governor shall appoint a Committee of the Executive Council to investigate the charges made and to make a full report to the Executive Council. The Governor shall forthwith cause such report to be considered by the Council, and shall cause to be recorded in the minutes whether the Council, or the majority thereof does or does not assent to the suspension, and if the Governor thereupon proceeds to such suspension he shall transmit the report of the Committee and the evidence taken by it, together with the minutes of the proceedings of the Council, to Us through one of Our Principal Secretaries of State at the earliest opportunity. But if in any case the interests of Our service shall appear to the Governor to demand that a person shall cease to exercise the powers and functions of his office instantly, or before there shall be time to take the proceedings hereinbefore directed, he shall then interdict such person from the exercise of the powers and functions of his office.

Regulation of power of pardon in capital cases. Judge's Report to be laid before Executive Council.

XXII. Whenever any offender shall have been condemned by the sentence of any Court to suffer death, the Governor shall call upon the Judge who presided at the trial to make to him a written Report of the case of such offender, and shall cause such Report to be taken into consideration at the first meeting of the Executive Council which may be conveniently held thereafter, and he may cause the said Judge to be specially summoned to attend at such meeting and to produce his notes thereat. The Governor shall not pardon or reprieve any such offender unless it shall appear to him expedient **Governor to take advice of Executive Council in such cases;** so to do, upon receiving the advice of the said Executive Council thereon; but in all such cases he is to decide either to extend or to withhold a **but to exercise his own judgment.** pardon or reprieve, according to his own deliberate judgment, whether the Members of the Executive Council concur therein or otherwise; entering, nevertheless, on the minutes of the said Executive Council a minute of his reasons at length in case he should decide any such question in opposition to the judgment of the majority of the Members thereof.

XXIII. The Governor shall punctually forward to Us from year to year, through one of Our Principal Secretaries of State, the annual Book of Returns for the Colony, commonly called the " Blue Book," relating to the revenue and expenditure, defence, public works, legislation, civil establishments, pensions, population, schools, course of exchange, imports and exports, agricultural produce, manufactures, and other matters in the said Blue Book more particularly specified, with reference to the state and condition of the Colony.

Blue Book.

XXIV. The Governor shall not, on any pretence whatever, quit the Colony without having first obtained leave from Us for so doing under Our Sign Manual and Signet, or through one of Our Principal Secretaries of State.

Governor's absence.

Given at Our Court at Saint James's this Twenty-fifth day of February, 1911, in the First year of Our Reign.

APPENDIX P

(See Part II, chapters xvi and xvii.)

ORDINANCE No. 1 OF 1891

(Ordinances No. 11 of 1891, No. 26 of 1891, No. 9 of 1896, No. 1 of 1898, No. 16 of 1898, No. 6 of 1901, No. 22 of 1902, No. 37 of 1903, No. 24 of 1909, No. 6 of 1914 and No. 34 of 1919 incorporated.) *

AN ORDINANCE to alter and amend the Political Constitution of this Colony.

[1st August, 1891.]

BE it enacted by the Governor of British Guiana, with the advice and consent of the Court of Policy thereof, as follows :—

Short title. **1.** This Ordinance may be cited as the British Guiana Constitution Ordinance 1891.

PART I.

THE COURT OF POLICY.

Composition of the Court of Policy. **2.** From and after the issue of the writs for the first general election of members of the Court of Policy under this Ordinance, the Court of Policy shall consist of sixteen members, namely, the Governor, seven official members, and eight elected members.

Official Members.

Official members.
Amd. 6 of 1914, s. 2, and 23 of 1914.
3. The official members of the Court of Policy shall be the Colonial Secretary, the Attorney General, the Immigration Agent General, the Colonial Treasurer (hereinafter referred to as " *ex officio* members ") and such three other persons holding public offices in this Colony as His Majesty may from time to time appoint or as the Governor may, in the exercise of the power vested in him by this Ordinance, from to time provisionally appoint.

* I have not incorporated the Register of Voters (Electoral District No. 1) Ordinance of 1927 (*vide supra*, p. 319), because it was only passed in the year immediately preceding the 1928 reforms and, therefore, did not really affect the practice under the pre-reform constitution.

493

Precedence of ex officio members.

4. The *ex officio* members of the Court of Policy shall take precedence of the other members of the Court, except the Governor, and shall rank amongst themselves in the order in which they are named in the last preceding section.

Precedence of official members.

5. The official members of the Court of Policy, other than the *ex officio* members, shall take precedence of the elected members, and shall rank amongst themselves in the order of date of their appointment : Provided that a member appointed by His Majesty shall rank before a member provisionally appointed by the Governor : Provided, also, that if any two or more members are appointed by His Majesty, or provisionally appointed by the Governor, on the same date, they shall rank amongst themselves as His Majesty or the Governor may direct, and, in default of such direction, in the alphabetical order of their names.

Vacation of office by public officer appointed as official member and refusing to act.

6. If any person holding a public office in this Colony, to which he has been appointed after the commencement of this Ordinance, who may be appointed by His Majesty, or provisionally appointed by the Governor, to be an official member of the Court of Policy, refuses or neglects to act in that capacity he shall *ipso facto* vacate his office.

Tenure of seat of official member.

7. An official member of the Court of Policy, other than an *ex officio* member, may at any time be removed by His Majesty and shall vacate his seat upon a dissolution of the Court of Policy, but may be reappointed.

Power to the Governor to suspend official member.

8.—(1) The Governor may at any time, by an instrument under the Public Seal of the Colony, suspend any official member of the Court of Policy, other than an *ex officio* member, from the exercise of his functions as a member of the said Court.

(2) Every such suspension shall be forthwith reported by the Governor to one of His Majesty's Principal Secretaries of State, and shall remain in force unless and until it is either removed by the Governor, by an instrument under the said Seal, or disallowed by His Majesty.

Provisional appointment of official member.

9.—(1) Whenever any official member of the Court of Policy, other than an *ex officio* member, is suspended from the exercise of his functions as a member of the Court, or is declared by the Governor, by an instrument under the Public Seal of the Colony, to be incapable of exercising his functions as a member of the Court, or is temporarily absent from the Colony, or is acting in an office of which the holder is, by the provisions of this Ordinance, an *ex officio*

Amd. 6 of 1914, s. 3.

member of the Court of Policy, or has ceased to hold a public office in the Colony, the Governor may, by an instrument under the said Seal, appoint some other person holding a public office in the Colony to be provisionally a member of the Court of Policy in the place of the member so suspended, or declared incapable, or temporarily absent, or acting as aforesaid, or who has ceased to hold a public office in the Colony. (Amd. 6 of 1901, s. 2.)

(2) Every such provisional appointment may be disallowed by His Majesty or may be revoked by the Governor by an instrument under the said Seal.

(3) Every person so provisionally appointed shall be, to all intents and purposes, an official member of the Court of Policy until his appointment is disallowed, or revoked, or superseded by the permanent appointment of an official member of the said Court, or until the person in whose place he has been appointed is relieved from suspension, or is declared by the Governor, by an instrument under the said Seal, to be capable of exercising the functions of a member of the Court, or returns to the Colony, as the case may be.

Elected Members.

Elected members.

10. The elected members of the Court of Policy shall be persons duly qualified and elected as hereinafter mentioned.

Precedence of elected members.

11. The elected members of the Court of Policy shall rank amongst themselves in the order of date of their election, and if two or more members are elected on the same day, they shall rank amongst themselves in the alphabetical order of their names.

Amd. 24 of 1909, s. 3.

Notwithstanding anything contained in this section, where two elected members of the Court of Policy are returned for the same Electoral District or Division on the same day, the member who received the largest number of votes shall rank before the other member.

Qualification of elected members. (S. 4 of 24 of 1909 replaces s. 12 of 1 of 1891.)

12. No person shall be capable of being elected a member of the Court of Policy, or, having been so elected, shall sit or vote in the said Court, who—

(1) Is not entitled to vote at the election of a member of the said Court for any Electoral District or Division ; or

(2) Is a Minister of Religion ; or

(3) Is the holder of any office of emolument under the Crown or under the Government of this Colony ; or

(4) Has failed for the space of three months to comply with any order of the Supreme Court made after the commencement of this Ordinance, directing him to pay any money held or received by him in a fiduciary capacity ; or

(5) Does not possess some one of the following property qualifications, namely,—

(a) Ownership, under a title by grant from the Crown, transport, letters of decree, inheritance *ab intestato vel ex testamento*, devise, or marriage, or possession under a licence of occupancy from the Crown, of not less than eighty acres of land unencumbered by mortgage situate in the Colony, of which not less than forty acres are actually and *bona fide* under cultivation; or

(*b*) Ownership of immovable property situate in the Colony, under any such title as aforesaid, of the value over and above the amount of any mortgage of not less than five thousand dollars; or

(*c*) Ownership, or possession under a lease for twenty years or upwards, of any house or house and land situate in the Colony, the annual rental or value whereof over and above the interest payable under any mortgage is not less than twelve hundred dollars.

Provision as to joint owners or tenants.

13.—(1) Where any land, or immovable property, or house, or house and land situate in the Colony is or are jointly owned or occupied by more persons than one as joint owners or tenants, each of such joint owners or tenants shall be deemed to have the property qualification for an elected member of the Court of Policy in case the total area of the land owned or occupied and the part thereof actually and *bona fide* under cultivation or the value of such land, or immovable property, or house, or house and land are or is such as when divided by the number of such owners or tenants, gives a qualification for each of such owners or tenants, but not otherwise.   (Amd. 1 of 1898, s. 3.)

Qualification by shares in a company. (S. 5 of 24 of 1909 replaces s. 13 (2) of 1 of 1891.)

(2) Where any land, or immovable property, or house and land, situate in the Colony is owned or occupied by any Company every shareholder in such Company shall be deemed to have the property qualification for an elected member of the Court of Policy in case—

(*a*) The total area of the land so owned or occupied and the part thereof actually and *bona fide* under cultivation unencumbered by any mortgage; or

(*b*) The value of such land or immovable property over and above the amount of any mortgage; or

(*c*) The annual rental or value of such house, or house and land over and above the interest payable under any mortgage

are or is such as when divided by the number of shares into which the capital of the said Company is divided and multiplied by the number of shares held by such shareholder gives a qualification for such shareholder.

Penalty on
elected mem-
ber sitting
or voting
without
qualification,
etc.

14. Every person who—

(1) Having been returned as an elected member of the Court of Policy, but not having been, at the time of his election, qualified to be an elected member, sits or votes in the said Court; or

(2) Having been duly returned as an elected member of the said Court, sits or votes in the said Court after his seat has become vacant,

shall be liable to a penalty of two hundred and fifty dollars for every day on which he so sits and votes; and such penalty may be recovered, with costs, by an action in the Supreme Court of British Guiana in its civil jurisdiction by any person who may sue for the same.

Vacation of
seat by elected
member.

15. If any elected member of the Court of Policy—

(1) Dies or, by writing under his hand addressed to the Governor, resigns his seat in the said Court; or

(2) Departs from the Colony without the leave of the said Court or of the Governor; or

(3) Having departed from the Colony with such leave, remains out of the Colony after such leave has expired; or

(4) Fails without reasonable excuse (the sufficiency whereof shall be determined by the said Court) to attend any six consecutive sittings of the said Court; or

(5) Ceases to possess a property qualification mentioned in section 12; or

(6) Makes any declaration or acknowledgment of allegiance to any Foreign State or Power; or

(7) Becomes a citizen or subject of any Foreign State or Power; or

(8) Becomes a Minister of Religion; or

(9) Accepts any office of emolument under the Crown or under the Government of this Colony; or

(10) Is adjudicated a bankrupt in the United Kingdom of Great Britain and Ireland or an insolvent in this Colony; or

(11) Is declared by any competent Court to be *non compos mentis*; or

(12) Is sentenced in any part of His Majesty's Dominions to death, penal servitude, or imprisonment with hard labour for any term exceeding twelve months; or

Supplemented
by 24 of 1909,
s. 6.

(13) Fails for the space of three months to comply with any order of the Supreme Court made after the commencement of this Ordinance, directing him to pay any money held or received by him in a fiduciary capacity,

K K

his seat in the said Court shall thereupon *ipso facto* become vacant. (Amd. 1 of 1898, s. 33, and 22 of 1902, s. 2.)

Issue of writ for election of new member.

16. Whenever it is shown, to the satisfaction of the Governor, that the seat of an elected member of the Court of Policy has become vacant, the Governor shall, within one month thereafter, issue a writ for the election of a new member of the said Court in the place of the member whose seat has become vacant; but if any question arises as to the the fact of such vacancy, it shall be referred to and decided by the said Court.

Taking of oath by elected member.

17. Every elected member of the Court of Policy shall, before he sits or votes in the Court, take and subscribe the oath of allegiance to His Majesty : Provided that every person authorized by law to make an affirmation instead of taking an oath may make such affirmation instead of taking the said oath.

Granting of leave of absence to elected member. (S. 7 of 24 of 1909 replaces s. 18 of 1 of 1891.) Supplemented by 34 of 1919, s. 2.

18. The Court of Policy, or, in non-session of the said Court, the Governor, may grant to any elected member leave of absence, not exceeding six months at any one time, from the service of the said Court, whether such member does or does not remain in the Colony :

Provided always that it shall be lawful for the Governor with the consent of the Combined Court to grant leave of absence for any period or extended period beyond six months to any elected member of the Court of Policy who may in the opinion of the Combined Court be engaged beyond the Colony in any matter of public concern to the Colony.

Sessions and Meetings.

Prorogation and dissolution.

19. The Governor may at any time, by Proclamation, prorogue or dissolve the Court of Policy.

Duration of the Court.

20. The Governor shall dissolve the Court of Policy at the expiration of five years from the date of the return of the first writ for the election of elected members at the last preceding general election, if the said Court has not been sooner dissolved.

Time of holding general election.

21. A general election of members of the Court of Policy shall be held at such time within two months after every dissolution of the said Court as the Governor may, by Proclamation, appoint.

Holding of sessions.

22.—(1) The sessions of the Court of Policy shall be held at such times and places as the Governor may from time to time, by Proclamation, appoint.

(2) There shall be at least two sessions of the said Court in every year, and there shall not be an interval of more than eight months between the last sitting in one session and the first sitting in the next session.

Vacancy among members not to affect proceedings.

23. The existence of any vacancy or vacancies among the members of the Court of Policy shall not affect the validity of any proceeding of the said Court.

Quorum.

24.—(1) No business, except that of adjournment, shall be transacted at any meeting of the Court of Policy unless there are present nine members besides the Governor or other presiding member.

(2) No member of the Court of Policy shall be entitled, after having taken his seat at any meeting of the Court, to withdraw himself from such meeting without the leave of the Governor or other presiding member, and if any member so withdraws himself without such leave, it shall be lawful for the remaining members, not being less than seven in number besides the Governor or other presiding member, to proceed with and transact business in the same manner as if a quorum had been present.

President of the Court.

25.—(1) The Governor, if present, or, in his absence, the member present who stands first in order of precedence, shall preside at the meetings of the Court of Policy.

(2) The Governor or other presiding member shall be the sole judge of order at any meeting of the said Court.

Voting.

26.—(1) Every question before the Court of Policy shall be determined by the votes of a majority of the members present.

(2) The Governor or other presiding member shall have an original vote on all such questions and also a casting vote, if the votes are equally divided.

(3) The votes of members of the said Court shall be taken in the inverse order of their precedence.

Adjournment.

27. The Governor or other presiding member may at any time adjourn any meeting of the Court of Policy, and no motion for adjournment shall be in order.

Legislation.

Publication of Ordinances.

28.—(1) Every Ordinance enacted by the Governor with the advice and consent of the Court of Policy shall be published in *The Official Gazette* and in a newspaper of the Colony as soon as possible after it has received the assent of the Governor or of His Majesty, and shall, unless some other time is therein specified for its coming into force, come into force on such publication in *The Official Gazette*.

(2) The date of such publication in *The Official Gazette* shall be printed in some convenient place on each copy of the Ordinance, and shall be taken notice of, in all Courts and for all other purposes, as the date of such Ordinance becoming law.

Enrolling of Ordinances.
Amd. 6 of 1914, s. 5, and 23 of 1914.

29.—(1) So soon as an Ordinance enacted by the Governor with the advice and consent of the Court of Policy becomes law, a copy thereof, signed by the Governor, shall be delivered by the Clerk of the Court to the Colonial Secretary.

(2) The Colonial Secretary shall cause such copy to be impressed with the Public Seal of the Colony and to be deposited in a fireproof safe to be provided for that purpose.

(3) The Colonial Secretary shall be personally responsible for the safe keeping of all such copies of Ordinances, which shall be styled and known as " Rolls of the Court of Policy."

PART II.

THE COMBINED COURT.

Composition of the Combined Court.

30. The Combined Court shall consist of the members of the Court of Policy and six Financial Representatives.

Precedence of members.

31. In the Combined Court the Members of the Court of Policy shall take precedence of the Financial Representatives and shall rank amongst themselves in the order hereinbefore mentioned. The Financial Representatives shall rank amongst themselves in the order of date of their election, and if two or more Financial Representatives are elected on the same day, they shall rank amongst themselves in the alphabetical order of their names.

The Financial Representatives.

The Financial Representatives.

32. The Financial Representatives shall be persons qualified and elected as hereinafter mentioned.

Qualification of Financial Representative.
(S. 8 of 24 of 1909 replaces s. 33 of 1 of 1891.)

33. The qualifications for election as a Financial Representative shall be the qualifications hereinbefore prescribed for election as an elected member of the Court of Policy : Provided that either of the following property qualifications shall be a sufficient property qualification in lieu of those specified in sub-section five of section twelve of this Ordinance :—

(a) Receipt of a clear annual income of not less than one thousand four hundred and forty dollars arising from any kind of property in the Colony not mentioned in the other property qualifications over and above any interest payable under any mortgage thereon ; or

(b) Receipt of a clear annual income of not less than one thousand four hundred and forty dollars from any profession, business, or trade carried on in the Colony.

Penalty on
Financial Re-
presentative
sitting or vot-
ing without
qualification.

34. Every person who—

(1) Having been returned as a Financial Representative, but not having been, at the time of his
election, qualified to be a Financial Representative, sits or votes in the Combined Court ; or

(2) Having been duly returned as a Financial Representative, sits or votes in the said Court after
his seat has become vacant,

shall be liable to a penalty of two hundred and forty
dollars for every day on which he so sits or votes ; and
such penalty may be recovered, with costs, by an action
in the Supreme Court of British Guiana in its civil jurisdiction by any person who may sue for the same.

Vacation of
seat by
Financial
Representa-
tive.

35. If any Financial Representative—

(1) Dies or by writing under his hand addressed to the
Governor, resigns his seat in the Combined Court ;
or

(2) Departs from the Colony without the leave of the
said Court or of the Governor ; or

(3) Having departed from the Colony with such leave,
remains out of the Colony after such leave has
expired ; or

(4) Fails without reasonable excuse (the sufficiency
whereof shall be determined by the said Court)
to attend any six consecutive sittings of the said
Court ; or

(5) Ceases to possess a property qualification hereinbefore prescribed for a Financial Representative ; or

(6) Makes any declaration or acknowledgment of
allegiance to any Foreign State or Power ; or

(7) Becomes a citizen or subject of any Foreign State or
Power ; or

(8) Becomes a Minister of Religion ; or

(9) Accepts any office of emolument under the Crown or
under the Government of this Colony ; or

(10) Is adjudicated a bankrupt in the United Kingdom
of Great Britain and Ireland or an insolvent in
this Colony ; or

(11) Is declared by any competent Court to be *non
compos mentis* ; or

(12) Is sentenced in any part of His Majesty's Dominions
to death, penal servitude, or imprisonment with
hard labour for any term exceeding twelve
months ; or

Supplemented
by 24 of 1909,
s. 9.

(13) Fails for the space of three months to comply with
any order of the Supreme Court made after the
commencement of this Ordinance, directing him

to pay any money held or received by him in a fiduciary capacity,

his seat in the said Court shall thereupon *ipso facto* become vacant. (Amd. 1 of 1898, s. 33, and 22 of 1902, s. 2.)

36. Whenever it is shown to the satisfaction of the Governor, that the seat of a Financial Representative has become vacant, the Governor shall within one month thereafter, issue a writ for the election of a Financial Representative in the place of the Financial Representative whose seat has become vacant; but if any question arises as to the fact of such vacancy, it shall be referred to and decided by the Combined Court.

37. Every Financial Representative shall, before he sits and votes in the Combined Court, take and subscribe the oath of allegiance to His Majesty : Provided that every person authorized by law to make an affirmation instead of taking an oath may make such affirmation instead of taking the said oath.

38. The Combined Court, or, in non-session of the said Court, the Governor, may grant to any Financial Representative leave of absence, not exceeding six months at any one time, from the service of the said Court, whether such Financial Representative does or does not remain in the Colony :

Provided always that it shall be lawful for the Governor with the consent of the Combined Court to grant leave of absence for any period or extended period beyond six months to any Financial Representative who may in the opinion of the Combined Court be engaged beyond the Colony in any matter of public concern to the Colony.

39. The Financial Representatives shall vacate their seats on the dissolution of the Court of Policy.

Sessions and Meetings.

40.—(1) The sessions of the Combined Court shall be held at such times and places as the Governor may from time to time, by Proclamation, appoint.

(2) There shall be at least one session of the said Court in every year, and there shall not be an interval of twelve months between the last sitting in one session and the first sitting in the next session.

41. The existence of any vacancy or vacancies among the members of the Combined Court shall not affect the validity of any proceeding of the said Court.

42.—(1) No business, except that of adjournment, shall be transacted at any meeting of the Combined Court unless

Marginalia: Fresh election on vacation of seat of Financial Representative. — Taking of oath by Financial Representative. — Granting of leave of absence to Financial Representative. — Supplemented by 34 of 1919, s. 3. — Tenure of seat of Financial Representative. — Holding of sessions. — Vacancy among members not to affect proceedings. — Quorum.

there are present eleven members besides the Governor or other presiding member.

(2) No member of the Combined Court shall be entitled after having taken his seat at any meeting of the Court, to withdraw himself from such meeting without the leave of the Governor or other presiding member, and if any member so withdraws himself without such leave, it shall be lawful for the remaining members, not being less than seven in number besides the Governor or other presiding member, to proceed with and transact business in the same manner as if a quorum had been present.

President of the Court.

43.—(1) The Governor, if present, or, in his absence, the member present who stands first in order of precedence, shall preside at the meetings of the Combined Court : Provided that when in Committee of Ways and Means the Combined Court may elect any member of such Court to be Chairman of such Committee.   (Amd. 37 of 1903, s. 5.)

(2) The Governor or other presiding member shall be the sole judge of order at any meeting of the said Court.

Voting.

44.—(1) Every question before the Combined Court shall be determined by the votes of the majority of the members present.

(2) The Governor or other presiding member shall have an original vote on all such questions and also a casting vote, if the votes are equally divided.

(3) The votes of members of the said Court shall be taken in the inverse order of their precedence.

Adjournment.

45. The Governor or other presiding member may at any time adjourn any meeting of the Combined Court, and no motion for adjournment shall be in order.

Prorogation, etc.

Prorogation and dissolution.

46. The Governor may at any time, by Proclamation, prorogue the Combined Court, and the said Court shall *ipso facto* be dissolved by the dissolution of the Court of Policy.

General election after dissolution.

47. A general election of the Financial Representatives shall be held at such time within two months after every dissolution of the Court of Policy as the Governor may by Proclamation appoint.

Clerk of the Combined Court.

48. The Clerk of the Court of Policy shall also be the Clerk of the Combined Court.

PART III.

ELECTION OF MEMBERS AND FINANCIAL REPRESENTATIVES.

Electoral Districts and Divisions.

Division of the Colony into Electoral Districts and Divisions.

49 For the purposes of the election of members of the Court of Policy and of Financial Representatives, the Colony shall be divided into five Electoral Districts, with two Divisions in each of two of such Districts, as follows, that is to say,—

No. 1.—The County of Demerara, exclusive of the City of Georgetown :
 (*a*) Eastern Division, and
 (*b*) Western Division.
No. 2.—The County of Essequebo;
 (*a*) North-Western Division, and
 (*b*) South-Eastern Division.
No. 3.—The County of Berbice, exclusive of the Town of New Amsterdam.
No. 4.—The City of Georgetown.
No. 5.—The Town of New Amsterdam.

Boundaries of Divisions.

50.—(1) The Eastern Division of the County of Demerara shall comprise all that portion of the County, excepting the City of Georgetown, lying to the East of the River Demerara, and the Western Division shall comprise all that portion of the County lying to the West of the said River. The islands in the said River shall form part of the Eastern Division.

(2) The North-Western Division of the County of Essequebo shall comprise all that portion of the County lying to the West and North-West of the River Essequebo as far as its junction with the River Massaruni, and thence all that part of the County lying to the West of the River Massaruni, and the South-Eastern Division shall comprise all the remainder of the County, including the Islands.

Distribution of seats of the elected members.

51. For each of the Electoral Districts No. 3 and No. 5 and for each Division of the Electoral Districts No. 1 and No. 2 there shall be returned one elected member of the Court of Policy, and for Electoral District No. 4 there shall be returned two elected members of the said Court.

Distribution of seats of the Financial Representatives.

52. For each of the Electoral Districts No. 1, No. 3, No. 4, and No. 5, and for each Division of the Electoral District No. 2 there shall be returned one Financial Representative.

The Franchise.

General qualification of voter.

53. Subject to the provisions hereinafter contained, every male person shall be entitled to be registered in any year as a voter, and, when registered, to vote at the election of a member of the Court of Policy or of a Financial Representative for an Electoral District or Division, as the case may be, who is qualified as follows, that is to say,—

(1) Has attained the age of twenty-one years;
(2) Is under no legal incapacity;
(3) Is a British subject by birth or naturalization; and
(4) Possesses within the District or Division some one of the following property qualifications hereinafter mentioned.

Property qualifications for County voter.

54. The property qualifications for a County voter shall be—

(1) Ownership, during the six months previous to registration, under a title by grant from the Crown, transport, letters of decree, inheritance *ab intestato vel ex testamento*, devise, or marriage, or possession under a licence of occupancy from the Crown, of not less than three acres of land actually and *bona fide* under cultivation; or

(2) Ownership, during the six months previous to registration, of a house or of a house and land, of the annual rental or value of not less than ninety-six dollars; or

(3) Occupation or tenancy, during the six months previous to registration, of not less than six acres of land actually and *bona fide* under cultivation, secured by lease or any document in writing for three years or upwards, such lease or document being deposited or recorded in the Registrar's Office; or

(4) Occupation or tenancy, during the six months previous to registration, of a house or of a house and land, of the annual rental or value of not less than one hundred and ninety-two dollars, secured by lease or any document in writing for one year or upwards, deposited or recorded as aforesaid; or

(5) Possession or enjoyment of an annual income or salary which (together with any sum paid or allowed to him or on his behalf for board or lodging or board and lodging) amounts to not less than three hundred dollars, coupled with residence in the District or Division, such possession or enjoyment and residence having subsisted during the six months previous to registration; or

Amd. by 24 of 1909, s. 10, to $300.

(6) Payment, during the twelve months previous to registration, of direct taxes to the Colonial Revenue of twenty dollars or upwards, coupled with residence in the District or Division during

the six months previous to registration : Provided that no licence duty of any kind shall be deemed to be within the meaning of the term " direct taxes." (Amd. 1 of 1898, ss. 4 and 33.)

Property qualifications for City or Town Voter. (S. 11 of 24 of 1909 replaces s. 55 of 1 of 1891.)

55. The property qualifications for a City or Town voter shall be—

(1) Ownership, during the six months previous to registration, under a title by grant from the Crown, transport, letters of decree, inheritance *ab intestato vel ex testamento*, devise, or marriage, of a house or land or of land with a house or other erections thereon, of the value of not less than five hundred dollars as appraised for local taxation; or

(2) Occupation or tenancy, during the six months previous to registration, of a house or land or of land with a house or other erections thereon of the annual rental or value of not less than one hundred and twenty dollars, secured by lease or any document in writing for one year or upwards, such lease or document being deposited or recorded in the Registrar's Office of the County in which the City or Town is situated; or

(3) Possession or enjoyment of an annual income or salary which (together with any sum paid or allowed to him or on his behalf for board or lodging or board and lodging) amount to not less than three hundred dollars, coupled with residence in the District, such possession or enjoyment and residence having subsisted during the six months previous to registration; or

(4) Payment, during the twelve months previous to registration, of direct taxes to the Colonial Revenue of twenty dollars or upwards, coupled with residence in the District during the six months previous to registration : Provided that no licence duty of any kind shall be deemed to be within the meaning of the term " direct taxes." (1 of 1898, ss. 4 and 5.)

Provision as as to joint owners and tenants.

56.—(1) Where any land, or house, or house and land, or house and land or appurtenances in any Electoral District of Division is or are jointly owned or occupied by more persons than one as owners or tenants, each of such joint owners or tenants shall be entitled to be registered as a voter for such Electoral District or Division in respect of such land, or house, or house and land, or house and land or appurtenances, in case the area of the land actually and *bona fide* under cultivation or the value of such land, or house, or house and land, or house and land or appurtenances is such as when divided by the number of such owners or tenants, gives a qualification for each and every such owner or tenant, but not otherwise.   (Amd. 1 of 1898, s. 5.)

(2) Where any land, or house, or house and land, or house and land or appurtenances in any Electoral District or Division is owned or occupied by any Company, every shareholder in such Company shall be entitled to be registered as a voter for such Electoral District or Division in respect of such land, or house, or house and land, or house and land or appurtenances in case the area of land actually and *bona fide* under cultivation or the value of such land or house, or house and land, or house and land or appurtenances is such as when divided by the number of shares into which the capital of the said Company is divided and multiplied by the number of shares held by such shareholder gives a qualification for such shareholder.   (37 of 1903, s. 4.)

Disqualifications for being voter.

57. No person shall be entitled to be registered as a voter who—

(1) Cannot read and write some language, provided always that any person who knows how to read and write but is incapacitated by blindness or other physical cause from reading or writing or reading and writing shall not be disqualified from being a voter ; or

(2) Has, within the twelve months previous to registration, received any relief from public or parochial funds ; or

(3) Has been sentenced in any part of His Majesty's Dominions to death, or penal servitude, or imprisonment with hard labour, or for any term exceeding twelve months, and has not either suffered the punishment to which he was sentenced or such other punishment as by competent authority may have been substituted for the same, or received a free pardon from His Majesty. (Amd. 1 of 1898, s. 6.)

Registration of Voters.

Making of annual Register of Voters.

58.—(1) In each Electoral District or Division a Register shall be made in every year of the persons entitled to vote at the election of a member of the Court of Policy or of a Financial Representative for such District or Division.

(2) The Register to be made in every year shall come into force on the first day of October in the same year, and shall remain in force for one year from that date.   (1 of 1898, s. 7.)

Appointment of Registering Officers.

59. The Governor may from time to time appoint a Stipendiary Magistrate or any other fit and proper person to be the Registering Officer of each Electoral District or Division. (1 of 1898, s. 8, amd. 6 of 1901, s. 3.)

Notice to persons entitled to register to make claim. Amd. 6 of 1914, s. 6.

60. On or before the first day of April in each year the Registering Officer of each Electoral District or Division shall cause to be published in the *Gazette* and to be posted on or near the doors of such Churches and Chapels as he may deem necessary, and the Police Stations in his District or Division, a notice requiring every person in his District or Division who may be entitled to vote at the election of a member of the Court of Policy or of a Financial Representative to deliver or cause to be delivered to him, on or before the first day of May then next ensuing, a notice of his claim to be registered as a voter : Provided that no person whose name is placed upon the Register of Voters for the time being in force under this Ordinance for any Electoral District or Division shall be required thereafter to make any such claim as aforesaid, so long as he retains the same qualification. (1 of 1898, s. 9.)

Proceedings preliminary to making up list of voters. Amd. 6 of 1914, s. 6 (1).

First Schedule : Form 1.

61.—(1) Between the first day of April and the first day of May both inclusive, in each year, every person who is entitled to be registered as a voter in any District or Division shall deliver or cause to be delivered to the Registering Officer of the District or Division a notice of his claim to be registered as a voter, according to the Form contained in the First Schedule to this Ordinance, and shall produce or cause to be produced such deeds or documents or such other evidence as may be necessary to establish his claim to be so registered.

(2) The Registering Officer shall inquire into, examine and investigate the qualification in respect of which such claim is made, and shall receive such evidence as may be necessary to prove to his satisfaction that the person making such claim possesses the qualification in respect of which he claims to be registered as a voter. Every person who in support of any such claim knowingly swears or affirms anything material to the validity thereof which is false or incorrect shall be deemed guilty of wilful and corrupt perjury and be liable to be prosecuted and, if convicted, punished accordingly.

(3) If the Registering Officer is satisfied that the person making such claim possesses the qualification in respect of which such claim is made, he shall register such person in the manner hereinafter provided, otherwise he shall disallow such claim.

Amd. 6 of 1914, s. 6 (2).

(4) The Registering Officer shall before the first day of June, in each year, ascertain whether any of the persons admitted and registered as voters in the list made up as hereinafter mentioned, in the year immediately preceding,

have ceased to retain the qualifications in respect of which they were registered or have become disqualified by being convicted of an offence relating to elections under this Ordinance or whether any of them are dead ; and he shall, in the next List of Voters to be made up by him as hereinafter provided, write the words " objected to " against the name of every person who he has cause to believe has ceased to retain the qualification in respect of which he was registered, or become disqualified as aforesaid, and shall write the word " dead " against the name of every person whom he has grounds for believing to be dead.

(5) Any person in the public service of the Colony shall, on being required by the Registering Officer to do so, furnish him with such information and assistance as the Registering Officer may consider necessary for the purposes of any inquiry, examination and investigation under this section and generally for the purpose of preparing the list of voters hereinafter mentioned. (1 of 1898, s. 10.)

Making up and publication of list of voters. Amd. 6 of 1914, s. 7, and 24 of 1909, s. 12.

62.—(1) The Registering Officer shall, on or before the first day of June in each year, make out an alphabetical list, according to Form 2 contained in the First Schedule to this Ordinance, of all persons registered as voters in the Register of Voters then in force, and of all persons claiming to be registered as voters whose claim he has allowed, and also showing the names of persons against which he has written the words " objected to " and " dead " respectively,

First Schedule : Form 2.

and shall cause a copy of such list, signed by him, to be published in the *Gazette* ,and also to be posted in the manner mentioned in section 60 until the twenty-second day of July then next ensuing. (1 of 1898, s. 11.)

Ord. 6 of 1914, s. 7.

(2) In case any Electoral District or Division is divided into Polling Areas the Registering Officer shall make out a separate alphabetical list of voters resident within any Polling Area in existence at that date.

Making of objections to list.

63.—(1) Every person whose name has been omitted from any such List of Voters, and who claims to have his name inserted therein, shall, on or before the twenty-second day of July, give notice thereof in writing to the Registering Officer, according to Form 3 contained in the First Schedule to this Ordinance ; and every person whose name appears in any such list may object to any person whose name also appears therein as not being entitled to have his name inserted therein.

First Schedule : Form 3.

(2) Every person so objecting shall, on or before the twenty-second day of July, give or cause to be given to the Registering Officer and to the person objected to, or leave or cause to be left at the usual or last known place of abode of such person, notice of such objection in writing, according to Form 4 contained in the First Schedule to this Ordinance.

First Schedule : Form 4.

(3) It shall be sufficient in every case of notice to any person objected to in any List of Voters if the notice so required to be given as aforesaid shall be sent as hereinafter provided by the post directed to the person to whom the same is sent, at his place of abode, as described in such List of Voters, and where any person shall be desirous of sending any such notice of objection by post, he shall deliver the same duly directed, open and in duplicate, to the Postmaster of any post office where money orders are received or paid within such hours as shall have been previously given notice of at such post office, and under such regulations with respect to the registration of such letters and the fee to be paid for such registration as shall from time to time be made by the Postmaster-General in that behalf; and in all cases in which such fee is duly paid, the Postmaster shall compare the said notice and the duplicate, and on being satisfied that they are alike in their address and contents, shall forward one of them to its address by the post and shall return the other to the party bringing the same, duly stamped with the stamp of the said post office, and the production by the party who posted such notice of such stamped duplicate shall be evidence of the notice having been given to the person at the place mentioned in such duplicate on the date purporting to be the date of such acknowledgment of receipt; provided always that if such place of abode is out of this Colony then it shall be sufficient if such notice is sent as aforesaid to the duly constituted attorney (if any) of the person objected to.

(4) Immediately after the twenty-second day of July, the Registering Officer shall prepare a list of all such claims and objections and of the names of the persons who have made the same. (1 of 1898, s. 12.) Every list of claims and objections prepared by a Registering Officer under this sub-section shall be published by him in the *Gazette* and shall be posted on or near the doors of such Churches and Chapels as he may deem necessary, and at the Police Stations in his Electoral District or Division.

64.—(1) In each year the Governor shall appoint Barristers-at-Law or Advocates to be Revising Barristers for the purpose of revising the Lists of Voters in the several Electoral Districts and Divisions.

(2) A Revising Barrister may act for more Electoral Districts or Divisions than one. (1 of 1898, s. 13, amd. 22 of 1902, s. 4.)

65.—(1) Between the twenty-second day of July, and the seventh day of September, both inclusive, in each year, the Revising Barrister for each Electoral District or Division

Amd. 24 of 1909, s. 21 (2).

Amd. 24 of 1909, s. 21 (2).

Publication of lists of claims and objections to voters list. Added by 24 of 1909, s. 13.

Appointment of Revising Barristers.

Revision of list.

shall hold an open Court in such District or Division for the purpose of revising the said List of Voters.

(2) The said Court shall be held on such days and at such places as may be fixed by the Revising Barrister, and not less than six days' notice of the holding of such Court, and of the place at which the same is to be held, shall be given in *The Official Gazette* and by posting such notice in the manner mentioned in section 60.

(3) The Registering Officer shall deliver or cause to be delivered to the Revising Barrister, before the holding of the said Court, the List of Voters made out by him as aforesaid, and the list of persons claiming to be registered as voters and of those objected to as such.

(4) The Revising Barrister shall with respect to the List of Voters which he is appointed to revise, perform the duties and have the powers following :—

(a) He shall correct any mistake which is proved to him to have been made in the list ;

(b) He may correct any mistake which is proved to him to have been made in any claim or notice of objection ;

(c) He shall expunge the name of every person whether objected to or not, whose qualification as stated in the list is insufficient in law to entitle such person to be included therein ;

(d) He shall expunge the name of every person who, whether objected to or not, is proved to the Revising Barrister to be dead, or disqualified by having been convicted of an offence relating to elections ;

(e) The Revising Barrister shall expunge the name of every person whether objected to or not, whose name or place of abode or the nature of whose qualification, or the name or situation of whose qualifying property, if the qualification is in respect of property, or any other particulars respecting whom by law required to be stated in the list is or are either wholly omitted or in the judgment of the Revising Barrister insufficiently described for the purpose of being identified, unless the matter or matters so omitted or insufficiently described be supplied to the satisfaction of the Revising Barrister, before he has completed the revision of the list in which the omission or insufficient description occurs, and in case such matter or matters shall be so supplied, he shall then and there insert the same in such list ;

(f) He shall expunge the name of every person whether objected to or not, where it is proved to the

Revising Barrister that such person was on the
last day on which his name could have been
inserted by the Registering Officer in the list
incapacitated by any law or Ordinance from voting
at an election for the electoral district or division
to which the list relates;

(g) Before expunging from a list the name of any person
not objected to, the Revising Barrister shall cause
such notice (if any) as shall appear to him necessary
or proper under the circumstances, of the proposal
to expunge the name, to be given to or left at the
usual or last known place of abode of such person,
and the provisions of section 63 sub-section (3)
shall apply to any such notice;

(h) Subject as herein otherwise provided the Revising
Barrister shall retain the name of every person
not objected to and also of every person objected
to unless the objector appears by himself or by
some person on his behalf in support of his
objection;

(i) If the objector so appears the Revising Barrister shall
require him to prove that he gave the notice or
notices of objection required by law to be given by
him and to give *prima facie* proof of the ground of
objection, and for that purpose may himself
examine and allow the objector to examine any
person on oath touching the alleged ground of
objection, and, unless such proof is given to his
satisfaction, shall subject as herein otherwise
provided retain the name of the person objected
to;

(j) The *prima facie* proof shall be deemed to be given by
the objector if it is shown to the satisfaction of the
Revising Barrister by evidence, repute or otherwise that there is reasonable ground for believing
that the objection is well founded and that by
reason of the person objected to not being present
for examination or some other reason, the objector
is prevented from discovering or proving the truth
respecting the entry objected to;

(k) If such proof is given by the objector as herein prescribed, then unless the person objected to appears
by himself or by some person on his behalf and
proves that he was entitled on the last day on
which his name could have been inserted by the
Registering Officer in the list, to have his name
inserted in the list in respect of the qualification
described in such list, the Revising Barrister shall
expunge the name of the person objected to;

(*l*) Where the matter stated in a list or claim, or proved to the Revising Barrister in relation to any alleged right to be on the list, is in the judgment of the Revising Barrister insufficient in law to constitute a qualification of the nature or description stated or claimed, but sufficient in law to constitute a qualification of some other nature or description, the Revising Barrister shall (as the case may be) correct such list by inserting such qualification accordingly, or insert such name in the list with such qualification;

(*m*) Except as herein provided, and whether any person is objected to or not, no evidence shall be given of any other qualification than that which is described in the list or claim as the case may be, nor shall the Revising Barrister be at liberty to change the description of the qualification as it appears on the list except for the purpose of more clearly and accurately defining the same;

(*n*) If any person who has given to the Registering Officer of any electoral district or division due notice of his claim to have his name inserted in the List of Voters for that district or division has been omitted from such list, the Revising Barrister upon the revision of such list shall insert therein the name of the person so omitted in case it is proved to the satisfaction of such Barrister that such person gave due notice of such his claim to the said Registering Officer, and that on the last day on which the Registering Officer could have inserted his name in such list he was entitled to have his name inserted therein;

(*o*) Any person whose name is on any List of Voters may oppose the claim of any person so omitted as aforesaid to have his name inserted in such list; and such person intending to oppose any such claim shall, in the Court holden for the revision of such list and before the hearing of the said claim, give notice in writing to the Revising Barrister of his intention to oppose the said claim, and shall thereupon be admitted to oppose the same by evidence or otherwise without any previous or other notice, and shall have the same rights, powers and liabilities as to costs, appeal and other matters relating to the hearing and determination of the said claim as any person who has duly objected to the name of any other person being retained on the List of Voters, and who appears and proves the requisite notices as hereinbefore mentioned.

L L

(*p*) The Revising Barrister shall expunge from the List of Voters the name of every person against which the Registering Officer has written the words "objected to" or the word "dead," unless it is proved to his satisfaction that such person is entitled to have his name retained in the list; and the Registering Officer shall not, in respect of any such person, be deemed to be a "person objecting" or an "objector" within the meaning of this section or of section 63 of this Ordinance.

(*q*) In acting under this section the Revising Barrister shall not, in the case of any person objected to as disqualified by being convicted of an offence relating to elections, and claiming to be entitled to have his name inserted in the list, determine whether he has or has not been guilty of such offence, but only whether he has been so convicted as aforesaid. (1 of 1898, s. 14.)

Powers of Revising Barrister.

66.—(1) Every Revising Barrister holding a Court under this Ordinance shall have power to adjourn the same to such time and place and as often as may be necessary.

(2) The Revising Barrister shall also have power to require the Registrar of the Supreme Court to produce or cause to be produced before him any Register of Voters for the District or Division, and the Revising Barrister shall have a right to inspect the said Register of Voters, as occasion may require, at any Court to be held by him for the revision of the list of voters.

(3) The Revising Barrister shall also have power to administer oaths to the Registrar or other person producing any Register of Voters, and to all persons claiming to be registered as voters or claiming to have any mistake or omission corrected in the list of voters, and to all witnesses produced on either side.

(4) Every person who is authorized by law to make an affirmation instead of taking an oath, may make such an affirmation in every case in which by this Ordinance an oath is required to be taken; and if any person taking any oath required by this Ordinance, or making any affirmation in lieu of such oath, wilfully swears or affirms falsely, such person shall be deemed guilty of perjury, and shall be liable to be indicted and punished accordingly.

(5) In all proceedings before the Revising Barrister the law and rules of evidence to be complied with shall be the same as the law and rules of evidence observed by the Supreme Court in cases within its civil jurisdiction, and the practice and procedure on the hearing of claims and objections shall as nearly as may be conform to the practice and

procedure of the Supreme Court on the hearing of cases within its civil jurisdiction.

(6) The Revising Barrister may at the request of either party by summons under his hand require any person to attend at the Court and give evidence or produce documents for the purpose of the revision, and any person who after the tender to him of a reasonable amount for his expenses fails so to attend or who fails to answer any question put to him by the Revising Barrister in pursuance of this section, or to produce any documents which he is required in pursuance of this section to produce shall be liable to pay such fine not exceeding twenty-four dollars as may be imposed by the Revising Barrister, and the Revising Barrister shall forward to the Stipendiary Magistrate of the District an order in writing imposing such fine, and thereupon the payment of such fine shall be enforced by such Stipendiary Magistrate in all respects as if it were a penalty imposed by him in the exercise of his summary jurisdiction.

(7) The Revising Barrister may order any person to be removed from his Court who interrupts the business of his Court or refuses to obey his lawful orders in respect of the same, and it shall be the duty of the Inspector-General of Police to take care that a Police Constable attends the Revising Barrister's Court during its sittings for the purpose of keeping order therein and of carrying into effect any such order of the Revising Barrister as aforesaid. (1 of 1898, s. 15.)

Settlement of list. **67.**—(1) The Revising Barrister shall, in open Court, determine all claims or objections made before him, and shall write his initials against each name struck out of the List of Voters or inserted therein, and against any mistake or omission corrected, and shall sign his name to every page of the list when the same is finally settled.

(2) If the Revising Barrister is of opinion that the claim or the objection of any person is without foundation or frivolous, he may order such person to pay the costs of the inquiry, including the costs of witnesses, and in every such case the said barrister shall make an order in writing specifying the sum to be paid for such costs (which sum shall not in the case of any one vote exceed the sum of twenty-four dollars), and by and to whom and when and where the said sum is to be paid, and shall date and sign the said order, and deliver it to the person to whom such sum is to be paid or to his representative; and if such sum shall not be paid in accordance with such order, the Stipendiary Magistrate of the District upon proof before him that a true copy of the said order has been served upon or left at the last or usual place of abode of the person ordered to pay such sum, and

that demand of payment having been made he has refused
or neglected to pay the same, shall enforce payment of such
sum as if such order had been a judgment given by him under
No. 11 of 1893. the Petty Debts Recovery Ordinance, 1893 :

Provided always that any such order for the payment of
costs as aforesaid may be made in any case, notwithstanding any party has given notice of his intention to
appeal against any decision of the Revising Barrister in the
same case, but in case of such appeal the said order for the
payment of costs shall be suspended and shall abide the
event of such appeal unless the Supreme Court otherwise
directs, but no appeal shall be allowed or entertained against
or only in respect of any such order for the payment of
costs : Provided also that whenever the Revising Barrister
has made any such order for the payment of costs by any
person who has made any objection as aforesaid, it shall not
be lawful for the Revising Barrister to hear or admit proof of
any other objection or notice of objection made or signed
by the same person until the sum of money ordered to be
paid by him for costs be paid to the person entitled to receive
the same or deposited in the hands of the Revising Barrister
in court for the use of the person so entitled. (1 of 1898
s. 16.)

**Making up of
Register of
Voters.**　　68.—(1) The List of Voters, when finally settled and
signed as aforesaid, shall be delivered or transmitted by the
Revising Barrister to the Registrar, who shall keep the same,
and shall cause the names in such list to be fairly and truly
recorded in alphabetical order in a book to be by him
provided for that purpose, with every name therein
numbered, beginning the numbers from the first name and
continuing them in a regular series to the last name, and
shall cause such recording to be completed within ten days
after the delivering to him of such revised list by the
Revising Barrister.

(2) The book in which such revised list is copied shall be
the Register of Voters for the particular Electoral District
or Division for the twelve months from the first day of
October next ensuing such delivery of such list entitled to
vote at the election of any member of the Court of Policy
or of any Financial Representative for such District or
Division, and all persons whose names are therein, but no
others, shall be entitled to vote at any such election during
such twelve months.

(3) The Registrar shall cause a copy, certified by him to
be correct, of each Register of Voters to be published in *The
Official Gazette* and shall transmit a copy of such *Gazette*
to the Registering Officer of the Electoral District or
Division for his use in preparing the next list of voters.

(4) A copy of *The Official Gazette* containing such copy of any Register of Voters or any document purporting to be a copy of or extract from any Register of Voters, and purporting to be certified by the Registrar as being correct, shall on production be admissible in evidence of the existence and contents of such Register in all Courts in any proceedings under this Ordinance. (1 of 1898, s. 17.)

Appeals from the Revising Barrister.

Who may appeal.

69.—(1) Any person who has made any claim as hereinbefore provided to have his name inserted in any list or made any objection to any other person as not entitled to have his name inserted in any list, or whose name has been expunged from any list and who is dissatisfied with any decision of the Revising Barrister on any point of law material to the result of the case, may either in person or by some person on his behalf give to the Revising Barrister before the rising of the Court on the day on which the decision is given, a notice in writing stating that he desires to appeal and shortly stating the decision against which he desires to appeal.

Statement of case.

(2) The Revising Barrister thereupon shall state in writing the facts which in his judgment have been established by evidence in the case and are material to the matter in question, and shall also state in writing his decision upon the whole case and upon the point of law in question appealed against, and such statement shall be made as nearly as conveniently may be in like manner as is now usual in stating any special case without pleadings for the opinion of the Supreme Court on any question of law arising in any civil action, and the Revising Barrister shall within four days submit the same to the appellant, who shall return the same (having previously if he approves thereof signed the same) to the Revising Barrister, who shall thereupon sign the same and endorse thereon the name of the Electoral District or Division to which the same relates and the respective Christian names and Surnames and places of abode of the appellant and respondent (if any), and shall sign and date such endorsement, and shall deliver such statement so endorsed to the appellant for transmission to the Registrar of the Supreme Court, and the Revising Barrister shall also deliver a copy of such statement so endorsed to the respondent (if any) in such appeal if he requires the same.

Respondents.

(3) The party in whose favour the decision appealed against is given shall be the respondent, but if there is no such party, or if such party or someone on his behalf in open Court declines to support the decision appealed against, the Revising Barrister may name as respondent any voter

for the same District or Division who may consent, and such person so named shall for all purposes be deemed to be the respondent in such appeal, and if no such person consents, the appeal shall proceed without any respondent being necessary. (1 of 1898, s. 18.)

Amendment
as to time
for appealing
against
decision of
Revising
Barrister.
Added by 24
of 1909, s. 4.

Notwithstanding anything contained in this section any person who desires to appeal from a decision of a Revising Barrister under the provisions of this section may give notice of his desire to do so at any time within four days after the day on which the decision is given and a statement of the decision against which he desires to appeal shall not be necessary.

Consolidation
of appeals.

70.—(1) If it appears to the Revising Barrister that the validity of more than one such claim or objection determined by him depends and has been decided by him upon the same point of law, and more parties than one dissatisfied with his decision thereon have given notice of appeal therefrom, the Revising Barrister may declare that the appeals against such decision ought to be consolidated, and after stating a case as hereinbefore provided, shall add thereto a statement that several appeals depend on the same decision and ought to be consolidated, and shall name any person interested and consenting to be the appellant or respondent in such appeal for and on behalf of himself and all other persons in like manner interested, and to prosecute or answer the said appeal, and the persons so named as appellant and respondent, respectively, may in all respects prosecute or appear and answer such appeal as if it were an appeal in which they alone were interested.

(2) The Christian names and Surnames and places of abode of all persons interested in the said appeal shall be endorsed by the Revising Barrister on the said case after the names and places of abode of the persons so named as appellant and respondent as aforesaid.

(3) Every such consolidated appeal shall be prosecuted in like manner and be subject to the same statutory provisions and to the same rules and regulations as any other appeal under this Ordinance, and every decision or order of the Supreme Court in respect thereof shall be binding and conclusive on all parties named or referred to as parties to or interested in such appeal.

(4) If any such consolidated appeal is not duly prosecuted or answered, the Supreme Court may give to any party interested in such appeal, upon his application, the conduct and direction of the said appeal or of the answer thereto as the case may require, instead of or in addition to any person named as aforesaid as appellant or respondent, and in such manner and upon such terms as the Court may think

fit, or may make such other order in the case as may seem meet.

(5) If after the Revising Barrister has declared that an appeal in any case ought to be consolidated with others any party interested in such appeal objects to be a party to or be bound by such consolidated appeal, then and in such case the appeal in which such person is interested may proceed separately, but such person so refusing or objecting shall be liable to pay costs to the other party, but shall not be entitled to receive any costs of or in such appeal unless the Supreme Court otherwise orders. (1 of 1898, s. 19.)

Prosecution, etc., of appeal.

71. Every appeal shall be prosecuted, heard and determined by the Supreme Court in accordance with such rules and regulations as to the practice and procedure in such cases as the said Court may from time to time make, and in default of such rules and regulations according to the rules and regulations, statutory or other, of the said Court in special cases without pleadings for the opinion of the Supreme Court on questions of law arising in any civil action so far as such rules and regulations are applicable thereto. (1 of 1898, s. 20.)

Decisions from which no appeal is allowed.

72. No appeal or notice of appeal shall be received or allowed against any decision of any Revising Barrister upon any question of fact only or upon the admissibility or effect of any evidence or admission adduced or made in any case to establish any matter of fact only, provided always that if the Supreme Court shall be of opinion in any case that the statement of the matter of the appeal is not sufficient to enable it to give judgment in law, the Court may remit the said statement to the Revising Barrister in order that the case may be more fully stated. (1 of 1898, s. 21.)

Effect of decision.

73. Every judgment or decision of the Supreme Court shall be final and conclusive in the case upon the point of law adjudicated upon and shall be binding on any Judge trying any Election Petition. (1 of 1898, s. 22.)

Alteration of registers after decision.

74. Whenever by any judgment or Order of the Supreme Court any decision or order of a Revising Barrister is reversed or altered so as to necessitate any alteration or correction of any Register of Voters, the Registrar shall forthwith alter or correct the said register accordingly and shall sign his name against every such alteration or correction, and notice of such alteration or correction shall without delay be published in the *Gazette*. (1 of 1898, s. 23.)

Effect of pending appeals on right of voting.

75. No right of voting at any election shall be affected by any appeal pending at the time of the issuing of the writ for such election, but every person may exercise the right of voting at such election as effectually, and every vote tendered thereat shall be as good, as if no such appeal were pending, and the subsequent decision of any appeal pending at the time of issuing the writ for any such election shall not in any way whatever alter or affect the poll taken at such election nor the return made thereat by the Returning Officer. (1 of 1898, s. 24.)

Costs of appeals.

76.—(1) The Supreme Court may make such order respecting the payment of the costs of any appeal or of any part of such costs as to the said Court seems meet : Provided always that the said Court shall not in any case make any order for costs against or in favour of any respondent or person named as respondent as aforesaid unless he appears before the said Court in support of the decision of the Revising Barrister which is in question.

(2) In the case of any consolidated appeal the Court may make such order as it thinks fit as to the mode of payment of and proportions in which the several parties interested in such appeal shall contribute among themselves to the costs of such appeal. (1 of 1898, s. 25.)

Returning Officers, etc.

Appointment of Returning Officer.

77.—(1) The Governor shall from time to time appoint some fit and proper person to be the Returning Officer of each Electoral District or Division, and may at any time cancel any such appointment.

(2) If any Returning Officer is prevented, by sickness or any other cause, from acting, or refuses or neglects to act, at any election, the Governor may at any time appoint some other fit and proper person to act in the place of such Returning Officer at such election.

(3) Every appointment of a Returning Officer shall, unless made *ex officio*, be valid until his death or until such appointment is cancelled by the Governor.

(4) Every appointment or cancellation of appointment of a Returning Officer shall be notified in *The Official Gazette.*

Issue of writs for holding elections.

78.—(1) For the purpose of every general election of Members of the Court of Policy and Financial Representatives, and for the purpose of the election of Members or Financial Representatives to supply vacancies caused by death, resignation, or otherwise, the Governor shall issue writs of election, under the Public Seal of the Colony, addressed to the Returning Officers of the respective Electoral Districts or Divisions for which Members or Financial Representatives are to be returned.

(2) Every such writ shall specify the place of election and the date on or before which it is returnable to the Governor.

(3) On receipt of such writ, every Returning Officer shall proceed to hold the election thereby directed and in accordance therewith after giving notice, in the manner mentioned in section 60, of the time and place of election.

Delivery to Returning Officer of Register of Voters.

79. Before the day of election the Registrar shall cause to be delivered to the Returning Officer the Register of Voters for the time being in force for the Electoral District or Division.

Appointment of polling stations. (S. 15 of 24 of 1909 replaces s. 80 of 1 of 1891.)

80.—(1) The Governor may, from time to time, appoint suitable places as polling stations for the election of Members of the Court of Policy and Financial Representatives and may at any time cancel the appointment of any such place and such place shall thereupon cease to be a polling station; but the number of polling stations shall not be less than four nor more than eight in any Electoral District or Division.

(2) Every place so appointed shall remain a polling station until such cancelment.

(3) Notice of any such appointment or cancelment shall be published in the *Gazette*.

Added by 6 of 1914, s. 4.

(4) The Governor may from time to time by notice in the *Gazette* divide any Electoral District or Division into a number of Polling Areas corresponding to the number of Polling Stations appointed for such Electoral District or Division and after such notice the voters resident within any Polling Area at the date of the making up of the Register of Voters shall vote only at the Polling Station corresponding to the said Polling Area. The Governor may at any time by notice in the *Gazette* alter or cancel any such division into Polling Areas.

Proceedings at Election.

Appointment of day of nomination and election.

81.—(1) On receiving a writ for the election of a Member of the Court of Policy or of a Financial Representative, the Returning Officer shall give notice, in the manner mentioned in section 60, of the day and place on and at which he will receive the nomination of a candidate or candidates for the seat or seats to be filled by election.

(2) The day so fixed shall be not less than five or more than ten days after the day on which the writ was received.

Nomination of candidates. (S. 16 of 24 of 1909 replaces s. 82 of 1 of 1891.)

82.—(1) On the day and at the place fixed by the Returning Officer under section eighty-one of this Ordinance to receive the nomination of a candidate or candidates, the Returning Officer shall attend at nine o'clock in the morning, and receive the nomination of any duly qualified candidate or candidates for the seat or seats to be filled.

(2) Every candidate shall be proposed and seconded by

two persons whose names appear on the Register of Voters for the Electoral District or Division.

(3) If at the hour of ten of the clock in the morning of the said day only one candidate has been nominated for each or any seat to be filled, the Returning Officer shall declare such candidate to have been duly elected.

(4) If more candidates than one are nominated for each or any seat to be filled, or if, in a case where two seats are to be filled, more than two candidates are nominated, the Returning Officer shall thereupon appoint a day, being not more than ten days thereafter, for the holding of the election.

(5) If any candidate duly nominated desires to withdraw from his candidature before the day fixed for the holding of the election, he may do so on giving notice in writing to that effect to the Returning Officer, and if on such withdrawal there remains only one candidate for each or any seat to be filled, or if, in a case where two seats are to be filled, only two candidates remain, the Returning Officer shall thereupon declare such candidate or candidates to have been duly elected.

Appointment of substitutes and clerks by Returning Officer.

83.—(1) On the day of election, the Returning Officer shall himself attend at the principal polling station of his Electoral District or Division, and shall appoint fit and proper persons to be his substitutes at the other polling stations of the said District or Division.

(2) The Returning Officer may also appoint fit and proper persons to be clerks for attendance at the several polling stations.

Copy of Register of Voters to be provided.

84. The Returning Officer shall take care that each substitute is provided with a certified copy of the Register of Voters for the Electoral District or Division for which he acts.

Presiding Officer at election.

85. The Returning Officer or his substitute shall preside at and conduct the election at each polling station.

Hours of voting.

86. The voting shall commence at each polling station at nine o'clock in the morning of the day appointed for the holding of the election, and shall close at five o'clock in the afternoon of the same day.

Vote by Ballot.

87. In case of a poll at an election of a Member of the Court of Policy or of a Financial Representative, the votes shall be given by ballot. The ballot of each voter shall consist of a paper (in this Ordinance called a Ballot Paper) showing the names and description of the candidates. Each Ballot Paper shall have a number printed on the back, and shall have attached to it a counterfoil with the same number printed on the face. (9 of 1896, s. 11.)

88. In cases where a poll is to take place the Returning Officer shall take care beforehand that each polling-place is provided with proper doors, barriers, tables, chairs and other conveniences, and that the same are properly arranged for carrying out the provisions of this Ordinance, and he shall also provide each polling-place with a proper ballot box, and a sufficient number of voting papers, in conformity with the provisions of this Ordinance, and such other convenience for taking the poll as may be necessary. (9 of 1896, s. 12.)

Preparing Polling-places and making arrangements for taking the Poll.

89. The Returning Officer shall, on or before the day fixed for the taking of the poll, visit each polling station, and see that each such station is provided with the proper conveniences as aforesaid for taking the poll (9 of 1896, s. 13) :

Inspection of Polling Stations.

Provided that in the Electoral District of North-West Essequebo, the Commissioner for the North-West District may exercise all or any of the powers of the Returning Officer in his name and in his stead in regard to any Polling Station at Morawhanna or elsewhere within the North-West District.

Ord. 6 of 1914, s. 8.

90. For the guidance of electors in voting, notices shall be printed in conspicuous characters and placarded in various places, outside and inside of every polling station, in the following form :—

Directions to voters.

Directions.

(1) To mark your vote, you must draw your pen through the names of all the candidates other than the one (or two as the case may be) for whom you wish to vote.

(2) You can vote for one (or two as the case may be) candidate (or candidates) at this election.

(3) When you have marked your vote, fold up your ballot paper so as to conceal your vote, but so as to show the official mark on the back, show the officer in charge the official mark, and then put your ballot paper in the ballot box and leave the room.   (9 of 1896, s. 37.)

91. Each person on coming to vote shall address himself to the Returning Officer or his substitute, and shall state his name and address in an audible voice.   (9 of 1896, s. 14.)

Duty of voter on coming to vote.

92. The Returning Officer or his substitute shall proceed to write the number of such Elector on the Register of Voters on the Counterfoil of a Voting paper, mark the same with an official mark and, calling out the name of the Voter in an audible voice, deliver such paper to the Voter within

Duty of Returning Officer.

the Polling Station. The Voter shall then retire to a table apart, but within the Polling Station, and having secretly marked his vote on the paper, and folded it up so as to conceal his Vote but so as to show the official mark at the back, shall place it in the Ballot Box in the presence of the Returning Officer or his substitute after having shown to him the official mark at the back. The Voter having voted shall forthwith leave the Polling Station. The Returning Officer or his substitute after having delivered to the Voter a Ballot Paper, and while the Voter is recording his Vote, shall make a mark against the name of such Voter on his copy of the Register of Voters to indicate that such Voter has voted at the Election, but not so as to show the particular Voting Paper given to such Voter. (9 of 1896, s. 15.)

How to mark a vote. **93.** The Voter shall mark his Vote upon the Voting Paper by drawing his pen through the names of all the Candidates other than that of the person for whom he wishes to vote. (9 of 1896, s. 16.)

Who are to be admitted within the Polling-place. **94.** No person shall be admitted within any Polling-place during the hours appointed for taking the Poll, except the Returning Officer or his substitute, the Clerk at such place, one Agent for each Candidate appointed by such Candidate in writing, and one Voter at a time. (9 of 1896, s. 17, amd. 1 of 1898, s. 28.)

Agents, how to be placed. **95.** The Agents aforesaid shall be posted in such a place that they can see each person who presents himself as a Voter, and hear his name as given in by him, and interfere in the proceedings to the extent allowed by this Ordinance, but so that they cannot see how any Voter votes or otherwise interfere. (9 of 1896, s. 18.)

Preservation of order. **96.** If any Agent persists, after being warned, in contravening these Provisions, it shall be lawful for the Returning Officer or his substitute to have him turned out of the Polling-place. The Returning Officer or his substitute may any time summon Constables within the Polling-place for the purposes of preserving order. (9 of 1896, s. 19.)

Instructions by Returning Officers. **97.** The Returning Officer or his substitute shall, on request, give such instructions as may appear to be necessary to any Voter as to the manner in which he should record his Vote. (9 of 1896, s. 20.)

Questions allowed to be put to voter about to vote. **98.**—(1) The Returning Officer or his substitute may in his discretion, and shall, if required by any candidate or any person representing a candidate at an election, put to any Voter, at the time of his applying for a Ballot Paper, the following questions or either of them, and no other :—

1st. Are you the same person whose name appears as *A. B.* on the Register of Voters now in force for this District [*or* Division]?

2nd. Have you already voted, either here or elsewhere, in this District [*or* Division] for the election of a Member of the Court of Policy [*or* of a Financial Representative]?

(2) If any person refuses to answer any such question so put to him, the Returning Officer or his substitute may refuse to give him a Ballot Paper.

(3) If any person wilfully makes a false answer to any such question so put to him, he shall be guilty of a misdemeanour, and, being convicted thereof, shall be liable to imprisonment, with or without hard labour, for any term not exceeding one year.   (Amd. 1 of 1898, s. 27.)

As to a person claiming to vote as an Elector after another person has voted as such Elector. **99.** If a person representing himself to be a particular Elector named on the Register applies for a Ballot Paper after another person has voted as such Elector, the applicant shall, upon duly answering the questions set forth in section 98 of this Ordinance, be entitled to mark a Ballot Paper in the same manner as any other Voter; but the Ballot Paper (hereinafter called a Tendered Ballot Paper) shall be of a colour differing from the other Ballot Papers, and, instead of being put into the Ballot Box, shall be given to the Returning Officer or his substitute, and endorsed by him with the name of the Voter and his number in the Register of Voters, and set aside in a separate packet, and shall not be counted by the Returning Officer. And the name of the Voter and his number on the Register shall be **The Tendered Votes List.** entered on a list to be called " The Tendered Votes List." (9 of 1896, s. 21.)

As to spoilt Ballot Papers **100.**—(1) A Voter who has inadvertently dealt with his Ballot Paper in such manner that it cannot be conveniently used as a Ballot Paper may, on delivering to the Returning Officer or his substitute the Ballot Paper so inadvertently dealt with, and proving the fact of the inadvertence to the satisfaction of the Returning Officer or his substitute, obtain another Ballot Paper in the place of the Ballot Paper so delivered up (hereinafter called a spoilt Ballot Paper), and the spoilt Ballot Paper shall be immediately cancelled by the Returning Officer or his substitute writing the word " cancelled " across the face of the same.

(2) All papers cancelled by any substitute of the Returning Officer shall be preserved and given up by him at the close of the Poll to the Returning Officer as hereinafter mentioned.   (9 of 1896, s. 22.)

Cases of voters who are blind or unable to vote. **101.** If any Voter is incapacitated by blindness or other physical cause from voting in the manner prescribed by this or any Ordinance in force for the time being, the

Presiding Officer shall, at the request of such Voter, in the presence of the Agents of the Candidates, cause his vote to be marked on a Ballot Paper in manner directed by such Voter, and the Ballot Paper so marked to be placed in the Ballot Box; and the name and number on the Register of Voters of every Voter whose vote is so marked for him, and the reason why it is so marked, shall be entered on a List which shall be kept by or delivered to the Returning Officer. (9 of 1896, s. 23, amd. 1 of 1898, s. 33.)

Ballot Box : particulars as to same.

102. The Ballot Box shall be of convenient size, and shall be so constructed that the Ballot Paper can be introduced therein but cannot be withdrawn without the box being unlocked. It shall be provided with a lock and key. (9 of 1896, s. 24.)

Exhibition thereof.

103. It shall be exhibited empty to such persons as may be in the Polling-place immediately before the taking of the Poll, and shall then be securely locked, and not be again unlocked except by the Returning Officer at the close of the Poll in manner hereinafter mentioned. (9 of 1896, s. 25.)

Procedure in case of obstruction of election.

104. In any case where the proceedings at an election are interrupted or obstructed by any riot or open violence at any polling station, the Returning Officer or his substitute may adjourn the further holding of the election at such polling station until the next working day, and so on as often as may be necessary, but subject to the provision that such adjournment shall not continue to be made beyond the day on which it is necessary to close the election in order that a return thereof may be made in accordance with the tenor of the writ.

Duty of Presiding Officer at each station on close of the poll.

105. The substitute of the Returning Officer at each Station, as soon as practicable after the close of the Poll, shall, in the presence of the Agents of the Candidates, make up into separate packets, sealed with his own seal and the seals of such Agents of the Candidates as desire to affix their seals,—

(1) The Ballot Box in use at his Station, unopened but with the key attached which shall be so sealed as to prevent the introduction of additional Ballot Papers, and

(2) The unused and spoilt Ballot Papers placed together, and

(3) The tendered Ballot Papers, and

(4) The Counterfoils of all used, spoilt and tendered Ballot Papers, and

(5) The marked copies of the Register of Voters, and

(6) The Tendered Votes List, and the List of the Voters whose Votes were marked by him. (1 of 1898, s. 29.)

Duty of
Returning
Officer after
close of the
poll.

106. The Returning Officer, as soon as practicable after the close of the poll, shall in the presence of the candidates or their agents appointed as aforesaid proceed as follows :—

(1) He shall before opening any ballot box compare the several marked copies of the Register of Voters used at the polling stations, so as to ascertain whether a vote has been taken in the name of the same voter at more stations than one, and if any vote has been so taken, shall record in writing the stations at which it has been taken and the number of the voter on the Register of Voters.

(2) He shall then proceed to deal with the ballot box, papers and documents from each polling station in the following manner : dealing with the ballot box, papers and documents from one station at a time :

(a) He shall count the ballot papers in such box and the unused and spoilt ballot papers, so as to ascertain whether those papers, together with those which from the Tendered Votes List appear to have been used for Tendered Votes, account for all the ballot papers with which such polling station was provided by him, and shall record in writing the result of such examination.

(b) If from the comparison mentioned in sub-section (1), it appears that no vote has been taken at such polling station in the name of a voter who has voted at some other station, or such vote at such other station has not be counted, the Returning Officer shall count the votes contained in such ballot box, recording as he proceeds, the number of votes given for each candidate.

(c) If from such comparison it appears that any such vote has been taken at such polling station, and a vote in the name of such voter at another station has been counted, the Returning Officer shall open the sealed packet of counterfoils and refer to the numbers thereon, and on the back of the ballot papers so as to ascertain which ballot paper is to be rejected, and having excluded such paper shall proceed to count and record the votes as hereinbefore provided.

(d) The Returning Officer after counting the votes in any ballot box as aforesaid shall make up into one packet the ballot papers and all other papers and documents from the same polling station, and the record of the result of the examination mentioned in this sub-section, and shall write on such packet the name of the polling station from which such papers and documents came, and shall seal up such packet so that the same cannot be opened without breaking the seals.

(e) While counting the ballot papers and in counting the votes, the Returning Officer shall keep the ballot papers with their faces upwards, and take all proper precautions for preventing any person from seeing the numbers printed on the backs of such papers.

(f) Save and except in cases provided for in clause (c) of this sub-section, and so far as is necessary to comply with that clause, the Returning Officer shall not open the sealed packet of counterfoils coming from any station or refer to the numbers thereon or to the numbers on the backs of the ballot papers.

(g) The Returning Officer shall not open the sealed packet of Tendered Ballot Papers coming from any station. (1 of 1898, s. 30.)

What ballot papers are not to be counted. **107.** Any Ballot Paper which has not on its back the official mark, or on which votes are given to more Candidates than the Voter is entitled to vote for, or on which anything except the said number on the back is written or marked by which the Voter can be identified, shall be void and not counted. (9 of 1896, s. 28.)

Rejected ballot papers. **108.**—(1) The Returning Officer shall endorse " rejected " on any Ballot Paper which he may reject as invalid, and shall add to the endorsement " rejection objected to " if an objection be in fact made by any Agent to his decision. **Report as to same.** The Returning Officer shall report to the Governor the number of Ballot Papers rejected and not counted by him under the several heads of—

1. Want of official mark,—
2. Voting for more Candidates than entitled to,—
3. Writing or mark by which Voter could be identified,—
4. Unmarked or void for uncertainty,—
5. Voting at more polling stations than one,—

and shall, on request, allow any Agents of the Candidates before such Report is sent to copy it.

(2) The Governor shall cause such Report as aforesaid to be published in *The Official Gazette*. (9 of 1896, s. 29, amd. 1 of 1898, s. 31.)

How far decision of Returning Officer final. **109.** The decision of the Returning Officer as to any question arising in respect of any Ballot Paper shall be final, subject to reversal on Petition questioning the Election or Return. (9 of 1896, s. 30.)

110. When the Ballot Boxes and Papers aforesaid have been received from each Polling-place, and the Ballot Papers have been counted, compared and recorded in manner aforesaid the Returning Officer shall proceed to add up the number of Votes given to each Candidate. (9 of 1896, s. 31.)

Case of equality of votes.

111.—(1) Where two or more candidates have an equal number of votes, and the addition of a vote would entitle one of such candidates to be declared elected, the Returning Officer, if he is a registered voter for the Electoral District or Division, may give such additional vote, but the Returning Officer shall not in any other case be entitled to vote at an election for which he is the Returning Officer.

(2) If, in any such last-mentioned case, the Returning Officer is not a registered voter as aforesaid, or if, being such registered voter, he declines to vote, he shall make a special return of the result of the election, and the Court of Policy or the Combined Court, as the case may be, shall have the right of choosing one of such candidates to be a Member of the Court of Policy or to be a Financial Representative.

Declaration of result of poll.

112. On the working day next after he has received the Ballot Boxes from the several polling stations at eleven o'clock in the morning, the Returning Officer shall attend at the principal polling station of the Electoral District or Division, and shall publicly state the result of the poll and make declaration of the person or persons elected to be a Member or Members of the Court of Policy or to be a Financial Representative, as the case may be.   (Amd. 9 of 1896, s. 40.)

Return of person elected.

113.—(1) On or before the date appointed for the return of the writ of election, the Returning Officer shall appear before the Governor and make a return of the person or persons elected to be a Member or Members of the Court of Policy or to be a Financial Representative, as the case may be ; or in lieu of appearing before the Governor the Returning Officer may, if he thinks fit, after filling in and signing the return endorsed thereon, send the writ as a registered letter by post free of charge to the Colonial Secretary, so that the same may be received by him on or before the date appointed for the return of the said writ.

(2) If any Returning Officer wilfully makes a false return, he shall forfeit the sum of one thousand dollars, which may be recovered, with costs, by an action in the Supreme Court of British Guiana in its civil jurisdiction at the suit of any person aggrieved.   (Amd. 9 of 1896, s. 10.)

M M

Returns of particulars of voting to be sent to the Governor.

114. The Returning Officer shall, as soon as may be after any election, make a return to the Governor, shewing the number of persons who appear to have voted at each Voting-place, and the number of Spoilt Ballot Papers delivered to him from such place.   (9 of 1896, s. 32, amd. 37 of 1903, s. 7.)

Papers to be sent to the Colonial Secretary.

115. The Returning Officer shall, as soon as may be after making the return, make up into one parcel the different parcels of Voting Papers, Counterfoils, marked copies of registers, and other papers used at the said Election, and seal up the same so that such parcel cannot be opened without breaking the seals and send the same to the Colonial

His duty and powers as to same.

Secretary, who shall keep the same in safe custody, and shall allow no person to have access to the same : Provided always that, when an Election Petition has been presented questioning the validity of any Election or return, the Colonial Secretary shall, on the order of a Judge of the Supreme Court, deliver to such Judge the parcel of papers relating to the Election that is in dispute : Provided also that after the expiration of twelve months from the day of any Election it shall be lawful for the Colonial Secretary to burn the said parcel of papers used at such Election. (9 of 1896, s. 33.)

Delivery by candidate of declaration of his qualification. (Ss. 17, 18 and 19 of 24 of 1909 replace s. 116 of 1 of 1891.)

116.—(1) Every candidate nominated at any election of a member of the Court of Policy or of a Financial Representative, shall at the time of nomination or within forty-eight hours thereafter deliver or cause to be delivered to the Returning Officer a statutory declaration made and subscribed by such candidate of his qualification in the form contained in the Second Schedule to this Ordinance. If such statutory declaration is not delivered as aforesaid the

Second Schedule.

nomination or election as the case may be of such candidate shall be deemed to be void and the Returning Officer shall thereupon proceed as if such candidate had withdrawn from his candidature, or had not been elected.

(2) The Returning Officer after the election shall forward the statutory declaration of the candidate elected, or the statutory declaration of both candidates, if more than one is elected, to the Clerk of the Court.

Penalty on member of Court of Policy or Financial Representative who sits or votes without being qualified. Ord. 24 of 1909, s. 18.

(3) Every person elected a member of the Court of Policy or as a Financial Representative who sits or votes at any meeting of the Court of Policy or of the Combined Court without being duly qualified as such member or Financial Representative shall forfeit and pay the sum of five hundred dollars to His Majesty, one half of which shall be payable to any voter who may sue for the same, and the other half to the Colonial Treasurer for the public use of the Colony, and such sum shall be recoverable with costs, before the Supreme Court in its Civil Jurisdiction by an action in the

name of the Colonial Treasurer : Provided that no person shall be liable to be sued under this section and also to be prosecuted for making a false statutory declaration under sub-section one of this section.

Person convicted of making false declaration as to qualification not to be eligible for election.
Ord. 24 of 1909, s. 19.

(4) Any person who is convicted of making a false statutory declaration under sub-section one of this section shall not thereafter be eligible to be elected as a member of the Court of Policy or as a Financial Representative, for the period of seven years.

Offences Relating to Elections.

Punishment of bribery, treating and undue influence.

117. Every person who is guilty of bribery, treating or undue influence shall be guilty of a misdemeanour, and, being convicted thereof, shall be liable to a fine not exceeding one thousand dollars or to imprisonment, with or without hard labour, for any term not exceeding one year.

Punishment of personation.

118. Every person who is guilty of personation, or of aiding, abetting, counselling, or procuring the commission of the offence of personation, shall be guilty of a misdemeanour, and, being convicted thereof, shall be liable to imprisonment, with or without hard labour, for any term not exceeding two years.

Incapacity entailed by conviction for bribery, etc.

119. Every person who is convicted of bribery, treating, undue influence, or personation, or of aiding, abetting, counselling, or procuring the commission of the offence of personation, shall (in addition to any other punishment) be incapable, during a period of seven years from the date of his conviction,

(1) Of being registered as a voter or voting at any election of a member of the Court of Policy or of a Financial Representative; and

(2) Of being elected as a member of the Court of Policy or as a Financial Representative, or, if elected before his conviction, of retaining his seat as such member or Financial Representative.

Persons to be deemed guilty of bribery.

120. The following persons shall be deemed guilty of bribery within the meaning of this Ordinance :—

(1) Every person who directly or indirectly, by himself or by any other person on his behalf, gives, lends, or agrees to give or lend, or offers, promises, or promises to procure or to endeavour to procure, any money or valuable consideration to or for any voter, or to or for any person on behalf of any voter, or to or for any other person, in order to induce any voter to vote or refrain from voting, or corruptly does any such act as aforesaid on account

of such voter having voted or refrained from
voting, at any election ;

(2) Every person who directly or indirectly, by himself or
by any other person on his behalf, gives or procures,
or agrees to give or procure, or offers, promises, or
promises to procure or to endeavour to procure,
any office, place or employment to or for any voter,
or to or for any person on behalf of any voter, or
to or for any other person, in order to induce such
voter to vote or refrain from voting, or corruptly
does any such act as aforesaid on account of any
voter having voted or refrained from voting, at
any election ;

(3) Every person who directly or indirectly, by himself or
by any other person on his behalf, makes any such
gift, loan, offer, promise, procurement, or agreement as aforesaid to or for any person, in order to
induce such person to procure, or to endeavour to
procure, the return of any person as an elected
member of the Court of Policy or as a Financial
Representative or the vote of any voter at any
election ;

(4) Every person who, upon or in consequence of any
such gift, loan, offer, promise, procurement, or
agreement, procures, or engages, promises, or
endeavours to procure, the return of any person
as an elected member of the Court of Policy or as
a Financial Representative or the vote of any
voter at any election ;

(5) Every person who advances or pays, or causes to be
paid, any money to or to the use of any other
person, with the intent that such money, or any
part thereof, shall be expended in bribery at any
election, or who knowingly pays, or causes to be
paid, any money to any person, in discharge or
repayment of any money wholly or in part expended in bribery at any election ;

(6) Every voter who, before or during any election,
directly or indirectly, by himself or by any other
person on his behalf, receives, agrees, or contracts
for any money, gift, loan, or valuable consideration,
office, place or employment, for himself or for any
other person, for voting or agreeing to vote, or for
refraining or agreeing to refrain from voting, at any
election ;

(7) Every person who, after any election, directly or
indirectly, by himself or by any other person on
his behalf, receives any money or valuable consideration on account of any person having voted

or refrained from voting, or having induced any other person to vote or refrain from voting, at any election; and

(8) Every person who, directly or indirectly, corruptly pays any rate or tax on behalf of any other person, for the purpose of enabling him to be registered as a voter in order thereby to influence his vote at any future election, and every person on whose behalf, and with whose privity, any such payment as last aforesaid is made.

Persons to be deemed guilty of treating

121. The following persons shall be deemed guilty of treating within the meaning of this Ordinance :—

(1) Every person who corruptly, by himself or by any other person, either before, during, or after an election, directly or indirectly gives or provides, or pays, wholly or in part, the expense of giving or providing, any food, drink, entertainment, or provision to or for any person for the purpose of corruptly influencing that person, or any other person, to vote or refrain from voting at such election, or on account of such person or any other person having voted or refrained from voting at such election; and

(2) Every voter who corruptly accepts or takes any such food, drink, entertainment, or provision.

Persons to be deemed guilty of undue influence.

122. Every person who directly or indirectly, by himself or by any other person on his behalf, makes use of, or threatens to make use of, any force, violence, or restraint, or inflicts or threatens to inflict, by himself or by any other person, any temporal or spiritual injury, damage, harm, or loss upon or against any person, in order to induce or compel such person to vote or refrain from voting, or on account of such person having voted or refrained from voting, at any election, or who, by abduction, duress, or any fraudulent contrivance, impedes or prevents the free exercise of the franchise of any voter, or thereby compels, induces, or prevails upon any voter either to give or refrain from giving his vote at any election, shall be guilty of undue influence within the meaning of this Ordinance.

Persons to be deemed guilty of personation.

123.—(1) Every person who at any election tenders a vote in the name of another person, whether that name is the name of a person living or dead or of a fictitious person, or who, having voted once at any election, tenders a vote at the same election, in his own name, shall be guilty of personation within the meaning of this Ordinance.

(2) Every person who at any election applies for a ballot paper in the name of another person, whether that name be

the name of a person living or dead, or of a fictitious person, or who having voted once at any election applies at the same election for a ballot paper in his own name, shall be guilty of personation within the meaning of this Ordinance. (9 of 1896, s. 34.)

Punishment of persons guilty of certain illegal practices.

124.—(1) Every person who—

(a) Votes, or induces or procures any person to vote, at any election, knowing that he or such other person is prohibited by this Ordinance, or by any other law, from voting at such election; or

(b) Before or during an election, knowingly publishes any false statement of the withdrawal of a candidate at such election for the purpose of promoting or procuring the election of another candidate,

shall be guilty of an illegal practice, and, being convicted thereof, shall be liable to a fine not exceeding five hundred dollars and be incapable, during a period of five years from the date of his conviction, of being registered as a voter or voting at any election of a member of the Court of Policy or of a Financial Representative for the Electoral District or Division in which the illegal practice was committed.

(2) Any such fine may be sued for by any person before any Stipendiary Magistrate, and the procedure shall be in accordance with any Ordinances for the time being in force regulating procedure before Stipendiary Magistrates in the exercise of their summary jurisdiction and appeals from the decisions of Stipendiary Magistrates.

See Ordinances No. 12 of 1893 and No. 13 of 1893.

(3) If such fine is paid on conviction of the offender, the person suing for the same shall be entitled to a moiety thereof.

Specified misdemeanors.

125.—(1) Every person who—

(1) Forges or counterfeits, or fraudulently defaces or destroys, any ballot paper or the official mark on any ballot paper, or

(2) Without due authority supplies a ballot paper to any person, or

(3) Fraudulently puts into any ballot box any paper other than the ballot paper which he is authorized by law to put in, or

(4) Fraudulently takes out of the polling station any ballot paper, or

(5) Without due authority destroys, takes, opens, or otherwise interferes with, any ballot box or packet of ballot papers then in use for the purposes of an election,

shall be guilty of misdemeanor, and be liable, if he is the Returning Officer or his substitute, or Clerk employed at a

Penalty therefor.

polling station, to imprisonment for any term not exceeding two years, with or without hard labour, or to a fine not exceeding one thousand dollars, and if he is any other person, to imprisonment to any term not exceeding six months, with or without hard labour, or to a fine not exceeding two hundred and fifty dollars.

Attempts.

(2) Any attempt to commit any offence specified in this section shall be punishable in the manner in which the offence itself is punishable.

(3) In any information or prosecution for an offence in relation to the ballot boxes, ballot papers, and other things in use at an election, the property in such ballot boxes, ballot papers or things, may be stated to be in the Returning Officer at such Election.   (9 of 1896, s. 35.)

Duty of secrecy.

126.—(1) Every Officer, Clerk and Agent, in attendance at a polling station shall maintain and aid in maintaining the secrecy of the voting in such station, and shall not communicate, except for some purpose authorized by law, before the poll is closed, to any person any information as to the name or number on the register of voters of any voter who has or has not applied for a ballot paper or voted at that station ; and no person whosoever shall interfere with or attempt to interfere with a voter when marking his vote, or otherwise attempt to obtain in the polling station any information as to the candidate for whom any voter in such station is about to vote or has voted, or as to the number on the back of the ballot paper given to any voter at such station.

(2) Every Officer, Clerk and Agent, in attendance at the counting of the votes shall maintain and aid in maintaining the secrecy of the voting, and shall not attempt to ascertain at such counting the number on the back of any ballot paper, or communicate any information obtained at such counting as to the candidate for whom any vote is given in any particular ballot paper.

(3) No person shall, directly or indirectly, induce any voter to display his ballot paper after he has marked it, so as to make known to any person the name of the candidate for or against whom he has so marked his vote.

Penalty on breach of this section.

(4) Every person who acts in contravention of the provisions of this section shall be liable, on summary conviction before a Stipendiary Magistrate, to imprisonment for any term not exceeding six months, with or without hard labour.   (9 of 1896, s. 36.)

Employment of hackney carriages, or of carriage and horses

126A.—(1) In the City of Georgetown and Town of New Amsterdam, a person shall not let, lend, or employ for the purpose of the conveyance of electors to or from the poll, any public stage or hackney carriage, or any horse or other kept for hire.
Ord. 6 of
1914, s. 9.

animal kept or used for drawing the same, or any carriage, horse, or other animal which he keeps or uses for the purpose of letting out for hire, and if he lets, lends, or employs such carriage, horse, or other animal, knowing that it is intended to be used for the purpose of the conveyance of electors to or from the poll, he shall be guilty of an offence, and, on summary conviction shall be liable to a fine not exceeding five hundred dollars or to imprisonment not exceeding six months.

(2) A person shall not hire, borrow, or use for the purpose of the conveyance of electors to or from the poll any carriage, horse, or other animal which he knows the owner thereof is prohibited by this section to let, lend, or employ for that purpose, and if he does so he shall be guilty of an offence, and, on summary conviction shall be liable to a fine not exceeding five hundred dollars or to imprisonment not exceeding six months.

(3) Nothing in this Ordinance shall prevent a carriage, horse, or other animal being let to or hired, employed, or used by an elector or several electors at their joint cost, for the purpose of being conveyed to or from the poll.

(4) No person shall be liable to pay any duty or to take out a licence for any carriage by reason only of such carriage being used without payment or promise of payment for the conveyance of electors to or from the poll at an election.

(5) In this section the words hackney carriage shall be deemed to include a motor car or motor bus kept for hire.

Election Petition.

Presentation
of election
petition.

127. A petition complaining of an undue return or undue election of a member of the Court of Policy or of a Financial Representative, hereinafter called an election petition, may be presented to the Supreme Court of British Guiana in its civil jurisdiction by any one or more of the following persons, that is to say,—

(1) Some person who voted or had a right to vote at the election to which the petition relates; or

(2) Some person who claims to have had a right to be returned or elected at such election; or

(3) Some person who alleges himself to have been a candidate at such election.

Added by 6
of 1914, s. 10.

Provided that any person presenting a petition shall be obliged to deposit with the Registrar of the Supreme Court of British Guiana the sum of two hundred dollars as security for costs.

Provided also that such petition shall be presented within twenty-one days after the return has been made to the Governor of the person or persons selected to be a member or members of the Court of Policy or to be a Financial Representative, as the case may be, unless it questions the return or election upon an allegation of corrupt practices, and specifically alleges a payment of money or other award to have been made by any member or Financial Representative, or on his account or with his privity, since the time of such return, in pursuance or in furtherance of such corrupt practice, in which case the petition may be presented at any time within twenty-eight days after the date of such payment.

Trial of election petition.

128.—(1) Every election petition shall be tried by a Judge of the Supreme Court, sitting alone without a jury, in open Court.

(2) At the conclusion of the trial, the Judge shall determine whether the member of the Court of Policy or the Financial Representative whose return or election is complained of, or any other and what person, was duly returned or elected, or whether the election was void, and shall certify such determination to the Governor; and, upon such certificate being given, such determination shall be final; and the return shall be confirmed or altered, or a writ for a new election shall be issued, as the case may require, in accordance with such certificate.

Procedure at trial of election petition.

129. At the trial of an election petition, the procedure shall, as near as circumstances will admit, be the same, and the Judge shall have the same powers, jurisdiction and authority, as if he were trying a civil action without a jury; and witnesses shall be subpœnaed and sworn in the same manner, as near as circumstances will admit, as in the trial of a civil action in the Supreme Court, and shall be subject to the same penalties for perjury.

Disallowance of vote corruptly given, etc.

130. Where on the trial of any election petition, a candidate is proved to have been guilty, by himself or by any other person on his behalf, of bribery, treating, or undue influence in respect of any person who voted for him at such election, or where any person retained or employed for reward by or on behalf of such candidate, for all or any of the purposes of such election, as agent, clerk, messenger, or in any other capacity, is proved on such trial to have voted for such candidate at such election, the vote of every person who voted for such candidate at such election and is proved to have been so bribed, treated, or unduly influenced, or so retained or employed for reward as aforesaid, shall be struck out.

Protection to voter.

131. No voter who has voted at any election shall in any proceeding to question the election be required to state for whom he has voted. (9 of 1896, s. 39.)

PART IV.

MISCELLANEOUS PROVISIONS.

Candidates to have same privileges as agents.

132. Any candidate may himself do or aid in doing anything which his agent may do under any Ordinance and may be present at any place at which his agent may under any Ordinance be present. (1 of 1898, s. 32.)

Effect of non-attendance of candidate.

133. The non-attendance of any candidate or of any agent nominated by him shall not in any wise invalidate any act or thing done under this Ordinance if such act or thing is otherwise duly done, notwithstanding such act or thing is required or authorized done in the presence of such candidate or of his duly authorized agent. (9 of 1896, s. 38.)

Payment of moneys from the Treasury.

134. All moneys paid from the Treasury shall be paid on a warrant under the hand of the Governor.

Power to expel member of the Court of Policy or of the Combined Court for disobedience to rules.

135. If any member of the Court of Policy, not being an *ex officio* member, or of the Combined Court obstinately refuses to yield due obedience and conform himself to the rules and standing orders of such Court, it shall be lawful for such Court, after affording such member a full opportunity of defending himself, by resolution to expel such member from such Court, and to declare his seat vacant and his seat shall thereupon become vacant accordingly.

Power to commit person guilty of improper conduct to the Court of Policy or to the Combined Court.

136. If any person being present in the assembly hall of the Court of Policy or of the Combined Court and while such Court is sitting, is guilty of any improper conduct towards such Court, or any member thereof, it shall be lawful for such Court, after affording such person a full opportunity of defending himself, either forthwith or at any adjourned sitting of such Court, by resolution to declare and adjudge such person to have been guilty of a contempt of such Court; and thereupon it shall be lawful for the Governor or other presiding member of such Court, by warrant under his hand, to commit such person to any prison in this Colony, there to remain without bail until he makes his submission to such Court and is released by order under the hand of the Governor or other presiding member of such Court : Provided that no person shall be detained in prison under this section for a longer term than six months.

Exemption from service on juries.

137. Every member of the Court of Policy and every Financial Representative is hereby exempted from serving on any jury.

Prohibition of voting by members personally interested.

138. No member of the Court of Policy or of the Combined Court shall vote on any question before the Court of which he is a member in which he has a direct personal pecuniary interest : Provided always that this enactment shall not be deemed to preclude any officer of the Government from voting on any motion for a reduction of the salary of the office held by him or of the salaries of such office and of any other office. (16 of 1898, s. 2.)

Temporary Provision.

Preservation of rights of members of the College of Electors.

139. Every person who, at the time of the abolition of the College of Electors of this Colony taking effect by virtue of this Ordinance is a member of the said College shall, during the term of his natural life, have and enjoy all the rights, privileges, and immunities at present had and enjoyed by a member of the said College in as full and ample a manner as if the said College had not been abolished.

FIRST SCHEDULE

Section 61.

FORM No. 1.

NOTICE OF CLAIM TO BE REGISTERED AS A VOTER.

BRITISH GUIANA.

To   *Registering Officer of Electoral District*
No.   [*or* the   Division of Electoral District
No.   ].

I, *A . B .*, of   in the   of
hereby give you notice that I claim to have my name inserted in the List of Voters for Electoral District No.   ; [*or* the   Division of Electoral District No.   ] and the particulars of my qualification, and the proof thereof which I produce, are as follows :—[*Here state the qualification and the evidence produced to prove it*].

Dated this   day of   1   .

(Signed.)

—————————————   *A . B .*

Section 62.

FORM No. 2.

BRITISH GUIANA.

LIST OF PERSONS ENTITLED TO VOTE IN THE ELECTION OF MEMBERS OF THE COURT OF POLICY AND FINANCIAL REPRESENTATIVES FOR ELECTORAL DISTRICT No.   ; [*or* FOR THE   DIVISION OF ELECTORAL DISTRICT No.   ]

FOR THE YEAR 1   .

No.	Date of Registration.	Surname and Christian Name.	Residence.	Nature of Qualification.	Local or other Description of Land, etc.

Section 63 (1).

Form No. 3.

Notice of Objection by Person omitted from the List of Voters.

British Guiana.

To *Registering Officer of Electoral District*
No. [*or* the Division of Electoral
District No.].

I, *A. B.*, of in the of
hereby give you notice that I object to the
omission of my name from the List of Voters for Electoral
District No. [*or* for the Division of
Electoral District No.] for the year 1 ; and that
I claim to have my name inserted in the said List on the
following qualification of which I produce proof as follows :—
[*Here state the qualification and the evidence produced to prove it.*]

[N.B.—*In case of person omitted as disqualified by conviction*
substitute for " qualification " wherever that word occurs the
words " ground namely " and *add* the ground and also state
the evidence produced.]

Dated this day of 1 .

(Signed.)
A. B.

Section 63 (2).

Form No. 4.

Notice of Objection to Retention of Name in the List of Voters.

1. *Notice to the Registering Officer.*

British Guiana.

To *Registering Officer of Electoral District*
No. [*or* the Division of Electoral
District No.].

I, *A. B.*, of in the of
being a person whose name appears in the
List of Voters for the said Electoral District [*or* the said
Division of the said Electoral District] hereby give you notice
that I object to the name of *C. D.*, of in the
of being retained in the said
List on the ground that [*here state shortly the grounds on which
the objection is based*].

Dated this day of 1 .

(Signed.)
A. B.

2. *Notice to the person objected to.*

BRITISH GUIANA.

To

I, *A. B.,* of   in the   of
being a person whose name appears in the
List of Voters for Electoral District No.   [*or* the
Division of Electoral District No.   ] for
the year 1   , hereby give you notice that I object to your
name being retained on the said List on the ground that [*here
state shortly the grounds on which the objection is based*].

Dated this   day of   19   .

(Signed.)
A. B.

Section 116.   SECOND SCHEDULE

STATUTORY DECLARATION OF A PERSON NOMINATED AS A
CANDIDATE FOR ELECTION AS A MEMBER OF THE COURT
OF POLICY [*or* AS A FINANCIAL REPRESENTATIVE].

Qualification of *A. B.* of   in the
of   nominated as a candidate for election as
a member of the Court of Policy [*or* a Financial Representa-
tive] for Electoral District No.   [*or* the
Division of Electoral District No.   ].

I, *A. B.,* of   in the   of
do solemnly and sincerely declare as
follows :—

That I am duly qualified to be elected a member of the
Court of Policy [*or* a Financial Representative] and that my
qualification is,—

[*Here state the qualification.*]

I make this declaration conscientiously believing the same
to be true and according to the Statutory Declarations
Ordinance, 1893.

(Signed.)

_____
Declarant.

Declared before me
this   day of   1   .

(Signed) _____

APPENDIX Q

(See Part II, chapter xvi, p. 313.)

(i) COLONIAL REPRESENTATION PRIOR TO GENERAL ELECTION OF 1892

(a) *College of Electors*

Representative for	Name.	Race.	Occupation.
Demerara	W. H. Sherlock	White	Attorney of Messrs. Sandbach, Parker & Coy.
Georgetown	F. A. Mason	do.	Manager, Demerara Railway
do.	M. R. O'Maley	do.	Manager, Colonial Bank
Berbice	D. W. A. McKinnon	Coloured	Merchant
New Amsterdam	G. L. Davson	do.	Manager, British Guiana Bank
Essequebo	A. R. Gilzean	White	Planter
do.	H. B. Hunter	do.	Sugar Estates Proprietor

(b) *Court of Policy* *

Name.	Race.	Occupation.
Alexander Barr	White	Attorney of Messrs. Hogg, Curtis Campbell & Coy.
B. Howell Jones	do.	Sugar Estates' Proprietor
Hugh McN. Greene	do.	do.
Thos. Mulligan	do.	do.
Chas. Ross	do.	do.

* Prior to the enactment of Ordinance No. 1 of 1891 members of the Court of Policy did not represent different electoral divisions of the Colony.

(c) *College of Financial Representatives*

Representative for	Name.	Race.	Occupation.
Demerara	D. M. Hutson	Coloured	Barrister
Georgetown	Arthur Weber	White	Merchant
Berbice	N. R. McKinnon	Coloured	Barrister
New Amsterdam	R. J. v. R. de Groot	White	do.
Essequebo	R. G. Duncan	do.	Attorney, Colonial Coy., Ltd.
do.	Wm. Smith	Negro	Merchant

542

APPENDIX S

(See Part II, chapter ix, p. 173; Part III, chapter ii, p. 328; and Part IV, p. 399.)

JUDGMENT OF CHIEF JUSTICE LORD MANSFIELD IN CAMPBELL *versus* HALL: 1775

See (*a*) Report of Cases adjudged in the Court of King's Bench from Hilary Term, the 14th of George III, 1774, to Trinity Term, the 18th of George III, 1778, both inclusive: by Henry Cowper, Esq., Barrister-at-law, of the Middle Temple. Second edition: London, 1800, printed by A. Strahan. Vol. I, pp. 204–214: and (*b*) the Lives of the Chief Justices of England by John Lord Campbell: London, John Murray, 1849, Vol. II, pp. 410–413.

In the year 1722, the assembly of Jamaica being refractory, reference was made to Sir Philip Yorke and Sir Clement Wearge to know " what could be done if the assembly should obstinately continue to withhold all the usual supplies." They reported that, if Jamaica was still to be considered as a conquered island, the King had a right to levy taxes upon the inhabitants; but that, " if it was to be considered in the same light as the other colonies, no tax could be imposed on the inhabitants but by an assembly of the island or by an Act of Parliament."

In 1775, in the case of *Campbell* versus *Hall* (Michaelmas Term, the 15th of George III), Lord Mansfield, as Chief Justice, fully developed the law upon this subject and laid down the rules upon which our colonies have been governed ever since. The island of Grenada had been taken by Great Britain in the Seven Years' War and had been ceded to us by the peace of 1762. Next year the King of his own authority imposed by proclamation a tax of 4% on all exports from Grenada. Thereafter James Campbell, a British subject, who had subsequently purchased an estate and settled in the island, brought an action in the Court of King's Bench in England to recover back the sum he had been compelled to pay in respect of this tax for liberty to ship his sugar to London, maintaining that such a tax could only be imposed by the authority of Parliament. Lord Mansfield gave judgment in favour of Campbell, and in the course of his judgment laid down the following six propositions:

(1) A country conquered by the British arms becomes a dominion of the King in right of his crown and is therefore necessarily subject to the Parliament of Great Britain.

(2) The conquered inhabitants, once received under the King's protection, become subjects, and are universally to be considered in that light—not as enemies or aliens.

(3) The articles of capitulation upon which the country surrendered, and the articles of peace by which it is ceded, are sacred and inviolable according to their true meaning and intent.

(4) The law of every dominion annexed to the Crown equally affects all persons and all property within the limits thereof and is the rule of decision for all questions which arise therein. Whoever purchases, lives or sues there, puts himself under the law of the place.

(5) The laws of a conquered country continue in force until they are altered by the conqueror.

(6) If the King without the consent of Parliament has a power to alter the old and to introduce new laws in a conquered country, this legislation being subordinate, that is, subordinate to his own authority in Parliament, he cannot make any change contrary to fundamental principles : he cannot exempt an inhabitant from that particular dominion, as for instance, from the laws of trade or from the power of Parliament, or give him privileges exclusive of his other subjects.

Printed in Great Britain by Richard Clay & Sons, Limited,
BUNGAY, SUFFOLK.